Lecture Notes in Computer Science 8301

Commenced Publication in 1973
Founding and Former Series Editors:
Gerhard Goos, Juris Hartmanis, and Jan van Leeuwen

Chung-chieh Shan (Ed.)

Programming Languages and Systems

11th Asian Symposium, APLAS 2013
Melbourne, VIC, Australia, December 9-11, 2013
Proceedings

Springer

Volume Editor

Chung-chieh Shan
Indiana University
150 S. Woodlawn Avenue
Bloomington, IN 47405-7104, USA
E-mail: ccshan@indiana.edu

ISSN 0302-9743 e-ISSN 1611-3349
ISBN 978-3-319-03541-3 e-ISBN 978-3-319-03542-0
DOI 10.1007/978-3-319-03542-0
Springer Cham Heidelberg New York Dordrecht London

Library of Congress Control Number: 2013952464

CR Subject Classification (1998): D.3, D.2, F.3, F.4, D.4

LNCS Sublibrary: SL 2 – Programming and Software Engineering

Typesetting: Camera-ready by author, data conversion by Scientific Publishing Services, Chennai, India

Printed on acid-free paper

Springer is part of Springer Science+Business Media (www.springer.com)

Preface

Welcome to APLAS 2013, the 11th Asian Symposium on Programming Languages and Systems! APLAS aims to stimulate programming language research by providing a forum for foundational and practical issues in programming languages and systems. APLAS is based in Asia and sponsored by the Asian Association for Foundation of Software (AAFS), but it serves the worldwide programming language community. This latest APLAS was held in Melbourne, Australia, during December 9–11, 2013, after ten successful symposia and, before them, three informal workshops.

Our call for papers this year attracted 57 submissions from all around the globe. Each submission was reviewed by at least three Program Committee members, with the help of external reviewers. A total of 185 reviews were produced. The Program Committee then discussed the submissions during a 10-day electronic meeting. In the end, we accepted 20 regular research papers and three system and tool papers. (One of the papers was initially accepted on condition of being revised to address certain concerns. The final version of the paper was discussed and checked by a shepherd before being accepted.)

As usual, we rounded off the program with three invited talks:

– Nick Benton (Microsoft Research), "The proof assistant as an integrated development environment"
– Cristina Cifuentes (Oracle Labs Australia), "Internal deployment of the Parfait static code analysis tool at Oracle"
– Alexandra Silva (Radboud University Nijmegen), "Brzozowski's and up-to algorithms for must testing"

I am grateful to everyone who submitted to the symposium. Thanks also to all the Program Committee members and external reviewers, for their helpful reviews and thoughtful discussion. The EasyChair conference management system enabled the reviewing process as well as proceedings preparation. Thanks to the AAFS executive committee for their support, especially Kazunori Ueda for his sage advice. Finally, thanks to the general chair Peter Schachte and the poster chair Shin-ya Katsumata.

September 2013 Chung-chieh Shan

Organization

Program Committee

Filippo Bonchi	CNRS, ENS-Lyon, France
Yu-Fang Chen	Academia Sinica, Taiwan
Shigeru Chiba	The University of Tokyo, Japan
Jacques Garrigue	Nagoya University, Japan
Robert Glück	University of Copenhagen, Denmark
R. Govindarajan	Indian Institute of Science, India
Kazuhiro Inaba	Google, Inc., Japan
Jie-Hong Roland Jiang	National Taiwan University, Taiwan
Shin-ya Katsumata	Kyoto University, Japan
Gabriele Keller	University of New South Wales, Australia
Ana Milanova	Rensselaer Polytechnic Institute, USA
Keisuke Nakano	The University of Electro-Communications, Japan
Hakjoo Oh	Seoul National University, South Korea
Bruno Oliveira	National University of Singapore, Singapore
Kaushik Rajan	Microsoft Research, India
Max Schaefer	Nanyang Technological University, Singapore
Ulrich Schöpp	Ludwig-Maximilians-Universität München, Germany
Paula Severi	University of Leicester, UK
Chung-chieh Shan	Indiana University, USA
Gang Tan	Lehigh University, USA
Hiroshi Unno	University of Tsukuba, Japan
Meng Wang	Chalmers University of Technology, Sweden
Jingling Xue	University of New South Wales, Australia
Mingsheng Ying	University of Technology, Sydney, Australia
Kenny Zhu	Shanghai Jiao Tong University, China

Additional Reviewers

Abel, Andreas
Ahmed, Amal
Atkey, Robert
Axelsen, Holger Bock
Axelsson, Emil
Berger, Martin
Boldo, Sylvie
Bono, Viviana
Carayol, Arnaud
Chakravarty, Manuel
Chang, Bor-Yuh Evan
Cho, Sungkeun
D'Souza, Deepak
Espírito Santo, José Carlos
Fahrenberg, Uli
Filinski, Andrzej

Ganapathy, Vinod
Heo, Kihong
Holik, Lukas
Ilik, Danko
Jia, Xiao
Kameyama, Yukiyoshi
Komondoor, Raghavan
Lee, Wonchan
Leonardsson, Carl
Lescanne, Pierre
Lippmeier, Ben
Lo, David
Lu, Yi
Löh, Andres
Magalhães, José Pedro
Millstein, Todd
Mogensen, Torben
Møgelberg, Rasmus Ejlers
Müller, Norbert
Nagaraj, Vaivaswatha
Nanevski, Aleksandar
Nasre, Rupesh
O'Connor, Liam
Oliva, Paulo
Pearce, David
Radhakrishna, Arjun
Rezine, Ahmed
Rochel, Jan
Rogalewicz, Adam
Sato, Tetsuya
Schrijvers, Tom
Skalka, Christian
Smallbone, Nick
Sokolova, Ana
Terui, Kazushige
Thomsen, Michael Kirkedal
Wang, Bow-Yaw
Xian, Xu
Yu, Fang

Table of Contents

Brzozowski's and Up-To Algorithms for Must Testing

Filippo Bonchi[1], Georgiana Caltais[2], Damien Pous[1], and Alexandra Silva[3,*]

[1] ENS Lyon, U. de Lyon, CNRS, INRIA, UCBL
[2] Reykjavik University
[3] Radboud University Nijmegen

Abstract. Checking language equivalence (or inclusion) of finite automata is a classical problem in Computer Science, which has recently received a renewed interest and found novel and more effective solutions, such as approaches based on antichains or bisimulations up-to. Several notions of equivalence (or preorder) have been proposed for the analysis of concurrent systems. Usually, the problem of checking these equivalences is reduced to checking bisimilarity. In this paper, we take a different approach and propose to adapt algorithms for language equivalence to check one prime equivalence in concurrency theory, must testing semantics. To achieve this transfer of technology from language to must semantics, we take a coalgebraic outlook at the problem.

1 Introduction

Determining whether two systems exhibit the same behavior under a given notion of equivalence is a recurring problem in different areas from Computer Science, from compiler analysis, to program verification, to concurrency theory. A widely accepted notion of equivalence is that two systems are equivalent if they behave the same when placed in the same context.

We will focus on the equivalence problem in the context of concurrency theory and process calculi. Systems are processes and contexts will be given by sets of tests a process should obey. This leads us to consider standard behavioural equivalences and preorders for process calculi, in particular *must testing* [14]: two systems are equivalent if they pass exactly the same tests, in all their executions.

The problem of automatically checking such testing equivalences is usually reduced to the problem of checking bisimilarity, as proposed in [12] and implemented in several tools [13,10]. In a nutshell, equivalence is checked as follows. Two processes are considered, given by their labeled transition systems (LTS's). Then, the given LTS's are first transformed into "acceptance graphs", using a construction which is reminiscent of the *determinization* of non-deterministic automata (NDA). Finally, bisimilarity is checked via the *partition refinement*

* Also affiliated to Centrum Wiskunde & Informatica (Amsterdam, The Netherlands) and HASLab / INESC TEC, Universidade do Minho (Braga, Portugal).

C.-c. Shan (Ed.): APLAS 2013, LNCS 8301, pp. 1–16, 2013.

algorithm [17,22]. And one can answer the question of testing equivalence because gladly bisimilarity in acceptance graphs coincides with testing equivalence in the original LTS's.

The partition refinement algorithm, which is the best-known for minimizing LTS's w.r.t. bisimilarity, is analogous to Hopcroft's algorithm [16] for minimizing deterministic automatata (DA) w.r.t. language equivalence. In both cases, a partition of the state space is iteratively refined until a fixpoint is reached. Thus, the above procedure for checking testing semantics [12] is in essence the same as the classical procedure for checking language equivalence of NDA: first determinize and then compute a (largest) fixpoint.

In this work, we propose to transfer other algorithms for language equivalence, which are not available for bisimilarity, to the world of testing semantics. In order to achieve this, we take a coalgebraic perspective at the problem in hand, which allows us to study the constructions and the semantics in a uniform fashion. The abstract framework of *coalgebras* makes it possible to study different kinds of state based systems in a uniform way [26]. In particular, both the determinization of NDA's and the construction of acceptance graphs in [12] are instances of the generalized powerset construction [28,20,11]. This is the key observation of this work, which enables us to devise the presented algorithms.

First, we consider *Brzozowski's algorithm* [9] which transforms an NDA into the minimal deterministic automaton accepting the same language in a rather magical way: the input automaton is reversed (by swapping final and initial states and reversing its transitions), determinized, reversed and determinized once more. This somewhat intriguing algorithm can be explained in terms of duality and coalgebras [4,2]. The coalgebraic outlook in [4] has several generalization of Brzozowski's algorithm to other types of transition systems, including Moore machines. This paves the way to adapt Brzozowski's algorithm for checking must semantics, which we will do in this paper.

Next, we consider several more efficient algorithms that have been recently introduced in a series of papers [32,1,7]. These algorithms rely on different kinds of *(bi)simulations up-to*, which are proof techniques originally proposed for process calculi [21,27]. From these algorithms, we choose the one in [7] (`HKC`) which has been introduced by a subset of the authors and which, as we will show, can be adapted to must testing using a coalgebraic characterization of must equivalence, which we will also introduce.

Comparing these three families of algorithms (partition refinement [12], Brzozowski and bisimulations up-to) is not a simple task: both the problems of checking language and must equivalence are PSPACE-complete [17] but, in both cases, the theoretical complexity appears not to be problematic in practice, so that an empirical evaluation is more desirable. In [31,29], experiments have shown that Brzozowski's algorithm performs better than Hopcroft for "high-density" NDA's, while Hopcroft is more efficient for generic NDA's. Both algorithms appear to be rather inefficient compared to those of the new generation [32,1,7]. It is out of the scope of this paper to present an experimental comparison of these algorithms and we confine our work to showing concrete examples where

HKC and Brzozowski's algorithm are exponentially more efficient than the other approaches.

Contributions. The main contributions of this work are:

- The coalgebraic treatment of must semantics (preorder and equivalence).
- The adaptation of HKC and Brzozowski's algorithm for must semantics. For the latter, this includes an optimization which avoids an expensive determinization step.
- The evidence that the coalgebraic analysis of systems yields not only a good mathematical theory of their semantics but also a rich playground to devise algorithms.
- An interactive applet allowing one to experiment with these algorithms [6].

The full version of this paper [5] contains further optimizations for the algorithms, their proofs of correctness, the formal connections with the work in [12] and the results of experiments checking the equivalence of an ideal and a distributed multiway synchronisation protocol [23].

Related Work. Another coalgebraic outlook on must is presented in [8] which introduces a fully abstract semantics for CSP. The main difference with our work consists in the fact that [8] builds a coalgebra from the syntactic terms of CSP, while here we build a coalgebra starting from LTS's via the generalized powerset construction [28]. Our approach puts in evidence the underlying semilattice structure which is needed for defining bisimulations up-to and HKC. As a further coalgebraic approach to testing, it is worth mentioning test-suites [18], which however do not tackle must testing. A coalgebraic characterization of other semantics of the linear time/branching time spectrum is given in [3].

Notation. We denote sets by capital letters $X, Y, S, T \dots$ and functions by lower case letters $f, g, \dots$ Given sets X and Y, $X \times Y$ is the Cartesian product of X and Y, $X + Y$ is the disjoint union and X^Y is the set of functions $f\colon Y \to X$. The collection of *finite* subsets of X is denoted by $\mathcal{P}(X)$ (or just $\mathcal{P}X$). These operations, defined on sets, can analogously be defined on functions [26], yielding (bi-)functors on **Set**, the category of sets and functions. For a set of symbols A, A^* denotes the set of all finite words over A; ε the empty word; and $w_1 \cdot w_2$ (or $w_1 w_2$) the concatenation of words $w_1, w_2 \in A^*$. We use 2 to denote the set $\{0, 1\}$ and 2^{A^*} to denote the set of all formal languages over A. A *semilattice with bottom* $(X, \sqcup, 0)$ consists of a set X and a binary operation $\sqcup\colon X \times X \to X$ that is associative, commutative, idempotent (ACI) and has $0 \in X$ (the bottom) as identity. A *homomorphism* (of semilattices with bottom) is a function preserving $\sqcup$ and 0. Every semilattice induces a *partial order* defined as $x \sqsubseteq y$ iff $x \sqcup y = y$. The set 2 is a semilattice when taking $\sqcup$ to be the ordinary Boolean disjunction. Also the set of all languages 2^{A^*} carries a semilattice structure where $\sqcup$ is the union of languages and 0 is the empty language. More generally, for any set S, $\mathcal{P}(S)$ is a semilattice where $\sqcup$ is the union of sets and 0 is the empty set. In the rest of the paper we will indiscriminately use 0 to denote the element $0 \in 2$, the empty language in 2^{A^*} and the empty set in $\mathcal{P}(S)$. Analogously, $\sqcup$ will denote the "Boolean or" in 2, the union of languages in 2^{A^*} and the union of sets in $\mathcal{P}(S)$.

Acknowledgments. This work was supported by the LABEX MILYON (ANR-10-LABX-0070) of Université de Lyon, within the program Investissements dAvenir (ANR-11-IDEX-0007) operated by the French National Research Agency (ANR). In addition, Filippo Bonchi was partially supported by the projects PEPS-CNRS CoGIP, ANR-09-BLAN-0169-01, and ANR 12IS02001 PACE. Georgiana Caltais has been partially supported by the project 'Meta-theory of Algebraic Process Theories' (nr. 100014021) of the Icelandic Research Fund. Damien Pous was partially supported by the PiCoq project, ANR-10-BLAN-0305. Alexandra Silva was partially supported by the ERDF through the Programme COMPETE and by the Portuguese Government through FCT - Foundation for Science and Technology, project ref. `FCOMP-01-0124-FEDER-020537` and `SFRH/BPD/71956/2010`.

2 Background

The core of this paper is about the problem of checking whether two states in a transition system are testing equivalent by reducing it to the classical problem of checking language equivalence. We will consider different types of transition systems, deterministic and non-deterministic, which we will formally describe next, together with their language semantics.

A *deterministic automaton* (DA) over the alphabet A is a pair $(S, \langle o, t\rangle)$, where S is a set of states and $\langle o, t\rangle : S \to 2 \times S^A$ is a function with two components: o, the output function, determines whether a state x is final ($o(x) = 1$) or not ($o(x) = 0$); and t, the transition function, returns for each state and each input letter, the next state. From any DA, there exists a function $[\![-]\!] : S \to 2^{A^*}$ mapping states to languages, defined for all $x \in S$ as follows:

$$[\![x]\!](\varepsilon) = o(x) \qquad\qquad [\![x]\!](a \cdot w) = [\![t(x)(a)]\!](w) \tag{1}$$

The language $[\![x]\!]$ is called the language accepted by x. Given an automaton $(S, \langle o, t\rangle)$, the states $x, y \in S$ are said to be *language equivalent* iff they accept they same language.

A *non-deterministic automaton* (NDA) is similar to a DA but the transition function returns a set of next-states instead of a single state. Thus, an NDA over the input alphabet A is a pair $(S, \langle o, t\rangle)$, where S is a set of states and $\langle o, t\rangle : S \to 2 \times (\mathcal{P}(S))^A$. An example is depicted below (final states are overlined, labeled edges represent transitions).

(2)

Classically, in order to recover language semantics of NDA, one uses the *subset (or powerset) construction*, transforming every NDA $(S, \langle o, t\rangle)$ into the DA

$(\mathcal{P}(S), \langle o^\sharp, t^\sharp \rangle)$ where $o^\sharp \colon \mathcal{P}(S) \to 2$ and $t^\sharp \colon \mathcal{P}(S) \to \mathcal{P}(S)^A$ are defined for all $X \in \mathcal{P}(S)$ as

$$o^\sharp(X) = \bigsqcup_{x \in X} o(x) \qquad\qquad t^\sharp(X)(a) = \bigsqcup_{x \in X} t(x)(a) \ .$$

For instance with the NDA from (2), $o^\sharp(\{x,y\}) = 0 \sqcup 1 = 1$ (*i.e.*, the state $\{x,y\}$ is final) and $t^\sharp(\{x,y\})(a) = \{y\} \sqcup \{z\} = \{y,z\}$ (*i.e.*, $\{x,y\} \xrightarrow{a} \{y,z\}$).

Since $(\mathcal{P}(S), \langle o^\sharp, t^\sharp \rangle)$ is a deterministic automaton, we can now apply (1), yielding a function $[\![-]\!] \colon \mathcal{P}(S) \to 2^{A^*}$ mapping *sets* of states to languages. Given two states x and y, we say that they are language equivalent iff $[\![\{x\}]\!] = [\![\{y\}]\!]$. More generally, for two sets of states $X, Y \subseteq S$, we say that X and Y are language equivalent iff $[\![X]\!] = [\![Y]\!]$.

In order to introduce the algorithms in full generality, it is important to remark here that the sets 2, $\mathcal{P}(S)$, $\mathcal{P}(S)^A$, $2 \times \mathcal{P}(S)^A$ and 2^{A^*} carry semilattices with bottom and that the functions $\langle o^\sharp, t^\sharp \rangle \colon \mathcal{P}(S) \to 2 \times \mathcal{P}(S)^A$ and $[\![-]\!] \colon \mathcal{P}(S) \to 2^{A^*}$ are homomorphisms.

2.1 Checking Language Equivalence via Bisimulation Up-To

We recall the algorithm HKC from [7]. We first define a notion of bisimulation on sets of states. We make explicit the underlying notion of progression.

Definition 1 (Progression, Bisimulation). *Let $(S, \langle o, t \rangle)$ be an NDA. Given two relations $R, R' \subseteq \mathcal{P}(S) \times \mathcal{P}(S)$, R progresses to R', denoted $R \rightarrowtail R'$, if whenever $X \; R \; Y$ then*

1. $o^\sharp(X) = o^\sharp(Y)$ and 2. for all $a \in A$, $t^\sharp(X)(a) \; R' \; t^\sharp(Y)(a)$.

A bisimulation *is a relation R such that $R \rightarrowtail R$.*

This definition considers the states, the transitions and the outputs of the *determinized* NDA. For this reason, the bisimulation proof technique is sound and complete for language equivalence rather than for the standard notion of bisimilarity by Milner and Park [21].

Proposition 1 (Coinduction [7]). *For all $X, Y \in \mathcal{P}(S)$, $[\![X]\!] = [\![Y]\!]$ iff there exists a bisimulation that relates X and Y.*

For an example, we want to check the equivalence of $\{x\}$ and $\{u\}$ of the NDA in (2). The part of the determinized NDA that is reachable from $\{x\}$ and $\{u\}$ is depicted below. The relation consisting of dashed and dotted lines is a bisimulation which proves that $[\![\{x\}]\!] = [\![\{u\}]\!]$.

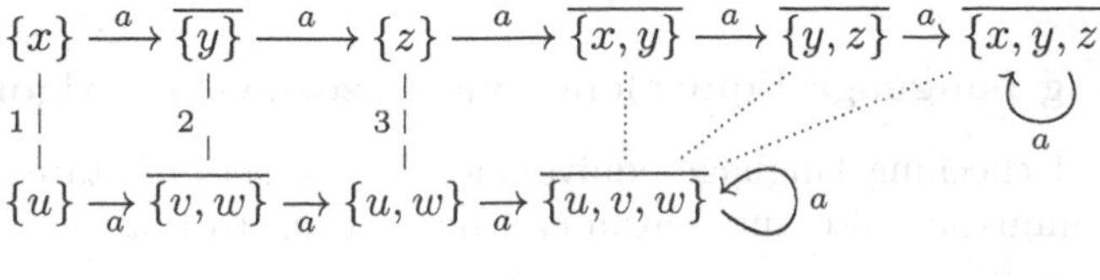

(3)

The dashed lines (numbered by 1, 2, 3) form a smaller relation which is not a bisimulation, but a *bisimulation up-to congruence*: the equivalence of $\{x, y\}$ and $\{u, v, w\}$ can be immediately deduced from the fact that $\{x\}$ is related to $\{u\}$ and $\{y\}$ to $\{v, w\}$. In order to formally introduce bisimulations up-to congruence, we need to define first the *congruence closure* $c(R)$ of a relation $R \subseteq \mathcal{P}(S) \times \mathcal{P}(S)$. This is done inductively, by the following rules:

$$\frac{X\;R\;Y}{X\;c(R)\;Y} \qquad \frac{}{X\;c(R)\;X} \qquad \frac{X\;c(R)\;Y}{Y\;c(R)\;X} \tag{4}$$

$$\frac{X\;c(R)\;Y\;\;Y\;c(R)\;Z}{X\;c(R)\;Z} \qquad \frac{X_1\;c(R)\;Y_1\;\;X_2\;c(R)\;Y_2}{X_1 \sqcup X_2\;c(R)\;Y_1 \sqcup Y_2}$$

Note that the term "congruence" here is intended w.r.t. the semilattice structure carried by the state space $\mathcal{P}(S)$ of the determinized automaton. Intuitively, $c(R)$ is the smallest equivalence relation containing R and which is closed w.r.t $\sqcup$.

Definition 2 (Bisimulation up-to congruence). *A relation* $R \subseteq \mathcal{P}(S) \times \mathcal{P}(S)$ *is a* bisimulation up-to c *if* $R \rightarrowtail c(R)$, i.e., *whenever* $X\;R\;Y$ *then*

1. $o^\sharp(X) = o^\sharp(Y)$ *and* *2. for all* $a \in A$, $t^\sharp(X)(a)\;c(R)\;t^\sharp(Y)(a)$.

Theorem 1 ([7]). *Any bisimulation up-to c is contained in a bisimulation.*

The corresponding algorithm (HKC) is given in Figure 1 (top). Starting from an NDA $(S, \langle o, t\rangle)$ and considering the determinized automaton $(\mathcal{P}(S), \langle o^\sharp, t^\sharp\rangle)$, it can be used to check language equivalence of two sets of states X and Y. Starting from the pair (X, Y), the algorithm builds a relation R that, in case of success, is a bisimulation up-to congruence. In order to do that, it employs the set *todo* which, intuitively, at any step of the execution, contains the pairs (X', Y') that must be checked: if (X', Y') already belongs to $c(R \cup todo)$, then it does not need to be checked. Otherwise, the algorithm checks if X' and Y' have the same outputs. If $o^\sharp(X') \neq o^\sharp(Y')$ then X and Y are different, otherwise the algorithm inserts (X', Y') in R and, for all $a \in A$, the pairs $(t^\sharp(X')(a), t^\sharp(Y')(a))$ in *todo*. The check $(X', Y') \in c(R \cup todo)$ at step 2.2 is done with the rewriting algorithm of [7, Section 3.4].

Proposition 2. *For all* $X, Y \in \mathcal{P}(S)$, $[\![X]\!] = [\![Y]\!]$ *iff* HKC(X, Y).

The iterations corresponding to the execution of HKC$(\{x\}, \{u\})$ on the NDA in (2) are concisely described by the numbered dashed lines in (3). Observe that only a small portion of the determinized automaton is explored; this fact usually makes HKC more efficient than the algorithms based on minimization, that need to build the whole reachable part of the determinized automaton.

2.2 Checking Language Equivalence via Brzozowski's Algorithm

The problem of checking language equivalence of two sets of states X and Y of a non-deterministic finite automaton can be reduced to that of building the minimal DA for $[\![X]\!]$ and $[\![Y]\!]$ and checking whether they are the same (up to isomorphism). The most well-known procedure consists in first determinizing the NDA and then minimizing it with the Hopcroft algorithm [16]. Another interesting solution is Brzozowski's algorithm [9].

To explain the latter, it is convenient to consider a set of *initial states* I. Given an NDA $(S, \langle o, t\rangle)$ and a set of states I, Brzozowski's algorithm computes the minimal automaton for the language $[\![I]\!]$ by performing the 4 steps in Figure 1 (bottom).

The operation `reverse and determinize` takes as input an NDA $(S, \langle o, t\rangle)$ and returns a DA $(\mathcal{P}(S), \langle \overline{o}_R, \overline{t}_R\rangle)$ where the functions $\overline{o}_R\colon \mathcal{P}(S) \to 2$ and $\overline{t}_R\colon \mathcal{P}(S) \to \mathcal{P}(S)^A$ are defined for all $X \in \mathcal{P}(S)$ as $\overline{o}_R(X) = 1$ iff $X \cap I \neq 0$ and $\overline{t}_R(X)(a) = \{x \in S \mid t(x)(a) \cap X \neq 0\}$. The new initial state is the set of accepting states of the original NDA: $\overline{I}_R = \{x \mid o(x) = 1\}$. The second step consists in taking the part of $(\mathcal{P}(S), \langle \overline{o}_R, \overline{t}_R\rangle)$ which is reachable from $\overline{I}_R$. The third and the fourth steps perform this procedure once more.

As an example, consider the NDA in (2) with the set of initial states $I = \{x\}$. Brzozowski's algorithm builds the minimal DA accepting $[\![\{x\}]\!]$ as follows. After the first two steps, it returns the following DA where the initial state is $\{y\}$.

$$\{y\} \xrightarrow{a} \overline{\{x,z\}} \xrightarrow{a} \{z,y\} \xrightarrow{a} \overline{\{x,y,z\}} \circlearrowleft a$$

After steps 3 and 4, it returns the DA below with initial state $\{\{x,z\}\{x,y,z\}\}$.

$$\{\{x,z\}\{x,y,z\}\} \xrightarrow{a} \overline{\{\{y\}\{x,y\}\{x,y,z\}\}} \xrightarrow{a} \{\{x,z\}\{z,y\}\{x,y,z\}\} \xrightarrow{a} \overline{\{\{y\}\{x,z\}\{z,y\}\{x,y,z\}\}} \circlearrowleft a$$

Computing the minimal NDA in (2) with the set of initial states $I = \{u\}$ results in an isomorphic automaton, showing the equivalence of x and u.

2.3 Generalized Powerset Construction

The notions introduced above can be easily described using *coalgebras*. Given a functor $F\colon \mathbf{Set} \to \mathbf{Set}$, an *F-coalgebra* is a pair (S, f) where S is a set of states and $f\colon S \to F(S)$ is its *transition structure*. F intuitively determines the "type" of the transitions. An *F-homomorphism* from an F-coalgebra (S, f) to an F-coalgebra (T, g) is a function $h\colon S \to T$ preserving the transition structure, *i.e.*, $g \circ h = F(h) \circ f$. An F-coalgebra (Ω, ω) is said to be *final* if for any F-coalgebra (S, f) there exists a unique F-homomorphism $[\![-]\!]\colon S \to \Omega$. Intuitively, Ω represents the universe of "F-behaviours" and $[\![-]\!]$ represents the semantic map associating states to their behaviours. Two states $x, y \in X$ are said *F-behaviourally equivalent* iff $[\![x]\!] = [\![y]\!]$. Such equivalence can be proved using *F-bisimulations* [26]. For lack of space, we refer the reader to [25] for their categorical definitions. Given a behaviour $b \in \Omega$, the *minimal coalgebra* realizing b is the part of (Ω, ω) that is reachable from b.

Let us exemplify for DA's how these abstract notions yield the expected concrete notions. DA's are coalgebras for the functor $F(S) = 2 \times S^A$. The final coalgebra of this functor is the set 2^{A^*} of formal languages over A, or more precisely, the pair $(2^{A^*}, \langle \epsilon, (-)_a \rangle)$ where $\langle \epsilon, (-)_a \rangle$, given a language L, determines whether or not the empty word is in the language ($\epsilon(L) = 1$ or $\epsilon(L) = 0$, resp.) and, for each input letter a, returns the *a-derivative* of L: $L_a = \{w \in A^* \mid aw \in L\}$. The unique map $[\![-]\!]$ into the final coalgebra 2^{A^*} is precisely the map which assigns to each state the language that it recognizes. For any language $L \in 2^{A^*}$, the minimal automaton for L is the part of $(2^{A^*}, \langle \epsilon, (-)_a \rangle)$ that is reachable from L.

In Section 3, we will use *Moore machines* which are coalgebras for the functor $F(S) = B \times S^A$. These are like DA's, but with outputs in a fixed set B. The unique F-homomorphism to the final coalgebra $[\![-]\!]: S \to B^{A^*}$ is defined exactly as for DA's by the equations in (1). Note that the behaviours of Moore machines are functions $\varphi: A^* \to B$, rather than subsets of A^*. For each behaviour $\varphi \in B^{A^*}$, there exists a minimal Moore machine realizing it.

Recall that an NDA is a pair $(S, \langle o, t \rangle)$, where $\langle o, t \rangle: S \to 2 \times (\mathcal{P}(S))^A$. As explained above, to recover language semantics one needs to use the subset construction, which transforms an NDA into a DA. More abstractly, this can be captured by observing that the type functor of NDA's – $2 \times \mathcal{P}(-)^A$ – is a composition of the functor $F(S) = 2 \times S^A$ (that is the functor for DA's) and the monad $T(S) = \mathcal{P}(S)$. $\mathcal{P}$-algebras are exactly semilattices with bottom and $\mathcal{P}$-algebra morphisms are the ones of semilattices with bottom. Now note that (a) the F-coalgebra $(\mathcal{P}(S), \langle o^\sharp, t^\sharp \rangle)$ resulting of the powerset construction is a morphism of semilattices, (b) 2^{A^*} carries a semilattice structure and (c) $[\![-]\!]: \mathcal{P}(S) \to 2^{A^*}$ is a morphism of semilattices. This is summarized by the following commuting diagram:

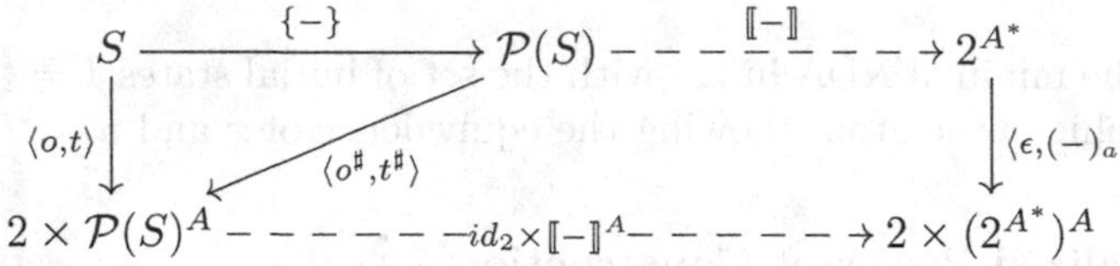

In the diagram above, one can replace $2 \times -^A$ and $\mathcal{P}$ by arbitrary F and T as long as $FT(S)$ *carries a T-algebra structure*. In fact, given an *FT-coalgebra*, that is $(S, f: S \to FT(S))$, if $FT(S)$ carries a T-algebra structure h, then (a) one can define an F-coalgebra $(T(S), f^\sharp = h \circ Tf)$ where $f^\sharp: T(S) \to FT(S)$ is a T-algebra morphism (b) the final F-coalgebra (Ω, ω) carries a T-algebra and (c) the F-homomorphism $[\![-]\!]: T(S) \to \Omega$ is a T-algebra morphism.

The F-coalgebra $(T(S), f^\sharp)$ is (together with the multiplication $\mu: TT(S) \to T(S)$) a *bialgebra* for some distributive law $\lambda: FT \Rightarrow TF$ (we refer the reader to [19] for a nice introduction on this topic). The behavioural equivalence of bialgebras can be proved either via bisimulation, or, like in Section 2.1, via *bisimulation up-to congruence* [20,25]: the result that justifies `HKC` (Theorem 1) generalises to this setting – the congruence being taken w.r.t. the algebraic structure μ. This is what allows us to move to must semantics.

```
HKC(X,Y):

(1) R is empty; todo is {(X',Y')};
(2) while todo is not empty, do
 (2.1) extract (X',Y') from todo;
 (2.2) if (X',Y') ∈ c(R ∪ todo) then continue;
 (2.3) if o♯(X') ≠ o♯(Y') then return false;
 (2.4) for all a ∈ A,
         insert (t♯(X')(a), t♯(Y')(a)) in todo;
 (2.5) insert (X',Y') in R;
(3) return true;
```

```
Brzozowski:

(1) reverse and determinize;
(2) take the reachable part;
(3) reverse and determinize;
(4) take the reachable part.
```

Fig. 1. Top: Generic HKC algorithm, parametric on $o^\sharp$, $t^\sharp$ and c. Bottom: Generic Brzozowski's algorithm, parametric on **reverse and determinize**. Instantiations to language and must equivalence in Sections 2 and 3.

3 Must Semantics

The operational semantics of concurrent systems is usually given by *labelled transition systems* (LTS's), labelled by actions that are either visible to an external observer or internal actions (usually denoted by a special symbol τ). Different kinds of semantics can be defined on these structures (*e.g.*, linear or branching time, strong or weak semantics). In this paper we consider *must semantics* [14] which, intuitively, equates those systems that pass exactly the same tests, in all their executions.

Before formally introducing *must semantics* as in [12], we fix some notations: $\stackrel{\varepsilon}{\Rightarrow}$ denotes $\stackrel{\tau}{\rightarrow}^*$ the reflexive and transitive closure of $\stackrel{\tau}{\rightarrow}$ and, for $a \in A$, $\stackrel{a}{\Rightarrow}$ denotes $\stackrel{\tau}{\rightarrow}^*\stackrel{a}{\rightarrow}\stackrel{\tau}{\rightarrow}^*$. For $w \in A^*$, $\stackrel{w}{\Rightarrow}$ is defined inductively, in the obvious way. The *acceptance set of x after w* is $A(x,w) = \{\{a \in A \mid x' \stackrel{a}{\rightarrow}\} \mid x \stackrel{w}{\Rightarrow} x' \wedge x' \stackrel{\tau}{\not\rightarrow}\}$. Intuitively, it represents the set of actions that can be fired after "maximal" executions of w from x, those that cannot be extended by some τ-labelled transitions. The possibility of executing τ-actions forever is referred to as *divergence*. We write $x \not\downarrow$ whenever x diverges. Dually, the convergence relation $x \downarrow w$ for a state x and a word $w \in A^*$ is inductively defined as follows: $x \downarrow \varepsilon$ iff x does not diverge and $x \downarrow aw'$ iff (a) $x \downarrow \varepsilon$ and (b) if $x \stackrel{a}{\Rightarrow} x'$, then $x' \downarrow w'$. Given two sets $B, C \in \mathcal{PP}(A)$, we write $B \subset\subset C$ iff for all $B_i \in B$, there exists $C_i \in C$ such that $C_i \subseteq B_i$. With these ingredients, it is possible to introduce must preorder and equivalence.

Definition 3 (Must semantics [12]). *Let x and y be two states of an LTS. We write $x \sqsubseteq_{mst} y$ iff for all words $w \in A^*$, if $x \downarrow w$ then $y \downarrow w$ and $A(y,w) \subset\subset A(x,w)$. We say that x and y are must-equivalent ($x \sim_{mst} y$) iff $x \sqsubseteq_{mst} y$ and $y \sqsubseteq_{mst} x$.*

As an example, consider the LTS depicted below. States x_4, x_5 and y_1 are divergent. All the other states diverge for words containing the letter b and converge for words on a^*. For these words and states x, x_1, x_2, x_3 and y, the corresponding acceptance sets are $\{\{a,b\}\}$. In particular, note that $A(x_2, \varepsilon)$ is $\{\{a,b\}\}$ and not $\{\{b\},\{a,b\}\}$. It is therefore easy to conclude that x, x_1, x_2, x_3 and y are all must equivalent.

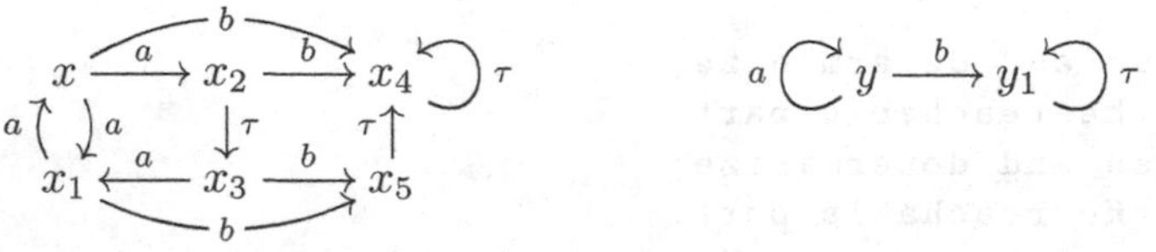

(5)

3.1 A Coalgebraic Characterization of Must Semantics

In what follows we show how $\sqsubseteq_{mst}$ can be captured in terms of coalgebras. This will further allow adapting the algorithms introduced in Section 2 for checking $\sim_{mst}$ and $\sqsubseteq_{mst}$.

First, we model LTS's in terms of coalgebras $(S, t\colon S \to (1+\mathcal{P}(S))^A)$, where $1 = \{\top\}$ is the singleton set, and for $x \in S$,

$$t(x)(a) = \top, \text{ if } x \not\downarrow a \qquad t(x)(a) = \{y \mid x \stackrel{a}{\Rightarrow} y\}, \text{ otherwise.}$$

Intuitively, a state $x \in S$ that displays divergent behaviour with respect to an action $a \in A$ is mapped to $\top$. Otherwise t computes the set of states that can be reached from x through a (by possibly performing a finite number of τ-transitions). At this point we need some additional definitions: for a function $\varphi\colon A \to \mathcal{P}(S)$, $I(\varphi)$ denotes the set of all labels "enabled" by φ, given by $I(\varphi) = \{a \in A \mid \varphi(a) \neq 0\}$, while $\mathit{Fail}(\varphi)$ denotes the set $\{Z \subseteq A \mid Z \cap I(\varphi) = 0\}$. With these definitions, we decorate the states of an LTS by means of an output function $o\colon S \to 1 + \mathcal{P}(\mathcal{P}(A))$ defined as follows:

$$o(x) = \top, \text{ if } x \not\downarrow \qquad o(x) = \bigcup_{x \stackrel{\tau}{\to} x'} o(x') \text{ if } x \stackrel{\tau}{\to}, \quad o(x) = \mathit{Fail}(t(x)), \text{ otherwise.}$$

Note that $(S, \langle o, t\rangle)$ is an FT-coalgebra for the functor $F(S) = (1 + \mathcal{PP}A) \times S^A$ and the monad $T(S) = 1 + \mathcal{P}(S)$. Algebras for such monad T are semilattices with bottom and an extra element $\top$ acting as *top* (*i.e.*, such that $x \sqcup \top = \top$ for all x). For any set U, $1+\mathcal{P}(U)$ carries a semilattice with bottom and top: bottom is the empty set; top is the element $\top \in 1$; $X \sqcup Y$ is defined as the union for arbitrary subsets $X, Y \in \mathcal{P}(U)$ and as $\top$ otherwise. Consequently, $1 + \mathcal{P}(\mathcal{P}A)$, $1 + \mathcal{P}(S)$, $(1 + \mathcal{P}(S))^A$ and $FT(S)$ carry a T-algebra structure as well. This enables the application of the generalized powerset construction (Section 2.3) associating to each FT-coalgebra $(S, \langle o, t\rangle)$ the F-coalgebra $(1 + \mathcal{P}(S), \langle o^\sharp, t^\sharp\rangle)$ defined for all $X \in 1 + \mathcal{P}(S)$ as expected:

$$o^\sharp(X) = \begin{cases} \top & \text{if } X = \top \\ \bigsqcup_{x \in X} o(x) & \text{if } X \in \mathcal{P}(S) \end{cases} \quad t^\sharp(X)(a) = \begin{cases} \top & \text{if } X = \top \\ \bigsqcup_{x \in X} t(x)(a) & \text{if } X \in \mathcal{P}(S) \end{cases}$$

Note that in the above definitions, $\sqcup$ is not simply the union of subsets, but it is the join operation in $1 + \mathcal{PP}A$ and $1 + \mathcal{P}(S)$. Moreover, $(1 + \mathcal{P}S, \langle o^\sharp, t^\sharp\rangle)$ is a Moore machine with output in $1 + \mathcal{PP}A$ and, therefore, the equations in (1) induce a function $[\![-]\!]\colon (1 + \mathcal{P}(S)) \to (1 + \mathcal{PP}A)^{A^*}$. The semilattice structure of $1 + \mathcal{PP}A$ can be easily lifted to $(1 + \mathcal{PP}A)^{A^*}$: bottom, top and $\sqcup$ are defined pointwise on A^*. If $\sqsubseteq_{\mathcal{M}}$ represents the preorder on $(1 + \mathcal{PP}A)^{A^*}$ induced by this semilattice, then the following theorem holds.

Theorem 2. *$x \sqsubseteq_{mst} y$ iff $[\![\{y\}]\!] \sqsubseteq_{\mathcal{M}} [\![\{x\}]\!]$ and $x \sim_{mst} y$ iff $[\![\{x\}]\!] = [\![\{y\}]\!]$.*

Note that according to the definition of $\sqsubseteq_{\mathcal{M}}$, $[\![\{y\}]\!] \sqsubseteq_{\mathcal{M}} [\![\{x\}]\!]$ iff $[\![\{y\}]\!] \sqcup [\![\{x\}]\!] = [\![\{x\}]\!]$, and since $[\![-]\!]$ is a T-homomorphism (namely it preserves bottom, top and $\sqcup$), the latter equality holds iff $[\![\{y, x\}]\!] = [\![\{x\}]\!]$. Summarizing,

$$x \sqsubseteq_{mst} y \text{ iff } [\![\{x, y\}]\!] = [\![\{x\}]\!].$$

Consider, once more, the LTS in (5). The part of the Moore machine $(1 + \mathcal{P}(S), \langle o^\sharp, t^\sharp\rangle)$ which is reachable from $\{x\}$ and $\{y\}$ is depicted below (the output function $o^\sharp$ maps $\top$ to $\top$ and the other states to $\{0\}$). The relation consisting of dashed and dotted lines is a bisimulation proving that $[\![\{x\}]\!] = [\![\{y\}]\!]$, *i.e.*, that $x \sim_{mst} y$.

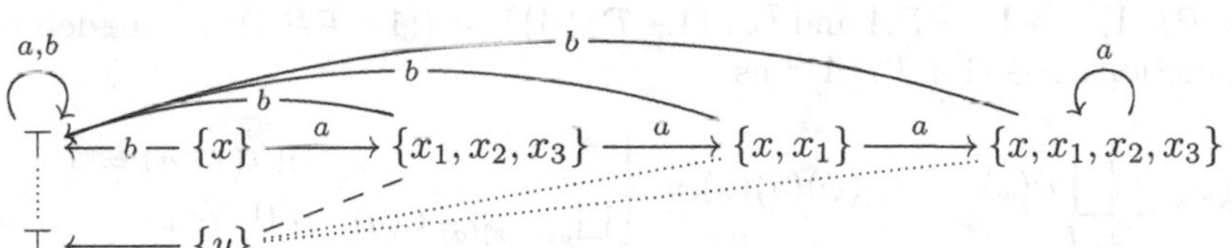

(6)

Our construction is closely related to the one in [12], that transforms LTS's into (deterministic) acceptance graphs. We refer the interested reader to a detailed comparison provided in the full version of this paper [5]. There we also show an optimization for representing outputs by means of $I(t(x))$ rather $Fail(t(x))$.

3.2 HKC for Must Semantics

The coalgebraic characterization discussed in the previous section guarantees soundness and completeness of bisimulation up-to congruence for must equivalence. Bisimulations are now relations $R \subseteq (1 + \mathcal{P}(S)) \times (1 + \mathcal{P}(S))$ on the state space $1 + \mathcal{P}(S)$ where $o^\sharp$ and $t^\sharp$ are defined as in Section 3.1. Now, the congruence closure $c(R)$ of a relation $R \subseteq (1 + \mathcal{P}(S)) \times (1 + \mathcal{P}(S))$ is defined by the rules in (4) where $\sqcup$ is the join in $(1 + \mathcal{P}(S))$ (rather than the union in

$\mathcal{P}(S)$). By simply redefining $o^\sharp$, $t^\sharp$ and $c(R)$, the algorithm in Figure 1 can be used to check must equivalence and preorder (the detailed proof can be found in the full version of the paper [5]). In particular, note that the check at step `2.1` can be done with the same algorithm as in [7, Section 3.4].

Suppose, for example, that we want to check whether the states x and y of the LTS in (5) are must equivalent. The relation $R = \{(\{x\},\{y\}),(\{x_1,x_2,x_3\},\{y\})\}$ depicted by the dashed lines in (6) is not a bisimulation, but a bisimulation up-to congruence, since both $(\top,\top) \in c(R)$ and $(\{x,x_1\},\{y\}) \in c(R)$. For the latter, observe that

$$\{x,x_1\}\ c(R)\ \{y,x_1\}\ c(R)\ \{x_1,x_2,x_3\}\ c(R)\ \{y\}.$$

It is important to remark here that HKC computes this relation without the need of exploring all the reachable part of the Moore machine $(1+\mathcal{P}(S),\langle o^\sharp,t^\sharp\rangle)$. So, amongst all the states in (6), HKC only explores $\{x\}$, $\{y\}$ and $\{x_1,x_2,x_3\}$.

3.3 Brzozowski's Algorithm for Must Semantics

A variation of the Brzozowski algorithm for Moore machines is given in [4]. We could apply such algorithm to the Moore machine $(1+\mathcal{P}(S),\langle o^\sharp,t^\sharp\rangle)$ which is induced by the coalgebra $(S,\langle o,t\rangle)$ introduced in Section 3.1. Here, we propose a more efficient variation that skips the first determinization from $(S,\langle o,t\rangle)$ to $(1+\mathcal{P}(S),\langle o^\sharp,t^\sharp\rangle)$.

The novel algorithm consists of the four steps described in Section 2.2, where the procedure `reverse and determinize` is modified as follows: $(S,\langle o,t\rangle)$ with the set of initial states I is transformed into $((1+\mathcal{P}\mathcal{P}(A))^S,\langle \overline{o}_R,\overline{t}_R\rangle)$ where $\overline{o}_R\colon (1+\mathcal{P}\mathcal{P}A)^S \to 1+\mathcal{P}\mathcal{P}A$ and $\overline{t}_R\colon (1+\mathcal{P}\mathcal{P}A)^S \to ((1+\mathcal{P}\mathcal{P}A)^S)^A$ are defined for all functions $\psi \in (1+\mathcal{P}\mathcal{P}A)^S$ as

$$\overline{o}_R(\psi) = \bigsqcup_{x\in I}\psi(x) \qquad \overline{t}_R(\psi)(a)(x) = \begin{cases}\top & \text{if } t(x)(a)=\top\\ \bigsqcup_{y\in t(x)(a)}\psi(y) & \text{otherwise}\end{cases}$$

and the new initial state is $\overline{I}_R = o$.

Note that the result of this procedure is a Moore machine. Brzozowski's algorithm in Section 2.2 transforms an NDA $(S,\langle o,t\rangle)$ with initial state I into the minimal DA for $[\![I]\!]$. Analogously, our algorithm transforms an LTS into the minimal Moore machine for $[\![I]\!]$.

Let us illustrate the minimization procedure by means of an example. Take the alphabet $A=\{a,b,c\}$ and the LTS depicted below on the left.

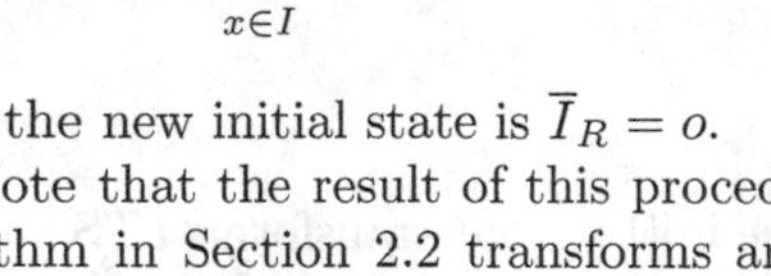

$$o(p)=\{0\} \quad o(s)=\{0\}$$
$$o(q)=\mathcal{P}(A) \quad o(u)=\mathcal{P}(A)$$
$$o(r)=\mathcal{P}(A) \quad o(v)=\mathcal{P}(A)$$

Since there are no τ transitions, the function $t\colon S\to(1+\mathcal{P}(S))^A$ is defined as on the left, and the function $o\colon S\to(1+\mathcal{P}\mathcal{P}A)$ (given on the right) assigns to each state x the set $Fail(t(x))$. Suppose we want to build the minimal Moore machine for the behaviour $[\![\{p\}]\!]\colon A^* \to 1 + \mathcal{PP}A$, which is the function

$$[\![\{p\}]\!]\colon a^* \mapsto \{0\},\, a^*b \mapsto \mathcal{P}(A),\, a^*c \mapsto \mathcal{P}(A),\, \_ \mapsto 0$$

where _ denotes all the words different from a^*, a^*b and a^*c. By applying our algorithm to the coalgebra $(S, \langle o, t\rangle)$, we first obtain the intermediate Moore machine on the left below, where a double arrow $\psi \Rightarrow Z$ means that the output of ψ is the set Z. The initial state is $\psi_1\colon S \to 1 + \mathcal{PP}A$ which, by definition, is the output function o above. The explicit definitions of the other functions ψ_i can be computed according to the definition of $\bar{t}_R$.

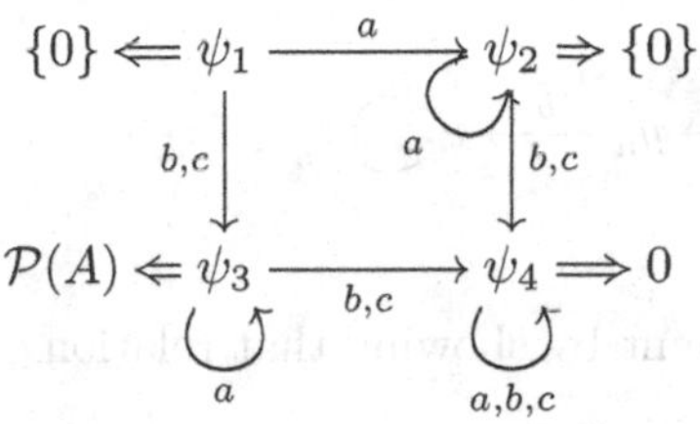

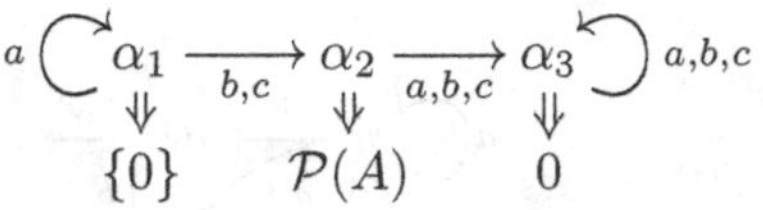

Observe that $[\![\psi_1]\!]$ is the "reversed" of $[\![\{p\}]\!]$. For instance, triggering ba^* from ψ_1 leads to ψ_3 with output $\mathcal{P}(A)$; this is the same output we get by executing a^*b from p, according to $[\![\{p\}]\!]$. Executing `reverse and determinize` once more (step 3) and taking the reachable part (step 4), we obtain the minimal Moore machine on the right, with initial state α_1.

We have proved the correctness of this algorithm in the full version of this paper [5]; it builds on the coalgebraic perspective on Brzozowski's algorithm given in [4].

4 A Family of Examples

As discussed in the introduction, the problem of checking must equivalence is PSPACE-complete [17]. Hence, a theoretical comparison of HKC, Brzozowski (BRZ) and the partition refinement (PR) of [12] will be less informative than a thorough experimental analysis. Designing adequate experiments is out of the scope of this paper. We will instead just show the reader some concrete examples. It is possible to show some concrete cases where (a) HKC takes polynomial time while BRZ and PR exponential time and (b) (BRZ) polynomial time while HKC and PR exponential time. There are also examples where (c) PR is polynomial and BRZ is exponential, but it is impossible to have PR polynomial and HKC exponential. Indeed, cycle 2 of HKC is repeated at most $1 + |A|\cdot|R|$ times where $|A|$ is the size of the alphabet and $|R|$ is the size of the produced relation R. Such relation always contains at most n pairs of states, for n being the size of the reachable part of the determinised system. Therefore, if HKC takes exponential time, then also PR takes exponential time since it always needs to build the reachable part of the determinised LTS.

In this section we show an example for (a). Examples for (b) and (c) can be found in the full version of this paper [5].

Consider the following LTS, where n is an arbitrary natural number. After the determinization, $\{x\}$ can reach all the states of the shape $\{x\} \cup X_N$, where $X_N = \{x_i \mid i \in N\}$ for any $N \subseteq \{1, \dots, n\}$. For instance for $n = 2$, $\{x\} \overset{aa}{\to} \{x\}$, $\{x\} \overset{ab}{\to} \{x, x_1\}$, $\{x\} \overset{ba}{\to} \{x, x_2\}$ and $\{x\} \overset{bb}{\to} \{x, x_1, x_2\}$. All those states are distinguished by must and, therefore, the minimal Moore machine for $[\![\{x\}]\!]$ has at least 2^n states.

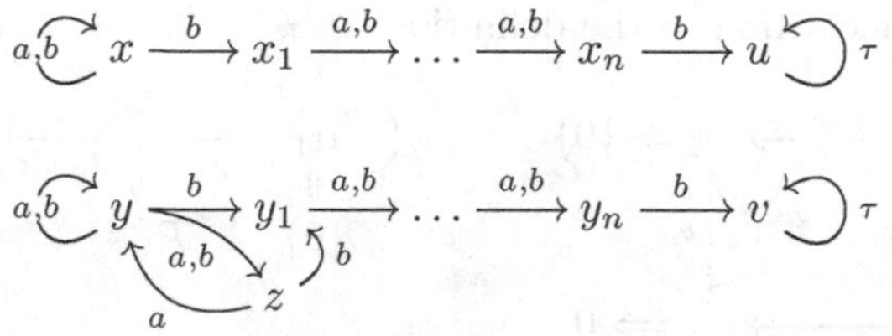

One can prove that x and y are must equivalent by showing that relation

$$R = \{(\{x\}, \{y\}), (\{x\}, \{y, z\}), (\top, \top)\} \\ \cup \{(\{x\} \cup X_N, \{y, z\} \cup Y_N) \mid N \subseteq \{1, \dots, n\}\}$$

is a bisimulation (here $Y_N = \{y_i \mid i \in N\}$). Note that R contains $2^n + 2$ pairs.

In order to check $[\![\{x\}]\!] = [\![\{y\}]\!]$, HKC builds the following relation,

$$R' = \{(\{x\}, \{y\}), (\{x\}, \{y, z\})\} \cup \{(\{x, x_i\}, \{y, z, y_i\}) \mid i \in \{1, \dots, n\}\}$$

which is a bisimulation up-to and which contains only $n + 2$ pairs. It is worth to observe that R' is like a "basis" of R: all the pairs $(X, Y) \in R$ can be generated by those in R' by iteratively applying the rules in (4). Therefore, HKC proves $[\![\{x\}]\!] = [\![\{y\}]\!]$ in polynomial time, while minimization-based algorithms (such as [12] or Brzozowski's algorithm) require exponential time.

5 Conclusions and Future Work

We have introduced a coalgebraic characterization of must testing semantics by means of the *generalized powerset construction* [28]. This allowed us to adapt proof techniques and algorithms that have been developed for language equivalence to must semantics. In particular, we showed that *bisimulations up-to congruence* (that was recently introduced in [7] for NDA's) are sound also for must semantics. This fact guarantees the correctness of a generalization of HKC [7] for checking must equivalence and preorder and suggests that the *antichains*-based algorithms [32,1] can be adapted in a similar way. We have also proposed a variation of Brzozowski's algorithm [9] to check must semantics, by exploiting the abstract theory in [4]. Our contribution is not a simple instantiation of [4], but developing our algorithm has required some ingenuity to avoid the preliminary determinization that would be needed to directly apply [4]. We implemented these algorithms together with an interactive applet available online [6].

We focused on must testing semantics because it is challenging to compute, but our considerations hold also for may testing and for several decorated trace semantics of the *linear time/branching time spectrum* [30] (namely, those that have been studied in [3]). Adapting these algorithms to check *fair testing* [24] seems to be more complicated: while it is possible to coalgebraically capture failure trees, we do not know how to model fair testing equivalence. We believe that this is a challenging topic to investigate in the future. Moreover, since coalgebras can easily model probabilistic systems, it is worth to investigate whether our approach can be extended to the testing semantics of probabilistic and non-deterministic processes (e.g. [15]).

References

1. Abdulla, P.A., Chen, Y.-F., Holík, L., Mayr, R., Vojnar, T.: When simulation meets antichains. In: Esparza, J., Majumdar, R. (eds.) TACAS 2010. LNCS, vol. 6015, pp. 158–174. Springer, Heidelberg (2010)
2. Bezhanishvili, N., Kupke, C., Panangaden, P.: Minimization via duality. In: Ong, L., de Queiroz, R. (eds.) WoLLIC 2012. LNCS, vol. 7456, pp. 191–205. Springer, Heidelberg (2012)
3. Bonchi, F., Bonsangue, M., Caltais, G., Rutten, J., Silva, A.: Final semantics for decorated traces. Elect. Not. in Theor. Comput. Sci. 286, 73–86 (2012)
4. Bonchi, F., Bonsangue, M.M., Rutten, J.J.M.M., Silva, A.: Brzozowski's algorithm (Co)Algebraically. In: Constable, R.L., Silva, A. (eds.) Kozen Festschrift. LNCS, vol. 7230, pp. 12–23. Springer, Heidelberg (2012)
5. Bonchi, F., Caltais, G., Pous, D., Silva, A.: Brzozowski's and up-to algorithms for must testing (full version), `http://www.alexandrasilva.org/files/brz-hkc-must-full.pdf`
6. Bonchi, F., Caltais, G., Pous, D., Silva, A.: Web appendix of this paper, with implementation of the algorithms (July 2013), `http://perso.ens-lyon.fr/damien.pous/brz`
7. Bonchi, F., Pous, D.: Checking NFA equivalence with bisimulations up to congruence. In: POPL, pp. 457–468. ACM (2013)
8. Boreale, M., Gadducci, F.: Processes as formal power series: a coinductive approach to denotational semantics. TCS 360(1), 440–458 (2006)
9. Brzozowski, J.A.: Canonical regular expressions and minimal state graphs for definite events. Mathematical Theory of Automata 12(6), 529–561 (1962)
10. Calzolai, F., De Nicola, R., Loreti, M., Tiezzi, F.: TAPAs: A tool for the analysis of process algebras. In: Jensen, K., van der Aalst, W.M.P., Billington, J. (eds.) ToPNoC I. LNCS, vol. 5100, pp. 54–70. Springer, Heidelberg (2008)
11. Cancila, D., Honsell, F., Lenisa, M.: Generalized coiteration schemata. Elect. Not. in Theor. Comput. Sci. 82(1) (2003)
12. Cleaveland, R., Hennessy, M.: Testing equivalence as a bisimulation equivalence. In: Sifakis, J. (ed.) CAV 1989. LNCS, vol. 407, pp. 11–23. Springer, Heidelberg (1990)
13. Cleaveland, R., Parrow, J., Steffen, B.: The Concurrency Workbench: A semantics-based tool for the verification of concurrent systems. TOPLAS 15(1), 36–72 (1993)

14. De Nicola, R., Hennessy, M.: Testing equivalences for processes. TCS 34, 83–133 (1984)
15. Deng, Y., van Glabbeek, R.J., Hennessy, M., Morgan, C.: Real-reward testing for probabilistic processes. In: QAPL. EPTCS, vol. 57, pp. 61–73 (2011)
16. Hopcroft, J.E.: An n log n algorithm for minimizing in a finite automaton. In: Proc. Int. Symp. of Theory of Machines and Computations, pp. 189–196. Academic Press (1971)
17. Kanellakis, P.C., Smolka, S.A.: CCS expressions, finite state processes, and three problems of equivalence. In: PODC 1983, pp. 228–240. ACM, New York (1983)
18. Klin, B.: A coalgebraic approach to process equivalence and a coinduction principle for traces. Elect. Not. in Theor. Comput. Sci. 106, 201–218 (2004)
19. Klin, B.: Bialgebras for structural operational semantics: An introduction. TCS 412(38), 5043–5069 (2011)
20. Lenisa, M.: From set-theoretic coinduction to coalgebraic coinduction: some results, some problems. Elect. Not. in Theor. Comput. Sci. 19, 2–22 (1999)
21. Milner, R.: Communication and Concurrency. Prentice Hall (1989)
22. Paige, R., Tarjan, R.E.: Three partition refinement algorithms. SIAM J. Comput. 16(6), 973–989 (1987)
23. Parrow, J., Sjödin, P.: Designing a multiway synchronization protocol. Computer Communications 19(14), 1151–1160 (1996)
24. Rensink, A., Vogler, W.: Fair testing. Inf. Comput. 205(2), 125–198 (2007)
25. Rot, J., Bonsangue, M., Rutten, J.: Coalgebraic bisimulation-up-to. In: van Emde Boas, P., Groen, F.C.A., Italiano, G.F., Nawrocki, J., Sack, H. (eds.) SOFSEM 2013. LNCS, vol. 7741, pp. 369–381. Springer, Heidelberg (2013)
26. Rutten, J.: Universal coalgebra: a theory of systems. TCS 249(1), 3–80 (2000)
27. Sangiorgi, D.: On the bisimulation proof method. Math. Struc. in CS 8, 447–479 (1998)
28. Silva, A., Bonchi, F., Bonsangue, M., Rutten, J.: Generalizing the powerset construction, coalgebraically. In: Proc. FSTTCS. LIPIcs, vol. 8, pp. 272–283 (2010)
29. Tabakov, D., Vardi, M.: Experimental evaluation of classical automata constructions. In: Sutcliffe, G., Voronkov, A. (eds.) LPAR 2005. LNCS (LNAI), vol. 3835, pp. 396–411. Springer, Heidelberg (2005)
30. van Glabbeek, R.: The linear time - branching time spectrum I. The semantics of concrete, sequential processes. In: Handbook of Process Algebra, pp. 3–99. Elsevier (2001)
31. Watson, B.W.: Taxonomies and Toolkits of Regular Language Algorithms. PhD thesis, Eindhoven University of Technology, the Netherlands (1995)
32. De Wulf, M., Doyen, L., Henzinger, T.A., Raskin, J.-F.: Antichains: A new algorithm for checking universality of finite automata. In: Ball, T., Jones, R.B. (eds.) CAV 2006. LNCS, vol. 4144, pp. 17–30. Springer, Heidelberg (2006)

Practical Alternating Parity Tree Automata Model Checking of Higher-Order Recursion Schemes

Koichi Fujima[1], Sohei Ito[2], and Naoki Kobayashi[1]

[1] The University of Tokyo
[2] National Fisheries University

Abstract. Higher-order (HO) model checking is the problem of deciding whether the tree generated by a higher-order recursion scheme (HORS) is accepted by an alternating parity tree automaton (APT). HO model checking has been shown to be decidable by Ong and recently applied to automated program verification. Practical HO model checkers have been, however, developed only for subclasses of APT such as trivial tree automata and weak APT. In this paper, we develop a practical model checking algorithm for the full class of APT, and implement an APT model checker for HORS. To our knowledge, this is the first model checker for HORS that can deal with the full class of APT. We also discuss its applications to program verification.

1 Introduction

The model checking of higher-order recursion schemes (HORS) has recently been drawing attention and applied to fully-automated verification of functional programs [8,11,10,12,17]. A HORS is a higher-order tree grammar for generating a single, possibly infinite tree, which can also be viewed as a term of the simply-typed call-by-name λ-calculus with recursion and tree constructors (but not destructors). Given a HORS $\mathcal{G}$ and an alternating parity tree automaton (APT) $\mathcal{A}$, the model checking of HORS [16] asks whether the tree generated by $\mathcal{G}$ is accepted by $\mathcal{A}$. Although the model checking problem is k-EXPTIME complete (for order-k HORS) [16], *practical* model checkers, which do not immediately suffer from the k-EXPTIME bottleneck, have been developed for subclasses of the APT model checking of HORS [8,12,7,15].

The previous studies on practical model checking algorithms for HORS and their applications have, however, not exploited the full power of APT model checking of HORS. Most of them [8,7,15] restricted tree automata (for expressing tree properties) to Aehlig's *trivial tree automata* [1], which can only express safety properties. Accordingly, applications have also been limited to verification of safety properties (that bad events will never happen). The only exception is the work of Lester et al.'s [12], who implemented a model checker for a larger subclass of APT called *weak alternating tree automata* [14], and applied it to verification of some liveness properties.

C.-c. Shan (Ed.): APLAS 2013, LNCS 8301, pp. 17–32, 2013.

The goal of the present paper is to develop a model checker for HORS that can deal with the *full* class of APT, and apply it to automated verification of functional programs. To this end, we propose a new APT model checking algorithm, which combines Kobayashi and Ong's reduction from APT model checking of HORS to a typability problem [9], and Kobayashi's algorithm for trivial automata model checking [8]. We use an extension of Kobayashi's algorithm to collect type candidates and decide whether a given HORS is typable under Kobayashi and Ong's type system. As the naive implementation of the algorithm suffers from the explosion of the number of type candidates, we also introduce a novel subtyping relation on Kobayashi and Ong's intersection types, and apply optimizations. To demonstrate the usefulness of the full APT model checking of HORS, we also discuss extensions of the two previous applications to program verification: resource usage verification and HMTT verification (verification of tree-processing programs) [8,11]. Thanks to the power of the full APT model checking, we can verify more elaborate properties of programs, like "does a program eventually close a file as long as the end of the file is eventually read?" and "does a tree-processing program generate a finite tree as long as the input tree is finite?"

Our contributions are: (i) the first practical, full APT model checking algorithm for HORS and its implementation. To our knowledge, ours is the first implementation of an APT model checker for HORS. (ii) Optimization based on a novel subtyping relation that respects priorities of APT. (iii) Applications to program verification, which take advantage of the full APT model checking.

In the rest of the paper, we first review basic definitions in Section 2. Sections 3 and 4 discuss our APT model checking algorithm and its optimizations. Section 5 discusses applications and Section 6 reports experiments. Section 7 discusses related work and Section 8 concludes the paper. A longer version of this paper is available from the first author's web page.

2 Preliminaries

We write $dom(f)$ and $codom(f)$ for the domain and codomain of a map f. A *ranked alphabet* Σ is a map from a finite set of symbols to non-negative integers (called *arities*). We write $ar(\Sigma)$ for the largest arity of symbols in Σ. Let **Pos** be the set of positive integers. An L*-labeled tree* is a partial map T from $\mathbf{Pos}^*$ to L, such that $\forall \pi \in \mathbf{Pos}^*.\forall i \in \mathbf{Pos}.(\pi i \in dom(T) \implies \{\pi\} \cup \{\pi j \mid 1 \leq j \leq i\} \subseteq dom(T))$. For a ranked alphabet Σ, a Σ*-labeled ranked tree* is a $dom(\Sigma)$-labeled tree T such that $\forall \pi \in \mathbf{Pos}^*.\{i \mid \pi i \in dom(T)\} = \{i \mid 1 \leq i \leq \Sigma(T(\pi))\}$.

HORS. The sets of *sorts* and *terms* are defined by:

$$\kappa \text{ (sorts) } ::= \mathsf{o} \mid \kappa_1 \to \kappa_2 \qquad t \text{ (terms) } ::= a \mid x \mid t_1 t_2 \mid \lambda x : \kappa.t.$$

Here, meta-variables a and x range over $dom(\Sigma)$ and a set of variables respectively. We call a term t an *applicative term* if it does not contain λ-abstractions. We often omit the sort annotation and write $\lambda x.t$ for $\lambda x : \kappa.t$.

Intuitively, o describes a tree, and $\kappa_1 \to \kappa_2$ describes a function that takes a value of sort κ_1 and returns a value of sort κ_2. The sort assignment relation $\mathcal{K} \vdash_\Sigma t : \kappa$ is defined by the following standard typing rules.

$$\frac{}{\mathcal{K} \vdash_\Sigma a : \underbrace{\mathsf{o} \to \cdots \mathsf{o}}_{\Sigma(a)} \to \mathsf{o}} \qquad \frac{}{\mathcal{K}, x : \kappa \vdash_\Sigma x : \kappa}$$

$$\frac{\mathcal{K} \vdash_\Sigma t_1 : \kappa' \to \kappa \qquad \mathcal{K} \vdash_\Sigma t_2 : \kappa'}{\mathcal{K} \vdash_\Sigma t_1 t_2 : \kappa} \qquad \frac{\mathcal{K}, x : \kappa' \vdash_\Sigma t : \kappa}{\mathcal{K} \vdash_\Sigma \lambda x : \kappa'.t : \kappa' \to \kappa}$$

The *order* and *arity* of a sort is defined by: $\mathit{ord}(\mathsf{o}) = \mathit{ar}(\mathsf{o}) = 0$, $\mathit{ord}(\kappa_1 \to \kappa_2) = \max(1 + \mathit{ord}(\kappa_1), \mathit{ord}(\kappa_2))$, and $\mathit{ar}(\kappa_1 \to \kappa_2) = \mathit{ar}(\kappa_2) + 1$.

Definition 1. *A* higher-order recursion scheme *(HORS) $\mathcal{G}$ is a quadruple $(\Sigma, \mathcal{N}, \mathcal{R}, S)$, where: (i) Σ is a ranked alphabet. (ii) $\mathcal{N}$ is a map from a finite set of symbols called* non-terminals *to sorts. (iii) $\mathcal{R}$ is a map from non-terminals to expressions of the form $\lambda x_1.\dots.x_\ell.t$ where t is an applicative term, and $\mathcal{N} \vdash_\Sigma \mathcal{R}(F) : \mathcal{N}(F)$ for every $F \in \mathit{dom}(\mathcal{N})$. (iv) S is a non-terminal called the start symbol, with $\mathcal{N}(S) = \mathsf{o}$. The order of a HORS $\mathcal{G}$ is the maximum order of the non-terminals.*

Intuitively, a HORS $\mathcal{G} = (\Sigma, \mathcal{N}, \mathcal{R}, S)$ is a tree-generating program that consists of a system of top-level function definitions $\{F_1 = \mathcal{R}(F_1), \dots, F_n = \mathcal{R}(F_n)\}$ with the "main" function $S \in \{F_1, \dots, F_n\}$. We define the reduction relation $\longrightarrow_\mathcal{G}$ by: (i) $F\, s_1 \cdots s_\ell \longrightarrow_\mathcal{G} [s_1/x_1, \dots, s_\ell/x_\ell]t$ if $\mathcal{R}(F) = \lambda x_1 \dots \lambda x_\ell.t$. (ii) If $t_i \longrightarrow_\mathcal{G} t'_i$, then $a\, t_1 \dots t_\ell \longrightarrow_\mathcal{G} a\, t_1 \dots t_{i-1}\, t'_i\, t_{i+1} \dots t_\ell$.

For an applicative term t of sort o, we write $t^\perp$ for the $(\Sigma\{\perp \mapsto 0\})$-labeled ranked tree defined inductively by: (i) $(F s_1 \dots s_n)^\perp = \perp$ and (ii) $(a s_1 \dots s_n)^\perp = a(s_1{}^\perp) \dots (s_n{}^\perp)$ (where $n \geq 0$). We define the binary relation $\sqsubseteq$ on $(\Sigma\{\perp \mapsto 0\})$-labeled ranked trees by: $t_1 \sqsubseteq t_2$ iff (i) $\mathit{dom}(t_1) \subseteq \mathit{dom}(t_2)$ and (ii) $\forall \pi \in \mathit{dom}(t_1).t_1(\pi) = t_2(\pi) \vee t_1(\pi) = \perp$. The *value tree* of $\mathcal{G}$, written $[\![\mathcal{G}]\!]$, is the least upper-bound of the set $\{t^\perp \mid S \longrightarrow^*_\mathcal{G} t\}$ with respect to $\sqsubseteq$.

Example 1.

Consider HORS $\mathcal{G}_1 = (\Sigma, \mathcal{N}, \mathcal{R}, S)$ where:

$$\Sigma = \{\mathsf{a} \mapsto 2, \mathsf{b} \mapsto 1, \mathsf{c} \mapsto 0\} \quad \mathcal{N} = \{S \mapsto \mathsf{o}, F \mapsto \mathsf{o} \to \mathsf{o}\}$$
$$\mathcal{R} = \{S \mapsto F\,\mathsf{c}, F \mapsto \lambda x.\mathsf{a}\, x\, (F\, (\mathsf{b}\, x))\}.$$

S is reduced as follows.

$$S \longrightarrow_{\mathcal{G}_1} F\,\mathsf{c} \longrightarrow_{\mathcal{G}_1} \mathsf{a}\,\mathsf{c}\,(F\,(\mathsf{b}\,\mathsf{c})) \longrightarrow_{\mathcal{G}_1} \cdots.$$

The tree $[\![\mathcal{G}_1]\!]$ is shown on the righthand side.

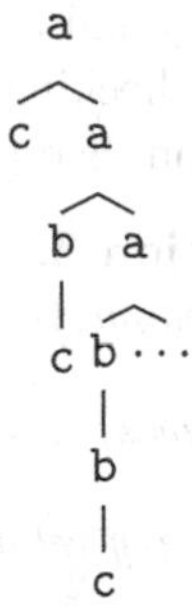

Alternating Parity Tree Automata (APT). Given a finite set X, the set $B^+(X)$ of positive Boolean formulas over X is given by (x ranges over X):

$$B^+(X) \ni \psi ::= \mathbf{true} \mid \mathbf{false} \mid x \mid \psi_1 \wedge \psi_2 \mid \psi_1 \vee \psi_2$$

For a set $Y \subseteq X$ and a formula $\psi \in B^+(X)$, $sat(Y, \psi)$ is defined by:

$$sat(Y, \mathbf{true}) = \mathbf{true} \qquad sat(Y, \mathbf{false}) = \mathbf{false} \quad sat(Y, x) = \begin{cases} \mathbf{true} & (x \in Y) \\ \mathbf{false} & (\text{otherwise}) \end{cases}$$
$$sat(Y, \psi_1 \wedge \psi_2) = sat(Y, \psi_1) \wedge sat(Y, \psi_2) \quad sat(Y, \psi_1 \vee \psi_2) = sat(Y, \psi_1) \vee sat(Y, \psi_2)$$

Definition 2. *An* alternating parity tree automaton *(APT for short) [3] is a 5-tuple $(\Sigma, Q, \delta, q_I, \Omega)$ where: (i) Σ is a ranked alphabet. (ii) Q is a finite set of states. (iii) δ is a map from $Q \times dom(\Sigma)$ to $B^+(\{1, ..., ar(\Sigma)\} \times Q)$, where $\delta(q, a) \in B^+(\{1, \ldots, \Sigma(a)\} \times Q)$ for each $a \in \Sigma$ and $q \in Q$. (iv) $q_I \in Q$ is an initial state. (v) Ω is a map from Q to natural numbers called* priorities. *A run-tree of an APT over a Σ-labeled tree T is a $(dom(T) \times Q)$-labeled tree R satisfying (i) $\varepsilon \in dom(R)$ and $R(\varepsilon) = (\varepsilon, q_I)$, and (ii) for every $\beta \in dom(R)$ with $R(\beta) = (\alpha, q)$ and $sat(\{(i, q') \mid \exists j.R(\beta j) = (\alpha i, q')\}, \delta(q, T(\alpha))) = \mathbf{true}$. A run-tree R is* accepting *if, for every infinite path of R, the largest priority of automaton states occurring infinitely often on the path is even. An APT $\mathcal{A}$* accepts *T if there exists an accepting run-tree of $\mathcal{A}$ over T.*

Example 2. Consider APT $\mathcal{A}_1 = (\Sigma = \{\mathtt{a} \mapsto 2, \mathtt{b} \mapsto 1, \mathtt{c} \mapsto 0\}, \{q_0, q_1\}, \delta, q_0, \Omega)$ where: $\delta(q_0, \mathtt{a}) = \delta(q_1, \mathtt{a}) = (1, q_0) \wedge (2, q_0) \quad \delta(q_0, \mathtt{b}) = \delta(q_1, \mathtt{b}) = (1, q_1)$
$\delta(q_0, \mathtt{c}) = \delta(q_1, \mathtt{c}) = \mathbf{true} \quad \Omega(q_0) = 0 \quad \Omega(q_1) = 1$
$\mathcal{A}_1$ accepts a Σ-labeled ranked tree T if and only if every path of T contains only finitely many $\mathtt{b}$. This property cannot be expressed by any non-deterministic Büchi tree automaton [20] or weak APT; note that the class of languages accepted by weak APT is a proper subclass of those accepted by non-deterministic Büchi automata [13].

APT Model Checking and Kobayashi and Ong's Type System
The *APT model checking problem of HORS* is, given a HORS $\mathcal{G}$ and an APT $\mathcal{A}$, the problem of checking whether $\mathcal{A}$ accepts $[\![\mathcal{G}]\!]$. Following [16], we assume (without loss of generality) that $[\![\mathcal{G}]\!]$ does not contain $\bot$.

Kobayashi and Ong [9] reduced the APT model checking problem above to a type checking problem (or, a type derivation game). We briefly review their reduction. See [9] for more details. We fix an APT $\mathcal{A} = (\Sigma, Q, \delta, q_0, \Omega)$ below.

Definition 3. *Let q and m range over the set Q of states and the set of priorities (i.e., $codom(\Omega)$). The set of types is defined by:*

$$\theta \text{ (types) } ::= q \mid \sigma \to \theta \qquad \sigma \text{ (intersections) } ::= \bigwedge\{(\theta_1, m_1), ..., (\theta_k, m_k)\}$$

The binary relation $\theta :: \kappa$ is defined by:

$$\frac{}{q :: \mathtt{o}} \qquad \frac{\theta :: \kappa_2 \quad \forall i \in \{1, \ldots, k\}.\theta_i :: \kappa_1}{(\bigwedge\{(\theta_1, m_1), ..., (\theta_k, m_k)\} \to \theta) :: (\kappa_1 \to \kappa_2)}$$

Intuitively, the type q describes a tree that is accepted by $\mathcal{A}$ from state q. The type $\bigwedge\{(\theta_1, m_1), ..., (\theta_k, m_k)\} \to \theta$ describes a function that takes an argument of types $\theta_1, \ldots, \theta_k$ and returns a value of type θ. The priority m_i represents the largest priority in the path from the root of the tree generated by the return value to the position where the argument is used as a value of type θ_i. We often write $\bigwedge_{i\in\{1,\ldots,k\}}(\theta_i, m_i)$ for $\bigwedge\{(\theta_1, m_1), \ldots, (\theta_k, m_k)\}$. We extend the priority function Ω on states to that on types by: $\Omega(\sigma \to \theta) = \Omega(\theta)$.

The type judgment relation $\Gamma \vdash_{\mathcal{A}} t : \theta$ is defined by:

$$\frac{}{x : (\theta, \Omega(\theta)) \vdash_{\mathcal{A}} x : \theta} \qquad \frac{\begin{array}{c} sat(\{(i, q_{ij}) \mid i \in \{1, \ldots, n\}, j \in J_i\}, \delta(q, a)) = \mathbf{true} \\ m_{ij} = \max(\Omega(q_{ij}), \Omega(q)) \text{ for each } i, j \end{array}}{\emptyset \vdash_{\mathcal{A}} a : \bigwedge_{j\in J_1}(q_{1j}, m_{1j}) \to \cdots \to \bigwedge_{j \in J_n}(q_{nj}, m_{nj}) \to q}$$

$$\frac{\begin{array}{c} \Gamma_0 \vdash_{\mathcal{A}} t_0 : \bigwedge_{i\in I}(\theta_i, m_i) \to \theta \\ \Gamma_i \vdash_{\mathcal{A}} t_1 : \theta_i \text{ for each } i \in I \end{array}}{\Gamma_0 \cup \bigcup_{i\in I}(\Gamma_i \Uparrow m_i) \vdash_{\mathcal{A}} t_0 t_1 : \theta} \qquad \frac{\begin{array}{c} \Gamma, x : \bigwedge_{i\in I}(\theta_i, m_i) \vdash_{\mathcal{A}} t : \theta \\ I \subseteq J \qquad \theta_i :: \kappa \end{array}}{\Gamma \vdash_{\mathcal{A}} (\lambda x : \kappa . t) : \bigwedge_{i\in J}(\theta_i, m_i) \to \theta}$$

Here, Γ is a set of type bindings of the form $x : (\theta, m)$ (where non-terminals are treated as variables). The operation $\Gamma \Uparrow m$ is defined by:

$$\Gamma \Uparrow m := \{F : (\theta, \max(m, m')) \mid F : (\theta, m') \in \Gamma\}.$$

The type judgment relation above induces the following parity game. A parity game [3] is a two-player game between a player $\exists$ and an opponent $\forall$ where each position of the game is associated with a priority, and the player wins an infinite play if the largest priority visited infinitely often is even. The edges $E_\exists$ and $E_\forall$ below represents the possible moves of the player and the opponent respectively.

Definition 4. *For a HORS $\mathcal{G} = (\Sigma, \mathcal{N}, \mathcal{R}, S)$ and an APT $\mathcal{A}$, the parity game $\mathbf{PG}_{\mathcal{G},\mathcal{A}}$ is $(V_\forall, V_\exists, v_0, E_\forall \cup E_\exists, \Omega)$, where $v_0 = (S, q_I, \Omega(q_I))$ and:*

$$V_\exists = \{(F, \theta, m) \mid F \in dom(\mathcal{N}), \theta :: \mathcal{N}(F), m \in dom(\Omega)\}$$
$$V_\forall = \{\Gamma \mid dom(\Gamma) \subseteq dom(\mathcal{N}), \forall F : (\theta, m) \in \Gamma. \theta :: \mathcal{N}(F)\}$$
$$E_\exists = \{((F, \theta, m), \Gamma) \mid \Gamma \vdash_{\mathcal{A}} \mathcal{R}(F) : \theta\} \quad E_\forall = \{(\Gamma, (F, \theta, m)) \mid F : (\theta, m) \in \Gamma\}$$

We write $\vdash_{\mathcal{A}} \mathcal{G}$ if Player $\exists$ has a winning strategy for $\mathbf{PG}_{\mathcal{G},\mathcal{A}}$.

In the game above, Player $\exists$ tries to show that the start symbol S has type q_I, and Opponent $\forall$ tries to disprove it. In the position (F, θ, m), the player must show why F has type θ by providing Γ such that $\Gamma \vdash \mathcal{R}(F) : \theta$.

The model checking problem for HORS is reduced to the parity game above.

Theorem 1. *[9] $[\![\mathcal{G}]\!]$ is accepted by $\mathcal{A}$ if and only if $\vdash_{\mathcal{A}} \mathcal{G}$.*

Example 3. Recall $\mathcal{G}_1$ in Example 1 and $\mathcal{A}_1$ in Example 2. Assume that the parity game is $(V_\exists, V_\forall, E, v_0, \Omega)$. One memoryless winning strategy for player $\exists$ is a (partial) map from $V_\exists$ to $V_\forall$, $\{(S, q_0, p) \mapsto \Gamma, (F, \theta, p) \mapsto \Gamma\}$ where $\theta = (q_0, 0) \wedge (q_1, 1) \to q_0$ and $\Gamma = \{F : (\theta, 0)\}$. Player $\exists$ wins because the game continues indefinitely and the maximum priority is 0.

3 Practical APT Model Checking Algorithm

Our algorithm is an extension of Kobayashi's algorithm for (deterministic) trivial automata model checking [8] that has been successfully used in the state-of-the-art model checker TRecS [8]. We extract candidates of types needed for constructing a winning strategy for the parity game $\mathbf{PG}_{\mathcal{G},\mathcal{A}}$, by partially reducing HORS and checking how each non-terminal is used in the partial reduction sequence. We then check whether a winning strategy can be constructed by using the type candidates. The type extraction phase is based on Kobayashi's algorithm [8], but has been extended to deal with priorities and alternations of the transition function. (Deterministic trivial automata are subclasses of APT, where every state has priority 0 and the image of the transition function is restricted to a formula of the form $(1, q_{i_1}) \wedge \cdots (k, q_{i_k})$.)

The overall structure of the (semi-)algorithm is given in Figure 1, which takes a HORS $\mathcal{G}$ and APT $\mathcal{A}$, and returns **true** if $\vdash_{\mathcal{A}} \mathcal{G}$ holds, and diverges otherwise. The whole algorithm runs two instances of the semi-algorithm concurrently, one for the input $(\mathcal{G}, \mathcal{A})$ and the other for $(\mathcal{G}, \overline{\mathcal{A}})$ where $\overline{\mathcal{A}}$ is an APT that accepts the complement of the tree language accepted by $\mathcal{A}$. Each step is described below.

$\mathcal{C} \Leftarrow$
  initial configuration tree
loop
  $\mathcal{C} \Leftarrow \mathit{Expand}(\mathcal{C})$
  $\Delta \Leftarrow \mathit{TypeCands}(\mathcal{C})$
  $\mathcal{J} \Leftarrow \mathit{EnumJudgments}(\Delta)$
  $P \Leftarrow \mathit{ConstructPG}(\mathcal{J})$
  if there is a winning strategy for player $\exists$ for P
    return true
end loop

Fig. 1. Pseudo code for the algorithm

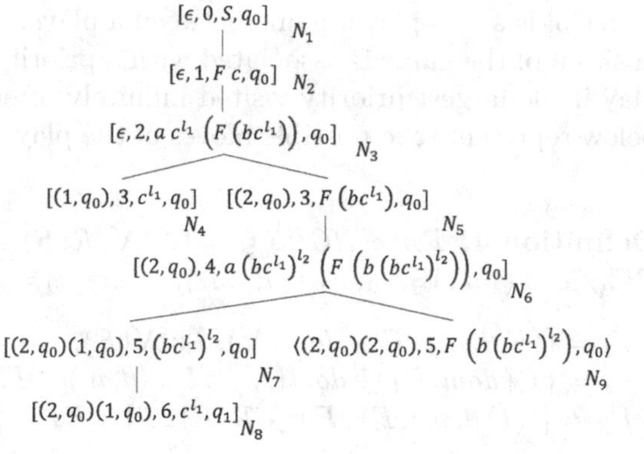

Fig. 2. A configuration tree for $\mathcal{G}_1$ and $\mathcal{A}_1$. $l_1 = \langle \epsilon, 1, 1 \rangle, l_2 = \langle (2, q_0), 3, 1 \rangle$

Construction of Configuration Trees. We introduce configuration trees, which describe how the start symbol S can be reduced to generate a tree, and how the (partially) generated tree can be accepted by the automaton. A *configuration tree* is a labeled tree consisting of nodes of the form (β, ℓ, t, q, b) where: (i) β is a sequence of pairs consisting of a natural number and a state of $\mathcal{A}$; (ii) ℓ is a natural number; (iii) t is a term of sort o; (iv) q is a state of $\mathcal{A}$; and (v) b is a boolean value that represents whether the node has been expanded ($b =$ **true**) or not ($b =$ **false**). We write $\langle \beta, \ell, t, q \rangle$ and $[\beta, \ell, t, q]$ for $(\beta, \ell, t, q, \mathbf{false})$

and $(\beta, \ell, t, q, \mathbf{true})$ and call them *open nodes* and *closed nodes* respectively. Intuitively, the label (β, ℓ, t, q, b) means that t is expected to generate a tree accepted from state q. The elements β and ℓ are used to uniquely identify a node of a configuration tree.

The *initial configuration tree* is the singleton tree $\langle \epsilon, 0, S, q_0 \rangle$, which represents the fact that S is expected to generate a tree that is accepted by $\mathcal{A}$ from q_0.

The sub-procedure *Expand* (on the third line in Figure 1) applies the following reduction rules in a finite number of steps (in a fair manner, so that every open node is eventually reduced in some iteration of the loop).

$$\frac{\mathcal{R}(F) = \lambda x_1. \cdots \lambda x_k.s}{\begin{array}{l} E[\langle \beta, \ell, F\, t_1 \cdots t_k, q \rangle] \rhd \\ \qquad E[[\beta, \ell, F\, t_1 \cdots t_k, q] \langle \beta, \ell+1, [t_1^{\langle \beta, \ell, k \rangle}/x_1, \ldots, t_k^{\langle \beta, \ell, 1 \rangle}/x_k]s, q \rangle] \end{array}}$$

$$\frac{\mathbf{Atoms}(\delta(q,a)) = \{(1, q_{1,1}), \ldots, (1, q_{1,n_1}), \ldots, (k, q_{k,1}), \ldots, (k, q_{k,n_k})\}}{\begin{array}{l} E[\langle \beta, \ell, a\, t_1 \cdots t_k, q \rangle] \rhd E[[\beta, \ell, a\, t_1 \cdots t_k, q] \\ \qquad \langle \beta(1, q_{1,1}), \ell+1, t_1^{\langle \beta, \ell, k \rangle}, q_{1,1} \rangle \cdots \langle \beta(1, q_{1,n_1}), \ell+1, t_1^{\langle \beta, \ell, k \rangle}, q_{1,n_1} \rangle \\ \qquad \ldots \langle \beta(k, q_{k,1}), \ell+1, t_k^{\langle \beta, \ell, 1 \rangle}, q_{k,1} \rangle \cdots \langle \beta(k, q_{k,n_k}), \ell+1, t_k^{\langle \beta, \ell, 1 \rangle}, q_{k,n_k} \rangle] \end{array}}$$

E denotes a tree context, defined by: $E ::= [\,] \mid a\, \mathcal{C}_1 \cdots \mathcal{C}_{i-1}\, E\, \mathcal{C}_{i+1} \cdots \mathcal{C}_n$. $\mathbf{Atoms}(\delta(q,a))$ denotes the set of atomic formulas of the form (i, q') in $\delta(q,a)$. Each term is annotated with labels of the form $\langle \beta, \ell, k \rangle$, which represent the origin of the term. For example, $s^{\langle \beta, \ell, k \rangle}$ means that s occurred as the k-th *rightmost* argument of the term in a node $[\beta, \ell, t, q]$. We often omit unimportant labels, so we may just write $t^{\langle \beta, \ell, i \rangle}$ for $((t^{\langle \beta', \ell', i' \rangle})^{\langle \beta, \ell, i \rangle})^{\langle \beta'', \ell'', i'' \rangle}$. In the second rule, a child node is created for every $(i, q') \in \mathbf{Atoms}(\delta(q,a))$, irrespectively of the shape of the formula. For example, if $\delta(q,a) = ((1, q_1) \wedge (2, q_2)) \vee ((1, q_1) \wedge (2, q_3))$, then a child node is created for each of $(1, q_1)$, $(2, q_2)$, and $(2, q_3)$. The shape of the formula $\delta(q,a)$ is taken into account in the type extraction phase. This design makes the construction of configuration trees deterministic up to the choice of expanded nodes, and postpones the treatment of non-determinism incurred by the transition function δ to the type extraction phase.

For example, a configuration tree for $\mathcal{G}_1$ and $\mathcal{A}_1$, obtained by reducing the initial configuration tree in 8 steps, is shown in Figure 2.

Extraction of Type Candidates. (procedure *TypeCands*) For each node $N = (\beta_N, \ell_N, t_N, q_N, b_N)$ of $\mathcal{C}$, we define the set Ξ_N of sets of type bindings of the form $\langle \beta', \ell', i \rangle : (\theta, m)$ or $\langle \beta', \ell', i \rangle : \alpha$ by:

$$\Xi''_N = \begin{cases} \{\langle \beta', \ell', i \rangle : \alpha \mid s^{\langle \beta', \ell', i \rangle} \text{ occurs in } t_N\} & \text{if } b_N = \mathbf{false} \\ \Xi_{N'} \quad \text{if } t_N = F\, s_1 \cdots s_n \text{ and } N' \text{ is the (unique) child node of } N \\ \delta(q,a)[\Xi_{N_1}/(i_1, q_{j_1}), \ldots, \Xi_{N_k}/(i_k, q_{j_k})] & \text{if } b_N = \mathbf{true} \text{ and} \\ \quad \text{if } t_N = a\, s_1 \cdots s_n \text{ and } \mathbf{Atoms}(\delta(q,a)) = \{(i_1, q_{j_1}), \ldots, (i_k, q_{j_k})\} \end{cases}$$

$$\begin{aligned}
&\Xi'_N = \\
&\quad \{\Delta \cup \{\langle\beta',\ell',i\rangle : (\sigma_1 \to \cdots \to \sigma_k \to q, \Omega(q)) \mid t_N = s^{\langle\beta',\ell',i\rangle} u_1 \cdots u_k \text{ and} \\
&\quad \sigma_i = \Delta(\langle\beta_N,\ell_N,k+1-i\rangle) \text{ for each } i \in \{1,\ldots,k\}\} \mid \Delta \in \Xi''_N \Uparrow \Omega(q)\} \\
&\Xi_N = \{\{\langle\beta',\ell',i\rangle : (\theta,m) \in \Delta \mid \ell' \text{ occurs in } N\} \mid \Delta \in \Xi'_N\}
\end{aligned}$$

Intuitively, $\langle\beta',\ell',i\rangle : (\theta,m) \in \Xi_N$ means that the term labeled by $\langle\beta',\ell',i\rangle$ (i.e., the term that occurs in the i-th rightmost argument of the term in the node indexed by (β',ℓ')) is used as a value of type θ in the subtree rooted by N, and that m is the largest priority in the path from the node (β',ℓ') to the node where the term is used as a value of type θ. In the definition above, $\Xi \Uparrow m = \{\Delta \Uparrow m \mid \Delta \in \Xi\}$, where $\Delta \Uparrow m = \{\langle\beta,\ell,i\rangle : (\theta,\max(m,m')) \mid \langle\beta,\ell,i\rangle : (\theta,m') \in \Delta\}$. The expression $\delta(q,a)[\Xi_{N_1}/(i_1,q_{j_1}),\ldots,\Xi_{N_k}/(i_k,q_{j_k})]$ represents the set obtained by replacing each atomic formula (i_m,q_{j_m}) with Ξ_{N_m}. Here, the formula consisting of Ξ_N is interpreted as a set of sets of type bindings by:

$$\begin{aligned}
&[\![\mathbf{true}]\!] = \{\emptyset\} \qquad [\![\mathbf{false}]\!] = \emptyset \qquad [\![\Xi_1 \vee \Xi_2]\!] = [\![\Xi_1]\!] \cup [\![\Xi_2]\!] \\
&[\![\Xi_1 \wedge \Xi_2]\!] = \{\Delta_1 \cup \Delta_2 \mid \Delta_1 \in [\![\Xi_1]\!], \Delta_2 \in [\![\Xi_2]\!]\}
\end{aligned}$$

Ξ''_N describes type bindings inherited from child nodes, and Ξ'_N describes those obtained by adding information on how head terms in the current node is used. Ξ_N is obtained from Ξ'_N by filtering out irrelevant type bindings.

Finally, *TypeCands*($\mathcal{C}$) returns:

$$\begin{aligned}
\{F : \theta \mid \sigma_i = \Xi_N(\langle\beta,\ell,k+1-i\rangle), \theta' = \sigma_1 \to \cdots \to \sigma_k \to q, \text{ and } \theta \in \mathit{Erase}(\theta') \\
\text{for some } N = (\beta,\ell,F\,u_1 \,\cdots\, u_k,q,b) \text{ and for each } i \in \{1,\cdots,k\}\ \}
\end{aligned}$$

Here, *Erase*(θ) [8] is the function to remove type variables, given by:

$$\begin{aligned}
&\mathit{Erase}(q) = \{q\} \\
&\mathit{Erase}((\tau_1,m_1) \wedge \cdots \wedge (\tau_k,m_k) \to \tau) = \mathit{Erase}((\tau_1,m_1) \wedge \cdots \wedge (\tau_k,m_k) \wedge \alpha \to \tau) \\
&= \{(\theta_1,m_1) \wedge \cdots \wedge (\theta_k,m_k) \to \theta \mid \theta_i \in \mathit{Erase}'(\tau_i), \theta \in \mathit{Erase}(\tau)\} \\
&\mathit{Erase}'(\tau) = \begin{cases} \mathit{Erase}(\tau) \cup \{\top\} & \text{if } \tau \text{ contains a type variable} \\ \mathit{Erase}(\tau) & \text{otherwise} \end{cases}
\end{aligned}$$

Example 4. Let $\mathcal{C}$ be the configuration tree in Figure 2. For each N, Ξ_N is given as follows.[1]

$$\begin{aligned}
&\Xi_{N_9} = \{\{l_2 : \alpha, l_1 : \alpha\}\}\ \Xi_{N_8} = \{\{l_1 : (q_1,1)\}\}\ \Xi_{N_7} = \{\{l_2 : (q_0,0), l_1 : (q_1,1)\}\} \\
&\Xi_{N_6} = \Xi_{N_5} = \{\{l_2 : (q_0,0), l_1 : (q_1,1), l_2 : \alpha, l_1 : \alpha\}\} \\
&\Xi_{N_4} = \{\{l_1 : (q_0,0)\}\}\ \Xi_{N_3} = \{\{l_1 : (q_1,1), l_1 : \alpha, l_1 : (q_0,0)\}\} \\
&\Xi_{N_2} = \{\{l_1 : (q_1,1), l_1 : \alpha, l_1 : (q_0,0)\}\}\ \Xi_{N_1} = \{\{\}\}
\end{aligned}$$

From N_1, N_2, N_5 and N_9, we obtain type candidates:

$$\mathit{TypeCands}(\mathcal{C}) = \{S : q_0,\ F : \top \to q_0,\ F : (q0,0) \to q0,\ F : (q0,0) \wedge (q1,1) \to q0\}$$

[1] Each Ξ_N is a singleton set because $\mathcal{A}_1$ is deterministic.

Construction of the Parity Game. The procedure *ConstructPG*(Δ) constructs the subgame (denoted by $\mathbf{PG}_{\mathcal{G},\mathcal{A},\Delta}$) of the parity game $\mathbf{PG}_{\mathcal{G},\mathcal{A}}$, obtained by replacing $E_\exists$ with:

$$E'_\exists = \{((F,\theta,m),\Gamma) \mid \Gamma \vdash_{\mathcal{A}} \mathcal{R}(F) : \theta \wedge \forall (F:(\theta,m')\in\Gamma).F:\theta \in \Delta\}$$

We can use a standard algorithm [6,19] to check the existence of a winning strategy for the parity game.

Example 5. Let Δ be the set of type candidates in Example 4. We obtain the following type judgments from Δ:

$$F:(\top \to q_0, 0) \vdash \mathcal{R}(S):q_0 \qquad F:((q_0,0)\to q_0, 0) \vdash \mathcal{R}(S):q_0$$
$$F:((q_0,0)\wedge(q_1,1)\to q_0,0) \vdash \mathcal{R}(S):q_0$$
$$F:((q_0,0)\wedge(q_1,1)\to q_0,0) \vdash \mathcal{R}(F):(q_0,0)\wedge(q_1,1)\to q_0$$

Then, from these type judgments, we obtain the following parity game.

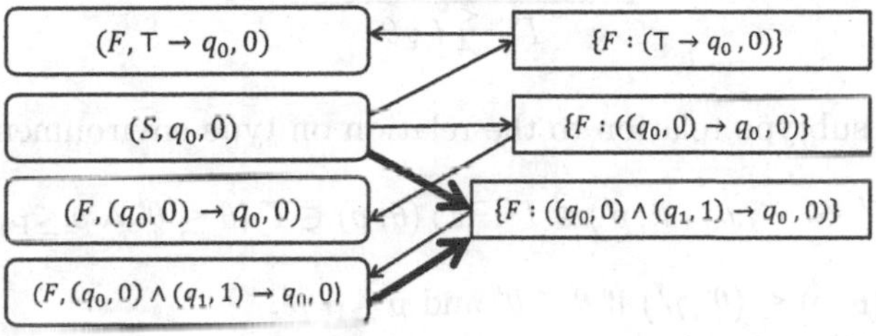

Here, rounded rectangles show Player's positions, and ordinary rectangles show Opponent's positions. The position $(S, q_0, 0)$ is the initial position and the thick arrows show a winning strategy of Player. □

Our algorithm is sound and complete in the following sense.

Theorem 2. *The procedure in Figure 1 eventually terminates and outputs* **true** *if and only if* $[\![\mathcal{G}]\!]$ *is accepted by* $\mathcal{A}$.

4 Optimization

The basic algorithm described in Section 3 still suffers from the blow-up of the size of the parity game $\mathbf{PG}_{\mathcal{G},\mathcal{A},\Delta}$. In this section, we introduce a novel subtype relation based on priorities, and then discuss two optimizations based on it.

Definition 5 (sub-priority and subtype relations). *The sub-priority relation* $\leq_{\mathbf{P}}$ *and the subtype relation* $\leq$ *are defined by (where* $\leq_{\mathbb{N}}$ *is the standard inequality relation on natural numbers):*

$$\frac{p \leq_{\mathbb{N}} p'}{2p \leq_{\mathbf{P}} 2p'} \qquad \frac{p \leq_{\mathbb{N}} p'}{2p'+1 \leq_{\mathbf{P}} 2p+1} \qquad \frac{}{2p+1 \leq_{\mathbf{P}} 2p'}$$

$$\frac{}{q \leq q} \qquad \frac{\theta \leq \theta' \qquad \forall i \in I.\exists j \in J.(\theta'_j \leq \theta_i \wedge p'_j \leq_{\mathbf{P}} p_i)}{\bigwedge_{i\in I}(\theta_i,p_i)\to\theta \leq \bigwedge_{j\in J}(\theta'_j,p'_j)\to\theta'}$$

For priorities, $\cdots \leq_{\mathbf{P}} 3 \leq_{\mathbf{P}} 1 \leq_{\mathbf{P}} 0 \leq_{\mathbf{P}} 2 \leq_{\mathbf{P}} 4 \leq_{\mathbf{P}} \cdots$ holds. Intuitively, $p \leq_{\mathbf{P}} p'$ means that the priority p' is more beneficial than p for the player of the parity game. The subtype relation is standard except for the condition on priorities. The relation $\theta \leq \theta'$ means that a value of type θ may be safely regarded as a value of type θ'. For example, $(q_1, 2) \to q_0 \leq (q_1, 0) \to q_0$ holds, since $(q_1, p) \to q_0$ means that an argument is used as a value of type q_1 when the largest priority visited is p, and it is safe to assume that p is 0 when p is actually 2, in the sense that if the largest priority in an infinite path is even under the assumption that $p = 0$, then that is also the case under the assumption that $p = 2$. The converse does not hold: for example, consider an infinite sequence of priorities $(p\,1)^\omega = p\,1\,p\,1 \cdots$. The largest priority is even if p is assumed to be 2, but that is odd (and the player loses) if p is actually 0.

We write $\Gamma \vdash^{\leq}_{\mathcal{A}} t : \theta$ if it is derivable from the rules for $\Gamma \vdash_{\mathcal{A}} t : \theta$ (with $\vdash_{\mathcal{A}}$ replaced by $\vdash^{\leq}_{\mathcal{A}}$) and the following subsumption rule:

$$\frac{\Gamma \vdash^{\leq}_{\mathcal{A}} t : \theta' \qquad \theta' \leq \theta}{\Gamma \vdash^{\leq}_{\mathcal{A}} t : \theta}$$

We extend the subtype relation to the relation on type environments by:

$$\Gamma \leq \Gamma' \iff \forall x : (\theta', p') \in \Gamma'. \exists x : (\theta, p) \in \Gamma. (\theta \leq \theta' \land p \leq_{\mathbf{P}} p').$$

We also write $(\theta, p) \leq (\theta', p')$ if $\theta \leq \theta'$ and $p \leq_{\mathbf{P}} p'$.

We write $\mathbf{PG}^{\leq}_{\mathcal{G},\mathcal{A}}$ for the parity game obtained by by replacing $\vdash_{\mathcal{A}}$ in the definition of $\mathbf{PG}_{\mathcal{G},\mathcal{A}}$ (Definition 4) with $\vdash^{\leq}_{\mathcal{A}}$, and write $\vdash^{\leq}_{\mathcal{A}} \mathcal{G}$ if there is a winning strategy for $\mathbf{PG}^{\leq}_{\mathcal{G},\mathcal{A}}$. The following theorem states the soundness of our notion of subtyping. The proof is almost the same as the proof of the soundness of Kobayashi and Ong's type system (without subtyping) [9]: By using the winning strategy for $\mathbf{PG}^{\leq}_{\mathcal{G},\mathcal{A}}$, we can construct an accepting run-tree of $\mathcal{A}$ over $[\![\mathcal{G}]\!]$.

Theorem 3. *If* $\vdash^{\leq}_{\mathcal{A}} \mathcal{G}$, *then* $[\![\mathcal{G}]\!]$ *is accepted by* $\mathcal{A}$.

We discuss two optimizations below.

Type Normalization Optimization $\mathbf{opt}_{\mathbf{TN}}$. A type $\bigwedge_{i \in \{1,\ldots,n\}} (\theta_i, p_i) \to \theta$ is *normalized* if for each i, there is no $j \neq i$ such that $(\theta_j, p_j) \leq (\theta_i, p_i)$. The function *normalize* on types is defined by:

$$nf(\theta) = \begin{cases} q & \text{if } \theta = q \\ \bigwedge\{(\theta_i, m_i) \in S' \mid & \\ \quad \neg\exists(\theta_j, m_j) \in S'.(\theta_j, m_j) \leq (\theta_i, m_i) \land (\theta_i, m_i) \not\leq (\theta_j, m_j)\} \to nf(\theta_0) & \\ \quad \text{if } \theta = \bigwedge S \to \theta_0 \text{ and } S' = \{(nf(\theta_i), m) \mid (\theta_i, m) \in S\} & \end{cases}$$

We extend the normalization operation nf pointwise to that on type environments by $nf(\Delta) = \{(F : nf(\theta) \mid (F : \theta) \in \Delta\}$ and $nf(\Gamma) = \{(F :$

$(nf(\theta), p) \mid (F : (\theta, p)) \in \Gamma\}$. Now, the optimized algorithm $\mathbf{opt_{TN}}$ is obtained by replacing the edge set $E'_{\exists}$ of $\mathbf{PG}_{\mathcal{G},\mathcal{A},\Delta}$ in Section 3 with:

$$E''_{\exists} = \{((F, \theta, m), \Gamma) \mid \Gamma \vdash^{\leq}_{\mathcal{A}} \mathcal{R}(F) : \theta \wedge \forall (F : (\theta, m') \in \Gamma).F : \theta \in nf(\Delta)\}.$$

We write $\mathbf{PG}^{\leq}_{\mathcal{G},\mathcal{A},\Delta}$ for the resulting parity game.

Type Environment Reduction Optimization $\mathbf{opt_{ER}}$. We remove weaker moves of the player from the parity game $\mathbf{PG}^{\leq}_{\mathcal{G},\mathcal{A},\Delta}$. For example, if there are two judgments $F' : (q_0, 0) \vdash^{\leq}_{\mathcal{A}} \mathcal{R}(F) : \theta$ and $F' : (q_0, 2) \vdash^{\leq}_{\mathcal{A}} \mathcal{R}(F) : \theta$, and the player must provide a witness for F having type θ, then choosing the environment $F' : (q_0, 2)$ is more advantageous since it has a larger even priority (so that it is more likely that the largest priority becomes even). Based on this observation, we define the reduced parity game $\mathbf{PGR}^{\leq}_{\mathcal{G},\mathcal{A},\Delta}$ by replacing $E''_{\exists}$ with:

$$E''_{\exists} = \{((F, \theta, m), \Gamma) \mid \Gamma \text{ is maximal with respect to } \leq \text{ among those that satisfy } \Gamma \vdash^{\leq}_{\mathcal{A}} \mathcal{R}(F) : \theta \text{ and } \forall (F : (\theta, m') \in \Gamma).F : \theta \in nf(\Delta)\}.$$

5 Applications

We discuss two applications of the full APT model checking (that cannot be handled by trivial automata or weak APT) to automated verification of functional programs.

Resource Usage Verification. The goal of resource usage verification [5,8] is to check that a given program accesses external resources (like files, networks, etc.) in a valid manner. For file-manipulating programs, a typical goal is to check that a file is eventually closed, and that no more access occurs afterwards. For example, consider the following OCaml-like (call-by-value) program.

```
let rec f x = let c = read x in if c=EOF then close x else f x
in f (open_in "foo")
```

It first defines a recursive function `f`, which takes a file pointer `x` as an argument, reads `x`, and depending on the character read, either closes `x` or recursively calls itself. The program then opens the file "foo" and calls `f`. For this program, the goal of resource usage verification would be to check that the file (pointer) is indeed used as a read-only file: the file is eventually closed, it is only read before being closed, and it is never accessed after being closed.

Kobayashi [8] presented a reduction from resource usage verification to a model checking problem for HORS. The idea was to transform a program into a HORS that generates a tree representing all the possible resource access sequences. For example, the above program can be transformed to the following HORS $\mathcal{G}_{\texttt{file}}$.

$$S \to F\ \texttt{end} \qquad F\ k \to \texttt{r}\ (\texttt{br}\ (\texttt{c}\ k)\ (F\ k))$$

Here, the second rule corresponds to the recursive definition of `f`. The parameter k is a kind of continuation parameter, which represents how the file "foo" is accessed after the function returns. The non-terminal symbols `r` and `c` represent read and close operations respectively, `br` represents a non-deterministic branch, and `end` represents program termination. The branch "`if c=EOF then ... else ...`" has been replaced by the non-deterministic branch (represented by `br`). The tree generated by the HORS $\mathcal{G}_{\mathtt{file}}$ is shown on the righthand side.

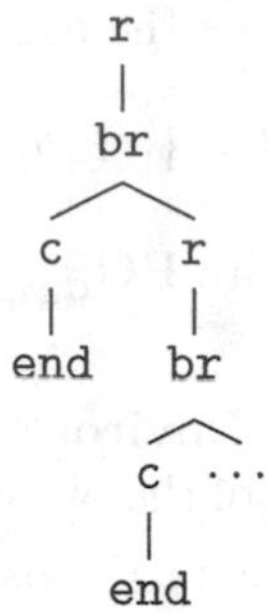

As expected, the tree represents the possible sequences of events (including read/write operations, branches, and termination) of the source program. By applying the trivial automata model checking to the HORS [8], one can verify the following properties of the source program: (i) The file is only read before a close operation (which corresponds to the property on the tree: "Only `r` and `br` may occur above `c`"). (ii) No file access occurs after the close operation. (iii) The file is closed before the program terminates. With the combination of the transformation above and trivial automata model checking, however, one cannot verify that the program eventually closes the file and terminates, for two reasons: First, to ensure that, one needs to make the assumption that the end of file (`EOF`) is eventually reached. Secondly, it is a liveness property, which cannot be verified by using trivial automata model checking. To address the first issue, we refine the transformation into HORS as follows.

$$S \rightarrow F\ \mathtt{d}\ \mathtt{end} \qquad F\ x\ k \rightarrow \mathtt{call}\ (\mathit{Read}\ (C\ x\ k))$$
$$C\ x\ k\ b \rightarrow b\ (\mathtt{c}\ k)\ (F\ x\ k)) \qquad \mathit{Read}\ k \rightarrow \mathtt{br}\ (\mathtt{r\_eof}\ (k\ \mathit{True}))\ (\mathtt{r}\ (k\ \mathit{False}))$$
$$\mathit{True}\ x\ y \rightarrow x \qquad \mathit{False}\ x\ y \rightarrow y$$

The read operation is now represented as the function *Read*, which returns whether EOF is read (through the continuation k), and at the same time records it by creating a node `r_eof` or `r`. The function F calls *Read*, passing to it the continuation $C\ x\ k$. We have also added a terminal symbol `call` to the rule of F to detect possible divergence involving no read operations. The tree generated by the refined HORS $\mathcal{G}'_{\mathtt{file}}$ is shown on the righthand side.
Now, in order to verify "As long as it is impossible to read a file infinitely often without reading the end of the file, the program eventually closes the file and terminates", it suffices to check "in any path of the tree, either `r` occurs infinitely often or both `c` and `end` occur", which can be performed by the APT model checking.

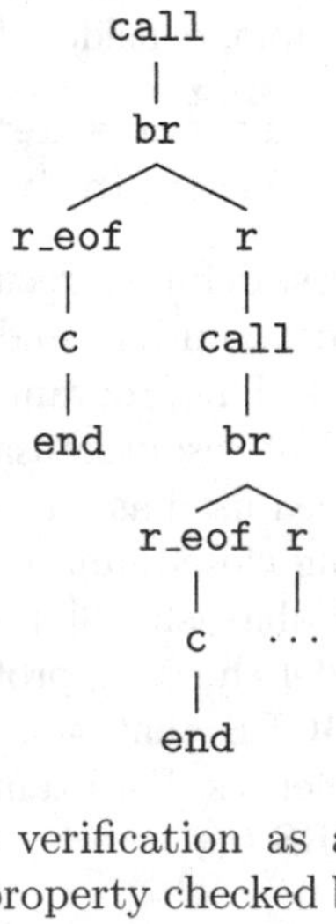

Remark 1. Lester et al. [12] also discussed resource usage verification as an application of the weak APT model checking of HORS. The property checked by

their method was not convincing enough: when applied to the above example, they only check that c occurs eventually if the branches of br are chosen in a fair manner.

HMTT Verification. An HMTT (higher order, multi-parameter tree transducer) [11] is a tree-processing, higher-order functional program. The aim of HMTT verification [11,22] is to check that a given HMTT satisfies a given input/output specification. The idea of their method [11,22] was to transform a given HMTT to a HORS that generates a tree that contains all the possible outputs of the HMTT, and to check that the tree contains only valid outputs. Since their method used trivial automata model checking, however, they could not check properties like "Given a *finite* input, does the HMTT always produces a *finite* output tree?" and "Is the HMTT productive, in the sense that it never diverges without producing any ouptut?" By using APT model checking and modifying the transformation of HMTT into HORS accordingly (so that we can talk about the finiteness of inputs), we can verify the properties mentioned above.

6 Experiments

We have implemented a full APT model checker based on the algorithm and optimizations in Sections 3 and 4. The implementation is still naive and we have not yet applied some of the optimizations (for trivial automata model checking) reported in [8], but we have confirmed that our algorithm works at least for small inputs (note that even for them, the naive algorithm [9] is not runnable at all).

Table 1 shows selected experimental results. The experiments were conducted under Ubuntu Linux 12.10 on a machine with Intel(R) Xeon(R) 3.30 GHz CPU and 16 GB memory. The columns O, P, and R describe the order of HORS, the number of priorities of APT, and the expected output. The column "no-opt" shows the result for the plain algorithm in Section 3. The columns $\mathbf{opt}_{\mathbf{TN}}$, $\mathbf{opt}_{\mathbf{ER}}$, and $\mathbf{opt}_{\mathbf{TN}}\&\mathbf{opt}_{\mathbf{ER}}$ show the results for the two optimizations and their combination (for $\mathbf{opt}_{\mathbf{ER}}$, $nf(\Delta)$ in the definition of $E''_{\exists}$ in Section 4 has been replaced by Δ). The subcolumns J and T show the number of type judgments (i.e., the number of possible moves of the player) and the running time (in seconds) of the model checker.

We used four categories of benchmarks (separated by double lines). The first category is from Lester et al.'s benchmark programs; they can be expressed by weak APT. The second category contains applications to the resource usage verification, which have been obtained by modifying the benchmark programs in [8] to check liveness properties, according to Section 5. The third category comes from those to the HMTT verification [11,22] discussed in Section 5. Finally, the fourth category contains benchmarks for a larger number of priorities.

With the two optimizations, the model checker successfully terminated. It should be noted that our model checker terminates for loop-dj-2, which uses 5 priorities. For the first category of benchmarks, our model checker seems still slower than Lester et al.' model checker THORS [12].[2] We expect that this inefficiency is due to the naive implementation of the type extraction phase, rather than the extra overhead to deal with priorities.

The comparison between the columns "no-opt" and "$\mathbf{opt_{TN}}$" show the effectiveness of the first optimization. In particular, the performance for imperative, intercept, var-dwt, and loop-dj-2 have been drastically improved. On the other hand, the effectiveness of $\mathbf{opt_{ER}}$ has not been confirmed in the experiments. This may be because the size of inputs and the number of priorities are too small in the benchmark programs, and larger experiments are required to check the effectiveness of $\mathbf{opt_{ER}}$.

Table 1. Benchmark results

				no-opt		$\mathbf{opt_{TN}}$		$\mathbf{opt_{ER}}$		$\mathbf{opt_{TN}}$& $\mathbf{opt_{ER}}$	
name	O	P	R	J	T	J	T	J	T	J	T
imperative	3	2	yes	268	10.780	28	0.220	262	10.69	26	0.96
intercept	4	2	yes	-	TO	37	22.73	-	TO	37	25.2
lock1	2	1	yes	63	0.080	24	0.027	35	0.089	23	0.04
var-dwt	5	2	yes	-	TO	266	44.24	-	TO	74	44.0
file	2	2	yes	7	0.044	7	0.044	7	0.044	7	0.06
twofiles	4	2	yes	39	0.272	39	0.260	39	0.272	39	0.62
twofilexn	4	2	no	18	2.692	18	2.496	18	2.608	18	2.55
reverse	2	2	yes	9	0.020	9	0.016	9	0.024	9	0.24
bsort	2	2	yes	5	0.012	5	0.016	5	0.016	5	0.24
merge	1	2	yes	34	0.116	34	0.088	34	0.100	34	0.86
homrep	4	2	yes	84	0.284	58	0.108	84	0.369	58	0.98
gcalloc	2	3	yes	10	0.141	8	0.096	10	0.180	8	0.065
loop-dj-2	5	5	no	-	TO	82	0.201	-	TO	78	0.306

7 Related Work

Previous algorithms for APT model checking of HORS [16,4,9,18] have been developed for the purpose of showing the decidability and/or discussing the complexity of the model checking, and have been only of theoretical interest. As already mentioned, previous practical model checking algorithms for HORS have focused on trivial automata [8,7,15] or weak APT [12]. Broadbent et al. [2] also introduced a model-checking algorithm for collapsible pushdown systems, but they also considered only trivial automata. Our algorithm extends Kobayashi's algorithm [8] used in the state-of-the-art model checker TRecS. Lester et al.'s

[2] As the source code of THORS is not available, we cannot perform detailed comparison.

algorithm [12] also works in a similar manner. The extension of Kobayashi's algorithm based on Kobayashi and Ong's type system [9] as described in Section 3 may be considered a folklore, but we are the first to actually implement a practical APT model checker for HORS. That required a non-trivial notion of subtyping based on priorities, as discussed in Section 4.

Applications of trivial automata model checking of HORS to safety property verification of functional programs have been well studied recently [8,11,10,17,21]. There were however few studies of applications of APT model checking of HORS to liveness property verification, probably partly because of the lack of practical model checkers. The only exception was the work of Lester et al. [12], who discussed an application of the weak APT model checking of HORS to resource usage verification. As mentioned in Remark 1, the properties they considered (like "a liveness property is guaranteed if the left branch of br is eventually taken") were not satisfactory.

8 Conclusion

We have proposed a practical algorithm for the full APT model checking of HORS, and implemented a model checker. To our knowledge, this is the first practical APT model checker for HORS. In order to achieve the practical performance, we have introduced optimizations based on a novel subtyping relation that respects priorities. Experimental results suggest that our model checker works reasonably well for typical small inputs. We have also proposed applications of the APT model checking of HORS to automated verification of functional programs. Further optimization of our implementation is left for future work.

Acknowledgment. We thank anonymous referees for useful comments. This work was partially supported by Kakenhi 23220001 and the Mitsubishi Foundation.

References

1. Aehlig, K., de Miranda, J.G., Ong, C.-H.L.: The monadic second order theory of trees given by arbitrary level-two recursion schemes is decidable. In: Urzyczyn, P. (ed.) TLCA 2005. LNCS, vol. 3461, pp. 39–54. Springer, Heidelberg (2005)
2. Broadbent, C., Carayol, A., Hague, M., Serre, O.: A saturation method for collapsible pushdown systems. In: Czumaj, A., Mehlhorn, K., Pitts, A., Wattenhofer, R. (eds.) ICALP 2012, Part II. LNCS, vol. 7392, pp. 165–176. Springer, Heidelberg (2012)
3. Grädel, E., Thomas, W., Wilke, T. (eds.): Automata, Logics, and Infinite Games. LNCS, vol. 2500. Springer, Heidelberg (2002)
4. Hague, M., Murawski, A., Ong, C.-H.L., Serre, O.: Collapsible pushdown automata and recursion schemes. In: Proc. of LICS, pp. 452–461 (2008)
5. Igarashi, A., Kobayashi, N.: Resource usage analysis. ACM Trans. Prog. Lang. Syst. 27(2), 264–313 (2005)

6. Jurdziński, M.: Small progress measures for solving parity games. In: Reichel, H., Tison, S. (eds.) STACS 2000. LNCS, vol. 1770, pp. 290–301. Springer, Heidelberg (2000)
7. Kobayashi, N.: A practical linear time algorithm for trivial automata model checking of higher-order recursion schemes. In: Hofmann, M. (ed.) FOSSACS 2011. LNCS, vol. 6604, pp. 260–274. Springer, Heidelberg (2011)
8. Kobayashi, N.: Model checking higher-order programs. JACM 60(3) (2013)
9. Kobayashi, N., Ong, C.-H.L.: A type system equivalent to the modal mu-calculus model checking of higher-order recursion schemes. Summary appeared in Proceedings of LICS 2009 (2013) Available from the last author's web page
10. Kobayashi, N., Sato, R., Unno, H.: Predicate abstraction and CEGAR for higher-order model checking. In: Proc. of PLDI, pp. 222–233 (2011)
11. Kobayashi, N., Tabuchi, N., Unno, H.: Higher-order multi-parameter tree transducers and recursion schemes for program verification. In: Proc. of POPL, pp. 495–508 (2010)
12. Lester, M.M., Neatherway, R.P., Ong, C.-H.L., Ramsay, S.J.: Model checking liveness properties of higher-order functional programs. In: Proceedings of ML Workshop (2011)
13. Muller, D.E., Saoudi, A., Schupp, P.E.: Alternating automata. the weak monadic theory of the tree, and its complexity. In: Kott, L. (ed.) ICALP 1986. LNCS, vol. 226, pp. 275–283. Springer, Heidelberg (1986)
14. Muller, D.E., Saoudi, A., Schupp, P.E.: Alternating automata, the weak monadic theory of trees and its complexity. Theor. Comput. Sci. 97(2), 233–244 (1992)
15. Neatherway, R.P., Ramsay, S.J., Ong, C.-H.L.: A traversal-based algorithm for higher-order model checking. In: ACM SIGPLAN International Conference on Functional Programming (ICFP 2012), pp. 353–364 (2012)
16. Ong, C.-H.L.: On model-checking trees generated by higher-order recursion schemes. In: LICS 2006, pp. 81–90. IEEE Computer Society Press (2006)
17. Ong, C.-H.L., Ramsay, S.: Verifying higher-order programs with pattern-matching algebraic data types. In: Proc. of POPL, pp. 587–598 (2011)
18. Salvati, S., Walukiewicz, I.: Krivine machines and higher-order schemes. In: Aceto, L., Henzinger, M., Sgall, J. (eds.) ICALP 2011, Part II. LNCS, vol. 6756, pp. 162–173. Springer, Heidelberg (2011)
19. Schewe, S.: Solving parity games in big steps. In: Arvind, V., Prasad, S. (eds.) FSTTCS 2007. LNCS, vol. 4855, pp. 449–460. Springer, Heidelberg (2007)
20. Thomas, W.: Languages, automata, and logic. In: Handbook of formal languages, vol. 3, pp. 389–455 (1997)
21. Tobita, Y., Tsukada, T., Kobayashi, N.: Exact flow analysis by higher-order model checking. In: Schrijvers, T., Thiemann, P. (eds.) FLOPS 2012. LNCS, vol. 7294, pp. 275–289. Springer, Heidelberg (2012)
22. Unno, H., Tabuchi, N., Kobayashi, N.: Verification of tree-processing programs via higher-order model checking. In: Ueda, K. (ed.) APLAS 2010. LNCS, vol. 6461, pp. 312–327. Springer, Heidelberg (2010)

Model Checking Dynamic Pushdown Networks★

Fu Song[1] and Tayssir Touili[2]

[1] Shanghai Key Laboratory of Trustworthy Computing, East China Normal University
fsong@sei.ecnu.edu.cn

[2] LIAFA, CNRS and Université Paris Diderot
touili@liafa.univ-paris-diderot.fr

Abstract. A Dynamic Pushdown Network (DPN) is a set of pushdown systems (PDSs) where each process can dynamically create new instances of PDSs. DPNs are a natural model of multi-threaded programs with (possibly recursive) procedure calls and thread creation. Thus, it is important to have model-checking algorithms for DPNs. We consider in this work model-checking DPNs against single-indexed LTL and CTL properties of the form $\bigwedge f_i$ s.t. f_i is a LTL/CTL formula over the PDS i. We consider the model-checking problems w.r.t. simple valuations (i.e, whether a configuration satisfies an atomic proposition depends only on its control location) and w.r.t. regular valuations (i.e., the set of the configurations satisfying an atomic proposition is a regular set of configurations). We show that these model-checking problems are decidable. We propose automata-based approaches for computing the set of configurations of a DPN that satisfy the corresponding single-indexed LTL/CTL formula.

1 Introduction

Multithreading is a commonly used technique for modern software. However, multithreaded programs are known to be error prone and difficult to analyze. Dynamic Pushdown Networks (DPN) [4] are a natural model of multi-threaded programs with (possibly recursive) procedure calls and thread creation. A DPN consists of a finite set of pushdown systems (PDSs), each of them models a sequential program (process) that can dynamically create new instances of PDSs. Therefore, it is important to investigate automated methods for verifying DPNs. While existing works concentrate on the reachability problem of DPNs [4,18,17,9,15,24], model checking for the Linear Temporal Logic (LTL) and the Computation Tree Logic (CTL) which can describe more interesting properties of program behaviors has not been tackled yet for DPNs.

In general, the model checking problem is undecidable for double-indexed properties, i.e., properties where atomic propositions are interpreted over the control states of two or more threads [11]. This undecidability holds for pushdown networks even without thread creation. To obtain decidable results, in this paper, we consider single-indexed LTL and CTL model checking for DPNs, where a single-index LTL or CTL formula is a formula of the form $\bigwedge f_i$ such that f_i is a LTL/CTL formula over the PDS i.

★ This work is partially funded by ANR grant ANR-08-SEGI-006, Shanghai Knowledge Service Platform for Trustworthy Internet of Things No. ZF1213, NSFC Project No.91118007, Civil Aerospace Project 125 and NSFC Project No.61021004.

C.-c. Shan (Ed.): APLAS 2013, LNCS 8301, pp. 33–49, 2013.

A DPN satisfies $\bigwedge f_i$ iff every PDS i that runs in the network satisfies the subformula f_i. We first consider LTL model-checking for DPNs with simple valuations where whether a configuration of a PDS i satisfies an atomic proposition depends only on the control state of the configuration. Then, we consider LTL model-checking for DPNs with regular valuations where the set of configurations of a PDS satisfying an atomic proposition is a regular set of configurations. Finally, we consider CTL model-checking for DPNs with simple and regular valuations. We show that these model-checking problems are decidable. We propose automata-based approaches for computing the set of configurations of a DPN that satisfy the corresponding single-indexed LTL/CTL formula.

It is non-trivial to do LTL/CTL model checking for DPNs, since the number of instances of PDSs can be unbounded. Checking independently whether all the different PDSs satisfy the corresponding subformula f_i is not correct. Indeed, we do not need to check whether an instance of a PDS j satisfies f_j if this instance is not created during a run. To solve this problem, we extend the automata-based approach for standard LTL/CTL model-checking for PDSs [2,8,7,20]. For every process i, we compute a finite automaton $\mathcal{A}_i$ recognizing all the configurations from which there exists a run σ of the process i that satisfies f_i. $\mathcal{A}_i$ also memorizes the set of all the initial configurations of the instances of PDSs that are dynamically created during the run σ. Then, to check whether a DPN satisfies a single-indexed LTL/CTL formula, it is sufficient to check whether the initial configurations of the processes are recognized by the corresponding finite automata and whether the set of generated instances of PDSs that are stored in the automata also satisfy the formula. This condition is recursive. To solve it, we compute the largest set $\mathcal{D}_{fp}$ of the dynamically created initial configurations that satisfy the formula f. Then, to check whether a DPN satisfies f, it is sufficient to check whether the initial configurations of the different processes are recognized by the corresponding finite automata and whether the dynamically created initial configurations that are stored in the automata are in $\mathcal{D}_{fp}$.

To compute the finite automata $\mathcal{A}_i$s, we extend the automata-based approaches for standard LTL [2,7,8] and CTL [20] model-checking for PDSs. For every i, $1 \leq i \leq n$, we construct a Büchi Dynamic PDS (resp. alternating Büchi Dynamic PDS) which is a synchronization of the PDS i and the LTL (resp. CTL) formula f_i. Büchi Dynamic PDS (resp. alternating Büchi Dynamic PDS) is an extension of Büchi PDS (resp. alternating Büchi PDS) with the ability to create new instances of PDSs during the run. The finite automata $\mathcal{A}_i$s we are looking for correspond to the languages accepted by these Büchi Dynamic PDSs (resp. alternating Büchi Dynamic PDSs). Then, we show how to solve these language problems and compute the finite automata $\mathcal{A}_i$s.

Related Work. The DPN model was introduced in [4]. Several other works use DPN and its extensions to model multi-threaded programs [4,9,17,18,24]. All these works only consider reachability issues. Ground Tree Rewrite Systems [10] and process rewrite systems [5,19] are two models of multi-threaded programs with procedure calls and threads creation. However, [19] only considers reachability problem and [10,5] only consider subclasses of LTL. We consider LTL and CTL model checking problems.

Pushdown networks with communication between processes are studied in [3,6,1,22]. These works consider systems with a fixed number of threads. [15,16] use parallel flow graphs to model multi-threaded programs. However, all these works only consider reachability. [25] considers safety properties of multi-threaded programs.

[11,12,13] study single-index LTL/CTL and double-indexed LTL model checking problems for networks of pushdown systems that synchronize via a finite set of nested locks. [14] considers model-checking on properties that are expressed in a kind of finite automata for such networks of pushdown systems. These works don't consider dynamic threads creation.

Outline. Section 2 gives the basic definitions. Section 3 and Section 4 show LTL and CTL model-checking for DPNs, respectively. Due to lack of space, proofs are omitted and can be found in the full version of this paper [21].

2 Preliminaries

2.1 Dynamic Pushdown Networks

Definition 1. *A Dynamic Pushdown Network (DPN) $\mathcal{M}$ is a set $\{\mathcal{P}_1, ..., \mathcal{P}_n\}$ s.t. for every i, $1 \leq i \leq n$, $\mathcal{P}_i = (P_i, \Gamma_i, \Delta_i)$ is a dynamic pushdown system (DPDS), where P_i is a finite set of control locations s.t. $P_k \cap P_i = \emptyset$ for $k \neq i$, Γ_i is the stack alphabet, and Δ_i is a finite set of transition rules in the following forms: (a) $q\gamma \hookrightarrow p_1\omega_1$ or (b) $q\gamma \hookrightarrow p_1\omega_1 \rhd p_2\omega_2$ s.t. $q, p_1 \in P_i, \gamma \in \Gamma_i, \omega_1 \in \Gamma_i^*, p_2\omega_2 \in P_j \times \Gamma_j^*$ for some j, $1 \leq j \leq n$.*

A *global configuration* of $\mathcal{M}$ is a *multiset* $\mathcal{G}$ over $\bigcup_{i=1}^n P_i \times \Gamma_i^*$. Each element $q\omega \in P_i \times \Gamma_i^* \cap \mathcal{G}$ denotes that an instance of $\mathcal{P}_i$ running in parallel in the network is at the *local configuration* $q\omega$, i.e., $\mathcal{P}_i$ is at the control location q and its stack content is ω. If $\omega = \gamma u$ for $\gamma \in \Gamma_i$ and there is in Δ_i a transition (a) $q\gamma \hookrightarrow p_1\omega_1$ or (b) $q\gamma \hookrightarrow p_1\omega_1 \rhd p_2\omega_2$ s.t. $p_2\omega_2 \in P_j \times \Gamma_j$, then the instance of $\mathcal{P}_i$ can move from $q\omega$ to the control location p_1 and replace γ by ω_1 at the top of its stack, i.e., $\mathcal{P}_i$ moves to $p_1\omega_1 u$. The other instances in parallel in the network stay at the same local configurations. In addition, transition (b) will create a new instance of $\mathcal{P}_j$ starting from $p_2\omega_2$. Formally, a DPDS $\mathcal{P}_i$ induces an *immediate successor relation* $\Longrightarrow_i$ as follows: for every $\omega \in \Gamma_i^*$, if $q\gamma \hookrightarrow p_1\omega_1 \in \Delta_i$, then $q\gamma\omega \Longrightarrow_i p_1\omega_1\omega$; if $q\gamma \hookrightarrow p_1\omega_1 \rhd p_2\omega_2 \in \Delta_i$, then $q\gamma\omega \Longrightarrow_i p_1\omega_1\omega \rhd \{p_2\omega_2\}$. To unify the presentation, if $q\gamma\omega \Longrightarrow_i p_1\omega_1\omega$, we sometimes write $q\gamma\omega \Longrightarrow_i p_1\omega_1\omega \rhd \emptyset$ instead. The transitive and reflexive closure of $\Longrightarrow_i$ is denoted by $\Longrightarrow_i^*$. Formally, for every $p\omega \in P_i \times \Gamma_i^*$, $p\omega \Longrightarrow_i^* p\omega \rhd \emptyset$; and if $p\omega \Longrightarrow_i p_1\omega_1 \rhd D_1$ and $p_1\omega_1 \Longrightarrow_i^* p_2\omega_2 \rhd D_2$, then $p\omega \Longrightarrow_i^* p_2\omega_2 \rhd D_1 \cup D_2$. $\Longrightarrow_i^+$ is defined as usual.

A DPDS $\mathcal{P}_i$ can be seen as a pushdown system (PDS) with the ability of dynamically creating new instances of PDSs. The initial local configuration of a newly created instance is called DCLIC (for Dynamically Created Local Initial Configuration).

A local run of an instance of $\mathcal{P}_i$ from a local configuration c_0 is a sequence of local configurations $c_0c_1...$ over $\mathcal{P}_i \times \Gamma_i^*$ s.t. for every $j \geq 0$, $c_j \Longrightarrow_i c_{j+1} \rhd D$ for some D. A global run ρ of $\mathcal{M}$ from a global configuration $\mathcal{G}$ is a (potentially infinite) set of local runs. Initially, ρ contains exactly the local runs starting from the local configurations in $\mathcal{G}$. Whenever a DCLIC c is created by some local run of ρ, a new local run starting from c is added into ρ. For every i, $1 \leq i \leq n$, let $\wp(\sigma) = i$ iff σ is a local run of an instance of $\mathcal{P}_i$, and $\wp(p\omega) = \wp(p) = i$ iff $p \in P_i$. Let $\mathcal{D}_i = \{p_2\omega_2 \in \bigcup_{i=1}^n P_i \times \Gamma_i^* \mid q\gamma \hookrightarrow p_1\omega_1 \rhd p_2\omega_2 \in \Delta_i\}$ be the set of potential DCLICs of the DPDS $\mathcal{P}_i$.

2.2 LTL and Büchi Automata

From now on, we fix a set of atomic propositions AP.

Definition 2. *The set of LTL formulas is given by (where $a \in$ AP):*

$$\psi ::= a \mid \neg\psi \mid \psi \wedge \psi \mid X\psi \mid \psi U \psi.$$

Given an ω-word $\eta = \alpha_0\alpha_1...$ over 2^{AP}, let $\eta(k)$ denote α_k, and η_k denote the *suffix* of η starting from α_k. $\eta \models \psi$ (η satisfies ψ) is inductively defined as follows: $\eta \models a$ iff $a \in \eta(0)$; $\eta \models \neg\psi$ iff $\eta \not\models \psi$; $\eta \models \psi_1 \wedge \psi_2$ iff $\eta \models \psi_1$ and $\eta \models \psi_2$; $\eta \models \mathbf{X}\psi$ iff $\eta_1 \models \psi$; $\eta \models \psi_1 \mathbf{U} \psi_2$ iff there exists $k \geq 0$ such that $\eta_k \models \psi_2$ and for every j, $1 \leq j < k$, $\eta_j \models \psi_1$.

Definition 3. *A* Büchi automaton *(BA) $\mathcal{B}$ is a tuple $(G, \Sigma, \theta, g^0, F)$ where G is a finite set of states, Σ is the input alphabet, $\theta \subseteq G \times \Sigma \times G$ is a finite set of transitions, $g^0 \in G$ is the initial state and $F \subseteq G$ is a finite set of accepting states.*

A run of $\mathcal{B}$ over an ω-word $\alpha_0\alpha_1...$ is a sequence of states $q_0q_1...$ s.t. $q_0 = g^0$ and $(q_i, \alpha_i, q_{i+1}) \in \theta$ for every $i \geq 0$. A run is accepting iff it infinitely often visits some states in F.

It is well-known that given a LTL formula f, one can construct a BA B_f s.t. $\Sigma = 2^{AP}$ recognizing all the ω-words that satisfy f [23].

2.3 Single-Indexed LTL for DPNs

Let $\mathcal{M} = \{\mathcal{P}_1, ..., \mathcal{P}_n\}$ be a DPN. A *single-indexed* LTL formula is a formula f of the form $\bigwedge_{i=1}^n f_i$ s.t. for every i, $1 \leq i \leq n$, f_i is a LTL formula in which the validity of the atomic propositions depends only on the DPDS $\mathcal{P}_i$. Let $\lambda : AP \longrightarrow 2^{\bigcup_{i=1}^n P_i \times \Gamma_i^*}$ be a valuation which assigns to each atomic proposition a set of local configurations. A local run $p_0\omega_0p_1\omega_1...$ of $\mathcal{P}_i$ satisfies f_i iff the ω-word $\alpha_0\alpha_1...$ where for every $j \geq 0$, $\alpha_j = \{a \in AP \mid p_j\omega_j \in \lambda(a)\}$, satisfies f_i. A local configuration c of $\mathcal{P}_i$ satisfies f_i iff $\mathcal{P}_i$ has a local run σ from c that satisfies f_i. If D is the set of DCLICs created during the run σ, we write $c \models_D f_i$. $\mathcal{M}$ satisfies f iff it has a global run ρ such that for every i, $1 \leq i \leq n$, each local run of $\mathcal{P}_i$ in ρ satisfies the formula f_i.

2.4 Multi-automata and Predecessors

From now on, we fix a DPN $\mathcal{M} = \{\mathcal{P}_1, ..., \mathcal{P}_n\}$ where for every i, $1 \leq i \leq n$, $\mathcal{P}_i = (P_i, \Gamma_i, \Delta_i)$, and a single-indexed LTL formula $f = \bigwedge_{i=1}^n f_i$. To check whether $\mathcal{M}$ satisfies f is non-trivial. Indeed, it is not correct to check independently whether each $\mathcal{P}_i$ satisfies f_i. Instead, we need to check whether there exists a global run ρ from a global configuration $\mathcal{G}$ s.t. an instance of $\mathcal{P}_i$ satisfies the formula f_i only if it is an instance in $\mathcal{G}$ or it is dynamically created during the run ρ. Thus, it is important to memorize the set of DCLICs that are created during a run. To this aim, we introduce the function $pre_{\mathcal{P}_i} : 2^{P_i \times \Gamma_i^* \times 2^{\mathcal{D}_i}} \longrightarrow 2^{P_i \times \Gamma_i^* \times 2^{\mathcal{D}_i}}$ as follows. $pre_{\mathcal{P}_i}(U) = \{(c, D_1 \cup D_2) \mid \exists c' \in P_i \times \Gamma_i^*,\ s.t.\ c \Longrightarrow_i c' \rhd D_1$ and $(c', D_2) \in U\}$. Intuitively, if $\mathcal{P}_i$ moves from c to c' and generates the DCLIC D_1 and $(c', D_2) \in U$, then $(c, D_1 \cup D_2) \in pre_{\mathcal{P}_i}(U)$. The transitive and reflexive closure of $pre_{\mathcal{P}_i}$ is denoted by $pre^*_{\mathcal{P}_i}$. Formally, $pre^*_{\mathcal{P}_i}(U) = \{(c, D_1 \cup D_2) \mid \exists c' \in P_i \times \Gamma_i^*,\ s.t.\ c \Longrightarrow_i^* c' \rhd D_1$ and $(c', D_2) \in U\}$. Let $pre^+_{\mathcal{P}_i}(U) = pre^*_{\mathcal{P}_i}(pre_{\mathcal{P}_i}(U))$.

To finitely represent (infinite) sets of local configurations of DPDSs and DCLICs generated by DPDSs, we use Multi-automata and Alternating Multi-automata.

Definition 4. *An Alternating Multi-automaton* (AMA) *is a tuple* $\mathcal{A}_i = (Q_i, \Gamma_i, \delta_i, I_i, Acc_i)$*, where* Q_i *is a finite set of states,* $I_i \subseteq P_i$ *is a finite set of initial states corresponding to the control locations of the DPDS* $\mathcal{P}_i$*,* $Acc_i \subseteq Q_i$ *is a finite set of final states,* $\delta_i \subseteq (Q_i \times \Gamma_i) \times 2^{\mathcal{D}_i} \times 2^{Q_i}$ *is a finite set of transition rules.*
A MA is a AMA $\mathcal{A}_i$ *s.t.* $\delta_i \subseteq (Q_i \times \Gamma_i) \times 2^{\mathcal{D}_i} \times Q_i$*.*

We write $p \xrightarrow{\gamma/D}_i \{q_1, ..., q_m\}$ instead of $(p, \gamma, D, \{q_1, ..., q_m\}) \in \delta_i$, where D is a set of DCLICs. We define the relation $\longrightarrow_i^* \subseteq (Q_i \times \Gamma_i^*) \times 2^{\mathcal{D}_i} \times 2^{Q_i}$ as the smallest relation s.t.: (1) $q \xrightarrow{\epsilon/\emptyset}_i^* \{q\}$ for every $q \in Q_i$, (2) if $q \xrightarrow{\gamma/D}_i \{q_1, ..., q_m\}$ and $q_k \xrightarrow{\omega/D_k}_i^* S_k$ for k, $1 \leq k \leq m$, then $q \xrightarrow{\gamma\omega/D \cup \bigcup_{k=1}^m D_k}_i^* \bigcup_{k=1}^m S_k$. Let $L(\mathcal{A}_i)$ be the set of tuples $(p\omega, D) \in P_i \times \Gamma_i^* \times 2^{\mathcal{D}_i}$ s.t. $p \xrightarrow{\omega/D}_i^* S$ for some $S \subseteq Acc_i$. A set $W \subseteq P_i \times \Gamma_i^* \times 2^{\mathcal{D}_i}$ is *regular* iff there exists an AMA $\mathcal{A}_i$ s.t. $L(\mathcal{A}_i) = W$. A set of local configurations $C \subseteq P_i \times \Gamma_i^*$ is *regular* iff $C \times \{\emptyset\}$ is a regular set.

Given a DPDS $\mathcal{P}_i$ and a regular set $W \subseteq P_i \times \Gamma_i^* \times 2^{\mathcal{D}_i}$ accepted by a MA $A_i = (Q_i, \Gamma_i, \delta_i, I_i, Acc_i)$, we can construct a MA $A_i^{pre^*} = (Q_i, \Gamma_i, \delta'_i, I_i, Acc_i)$ that exactly accepts $pre^*_{\mathcal{P}_i}(W)$. W.l.o.g., we assume that A_i has no transition leading to an initial state and that $P_i = I_i$. $A_i^{pre^*}$ is constructed by the following saturation procedure (an adaption of the saturation procedure of [2]).

- *For every* $p\gamma \hookrightarrow p_1\omega_1 \in \Delta_i$ *and* $p_1 \xrightarrow{\omega_1/D}_i^* q$*, add a new rule* $p \xrightarrow{\gamma/D}_i q$*;*
- *For every* $p\gamma \hookrightarrow p_1\omega_1 \rhd p_2\omega_2 \in \Delta_i$ *and* $p_1 \xrightarrow{\omega_1/D}_i^* q$*, add a new rule* $p \xrightarrow{\gamma/D \cup \{p_2\omega_2\}}_i q$*.*

The procedure adds only new transitions to A_i. Since the number of states is fixed, the number of possible new transitions is finite. Thus, the saturation procedure always terminates. We can show that each transition can be processed only once. Thus, the number of transition rules added into $A_i^{pre^*}$ is at most $O(|\Delta_i| \cdot |Q_i|^2 \cdot 2^{|\mathcal{D}_i|})$. The intuition behind this procedure is that, for every $\omega' \in \Gamma_i^*$: suppose $p\gamma \hookrightarrow p_1\omega_1 \rhd p_2\omega_2 \in \Delta_i$ and the tuple $(p_1\omega_1\omega', D)$ is accepted by the automaton, i.e., $p_1 \xrightarrow{\omega_1/D_1}_i^* q \xrightarrow{\omega'/D_2}_i^* g$ for some $g \in Acc_i$ and $D = D_1 \cup D_2$. Then, we add the new transition rule $p \xrightarrow{\gamma/D_1 \cup \{p_2\omega_2\}}_i q$ that allows the automaton to accept $(p\gamma\omega', D \cup \{p_2\omega_2\})$, i.e., $p \xrightarrow{\gamma/D_1 \cup \{p_2\omega_2\}}_i q \xrightarrow{\omega'/D_2}_i^* g$. The case $p\gamma \hookrightarrow p_1\omega_1 \in \Delta_i$ is similar. Thus, we obtain the following theorem.

Theorem 1. *Given a MA* A_i *recognizing a regular set* W *of the DPDS* $\mathcal{P}_i$*, we can construct a MA* $A_i^{pre^*}$ *recognizing* $pre^*_{\mathcal{P}_i}(W)$ *in time* $O(|\Delta_i| \cdot |Q_i|^2 \cdot 2^{|\mathcal{D}_i|})$*.*

3 Single-Indexed LTL Model-Checking for DPNs

In this section, we consider LTL model checking w.r.t. a labeling function $l : \bigcup_{i=1}^n P_i \longrightarrow 2^{AP}$ assigning to each control location a set of atomic propositions. In this case, the valuation λ_l (called simple valuation) is defined as follows: for every $a \in AP$, $\lambda_l(a) = \{p\omega \in \bigcup_{i=1}^n P_i \times \Gamma_i^* \mid a \in l(p)\}$. A global configuration $\mathcal{G}$ satisfies $f = \bigwedge f_i$ iff $\mathcal{M}$

has a global run ρ from $\mathcal{G}$ s.t. every local run σ of ρ satisfies $f_{\wp(\sigma)}$ where $\wp(\sigma)$ denotes the index of the DPDS which corresponds to the local run σ. Checking whether $\mathcal{G}$ satisfies f is non-trivial since the number of local runs of ρ can be unbounded. We cannot check all the different instances of the DPDSs independently. Indeed, we don't have to check whether an instance of $\mathcal{P}_i$ (for some $i, 1 \leq i \leq n$) satisfies f_i if this instance is not created during the execution. We can solve this problem in a naive way as follows: Given an initial global configuration $\mathcal{G}$, we can guess the set of DCLICs $D \subseteq \bigcup_{i=1}^{n} \mathcal{D}_i$ which are created in a global run from $\mathcal{G}$ such that the global run satisfies f. Then, it is sufficient to check that every local configuration $c \in \mathcal{G} \cup D$ satisfies the LTL formula $f_{\wp(c)}$ when disallowing the transition rules which create a DCLIC outside of D and discarding the DCLICs inside of D. Checking whether c satisfies $f_{\wp(c)}$ could be solved by LTL model-checking for PDSs [2,7] if we discard the DCLICs of the DPDS. However, this naive technique is very complicated as it necessitates an exponential number of calls to the LTL model checking algorithm of PDSs. Moreover, it is very complex. We have to consider all the possible sets of DCLICs whose number is at most $O(2^{|\bigcup_{i=1}^{n} \mathcal{D}_i|})$, and for each set D of DCLICs, we have to perform at most $O(|\bigcup_{i=1}^{n} \mathcal{D}_i|)$ times of LTL model-checking algorithm for PDSs, where LTL model-checking for PDSs is in time $O(|P_{\wp(d)}|^2 \cdot |\Delta_{\wp(d)}| \cdot 2^{|f_{\wp(d)}|})$ [2,7]. Thus, the complexity of checking whether $\mathcal{G}$ satisfies f or not will be $O(2^{|\bigcup_{i=1}^{n} \mathcal{D}_i|} \cdot \sum_{d \in \bigcup_{i=1}^{n} \mathcal{D}_i \cup \mathcal{G}} (|P_{\wp(d)}|^2 \cdot |\Delta_{\wp(d)}| \cdot 2^{|f_{\wp(d)}|}))$.

To overcome these problems, we propose in this section a *direct* algorithm. We compute for every $i, 1 \leq i \leq n$, a MA $\mathcal{A}_i$ such that $(c, D) \in L(\mathcal{A}_i)$, where c is a local configuration of $\mathcal{P}_i$ and $D \subseteq \mathcal{D}_i$ is a set of DCLICs, iff $\mathcal{P}_i$ has a local run σ from c that satisfies f_i such that D is the set of DCLICs created during the local run σ. Then, a global configuration $\mathcal{G}$ satisfies $f = \bigwedge f_i$ iff for every configuration $c \in \mathcal{G}$, there exists a set of DCLICs D_c s.t. $(c, D_c) \in L(\mathcal{A}_{\wp(c)})$ and every $d \in D_c$ satisfies f. This condition is recursive. However, it can be effectively checked since there is only a finite number of DCLICs. Checking this condition naively is not efficient. To obtain a more efficient procedure, we compute the largest set $\mathcal{D}_{fp} \subseteq \bigcup_{i=1}^{n} \mathcal{D}_i$ of DCLICs such that $d \in \mathcal{D}_{fp}$ iff d is a DCLIC and there exists a global run of $\mathcal{M}$ starting from d that satisfies f. Then, to check whether a global configuration $\mathcal{G}$ satisfies f, it is sufficient to check for every $c \in \mathcal{G}$ whether there exists $D_c \subseteq \mathcal{D}_{fp}$ s.t. $(c, D_c) \in L(\mathcal{A}_{\wp(c)})$.

3.1 Computing the MAs $\mathcal{A}_i$

To compute the MAs $\mathcal{A}_i$, for i, $1 \leq i \leq n$, we extend the automata-based approach for standard LTL model-checking for PDSs [2,7]. We first compute a Büchi automaton (BA) $\mathcal{B}_i$ that corresponds to the formula f_i, for i, $1 \leq i \leq n$. Then, we synchronize the BAs with the DPDSs to obtain Büchi DPDSs. The MAs $\mathcal{A}_i$ we are looking for correspond to the languages accepted by these Büchi DPDSs.

Definition 5. *A Büchi DPDS (BDPDS) is a tuple* $\mathcal{BP}_i = (P_i, \Gamma_i, \Delta_i, F_i)$*, where* $(P_i, \Gamma_i, \Delta_i)$ *is a DPDS and* $F_i \subseteq P_i$ *is a finite set of accepting control locations.*

A BDPDS is a kind of DPDS with a Büchi acceptance condition F_i. Runs of a BDPDS are defined as local runs for DPDSs. A run σ of $\mathcal{BP}_i$ is accepting iff σ *infinitely often* visits some control locations in F_i. Let $L(\mathcal{BP}_i)$ be the set of all the pairs $(c, D) \in P_i \times$

$\Gamma_i^* \times 2^{\mathcal{D}_i}$ s.t. $\mathcal{BP}_i$ has an accepting run from c and the run generates the set of DCLICs D.

Let $\mathcal{B}_i = (G_i, 2^{AP}, \theta_i, g_i^0, F_i)$ be the BA recognizing all the ω-words that satisfy f_i. We compute a BDPDS $\mathcal{BP}_i$ such that $\mathcal{P}_i$ has a local run from $p\omega$ that satisfies f_i and generates a set of DCLICs D iff $([p, g_i^0]\omega, D) \in L(\mathcal{BP}_i)$. We define $\mathcal{BP}_i = (P_i \times G_i, \Gamma_i, \Delta_i', F_i')$ as follows: for every $p \in P_i$, $[p, g] \in F_i'$ iff $g \in F_i$; and for every $(g_1, l(p), g_2) \in \theta_i$, we have:

1. $[p, g_1]\gamma \hookrightarrow [p_1, g_2]\omega_1 \in \Delta_i'$ iff $p\gamma \hookrightarrow p_1\omega_1 \in \Delta_i$;
2. $[p, g_1]\gamma \hookrightarrow [p_1, g_2]\omega_1 \rhd D \in \Delta_i'$ iff $p\gamma \hookrightarrow p_1\omega_1 \rhd D \in \Delta_i$.

Intuitively, $\mathcal{BP}_i$ is a product of $\mathcal{P}_i$ and the BA $\mathcal{B}_i$. $\mathcal{B}_i$ has an accepting run $g_0 g_1 ...$ over an ω-word $l(p_0)l(p_1)...$ that corresponds to a local run $\sigma = p_0\omega_0\ p_1\omega_1 ...$ of $\mathcal{P}_i$ iff $\mathcal{BP}_i$ has an accepting run $\sigma' = [p_0, g_0]\omega_0\ [p_1, g_1]\omega_1 ...$, and D is the set of DCLICs created during the run σ iff D is the set of DCLICs created during the run σ'. Suppose the run of $\mathcal{P}_i$ is at $p_j\omega_j$, then the run of $\mathcal{B}_i$ can move from g_j to g_{j+1} iff $(g_j, l(p_j), g_{j+1}) \in \theta_i$. This is ensured by Items 1 and 2 expressing that $\mathcal{BP}_i$ can move from $[p_j, g_j]\omega_j$ to $[p_{j+1}, g_{j+1}]\omega_{j+1}$ iff $(g_j, l(p_j), g_{j+1}) \in \theta_i$. The accepting control locations $F_i' = \{[p, g] \mid p \in P_i, g \in F_i\}$ ensures that the run of $\mathcal{B}_i$ visits infinitely often some states in F_i iff the run of $\mathcal{BP}_i$ visits infinitely often some control locations F_i'. Item 2 ensures that the run of $\mathcal{P}_i$ creates a DCLIC $p_2\omega_2$ iff the run of $\mathcal{BP}_i$ creates this DCLIC. Thus, we obtain the following theorem.

Lemma 1. *$\mathcal{P}_i$ has a local run from $p\omega$ that satisfies f_i and creates a set of DCLICs D iff $([p, g_i^0]\omega, D) \in L(\mathcal{BP}_i)$, where $\mathcal{BP}_i$ can be constructed in time $O(|\Delta_i| \cdot 2^{|f_i|})$.*

The complexity follows from the fact that the number of transition rules of $\mathcal{BP}_i$ is at most $O(|\Delta_i| \cdot 2^{|f_i|})$.

Computing $L(\mathcal{BP}_i)$: Let us fix an index i, $1 \le i \le n$. We show that computing $L(\mathcal{BP}_i)$ boils down to $pre^*_{\mathcal{P}_i}$ computations.

Proposition 1. *Let $\mathcal{BP}_i = (P_i, \Gamma_i, \Delta_i, F_i)$ be a BDPDS, $\mathcal{BP}_i$ has an accepting run from $c \in P_i \times \Gamma_i^*$ and D is the set of DCLICs created during this run iff $\exists D_1, D_2, D_3 \subseteq \mathcal{D}_i$ s.t. $D = D_1 \cup D_2 \cup D_3$, and*
$(\alpha_1) : c \Longrightarrow_i^* p\gamma\omega \rhd D_1$ for some $\omega \in \Gamma_i^*$;
$(\alpha_2) : p\gamma \Longrightarrow_i^+ gu \rhd D_2$ and $gu \Longrightarrow_i^* p\gamma v \rhd D_3$, for some $g \in F_i, v \in \Gamma_i^*$.

Intuitively, an accepting run from c will reach a configuration $p\gamma\omega$ (Item α_1) followed by a repeatedly executed cycle (Item α_2) which is a sequence of configurations with an accepting location g. The execution of the cycle returns to the control location p with the same symbol γ at the top of the stack. The rest of the stack will never be popped during this cycle. Repeatedly executing the cycle yields an accepting run (since $g \in F_i$) and the set of DCLICs generated during this cycle is $D_2 \cup D_3$. Thus, the set of DCLICs created by the accepting run starting from c is $D_1 \cup D_2 \cup D_3$. To compute $L(\mathcal{BP}_i)$, we reformulate the above conditions as follows:

Proposition 2. *Let $\mathcal{BP}_i = (P_i, \Gamma_i, \Delta_i, F_i)$ be a BDPDS, $\mathcal{BP}_i$ has an accepting run from $c \in P_i \times \Gamma_i^*$ and D is the set of DCLICs created during this run iff $\exists D_1, D_2' \subseteq \mathcal{D}_i$ s.t. $D = D_1 \cup D_2'$, and*

$(\beta_1) : (c, D_1) \in pre^*_{\mathcal{P}_i}(\{p\} \times \gamma\Gamma_i^* \times \{\emptyset\})$;

$(\beta_2) : (p\gamma, D_2') \in pre^+_{\mathcal{P}_i}((F_i \times \Gamma_i^* \times 2^{\mathcal{D}_i}) \cap pre^*_{\mathcal{P}_i}(\{p\} \times \gamma\Gamma_i^* \times \{\emptyset\}))$ (note that $D_2' = D_2 \cup D_3$).

Intuitively, items β_1 and β_2 are reformulations of items α_1 and α_2, respectively. By Proposition 2, we can get that $L(\mathcal{BP}_i) = \{(c, D_1 \cup D_2') \in P_i \times \Gamma_i \times 2^{\mathcal{D}_i} \mid$ Items β_1 and β_2 hold$\}$. Since $F_i \times \Gamma_i^* \times 2^{\mathcal{D}_i}$ and $\{p\} \times \gamma\Gamma_i^* \times \{\emptyset\}$ are regular sets, using Theorem 1, we can construct two MAs A' and A'' accepting $pre^+_{\mathcal{P}_i}((F_i \times \Gamma_i^* \times 2^{\mathcal{D}_i}) \cap pre^*_{\mathcal{P}_i}(\{p\} \times \gamma\Gamma_i^* \times \{\emptyset\}))$ and $pre^*_{\mathcal{P}_i}(\{p\} \times \gamma\Gamma_i^* \times \{\emptyset\})$. The intersection $(F_i \times \Gamma_i^* \times 2^{\mathcal{D}_i}) \cap pre^*_{\mathcal{P}_i}(\{p\} \times \gamma\Gamma_i^* \times \{\emptyset\})$ is easy to compute. Since $F_i \times \Gamma_i^* \times 2^{\mathcal{D}_i}$ denotes all the configurations whose control locations are accepting, we only need to let the initial states of A'' be the states of F_i. Since the set $P_i \times \Gamma_i \times 2^{\mathcal{D}_i}$ is finite, we can determine all the tuples $(p\gamma, D_2') \in P_i \times \Gamma_i \times 2^{\mathcal{D}_i}$ s.t. Item β_2 holds. The set of pairs (c, D_1) is the union of all the sets $pre^*_{\mathcal{P}_i}(\{p\} \times \gamma\Gamma_i^* \times \{\emptyset\})$. Thus, we can get $L(\mathcal{BP}_i)$. For every BDPDS $\mathcal{P}_i$ and MA A_i, $pre^*_{\mathcal{P}_i}(L(A_i))$ and $pre^+_{\mathcal{P}_i}(L(A_i))$ can be computed in time $O(|\Delta_i| \cdot |Q_i|^2 \cdot 2^{|\mathcal{D}_i|})$, where $|Q_i| = O(|P_i|)$. Thus, we get that:

Lemma 2. *For every BDPDS $\mathcal{BP}_i = (P_i, \Gamma_i, \Delta_i, F_i)$, we can construct a MA $\mathcal{A}_i$ in time $O(|\Delta_i| \cdot |\Gamma_i| \cdot |P_i|^3 \cdot 2^{|\mathcal{D}_i|})$ such that $L(\mathcal{A}_i) = L(\mathcal{BP}_i)$.*

From Lemma 1 and Lemma 2, we get:

Theorem 2. *Given a DPN $\mathcal{M} = \{\mathcal{P}_1, ..., \mathcal{P}_n\}$, a single-indexed LTL formula $f = \bigwedge_{i=1}^n f_i$ and a labelling function l, we can compute MAs $\mathcal{A}_1, ..., \mathcal{A}_n$ in time $O(\sum_{i=1}^n (|\Delta_i| \cdot 2^{|f_i|} \cdot |\Gamma_i| \cdot |P_i|^3 \cdot 2^{|\mathcal{D}_i|}))$ s.t. for every i, $1 \le i \le n$, every $p\omega \in P_i \times \Gamma_i^*$ and $D \subseteq \mathcal{D}_i$, $p\omega \models_D f_i$ iff $([p, g_i^0]\omega, D) \in L(\mathcal{A}_i)$.*

3.2 Single-Indexed LTL Model-Checking for DPNs with Simple Valuations

Given a DPN $\mathcal{M} = \{\mathcal{P}_1, ..., \mathcal{P}_n\}$ and a single-indexed LTL formula $f = \bigwedge_{i=1}^n f_i$, by Theorem 2, we can construct a set of MAs $\{\mathcal{A}_1, ..., \mathcal{A}_n\}$ s.t. for every i, $1 \le i \le n$, and every local configuration $p\omega \in P_i \times \Gamma_i^*$, $p\omega \models_D f_i$ iff $([p, g_i^0]\omega, D) \in L(\mathcal{A}_i)$. Then, to check whether a global configuration $\mathcal{G}$ satisfies f, we need to check whether for every local configuration $c \in \mathcal{G}$, there exists a set of DCLICs D_c s.t. $(c, D_c) \in L(\mathcal{A}_{\varphi(c)})$ and every DCLIC $d \in D_c$ satisfies f, i.e., there exists a set of DCLICs D_d s.t. $(d, D_d) \in L(\mathcal{A}_{\varphi(d)})$, etc. This condition is recursive. It can be solved, because the number of DCLICs is finite. To obtain a more efficient procedure, we compute the maximal set of DCLICs $\mathcal{D}_{fp}$ s.t. for every $d \in \bigcup_{i=1}^n \mathcal{D}_i$, d satisfies f iff $d \in \mathcal{D}_{fp}$. Then, to check whether $\mathcal{G}$ satisfies f, it is sufficient to check whether for every $c \in \mathcal{G}$, there exists $D_c \subseteq \mathcal{D}_{fp}$ s.t. $(c, D_c) \in L(\mathcal{A}_{\varphi(c)})$.

Let $\{\mathcal{A}_1, ..., \mathcal{A}_n\}$, s.t. for every i, $1 \le i \le n$, $\mathcal{A}_i = (Q_i, \Gamma_i, \delta_i, I_i, Acc_i)$, be the set of the computed MAs. Intuitively, $\mathcal{D}_{fp}$ should be equal to the set of local configurations $p\omega \in \bigcup_{i=1}^n \mathcal{D}_i$ s.t. there exists $D \subseteq \mathcal{D}_{fp}$ s.t. $p\omega \models_D f_{\varphi(p)}$, i.e., $([p, g^0_{\varphi(p)}]\omega, D) \in L(\mathcal{A}_{\varphi(p)})$. Thus, $\mathcal{D}_{fp}$ can be defined as the greatest fixpoint of the function $F(X) = \{p\omega \in \mathcal{D}_I \mid \exists D \subseteq X \text{ s.t. } ([p, g^0_{\wp(p)}]\omega, D) \in L(\mathcal{A}_{\wp(p)})\}$. This set can then be computed iteratively as follows: $\mathcal{D}_{fp} = \bigcap_{j\geq 0} D_j$, where $D_0 = \mathcal{D}_I$ and $D_{j+1} = \{p\omega \in \mathcal{D}_I \mid \exists D \subseteq D_j,\ ([p, g^0_{\wp(p)}]\omega, D) \in L(\mathcal{A}_{\wp(p)})\}$ for every $j \geq 0$. Since $\bigcup_{i=1}^n \mathcal{D}_i$ is a finite set, and for every $j \geq 0$, D_{j+1} is a subset of D_j, there always exists a fixpoint $m \geq 0$ such that $D_m = D_{m+1}$. Then, we can get that $\mathcal{D}_{fp} = D_m$.

For every $p\omega \in \bigcup_{i=1}^n \mathcal{D}_i$ and $D \subseteq \mathcal{D}_{\wp(p)}$, to avoid checking whether $([p, g^0_{\wp(p)}]\omega, D) \in L(\mathcal{A}_{\wp(p)})$ at each step when computing $D_0, D_1, ...,$ we can compute all these tuples that satisfy this condition once and store them in a hash table. We can show that whether or not $([p, g^0_{\wp(p)}]\omega, D) \in L(\mathcal{A}_{\wp(p)})$ can be decided in time $\mathbf{O}(|\omega| \cdot |\delta_{\wp(p)}| \cdot |Q_{\wp(p)}| \cdot 2^{|\mathcal{D}_{\wp(p)}|})$. Thus, we can get the hash table in time $\mathbf{O}(\sum_{p\omega \in \bigcup_{i=1}^n \mathcal{D}_i} (|\omega| \cdot |\delta_{\wp(p)}| \cdot |Q_{\wp(p)}| \cdot 2^{|\mathcal{D}_{\wp(p)}|}))$. Given D_j and the hash table, we can compute D_{j+1} in time $\mathbf{O}(\sum_{p\omega \in \bigcup_{i=1}^n \mathcal{D}_i} 2^{|\mathcal{D}_{\wp(p)}|})$. Thus we can get $\mathcal{D}_{fp}$ in time $\mathbf{O}(\sum_{p\omega \in \mathcal{D}_I} (|\omega| \cdot |\delta_{\wp(p)}| \cdot |Q_{\wp(p)}| \cdot 2^{|\mathcal{D}_I|}) + |\mathcal{D}_I|^2 \cdot 2^{|\mathcal{D}_I|})$.

Theorem 3. *We can compute $\mathcal{D}_{fp}$ in time $\mathbf{O}(\sum_{p\omega \in \bigcup_{i=1}^n \mathcal{D}_i} (|\omega| \cdot |\delta_{\wp(p)}| \cdot |Q_{\wp(p)}| \cdot 2^{|\mathcal{D}_{\wp(p)}|} + |\bigcup_{i=1}^n \mathcal{D}_i| \cdot 2^{|\mathcal{D}_{\wp(p)}|}))$ s.t. for every $c \in \bigcup_{i=1}^n \mathcal{D}_i$, c satisfies the single-indexed LTL formula f iff $c \in \mathcal{D}_{fp}$.*

Then, from Theorem 3 and Theorem 2, we get the following theorem.

Theorem 4. *Given a DPN $\mathcal{M} = \{\mathcal{P}_1, ..., \mathcal{P}_n\}$, a single-indexed LTL formula $f = \bigwedge_{i=1}^n f_i$ and a labelling function l, we can compute MAs $\mathcal{A}_1, ..., \mathcal{A}_n$ in time $O(\sum_{i=1}^n (|\Delta_i| \cdot 2^{|f_i|} \cdot |\Gamma_i| \cdot |P_i|^3 \cdot 2^{|\mathcal{D}_i|}))$ s.t. for every global configuration $\mathcal{G}$, $\mathcal{G}$ satisfies f iff for every $p\omega \in \mathcal{G}$, there exists $D \subseteq \mathcal{D}_{fp}$ s.t. $([p, g^0_{\wp(p)}]\omega, D) \in L(\mathcal{A}_{\wp(p)})$.*

You can see that the complexity of our technique is better than the one of the naive approach given at the beginning of Section 3.

3.3 Single-Indexed LTL Model-Checking with Regular Valuations

We generalize single-indexed LTL model checking for DPNs w.r.t. simple valuations to a more general model checking problem where the set of configurations in which an atomic proposition holds is a regular set of local configurations. Formally, a regular valuation is a function $\lambda : AP \longrightarrow 2^{\bigcup_{i=1}^n P_i \times \Gamma_i^*}$ s.t. for every $a \in AP$, $\lambda(a)$ is a regular set of local configurations of $\mathcal{P}_i$ for i, $1 \leq i \leq n$. The previous construction can be extended to deal with this case. For this, we follow the approach of [8]. We compute, for i, $1 \leq i \leq n$, a new DPDS $\mathcal{P}'_i$, which is a kind of synchronization of the DPDS $\mathcal{P}_i$ and the *deterministic* finite automata corresponding to the regular valuations. This allows to determine whether atomic propositions hold at a given step by looking only at the top of the stack of $\mathcal{P}'_i$, for every i, $1 \leq i \leq n$. By doing this, we can reduce single-indexed LTL model checking for DPNs with regular valuations to single-indexed LTL model checking for DPNs with simple valuations. Due to lack of space, we omit the details. They can be found in the full version of this paper [21].

Theorem 5. *Given a DPN $\mathcal{M} = \{\mathcal{P}_1, ..., \mathcal{P}_n\}$, a single-indexed LTL formula $f = \bigwedge_{i=1}^n f_i$ and a regular valuation λ, we can compute MAs $\mathcal{A}_1, ..., \mathcal{A}_n$ in time $\mathbf{O}(\sum_{i=1}^n (|\Delta_i| \cdot 2^{|f_i|} \cdot |\Gamma_i| \cdot |States_i| \cdot |P_i|^3 \cdot 2^{|\mathcal{D}_i|}))$ s.t. for every global configuration $\mathcal{G}$, $\mathcal{G}$ satisfies f iff for every $p\omega \in \mathcal{G}$, there exists $D \subseteq \mathcal{D}_{fp}$ s.t. $([p, g^0_{\wp(p)}]\omega, D) \in L(\mathcal{A}_{\wp(p)})$, where $|States_i|$ denotes the number of states of the automata corresponding to the regular valuation λ.*

4 Single-Indexed CTL Model Checking for DPNs

In this section, we consider single-indexed CTL model-checking for DPNs with regular valuations. Single-indexed CTL model-checking for DPNs with simple valuations is a special case.

4.1 Single-Indexed CTL

For technical reasons, we suppose that CTL formulas are given in positive normal form, i.e., only atomic propositions are negated. Indeed, any CTL formula can be translated into positive normal form by pushing the negations inside. Moreover, we use the *release* operator **R** as the dual of the until operator **U**. Let AP be a finite set of atomic propositions. The set of CTL formulas is given by (where $a \in AP$):

$$\psi ::= a \mid \neg a \mid \psi \wedge \psi \mid \psi \vee \psi \mid \mathbf{AX}\psi \mid \mathbf{EX}\psi \mid \mathbf{A}[\psi\mathbf{U}\psi] \mid \mathbf{E}[\psi\mathbf{U}\psi] \mid \mathbf{A}[\psi\mathbf{R}\psi] \mid \mathbf{E}[\psi\mathbf{R}\psi].$$

The other standard CTL operators can be expressed by the above operators. E.g., $\mathbf{EF}\psi = \mathbf{E}[true\mathbf{U}\psi]$, $\mathbf{AF}\psi = \mathbf{A}[true\mathbf{U}\psi]$, $\mathbf{EG}\psi = \mathbf{E}[false\mathbf{R}\psi]$ and $\mathbf{AG}\psi = \mathbf{A}[false\mathbf{R}\psi]$. The closure $cl(\psi)$ of ψ is the set of all the subformulas of ψ including ψ. Let $At(\psi) = \{a \in AP \mid a \in cl(\psi)\}$ and $cl_{\mathbf{R}}(\psi) = \{\phi \in cl(\psi) \mid \phi = \mathbf{E}[\psi_1\mathbf{R}\psi_2] \text{ or } \phi = \mathbf{A}[\psi_1\mathbf{R}\psi_2]\}$.

Let $\lambda : AP \rightarrow 2^{\bigcup_{i=1}^{n} P_i \times \Gamma_i^*}$ a regular valuation assigning to each atomic proposition a regular set of local configurations. A local configuration c satisfies a CTL formula f_i, (denoted $c \models^{\lambda} f_i$), iff there exists $D \subseteq \mathcal{D}_i$ s.t. $c \models_D^{\lambda} f_i$ holds, where $\models_D^{\lambda}$ is inductively defined in Figure 1. Intuitively, $c \models_D^{\lambda} f_i$ means that c satisfies f_i and the executions that made c satisfy f_i create the set of DCLICs D, i.e., when a transition rule $q\gamma \hookrightarrow p_1\omega_1 \rhd p_2\omega_2$ is used to make f_i satisfied, $p_2\omega_2$ is in D. We write $c \models_D f_i$ instead of $c \models_D^{\lambda} f_i$ when λ is clear from the context.

A *single-indexed* CTL formula f is a formula of the form $\bigwedge f_i$ s.t. for every i, $1 \leq i \leq n$, f_i is a CTL formula in which the validity of the atomic propositions depends only on the DPDS $\mathcal{P}_i$. A global configuration $\mathcal{G}$ satisfies $f = \bigwedge f_i$ iff for every $c \in \mathcal{G}$, there exists a set of DCLICs $D \subseteq \mathcal{D}_{\wp(c)}$ s.t. $c \models_D f_{\wp(c)}$ and for every $d \in D$, d also satisfies f.

4.2 Alternating BDPDSs

Definition 6. *An Alternating BDPDS (ABDPDS) is a tuple $\mathcal{BP}'_i = (P'_i, \Gamma_i, \Delta'_i, F_i)$, where P'_i is a finite set of control locations, Γ_i is the stack alphabet, $F_i \subseteq P'_i$ is a set of accepting control locations, Δ'_i is a finite set of transition rules in the form of $p\gamma \hookrightarrow \{p_1\omega_1, ..., p_h\omega_h\} \rhd \{q_1u_1, ..., q_ku_k\}$ s.t. $p\gamma \in P'_i \times \Gamma_i, \{p_1\omega_1, ..., p_h\omega_h\} \subseteq P'_i \times \Gamma_i^*$ and $\{q_1u_1, ..., q_ku_k\} \subseteq \mathcal{D}_i$.*

An ABDPDS $\mathcal{BP}'_i$ induces a relation $\mapsto_i \subseteq (P'_i \times \Gamma_i^*) \times (2^{P'_i \times \Gamma^*} \times 2^{\mathcal{D}_i})$ defined as follows: for every $\omega \in \Gamma_i^*$, if $p\gamma \hookrightarrow \{p_1\omega_1, ..., p_h\omega_h\} \rhd \{q_1u_1, ..., q_ku_k\} \in \Delta_i$, then $p\gamma\omega \mapsto_i \{p_1\omega_1\omega, ..., p_h\omega_h\omega\} \rhd \{q_1u_1, ..., q_ku_k\}$. Intuitively, if $\mathcal{BP}'_i$ is at the configuration $p\gamma\omega$, it can fork into h copies in the configurations $p_1\omega_1\omega, ..., p_h\omega_h\omega$ and creates k new instances of ABDPDSs starting from the DCLICs $q_1u_1, ..., q_ku_k$, respectively. We sometimes write $p\gamma \hookrightarrow \{p_1\omega_1, ..., p_h\omega_h\}$ if $p\gamma \hookrightarrow \{p_1\omega_1, ..., p_h\omega_h\} \rhd \emptyset \in \Delta_i$.

$c \models^{\lambda}_{\emptyset} a$	$\Longleftrightarrow$	$c \in \lambda(a)$;
$c \models^{\lambda}_{\emptyset} \neg a$	$\Longleftrightarrow$	$c \notin \lambda(a)$;
$c \models^{\lambda}_{D} \psi_1 \wedge \psi_2$	$\Longleftrightarrow$	$\exists D_1, D_2 \subseteq \bigcup_{i=1}^{n} \mathcal{D}_i$ *s.t.* $D = D_1 \cup D_2$, $c \models^{\lambda}_{D_1} \psi_1$ and $c \models^{\lambda}_{D_2} \psi_2$;
$c \models^{\lambda}_{D} \psi_1 \vee \psi_2$	$\Longleftrightarrow$	$c \models^{\lambda}_{D} \psi_1$ or $c \models^{\lambda}_{D} \psi_2$;
$c \models^{\lambda}_{D} \mathbf{AX}\,\psi$	$\Longleftrightarrow$	For every $c_1, ..., c_m \in P_i \times \Gamma_i^*$ s.t. for $j, 1 \leq j \leq m, \exists D_j, D'_j \subseteq \bigcup_{i=1}^{n} \mathcal{D}_i$, $c \Longrightarrow_i c_j \triangleright D'_j$, $c_j \models^{\lambda}_{D_j} \psi$ and $D = \bigcup_{j=1}^{m} (D_j \cup D'_j)$;
$c \models^{\lambda}_{D} \mathbf{EX}\,\psi$	$\Longleftrightarrow$	There exist $c' \in P_i \times \Gamma_i^*$, $D', D'' \subseteq \bigcup_{i=1}^{n} \mathcal{D}_i$ *s.t.* $c \Longrightarrow_i c' \triangleright D''$, $c' \models^{\lambda}_{D'} \psi$ and $D = D' \cup D''$;
$c \models^{\lambda}_{D} \mathbf{A}[\psi_1 \mathbf{U} \psi_2]$	$\Longleftrightarrow$	For every path $\sigma = c_0 c_1 ...$ with $c_0 = c$, for every $m \geq 1, \exists D'_m \subseteq \bigcup_{i=1}^{n} \mathcal{D}_i$, *s.t.* $c_{m-1} \Longrightarrow c_m \triangleright D'_m$, and $\exists k \geq 0$, *s.t.* $\exists D_k \subseteq \bigcup_{i=1}^{n} \mathcal{D}_i, c_k \models^{\lambda}_{D_k} \psi_2, \forall j, 0 \leq j < k, c_j \models^{\lambda}_{D_j} \psi_1$ and $D = \bigcup_{\sigma} (\bigcup_{j=1}^{k} D'_j \cup \bigcup_{j=0}^{k} D_j)$;
$c \models^{\lambda}_{D} \mathbf{E}[\psi_1 \mathbf{U} \psi_2]$	$\Longleftrightarrow$	There exists a path $\sigma = c_0 c_1 ...$ with $c_0 = c$, for every $m \geq 1$, $\exists D'_m \subseteq \bigcup_{i=1}^{n} \mathcal{D}_i$, such that $c_{m-1} \Longrightarrow c_m \triangleright D'_m$, and $\exists k \geq 0$, *s.t.* $\exists D_k \subseteq \bigcup_{i=1}^{n} \mathcal{D}_i$, $c_k \models^{\lambda}_{D_k} \psi_2, \forall j, 0 \leq j < k, c_j \models^{\lambda}_{D_j} \psi_1$, and $D = \bigcup_{j=1}^{k} D'_j \cup \bigcup_{j=0}^{k} D_j$;
$c \models^{\lambda}_{D} \mathbf{A}[\psi_1 \mathbf{R} \psi_2]$	$\Longleftrightarrow$	For every path $\sigma = c_0 c_1 ...$ with $c_0 = c$, for every $m \geq 1$, $\exists D'_m \subseteq \bigcup_{i=1}^{n} \mathcal{D}_i$, such that $c_{m-1} \Longrightarrow c_m \triangleright D'_m$, and either $\forall j \geq 0, \exists D_j \subseteq \bigcup_{i=1}^{n} \mathcal{D}_i$, $c_j \models^{\lambda}_{D_j} \psi_2$ and $D_\sigma = \bigcup_{j \geq 1} D'_j \cup \bigcup_{j \geq 0} D_j$, or $\exists k \geq 0$, $\exists D''_k \subseteq \bigcup_{i=1}^{n} \mathcal{D}_i$ *s.t.* $c_k \models^{\lambda}_{D''_k} \psi_1$ and $\forall j$, $0 \leq j \leq k$, $\exists D_j \subseteq \bigcup_{i=1}^{n} \mathcal{D}_i, c_j \models^{\lambda}_{D_j} \psi_2$, $D_\sigma = \bigcup_{j=0}^{k} D_j \cup D''_k \cup \bigcup_{j=1}^{k} D'_j . D = \bigcup_{\sigma} D_\sigma$;
$c \models^{\lambda}_{D} \mathbf{E}[\psi_1 \mathbf{R} \psi_2]$	$\Longleftrightarrow$	There exists a path $\sigma = c_0 c_1 ...$ with $c_0 = c$, for every $m \geq 1, \exists D'_m \subseteq \bigcup_{i=1}^{n} \mathcal{D}_i$, such that $c_{m-1} \Longrightarrow c_m \triangleright D'_m$, and either $\forall j \geq 0$, $\exists D_j \subseteq \bigcup_{i=1}^{n} \mathcal{D}_i, c_j \models^{\lambda}_{D_j} \psi_2$ and $D = \bigcup_{j \geq 1} D'_j \cup \bigcup_{j \geq 0} D_j$, or $\exists k \geq 0, \exists D''_k \subseteq \bigcup_{i=1}^{n} \mathcal{D}_i$ *s.t.* $c_k \models^{\lambda}_{D''_k} \psi_1$ and $\forall j$, $0 \leq j \leq k, \exists D_j \subseteq \bigcup_{i=1}^{n} \mathcal{D}_i, c_j \models^{\lambda}_{D_j} \psi_2$, and $D = \bigcup_{j=0}^{k} D_j \cup D''_k \cup \bigcup_{j=1}^{k} D'_j$.

Fig. 1. Semantics of CTL

A run of $\mathcal{BP}'_i$ from a configuration $p\omega \in P'_i \times \Gamma_i^*$ is a tree rooted by $p\omega$, the other nodes are labeled by elements of $P'_i \times \Gamma_i^*$. If a node is labelled by qu whose children are $p_1\omega_1, ..., p_m\omega_m$, then, necessarily, $qu \mapsto \{p_1\omega_1, ..., p_m\omega_m\} \triangleright D$ for some $D \subseteq \mathcal{D}_i$. The run is *accepting* iff each branch of this run *infinitely often* visits some control locations in F_i. Let $L(\mathcal{BP}'_i)$ be the set of all the pairs $(c, D) \in P'_i \times \Gamma_i^* \times 2^{\mathcal{D}_i}$ s.t. $\mathcal{BP}'_i$ has an accepting run from c and that creates the set of DCLICs D.

4.3 Computing Corresponding Alternating BDPDSs

To perform single-indexed CTL model-checking for DPNs with regular valuations, we follow the approach for LTL model-checking for DPNs. But, in this case, we need alternating MAs and Alternating BDPDSs, since CTL formulas can be translated to alternating Büchi automata. We compute a set of AMAs $\mathcal{A}'_1, ..., \mathcal{A}'_n$ s.t. for every i, $1 \leq i \leq n$ and every local configuration $p\omega$ of $\mathcal{P}_i$, $p\omega \models_D f_i$ iff $([p, f_i]\omega, D) \in L(\mathcal{A}'_i)$. Later, we compute the largest set of DCLICs $\mathcal{D}'_{fp}$ such that a DCLIC d satisfies f iff $d \in \mathcal{D}'_{fp}$. Then, to check whether a global configuration $\mathcal{G}$ satisfies f, it is sufficient to check whether for every $p\omega \in \mathcal{G}$, there exists $D \subseteq \mathcal{D}'_{fp}$ s.t. $([p, f_{\wp(p)}]\omega, D) \in L(\mathcal{A}'_{\wp(p)})$. To compute the AMAs, we construct a set of alternating BDPDSs $\mathcal{BP}'_i$ which are synchronizations of the DPDSs $\mathcal{P}_i$ with formulas f_i s.t. the AMAs we are looking for correspond to the languages accepted by these alternating BDPDSs $\mathcal{BP}'_i s$. We first show how to compute the alternating BDPDSs $\mathcal{BP}'_i$. Then, we show how to compute the languages of these alternating BDPDSs $\mathcal{BP}_i s$, i.e. the AMAs.

We fix an index i, $1 \leq i \leq n$. We construct an ABDPDS $\mathcal{BP}'_i$ s.t. for every $p\omega \in P'_i \times \Gamma_i^*$, $p\omega \models_D f_i$ iff $([p, f_i]\omega, D) \in L(\mathcal{BP}'_i)$. We suppose w.l.o.g. that the DPDS $\mathcal{P}_i$ has a bottom-of-stack $\sharp$ which is never popped from the stack. For every $a \in At(f_i)$, since

$\lambda(a)$ is a regular set of local configurations of $\mathcal{P}_i$, let $M_a = (Q_a, \Gamma_i, \delta_a, I_a, Acc_a)$ be a MA s.t. $L(M_a) = \lambda(a) \times \{\emptyset\}$, and $M_{\neg a} = (Q_{\neg a}, \Gamma_i, \delta_{\neg a}, I_{\neg a}, Acc_{\neg a})$ a MA s.t. $L(M_{\neg a}) = (P_i \times \Gamma_i^* \setminus \lambda(a)) \times \{\emptyset\}$, i.e., the set of configurations where a does not hold. To distinguish between all the initial states p in M_a and $M_{\neg a}$, we write p_a and $p_{\neg a}$ instead. W.l.o.g., we assume that the set of states Q_as, and $Q_{\neg a}$s are disjoint for every $a \in At(f_i)$.

Let $\mathcal{BP}'_i = (P'_i, \Gamma_i, \Delta'_i, F_i)$ be the ABDPDS such that $P'_i = P_i \times cl(f_i) \cup \bigcup_{a \in At(f_i)}(Q_a \cup Q_{\neg a})$; $F_i = P_i \times cl_{\mathbf{R}}(f_i) \cup \bigcup_{a \in At(f_i)}(Acc_a \cup Acc_{\neg a})$; and Δ'_i is the smallest set of transition rules s.t. for every control location $p \in P_i$, every subformula $\psi \in cl(f_i)$ and every $\gamma \in \Gamma_i$, we have:

1. if $\psi = a$ or $\psi = \neg a$, where $a \in At(f_i)$; $[p, \psi]\gamma \hookrightarrow \{p_\psi \gamma\} \in \Delta'_i$;
2. if $\psi = \psi_1 \wedge \psi_2$; $[p, \psi]\gamma \hookrightarrow \{[p, \psi_1]\gamma, [p, \psi_2]\gamma\} \in \Delta'_i$;
3. if $\psi = \psi_1 \vee \psi_2$; $[p, \psi]\gamma \hookrightarrow \{[p, \psi_1]\gamma\} \in \Delta'_i$ and $[p, \psi]\gamma \hookrightarrow \{[p, \psi_2]\gamma\} \in \Delta'_i$;
4. if $\psi = \mathbf{EX}\psi_1$; $[p, \psi]\gamma \hookrightarrow \{[p', \psi_1]\omega\} \rhd \{p''\omega'\} \in \Delta'_i$ if $p\gamma \hookrightarrow p'\omega \rhd p''\omega' \in \Delta_i$; $[p, \psi]\gamma \hookrightarrow \{[p', \psi_1]\omega\} \in \Delta'_i$ if $p\gamma \hookrightarrow p'\omega \in \Delta_i$;
5. if $\psi = \mathbf{AX}\psi_1$; $[p, \psi]\gamma \hookrightarrow \{[p', \psi_1]\omega \mid p\gamma \hookrightarrow p'\omega \rhd p''\omega' \in \Delta_i\} \rhd \{p''\omega' \mid p\gamma \hookrightarrow p'\omega \rhd p''\omega' \in \Delta_i\} \in \Delta'_i$;
6. if $\psi = \mathbf{E}[\psi_1 \mathbf{U} \psi_2]$; $[p, \psi]\gamma \hookrightarrow \{[p, \psi_2]\gamma\} \in \Delta'_i$, and $[p, \psi]\gamma \hookrightarrow \{[p, \psi_1]\gamma, [p', \psi]\omega\} \rhd \{p''\omega'\} \in \Delta'_i$ if $p\gamma \hookrightarrow p'\omega \rhd p''\omega' \in \Delta_i$, $[p, \psi]\gamma \hookrightarrow \{[p, \psi_1]\gamma, [p', \psi]\omega\} \in \Delta'_i$ if $p\gamma \hookrightarrow p'\omega \in \Delta_i$;
7. if $\psi = \mathbf{A}[\psi_1 \mathbf{U} \psi_2]$; $[p, \psi]\gamma \hookrightarrow \{[p, \psi_2]\gamma\} \in \Delta'_i$ and $[p, \psi]\gamma \hookrightarrow \{[p, \psi_1]\gamma, [p', \psi]\omega \mid p\gamma \hookrightarrow p'\omega \rhd p''\omega' \in \Delta_i\} \rhd \{p''\omega' \mid p\gamma \hookrightarrow p'\omega \rhd p''\omega' \in \Delta_i\} \in \Delta'_i$;
8. if $\psi = \mathbf{E}[\psi_1 \mathbf{R} \psi_2]$; $[p, \psi]\gamma \hookrightarrow \{[p, \psi_2]\gamma, [p, \psi_1]\gamma\} \in \Delta'_i$, and $[p, \psi]\gamma \hookrightarrow \{[p, \psi_2]\gamma, [p', \psi]\omega\} \rhd \{p''\omega'\} \in \Delta'_i$ if $p\gamma \hookrightarrow p'\omega \rhd p''\omega' \in \Delta_i$, $[p, \psi]\gamma \hookrightarrow \{[p, \psi_2]\gamma, [p', \psi]\omega\} \in \Delta'_i$ if $p\gamma \hookrightarrow p'\omega \in \Delta_i$;
9. if $\psi = \mathbf{A}[\psi_1 \mathbf{R} \psi_2]$; $[p, \psi]\gamma \hookrightarrow \{[p, \psi_2]\gamma, [p, \psi_1]\gamma\} \in \Delta'_i$ and $[p, \psi]\gamma \hookrightarrow \{[p, \psi_2]\gamma, [p', \psi]\omega \mid p\gamma \hookrightarrow p'\omega \rhd p''\omega' \in \Delta_i\} \rhd \{p''\omega' \mid p\gamma \hookrightarrow p'\omega \rhd p''\omega' \in \Delta_i\} \in \Delta'_i$.
10. for every transition (q_1, γ, q_2) in $\bigcup_{a \in At(f_i)}(\delta_a \cup \delta_{\neg a})$; $q_1\gamma \hookrightarrow \{q_2\epsilon\} \in \Delta'_i$,
11. for every $q \in \bigcup_{a \in At(f_i)}(Acc_a \cup Acc_{\neg a})$; $q\sharp \hookrightarrow \{q\sharp\} \in \Delta'_i$.

For every $p\omega \in P'_i \times \Gamma_i^*$, $\mathcal{BP}'_i$ has an accepting run σ from $[p, f_i]\omega$ and D is the set of DCLICs created by σ iff $p\omega \models_D f_i$. The intuition behind each rule is explained as follows.

If $\psi = a \in At(f_i)$, for every $p\omega \in P'_i \times \Gamma_i^*$, $p\omega$ satisfies ψ iff $\mathcal{BP}'_i$ has an accepting run from $[p, a]\omega$. To check this, $\mathcal{BP}'_i$ moves to the initial state corresponding to p in M_a (i.e. p_a) by Item 1 allowing to check whether M_a accepts ω. Then the run of $\mathcal{BP}'_i$ from $p_a\omega$ mimics the run of M_a from the initial state p. Checking whether M_a accepts ω is ensured by Item 10. If $\mathcal{BP}'_i$ is at state q_1 with γ on the top of the stack and $q_1 \xrightarrow{\gamma} q_2$ is a transition of M_a, then $\mathcal{BP}'_i$ pops γ from the stack and moves the control location from q_1 to q_2. Popping γ from the stack allows to check the rest of the stack content. The configuration $p\omega$ is accepted by M_a iff the run of M_a reaches a final state $q \in Acc_a$, i.e., the run of $\mathcal{BP}'_i$ from $p\omega$ reaches the control location q with the empty stack, i.e., the stack only contains $\sharp$. Thus, $\mathcal{BP}'_i$ should have an infinite run from $q\sharp$ which infinitely often visits some control locations in F_i. This is ensured by adding a loop on the configuration $q\sharp$ (Item 11) and adding q into F_i. The case $\psi = \neg a$ s.t. $a \in At(f_i)$ is similar.

If $\psi = \psi_1 \wedge \psi_2$, then, for every $p\omega \in P_i' \times \Gamma_i^*$, $p\omega$ satisfies ψ iff $p\omega$ satisfies ψ_1 and ψ_2. This is ensured by Item 2 stating that $\mathcal{BP}_i'$ has an accepting run from $[p, \psi_1 \wedge \psi_2]\omega$ iff $\mathcal{BP}_i'$ has an accepting run from $[p, \psi_1]\omega$ and $[p, \psi_2]\omega$. Item 3 is similar to Item 2.

Item 4 expresses that if $\psi = \mathbf{EX}\psi_1$, then, for every $p\gamma u \in P_i' \times \Gamma_i^*$ s.t. $\gamma \in \Gamma_i$, $p\gamma u$ satisfies ψ iff there exists a transition $t_1 = p\gamma \hookrightarrow p'\omega \in \Delta_i$ or $t_2 = p\gamma \hookrightarrow p'\omega \rhd p''\omega' \in \Delta_i$ such that $p'\omega u$ satisfies ψ_1. Thus, $\mathcal{BP}_i'$ should have an accepting run from $[p, \psi]\gamma u$ iff $\mathcal{BP}_i'$ has an accepting run from $[p', \psi_1]\omega u$. Moreover, if t_2 is the fired transition rule, the created DCLIC $p''\omega'$ should also be created by $\mathcal{BP}_i'$. Item 5 is analogous.

If $\psi = \mathbf{E}[\psi_1 \mathbf{U} \psi_2]$, then, for every $p\gamma u \in P_i' \times \Gamma_i^*$ s.t. $\gamma \in \Gamma_i$, $p\gamma u$ satisfies ψ iff either it satisfies ψ_2, or it satisfies ψ_1 and there exists a transition $t_1 = p\gamma \hookrightarrow p'\omega \in \Delta_i$ or $t_2 = p\gamma \hookrightarrow p'\omega \rhd p''\omega' \in \Delta_i$ such that $p'\omega u$ satisfies ψ. Thus, $\mathcal{BP}_i'$ has an accepting run from $[p, \psi]\gamma u$ iff either $\mathcal{BP}_i'$ has an accepting run from $[p, \psi_2]\gamma u$ or $\mathcal{BP}_i'$ has an accepting run from $[p, \psi_1]\gamma u$ and $[p', \psi]\omega u$. This is ensured by Item 6. Moreover, if t_2 is the fired transition rule, the created DCLIC $p''\omega'$ should also be created by $\mathcal{BP}_i'$. The case $\psi = \mathbf{A}[\psi_1 \mathbf{U} \psi_2]$ is analogous.

Item 8 expresses that if $\psi = \mathbf{E}[\psi_1 \mathbf{R} \psi_2]$, then, for every $p\gamma u \in P_i' \times \Gamma_i^*$ s.t. $\gamma \in \Gamma_i$, $p\gamma u$ satisfies ψ iff it satisfies ψ_2, and either it satisfies also ψ_1, or there exists a transition $t_1 = p\gamma \hookrightarrow p'\omega \in \Delta_i$ or $t_2 = p\gamma \hookrightarrow p'\omega \rhd p''\omega' \in \Delta_i$ such that $p'\omega u$ satisfies ψ. This guarantees that ψ_2 holds either always, or until both ψ_1 and ψ_2 hold. The fact that the state $[p, \psi]$ is in F_i ensures that paths where ψ_2 always hold are accepting. If t_2 is the fired transition rule, the created DCLIC $p''\omega'$ should also be created by $\mathcal{BP}_i'$. The intuition behind Item 9 is analogous to Item 8. Then, we obtain the following lemma.

Lemma 3. *For every i, $1 \leq i \leq n$, we can compute an ABDPDS $\mathcal{BP}_i'$ with $O(|P_i| \cdot |f_i| + \sum_{a \in At(f_i)}(|Q_a| + |Q_{\neg a}|))$ states and $O((|P_i| \cdot |\Gamma_i| + |\Delta_i|)|f_i| + \sum_{a \in At(f_i)}(|\delta_a| + |\delta_{\neg a}|))$ transition rules such that for every $(p\omega, D) \in P_i \times \Gamma_i^* \times 2^{\mathcal{D}_i}$, $p\omega \models_D f_i$ iff $([p, f_i]\omega, D) \in L(\mathcal{BP}_i')$.*

4.4 Computing $L(\mathcal{BP}_i')$

Let us fix an index i, $1 \leq i \leq n$, the AMA $\mathcal{A}_i'$ we are looking for corresponds to $L(\mathcal{BP}_i')$. To compute this language, it is insufficient to simply compute the set of configurations from which $\mathcal{BP}_i'$ has an accepting run, since we also need to memorize the set of DCLICs created during the run of $\mathcal{BP}_i'$. To this aim, we follow the automata-based approach for CTL model-checking of PDSs presented in [20]. We first characterize the set $L(\mathcal{BP}_i')$, then we compute the AMA $\mathcal{A}_i'$ such that $L(\mathcal{A}_i') = L(\mathcal{BP}_i')$.

Characterizing $L(\mathcal{BP}_i')$**:** To characterize $L(\mathcal{BP}_i')$, we introduce the function $pre_{\mathcal{BP}_i'} : 2^{P_i' \times \Gamma_i^* \times 2^{\mathcal{D}_i}} \longrightarrow 2^{P_i' \times \Gamma_i^* \times 2^{\mathcal{D}_i}}$ as follows: $pre_{\mathcal{BP}_i'}(U) = \{(c, D) \mid c \mapsto_i \{c_1, ..., c_m\} \rhd D_0, \forall j : 1 \leq j \leq m, (c_j, D_j) \in U, \text{and } D = \bigcup_{j=0}^m D_j\}$. The transitive and reflexive closure of $pre_{\mathcal{BP}_i'}$ is denoted by $pre^*_{\mathcal{BP}_i'}$. Formally, $pre^*_{\mathcal{BP}_i'}(U) = \{(c, D) \mid (c, D) \in U$ or there exist $c_1, ..., c_m$ *s.t.* $c \mapsto_i \{c_1, ..., c_m\} \rhd D_0, \forall j : 1 \leq j \leq m, (c_j, D_j) \in pre^*_{\mathcal{BP}_i'}(U)$, and $D = \bigcup_{j=0}^m D_j\}$. Let $pre^+_{\mathcal{BP}_i'}(U) = pre^*_{\mathcal{BP}_i'}(pre_{\mathcal{BP}_i'}(U))$.

Let $Y_{\mathcal{BP}_i'} = \bigcap_{j \geq 1} Y_j$ where $Y_0 = P_i' \times \Gamma_i^* \times \{\emptyset\}$, $Y_{j+1} = pre^+_{\mathcal{BP}_i'}(Y_j \cap F_i \times \Gamma_i^* \times 2^{\mathcal{D}_i})$ for every $j \geq 0$. Intuitively, $(c, D) \in Y_1$ iff $\mathcal{BP}_i'$ has a run from c s.t. each path of this

Algorithm 1. Computation of $Y_{\mathcal{BP}'_i}$.

Input : An ABDPDS $\mathcal{BP}'_i = (P'_i, \Gamma_i, \Delta'_i, F_i)$;
Output: An AMA $\mathcal{A}'_i = (Q_i, \Gamma_i, \delta_i, I_i, \{q_f\})$ s.t. $L(\mathcal{A}'_i) = Y_{\mathcal{BP}'_i}$;

1 Let $k := 0, \delta_i := \{(q_f, \gamma, \emptyset, \{q_f\})$ for every $\gamma \in \Gamma_i\}$, and $\forall p \in P'_i$, $p^0 := q_f$;
2 **repeat** we call this loop $loop_1$
3 $\quad k := k + 1$;
4 $\quad$ Add a new transition rule $p^k \xrightarrow{\epsilon/\emptyset}_i \{p^{k-1}\}$ in δ_i for every $p \in F_i$;
5 $\quad$ **repeat** we call this loop $loop_2$
6 $\quad\quad$ For every $p\gamma \hookrightarrow \{p_1\omega_1, ..., p_h\omega_h\} \rhd D$ in Δ'_i,
7 $\quad\quad$ and every case $p_j^k \xrightarrow{\omega_j/D_j}{}^*_i R_j$ for all j, $1 \leq j \leq h$;
8 $\quad\quad\quad p^k \xrightarrow{\gamma/D \cup \bigcup_{j=1}^h D_j}_i \bigcup_{j=1}^h R_j$ in δ_i
9 $\quad$ **until** *No new transition rule can be added*;
10 $\quad$ Remove from δ_i the transition rules $p^k \xrightarrow{\epsilon/\emptyset}_i \{p^{k-1}\}$, $\forall p \in F_i$;
11 $\quad$ Replace in δ_i transition rule $p^k \xrightarrow{\gamma/D}_i R$ by $p^k \xrightarrow{\gamma/D}_i \pi^k(R)$, $\forall p \in P'_i, \gamma \in \Gamma_i, R \subseteq Q_i$;
12 **until** $k > 1$ *and* $\forall p \in P'_i, \gamma \in \Gamma_i, R \subseteq P'_i \times \{k\} \cup \{q_f\}, D \subseteq \mathcal{D}_i$, $p^k \xrightarrow{\gamma/D}_i R \in \delta_i$ *iff* $p^{k-1} \xrightarrow{\gamma/D}_i \pi^{-1}(R) \in \delta_i$;

run visits accepting control locations at least *once* and D is the set of DCLICs created during this run. $(c, D) \in Y_j$ iff $\mathcal{BP}'_i$ has a run from c s.t. each path of this run visits some control locations in F_i at least j times and D is the set of DCLICs created during this run. Since $Y_{\mathcal{BP}'_i} = \bigcap_{j\geq 1} Y_j$, for every $(c, D) \in Y_{\mathcal{BP}'_i}$, $\mathcal{BP}'_i$ has a run from c s.t. each path visits some control locations in F_i infinitely often and D is the set of all the DCLICs created during this run. Thus, we get:

Proposition 3. $L(\mathcal{BP}'_i) = Y_{\mathcal{BP}'_i}$.

Computing $Y_{\mathcal{BP}'_i}$**:** We show that $Y_{\mathcal{BP}'_i}$ can be represented by an AMA $\mathcal{A}'_i = (Q_i, \Gamma_i, \delta_i, I_i,$
$Acc_i)$ where $Q_i \subseteq P'_i \times \mathbb{N} \cup \{q_f\}$ and q_f is the unique final state, i.e., $Acc_i = \{q_f\}$. Let q^k denote $(q, k) \in P'_i \times \mathbb{N}$. Intuitively, to compute $Y_{\mathcal{BP}'_i}$, we will compute iteratively the different Y_js. The iterative procedure computes different AMAs. To force termination, we use an acceleration based on the projection functions π^{-1} and π^k: for every $S \subseteq Q_i$,

$$\pi^{-1}(S) = \begin{cases} \{q^k \mid q^{k+1} \in S\} \cup \{q_f\} \text{ if } q_f \in S \text{ or } \exists q^1 \in S, \\ \{q^k \mid q^{k+1} \in S\} \quad\quad \text{else.} \end{cases}$$

$$\pi^k(S) = \{q^k \mid \exists j, 1 \leq j \leq k \text{ s.t. } q^j \in S\} \cup \{q_f \mid q_f \in S\}.$$

Algorithm 1 computes an AMA $\mathcal{A}'_i$ recognizing $Y_{\mathcal{BP}'_i}$. Let us explain the intuition behind the different lines of this algorithm. Let A_0 be the automaton obtained after the initialization (Line 1). It is clear that A_0 accepts Y_0. Let A_k be the AMA obtained at step k (a step starts at Line 3). For every $p \in P'_i$, state p^k denotes state p at step k, i.e., A_k recognizes a tuple $(p\omega, D)$ iff $p^k \xrightarrow{\omega/D}{}^*_i \{q_f\}$. Suppose the algorithm is at the beginning of the kth step ($loop_1$). Line 4 adds the ϵ-transition $p^k \xrightarrow{\epsilon/\emptyset}_i \{p^{k-1}\}$ for every $p \in F_i$. Then, we obtain $L(A_{k-1}) \cap F_i \times \Gamma_i^* \times 2^{\mathcal{D}_i}$. $loop_2$ (Lines 5-9) is the saturation procedure that computes $pre^*_{\mathcal{BP}'_i}(L(A_{k-1}) \cap F_i \times \Gamma_i^* \times 2^{\mathcal{D}_i})$. Line 10 removes the ϵ-transition $p^k \xrightarrow{\epsilon/\emptyset}_i \{p^{k-1}\}$ for every $p \in F_i$. After this, we obtain $pre^+_{\mathcal{BP}'_i}(L(A_{k-1}) \cap F_i \times \Gamma_i^* \times 2^{\mathcal{D}_i})$. Thus, in case of termination, the algorithm outputs $Y_{\mathcal{BP}'_i}$. The substitution at Line 11 is used to force termination. Thus, we can show the following theorem.

Theorem 6. *Algorithm 1 always terminates and produces* $Y_{\mathcal{BP}'_i}$.

Proof Sketch. The proof follows the proof of [20]. Algorithm 1 follows the idea of the algorithm of [20]. computing an AMA recognizing the language of an ABDPDS when transition rules are in the form of $p\gamma \hookrightarrow \{p_1\omega_1, ..., p_h\omega_h\}$, i.e., $\mathcal{D}_i = \emptyset$. The main differences are:

To compute $pre^*_{\mathcal{BP}'_i}(L(A_{k-1}) \cap F_i \times \Gamma_i^* \times 2^{\mathcal{D}_i})$, instead of using the following saturation procedure given in [2] that computes reachable configurations of *Alternating* PDSs:

If $p\gamma \hookrightarrow \{p_1\omega_1, ..., p_m\omega_m\} \in \Delta'_i$ and $p_j^k \xrightarrow{\omega_j/\emptyset}{}^*_i R_j$, for j, $1 \leq j \leq m$, add $p^k \xrightarrow{\gamma/\emptyset}_i \cup_{j=1}^m R_j$ in δ_i.

We use the following saturation procedure:

If $p\gamma \hookrightarrow \{p_1\omega_1, ..., p_h\omega_h\} \rhd D \in \Delta'_i$ and $p_j^k \xrightarrow{\omega_j/D_j}{}^*_i R_j$ for j, $1 \leq j \leq h$, add $p^k \xrightarrow{\gamma/D \cup \bigcup_{j=1}^h D_j} \cup_{j=1}^h R_j$ in δ_i.

The idea behind our saturation procedure is the following: suppose $p\gamma \hookrightarrow \{p_1\omega_1, ..., p_h\omega_h\} \rhd D \in \Delta'_i$ and for every j, $1 \leq j \leq h$, $(p_j\omega_j\omega', D_j)$ is in $L(A'_{k-1}) \cap F_i \times \Gamma_i^* \times 2^{\mathcal{D}_i}$ (i.e., $p_j^k \xrightarrow{\omega_j/D'_j}{}^*_i R_j \xrightarrow{\omega'/D''_j}{}^*_i \{q_f\}$ and $D_j = D'_j \cup D''_j$). Then, Lines 3-6 add the new transition rule $p^k \xrightarrow{\gamma(D \cup \bigcup_{j=1}^h D_j)}_i \bigcup_{j=1}^h R_j$ that allows to accept $(p\gamma\omega', D \cup \bigcup_{j=1}^h D_j)$, i.e., $(p\gamma\omega', D \cup \bigcup_{j=1}^h D_j) \in pre^*_{\mathcal{BP}'_i}(\{(p_1\omega_1\omega', D_1), ..., (p_j\omega_j\omega', D_j)\})$. □

Complexity. Following [20], we can show that $loop_2$ can be done in time $O(|P'_i| \cdot |\Delta'_i| \cdot 2^{4|P'_i|+|\mathcal{D}_i|})$. The substitution (Line 11) and termination condition (Line 12) can be done in time $O(|\Gamma_i| \cdot |P'_i| \cdot 2^{2|P'_i|+|\mathcal{D}_i|})$ and $O(|\Gamma_i| \cdot |P'_i| \cdot 2^{|P'_i|+|\mathcal{D}_i|})$, respectively. Putting all these estimations together, the global complexity of Algorithm 1 is $O(|P'_i|^2 \cdot |\Delta'_i| \cdot |\Gamma_i| \cdot 2^{5|P'_i|+|\mathcal{D}_i|})$.

By Proposition 3 and Theorem 6, we get:

Lemma 4. *Given an ABDPDS* $\mathcal{BP}'_i$, *we can construct an AMA* $\mathcal{A}'_i$ *with* $O(|\Gamma_i| \cdot |P'_i| \cdot 2^{|P'_i|+|\mathcal{D}_i|})$ *transitions and* $O(|P'_i|)$ *states in time* $O(|P'_i|^2 \cdot |\Delta'_i| \cdot |\Gamma_i| \cdot 2^{5|P'_i|+|\mathcal{D}_i|})$ *s.t.* $L(\mathcal{BP}'_i) = L(\mathcal{A}'_i)$.

From Lemma 4 and Lemma 3, we get:

Lemma 5. *We can compute AMAs* $\mathcal{A}'_1, ..., \mathcal{A}'_n$ *in time* $O(\sum_{i=1}^n ((|P_i| \cdot |f_i| + k)^2 \cdot ((|P_i| \cdot |\Gamma_i| + |\Delta_i|)|f_i| + d) \cdot |\Gamma_i| \cdot 2^{5(|P_i| \cdot |f_i| + k) + |\mathcal{D}_i|}))$ *s.t. for every* i, $1 \leq i \leq n$, $p\omega \in P_i \times \Gamma_i^*$, $p\omega \models_D f_i$ *iff* $([p, f_i], D) \in L(\mathcal{A}'_i)$, *where* $k = \sum_{a \in At(f_i)}(|Q_a| + |Q_{\neg a}|)$ *and* $d = \sum_{a \in At(f_i)}(|\delta_a| + |\delta_{\neg a}|)$.

4.5 CTL Model-Checking For DPNs with Regular Valuations

By Lemma 5, we obtain a set of AMAs $\{\mathcal{A}'_1, ..., \mathcal{A}'_n\}$ s.t. for every i, $1 \leq i \leq n$ and every local configuration $p\omega \in P_i \times \Gamma_i^*$, $p\omega \models_D f_i$ iff $([p, f_i]\omega, D) \in L(\mathcal{A}'_i)$. Following the approach for single-indexed LTL model-checking for DPNs, to obtain an efficient procedure, we compute the largest set $\mathcal{D}'_{fp}$ of DCLICs s.t. for every $d \in \bigcup_{i=1}^{n} \mathcal{D}_i$, d satisfies f iff $d \in \mathcal{D}'_{fp}$. Then, to check whether a global configuration $\mathcal{G}$ satisfies f, it is sufficient to check whether for every $p\omega \in \mathcal{G}$, there exists $D \subseteq \mathcal{D}'_{fp}$ s.t. $([p, f_{\wp(p)}]\omega, D) \in L(\mathcal{A}'_{\wp(p)})$. $\mathcal{D}'_{fp}$ can be computed as done in Section 3.2. We can show that:

Theorem 7. *We can compute AMAs $\mathcal{A}'_1, ..., \mathcal{A}'_n$ in time $O(\sum_{i=1}^{n}((|P_i| \cdot |f_i| + k)^2 \cdot ((|P_i| \cdot |\Gamma_i| + |\Delta_i|)|f_i| + d) \cdot |\Gamma_i| \cdot 2^{5(|P_i| \cdot |f_i| + k) + |\mathcal{D}_i|}))$ s.t. for every global configuration $\mathcal{G}$, $\mathcal{G}$ satisfies f iff for every $p\omega \in \mathcal{G}$, there exists $D \subseteq \mathcal{D}'_{fp}$ such that $([p, f_{\wp(p)}]\omega, D) \in L(\mathcal{A}'_{\wp(p)})$, where $k = \sum_{a \in At(f_i)}(|Q_a| + |Q_{\neg a}|)$ and $d = \sum_{a \in At(f_i)}(|\delta_a| + |\delta_{\neg a}|)$.*

References

1. Atig, M.F., Bouajjani, A., Touili, T.: On the reachability analysis of acyclic networks of pushdown systems. In: van Breugel, F., Chechik, M. (eds.) CONCUR 2008. LNCS, vol. 5201, pp. 356–371. Springer, Heidelberg (2008)
2. Bouajjani, A., Esparza, J., Maler, O.: Reachability Analysis of Pushdown Automata: Application to Model Checking. In: Mazurkiewicz, A., Winkowski, J. (eds.) CONCUR 1997. LNCS, vol. 1243, pp. 135–150. Springer, Heidelberg (1997)
3. Bouajjani, A., Esparza, J., Touili, T.: A generic approach to the static analysis of concurrent programs with procedures. In: POPL, pp. 62–73 (2003)
4. Bouajjani, A., Müller-Olm, M., Touili, T.: Regular symbolic analysis of dynamic networks of pushdown systems. In: Abadi, M., de Alfaro, L. (eds.) CONCUR 2005. LNCS, vol. 3653, pp. 473–487. Springer, Heidelberg (2005)
5. Bozzelli, L., Kretínský, M., Rehák, V., Strejcek, J.: On decidability of LTL model checking for process rewrite systems. Acta Inf. 46(1) (2009)
6. Chaki, S., Clarke, E., Kidd, N., Reps, T., Touili, T.: Verifying concurrent message-passing C programs with recursive calls. In: Hermanns, H., Palsberg, J. (eds.) TACAS 2006. LNCS, vol. 3920, pp. 334–349. Springer, Heidelberg (2006)
7. Esparza, J., Hansel, D., Rossmanith, P., Schwoon, S.: Efficient algorithm for model checking pushdown systems. In: Emerson, E.A., Sistla, A.P. (eds.) CAV 2000. LNCS, vol. 1855, pp. 232–247. Springer, Heidelberg (2000)
8. Esparza, J., Kucera, A., Schwoon, S.: Model checking LTL with regular valuations for pushdown systems. Inf. Comput. 186(2), 355–376 (2003)
9. Gawlitza, T.M., Lammich, P., Müller-Olm, M., Seidl, H., Wenner, A.: Join-lock-sensitive forward reachability analysis for concurrent programs with dynamic process creation. In: VMCAI, pp. 199–213 (2011)
10. Göller, S., Lin, A.W.: The complexity of verifying ground tree rewrite systems. In: LICS, pp. 279–288 (2011)
11. Kahlon, V., Gupta, A.: An Automata-Theoretic Approach for Model Checking Threads for LTL Properties. In: LICS, pp. 101–110 (2006)
12. Kahlon, V., Gupta, A.: On the analysis of interacting pushdown systems. In: POPL, pp. 303–314 (2007)
13. Kahlon, V., Ivančić, F., Gupta, A.: Reasoning about threads communicating via locks. In: Etessami, K., Rajamani, S.K. (eds.) CAV 2005. LNCS, vol. 3576, pp. 505–518. Springer, Heidelberg (2005)
14. Kidd, N., Lammich, P., Touili, T., Reps, T.: A decision procedure for detecting atomicity violations for communicating processes with locks. In: Păsăreanu, C.S. (ed.) Model Checking Software. LNCS, vol. 5578, pp. 125–142. Springer, Heidelberg (2009)

15. Lammich, P., Müller-Olm, M.: Precise fixpoint-based analysis of programs with thread-creation and procedures. In: Caires, L., Vasconcelos, V.T. (eds.) CONCUR 2007. LNCS, vol. 4703, pp. 287–302. Springer, Heidelberg (2007)
16. Lammich, P., Müller-Olm, M.: Conflict analysis of programs with procedures, dynamic thread creation, and monitors. In: Alpuente, M., Vidal, G. (eds.) SAS 2008. LNCS, vol. 5079, pp. 205–220. Springer, Heidelberg (2008)
17. Lammich, P., Müller-Olm, M., Wenner, A.: Predecessor sets of dynamic pushdown networks with tree-regular constraints. In: Bouajjani, A., Maler, O. (eds.) CAV 2009. LNCS, vol. 5643, pp. 525–539. Springer, Heidelberg (2009)
18. Lugiez, D.: Forward analysis of dynamic network of pushdown systems is easier without order. Int. J. Found. Comput. Sci. 22(4), 843–862 (2011)
19. Mayr, R.: Process rewrite systems. Inf. Comput. 156(1-2), 264–286 (2000)
20. Song, F., Touili, T.: Efficient CTL model-checking for pushdown systems. In: Katoen, J.-P., König, B. (eds.) CONCUR 2011. LNCS, vol. 6901, pp. 434–449. Springer, Heidelberg (2011)
21. Song, F., Touili, T.: Model Checking Dynamic Pushdown Networks. Research report (2012), `http://www.liafa.univ-paris-diderot.fr/~song/dpn-full.pdf`
22. Touili, T., Atig, M.F.: Verifying parallel programs with dynamic communication structures. Theor. Comput. Sci. 411(38-39), 3460–3468 (2010)
23. Vardi, M.Y., Wolper, P.: Automata-theoretic techniques for modal logics of programs. J. Comput. Syst. Sci. 32(2), 183–221 (1986)
24. Wenner, A.: Weighted dynamic pushdown networks. In: Gordon, A.D. (ed.) ESOP 2010. LNCS, vol. 6012, pp. 590–609. Springer, Heidelberg (2010)
25. Yahav, E.: Verifying safety properties of concurrent java programs using 3-valued logic. In: POPL, pp. 27–40 (2001)

Robustness Analysis of Finite Precision Implementations

Eric Goubault and Sylvie Putot

CEA Saclay Nano-INNOV, CEA LIST, Laboratory for the Modelling and Analysis of Interacting Systems, Point Courrier 174, 91191 Gif sur Yvette CEDEX
{Eric.Goubault,Sylvie.Putot}@cea.fr

Abstract. A desirable property of control systems is robustness to inputs, when small perturbations of the inputs of a system will cause only small perturbations on outputs. This property should be maintained at the implementation level, where close inputs can lead to different execution paths. The problem becomes crucial for finite precision implementations, where any elementary computation is affected by an error. In this context, almost every test is potentially unstable, that is, for a given input, the finite precision and real numbers paths may differ. Still, state-of-the-art error analyses rely on the stable test hypothesis, yielding unsound error bounds when the conditional block is not robust to uncertainties. We propose a new abstract-interpretation based error analysis of finite precision implementations, which is sound in presence of unstable tests, by bounding the discontinuity error for path divergences. This gives a tractable analysis implemented in the FLUCTUAT analyzer.

1 Introduction

In the analysis of numerical programs, a recurrent difficulty when we want to assess the influence of finite precision on an implementation, is the possibility for a test to be unstable: when, for a given input, the finite precision control flow can differ from the control flow that would be taken by the same execution in real numbers. Not taking this possibility into account may be unsound if the difference of paths leads to a discontinuity in the computation, while taking it into account without special care soon leads to large over-approximations.

This unstable test problem is thus closely related to the notion of continuity/discontinuity in programs, first introduced in [13]. Basically, a program is continuous if, when its inputs are slightly perturbed, its output is also only slightly perturbed, very similarly to the concept of a continuous function. Discontinuity in itself can be a symptom of a major bug in some critical systems, such as the one where a F22 Raptor military aircraft almost crashed after crossing the international date line in 2007, due to a discontinuity in the treatment of dates. We thus want to automatically characterize conditional blocks that perform a continuous treatment of inputs, and are thus robust, and those that do not. Consider the program presented on the left hand side of Figure 1, where input x takes its real value in $[1, 3]$, with an error $0 < u << 1$, that can come from

C.-c. Shan (Ed.): APLAS 2013, LNCS 8301, pp. 50–57, 2013.

previous finite precision computations or from any uncertainty such as sensor imperfection. The test is potentially unstable: for instance, if the real value of x at control point [1] is $r^x_{[1]} = 2$, then its floating-point value is $f^x_{[1]} = 2 + u$. Thus the execution in real numbers would take the **then** branch and lead at control point [2] to $r^y_{[2]} = r^x_{[1]} + 2 = 4$, whereas the floating-point execution would take the **else** branch and lead to $f^y_{[4]} = f^x_{[1]} = 2 + u$. The test is not only unstable, but also introduces a discontinuity around the test condition ($x == 2$). Indeed, for $r^x_{[1]} = 2$, there is an error due to discontinuity of $f^y_{[4]} - r^y_{[2]} = -2 + u$.

In the rest of the paper, we propose a new analysis, that enhances earlier work by the authors [11], by computing and propagating bounds on those discontinuity errors. This previous work characterized the computation error due to the implementation in finite precision, by comparing the computations in real-numbers with the same computations in the floating-point semantics, relying on the stable test assumption: the floating-point number control flow does not diverge from the real number control flow. When this assumption is not satisfied, the comparison between the two semantics (the error bounds) could be unsound. This issue appears in all other (static or dynamic) existing analyzes of numerical error propagation; the expression unstable test is actually taken from CADNA [4], a stochastic arithmetic instrumentation of programs, to assert their numerical quality. In Hoare provers dealing with both real number and floating-point number semantics, e.g. [1] this issue has to be sorted out by the user, through suitable assertions and lemmas.

Here as in previous work, we rely on the relational abstractions of real number and floating numbers semantics using affine sets (concretized as zonotopes) [9,10,5,6,11]. But we now also, using these abstractions, compute and solve constraints on inputs such that the execution potentially leads to unstable tests, and thus accurately bound the discontinuity errors, computed as the difference of the floating-point value in one branch and the real value in another, when the test distinguishing these two branches can be unstable.

x := [1,3] + u; // [1]
/* $\hat{r}^x_{[1]} = 2 + \varepsilon^r_1$; $\hat{e}^x_{[1]} = u$ */
if (x ≤ 2)
y = x+2; // [2]
/* $\hat{r}^y_{[2]} = 4 + \varepsilon^r_1$;
$\hat{e}^y_{[2]} = u + \delta\varepsilon^e_2$ */
else
y = x; // [3]
/* $\hat{r}^y_{[4]} = 2 + \varepsilon^r_1$;
/* $\hat{e}^y_{[4]} = u$ */
// [4] /* $\hat{r}^y_{[4]} = \hat{r}^y_{[2]} \sqcup \hat{r}^y_{[4]}$
$\hat{e}^y_{[4]} = \hat{e}^y_{[2]} \sqcup \hat{e}^y_{[3]} + d^y_{[4]}$ */

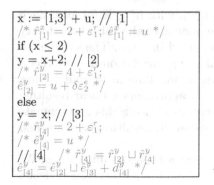

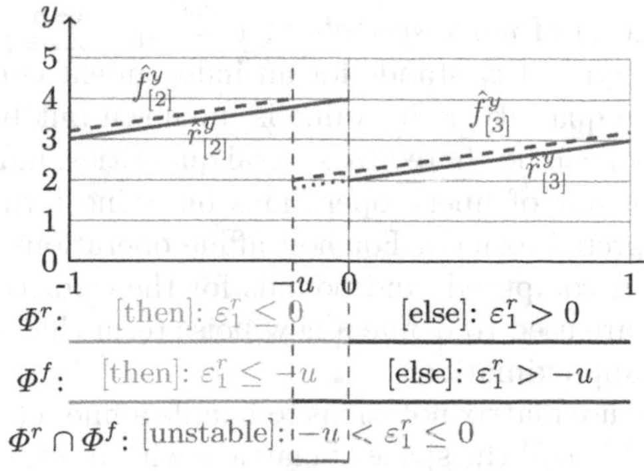

Fig. 1. Running example

Related Work. In [2], the authors introduce a continuity analysis of programs. This approach is pursued in particular in [3], where several refinements of the notion of continuity or robustness of programs are proposed, another one being introduced in [14]. In [14], the algorithm proposed by the authors symbolically traverses program paths and collects constraints on input and output variables. Then for each pair of program paths, the algorithm determines values of input variables that cause the program to follow these two paths and for which the difference in values of the output variable is maximized. One difference between the approaches is that we give extra information concerning the finite precision flow divergence with respect to the real number control flow, potentially exhibiting flawed behaviors. Also, their path-sensitive analysis can exhibit witnesses for worst discontinuity errors, but at the expense of a much bigger combinatorial complexity. Robustness has also been discussed in the context of synthesis and validation of control systems, for instance in [16]. Indeed, robustness has long been central in numerical mathematics, in particular in control theory. The field of robust control is actually concerned in proving stability of controlled systems where parameters are only known in range.

Contents. Our main contribution is a tractable analysis that generalizes both the abstract domain of [11] and the continuity or robustness analyses: it ensures the finite precision error analysis is now sound even in the presence of unstable tests, by computing and propagating discontinuity error bounds for these tests. More details on this analysis and further experiments are available in [12].

2 Preliminaries: Affine Sets for Real Valued Analysis

We sketch here some basics on the abstract domains based on affine sets for the abstraction of real number semantics, necessary to understand the robustness analysis presented here. We refer to [8,9,10,5,6] for more details.

Affine arithmetic is a more accurate extension of interval arithmetic, that takes into account affine correlations between variables. An *affine form* is a formal sum over a set of *noise symbols* ε_i, $\hat{x} \stackrel{\text{def}}{=} \alpha_0^x + \sum_{i=1}^n \alpha_i^x \varepsilon_i$, with $\alpha_i^x \in \mathbb{R}$ for all i. Each noise symbol ε_i stands for an independent component of the total uncertainty on the quantity $\hat{x}$, its value is unknown but bounded in [-1,1]. The same noise symbol can be shared by several quantities, indicating correlations among them. The result of linear operations on affine forms is an affine form, and is thus interpreted exactly. For non affine operations, an approximate linear resulting form is computed, and bounds for the error committed using this approximate form are used to define a new noise term that makes the resulting form a sound over-approximation.

We use matrix notations to handle affine sets, that is tuples of affine forms. We note $\mathcal{M}(n,p)$ the space of matrices with n lines and p columns of real coefficients. A tuple of affine forms expressing the set of values taken by p variables over n noise symbols ε_i, $1 \leq i \leq n$, is represented by a matrix $A \in \mathcal{M}(n+1,p)$.

Constrained Affine Sets. As described in [6], tests are interpreted by leaving affine sets unchanged and adding some constraints on the ε_i noise symbols, instead of having them vary freely into [-1,1]: we restrain ourselves to executions (or inputs) that can take the considered branch. These constraints can be abstracted in any abstract domain, the simplest being intervals. We note $\mathcal{A}$ for this abstract domain, and use $\gamma : \mathcal{A} \to \wp(\mathbb{R}^n)$ for the concretisation operator, and $\alpha : \wp(\mathbb{R}^n) \to \mathcal{A}$ for some abstraction operator.

This means that abstract values X are now composed of a zonotope identified with its matrix $R^X \in \mathcal{M}(n+1,p)$, together with an abstraction Φ^X of the constraints on the noise symbols, $X = (R^X, \Phi^X)$. The concretisation of such constrained zonotopes or affine sets is $\gamma(X) = \left\{ {}^tC^X\epsilon \mid \epsilon \in \gamma(\Phi^X) \right\}$. For $\Phi^X \in \mathcal{A}$, and $\hat{x}$ an affine form, we note $\Phi^X(\hat{x})$ the interval $[\inf_{\varepsilon\in\gamma(\Phi^X)} \hat{x}(\varepsilon), \sup_{\varepsilon\in\gamma(\Phi^X)} \hat{x}(\varepsilon)]$.

Example 1. On the running example from Figure 1, the real value of input `x`, given in $[1,3]$, will be abstracted by the affine form $\hat{r}^x_{[1]} = 2 + \varepsilon^r_1$, where ε^r_1 is a symbolic variable with values in $[-1,1]$. We associate the abstract value X with $R^X = (2\ 1)$, i.e. $\hat{x} = 2 + \varepsilon_1$, and $\gamma(\Phi^X) = \gamma(\varepsilon_1) = [-1,1]$.

Note the functional abstraction: affine forms represent a function from inputs to variable values. We will use this to interpret tests, and in particular to compute unstable tests conditions. Here, the interpretation of the test `if (x<=2)` in the **then** branch is translated into constraint $2+\varepsilon^r_1 \leq 2$, that is $\varepsilon^r_1 \leq 0$, thus $\gamma(\Phi^X) = [-1,0]$. Then, the interval concretisation of $\hat{x}$ is $\gamma(\hat{x}) = [2-1,2] = [1,2]$.

We also need an upper bound operator to combine abstract values coming from different branches. The computation of upper bounds (and if possible minimal ones) on constrained affine sets is a difficult task, already discussed in several papers [9,10,6,7], and orthogonal to the robustness analysis presented here. We will thus consider we have an upper bound operator on constrained affine sets we note $\sqcup$, and focus on the additional term due to discontinuity in tests.

3 Robustness Analysis of Finite Precision Computations

We now introduce an analysis of finite precision computations, based on an abstraction similar to some previous work [11], but refined to be sound in presence of unstable tests, and to exhibit the potential discontinuity errors due to these tests. For more concision, we insist here on what is directly linked to an accurate treatment of these discontinuities, and rely as much as possible on [11].

Floating-point computation is considered as a perturbation of the same computation in real numbers, and we use zonotopic abstractions of real computations and errors (introducing respectively noise symbols ε^r_i and ε^e_j), from which we get an abstraction of floating point computations. But we make here no assumptions on control flows in tests and will compute branch conditions independently on the real value and the floating-point value. For each branch, we thus get two sets of constraints: $\varepsilon^r = (\varepsilon^r_1, \ldots, \varepsilon^r_n) \in \Phi^X_r$ for the real control flow (test computed on real values R^X), and $(\varepsilon^r, \varepsilon^e) = (\varepsilon^r_1, \ldots, \varepsilon^r_n, \varepsilon^e_1, \ldots, \varepsilon^e_m) \in \Phi^X_f$ for the finite precision control flow (test computed on float values $R^X + E^X$).

Definition 1. *An abstract value X, defined at a given control point, for a program with p variables $x_1, \ldots, x_p$, is thus a tuple $X = (R^X, E^X, D^X, \Phi_r^X, \Phi_f^X)$ composed of the following affine sets and constraints, for all $k = 1, \ldots, p$:*

$$\begin{cases} R^X \;:\; \hat{r}_k^X = r_{0,k}^X + \sum_{i=1}^n r_{i,k}^X \varepsilon_i^r & \text{where } \varepsilon^r \in \Phi_r^X \\ E^X \;:\; \hat{e}_k^X = e_{0,k}^X + \sum_{i=1}^n e_{i,k}^X \varepsilon_i^r + \sum_{j=1}^m e_{n+j,k}^X \varepsilon_j^e & \text{where } (\varepsilon^r, \varepsilon^e) \in \Phi_f^X \\ D^X \;:\; \hat{d}_k^X = d_{0,k}^X + \sum_{i=1}^o d_{i,k}^X \varepsilon_i^d & \\ \quad\;\;\; \hat{f}_k^X = \hat{r}_k^X + \hat{e}_k^X & \text{where } (\varepsilon^r, \varepsilon^e) \in \Phi_f^X \end{cases}$$

where $R^X \in \mathcal{M}(n+1, p)$ defines the real values of variables, and $\hat{r}_k^X$ giving the real value of x_k is defined on the ε_i^r; $E^X \in \mathcal{M}(n+m+1, p)$ defines the rounding errors (or initial uncertainties) and their propagation through computations using the ε_i^r which handle the uncertainty on the real value and the ε_i^e which handle the uncertainty on the rounding errors; $D^X \in \mathcal{M}(o+1, p)$ defines the discontinuity errors, using noise symbols ε_i^d; Φ_r^X abstracts the set of constraints such that the real control flow reaches the control point, $\varepsilon^r \in \Phi_r^X$, and Φ_f^X abstracts the set of constraints for the finite precision control flow, $(\varepsilon^r, \varepsilon^e) \in \Phi_f^X$.

Example 2. Let us consider the running example. We already saw that the real value of input `x` is abstracted by the affine form $\hat{r}_{[1]}^x = 2 + \varepsilon_1^r$. Its error is $\hat{e}_{[1]}^x = u$ and its finite precision value is $\hat{f}_{[1]}^x = \hat{r}_{[1]}^x + \hat{e}_{[1]}^x = 2 + \varepsilon_1^r + u$.

Test Interpretation. A test `e1 op e2`, where `e1` and `e2` are two arithmetic expressions, and `op` an operator among $\leq, <, \geq, >, =, \neq$, is interpreted as `z op 0`, where `z` is the abstraction of expression `e1 - e2` with affine sets. We interpret this test independently for real and floating-point value, relying on the test interpretation on constrained affine sets introduced in [6]:

Definition 2. *Let $X = (R^X, E^X, D^X, \Phi_r^X, \Phi_f^X)$ a constrained affine set. We define $Z = ([\![x_k \text{ op } 0]\!]X$ by*

$$\begin{cases} (R^Z, E^Z, D^Z) = (R^X, E^X, D^X) \\ \Phi_r^Z = \Phi_r^X \bigcap \alpha\left(\varepsilon^r \mid r_{0,k}^X + \sum_{i=1}^n r_{i,k}^X \varepsilon_i^r \text{ op } 0\right) \\ \Phi_f^Z = \Phi_f^X \bigcap \alpha\left((\varepsilon^r, \varepsilon^e) \mid r_{0,k}^X + e_{0,k}^X + \sum_{i=1}^n (r_{i,k}^X + e_{i,k}^X)\varepsilon_i^r + \sum_{j=1}^m e_{n+j,k}^X \varepsilon_j^e \text{ op } 0\right) \end{cases}$$

Example 3. Consider the running example. We start with $\hat{r}_{[1]}^x = 2 + \varepsilon_1^r$, $\hat{e}_{[1]}^x = u$. The condition for the real control flow to take the `then` branch is $\hat{r}_{[1]}^x = 2 + \varepsilon_1^r \leq 2$, thus Φ^r is $\varepsilon_1^r \in [-1, 0]$. The condition for the finite precision control flow to take the `then` branch is $\hat{f}_{[1]}^x = \hat{r}_{[1]}^x + \hat{e}_{[1]}^x = 2 + \varepsilon_1^r + u \leq 2$, thus Φ^f is $\varepsilon_1^r \in [-1, -u]$. Thus, the unstable test condition being that for the same input the real and float control flow are different, this amounts to intersecting these two conditions on ε_1^r, and yields $-u < \varepsilon_1^r \leq 0$. These constraints are illustrated on Figure 1, with $u = 0.2$: Φ_r denotes the constraints on the real value, Φ_f, the constraints on the finite precision value, and $\Phi^r \cap \Phi^f$, the unstable test condition. For the other possibility for an unstable test, that is the execution in real numbers takes the `else` branch while the float execution takes the `then` branch, the constraints are $\varepsilon_1^r < 0$ and $\varepsilon_1^r \leq -u$, which are incompatible. This possibility is thus excluded.

Interval Concretisation. The interval concretisation of the value of program variable x_k defined by the abstract value $X = (R^X, E^X, D^X, \Phi_r^X, \Phi_f^X)$, is, with the notations of Section 2:

$$\begin{cases} \gamma_r(\hat{r}_k^X) = \Phi_r^X(r_{0,k}^X + \sum_{i=1}^n r_{i,k}^X \varepsilon_i^r) \\ \gamma_e(\hat{e}_k^X) = \Phi_f^X(e_{0,k}^X + \sum_{i=1}^n e_{i,k}^X \varepsilon_i^r + \sum_{j=1}^m e_{n+j,k}^x \varepsilon_j^e) \\ \gamma_d(\hat{d}_k^X) = \Phi_f^X(d_{0,k}^X + \sum_{l=1}^o d_{l,k}^x \varepsilon_l^d) \\ \gamma_f(\hat{f}_k^X) = \Phi_f^X(r_{0,k}^X + e_{0,k}^X + \sum_{i=1}^n (r_{i,k}^X + e_{i,k}^X) \varepsilon_i^r + \sum_{j=1}^m e_{n+j,k}^x \varepsilon_j^e) \end{cases}$$

Example 4. Take variable y in the running example. In the **then** branch, its real value is $\hat{r}_{[2]}^y = \hat{r}_{[1]}^x + 2 = 4 + \varepsilon_1^r$, the error $\hat{e}_{[2]}^y = \hat{e}_{[1]}^x + \delta\varepsilon_2^e$, where δ is the bound on the elementary rounding error on y, due to the addition, we deduce $\hat{f}_{[2]}^y = \hat{r}_{[2]}^y + \hat{e}_{[2]}^y$. In the **else** branch, the real value is $\hat{r}_{[3]}^y = \hat{r}_{[1]}^x = 2 + \varepsilon_1^r$, the error $\hat{e}_{[3]}^y = \hat{e}_{[1]}^x$, and we deduce $\hat{f}_{[3]}^y = \hat{r}_{[3]}^y + \hat{e}_{[3]}^y$. In Figure 1, we represent in solid lines the real value of y and in dashed lines its finite precision value. The interval concretisation of its real value on Φ_r^X, is $\gamma_r(\hat{r}_{[3]}^y) = \Phi_r^X(2 + \varepsilon_1^r) = 2 + [0, 1] = [2, 3]$. The interval concretisation of its floating-point value on Φ_f^X, is $\gamma_f(\hat{f}_{[3]}^y) = \Phi_f^X(\hat{r}_{[3]}^y + u) = 2 + [-u, 1] + u = [2, 3 + u]$. Actually, $\hat{r}_{[3]}^y$ is defined on $\Phi_r^X \cup \Phi_f^X$, as illustrated on Figure 1, because it is both used to abstract the real value, or, perturbed by an error term, to abstract the finite precision value.

Join. If the test distinguishing two branches can be unstable, then when we join abstract values X and Y coming from the two branches, the difference between the floating-point value of X and the real value of Y, $(R^X + E^X) - R^Y$, and the difference between the floating-point value of X and the real value of Y, $(R^Y + E^Y) - R^X$, are also errors due to finite precision. The join of all error terms can then be expressed as $E^Z + D^Z$, where $E^Z = E^X \sqcup E^Y$ is the propagation of classical rounding errors, and D^Z expresses the discontinuity errors.

A key point for an accurate computation of these discontinuity terms, is to express the unstable tests conditions as an intersection of constraints on the ε_i^r noise symbols, yielding a restriction of the sets of inputs (or equivalently the ε_i^r). It is thus crucial that these ε_i^r are shared by affine sets for real and float values.

Definition 3. *We join two abstract values* X *and* Y *by* $Z = X \sqcup Y$ *defined as* $Z = (R^Z, E^Z, D^Z, \Phi_r^X \cup \Phi_r^Y, \Phi_f^X \cup \Phi_f^Y)$ *where*

$$\begin{cases} (R^Z, \Phi_r^Z \cup \Phi_f^Z) = (R^X, \Phi_r^X \cup \Phi_f^X) \sqcup (R^Y, \Phi_r^Y \cup \Phi_f^Y) \\ (E^Z, \Phi_f^Z) = (E^X, \Phi_f^X) \sqcup (E^Y, \Phi_f^Y) \\ D^Z = D^X \sqcup D^Y \sqcup (R^X - R^Y, \Phi_f^X \sqcap \Phi_r^Y) \sqcup (R^Y - R^X, \Phi_f^Y \sqcap \Phi_r^X) \end{cases}$$

Example 5. Consider variable y in the example. We join $X = (\hat{r}_{[2]}^y = 4 + \varepsilon_1^r, \hat{e}_{[2]}^y = u + \delta\varepsilon_2^e, 0, \varepsilon_1^r \in [-1, 0], (\varepsilon_1^r, \varepsilon_2^e) \in [-1, -u] \times [-1, 1])$ from the **then** branch with $Y = (\hat{r}_{[3]}^y = 2 + \varepsilon_1^r, \hat{e}_{[3]}^y = u, 0, \varepsilon_1^r \in [0, 1], \varepsilon_1^r \in [-u, 1])$ from the **else** branch.

With the analysis of [11] that makes the stable test assumption, we get when joining branches at control point [4], $\hat{r}_{[4]}^y = \hat{r}_{[2]}^y \sqcup \hat{r}_{[3]}^y = 3 + \varepsilon_4^r \in [2, 4]$ with new noise symbol ε_4^r (we do not detail here the upper bound operator on affine forms), $\hat{e}^y_{[4]} = \hat{e}^y_{[2]} \sqcup \hat{e}^y_{[3]} = u + \delta\varepsilon_2^e \in [u-\delta, u+\delta]$, and $\hat{f}^y_{[4]} = \hat{r}^y_{[4]} + \hat{e}^y_{[4]} = 3 + u + \varepsilon_4^r + \delta\varepsilon_2^e$. This is sound for the real and float values $\hat{r}^y_{[4]}$ and $\hat{f}^y_{[4]}$, but unsound for the error.

The new analysis also computes bounds for discontinuity errors. The discontinuity due to the first possible unstable test, when the real takes the `then` branch and float takes the `else` branch is: $\hat{r}^y_{[3]} - \hat{r}^y_{[2]} = 2 + \varepsilon_1^r - 4 + \varepsilon_1^r = -2$, for $\varepsilon_1^r \in \Phi_f^Y \cap \Phi_r^X = [-u, 1] \cap [-1, 0] = [-u, 0]$. As already seen, the other possibility of an unstable test is excluded. The error is now $\hat{e}^y_{[4]} + d^y_{[4]}$ where $d^y_{[4]} = -2\chi_{[-u,0]}(\varepsilon_1)$ and $\chi_{[a,b]}(x)$ equals 1 if x is in $[a, b]$ and 0 otherwise.

4 Experiments

We experimented some small examples inspired by industrial codes, using our implementation of this abstraction in our static analyzer FLUCTUAT. More experiments are described in [12].

A Simple Interpolator. The following example implements an interpolator, affine by sub-intervals, as classically found in critical embedded software. It is a robust implementation indeed. In the code below, we used the FLUCTUAT assertion `FREAL_WITH_ERROR(a,b,c,d)` to denote an abstract value (of resulting type `float`), whose corresponding real values are $x \in [a, b]$, and whose corresponding floating-point values are of the form $x + e$, with $e \in [c, d]$.

```
float R1[3], E, res;
R1[0] = 0;  R1[1] = 5 * 2.25; R1[2] = R1[1] + 20 * 1.1;
E = FREAL_WITH_ERROR(0.0,100.0,-0.00001,0.00001);
if (E < 5)
  res = E*2.25 + R1[0];
else if (E < 25)
  res = (E-5)*1.1 + R1[1];
else
  res = R1[2];
return res;
```

The analysis proves `res` in [-2.25e-5,33.2], with an error in [-3.5e-5,2.4e-5], thus of the order of magnitude of the input error, despite unstable tests.

A Simple Square Root Function. This example is a rewrite in some particular case, of an actual implementation of a square root function, in an industrial context:

```
double sqrt2 = 1.414213538169860839843750;
double S, I;   I = DREAL_WITH_ERROR(1,2,0,0.001);
if (I>=2)
  S = sqrt2*(1+(I/2-1)*(.5-0.125*(I/2-1)));
else
  S = 1+(I-1)*(.5+(I-1)*(-.125+(I-1)*.0625));
```

With the former type of analysis within FLUCTUAT, we get the unsound result that `S` is proven in the real number semantics to be in [1,1.4531] with a global error in [-0.0005312,0.00008592]. The function does not exhibit a big discontinuity, but still larger than these bounds. For I=2 for instance, the `then` branch computes `sqrt2` which is approximately 1.4142, whereas the `else` branch computes 1+0.5-0.125+0.0625=1.4375. With our present analysis, FLUCTUAT proves that S in the real number semantics is in [1,1.4531] with an error in [-0.0394,0.0389], the test discontinuity accounting for most of it ([-0.0389,0.0389], coherent with the above rough estimate of 0.0233).

5 Conclusion

We have proposed an abstract interpretation based static analysis of the robustness of finite precision implementations, as a generalization of both software robustness or continuity analysis and finite precision error analysis, by abstracting the impact of finite precision in numerical computations and control flow divergences. Future work includes going along the lines of [15] and resorting to more sophisticated constraint solving: indeed our analysis can generate constraints on noise symbols, which we only partially use for the time being.

References

1. Boldo, S., Filliâtre, J.-C.: Formal Verification of Floating-Point Programs. In: 18th IEEE International Symposium on Computer Arithmetic (June 2007)
2. Chaudhuri, S., Gulwani, S., Lublinerman, R.: Continuity analysis of programs. In: POPL, pp. 57–70 (2010)
3. Chaudhuri, S., Gulwani, S., Lublinerman, R.: Continuity and robustness of programs. Commun. ACM 55(8), 107–115 (2012)
4. Chesneaux, J.-M., Lamotte, J.-L., Limare, N., Lebars, Y.: On the new cadna library. In: SCAN (2006)
5. Ghorbal, K., Goubault, E., Putot, S.: The zonotope abstract domain taylor1+. In: Bouajjani, A., Maler, O. (eds.) CAV 2009. LNCS, vol. 5643, pp. 627–633. Springer, Heidelberg (2009)
6. Ghorbal, K., Goubault, E., Putot, S.: A logical product approach to zonotope intersection. In: Touili, T., Cook, B., Jackson, P. (eds.) CAV 2010. LNCS, vol. 6174, pp. 212–226. Springer, Heidelberg (2010)
7. Goubault, E., Le Gall, T., Putot, S.: An accurate join for zonotopes, preserving affine input/output relations. In: Proceedings of NSAD 2012. ENTCS, pp. 65–76 (2012)
8. Goubault, E., Putot, S.: Static analysis of numerical algorithms. In: Yi, K. (ed.) SAS 2006. LNCS, vol. 4134, pp. 18–34. Springer, Heidelberg (2006)
9. Goubault, E., Putot, S.: Perturbed affine arithmetic for invariant computation in numerical program analysis. CoRR, abs/0807.2961 (2008)
10. Goubault, E., Putot, S.: A zonotopic framework for functional abstractions. CoRR, abs/0910.1763 (2009)
11. Goubault, E., Putot, S.: Static analysis of finite precision computations. In: Jhala, R., Schmidt, D. (eds.) VMCAI 2011. LNCS, vol. 6538, pp. 232–247. Springer, Heidelberg (2011)
12. Goubault, E., Putot, S.: Robustness analysis of finite precision implementationss. CoRR, abs/1309.3910 (2013)
13. Hamlet, D.: Continuity in software systems. In: ISSTA, pp. 196–200 (2002)
14. Majumdar, R., Saha, I.: Symbolic robustness analysis. In: RTSS (2009)
15. Ponsini, O., Michel, C., Rueher, M.: Refining abstract interpretation based value analysis with constraint programming techniques. In: Milano, M. (ed.) CP 2012. LNCS, vol. 7514, pp. 593–607. Springer, Heidelberg (2012)
16. Tabuada, P., Balkan, A., Caliskan, S.Y., Shoukry, Y., Majumdar, R.: Input-output robustness for discrete systems. In: EMSOFT, pp. 217–226 (2012)

A Hoare Logic for SIMT Programs

Kensuke Kojima[1,2] and Atsushi Igarashi[1,2]

[1] Kyoto University, Japan
[2] JST CREST, Japan

Abstract. We study a Hoare Logic to reason about GPU kernels, which are parallel programs executed on GPUs. We consider the SIMT (Single Instruction Multiple Threads) execution model, in which multiple threads execute in lockstep (that is, execute the same instruction at a time). When control branches both branches are executed sequentially but during the execution of each branch only those threads that take it are enabled; after the control converges, all threads are enabled and execute in lockstep again. In this paper we adapt Hoare Logic to the SIMT setting, by adding an extra component representing the set of enabled threads to the usual Hoare triples. It turns out that soundness and relative completeness do not hold for all programs; a difficulty arises from the fact that one thread can invalidate the loop termination condition of another thread through shared memory. We overcome this difficulty by identifying an appropriate class of programs for which soundness and relative completeness hold.

1 Introduction

General purpose computing on graphics processing units (GPGPU) has recently become widely available even to end-users, enabling us to utilize computational power of GPUs for solving problems other than graphics processing. Application areas include physics simulation, signal and image processing, etc. [1]. However, writing and optimizing GPU kernels, which are parallel programs executed on GPUs, is still a hard task and error-prone. For example, in programming in CUDA, a parallel computing platform and programming model on GPU [2], we have to care about synchronization and data races so that many threads cooperate correctly. Moreover, to obtain the best performance, we usually have to take into account more low-level mechanisms, to optimize memory access pattern, increase occupancy, etc.

Much effort has recently been made to develop automated verification tools for GPU kernels [3–11]. These tools try to automate detections of synchronization errors, data races, and inefficiency, as well as checking functional correctness and generating test cases. They, although automation is a great advantage, tend to suffer false positives/negatives because of approximation, as well as combinatorial explosion.

Another approach to formal verification is deductive verification, in which the correctness of a program is verified by formally proving (using a fixed set

C.-c. Shan (Ed.): APLAS 2013, LNCS 8301, pp. 58–73, 2013.

of deduction rules) that it is indeed correct. The relative completeness of the inference rules guarantee that all correct programs can be proved to be correct, although much effort is often required to complete the correctness proof. Deductive approach has been implemented as tools that can be applied to real-world programs (Why3[1], for example). However, in the context of GPU programming, this approach is not extensively studied yet (at the time of writing, we are only aware of the ongoing work using separation logic by Huisman and Mihelčić [12]).

In this work, we study a deductive verification method for GPU programs. We focus on the SIMT execution model (described in Section 1.1), and demonstrate that Hoare Logic, one of the traditional approaches to deductive verification, can be applied to GPU kernels with few modifications. Our contributions are (1) an extension of Hoare Logic to GPU kernels, and (2) proofs of its soundness and relative completeness for a large class of GPU kernels.

Generally speaking, reasoning about parallel programs requires much more sophisticated techniques than the sequential ones, because threads can interfere with each other through shared resources [13]. Although existing techniques could be applied to GPU kernels, we take advantage of the so-called lockstep semantics of SIMT to obtain simpler inference rules. In fact, our inference rules are similar to the usual Hoare Logic, and the soundness and relative completeness hold under a very mild restriction.

In the rest of this section we describe how SIMT works, and how we can extend Hoare Logic to the SIMT setting.

1.1 Overview of the SIMT Execution Model

SIMT (Single Instruction Multiple Threads) is a parallel execution model of GPUs employed by CUDA. A CUDA program is written in CUDA C, an extension of C language, and run on GPUs as specified in the SIMT execution model. In the SIMT execution model, multiple (typically thousands of) threads are launched and execute in lockstep, i.e., execute the same instruction at a time.

When a conditional branch is encountered during the lockstep execution, and the decisions on which branch to be taken vary among threads, then both branches are executed sequentially. During the execution of each branch, only those threads that take it are enabled. After all branches are completed, all threads are enabled and executed in lockstep again.

Therefore, in SIMT, some statements actually may be executed by only some of the threads, depending on the branching. We say that a thread is *active* if it is currently enabled, and *inactive* otherwise. A *mask* is a piece of data (typically a bit mask) that describe which thread is active. The state of a mask may change during execution, and the result of executing a statement may depend on a mask.

As an example, let us consider the following program.

```
k = tid;  while (k < n) { c[k] = a[k] + b[k];  k = k + ntid; }
```

[1] http://why3.lri.fr/

Here we assume that `k` is a thread local variable, `a`, `b`, and `c` are shared arrays of length `n`, and `ntid` is a constant whose value is the number of threads. The constant `tid` represents the thread identifier, ranging from 0 to `ntid - 1`. Let us suppose that this program is launched with 4 threads, and `n` equals 6. In the first iteration, the condition `k < n` holds in all threads, so the mask is $\{0, 1, 2, 3\}$, and all threads execute the loop body. In the second iteration, however, the values of `k` in threads 0, 1, 2, 3 are 4, 5, 6, 7 respectively, so the condition `k < n` does not hold in threads 2 and 3. Therefore these threads are deactivated, and the loop body is executed with mask $\{0, 1\}$. After that all threads exit the loop, and program terminates. The final value of `c` is the sum of `a` and `b`.

Although the way SIMT executes threads looks similar to SIMD (Single Instruction Multiple Data) in that a single instruction operates on multiple data, they are different in that parallel operations on vectors are explicitly specified in SIMD while it is not the case for SIMT. Indeed, when programming in CUDA C we only specify a behavior of a single scalar thread, like a usual sequential program written C or C++.

1.2 Extending Hoare Logic

Next we consider a Hoare Logic for the SIMT execution model. The programs we are going to reason about is a single GPU kernel, like the example above.

Actually, we can employ many of the inference rules from the ordinary Hoare Logic without significant changes, although Hoare triples have to be changed. As explained above, in SIMT the effect of the execution of a statement depends on the mask. Since the usual Hoare triple $\{\varphi\}\, P\, \{\psi\}$ does not contain the information about a mask, it cannot fully specify a program. Therefore we augment the usual Hoare triple with another piece of information, and consider a Hoare *quadruple* of the form $\{\varphi\}\, m \mid P\, \{\psi\}$, where m denotes a mask. Intuitively this quadruple means that "if an initial state satisfies φ, and we execute a program P *with a mask denoted by* m, then after termination the state satisfies ψ."

However, a difficulty arises from `while` loops. We found that, in some corner cases, it is difficult to reason about `while` loops correctly. Although it would be possible to modify the inference rule so that we can handle all programs soundly, we decided to keep simplicity by making some assumption on the program we deal with. As a result we consider a certain class of programs, which we call *regular* programs, and obtain the soundness and relative completeness for regular programs. However, this is not a serious restriction because any program can be transformed into a regular one without changing the behavior (with respect to our operational semantics).

Interestingly, the resulting Hoare Logic is quite similar to the ordinary one, despite the parallel nature of GPU programs. It seems that this simplicity is a result of the fact that in SIMT dependency between threads is relatively weak. Threads basically work independently, and only at synchronization points they have to wait for each other. As a result the execution of a SIMT program is very similar to a sequential program.

1.3 Organization of the Paper

The rest of the paper is organized as follows. In Section 2 we formalize the SIMT execution model by extending the usual while-language. Section 3 describes our Hoare Logic. Section 4 introduces the notion of regular programs, and prove soundness and relative completeness of our Hoare Logic for regular programs. In Section 5 we discuss some variants of our system. Section 6 mentions related work and Section 7 concludes the paper.

We omit the detailed proofs for brevity. They are available in the full version of the paper (`http://www.fos.kuis.kyoto-u.ac.jp/~kozima/hl-simt-full.pdf`).

2 SIMT Execution Model

In this section we formalize SIMT execution model. Our formalization is based on Habermaier and Knapp [14], but there are some differences. First, we omit `break`, function calls, and `return`. Second, we include arrays, which is almost always used in CUDA programs, and barrier synchronization.

In the semantics formalized here, the execution is in complete lockstep, but the actual GPU program is not necessarily executed in this manner. Possible approaches to filling this gap will be discussed in Section 7.

2.1 Formal Syntax

We assume countable, disjoint sets of variables LV_n and SV_n for each nonnegative integer n. Elements of LV_n and SV_n are thread local and shared variables of arrays of dimension n respectively (when $n = 0$ they are considered as scalars). We also fix the set of n-ary operations Op_n for each n. We assume that the standard arithmetic and logical operations such as `+`, `<`, `&&` and `!` are included in the language.

Well-formed expressions e and programs P are defined as follows:

$$e ::= \texttt{tid} \mid \texttt{ntid} \mid x_n\,\texttt{[}\bar{e}\texttt{]} \mid f_n(\bar{e})$$
$$P ::= x_n\,\texttt{[}\bar{e}\texttt{]} \texttt{ := } e \mid \texttt{skip} \mid \texttt{sync} \mid P;\ P' \mid \texttt{if}\ e\ \texttt{then}\ P\ \texttt{else}\ P' \mid \texttt{while}\ e\ \texttt{do}\ P$$

where x_n and f_n range over $LV_n \cup SV_n$ and Op_n, respectively, and $\bar{e}$ stands for the sequence $e_1, \ldots, e_n$.

Expressions include special constants `tid`, thread identifier, and `ntid`, the number of threads[2]. If a variable x is of dimension 0, we write x instead of $x\texttt{[]}$.

$x_n\,\texttt{[}e_1\texttt{, ... , }e_n\texttt{]} \texttt{ := } e$ is an assignment, which is performed by all active threads in parallel. `skip` is a statement that has no effect. `sync` is a barrier, typically used to avoid data races in CUDA. Although in our formalization a barrier does

[2] The name of this constant is taken from a special register in PTX [15]. In our formalization this is the same as the number of threads, although this is not always the case for PTX.

not play a significant role, we include it so that we can reason about deadlocks (sometimes called barrier divergence) caused by a barrier. The remaining constructs are the same as the usual while-language. Note that we do not have boolean expressions, so we use integer expressions for conditions of `if` and `while` statements, and regard any nonzero value as true.

2.2 Operational Semantics

Next we define a formal semantics of SIMT. For simplicity, arrays are represented simply by total maps from tuples of integers to integers, so we do not care about array bounds, and negative indices are also allowed. Our operational semantics basically follows the standard evaluation rules, but one of the main differences is that it is nondeterministic because multiple threads may try to write into the same shared variables simultaneously.

Below we fix a positive integer N which is the number of threads, and therefore is an interpretation of the constant `ntid`. We also assume for each n-ary operation f_n, a map from $\mathbb{Z}^n$ to $\mathbb{Z}$ (also denoted by f_n) is assigned. We denote the set of threads $\{0, 1, \ldots, N-1\}$ by $\mathbb{T}$.

Definition 1. *A state σ consists of a map $\sigma(x) : \mathbb{T} \to \mathbb{Z}^n \to \mathbb{Z}$ for each $x \in LV_n$, and $\sigma(y) : \mathbb{Z}^n \to \mathbb{Z}$ for each $y \in SV_n$.*

Given a state σ, we naturally interpret $\sigma(x)$ as the value of x.

The denotation of an expression e under a state σ is a map $\sigma\,[\![e]\!] : \mathbb{T} \to \mathbb{Z}$ defined by:

$$\sigma\,[\![\texttt{tid}]\!]\,(i) = i \qquad\qquad \sigma\,[\![\texttt{ntid}]\!]\,(i) = N$$

$$\sigma\,[\![x\texttt{[}e_1, \ldots, e_n\texttt{]}]\!]\,(i) = \begin{cases} \sigma(x)(i)(\sigma\,[\![e_1]\!]\,(i), \ldots, \sigma\,[\![e_n]\!]\,(i)) & \text{if } x \text{ is local} \\ \sigma(x)(\sigma\,[\![e_1]\!]\,(i), \ldots, \sigma\,[\![e_n]\!]\,(i)) & \text{if } x \text{ is shared} \end{cases}$$

$$\sigma\,[\![f(e_1, \ldots, e_n)]\!]\,(i) = f(\sigma\,[\![e_1]\!]\,(i), \ldots, \sigma\,[\![e_n]\!]\,(i))$$

Notation 1. *For a state σ, we define $\sigma[x \mapsto a]$ to be the state σ' such that: $\sigma'(x) = a$ and $\sigma'(y) = \sigma(y)$ for each $y \neq x$.*

When an expression is used as a predicate (e.g. the condition part of an `if`-statement), we regard $\sigma\,[\![e]\!]$ as a set of threads satisfying the condition e, that is, the set $\{i \in \mathbb{T} \mid \sigma\,[\![e]\!]\,(i) \neq 0\}$. We also use the notation $\sigma\,[\![e]\!]$ to denote this set, when no confusion arises.

The execution of a program is defined as a relation of the form

$$P, \mu, \sigma \Downarrow \sigma',$$

where P is a program, $\mu \subseteq \mathbb{T}$, and σ, σ' are states. This relation means that "if P is executed with mask μ and initial state σ, then the resulting state is σ'."

Evaluation rules are listed in Figure 1. The rule E-INACTIVE means that, if there is no active thread, the execution has no effect. A barrier synchronization succeeds only if all threads are active (or no thread is active, in which case

$$P, \emptyset, \sigma \Downarrow \sigma \text{ (E-INACTIVE)} \qquad \texttt{skip}, \mu, \sigma \Downarrow \sigma \text{ (E-SKIP)} \qquad \texttt{sync}, \mathbb{T}, \sigma \Downarrow \sigma \text{ (E-SYNC)}$$

$$\frac{\begin{array}{c} x \text{ is local} \quad \sigma'(y) = \sigma(y) \text{ for each variable } y \neq x \\ \sigma'(x)(i) = \sigma(x)(i) \text{ for each } i \notin \mu \\ \sigma'(x)(i) = \sigma(x)(i)\,[\sigma\,[\![\bar{e}]\!]\,(i) \mapsto \sigma\,[\![e]\!]\,(i)] \text{ for each } i \in \mu \end{array}}{x\,[\bar{e}] := e, \mu, \sigma \Downarrow \sigma'} \text{ (E-LASSIGN)}$$

$$\frac{\begin{array}{c} x \text{ is shared} \quad \sigma'(y) = \sigma(y) \text{ for each variable } y \neq x \\ \text{if } \forall i \in \mu. \sigma\,[\![\bar{e}]\!]\,(i) \neq \bar{n}, \text{ then } \sigma'(x)(\bar{n}) = \sigma(x)(\bar{n}) \\ \text{otherwise } \exists i \in \mu. \sigma\,[\![\bar{e}]\!]\,(i) = \bar{n} \text{ and } \sigma'(x)(\bar{n}) = \sigma\,[\![e]\!]\,(i) \end{array}}{x\,[\bar{e}] := e, \mu, \sigma \Downarrow \sigma'} \text{ (E-SASSIGN)}$$

$$\frac{P, \mu, \sigma \Downarrow \sigma' \qquad Q, \mu, \sigma' \Downarrow \sigma''}{P;\ Q, \mu, \sigma \Downarrow \sigma''} \text{ (E-SEQ)}$$

$$\frac{P, \mu \cap \sigma\,[\![e]\!], \sigma \Downarrow \sigma' \qquad Q, \mu \setminus \sigma\,[\![e]\!], \sigma' \Downarrow \sigma''}{\texttt{if}\ e\ \texttt{then}\ P\ \texttt{else}\ Q, \mu, \sigma \Downarrow \sigma''} \text{ (E-IF)}$$

$$\frac{P, \mu \cap \sigma\,[\![e]\!], \sigma \Downarrow \sigma' \qquad \texttt{while}\ e\ \texttt{do}\ P, \mu \cap \sigma\,[\![e]\!], \sigma' \Downarrow \sigma''}{\texttt{while}\ e\ \texttt{do}\ P, \mu, \sigma \Downarrow \sigma''} \text{ (E-WHILE)}$$

Fig. 1. Operational semantics of SIMT programs

E-INACTIVE is applicable), hence the set of active thread should be $\mathbb{T}$ in the rule E-SYNC. A synchronization does not change the state.

Nondeterministic behavior can arise from E-SASSIGN; there can be more than one choice of σ', in case of a data race. More precisely, by a data race here we mean a situation that there exist two (or more) distinct active threads i and j where the index $\bar{e}$ takes the same value on i and j, while e does not (formally, $\sigma\,[\![\bar{e}]\!]\,(i) = \sigma\,[\![\bar{e}]\!]\,(j)$ and $\sigma\,[\![e]\!]\,(i) \neq \sigma\,[\![e]\!]\,(j)$). In such a case, following Habermaier and Knapp [14], we allow to choose either $\sigma\,[\![e]\!]\,(i)$ or $\sigma\,[\![e]\!]\,(j)$, and set its value to $x\,[\bar{e}]$. As discussed in Section 5.1, it is possible to define a semantics which raises an error in such cases.

3 Reasoning about SIMT Programs

In this section we describe how to extend Hoare Logic to the SIMT setting formalized in the previous section.

3.1 Assertion Language

Our assertion language is based on first-order logic with function variables. We assume as many n-ary variables as we want for each nonnegative integer n. Formally, the syntax is as follows:

$$\text{terms } t ::= c \mid f_n(t_1, ..., t_n) \mid x_n(t_1, ..., t_n)$$
$$\text{formulas } \varphi ::= p_n(t_1, ..., t_n) \mid \varphi_1 \wedge \varphi_2 \mid \varphi_1 \vee \varphi_2 \mid \varphi_1 \rightarrow \varphi_2 \mid \neg\varphi \mid \forall x.\varphi \mid \exists x.\varphi$$

Here c ranges over constant symbols, and f_n, x_n, and p_n range over n-ary function symbols, variables, and predicate symbols, respectively.

We assume our assertion language contain N (the number of threads) as a constant symbol, and each operation $f \in Op_n$ as an n-ary function symbol. Extra constants and function symbols are allowed. We also assume that standard predicates on integers such as $\leq$ are included.

We associate a unique variable to each program variable. A variable that is not associated to any program variable is called a specification variable. We denote the variable corresponding to a program variable x again by x. Each $x \in SV_n$ is n-ary, and each $x \in LV_n$ is $(n+1)$-ary. This is because a local variable's value varies among threads, so has to receive one extra argument as thread identifier to determine its value. The first argument of a local variable represents a thread identifier.

An assertion is just a formula of the first-order logic. We briefly describe how to interpret it. First, we fix a model $\mathcal{M}$ of our first-order signature, with domain $\mathbb{Z}$, such that the interpretation of `ntid` is N that we fixed above, and the interpretation of each $f_n \in Op_n$ also equals the function used to define the denotation of an expression. An *assignment*, ranged over by ρ, is a map which assigns to (both program and specification) variables of arity n a map $\mathbb{Z}^n \to \mathbb{Z}$. The satisfaction relation $\rho \models \varphi$ for each assignment ρ and a formula φ is defined as usual.

By abuse of notation we write $P, \mu, \rho \Downarrow \rho'$ if and only if there exists σ' such that $P, \mu, \sigma \Downarrow \sigma'$, where σ is the restriction of ρ and ρ' equals σ' on program variables and ρ on specification variables. We also use the notation $\rho\,[\![e]\!]$ for the set $\{i \in \mathbb{T} \mid \rho\,[\![e]\!]\,(i) \neq 0\}$.

Definition 2. *A* Hoare quadruple *is of the form* $\{\varphi\}\, m \mid P\, \{\psi\}$, *where* P *is a program,* m *is a term built from specification variables, and* φ *and* ψ *are formulas. Note that no variable occurring in* m *occurs in* P.

Definition 3. *A Hoare quadruple* $\{\varphi\}\, m \mid P\, \{\psi\}$ *is* valid *if, for every assignment* ρ *satisfying* φ *and every* ρ' *such that* $P, \rho\,[\![m]\!]\,, \rho \Downarrow \rho'$, *it holds that* $\rho' \models \psi$.

Precisely speaking we have to distinguish states σ and assignments ρ but for brevity we will not distinguish them, if no confusion arises.

Definition 4. *For an expression* e *and a term* t, *we define a term* $e@t$ *as follows:*

$$\texttt{tid}@t = t \qquad\qquad \texttt{ntid}@t = N$$

$$(x\,[e_1, \ldots, e_n])@t = \begin{cases} x(t, e_1@t, \ldots, e_n@t) & \text{if } x \text{ is local} \\ x(e_1@t, \ldots, e_n@t) & \text{if } x \text{ is shared} \end{cases}$$

$$(f(e_1, \ldots, e_n))@t = f(e_1@t, \ldots, e_n@t)$$

The intended meaning of $e@t$ *is the value of* e *at thread* t.

Notation 2. *We occasionally use* $\mathbb{T}$ *in place of* m *when* m *is an expression always nonzero in all threads (*1*, for example).*

Definition 5. *We use the following abbreviations.*

- $all(e) := (\forall i.0 \le i < N \to e@i \ne 0)$
- $none(e) := (\forall i.0 \le i < N \to e@i = 0)$
- $i \in m := (m@i \ne 0)$
- $\forall i \in m.\varphi := (\forall i.0 \le i < N \to m@i \ne 0 \to \varphi)$. *Similarly for* $\exists$ *and other variants.*
- *If* x *is a shared variable,* $assign(x', m, x, \bar{e}, e)$ *is defined to be*

$$\forall \bar{n}.\, ((\forall i \in m.\bar{e}@i \ne \bar{n}) \wedge x'(\bar{n}) = x(\bar{n})) \vee (\exists i \in m.\bar{e}@i = \bar{n} \wedge x'(\bar{n}) = e@i)\,,$$

and if x *is local,*

$$\begin{aligned}\forall \bar{n}, i.\, (i \notin m \vee \bar{e}@i \ne \bar{n} \to x'(i, \bar{n}) = x(i, \bar{n})) \wedge \\ (i \in m \wedge \bar{e}@i = \bar{n} \to x'(i, \bar{n}) = e@i)\,.\end{aligned}$$

The last one of the definitions above would require some explanation. Intuitively, $assign(x', m, x, \bar{e}, e)$ is true when x' is (one of) the result(s) of executing $x\,[\bar{e}]$:= e with mask m. If x is shared this is the case if for each index $\bar{n}$, either

- no thread modifies $x(\bar{n})$ and $x'(\bar{n})$ equals the the original value $x(\bar{n})$, or
- some (possibly multiple) threads try to modify $x(\bar{n})$, and $x'(\bar{n})$ equals a value written by one of these threads.

The description is complicated because of possible data races. The case x is local is similar, but the situation is simpler because there is no data race.

We can state the meaning of *assign* formally as follows:

Lemma 1. $x\,[\bar{e}]$:= $e, \sigma\, [\![m]\!]\,, \sigma \Downarrow \sigma'$ *holds if and only if there exists* a *such that* $\sigma' = \sigma[x \mapsto a]$, *and* $\sigma[x' \mapsto a] \models assign(x', m, x, \bar{e}, e)$.

3.2 Inference Rules

Inference rules are listed in Figure 2. We write $\vdash \{\varphi\}\, m \mid P\, \{\psi\}$ if the quadruple $\{\varphi\}\, m \mid P\, \{\psi\}$ is provable from the rules in Figure 2. The variables x' in H-Assign and z in H-If and H-While are fresh specification variables of an appropriate arity. The expression $e = z$ appearing in H-If and H-While is shorthand for $\forall i \in \mathbb{T}.e@i = z@i$.

Rules H-Conseq, H-Skip and H-Seq are standard. H-Assign looks different from the standard assignment rule of Hoare Logic, but in view of Lemma 1 this would be natural. H-Sync is also understood in a similar way.

Rules H-If and H-While are more interesting. Since an `if` statement executes both then- and else-branches sequentially, the precondition of the second premise is ψ (the postcondition of the first), not φ. In both rules, we have to remember the initial value of e into a fresh variable z (see Remark 1 below). Since the threads in which the condition is false do not execute the body, the mask part of the premises has to be m `&&` z (or m `&& !` z).

$$\{\varphi\}\, m \mid \texttt{skip}\, \{\varphi\} \tag{H-Skip}$$

$$\{\mathit{all}(m) \vee \mathit{none}(m) \to \varphi\}\, m \mid \texttt{sync}\, \{\varphi\} \tag{H-Sync}$$

$$\frac{\models \varphi' \to \varphi \qquad \{\varphi\}\, m \mid P\, \{\psi\} \qquad \models \psi \to \psi'}{\{\varphi'\}\, m \mid P\, \{\psi'\}} \tag{H-Conseq}$$

$$\frac{\{\varphi\}\, m \mid P\, \{\psi\} \qquad \{\psi\}\, m \mid Q\, \{\chi\}}{\{\varphi\}\, m \mid P;\; Q\, \{\chi\}} \tag{H-Seq}$$

$$\{\forall x'.\mathit{assign}(x', m, x, \bar{e}, e) \to \varphi[x'/x]\}\, m \mid x\,[\bar{e}] \texttt{ := } e\, \{\varphi\} \tag{H-Assign}$$

$$\frac{\{\varphi \wedge e = z\}\, m \;\texttt{\&\&}\; z \mid P\, \{\psi\} \qquad \{\psi\}\, m \;\texttt{\&\&}\; \texttt{!}\, z \mid Q\, \{\chi\}}{\{\varphi\}\, m \mid \texttt{if}\; e\; \texttt{then}\; P\; \texttt{else}\; Q\, \{\chi\}} \tag{H-If}$$

$$\frac{\{\varphi \wedge e = z\}\, m \;\texttt{\&\&}\; z \mid P\, \{\varphi\}}{\{\varphi\}\, m \mid \texttt{while}\; e\; \texttt{do}\; P\, \{\varphi \wedge \mathit{none}(m \;\texttt{\&\&}\; e)\}} \tag{H-While}$$

Fig. 2. Inference rules

Remark 1. We introduce a fresh variable z in rules H-If and H-While. To see that this is indeed necessary, suppose the rule were of the following form (although this is actually ill-formed because the mask part contain a program variable).

$$\frac{\{\varphi\}\, m \;\texttt{\&\&}\; e \mid P\, \{\psi\} \qquad \{\psi\}\, m \;\texttt{\&\&}\; \texttt{!}\, e \mid Q\, \{\chi\}}{\{\varphi\}\, m \mid \texttt{if}\; e\; \texttt{then}\; P\; \texttt{else}\; Q\, \{\chi\}}$$

Let x and y be shared variables and $e = (x \texttt{>} 0)$, $P = (x \texttt{ := } 0;\;\; y \texttt{ := } 1)$, and $Q = \texttt{skip}$. Then the following is valid:

$$\{x@0 > 0\}\, \mathbb{T} \mid \texttt{if}\; e\; \texttt{then}\; P\; \texttt{else}\; Q\, \{y@0 = 1\}\,.$$

To prove this by using the above rule, we try to prove

$$\{x@0 > 0\}\, x \texttt{>} 0 \mid P\, \{y@0 = 1\}$$

but this is impossible because the verification condition would be

$$x@0 > 0 \to \forall x'.\mathit{assign}(x', x \texttt{>} 0, x, \cdot, 0) \to \forall y'.\mathit{assign}(y', x' \texttt{>} 0, y, \cdot, 1) \to y'@0 = 1$$

which is not true: $x@0 > 0$ implies $x'@0 = 0$, but we can prove $y'@0 = 1$ only if $x'@0 > 0$.

The problem is that, when executing $y \texttt{ := } 1$, the actual mask is represented by $x \texttt{>} 0$, whereas in the above verification condition it is incorrectly replaced by $x' \texttt{>} 0$. This does not happen in the actual rule H-If because instead of directly evaluating e the value of e at the point of the execution branch is referenced through a fresh variable z.

3.3 Examples

Vector Addition. Let us consider the program having appeared in Section 1.1. When this program is called with N threads, each thread i writes $a\texttt{[}k\texttt{]} \texttt{ + } b\texttt{[}k\texttt{]}$

into c[k] for $k = i, N + i, 2N + i, \ldots$ until k exceeds the length n of the arrays. Therefore after this program terminates, the value of c should be the sum of a and b. More precisely, letting P be the above program, the following holds:

$$\{\}\,\mathbb{T} \mid P\,\{\forall i.0 \le i < n \to c(i) = a(i) + b(i)\}\,.$$

Note that in the postcondition we have to write $c(i)$, not $c@i$, because c is a shared variable and i is the index specified in the program (and similarly for a and b). We can prove this quadruple using the following loop invariant:

$$\forall i \in \mathbb{T}.\exists l.k@i = lN + i \wedge \forall l'.0 \le l' < l \to c(l'N + i) = a(l'N + i) + b(l'N + i).$$

This formula asserts that at the beginning and the end of each iteration, the value of k at thread i is of the form $lN + i$, and all elements of indices $i, N+i, \ldots, (l-1)N+i$ are processed correctly. Here l is actually the number of iterations having been performed by thread i.

Array Sum. For simplicity we assume the number of threads N is a power of 2, and a is an array of length $n = 2N$. Consider the following program P:

```
s = n / 2;
while (s > 0) {
  if (tid < s) a[i] = a[i] + a[i + s];
  s = s / 2;
  sync;
}
```

After executing this program the value of a[0] is the sum of all values in the original array a. Intuitively, this program implements the following algorithm. In each iteration, we split a given array into two arrays of equal lengths (s in the program), say a_1 and a_2. Then, compute the sum $a_1 + a_2$, and store the result into a_1. Continue this process until the length of the array becomes 1. The final value of 0-th element is the answer.

The following is an invariant:

$$\exists l \ge 0.\,(\forall i \in \mathbb{T}.s@i = 2^l/2) \wedge \forall j.\,(0 \le j < 2^l \to a(j) = \textstyle\sum_k a_0(j + 2^l k))\,.$$

Here a_0 denotes the initial value of a, and the variable k in $\sum_k a_0(i + 2^l k)$ ranges over all nonnegative integers such that $i + 2^l k < n$. The expression $2^l/2$ is interpreted to be 0 when $l = 0$. We can verify that

$$\{n = 2N = 2^{t+1} \wedge a = a_0\}\,\mathbb{T} \mid P\left\{a(0) = \textstyle\sum_{m=0}^{n-1} a_0(m)\right\}.$$

4 Soundness and Relative Completeness

We are going to prove soundness and relative completeness. Unfortunately, however, they do *not* hold for all programs. We first describe how soundness fails, and introduce the notion of regular programs, being based on this observation. After that we prove soundness and relative completeness for regular programs.

4.1 Regular Programs

As a counterexample for the soundness, let us consider the program

$$e = x\texttt{[tid]} \mathbin{\texttt{==}} \texttt{tid}, \quad P = \texttt{while}\, e\, \texttt{do}\, (x\texttt{[0]} \mathbin{\texttt{:=}} \texttt{1};\ x\texttt{[1]} \mathbin{\texttt{:=}} \texttt{1}),$$

where x is a shared variable and the assertion

$$\varphi = (\exists i \in \mathbb{T}. x(i) = i).$$

It can be verified that φ is an invariant:

$$\{\varphi \wedge z = e\}\, z \mid x\texttt{[0]} \mathbin{\texttt{:=}} \texttt{1};\ x\texttt{[1]} \mathbin{\texttt{:=}} \texttt{1}\, \{\varphi\},$$

and therefore we can prove $\{\varphi\}\, \mathbb{T} \mid P\, \{\varphi \wedge \mathit{none}(e)\}$. However, this is not a valid quadruple. Suppose that the initial value of x is $x\texttt{[0]} = x\texttt{[1]} = 0$. Starting from such a state, it is easy to see that P terminates with some state, say σ'. If the quadruple above is valid, it means that σ' satisfies $\varphi \wedge \mathit{none}(e)$. However, this formula is inconsistent, so this is a contradiction. It follows that the rule H-WHILE is not sound for this example.

The problem is that initially the condition e is false in thread 1, but after the body is executed by thread 0, it becomes true at thread 1. In general, a difficulty arises when

- thread i has already exited the loop,
- another active thread j modifies some shared variable, and
- as a result the condition e becomes true at thread i.

Actually, this is the only obstacle to proving soundness and relative completeness. We will restrict our attention to programs that do not cause this situation.

First we define the notion of a stable expression under a given program. We say that e is stable under P, if the value of e at thread i does not change by executing P with i being disabled. More precisely:

Definition 6. *Let P be a program and e an expression. We say that e is* stable *under P if for all μ, σ and σ' such that $P, \mu, \sigma \Downarrow \sigma'$, it holds that $\sigma\, [\![e]\!]\, (i) = \sigma'\, [\![e]\!]\, (i)$ for all $i \notin \mu$.*

If e is stable under P, the above difficulty would not arise during the execution of the loop $\texttt{while}\, e\, \texttt{do}\, P$. Formally this is stated as follows:

Lemma 2. *Suppose e is stable under P. Then for all μ, σ and σ' such that $P, \mu \cap \sigma\, [\![e]\!], \sigma \Downarrow \sigma'$, it holds that $\mu \cap \sigma'\, [\![e]\!] \subseteq \mu \cap \sigma\, [\![e]\!]$.*

Definition 7. *Let us say a loop $\texttt{while}\, e\, \texttt{do}\, P$ is* regular *if e is stable under P. A program is said to be regular if any* `while`*-loop contained in it is regular.*

The following lemma gives a reasonable sufficient condition for the regularity.

Lemma 3. *Let P be a program and e an expression. Suppose that any shared variable occurring in e does not occur on the left-hand side of any assignment in P. Then e is stable under P.*

Proof. It suffices to show that if $P, \mu, \sigma \Downarrow \sigma'$ then

- $\sigma(x)(i) = \sigma'(x)(i)$ for all local x and $i \notin \mu$, and
- $\sigma(x) = \sigma'(x)$ for all shared x not occurring on the left-hand side of any assignment in P.

This is done by induction on the derivation of $P, \mu, \sigma \Downarrow \sigma'$.

Lemma 4. *Let P be a program, and assume that for any subprogram of the form* `while` e `do` Q, *e and Q satisfy the condition of Lemma 3. Then P is regular.*

Below we consider regular programs. However, this is not actually a problem because it is possible to transform a program into a regular one, which is equivalent (in the sense that if they are executed under the same state with the same mask, then the set of resulting states are also the same).

To do this, given a program, replace its subprograms of the form `while` e `do` P with z `:=` e; `while` z `do` $(P;\ z$ `:=` $e)$, where z is a fresh local variable. The program obtained by this transformation satisfies the condition of Lemma 4.

4.2 Soundness and Relative Completeness for Regular Programs

After restricting our attention to regular programs, we can prove the soundness by verifying that each rule preserves validity. H-While can be checked by induction on the number of iterations (more precisely, the height of the derivation tree of the execution relation $\Downarrow$).

Theorem 1 (Soundness). *If P is a regular program and $\{\varphi\}\, m \mid P\, \{\psi\}$ is derivable from the rules in Figure 2, then it is valid.*

Next we consider relative completeness. The statement and proof strategy is mostly standard, except that masks are involved in the weakest preconditions.

Definition 8 (Weakest Liberal Precondition). *The weakest liberal precondition $wlp(m, P, \varphi)$ is defined as follows:*

$$wlp(m, P, \varphi) = \{\sigma \mid \forall \sigma'. P, \sigma(m), \sigma \Downarrow \sigma' \implies \sigma' \models \varphi\}.$$

If this set is definable in the assertion language, we also use $wlp(m, P, \varphi)$ to denote a formula defining this set.

To prove the relative completeness, by the standard argument it suffices to show that $\vdash \{wlp(m, P, \varphi)\}\, m \mid P\, \{\varphi\}$. We can prove this by induction on P. When P is a `while`-statement, we can use the formula $\exists z. e = z \wedge wlp(m \,\&\&\, z, P, \varphi)$ as an invariant.

Theorem 2 (Relative Completeness). *Suppose that the weakest liberal preconditions are definable in the assertion language. If P is a regular program and $\{\varphi\}\, m \mid P\, \{\psi\}$ is valid, then it is derivable.*

5 Extensions

In GPU programs, there are two kinds of errors that are intensively studied: data race and barrier divergence. In the above development we did not consider these errors explicitly. Below we discuss how our framework can be modified to detect these errors.

5.1 A Variant of the Assignment Rule

In rule E-SASSIGN, conflicting writes on a shared variable result in a nondeterministic behavior. Although this is consistent with NVIDIA's specification [15], such a conflict is often unintended. Thus it would be useful to regard such a situation as an error, so that a Hoare Logic can detect this data race. One of such semantics has been considered by Betts et al. [3]. (Below, we limit our attention to a data race of this type, although other types of data races may arise when lockstep execution is not assumed.)

Let us consider the following variant of E-SASSIGN:

$$\frac{\begin{array}{c} x \text{ is shared} \qquad \sigma'(y) = \sigma(y) \text{ for each variable } y \neq x \\ (\forall i \in \mu.\sigma\,[\![\bar{e}]\!]\,(i) \neq \bar{n}) \implies \sigma'(x)(\bar{n}) = \sigma(x)(\bar{n}) \\ \forall i \in \mu.(\sigma\,[\![\bar{e}]\!]\,(i) = \bar{n} \implies \sigma'(x)(\bar{n}) = \sigma\,[\![e]\!]\,(i)) \end{array}}{x\,[\bar{e}] := e, \mu, \sigma \Downarrow \sigma'} \quad \text{(E-SASSIGN')}$$

If we employ this rule, the execution gets stuck when there are conflicting writes. Indeed, if $\sigma\,[\![\bar{e}]\!]\,(i) = \bar{n}$ holds for multiple i's, with $\sigma\,[\![e]\!]\,(i)$ being distinct, then no σ' satisfy the last line of the premises. In other words, the premises require that all values being written into a certain location must be the same.

If we replace E-SASSIGN with E-SASSIGN', then the definition of *assign* in H-ASSIGN has to be modified accordingly. The definition would be as follows (here, we show the definition for shared variables):

$$\begin{aligned} assign'(x', m, x, \bar{e}, e) = \forall \bar{n}.\, ((\forall i \in m.\bar{e}@i \neq \bar{n}) \wedge x'(\bar{n}) = x(\bar{n})) \vee \\ (\forall i \in m.\bar{e}@i = \bar{n} \to x'(\bar{n}) = e@i). \end{aligned}$$

If there exist distinct active threads i, j such that $\bar{e}@i = \bar{e}@j (= \bar{n})$ and $e@i \neq e@j$ (that is, if two threads are trying to write different values to the same location), then there does not exist x' satisfying this formula. For example, if $x := \texttt{tid}$ is executed with mask $\mathbb{T}$, then $assign'(x', \mathbb{T}, x, \cdot, \texttt{tid})$ implies $\forall i \in \mathbb{T}.x' = i$ which is a contradiction (unless $N = 1$).

5.2 Treatment of Erroneous Situations

In the proof rules considered above (including E-SASSIGN' above), any postcondition can be proved if a program gets stuck. It may be desirable if the rules prevent us from proving such a consequence when a program may get stuck.

To handle such a situation explicitly, we can introduce a special state representing an error, denoted by $\bot$. We extend $\models$ so that $\bot$ do not satisfy any specification; in other words, $\bot \not\models \varphi$ for all φ.

Consider the following rule, which treats a data race as an error.

$$\frac{x \text{ is shared} \qquad i, j \in \mu \qquad \sigma\,[\![\bar{e}]\!]\,(i) = \sigma\,[\![\bar{e}]\!]\,(j) \qquad \sigma\,[\![e]\!]\,(i) \neq \sigma\,[\![e]\!]\,(j)}{x\,[\bar{e}] \;:=\, e, \mu, \sigma \Downarrow \bot} \quad \text{(E-SAssignRace)}$$

The following axiom would replace the original H-Assign.

$$\{\exists x'.\mathit{assign}'(x', m, x, \bar{e}, e) \wedge \varphi[x'/x]\}\, m \mid x\,[\bar{e}] \;:=\, e\, \{\varphi\}$$

Here we use assign' defined in Section 5.1. The precondition of this rule requires that there exists a result of the assignment, so if a program causes a data race, then the precondition becomes inconsistent. Therefore this rule prevents us from proving $\{\varphi\}\, m \mid x\,[\bar{e}] \;:=\, e\,\{\psi\}$, whenever there can be a data race, without φ being inconsistent. Also note that replacing $\forall x'$ in H-Assign with $\exists x'$ does not cause a problem, because E-SAssignRace excludes nondeterminism (there is at most one x' that has to be considered).

Similarly we can treat a so-called barrier divergence (a failure of synchronization) by modifying H-Sync. In the original rule H-Sync, similarly to H-Assign, the precondition is vacuously true for any state σ and a mask m such that $\sigma\,[\![m]\!] \neq \emptyset, \mathbb{T}$ (that is, a barrier divergence).

We add the following evaluation rule

$$\frac{\mu \neq \emptyset, \mathbb{T}}{\mathtt{sync}, \mu, \sigma \Downarrow \bot} \quad \text{(E-SyncDiv)}$$

and replace H-Sync with

$$\{(\mathit{all}(m) \vee \mathit{none}(m)) \wedge \varphi\}\, m \mid \mathtt{sync}\,\{\varphi\}\,.$$

Then, we can prove $\{\varphi\}\, m \mid \mathtt{sync}\,\{\psi\}$ only if φ implies $\mathit{all}(m) \vee \mathit{none}(m)$.

6 Related Work

Semantics of GPU Programs. Habermaier and Knapp [14] formalized both SIMT and interleaved multi-thread semantics, and discussed relationships between them. In particular, they proved that their SIMT semantics can be simulated by the interleaved semantics with an appropriate scheduling. Collingbourne et al. considered a lockstep execution of an unstructured programs based on control-flow graph [4]. They defined both interleaving and lockstep semantics, and proved that two semantics are equivalent in a certain sense under the assumption of race-freedom and termination. Betts et al. [3] defined another semantics, called synchronous, delayed visibility (SDV) semantics. The major difference from ours is that, in SDV semantics, a conflicting write results in an error, while in our semantics it is not. They developed a verification tool GPUVerify that detects race condition and barrier divergence, based on their SDV semantics.

Verification Tools. Verification tools for GPU programs are developed by several authors. Tripakis, Stergiou and Lublinerman developed a method to check determinism and equivalence of SPMD programs based on non-interference [16].

Collingbourne, Cadar and Kelly proposed a method of symbolic execution of SIMD programs based on KLEE symbolic execution tool [5, 6]. Li and Gopalakrishnan developed an SMT-based verification tools PUG [7] and PUG_{para} [8]. They first transform a CUDA program into a first-order formula, and detect assertion failures, barrier divergence and date races by using an SMT solver. Li et al. developed a concolic verification and test generation tool for GPU programs, called GKLEE [9]. Further optimizations and extensions of GKLEE are also considered [10, 11].

Deductive Verification. Huisman and Mihelčić suggest permission-based separation logic [12] for deductive verification of GPU programs. They demonstrated how they can verify race-freedom and functional correctness by separation logic. They consider an assignment of resources to threads, and use it to prove race-freedom. As discussed in Section 5, our approach can also be used to detect data races, although we did not consider explicit resource assignments. This is because in our language there is no pointers, and no two arrays can ovarlap. Moreover, in our semantics the execution is in lockstep, which implies that there is no data races between different instructions. Under these assumptions, absence of data races can be expressed without introducing a new construct like points-to relation in separation logic. Since Huisman and Mihelčić do not assume lockstep execution, the same method would not apply to their setting.

7 Conclusions and Future Work

We have formalized the SIMT execution model for while-language extended with arrays and SIMT constructs, and defined a Hoare Logic for this language. We also proved that the inference rules are sound and relatively complete for a regular program. This restriction is, as discussed above, not significant, because it is always possible to transform a given program into a regular one without changing the meaning of the program.

In our semantics, each program is executed in all threads in complete lockstep. However, actual execution on GPUs do not necessarily proceed in such a way. For example, CUDA has a thread hierarchy in its programming model, and the execution of threads may be interleaved [2]. One possible future direction would be to extend our framework so that it can handle this thread hierarchy.

However, there is another possible approach to fill the gap. Even if the actual thread execution is interleaved, if we restrict our attention to programs that are scheduling independent (that is, programs that produce the same result regardless of which scheduling is selected), it would be sound to assume that programs are executed in complete lockstep. So under such an assumption, our method can be applied to a more realistic programs such as CUDA without significant changes. Since, as far as we know, many GPU programs are intended to be scheduling independent, a detailed investigation is left for future work.

Acknowledgement. We thank Kohei Suenaga and anonymous reviewers for valuable comments.

References

1. Owens, J.D., Luebke, D., Govindaraju, N., Harris, M., Krüger, J., Lefohn, A., Purcell, T.J.: A survey of general-purpose computation on graphics hardware. Computer Graphics Forum 26(1), 80–113 (2007)
2. NVIDIA: NVIDIA CUDA C Programming Guide (2012)
3. Betts, A., Chong, N., Donaldson, A., Qadeer, S., Thomson, P.: GPUVerify: a verifier for GPU kernels. In: Proc. of the ACM International Conference on Object Oriented Programming Systems Languages and Applications. OOPSLA 2012, pp. 113–132. ACM, New York (2012)
4. Collingbourne, P., Donaldson, A.F., Ketema, J., Qadeer, S.: Interleaving and lock-step semantics for analysis and verification of GPU kernels. In: Felleisen, M., Gardner, P. (eds.) Programming Languages and Systems. LNCS, vol. 7792, pp. 270–289. Springer, Heidelberg (2013)
5. Collingbourne, P., Cadar, C., Kelly, P.H.: Symbolic crosschecking of floating-point and SIMD code. In: Proc. of the sixth conference on Computer systems, EuroSys 2011, pp. 315–328. ACM, New York (2011)
6. Collingbourne, P., Cadar, C., Kelly, P.H.J.: Symbolic testing of openCL code. In: Eder, K., Lourenço, J., Shehory, O. (eds.) HVC 2011. LNCS, vol. 7261, pp. 203–218. Springer, Heidelberg (2012)
7. Li, G., Gopalakrishnan, G.: Scalable SMT-based verification of GPU kernel functions. In: Proc. of the 18th ACM SIGSOFT International Symposium on Foundations of Software Engineering (FSE 2010), pp. 187–196. ACM (2010)
8. Li, G., Gopalakrishnan, G.: Parameterized verification of GPU kernel programs. In: 2012 IEEE 26th International Parallel and Distributed Processing Symposium Workshops & PhD Forum (IPDPSW), pp. 2450–2459 (May 2012)
9. Li, G., Li, P., Sawaya, G., Gopalakrishnan, G., Ghosh, I., Rajan, S.P.: GKLEE: concolic verification and test generation for GPUs. In: Proc. of the 17th ACM SIGPLAN Symposium on Principles and Practice of Parallel Programming. PPoPP 2012, pp. 215–224. ACM, New York (2012)
10. Li, P., Li, G., Gopalakrishnan, G.: Parametric flows: automated behavior equivalencing for symbolic analysis of races in CUDA programs. In: Proc. of the International Conference on High Performance Computing, Networking, Storage and Analysis (SC 2012), pp. 29:1–29:10. IEEE Computer Society Press (2012)
11. Chiang, W.-F., Gopalakrishnan, G., Li, G., Rakamarić, Z.: Formal analysis of GPU programs with atomics via conflict-directed delay-bounding. In: Brat, G., Rungta, N., Venet, A. (eds.) NFM 2013. LNCS, vol. 7871, pp. 213–228. Springer, Heidelberg (2013)
12. Huisman, M., Mihelčić, M.: Specification and verification of GPGPU programs using permission-based separation logic. In: Bytecode 2013, 8th Workshop on Bytecode Semantics, Verification, Analysis and Transformation (2013), `http://hgpu.org/?p=9099`
13. Apt, K.R., de Boer, F., Olderog, E.R.: Verification of Sequential and Concurrent Programs, 3rd edn. Springer Publishing Company, Incorporated (2009)
14. Habermaier, A., Knapp, A.: On the correctness of the SIMT execution model of GPUs. In: Seidl, H. (ed.) Programming Languages and Systems. LNCS, vol. 7211, pp. 316–335. Springer, Heidelberg (2012)
15. NVIDIA: Parallel Thread Execution ISA Version 3.1 (2012)
16. Tripakis, S., Stergiou, C., Lublinerman, R.: Checking equivalence of spmd programs using non-interference. Technical Report UCB/EECS-2010-11, EECS Department, University of California, Berkeley (January 2010)

The Undefined Domain: Precise Relational Information for Entities That Do Not Exist*

Holger Siegel, Bogdan Mihaila, and Axel Simon

Technische Universität München, Institut für Informatik II, Garching, Germany
firstname.lastname@in.tum.de

Abstract. Verification by static analysis often hinges on the inference of relational numeric information. In real-world programs, the set of active variables is often not fixed for a given program point due to, for instance, heap-allocated cells or recursive function calls. For these program points, an invariant has to summarize values for traces E where a variable x exists and values for traces N where x does not exist. Non-relational domains solve this problem by copying all information on x in traces E to those in N. Relational domains face the challenge that the relations in traces E between x and other variables cannot simply be replicated for the traces N. This work illustrates this problem and proposes a general solution in form of a co-fibered abstract domain that forwards each domain operation to operations on a child domain. By tracking which variables are undefined, it transparently stores suitable values in the child domain thus minimizing the loss of relational information. We present applications in heap abstractions and function summaries.

1 Introduction

Static analyses that are based on relational numeric domains are often restricted to programs with limited dynamic memory allocation and without recursive functions [2]. Analyses that explicitly target heap manipulating programs often represent their state using a logic formula, e.g. separation logic [7] or three-valued logic analysis (TVLA) [8]. Combining them with relational numeric domains is not straightforward. In particular, problems occur when the numeric domain has to track a changing number of memory cells or when it has to deal with uninitialized variables. The following examples illustrate these problems.

Non-Existing Memory Regions. In the C program in Fig. 1, a region x is allocated in one conditional branch but not in the other. When this program is analyzed using some abstract domain, the resulting abstract state of the then-branch has to be merged with that of the else-branch. The desired invariant is that x is initialized to 3 if p points to x. When using the Intervals domain, at least the fact that $x = 3$ can be inferred by allowing x to be mapped to an explicit empty interval $\bot$. Specifically, by using this bottom value $\bot$ as the value of x in the else-branch as shown in the first row of the table, the join of the branches retains

* This work was supported by DFG Emmy Noether programme SI 1579/1.

C.-c. Shan (Ed.): APLAS 2013, LNCS 8301, pp. 74–89, 2013.

```
if (rnd()) {
  p = malloc(4);
  *p = 3;
} else {
  p = NULL;
}
```

Intervals	$\{p = 1 \cdot \&x, x = 3\} \sqcup \{p = 0 \cdot \&x, x = \bot\}$ $= \{p \in \{0,1\} \cdot \&x, x = 3\}$
Polyhedra	$\{p = 1 \cdot \&x, x = 3\} \sqcup \{p = 0 \cdot \&x, x = \top\}$ $= \{p \in \{0,1\} \cdot \&x, x = \top\}$
Polyhedra as Undefined child	$\{p = 1 \cdot \&x, x = 3, f_x = 1\}$ $\sqcup \{p = 0 \cdot \&x, x = 3, f_x = 0\}$ $= \{p = f_x \cdot \&x, x = 3, f_x \in \{0, 1\}\}$

Fig. 1. Non-existing regions

```
if (rnd()) {
  x = 1;
  y = 2;
} else {
  x = 0;
}
```

Polyhedra/ Intervals	$\{x = 1, y = 2\} \sqcup \{x = 0, y = \top\}$ $= \{x \in \{0,1\}, y = \top\}$
Polyhedra as Undefined child	$\{x = 1, f_x = 1, y = 2, f_y = 1\}$ $\sqcup \{x = 0, f_x = 1, y = 2, f_y = 0\}$ $= \{x \in \{0,1\}, f_x = 1, y = 2, f_y = x\}$

Fig. 2. Non-initialized variables

the information that x can only contain value 3. However, relational numeric domains typically model *smash products*, i.e. they do not allow assigning the "empty" value $\bot$ to individual variables since this always implies an empty set of relations and, thus, a domain state that is $\bot$. Thus, in contrast to non-relational domains, x must map to a value. Consider choosing $x = \top$. In this case the second table row shows that the relational Polyhedra domain [4] loses the information that $x = 3$ in the else-branch. In order to retain as much information as possible, we propose a copy-and-paste operation that can be used to add missing variables with values that are more precise than $\top$, so that $x = 3$ is retained in the join.

Non-Initialized Variables. Now we consider a precision loss that occurs in the C program in Fig. 2. Here, one conditional branch initializes variables x and y, whereas the other branch only initializes variable x, leaving y undefined. When the resulting states are joined, y has to be introduced in the latter state with an unrestricted value $\top$, giving the joined state $\{x = 1, y = 2\} \cup \{x = 0, y = \top\}$. However, introducing variables with value $\top$ can lead to loss of precision. In particular, the implication $x = 1 \Rightarrow y = 2$ is lost in domains whose state is a convex set. For instance, when using the relational Polyhedra domain, the joined state $\{x \in \{0,1\}, y = \top\}$ (shown in the first row of the table) is only as precise as the join over the intervals, in that any relation between x and y is lost.

As a solution to these two problems of non-existing regions and of non-initialized variables, we propose a dedicated abstract domain called the *Undefined* domain which is parameterized over another numeric domain, that we call the *child domain*. The child can be an arbitrary numeric domain. We require that non-initialized *and* non-existent variables are introduced as $\top$. The Undefined domain then transparently inserts placeholder values using a so-called copy-and-paste operation. It additionally tracks a flag f_x that indicates if variable x is defined, thereby enabling the child domain to infer relations with this flag, e.g. "x is defined iff p points to x". In order to introduce the Undefined domain, we now exemplify how it can be employed to analyze the examples.

We illustrate the Undefined domain by performing an abstract interpretation of the program in Fig. 1. The resulting state of the then-branch is represented by the child state $s_t = \{p = \&x, x = 3, f_x = 1\}$, where x is the content of region x and f_x is a flag that indicates whether x is defined or not. Since flag f_x has value 1, variable x is defined and it has value 3 stored in the child domain. Furthermore, the state in the else-branch $\{p = 0\}$ does not contain the variable x, so that it has to be added with $x = \top$. The Undefined domain observes this undefined value of x and replaces it by a copy of x from s_t, yielding the child state $s_e = \{p = 0, x = 3, f_x = 0\}$. Note here that the Undefined domain has added $f_x = 0$, indicating that x is not defined, and the value of x that is stored in the child domain has to be ignored. As shown in the second row of the table, joining both states results in the child state $\{p = f_x \cdot \&x, x = 3, f_x \in \{0, 1\}\}$, where p can only point to x if f_x has value 1, which means that x is defined. The Undefined domain has retained the information that region x can only contain value 3, although the undefined value of x is modeled by $\top$ instead of $\bot$.

Now consider analyzing the program in Fig. 2 using the Undefined domain with the Polyhedra domain as its child. The resulting state of the then-branch is represented by the child state $\{x = 1, f_x = 1, y = 2, f_y = 1\}$. Here, flags f_x and f_y have value 1, indicating that x and y are defined. The resulting state of the else-branch is modeled by the child state $\{x = 0, f_x = 1, y = 2, f_y = 0\}$. Flag f_y has value 0, indicating that y appears to have the value $\top$ at the interface of the Undefined domain. As before, the Undefined domain has used the value of y from the then-branch as a placeholder value. As shown in the second row of the table, the joined child state $\{x \in \{0,1\}, f_x = 1, y = 2, f_y = x\}$ now indicates that $x = 1$ implies $f_y = 1$ and thus $y = 2$, an invariant that is retained although the state is approximated by the Polyhedra domain.

As shown in the examples, existing numeric domains can be wrapped by the Undefined domain. The resulting domain is a drop-in replacement for the original numeric domain. The Undefined domain transparently manages flags for all variables that may be undefined, thereby ensuring that all operations on the domain are sound even if some of the variables mentioned in the operations are undefined. We provide an implementation of the Undefined domain that partitions the flags into groups of flags with equal valuations. By collapsing each group into one single flag, it minimizes the required number of flag variables. In summary, this paper makes the following contributions:

- We describe how existing numeric domains can be enabled to incorporate program states of different size in one abstract state.
- We define the *Undefined* abstract domain that translates domain operations to operations on a child domain such that relational information can be inferred in these situations.
- We illustrate the precision of our approach by presenting examples that perform dynamic heap allocation and summarize calls to procedures.

After providing a formal basis, Sect. 3 defines the Undefined domain. Its utility for common analysis tasks is shown in Sect. 4 before Sect. 5 presents our experimental evaluation. Section 6 discusses related work and Sect. 7 concludes.

2 The *Undefined* Domain

Numeric domains may provide operations that change the *support set* of a numeric state, that is, the set of variables for which the domain holds numeric valuations. Joining and comparing states with different support sets is often preceeded by a process that makes their support sets equal. We follow [11] and describe domains with non-fixed support sets as *co-fibered domains*. This construction allows to systematically derive variants of the compare and join operations that adjust the support sets themselves. We first give a definition of numeric domains before we introduce the *Undefined* domain as an abstract numeric domain.

Definition 1 (Numeric Domain). *A* numeric domain *is given by a tuple* $(D, \sqsubseteq_D, \sqcup_D, T_D)$ *where* D *is the set of* states, $\sqsubseteq_D$ *is a pre-order,* $\sqcup_D$ *is a binary function, such that* $s \sqsubseteq_D s \sqcup_D t$ *and* $t \sqsubseteq_D s \sqcup_D t$ *for all* $s, t \in D$*, and* $T \subseteq D^D$ *is a set of monotonic* transfer functions.

Let $\mathbb{X}$ be the set of program variables. In this work, we assume that each numeric state $s \in D$ has a *support set* $\chi(s) \subseteq \mathbb{X}$ that represents the set of variables for which state s holds valuations. Then each state $s \in D$ represents a set of vectors of dimension $|\chi(s)|$. Since program variables may be introduced and removed during a program run, the numeric domain must provide operations that add or remove variables to and from the support set. Removing a variable x from a state $s \in D$ with $x \in \chi(s)$ is denoted by a function $drop_{D,x} : D \to D$. Adding an unrestricted variable x to a state $s \in D$ with $x \notin \chi(s)$ is denoted by a function $add_{D,x} : D \to D$. These functions are lifted to sets of variables by repeated application of *add* and *drop* operations, that is, $add_{D,X} := \bigcirc_{x \in X} add_{D,x}$ and $drop_{D,X} := \bigcirc_{x \in X} drop_{D,x}$ with $\bigcirc$ denoting function composition.

Comparing and joining two states $s \in D$ and $t \in D$ with different support sets requires to add missing variables to s and t beforehand. Following [11], we capture this behaviour by requiring that the pre-ordered set $(D, \sqsubseteq_D)$ together with the morphisms $add_{D,X}$, $drop_{D,X}$ for $X \subseteq \mathbb{X}$ forms a co-fibered domain. Specifically, we require the following equivalence:

$$s \sqsubseteq_D t \Leftrightarrow add_{D,\chi(t)\setminus\chi(s)}(s) \sqsubseteq_D add_{D,\chi(s)\setminus\chi(t)}(t).$$

For the sake of a generic presentation, we assume that all other transfer functions are divided into assignments $[\![y := f(x_1, \ldots, x_n)]\!]_D$ and tests $[\![f(x_1, \ldots, x_n) \leq 0]\!]_D$ with program variables $x_1, \ldots, x_n, y \in \mathbb{X}$ and an n-ary function f.

Example 1 (Concrete Domain). The *concrete domain* $(C, \sqsubseteq_C, \sqcup_C, T_C)$ models exact sets of vectors over $\mathbb{Z}$, that is, $C = \bigcup_{n \in \mathbb{N}} \wp(\mathbb{Z}^n)$. The join $s \sqcup_C t$ of two states s and t with $\chi(s) = \chi(t)$ is just the set union $s \cup t$. Analogously, for $\chi(s) = \chi(t)$ the comparison $s \sqsubseteq_C t$ is just $s \subseteq t$.

An abstract numeric domain over-approximates the state of another domain. Its semantics is determined by a *concretization function* γ that takes an abstract state to a concrete state.

Definition 2 (Abstract Domain). *A domain* $(A, \sqsubseteq_A, \sqcup_A, T_A)$ abstracts *a domain* $(D, \sqsubseteq_D, \sqcup_D, T_D)$ *if there is a* concretization *function* $\gamma : A \to D$, *such that* $s \sqsubseteq_A t \Rightarrow \gamma(s) \sqsubseteq_D \gamma(t)$ *and* $\gamma(s) \sqcup_D \gamma(t) \sqsubseteq_D \gamma(s \sqcup_A t)$ *for every* $s, t \in A$ *and for every* $\tau_D \in T_D$ *exists a* $\tau_A \in T_A$, *such that* $\tau_D \circ \gamma \sqsubseteq_D \gamma \circ \tau_A$.

This definition ensures that every domain operation of the abstract domain over-approximates the corresponding operation of the concrete domain.

Example 2. The previously mentioned domain of closed convex *Polyhedra* [4] abstracts the concrete domain C by over-approximating a set of vectors by the topological closure of their convex hull.

In Sect. 4 we will detail how the Undefined domain can improve the precision of the Polyhedra domain. In the remainder of this section, we assume an abstract domain $(A, \sqsubseteq_A, \sqcup_A, T_A)$ without making further assumptions about this domain.

2.1 The Undefined Domain

The *Undefined* domain is a functor domain [3]: Each state holds a state of a *child domain*, and domain operations are forwarded to domain operations on this child domain. Here, for each variable x of the Undefined domain, its child domain holds a variable x and a flag f_x. When $f_x = 1$ in the child domain, the value of x is given by the value of x in the child domain. When $f_x = 0$, variable x is unrestricted and the value stored for x in the child domain is just a placeholder. As a consequence, every numeric state of dimension n is modelled by a child state of dimension $2n$. We later detail how fewer dimensions suffice. We denote an Undefined domain that transforms a child domain $(D, \sqsubseteq_D, \sqcup_D, T_D)$ by $(U(D), \sqsubseteq_{U(D)}, \sqcup_{U(D)}, T_{U(D)})$. An element of the Undefined domain that has a child state $s \in D$ is denoted by $u \rhd s$ where u denotes the mapping from each x to its flag f_x. We fix the semantics of $U(D)$ by defining functions $\tilde{\gamma}_D$ that relate states of $U(D)$ to states of D.

Definition 3. *For every domain* $(D, \sqsubseteq_D, \sqcup_D, T_D)$, *function* $\tilde{\gamma}_D : U(D) \to D$ *is given by* $\tilde{\gamma}_D(u \rhd s) := (\bigcirc_{x \in \mathcal{X}(s)} \tilde{\gamma}_{D,x})(s)$ *where* $\tilde{\gamma}_{D,x} : D \to D$ *is defined by* $\tilde{\gamma}_{D,x}(s) := \mathit{drop}_{D,f_x}([\![f_x = 1]\!] s \sqcup_D (\mathit{add}_{D,x} \circ \mathit{drop}_{D,x})([\![f_x = 0]\!] s))$ *for each* $x \in \mathbb{X}$.

Adding and Removing Dimensions. Removing a variable x from a state $u \rhd s \in U(D)$ consists of straightforwardly removing variable x and the corresponding flag f_x from the child state. Thus, we define $\mathit{drop}_{U(D),x}(u \rhd s) := u \rhd \mathit{drop}_{D,\{x,f_x\}}(s)$. Adding a variable x to a state $u \rhd s \in U(D)$ can be done in two different ways: One way is to simply add an unrestricted variable x and the corresponding flag f_x with value one to the child state s. Another way is to add x with an arbitrary value and flag f_x with value zero to the child domain, indicating that x is undefined and the value held for x in the child domain has to be ignored. However, for abstract domains the chosen placeholder value of x can influence the precision of subsequent domain operations, namely join operations. In order to characterize the functions that may be used to introduce placeholder values for x, we first introduce the notion of X-Adders.

Definition 4. *A function* $\varphi : D \to D$ *is an* X-Adder *iff* $\chi(\varphi(d)) = \chi(d) \cup X$ *and* $drop_{D,X}(\varphi(d)) = d$ *for all sets of variables* $X \subseteq \mathbb{X}$ *and states* $d \in D$ *with* $\chi(d) \cap X = \emptyset$.

The intuition of an X-Adder φ is that it extends a state with new dimensions X that are bound to placeholder values. Given an X-Adder φ for domain D and variable set $x_1, \ldots, x_n$, we define operation $add^{\varphi}_{U(D),\{x_1,\ldots,x_n\}}(u \rhd s) := u \rhd [\![f_{x_1} = \cdots = f_{x_n} = 0]\!]\varphi(add_{D,f_{x_1},\ldots,f_{x_n}}(s))$. It remains to show that every operation $add_{D,X}$ on domain D has a corresponding operation on domain $U(D)$. Indeed, for every domain D and variable set X function $add_{D,X}$ itself is an X-Adder, and so $add^{add_{D,X}}_{U(D),X}$ corresponds to $add_{D,X}$.

Joining, Widening and Comparing States. Two states $u \rhd s$ and $u \rhd t$ with equal support sets $\chi(s) = \chi(t)$ are compared, joined or widened by simply performing these operations on their child states s and t. For states $u \rhd s$ and $u \rhd t$ with different support sets $\chi(s) \neq \chi(t)$, their support sets are made equal by performing add^{φ} operations on s and t before they can be compared, joined or widened. This allows for a degree of freedom, since an arbitrary X-Adder φ can be chosen for each add^{φ} operation. In the next section we will show how the precision of the Undefined domain can be improved by introducing an X-Addder that retains relational information between the variables X.

It is worth noting that the ordering given by this comparison operation slightly deviates from the pre-order obtained from constructing the co-fibered domain. There, the relation $u \rhd s \sqsubseteq u \rhd t$ holds for two states $u \rhd s$ and $u \rhd t$ with different support sets whenever two X-Adders φ and ψ *exist*, such that $add^{\varphi}_{D,\chi(t)\setminus\chi(s)}(s) \sqsubseteq_D add^{\psi}_{D,\chi(s)\setminus\chi(t)}(t)$, whereas the comparison operation only detects subset relations that can be established by a *previously chosen* pair of X-Adders. In fixpoint computations, this may lead to extra iterations, although termination is still guaranteed by widening. Consider, for example, the child states $s := \{x = 1, y = 1, f_y = 0\}$ and $t := \{x = 1\}$. Clearly, s and t describe the same state, but the comparison operation might obscure this by adjusting state t to $\{x = 1, y = 2, f_y = 0\}$, thereby necessitating one more fixpoint iteration.

Transfer Functions. An assignment $y := f(x_1, \ldots, x_n)$ is directly executed on the child domain. Since the resulting value y is only valid if all variables $x_1, \ldots, x_n$ are defined (that is, if all $f_i = 1$), the flag f_y is set to the conjunction $\bigwedge_{i=1}^{n} f_{x_i}$. A test $f(x_1, \ldots, x_n) \leq 0$ is performed by first splitting the state into one state where all $f_i = 1$ and one state where $f_i = 0$ for some i. The test is then performed on the former state, while the latter state remains unchanged. After that, both states are joined. Figure 3 shows the transfer functions for tests and assignments.

$$\llbracket y := f(x_1, \ldots, x_n) \rrbracket_{U(D)} u \rhd s$$
$$:= u \rhd \llbracket y := f(x_1, \ldots, x_n);\ f_y := \bigwedge_{i=1}^{n} f_{x_i} \rrbracket_D s$$
$$\llbracket f(x_1, \ldots, x_n) \leq 0 \rrbracket_{U(D)} u \rhd s$$
$$:= u \rhd \llbracket f(x_1, \ldots, x_n) \leq 0;\ \bigwedge_{i=1}^{n} f_{x_i} = 1 \rrbracket_D s \sqcup_D \llbracket \bigvee_{i=1}^{n} f_{x_i} = 0 \rrbracket_D s$$

Fig. 3. Transfer functions for unary operations

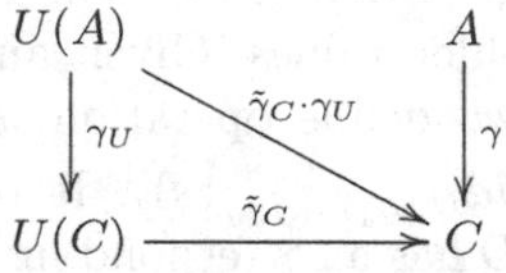

Fig. 4. Abstract domains and their concretizations

2.2 Correctness of the Undefined Domain

In order to verify that domain $U(A)$ is indeed an abstraction of domain C, we first show that $U(A)$ is an abstraction of domain $U(C)$, and then we show that $U(C)$ is an abstraction of C. As sketched in Fig. 4, it follows immediately that domain $U(A)$ is also an abstraction of domain C. In the first step, we observe that domain $U(A)$ is an abstraction of $U(C)$.

Lemma 1. *If domain A abstracts domain C, then $U(A)$ abstracts $U(C)$.*

Proof. Given an concretization function $\gamma : A \to C$, a concretization function $\gamma_U : U(A) \to U(C)$ is given by $\gamma_U(u \rhd s) := u \rhd \gamma(s)$.

In the second step, we observe that the domain $U(C)$ is an abstraction of C.

Lemma 2. *Domain $U(C)$ abstracts domain C.*

Proof. For every Domain $(D, \sqsubseteq_D, \sqcup_D, T_D)$ and every $x \in \mathbb{X}$, function $\tilde{\gamma}_{Dx}$ is a concretization function. In particular, every function $add^{\varphi}_{U(D),x}$ abstracts function $add_{D,x}$. As a composition of such functions, function $\tilde{\gamma}_C$ also is.

The following theorem states the desired property that domain $U(A)$ is an abstraction of the concrete domain C: all operations on domain $U(A)$ overaproximate the corresponding operations on the concrete domain C.

Theorem 1. *Domain $U(A)$ abstracts domain C.*

Proof. Since γ_U and $\tilde{\gamma}_C$ are concretization functions by Lemma 1 and 2, their composition $\tilde{\gamma}_C \circ \gamma_U : U(A) \to C$ also is.

The given semantics of the Undefined domain is still impractical, as it stores one additional flag variable for each variable in the child state, and it is incomplete, as it does not fully specify how missing variables are added. The next section describes how the number of flag variables can be reduced and suggests an X-Adder *copyAndPaste* that adds missing variables in a clever way: it copies relations between those variables that are missing in the respective other domain.

3 Practical Implementation of the *Undefined* Domain

In this section we propose an implementation of the Undefined domain that is practical in following two senses: firstly, it associates a flag with a set of variables rather than with each variable, thus yielding a scalable domain; secondly, it uses a copy-and-paste operation that transfers the valuations of whole sets of variables to another domain, thereby allowing for retaining relational information between variables of a partition. After some definitions, we consider each aspect in turn.

3.1 Definition of the Domain

Let $\mathcal{X} \subseteq \mathbb{X}$ denote the program variables and $\mathcal{F} \subseteq \mathbb{X} \setminus \mathcal{X}$ denote the variables used as flags. A state of the undefined domain $U(A)$ is given by $u \rhd a$ with child state $a \in A$ and a partial mapping $u : \mathcal{X} \dashrightarrow \mathcal{F}$. This mapping takes each variable in the state's support set to a flag that tracks whether this variable is defined. Thus, the support set of child state a is $\chi(a) = \text{dom}(u) \cup \text{img}(u)$ where $\text{dom}(u)$ denotes the domain of u and $\text{img}(u)$ denotes the image of u. We allow several program variables to map to the same flag variable, thereby inducing a partitioning of program variables. For each mapping u this partitioning is given by $\Pi(u) := \{u^{-1}(f) \mid f \in \text{img}(u)\}$, where $u^{-1} : \mathcal{F} \to \wp(\mathcal{X})$ is the reverse relation of u. For better legibility, we sometimes denote u by its reverse relation. Thus, for $u = [x_0 \mapsto f_0, x_1 \mapsto f_1, x_2 \mapsto f_0, x_3 \mapsto f_1]$ we write $[f_0 \mapsto \{x_0, x_2\}, f_1 \mapsto \{x_1, x_3\}]$. We now detail how to manage flags when partitions change.

3.2 Making Partitions Compatible

Whenever two states $u_1 \rhd a_1$ and $u_2 \rhd a_2$ are compared or joined, their partitionings $\Pi(u_1)$ and $\Pi(u_2)$ must agree. To this end, the coarsest partitioning $P := \{p_1 \cap p_2 \mid p_1 \in \Pi(u_1), p_2 \in \Pi(u_2)\}$ whose partitions can be merged to give either $\Pi(u_1)$ or $\Pi(u_2)$ is calculated. We then associate each partition $p \in P$ with a fresh flag f_p, thereby obtaining a new state $u_{12} = \bigcup_{p \in P}[f_p \mapsto p]$. Let $u_{12} = \mathit{common}(u_1, u_2)$ abbreviate this operation. Since u_{12} associates different (and possibly more) flags with its partitions than u_1 and u_2, the flags stored in a_1 and a_2 have to be adjusted. Thus, let $\mathit{trans}_{u_i}^{u_{12}}(f) := \{u_{12}(x) \mid x \in u_i^{-1}(f)\}$ denote the flags of those partitions in u_{12} whose union is associated with f in u_i. We transfer the value of f to the flags $\{f_1, \ldots, f_n\} \in \mathit{trans}_{u_i}^{u_{12}}(f)$ using the assignment $\mathit{adjOne}_{u_i}^{u_{12}}(f) := [\![f_1 := f]\!] \cdots [\![f_n := f]\!]$. The assignment for all partitions is then given by the composition $\mathit{adjust}_{u_i}^{u_{12}} := \bigcirc_{f \in \text{img}(u_i)} \mathit{adjOne}_{u_i}^{u_{12}}(f)$.

$x \in \mathcal{X}$	x_1	x_2	x_3	x_4	x_5	x_6	x_7	x_8	x_9	x_{10}
$u_1(x)$	f_1	f_1	f_1	f_1	f_2	f_2	f_2	f_2	f_3	f_3
$u_2(x)$	f_4	f_4	f_5	f_5	f_5	f_5	f_6	f_6	f_7	f_7
$u_{12}(x)$	f_8	f_8	f_9	f_9	f_{10}	f_{10}	f_{11}	f_{11}	f_{12}	f_{12}

Fig. 5. Partition $u_{12} = common(u_1, u_2)$ of Example 3

Making two child states a_1 and a_2 compatible with u_{12} requires that the flags $\text{img}(u_{12})$ are introduced, the renaming $adjust_{u_i}^{u_{12}}$ is applied, and that the now stale flags $\text{img}(u_i)$ are removed. These operations are aggregated by the function $compat_{u_i}^{u_{12}} = drop_{\text{img}(u_i)} \circ adjust_{u_i}^{u_{12}} \circ add_{\text{img}(u_{12})}$.

Example 3. Consider the task of making two domains, $u_1 \rhd a_1$ and $u_2 \rhd a_2$ compatible where u_1 and u_2 are given by the first two rows in Fig. 5. First, the new partition $u_{12} = common(u_1, u_2)$ is calculated as shown in the last line of Fig. 5. In order to adjust, a_1 to be compatible with u_{12}, we compute $a_1' = compat_{u_1}^{u_{12}}(a_1) = drop_{\{f_1,f_2,f_3\}}(adjust_{u_1}^{u_{12}}(add_{\{f_8,\ldots f_{12}\}}(a_1)))$. The function $adjust_{u_1}^{u_{12}}$ expands to $adjOne_{u_1}^{u_{12}}(f_1) \cdots adjOne_{u_1}^{u_{12}}(f_3) = [\![f_8 = f_1, f_9 = f_1]\!] \cdot [\![f_{10} = f_2, f_{11} = f_2]\!] \cdot [\![f_{12} = f_3]\!]$. Computing $a_2' = compat_{u_2}^{u_{12}}(a_2)$ analogously suffices to perform any operation that requires $\chi(a_1') = \chi(a_2')$, such as $(u_1 \rhd a_1) \sqcup_{U(A)} (u_2 \rhd a_2) = u_{12} \rhd (a_1' \sqcup_A a_2')$.

This concludes the process of making domains compatible which allows us to associate a flag with a partition rather than a single variable. While tracking fewer flags improves performance, we now detail how precision can be improved.

3.3 Rescuing Relational Information

Tracking whether a set of variables is undefined is only useful if the content of undefined variables is replaced by other values that lead to less precision loss. In order to distinguish variables that are always undefined, we use a special flag f_{undef} whose value is always zero in the child domain. The variables $u^{-1}(f_{undef})$ associated with f_{undef} are omitted from the child domain. Due to this, computing the join of two states $(u_1 \rhd a_1) \sqcup_{U(A)} (u_2 \rhd a_2)$ requires that the variables $X_{12} = u_1^{-1}(f_{undef}) \setminus u_2^{-1}(f_{undef})$ that are undefined in a_1 but not in a_2 are added to a_1 before the child states a_i can be joined (and vice-versa). To this end, define a function $copyAndPaste_{D,X} : D \times D \to D$ with $r = copyAndPaste_{D,X}(s, a)$ such that variables X are copied from s into a, yielding r where $X \subseteq \chi(s)$, $\chi(a) \cap X = \emptyset$ and $\chi(r) = \chi(a) \cup X$. We illustrate *copyAndPaste* with an example:

Example 4. Suppose the following modified version of the introductory example is given where `rnd(0,10)` returns a number between 0 and 10:

```
int x,y;
if (rnd()) {
  x = rnd(0,10);
  y = x;
}
```

$$
\begin{aligned}
(u_1 \rhd a_1) \boxdot_{U(A)} (u_2 \rhd a_2) &= \text{let for } i = 1,2 && (1)\\
&\quad X_i = u_i^{-1}(f_{undef})\\
&\quad u_i' = u_i[x \mapsto f_i]_{x \in X_i \setminus X_{3-i}} \text{ where } f_i \text{ fresh}\\
&\quad u_{12} = common(u_1', u_2')\\
&\quad a_i' = copyAndPaste_{A, X_{3-i} \setminus X_i}(a_{3-i}, a_i)\\
&\text{in } u_{12} \rhd (compat_{u_1}^{u_{12}}(a_1') \boxdot_A compat_{u_2}^{u_{12}}(a_2'))\\
add_x(u \rhd a) &= u[x \mapsto f_{undef}] \rhd a && (2)\\
drop_x(u \rhd a) &= \text{if } u(x) = f_{undef} \text{ then } (u \setminus x) \rhd a \text{ else} && (3)\\
&\quad \text{if } |\{y \in \text{dom}(u) \mid u(x) = u(y)\}| > 1\\
&\quad \text{then } (u \setminus x) \rhd drop_{A,x}(a)\\
&\quad \text{else } (u \setminus x) \rhd drop_{A,\{x,u(x)\}}(a) && (4)\\
[\![y := f(x_1, \ldots, x_n)]\!]_{U(A)} u \rhd a &= \text{let } \Phi := \{u(x_1), \ldots u(x_n)\} \text{ in} && (5)\\
&\quad \text{if } f_{undef} \in \Phi \text{ then } add_{U(A),y}(drop_{U(A),y}(u \rhd a)) \text{ else}\\
&\quad \text{if } \Phi = \{f\} \text{ then } u[y \mapsto f] \rhd [\![y := f(x_1, \ldots, x_n);]\!]_A a\\
&\quad \text{else let } f_y \text{ fresh and } u' = u[y \mapsto f_y] \text{ in} && (6)\\
&\quad u' \rhd [\![y := f(x_1, \ldots, x_n);\, f_y := \sum_{f \in \Phi} f = |\Phi|]\!]_A a && (7)\\
[\![f(x_1, \ldots, x_n) \le 0]\!]_{U(A)} u \rhd a &= \text{let } \Phi := \{u(x_1), \ldots u(x_n)\} \text{ and } \psi = \sum_{f \in \Phi} f \text{ in} && (8)\\
&\quad u \rhd [\![f(x_1, \ldots, x_n) \le 0; \psi = |\Phi|]\!]_A a \sqcup_A [\![\psi < |\Phi|]\!]_A a
\end{aligned}
$$

Fig. 6. Transfer functions for binary operations $\boxdot = \sqcup, \sqsubseteq, \nabla$, and unary operations

Consider analyzing this program with a state $u_1 \rhd a_1$ where $u_1 = [f_{undef} \mapsto \{x, y\}]$ and $a_1 = \{f_{undef} = 0\}$ is a convex polyhedron. Note that $\chi(a_1) = \{f_{undef}\}$ since the variables $x, y \in u_1^{-1}(f_{undef})$ are not stored in a_1 as explained above. The state at line 5 becomes $u_2 \rhd a_2$ where $u_2 = [f_{def} \mapsto \{x, y\}]$ and $a_2 = \{x = y, x \in [0, 10], f_{def} = 1\}$. The benefit of not storing x, y in a_1 is that they can be introduced using $a_1' = copyAndPaste_{A,\{x,y\}}(a_2, a_1) = \{x = y, x \in [0, 10], f_{undef} = 0\}$ that extracts all information over x, y in a_2 and adds it to a_1. In order to state that these variables are now explicitly stored in a_1', we rename f_{undef} to a new flag f_{xy}, yielding $u_2' \rhd a_2'$ with $u_2' = [f_{xy} \mapsto \{x, y\}]$ and $a_2' = \{x = y, x \in [0, 10], f_{xy} = 0\}$. Now the state after line 5 can be computed as $(u_1 \rhd a_1) \sqcup_{U(A)} (u_2' \rhd a_2') = u_{12} \rhd a_1' \sqcup_A a_2'$ where $u_{12} = u_2'$ and a_2' is a_2 in which f_{def} is renamed to f_{xy}. The result $a_1' \sqcup_A a_2' = \{x = y, x \in [0, 10], 0 \le f_{xy} \le 1\}$ retains the equality $x = y$, thereby improving the precision over copying intervals.

Figure 6 illustrates the implementation of the $\boxdot = \sqcup, \sqsubseteq, \nabla$ functions that use *copyAndPaste* on the child domain of type A. Here, we assume that $r = copyAndPaste_{D,X}(s, a)$ is defined as $r = s \sqcap_D drop_{D,\chi(a) \setminus X}(a)$ where $\sqcap_D$ is a greatest lower bound on two abstract states that adds missing dimensions as needed. The idea is to remove all dimensions from a that should not be copied before merging the remaining relations over X into s using the meet $\sqcap_D$. For each binary operation $\boxdot$, Eq. 1 shows how the states are made compatible as described above before applying $\boxdot$ on the child domains.

Figure 6 also defines other transfer functions of the Undefined domain. Adding an unrestricted dimension x using *add* merely adds a mapping $f_{undef} \mapsto x$ to the undefined mapping (Eq. 2). Removing a variable x using *drop* needs to check if x is not stored in a (Eq. 3), or if it was the last variable in its partition (Eq. 4). Assigning to a variable y computes the set of flags Ψ that must be one to make the result defined (Eq. 5). If $f_{undef} \in \Psi$ then y is always undefined and executing the assignment on the child is not necessary. If a single flag f suffices to make y defined, y is added to the partition of f. In the general case, a new flag f_y is created (Eq. 6) that represents the validity of the new partition $\{y\}$ (Eq. 7).

Applying a test (Eq. 8) partitions the child state a into one where all variables occurring in the test are defined ($\psi = |\Phi|$) and one where they are possibly undefined ($\psi < |\Phi|$). Only in the former case, the test is applied.

Analogously to Lemma 2, the following lemma states that with the concrete domain C as its child domain, the Undefined domain is an abstraction of C.

Lemma 3. *With the proposed implementation, domain $U(C)$ is an abstraction of the concrete domain C.*

Proof. Beneath the choice of function *copyAndPaste* for adding variables, the implementation only differs from the semantics given in the last section by the more efficient, but otherwise equivalent handling of flags. It remains to show that adding dimensions via function *copyAndPaste* is valid, which holds because for each domain D, state a and set of variables X, function $\lambda s.\mathit{copyAndPaste}_{D,X}(s,a)$ is an X-Adder since $\mathit{drop}_X(\mathit{copyAndPaste}_X(s,a)) = a$.

The following theorem states that the given implementation of the Undefined domain is indeed a sound approximation of the concrete domain.

Theorem 2. *Let A be an abstraction of the concrete domain C. Then, with the proposed implementation, domain $U(A)$ is an abstraction of C.*

Proof. Analogously to Theorem 1, the claim follows from Lemma 3.

4 Applications of the Undefined Domain

We now illustrate the utility of the Undefined domain by using examples from the analysis of function calls and of heap-allocated memory.

4.1 Merging Calls to Functions

For the sake of limiting the memory consumption of an analyzer, it is desirable to merge the states of certain call sites of a function `f` into one. To this end,

```
main() {            a(int x) {          b(int y) {          f(int z) {
    a(0);               f(x);               f(y);               ...
    b(1);           }                   }                   }
}
```

Fig. 7. Function calls example

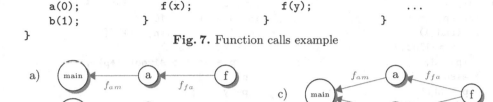

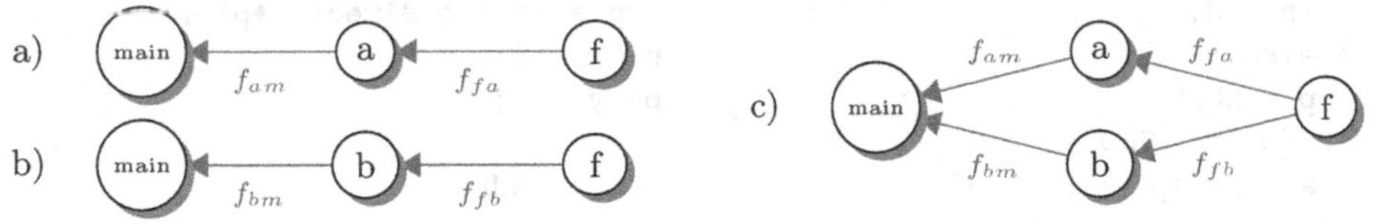

Fig. 8. Combining several call sites into one state

we use a stack functor domain $G(S)$ (with child state S) that manages a set of stack frames. Here, G tracks one dedicated *active* stack frame that represents the currently executed function `f`. In order to track to which stack frame the analysis has to return to when leaving the current function, the state $g \in G$ is a directed graph with stack frames as nodes, where the more recently called function points to its caller. Consider for example the program in Fig. 7. Here, function `f` is called twice. First, it is called by function `a`, which in turn is called from `main`. Figure 8a) shows how the first call path via `a` forms a linked list of stack frames, say g_a. Figure 8b) shows the graph of stack frames for the second call to `f` via `b`, say g_b.

In order to combine two graphs g_a and g_b, we follow [10] in qualifying the graph edges by numeric flags, that is, numeric variables that can take on the values 0 or 1. Let $g_a \triangleright s_a$ with $s_a = \{x = z = 0, f_{fa} = 1, f_{am} = 1\} \in S$ denote the abstract state (here $s_a \in S$ are convex polyhedra [4]) on entry to `f` for the path in Fig. 8a). In s_a, the flag f_{fa} has value one, indicating that the node (stack frame) of `a` is the predecessor of the node (stack frame) of `f`. Analogous for f_{am} that qualifies the edge between the stack frame of `f` and of `main`. Symmetrically, for the path shown in Fig. 8b) the state is $s_b = \{y = z = 1, f_{fb} = 1, f_{bm} = 1\}$.

The two graphs g_a and g_b are merged into the combined graph of stack frames g in Fig. 8c). In order to capture that the `b` node is not a predecessor of `f` in g_a, we add the flag $f_{fb} = 0$ to s_a and analogously we add $f_{bm} = 0$, yielding $s'_a = \{x = z = 0, f_{fa} = 1, f_{fb} = 0, f_{am} = 1, f_{bm} = 0\}$. Symmetrically, we enrich s_b to $s'_b = \{y = z = 1, f_{fa} = 0, f_{fb} = 1, f_{am} = 0, f_{bm} = 1\}$. Overall, we obtain the state $g \triangleright s'_a \sqcup_S s'_b = g \triangleright \{x = \top, y = \top, 0 \leq z \leq 1, z = f_{bm} = f_{fb} = 1 - f_{am} = 1 - f_{fa}\}$.

Note that all information within the stack frames, namely x and y is lost. The Undefined domain can improve this situation: we re-analyze the example using the domain $G(U(S))$. The net effect is that in the last step, instead of $g \triangleright s'_a \sqcup_S s'_b$ we compute $g \triangleright (u \triangleright s'_a) \sqcup_{U(S)} (u \triangleright s'_b)$ where $u \in U$ is the empty mapping (all variables are defined). By the definition of $\sqcup_{U(S)}$ the missing variable x is added to $u \triangleright s'_b$ giving $u_b \triangleright s'_b$ with $u_b = [x \mapsto f_{undef}]$ and, analogously, the left argument becomes $u_a \triangleright s'_a$ with $u_a = [y \mapsto f_{undef}]$. Computing the join $u_a \triangleright s'_a \sqcup_{U(S)} u_b \triangleright s'_b$ makes the two undefined states u_a and u_b compatible to $u = [x \mapsto f_x, y \mapsto f_y]$. The numeric state s'_a is modified by adding $f_x = 1, f_y = 0$

a)

```
main() {
  int *p;
  if (rnd()) {
    p = malloc(4);
    *p = 3;
  } else
    p = NULL;
  if (p != NULL)
    assert *p == 3;
  return 0;
}
```

b)

```
struct point {int x; int y;} *p;
int n = rnd(0, 100);
for (int i=0; i<n; i++) {
  if (p == NULL)
    p = malloc(sizeof (*p));
  p->x = i;
  p->y = i;
}
if (p != NULL)
  assert p->x == p->y;
```

Fig. 9. Heap allocation examples

and copying $y = 1$ from s'_b whereas s'_b is modified by adding $f_x = 0, f_y = 1$ and copying $x = 0$ from s'_a. The state that `f` is analyzed with is thus $g \rhd u \rhd \{x{=}0, y{=}1, 0 \leq z \leq 1, z = f_x{=}f_{bm} = f_{fb} = 1 - f_y = 1 - f_{am} = 1 - f_{fa}\}$.

The benefit of the Undefined domain is thus that, upon returning from `f`, the content of the predecessor stack frames is still available since $x = 0, y = 1$ is retained in the join of the two call sites. Our analysis infers more intricate invariants if pointers are passed, since the flags of the Undefined domain form an equality relation with the points-to flags, as detailed in the next section.

4.2 Application to Heap Analysis

We now detail how the Undefined domain can improve precision in the analysis of programs that use dynamically allocated memory. To this end, consider the program in Fig. 9a) that contains the conditional statement of Fig. 1 of the introduction. After executing the then-branch of the first conditional, the state consists of a dynamically allocated memory region x that contains a single memory cell of value 3 and a variable p that holds a pointer to region x. We model pointer expressions as linear combinations of abstract addresses where the coefficients are numeric flags. For example, the expression $c \cdot \&x$ is a pointer to l-value x if $c = 1$ and a `NULL` pointer if $c = 0$ holds [10]. Thus, the state is $S_1 := \{p = c \cdot \&x,\ c = 1,\ x = 3\}$. Analogously, after executing the else-branch, the numeric state is just $S_2 := \{p = 0\}$.

In order to join the resulting states S_1 and S_2 of both branches, they are made compatible by extending state S_2: the numeric variable x is introduced and the pointer expression stored for p is extended with $c \cdot \&x$ with flag $c = 0$, resulting in state $S'_2 := \{p = c \cdot \&x,\ c = 0,\ x \in \mathbb{Z}\}$. Approximating the join $S_1 \sqcup S'_2$ in the Polyhedra domain yields a state $\{p = c \cdot \&x,\ c \in [0, 1],\ x \in \mathbb{Z}\}$, thus losing the information that $c = 1$ implies $x = 3$.

Using the Undefined domain, the state after the then-branch is $\emptyset \rhd S_1$ with child state S_1 and an empty mapping from program variables to flags. Similarly, the state after the else-branch is $\emptyset \rhd S_2$. When both states are made compatible, a new flag f is introduced in both states that indicates whether variable x is

	U	instructions	time	memory	variables	undef. flags	warnings
heap 1	✓	12	19	19.0	14	1	0
	✗	12	18	17.8	13	–	1
heap 2	✓	24	35	23.2	23	2	0
	✗	24	32	21.7	21	–	1
call stack 1	✓	114	450	42.0	50	2	0
	✗	76	377	41.9	48	–	7
call stack 2	✓	254	641	42.0	74	2	0
	✗	178	416	42.6	72	–	7
call stack 3	✓	153	718	42.4	66	4	0
	✗	76	422	41.9	48	–	7
call stack 4	✓	128	702	42.2	54	2	0
	✗	88	920	42.5	52	–	8
call stack 5	✓	173	1455	47.3	75	4	0
	✗	90	709	42.0	54	–	8

Fig. 10. Evaluation of our implementation

defined. The value of x is copied from S_1 to S_2 by the *copyAndPaste* operation. The joined state is now $\{f \mapsto \{x\}\} \rhd \{p = c \cdot \&x,\ c = f,\ f \in [0,1],\ x = 3\}$. Since the child domain expresses the invariant $f = c$, the information that $c = 1$ implies $x = 3$ is maintained. Analogously, $c = 0$ implies that *p is unbounded, reflecting the fact that an uninitialized memory location can hold any value and thereby guaranteeing that the analysis is still sound.

Figure 9b) shows a similar scenario where the Undefined domain is able to preserve the relation between the contents of a possibly nonexisting memory region during a fixpoint computation. There, a struct is allocated on the heap inside a loop and the variables in the struct are assigned the same value. After the loop, if the pointer to the struct exists, the program tests that the equality between the struct members still holds.

5 Implementation and Experimental Results

We evaluated the Undefined domain in our analyzer for machine code [9], using a domain stack $G(U(P(A(C(I)))))$ where G maintains stack frames and dynamically allocated memory, U is the Undefined domain as described in Sect. 3, and P tracks points-to sets of variables. The remaining domains are numeric; they track affine equalities A, congruences C and intervals I. In order to estimate the performance of the Undefined domain, we also evaluated the examples with domain stack $G(P(A(C(I))))$, that is, without domain U.

Our tool analyzes Intel assembler programs and translates each x86 instruction into a sequence of instructions over an intermediate representation (IR) [9]. The stack domain G recognizes function boundaries by observing the stack pointer whenever the control flow changes through a jump, call or return instruction. An x86 return instruction is translated into a read access to the previous stack frame in order to retrieve the return address and a jump to this address.

The Undefined domain is thereby key to infer a precise address since, for Fig. 8, stack frames a and b are both read and joined before the jump is executed.

Figure 10 shows the experimental results. Column U indicates whether the Undefined domain is used, followed by the number of machine instructions in the program that were analyzed; columns *time* and *memory* show the runtime in milliseconds and the memory consumption in megabytes, averaged over several runs on a 3.2 GHz Core i7 Linux machine. The next column shows the total number of variables tracked, followed by the number of flag variables used by the Undefined domain and the number of warnings emitted by the analyzer.

The first two lines show the heap example from Fig. 9a) that has been discussed in Sect. 4.2. Our implementation using the Undefined domain is able to verify the assertion in the program. Without the Undefined domain it raises a warning as the value of the heap allocated variable is lost. The next two lines show the heap example from Fig. 9b) where our analysis is able to verify an assertion in the program only when using the Undefined domain as the relational information between the struct members is lost otherwise.

Next follows the call stack example of Sect. 4.1, followed by variations with more functions and call paths. Call stack examples 4 and 5 differ in that they use pointers to stack variables to pass parameter values. Note that the call stack examples exhibited shorter runtimes without the Undefined domain, because precision loss made it impossible to resolve the return addresses, so that the examples could only partially be analyzed. This is reflected in the number of analyzed instructions. For the same reason the number of total variables in the call stack of example 3 and 5 without the domain are much lower than with the Undefined domain. The examples show that the additional variables that are necessary as flags for the Undefined domain are only few compared to the total number of variables in the program.

6 Related Work

We addressed the challenge of tracking the content of memory that does not exist in all traces. Many existing analyses use some ad-hoc methods to approximate what we have put on a sound mathematical basis: the ability to store both, precise and undefined values for variables in a single state. For instance, recency abstraction [1] implicitly retains the defined value when the state is joined. When a purely logic description is used [7,8], the distinction between defined and undefined content is simply expressed using disjunction. In Astrée [2], disjunction is expressed using the decision tree domain that tracks two separate child domains depending on the value of a flag. The effect is similar to standard path-sensitive analyses in that tracking two states duplicates analysis time. More sophisticated analyses merge states on different paths if a finite abstraction determines that they are similar [5]. Future work will determine whether this technique can be implemented as a combinator in our domain stack.

The Undefined domain partially allows the encoding of conditional invariants. While this problem has been studied for logical domains [6], we provide a solution that enables existing numeric domains to infer certain conditional invariants, e.g. those guarded by the existence of objects. For overly complex invariants, our approach exploits the ability of numeric domains to gradually lose precision.

7 Conclusion

We addressed the task of storing a single state in cases where a piece of memory is non-existent in some of the traces. We introduced a generic functor domain that generalizes this approach to existent memory regions with undefined content. We illustrated the power of this domain by defining a specific instance, namely the Undefined domain, that improves precision in common program analysis tasks. Its novel copy-and-paste operation even retains relational information.

References

1. Balakrishnan, G., Reps, T.: Recency-abstraction for heap-allocated storage. In: Yi, K. (ed.) SAS 2006. LNCS, vol. 4134, pp. 221–239. Springer, Heidelberg (2006)
2. Blanchet, B., Cousot, P., Cousot, R., Feret, J., Mauborgne, L., Miné, A., Monniaux, D., Rival, X.: A Static Analyzer for Large Safety-Critical Software. In: Programming Language Design and Implementation, San Diego, California, USA. ACM (June 2003)
3. Cousot, P., Cousot, R., Feret, J., Mauborgne, L., Miné, A., Monniaux, D., Rival, X.: Combination of Abstractions in the ASTRÉE Static Analyzer. In: Okada, M., Satoh, I. (eds.) ASIAN 2006. LNCS, vol. 4435, pp. 272–300. Springer, Heidelberg (2008)
4. Cousot, P., Halbwachs, N.: Automatic Discovery of Linear Constraints among Variables of a Program. In: Principles of Programming Languages, Tucson, Arizona, USA, pp. 84–97. ACM (January 1978)
5. Das, M., Lerner, S., Seigle, M.: ESP: Path-Sensitive Program Verification in Polynomial Time. ACM SIGPLAN Notices 37(5), 57 (2002)
6. Gulwani, S., McCloskey, B., Tiwari, A.: Lifting abstract interpreters to quantified logical domains. In: Principles of Progamming Languages, vol. 43, pp. 235–246. ACM (January 2008)
7. Reynolds, J.C.: Separation logic: A logic for shared mutable data structures. In: Logic in Computer Science, Copenhagen, Denmark, pp. 55–74. IEEE (2002)
8. Sagiv, M., Reps, T., Wilhelm, R.: Parametric Shape Analysis via 3-Valued Logic. Transactions on Programming Languages and Systems 24(3), 217–298 (2002)
9. Sepp, A., Mihaila, B., Simon, A.: Precise Static Analysis of Binaries by Extracting Relational Information. In: Pinzger, M., Poshyvanyk, D. (eds.) Working Conference on Reverse Engineering, Limerick, Ireland. IEEE (October 2011)
10. Siegel, H., Simon, A.: FESA: Fold- and expand-based shape analysis. In: Jhala, R., De Bosschere, K. (eds.) Compiler Construction. LNCS, vol. 7791, pp. 82–101. Springer, Heidelberg (2013)
11. Venet, A.: Abstract Cofibered Domains: Application to the Alias Analysis of Untyped Programs. In: Cousot, R., Schmidt, D.A. (eds.) SAS 1996. LNCS, vol. 1145, pp. 366–382. Springer, Heidelberg (1996)

Separation Logic Modulo Theories

Juan Antonio Navarro Pérez[1] and Andrey Rybalchenko[2]

[1] University College London
[2] Microsoft Research Cambridge and Technische Universität München

Abstract. Logical reasoning about program behaviours often requires dealing with heap structures as well as scalar data types. Advances in Satisfiability Modulo Theories (SMT) offer efficient procedures for dealing with scalar values, yet they lack expressive support for dealing with heap structures. In this paper, we present an approach that integrates separation logic—a prominent logic for reasoning about linked data structures on the heap—and existing SMT solving technology. Our model-based approach communicates heap aliasing information between theory and separation logic reasoning, providing an efficient decision procedure for discharging verification conditions in program analysis and verification.

1 Introduction

Satisfiability Modulo Theory (SMT) solvers play an important role in the construction of abstract interpretation tools [11, 12]. They efficiently reason about various scalar data types, e.g., bit-vectors and numbers, as well as uninterpreted functions and arrays [1,7,14,15,18]. Today's SMT solvers, however, lack support for dealing with dynamically allocated heap data structures. Thus, a combination of theory reasoning with separation logic [25]—a successful logical formalism of resource allocation—has the potential to boost a wide range of program analysis systems: manual/tool assisted proof development [17, 21], extended static checking [5, 16], and automatic inference of heap shapes [2, 8].

In this paper we develop a method to augment an SMT solver with separation logic reasoning for linked list segments and their length. Our method decides the validity of entailments of the form $\Pi \wedge \Sigma \rightarrow \Pi' \wedge \Sigma'$, where Π, Π' are *arbitrary* theory assertions decided by the SMT solver, while Σ, Σ' symbolically describe a spatial conjunction of pointers and acyclic list segments. In contrast, existing decision procedures combine list segments with conjunctions of equality and disequality predicates only. Moreover, the length information on list segments allows our techniques to prove properties where a tight interaction between program data and the shape of heap structures is needed.

The crux of our method lies in an interaction of the model-based approach to theory combination [13] and a so-called *match* function that derives logical implication between pairs of spatial conjunctions. Models of Π, called stacks, guide the process of showing that all heaps satisfying Σ also satisfy Σ'. The *match* function produces an assertion describing a set of stacks for which the current derivation is applicable. This assertion is used to prune the search space

C.-c. Shan (Ed.): APLAS 2013, LNCS 8301, pp. 90–106, 2013.

and find more stacks for which the entailment has not been proved yet. Our method thus benefits from the efficiency of SMT solvers to maintain a logical representation of the search space already explored.

In summary, we present an efficient SMT-based decision procedure for separation logic with acyclic list segments with length. Our main contribution is the entailment checking algorithm for separation logic in combination with decidable theories, together with its formal proof of correctness.

Related Work. Our approach improves upon a previous separation logic proving method [22], which relied on paramodulation for equality reasoning [23] and provided improvements of several orders of magnitude on efficiency with respect to existing systems at the time. The current work extends this method, which only dealt with pure equalities, to support arbitrary theory expressions in both pure and spatial parts of the entailment. Our new *match* function generalises previous unfolding inference rules—in turn based on inferences from [3,4]—and runs in linear time avoiding case reasoning as performed by most other systems. The logic context of an SMT solver, rather than literals in a clausal representation, maintains the explored search space. Doing so we remove a technical limitation from the approach in [22]: spatial reasoning no longer requires access to equality reasoning steps, and off-the-shelf SMT solvers become directly applicable.

Separation logic entailment checking in the fragment limited to list segments and pure equalities was shown to be decidable in polynomial time [10], and a tool exploiting this result has been developed [19]. Although we are mainly interested in reasoning about rich theory assertions describing stacks, exploration of this polynomial time result is an interesting direction for future work. In the opposite direction, work such as that from Botinčan et al. [6] and Chin et al. [9] develop techniques for dealing with more general user-specified predicates beyond simple list segments. The former work, moreover, also relies on SMT for pure reasoning. The cost of this increased expressivity, however, is that such procedures become incomplete. Our logic is more restrictive, allowing us to develop a more efficient, sound, terminating and complete procedure for entailment checking.

Piskac et al. [24] also developed a decision procedure for the list segment fragment. Their approach translates entailments to an intermediate logic which, given suitable axioms, is then decided by an SMT solver. The technique works as well for slightly more general structures, such as sorted list segments and doubly linked lists, but further generalisations probably require changes and extensions in the intermediate logic. We believe that generalisations to our approach are more straightforward, since to support other predicates we only need to define a suitable *subtract* operator, as we discuss for the case of linked list segments with length later in Section 4 of this paper.

Finally, Iosif et al. [20] have recently proved a decidability result for a large class of separation logic formulas with recursive predicate definitions. Their result, which without a doubt represents a major advance in the theory of separation logic, is based on a monadic second order logic encoding where formulas with a bounded tree width are known to be decidable. Although their fragment considered still has a few limitations—unlike our algorithm, their decidability result does not apply for structures with dangling data pointers—these theoretical results have opened up exciting directions for future research.

2 Illustration

To motivate our work, we illustrate how our algorithm discharges a verification condition produced in the analysis of a program. Consider the following C++ snippet that retrieves data associated with the k-th element of a linked list.

```
struct node { int data; node* next };

node* get(node* p, int k) { /* assume: ∃n. 0 ≤ k < n ∧ lseg(p, nil, n) */
  node* q = p;
  for (int i = 0; i < k; i++) q = q->next;
  return q->data;
}
```

The implementation is memory safe only if the value of k is less than the length of the list rooted at p, as made explicit by the assumption at the beginning of the function. The $\mathsf{lseg}(p, \mathsf{nil}, n)$ predicate denotes that, starting from the location p in the heap and following an acyclic chain of exactly n next-pointers, we reach the end of the list, i.e., nil. When the start/finish locations are equal, and thus necessarily $n = 0$, the list is empty and no nodes are allocated.

We remark that, due to the crucial mix of arithmetic and spatial reasoning involved—on how indices relate to the length of chains of dynamic pointers—the automated verification of even such simple code is often beyond the capabilities of existing program analysers. An analyser would symbolically execute the code, producing a series of verification conditions to be discharged. At some point, for example, the analyser needs to establish the validity of the entailment

$$\overbrace{i \simeq i' + 1}^{\Pi} \land \overbrace{\mathsf{lseg}(p, q', i') * \mathsf{next}(q', q) * \mathsf{lseg}(q, \mathsf{nil}, n - i' - 1)}^{\Sigma} \\ \to \underbrace{\mathsf{lseg}(p, q, i) * \mathsf{lseg}(q, \mathsf{nil}, n - i)}_{\Sigma'} ,$$

explicating changes in the program state—respectively denoted by primed and regular variables—before and after the execution of each loop iteration. Note the use of '$\simeq$' for equality in the formal language, distinguished from '$=$' in the meta language. The star connective '$*$' states that memory cells allocated by the heap predicates are necessarily disjoint or *separated* from each other in memory; while $\mathsf{next}(q', q)$ represents a heap portion of exactly one node allocated at q' (the value of q before the loop execution) whose next pointer has the same value as q (after executing the loop).

Proving this entailment—which still involves a mix of arithmetic and spatial reasoning—shows that $\mathsf{lseg}(p, q, i) * \mathsf{lseg}(q, \mathsf{nil}, n - i)$ is a loop invariant. To this end, the algorithm performs the following key steps: First it enumerates pure models, assignments to program variables, that allow satisfying both Π and Σ in the antecedent. For each pure model s, the algorithm attempts to (symbolically) prove that every heap h satisfying the antecedent, $s, h \models \Pi \wedge \Sigma$, also satisfies the consequence, $s, h \models \Sigma'$. The assignment is generalised as an assertion M pruning models of Π that lead to similar reasoning steps as with s. The entailment is valid if and only if all models of the antecedent are successfully considered.

So, we first build a constraint characterising the satisfiability of the spatial part of the antecedent. This constraint requires each spatial predicate in Σ to be sound, e.g. list lengths are non-negative, and each pair of predicates to be separated from each other. In particular, if two predicates start at the same heap location, necessarily one of them must be an empty heap with no allocated nodes. For our example entailment, the soundness of $\mathsf{lseg}(p, q', i')$ requires that the length of the list segment is non-negative, i.e. $0 \leq i'$, and the start/finish locations coincide if and only if the length of the list is zero, i.e. $p \simeq q' \leftrightarrow i' \simeq 0$. The soundness condition of $\mathsf{lseg}(q, \mathsf{nil}, n - i' - 1)$ is similarly determined.

	soundness of ...
$0 \leq i' \wedge (p \simeq q' \leftrightarrow i' \simeq 0)$	$\mathsf{lseg}(p, q', i')$
$0 \leq n - i' - 1 \wedge (q \simeq \mathsf{nil} \leftrightarrow n - i' - 1 \simeq 0)$	$\mathsf{lseg}(q, \mathsf{nil}, n - i' - 1)$

Additionally, say, for the pair of predicates $\mathsf{lseg}(p, q', i')$ and $\mathsf{lseg}(q, \mathsf{nil}, n - i' - 1)$ their separation condition is represented as $p \simeq q \rightarrow (p \simeq q' \vee q \simeq \mathsf{nil})$, i.e., if the start location p of the first predicate is equal to the start location q of the second predicate then either one of them must represent an empty segment. The separation condition for each pair of predicates in Σ is similarly computed.

	separation of ...
$p \simeq q' \rightarrow p \simeq q'$	$\mathsf{lseg}(p, q', i')$ and $\mathsf{next}(q', q)$
$p \simeq q \rightarrow (p \simeq q' \vee q \simeq \mathsf{nil})$	$\mathsf{lseg}(p, q', i')$ and $\mathsf{lseg}(q, \mathsf{nil}, n - i' - 1)$
$q' \simeq q \rightarrow q \simeq \mathsf{nil}$	$\mathsf{next}(q', q)$ and $\mathsf{lseg}(q, \mathsf{nil}, n - i' - 1)$

Finally, to make sure that nothing is allocated at the nil location we have to assert, say for $\mathsf{lseg}(p, q', i')$, that if the start location p is nil then necessarily the finish location q' is also nil. For the case of $\mathsf{next}(q', q)$ we simply assert that q' is not nil. We thus obtain three additional assertions.

	nil is not allocated by ...
$p \simeq \mathsf{nil} \rightarrow q' \simeq \mathsf{nil}$	$\mathsf{lseg}(p, q', i')$
$q' \not\simeq \mathsf{nil}$	$\mathsf{next}(q', q)$
$q \simeq \mathsf{nil} \rightarrow \mathsf{nil} \simeq \mathsf{nil}$	$\mathsf{lseg}(q, \mathsf{nil}, n - i' - 1)$

We refer to the conjunction of all above assertions as *well-formed*(Σ).

Crucially, these assertions do not contain spatial predicates any more, so an SMT solver is used to search for models of $\Pi \wedge \textit{well-formed}(\Sigma)$. If no such model exists the entailment is vacuously true. In our example, however, the solver finds the model $s = \{p \mapsto 42, q' \mapsto 47, q \mapsto 29, i' \mapsto 1, i \mapsto 2, n \mapsto 3\}$. To show that, with respect to this assignment s, every heap h model of Σ is also a model of Σ', we try to establish a *match* between Σ and Σ'. Specifically for each predicate in Σ' we seek a matching 'chain' of predicates in Σ such that the finish and start location of adjacent predicates is equal with respect to s.

So, we first search for a match for $\mathsf{lseg}(p, q, i) \in \Sigma'$ connecting p to q in i steps within the antecedent Σ. Trivially, since $s(p) = s(p)$, the chain must begin with $\mathsf{lseg}(p, q', i')$ leaving us yet to connect q' with q in $i - i'$ steps. This issues a new request to match $\mathsf{lseg}(q', q, i - i')$ against the remaining predicates from Σ, namely, $\mathsf{next}(q', q) * \mathsf{lseg}(q, \mathsf{nil}, n - i' - 1)$. Similarly, the chain must now continue with $\mathsf{next}(q', q)$ and a new request to match $\mathsf{lseg}(q, q, i - i' - 1)$ is issued. This time, however, $s \models i - i' - 1 \simeq 0$ so the match is completed. In the same vein, we search for a match for $\mathsf{lseg}(q, \mathsf{nil}, n - i) \in \Sigma'$ against the only remaining $\mathsf{lseg}(q, \mathsf{nil}, n - i' - 1)$ in Σ. Luckily, since $s \models n - i \simeq n - i' - 1$, both connect q to nil in the same number of steps and the match quickly succeeds. Since all predicates of Σ' are matched, and all predicates in Σ were used in a match, we conclude that Σ and Σ' have match exactly with respect to the current s.

The algorithm keeps track of the assertions required on s for the match to succeed, namely $M = (i - i' - 1 \simeq 0 \wedge n - i \simeq n - i' - 1)$. The matching proof obtained for this particular assignment s is thus generalised to all models satisfying M, and we may continue the enumeration of models for the antecedent excluding those where M is true.

A second call to the SMT solver reveals that $\Pi \wedge \mathit{well\text{-}formed}(\Sigma) \wedge \neg M$ is now unsatisfiable. Although our spatial reasoning procedure is unaware of this fact, the arithmetic capabilities of the SMT solver easily figure out that the hypothesis $\Pi = (i \simeq i' + 1)$ forces M to be always true. Since matching is possible for all models of the antecedent, we thus conclude that the entailment is valid.

3 Preliminaries

We write $f \colon X \to Y$ to denote a *function* with domain $X = \operatorname{dom} f$ and range Y; and $f \colon X \rightharpoonup Y$ to denote a *finite partial function* with $\operatorname{dom} f \subseteq X$. We write $f_1 * \cdots * f_n$ to simultaneously assert the disjointness of the domains of n functions, namely $\operatorname{dom} f_i \cap \operatorname{dom} f_j = \emptyset$ when $i \neq j$, and denote the, therefore, well defined function $f = f_1 \cup \cdots \cup f_n$. We sometimes describe functions by explicitly enumerating their elements; for example $f = \{a \mapsto b, b \mapsto c\}$ is the function such that $\operatorname{dom} f = \{a, b\}$, $f(a) = b$, and $f(b) = c$.

Satisfiability Modulo Theories. We assume a first-order many-sorted language where each function symbol f of arity n has a signature $f \colon \tau_1 \times \cdots \times \tau_n \to \tau$, i.e. the symbol f takes n arguments of respective sorts τ_i and produces an expression of sort τ. A constant symbol is a 0-ary function symbol. Constant and function symbols are combined respecting their sorts to build syntactically valid *expressions*. We use $x \colon \tau$ to denote an expression x of sort τ. Each sort τ is associated with a set of values, for convenience also denoted τ. In particular we assume that booleans and integers, namely $\mathbb{B} = \{\mathit{true}, \mathit{false}\}$ and $\mathbb{Z} = \{\ldots, -1, 0, 1, \ldots\}$, are among the available sorts. We refer to a function symbol of boolean sort as a *predicate symbol*, and a boolean expression as a *formula*.

Some symbols have fixed predefined theory interpretations. For example the predicate $\simeq\colon \tau \times \tau \to \mathbb{B}$ tests equality between two expressions of the same sort; while theory symbols from the boolean domain, i.e. conjunction ($\wedge$), disjunction ($\vee$), negation ($\neg$), truth ($\top$), falsity ($\bot$), entailment ($\to$), boolean equivalence ($\leftrightarrow$), and first-order quantifiers ($\forall$, $\exists$), have their standard interpretations. We similarly assume theory symbols for integer arithmetic with their usual interpretation and use nil as an alias for the integer constant 0.

Some function symbols are also left uninterpreted. A *variable*, in particular, is an uninterpreted constant symbol. Interpretations map uninterpreted symbols to values of the appropriate sort. We write $s(x)$ to denote the result of evaluating the expression x under the interpretation s. For example, if $s = \{n \mapsto 2\}$ then $s(1+n) = 3$. A formula F is *satisfiable* if there is an s such that $s(F) = \mathit{true}$; in such case we also write $s \models F$ and say that s is a *model* of F. A formula is *valid* if it is satisfied by all interpretations. The job of an SMT solver is, given a formula F, to find a model such that $s \models F$ or prove that none exists.

Separation Logic. On top of the theories already supported by the SMT solver, we define *spatial symbols* to build expressions to describe properties about heaps. We thus introduce the spatial predicate symbols $\mathsf{emp}\colon \mathbb{B}$, $\mathsf{next}\colon \mathbb{Z} \times \mathbb{Z} \to \mathbb{B}$, $\mathsf{lseg}\colon \mathbb{Z}\times\mathbb{Z}\times\mathbb{Z} \to \mathbb{B}$, and $*\colon \mathbb{B}\times\mathbb{B} \to \mathbb{B}$ for, respectively, the empty heap, a points-to relation, an acyclic list segment with length, and the spatial conjunction. A *spatial formula* is one that may include spatial symbols, and a *pure formula* is one where no spatial symbols occur.

A *stack* is an interpretation for pure expressions, mapping uninterpreted symbols to suitable values. A *heap* is a partial finite map $h\colon \mathbb{Z} \rightharpoonup \mathbb{Z}$ that connects memory locations, represented as integers, and gives meaning to spatial symbols. Given a stack s, a heap h, and a spatial formula F we inductively define the spatial satisfaction relation $s, h \models F$ as $s, h \models \Pi$ if Π is pure and $s \models \Pi$, $s, h \models \mathsf{emp}$ if $h = \emptyset$, $s, h \models \mathsf{next}(x, y)$ if $h = \{s(x) \mapsto s(y)\}$, $s, h \models F_1 * F_2$ if $h = h_1 * h_2$ for some h_1 and h_2 such that $s, h_1 \models F_1$ and $s, h_2 \models F_2$. The acyclic list segment with length is inductively defined by

$$\begin{aligned}\mathsf{lseg}(x, z, n) = (x \simeq z \wedge n \simeq 0 \wedge \mathsf{emp}) \\ \vee (x \not\simeq z \wedge n > 0 \wedge \exists y.\ \mathsf{next}(x, y) * \mathsf{lseg}(y, z, n-1))\ .\end{aligned}$$

For example, given that $s = \{x \mapsto 3, y \mapsto 2, n \mapsto 1\}$ and $h = \{3 \mapsto 5, 5 \mapsto 2\}$, it follows that $s, h \models \mathsf{lseg}(x, y, n+1)$. As with pure formulas, we say that a spatial formula F is *satisfiable* if there is a pair (s, h) such that $s, h \models F$; and *valid* if it is satisfied by every stack-heap pair. In particular the entailment $F \to G$ is valid if and only if every model of F is also a model of G. For a spatial formula F, we write $s \models F$ to denote that $s, h \models F$ for all heaps h.

We remark that this definition does not treat nil in any special way. To regain its expected behaviour, i.e. on a spatial formula F *nothing* may be allocated at the nil location, it is enough to consider $F * \mathsf{next}(\mathsf{nil}, \mathsf{nil})$ instead. Furthermore,

function *prove*($\Pi \wedge \Sigma \to \Pi' \wedge \Sigma'$)
$\quad \Gamma := \Pi \wedge \mathit{well\text{-}formed}(\Sigma)$
$\quad \Delta := \mathit{alloc}(\Sigma)$
$\quad$ **if satisfiable** $\Gamma \wedge \neg\Pi'$ **return** *invalid*
$\quad$ **while exists** s **such that** $s \models \Gamma$ **do**
$\qquad M := \mathit{match}(s, \Delta, \Sigma, \Sigma')$
$\qquad$ **if** $s \not\models M$ **return** *invalid*
$\qquad \Gamma := \Gamma \wedge \neg M$
$\quad$ **return** *valid*

function *match*($s, \Delta, \Sigma, \Sigma'$)
$\quad$ **if exists** $S \in \Sigma$ **such that** $s \models \mathit{empty}(S)$
$\qquad$ **return** $\mathit{empty}(S) \wedge \mathit{match}(s, \Delta, \Sigma \setminus S, \Sigma')$
$\quad$ **if exists** $S' \in \Sigma'$ **such that** $s \models \mathit{empty}(S')$
$\qquad$ **return** $\mathit{empty}(S') \wedge \mathit{match}(s, \Delta, \Sigma, \Sigma' \setminus S')$
$\quad$ **if exists** $S \in \Sigma$ **and** $S' \in \Sigma'$ **such that** $s \not\models \mathit{separated}(S, S')$
$\qquad (S'', D) := \mathit{subtract}(\Delta, S', S)$
$\qquad$ **if** $s \models \mathit{sound}(S'') \wedge D$ **return** $\neg\mathit{separated}(S, S') \wedge \mathit{sound}(S'')$
$\qquad\qquad \wedge\, D \wedge \mathit{match}(s, \Delta, \Sigma \setminus S, (\Sigma' \setminus S') * S'')$
$\quad$ **if** $\Sigma = \emptyset$ **and** $\Sigma' = \emptyset$ **return** $\top$ **else return** $\bot$

Fig. 1. Model-driven entailment checker

although the language allows spatial conjunctions of arbitrary boolean formulas, we focus on the fragment where such conjuncts are restricted to spatial predicates. In the following when we say "a spatial conjunction" what we actually mean is "a spatial conjunction of spatial predicates". Also for convenience, a spatial conjunction $\Sigma = S_1 * \cdots * S_n$ is often treated in the meta level as a multi-set of boolean spatial predicates where $|\Sigma| = n$ is the number of conjuncts. We use set theory symbols, which are always to be interpreted as *multi*-set operations, to describe relations among spatial predicates and conjunctions. For example:

$$\mathsf{next}(y, z) \in \mathsf{lseg}(x, y) * \mathsf{next}(y, z) \qquad \mathsf{next}(x, y) * \mathsf{next}(x, y) \not\subseteq \mathsf{next}(x, y)$$
$$\mathsf{emp} * \mathsf{emp} * \mathsf{emp} \setminus \mathsf{emp} = \mathsf{emp} * \mathsf{emp}\ .$$

4 Decision Procedure for List Segments and Theories

We begin this section describing the building blocks that, when put together as shown in the *prove* and *match* functions of Figure 1, constitute a decision procedure for entailment checking. The procedure works for entailments of the form $\Pi \wedge \Sigma \to \Pi' \wedge \Sigma'$, where both Π and Π' are pure formulas, with respect to any background theory supported by the SMT solver, while both Σ and Σ' are spatial conjunctions.

To abstract away the specific details of individual spatial predicates, we first define *addr*(S), *sound*(S), and *empty*(S)—respectively the *address*, *soundness*, and *emptiness condition* of a spatial predicate S—as follows:

S	$addr(S)$	$sound(S)$	$empty(S)$
emp	nil	$\top$	$\top$
$\mathsf{next}(x, y)$	x	$\top$	$\bot$
$\mathsf{lseg}(x, y, n)$	x	$0 \leq n \land (x \simeq y \leftrightarrow n = 0)$	$x \simeq y$

The soundness condition is a formula that must be satisfied by any model of the spatial predicate, formally: if $s, h \models S$ then $s \models sound(S)$. If, furthermore, the emptiness condition is also true, then its corresponding heap model *must* be empty. Conversely, if the emptiness condition is false then the address of the predicate *must* necessarily occur in the domain of any heap satisfying the spatial predicate. Formally: given $s \models sound(S) \land empty(S)$ it follows $s, h \models S$ if and only if $h = \emptyset$; and if $s, h \models \neg empty(S) \land S$ then, necessarily, $s(addr(S)) \in \mathrm{dom}\, h$.

Separation. We begin defining the notion of *separation* which is used, in particular, at lines 13 and 15 of the algorithm in Figure 1. Given any two spatial predicates S and S', the formula

$$separated(S, S') = addr(S) \simeq addr(S') \to empty(S) \lor empty(S')$$

states that two predicates are separated if either their addresses are distinct or one of the two predicates is empty. Otherwise, if both predicates are non-empty and share the same address, the formula $S * S'$ would not be satisfied. More formally, if $s, h \models S * S'$ then necessarily $s \models separated(S, S')$. We also say that two spatial predicates S and S' collide, with respect to the given stack s, if it is the case that $s \not\models separated(S, S')$.

Well-Formedness. The *well-formedness condition*, found at line 1 in Figure 1, is defined for a spatial conjunction $\Sigma = S_1 * \cdots * S_n$ as the pure formula

$$well\text{-}formed(\Sigma) = \bigwedge_{1 \leq i \leq n} sound(S_i) \land \bigwedge_{1 \leq i < j \leq n} separated(S_i, S_j)\ ,$$

which states that all predicates are sound and every pair is separated. The reader might want to revisit the example in Section 2, where the well-formedness of $\Sigma = \mathsf{lseg}(p, q', i') * \mathsf{next}(q', q) * \mathsf{lseg}(q, \mathsf{nil}, n - i' - 1)$ is computed. In fact, since nil is not special in our definition of the semantics, what we computed was the well-formedness of $\Sigma * \mathsf{next}(\mathsf{nil}, \mathsf{nil})$, and the last three assertions for the non-allocation of nil are just the separation conditions with respect to the added $\mathsf{next}(\mathsf{nil}, \mathsf{nil})$. The importance of the well-formedness condition comes from the fact that, as the next theorem states, it characterises the satisfiability of spatial conjunctions.

Theorem 1. *A spatial conjunction Σ is satisfiable if, and only if, the pure formula well-formed(Σ) is satisfiable.*

Allocation. Given a stack s and a spatial conjunction $\Sigma = S_1 * \cdots * S_n$, the *allocated set* $alloc(\Sigma|s) = \{s(addr(S_i)) \mid s \not\models empty(S_i)\}$ is a set of locations necessarily allocated by any heap h satisfying Σ. That is, for all h such that $s, h \models \Sigma$ it follows that $alloc(\Sigma|s) \subseteq \operatorname{dom} h$.

The *allocation function*, found at line 2 in Figure 1, is defined without reference to any stack as

$$alloc(\Sigma) = \lambda x. \bigvee_{1 \leq i \leq n} \neg empty(S_i) \wedge x \simeq addr(S_i) ,$$

mapping a given variable x to a formula symbolically testing whether x should be allocated on heaps satisfying Σ. That is, if $\Delta = alloc(\Sigma)$ and s is any stack, we have that $s(x) \in alloc(\Sigma|s)$ if and only if $s \models \Delta(x)$. For instance, taking the same example Σ as before,

$$\Delta(x) = (p \not\simeq q' \wedge x = p) \vee (x \simeq q') \vee (q \not\simeq \mathsf{nil} \wedge x = q) \vee (x \simeq \mathsf{nil}) .$$

Thus x is considered allocated if it is equal to q' or nil; or if it is equal to the start location, p or q, of a non-empty list segment.

Subtraction. We now proceed towards the introduction of the *subtraction operation*, occurring at line 14 in Figure 1, which lies at the core of our matching function. When trying to prove an entailment $s \models \Sigma \to \Sigma'$, we want to show that any heap model of Σ is also a model of Σ'. Thus, if we find a pair of colliding predicates $S \in \Sigma$ and $S' \in \Sigma'$, the portion of the heap that satisfies S must overlap with the portion of the heap satisfying S'. In fact, it is not hard to convince oneself—for the list segment predicates considered—that the heap model of S' should match exactly that of S plus some extra surplus.

Given two spatial predicates S, S', and an allocation function Δ, the subtraction operation $(S'', D) := subtract(\Delta, S', S)$ returns a pair where S'' is the remainder of subtracting S from S', and D is an additional side condition. Intuitively, if D is not satisfied, then there is a counterexample for the subtraction (c.f. Proposition 2 later). Specifically, for each pair of predicates we have:

S'	S	S''	D
$\mathsf{next}(x', z)$	$\mathsf{next}(x, y)$	emp	$y \simeq z$
$\mathsf{lseg}(x', z, n)$	$\mathsf{next}(x, y)$	$\mathsf{lseg}(y, z, n-1)$	$\top$
$\mathsf{next}(x', z)$	$\mathsf{lseg}(x, y, n)$	emp	$y \simeq z \wedge n \simeq 1$
$\mathsf{lseg}(x', z, n)$	$\mathsf{lseg}(x, y, m)$	$\mathsf{lseg}(y, z, n-m)$	$y \not\simeq z \to \Delta(z) \vee m \simeq 1$

Formalising our stated intuition, the following proposition states how if S'' is obtained by subtracting S from S' then, under suitable assumptions, the spatial predicate S' is equivalent to $S * S''$. The validity of this statement, as well as the following proposition, is easily verified by inspection of the relevant definitions.

Proposition 1. *Let Σ be a spatial conjunction and S, S' a pair of spatial predicates. Let $\Delta = alloc(\Sigma)$, let $(S'', D) = subtract(\Delta, S', S)$, and let s be a stack such that $s \models \neg separated(S, S') \wedge sound(S'') \wedge D$. Then the following claims hold.*

1. $s, h \models \Sigma * S * S'' \to \Sigma * S'$ *for every heap* h.
2. *if* $s, h \models \Sigma * S'$ *and* $s, h_1 \models S$ *for some* $h_1 \subseteq h$ *then* $s, h \models \Sigma * S * S''$.

Conversely, the following proposition states that if S and S' collide, but the subtraction is not successful, i.e. D is not satisfied, then it is possible to build a counterexample to the original entailment.

Proposition 2. *Let* Σ *be a spatial conjunction and* S, S' *a pair of spatial predicates. Let* $\Delta = alloc(\Sigma)$, *let* $(S'', D) = subtract(\Delta, S', S)$, *and let* s *be a stack such that* $s \models \neg separated(S, S')$. *If* $s \not\models sound(S'') \wedge D$ *then there is a* h_1 *such that* $s, h_1 \models S$, *but for all* h *such that* $h_1 \subseteq h$ *we have* $s, h \not\models \Sigma * S'$.

As an example suppose we want to determine the validity of $\Sigma * S \to S'$, where each $\Sigma = \mathsf{lseg}(y, z, m)$, $S = \mathsf{lseg}(x, y, n)$, and $S' = \mathsf{lseg}(x, z, n + m)$. We would then have that $\Delta = \lambda v.\ (y \not\simeq z \wedge v \simeq y)$, $S'' = \mathsf{lseg}(y, z, n + m - n)$, and $D = (y \not\simeq z \to \Delta(z) \vee n \simeq 1) = (y \not\simeq z \to (y \not\simeq z \wedge z \simeq y) \vee n \simeq 1)$. Assume a stack $s = \{x \mapsto 1, y \mapsto 2, z, \mapsto 3, n \mapsto 2, m \mapsto 1\}$. With respect to s, it is clear that S and S' collide, as they are both non-empty lists starting on the same location $s(x) = 1$. However, $s \not\models D$, since $s \models y \not\simeq z$ but $s \not\models \Delta(z)$, because z is not necessarily allocated in Σ, and $s(n) = 2 \neq 1$. Proposition 2 asserts the existence of a heap, in this case say $h_1 = \{1 \mapsto 3, 3 \mapsto 2\}$, such that $s, h_1 \models \mathsf{lseg}(x, y, n)$ but cannot be extended into a model of $\mathsf{lseg}(x, z, n+m)$ as this would introduce a cycle. In particular with the heap $h = h_1 * \{2 \mapsto 3\}$ we have $s, h \not\models \Sigma * S \to S'$, providing a counterexample for the original entailment. We end this section with the remark that, in order to generalise our method to other inductive predicates, it is enough to find a suitable *subtract* operator satisfying the conditions imposed by Propositions 1 and 2.

Matching and Proving. To finalise the description of our decision procedure for entailment checking we have only left to put all the ingredients together, as shown in Figure 1, into the *match* and *prove* functions.

The *match* function tries to establish whether $s \models \Sigma \to \Sigma'$, in a context where Δ specifies heap locations that must be allocated. The function proceeds by matching predicates in Σ with those in Σ', reducing their number of conjuncts as progress is made, and succeeding if eventually both Σ and Σ' become empty. Furthermore, when successful, the function returns an assertion M generalising the matching proof to all stacks that, like s, also satisfy M.

The function begins by inspecting Σ and Σ' to discard, at lines 10 and 12, any predicates that are empty with respect to s, recursively calling itself to verify the rest of the entailment. After removing all such empty predicates, if a pair of colliding predicates $S \in \Sigma$ and $S' \in \Sigma'$ is found, on line 14 we then proceed to compute $subtract(\Delta, S', S) = (S'', D)$. If the subtraction is successful, signalled by the fact that $s \models sound(S'') \wedge D$, we may replace S' with $S * S''$ in Σ', before removing S from both Σ and Σ' and proceeding with the next recursive call. Alternatively, we reach the bottom of the recursion at line 16, succeeding only if both Σ and Σ' have become empty. This behaviour is formalised in the following theorem, proved later in Section 5.

Theorem 2. *Given three spatial conjunctions $\hat{\Sigma}$, Σ, Σ', let $\Delta = alloc(\hat{\Sigma} * \Sigma)$, and let s be a stack such that $s \models well\text{-}formed(\hat{\Sigma} * \Sigma)$. It follows that: 1) the function $match(s, \Delta, \Sigma, \Sigma')$ always terminates with a result M, 2) the execution requires $O(|\Sigma| + |\Sigma'|)$ recursive steps, 3) if $s \models M$ then the entailment $M \wedge \hat{\Sigma} * \Sigma \rightarrow \hat{\Sigma} * \Sigma'$ is valid, and 4) if $s \not\models M$ then $s \not\models \hat{\Sigma} * \Sigma \rightarrow \hat{\Sigma} * \Sigma'$.*

The main *prove* function, which determines whether $\Pi \wedge \Sigma \rightarrow \Pi' \wedge \Sigma'$ is valid, begins computing with the pure formula $\Gamma := \Pi \wedge well\text{-}formed(\Sigma)$ and the allocation function $\Delta := alloc(\Sigma)$. An SMT solver is first used to test whether there are any models for $\Gamma \wedge \neg\Pi'$ since, if this is the case, then it is possible to build a counterexample that satisfies the antecedent but not the consequence of the entailment. Otherwise the function proceeds iteratively using the SMT solver to find models of Γ to guide the search for a proof or a counterexample. Given one such stack s, the *match* function is called to check the validity of the entailment with respect to s. If successful, *match* returns a formula M generalising the conditions in which the entailment is valid, so the search may continue for models where M does not hold. Iterations proceed until either all models have been checked or a counterexample is found in the process. Formally we state the following theorem, whose proof is given in Section 5.

Theorem 3. *Given an entailment $\Pi \wedge \Sigma \rightarrow \Pi' \wedge \Sigma'$ we have: i) the function $prove(\Pi \wedge \Sigma \rightarrow \Pi' \wedge \Sigma')$ always terminates, and ii) the return value corresponds to the validity of $\Pi \wedge \Sigma \rightarrow \Pi' \wedge \Sigma'$.*

5 Proofs of Correctness

This section presents the main technical contribution of the paper, the proof of correctness of our entailment checking algorithm. The proof itself closely follows the structure of the previous section, filling in the technical details required to assert the statements of Theorem 1, on well-formedness, Theorem 2, on matching, and finally Theorem 3 on entailment checking.

Well-Formedness. Soundness of the well-formed condition $well\text{-}formed(\Sigma)$, the first half of Theorem 1, is easily shown by noting that if a spatial conjunction Σ is satisfiable with respect to some stack and a heap, the formula $well\text{-}formed(\Sigma)$ is also necessarily true with respect to the same stack.

Proposition 3. *Given $s, h \models \Sigma$ it follows $s \models well\text{-}formed(\Sigma)$.*

Proof. Let $\Sigma = S_1 * \cdots * S_n$. Since $s, h \models \Sigma$, there is a partition $h = h_1 * \cdots * h_n$ such that each $s, h_i \models S_i$. From the soundness definition it immediately follows that $s, h_i \models sound(S_i)$ for each predicate. For every pair S_i and S_j with $i < j$, if either $s \models empty(S_i)$ or $s \models empty(S_j)$, then trivially $s \models separated(S_i, S_j)$. Assume otherwise that $s \models \neg empty(S_i) \wedge \neg empty(S_j)$. It then follows that both $s(addr(S_i)) \in \text{dom}\, h_i$ and $s(addr(S_j)) \in \text{dom}\, h_j$. Since by construction h_i and h_j have disjoint domains, we have $s(addr(S_i)) \neq s(addr(S_j))$. This implies the fact that $s \models separated(S_i, S_j)$. □

For completeness of *well-formed*, the second half of Theorem 1, we prove a more general result. In particular if $s \models \textit{well-formed}(\Sigma)$ and R is a set of *reserved* locations, disjoint from the necessarily allocated $\textit{alloc}(\Sigma|s)$, then we show how to build a heap h such that $s, h \models \Sigma$ and $\operatorname{dom} h \cap R = \emptyset$.

Proposition 4. *Given a spatial conjunction Σ, a stack $s \models \textit{well-formed}(\Sigma)$, and a finite set of locations R such that $\textit{alloc}(\Sigma|s) \cap R = \emptyset$, there is a heap h such that $s, h \models \Sigma$ and $\operatorname{dom} h \cap R = \emptyset$.*

Proof. Let $\Sigma = S_1 * \cdots * S_n$. The proof is by induction on n and its base case, when $n = 0$, is trivially satisfied by $h = \emptyset$.

For $n > 1$, let $\Sigma' = \Sigma \setminus S_1 = S_2 * \cdots * S_n$ and let $R' = R \cup \textit{alloc}(S_1|s)$. By construction the formula $\textit{well-formed}(\Sigma) \rightarrow \textit{well-formed}(\Sigma')$ is valid so, in particular, we also have $s \models \textit{well-formed}(\Sigma')$. Furthermore, since $s \models \textit{separated}(S_1, S_j)$ for all $2 \leq j \leq n$, it follows that $\textit{alloc}(S_1|s) \cap \textit{alloc}(\Sigma'|s) = \emptyset$ and, moreover, we also obtain that $\textit{alloc}(\Sigma'|s) \cap R' = \emptyset$. Inductively applying the proposition on Σ' and the set R' we obtain a heap h' such that $s, h' \models \Sigma'$ and $\operatorname{dom} h' \cap R' = \emptyset$. Let

$$h_1 = \begin{cases} \emptyset & \text{if } S_1 = \mathsf{emp} \\ \{s(x) \mapsto s(y)\} & \text{if } S_1 = \mathsf{next}(x, y) \\ \{s(x) \mapsto \ell_1, \ell_1 \mapsto \ell_2, \ldots, \ell_{s(n)-1} \mapsto s(y)\} & \text{if } S_1 = \mathsf{lseg}(x, y, n) \end{cases}$$

where, if needed, the set of locations $\{\ell_1, \ldots, \ell_{s(n)-1}\} \cap (R \cup \operatorname{dom} h') = \emptyset$; since $R \cup \operatorname{dom} h'$ is finite but there are infinitely many locations, it is always possible to find suitable values. It is clear that $s, h_1 \models S_1$ and, furthermore, $\operatorname{dom} h_1 \cap \operatorname{dom} h'$ so $h = h_1 * h'$ is well defined. From these it follows that both $s, h \models \Sigma$ and $\operatorname{dom} h \cap R = \emptyset$. □

Theorem 1 follows as a corollary of Propositions 3 and 4.

Matching and Proving. The following proposition is the main ingredient required to establish the soundness and completeness of the *match* function of Figure 1. The proof, although quite long and rather technical, follows the intuitive description from Section 4 about the behaviour of *match*. Each of the main cases in the proof corresponds, respectively, to the conditions on lines 10 and 12, when discarding empty predicates, line 14, when a either a successful or unsuccessful subtraction is performed, and finally line 16, when the base case of the recursion is reached.

The first three cases are further divided each in two sub-cases, one for the situation when the recursive call is successful and a proof of validity is established, and one for the situation when a counterexample is built. The final case, the base of the recursion, is also divided into three sub-cases: when not all predicates in Σ' have been matched, when all predicates in Σ' were consumed but not all in Σ, and finally when both Σ and Σ' have become empty.

Proof (of Theorem 2). Termination of the function follows since, at each recursive call, the length of either Σ or Σ' is reduced. This also establishes the fact that there are $O(|\Sigma| + |\Sigma'|)$ recursive calls. Now, given that the function does terminate, the proof is by induction on the recursive definition of *match*.

Note that, during the inductive proof, the spatial conjunction $\hat{\Sigma} * \Sigma$ always remains invariant. When a predicate S is removed from Σ, we implicitly add it to $\hat{\Sigma}$, keeping track of the already matched fragment from the original antecedent. This also keeps $\Delta = alloc(\hat{\Sigma} * \Sigma)$ always invariant between calls.

- Suppose we reach line 10, with a predicate $S \in \Sigma$ such that $s \models empty(S)$. Recursively let $M' = match(s, \Delta, \Sigma \setminus S, \Sigma')$ and $M = empty(S) \wedge M'$. Since $s \models empty(S)$ we have $s \models M$ if and only if $s \models M'$.
  - if $s \models M'$, by induction the entailment $M' \wedge (\hat{\Sigma} * S) * (\Sigma \setminus S) \rightarrow \hat{\Sigma} * \Sigma'$ is valid. Since $M \rightarrow M'$ then $M \wedge \hat{\Sigma} * \Sigma \rightarrow \hat{\Sigma} * \Sigma'$ is also valid.
  - if $s \not\models M'$, by induction $s \not\models (\hat{\Sigma} * S) * (\Sigma \setminus S) \rightarrow \hat{\Sigma} * \Sigma'$, which is exactly the same as $s \not\models \hat{\Sigma} * \Sigma \rightarrow \hat{\Sigma} * \Sigma'$.
- Suppose we reach line 12 with a predicate $S' \in \Sigma$ such that $s \models empty(S')$. Recursively let $M' = match(s, \Delta, \Sigma, \Sigma' \setminus S')$ and also $M = empty(S') \wedge M'$. Again $s \models M$ if and only if $s \models M'$.
  - if $s \models M'$, by induction $M' \wedge \hat{\Sigma} * \Sigma \rightarrow \hat{\Sigma} * (\Sigma' \setminus S')$ is valid. To prove that $M \wedge \hat{\Sigma} * \Sigma \rightarrow \hat{\Sigma} * \Sigma'$ is also valid, take any pair $s', h \models M \wedge \hat{\Sigma} * \Sigma$. From the inductive entailment we have $s', h \models \hat{\Sigma} * (\Sigma' \setminus S')$ and from the fact that $s' \models empty(S')$ also $s', \emptyset \models S'$. Thus $s', h \models \hat{\Sigma} * \Sigma'$.
  - if $s \not\models M'$, by induction there is a heap h such that $s, h \models \hat{\Sigma} * \Sigma$ but $s, h \not\models \hat{\Sigma} * (\Sigma' \setminus S')$. If it were the case that $s, h \models \hat{\Sigma} * \Sigma'$, from the fact that $s \models empty(S')$ it would follow that $s, h \models \hat{\Sigma} * (\Sigma' \setminus S')$, contradicting the information from the inductive step. Thus $s, h \not\models \hat{\Sigma} * \Sigma'$.
- Suppose we reach line 13, with two of predicates $S \in \Sigma$ and $S' \in \Sigma'$, such that $s \not\models separated(S, S')$. We compute $(S'', D) := subtract(\Delta, S', S)$, and further suppose that $s \models sound(S'') \wedge D$ so that we reach the next recursive call at line 15. Recursively let $M' = match(s, \Delta, (\Sigma \setminus S), (\Sigma' \setminus S') * S'')$ and $M = \neg separated(S, S') \wedge sound(S'') \wedge D \wedge M'$. As before we have $s \models M$ if and only if $s \models M'$.
  - if $s \models M'$, by induction $M' \wedge (\hat{\Sigma} * S) * (\Sigma \setminus S) \rightarrow (\hat{\Sigma} * S) * ((\Sigma' \setminus S') * S'')$ is valid. To prove that $M \wedge \hat{\Sigma} * \Sigma \rightarrow \hat{\Sigma} * \Sigma'$ is also valid, now take any pair $s', h \models M \wedge \hat{\Sigma} * \Sigma$. Since $\hat{\Sigma} * \Sigma = (\hat{\Sigma} * S) * (\Sigma \setminus S)$, from the inductive entailment after some rearrangement $s', h \models \hat{\Sigma} * (\Sigma' \setminus S') * (S * S'')$ and from Proposition 1 also $s', h \models \hat{\Sigma} * (\Sigma' \setminus S') * S'$. Thus $s', h \models \hat{\Sigma} * \Sigma'$.
  - if $s \not\models M'$, by induction after some rearrangement there is a heap h such that $s, h \models \hat{\Sigma} * \Sigma$ but $s, h \not\models \hat{\Sigma} * (\Sigma' \setminus S') * (S * S'')$. Partition the heap $h = h_1 * h_2$ such that $s, h_1 \models S$ and $s, h_2 \models \hat{\Sigma} * (\Sigma \setminus S)$. If it were the case that $s, h \models \hat{\Sigma} * \Sigma'$, from the second item on Proposition 1 it follows that $s, h \models \hat{\Sigma} * (\Sigma' \setminus S') * (S * S'')$, contradicting the inductive step. We therefore have that $s, h \not\models \hat{\Sigma} * \Sigma'$
- Suppose again we reach line 13, with two colliding predicates S and S'; we compute $(S'', D) := subtract(\Delta, S', S)$; but this time $s \not\models sound(S'') \wedge D$ so we reach line 16 with non-empty Σ and Σ', returning $M = \bot$. Since $s \not\models M$ we have to show that $s \not\models \hat{\Sigma} * \Sigma \rightarrow \hat{\Sigma} * \Sigma'$.

From Proposition 2 there is a heap h_1 such that $s, h_1 \models S$ and for any extension h, i.e. $h_1 \subseteq h$, we have $s, h \not\models \hat{\Sigma} * (\Sigma' \setminus S') * S'$. Applying Proposition 4 with $R = \operatorname{dom} h_1$, it is possible to obtain another heap h_2 such that $s, h_2 \models \hat{\Sigma} * (\Sigma \setminus S)$ and $\operatorname{dom} h_1 \cap \operatorname{dom} h_2 = \emptyset$. Let $h = h_1 * h_2$, from this it follows that $s, h \models \hat{\Sigma} * \Sigma$, and we already knew that $s, h \not\models \hat{\Sigma} * \Sigma'$.

- Finally suppose that we reach line 16, with no remaining pairs of colliding predicates in Σ and Σ'. We may find ourselves in several situations:
  - $\Sigma' \neq \emptyset$, so there is a $S' \in \Sigma'$ with $s \not\models \mathit{empty}(S')$, but it does not collide with any $S \in \Sigma$, so the function returns $M = \bot$ and we have to prove that $s \not\models \hat{\Sigma} * \Sigma \to \hat{\Sigma} * \Sigma'$. If S collides with some predicate in $\hat{\Sigma}$, then the consequence is immediately unsatisfiable and from Proposition 4 we obtain a model for $\hat{\Sigma} * \Sigma$. Otherwise let $R = \{s(\mathit{addr}(S'))\}$, since S' does not collide with anything in $\hat{\Sigma} * \Sigma$, we have $R \cap \mathit{alloc}(\hat{\Sigma} * \Sigma | s) = \emptyset$ and again from Proposition 4 there is a h such that $s, h \models \hat{\Sigma} * \Sigma$ and $s(\mathit{addr}(S')) \notin \operatorname{dom} h$. Since $s(\mathit{addr}(S'))$ must be included, by necessity, on any model of $\hat{\Sigma} * \Sigma'$, it follows as we wanted that $s, h \not\models \hat{\Sigma} * \Sigma'$.
  - $\Sigma' = \emptyset$ but $\Sigma \neq \emptyset$, so there is a $S \in \Sigma$ with $s \not\models \mathit{empty}(S)$, the function returns $M = \bot$ and thus we have to prove that $s \not\models \hat{\Sigma} * \Sigma \to \hat{\Sigma}$. From Proposition 4 with $R = \emptyset$ there is a h such that $s, h \models \hat{\Sigma} * \Sigma$. Partition the heap $h = h_1 * h_2$ such that $s, h_1 \models \hat{\Sigma}$ and $s, h_2 \models \Sigma$. Since there is a non-empty S in Σ it must be the case that $h_2 \neq \emptyset$ and $h_1 \subset h$ is a strict subset. Because all our considered spatial predicates are precise, it therefore follows that $s, h \not\models \hat{\Sigma}$.
  - Both $\Sigma' = \emptyset$ and $\Sigma = \emptyset$, so the function returns $M = \top$. In this final case it is trivial that $s \models M$ and $M \wedge \hat{\Sigma} \to \hat{\Sigma}$ is valid. □

We are now ready to prove the termination and correctness of the main *prove* function as stated earlier in Theorem 3.

Proof (of Theorem 3). Termination is established since each iteration of the loop at line 4 strictly reduces the number satisfying models of Γ. Since there is only a finite number of distinct formulas that may be built by conjunctions of $\mathit{empty}(S)$, $\mathit{sound}(S)$, $\neg\mathit{separated}(S, S')$ and the side condition of $\mathit{subtract}(\Delta, S', S)$—the building blocks for the return value M of *match*—all combinations will be exhausted at some point.

For correctness we first note that, starting from line 1, it is established that the formula $\Gamma \to \Pi \wedge \mathit{well\text{-}formed}(\Sigma)$ is valid and, since later only more conjuncts are appended to Γ, this invariant is maintained throughout the execution.

If the formula $\Gamma \wedge \neg\Pi'$ in line 3 is satisfiable, then there is a stack s such that $s \models \Gamma$ but $s \not\models \Pi'$. From Proposition 4 there is a heap h such that $s, h \models \Pi \wedge \Sigma$ but, since it already fails on the pure part, $s, h \not\models \Pi' \wedge \Sigma'$ and the program reports that the entailment is invalid. Otherwise, if $\Gamma \wedge \neg\Pi'$ is unsatisfiable, it follows that $\Pi \wedge \Sigma \to \Pi'$ is valid. In order to show this take any $s', h \models \Pi \wedge \Sigma$, from Proposition 3 we have that $s' \models \Pi \wedge \mathit{well\text{-}formed}(\Sigma)$. It therefore must be the case that $s' \models \Pi'$ or s' would be a model of the unsatisfiable $\Gamma \wedge \neg\Pi'$.

To finalise we now prove that line 4 at the base of the loop always satisfies the invariants that if $\Gamma \wedge \Sigma \to \Sigma'$ is valid then also $\Pi \wedge \Sigma \to \Sigma'$ is. Just before entering the loop we have $\Gamma = \Pi \wedge \mathit{well\text{-}formed}(\Sigma)$. Assuming $\Gamma \wedge \Sigma \rightarrow \Sigma'$ is valid take any $s', h \models \Pi \wedge \Sigma$, from Proposition 3 it follows that $s' \models \mathit{well\text{-}formed}(\Sigma)$ and therefore, from our assumption, $s', h \models \Pi' \wedge \Sigma'$.

If we enter the code of the loop we have $s \models \Gamma$ and $M = \mathit{match}(s, \Delta, \Sigma, \Sigma')$. If $s \not\models M$ from Theorem 2 there is a heap h such that $s, h \models \Pi \wedge \Sigma$ but, however, $s, h \not\models \Sigma'$, providing as required a counterexample for the entailment. Alternatively, if $s \models M$, from $\Gamma \wedge \neg M \wedge \Sigma \rightarrow \Sigma'$ we have to prove $\Pi \wedge \Sigma \rightarrow \Sigma'$. Take any $s', h \models \Pi \wedge \Sigma$, if $s', h \models M$ then again from Theorem 2 the formula $M \wedge \Sigma \rightarrow \Sigma'$ is valid, and $s', h \models \Sigma'$. Otherwise, if $s', h \not\models M$, from our previous assumption it would also follow that $s', h \models \Sigma'$.

We reach the final line if Γ becomes unsatisfiable and, since $\Gamma \wedge \Sigma \rightarrow \Sigma'$ would then be trivially valid, we prove as desired the validity of $\Pi \wedge \Sigma \rightarrow \Sigma'$. □

6 Experiments

We implemented our entailment checking algorithm in a tool called Asterix using Z3 as the pure theory back-end. Due to the current lack of realistic benchmarks making use of such theory features, we only report the running times of our new implementation against already published benchmarks from [22].

These are benchmarks with a significant number of repeated spatial atoms in the entailment, generated by "cloning" multiple copies of verification conditions obtained when running Smallfoot [5] against its own benchmark suite. They are particularly difficult for the unfolding implemented in slp [22] and the match function in Asterix. We observe a significant improvement, since our match function collects constraints that are potentially useful for other applications of match and relies on the efficiency of a highly optimised SMT solver.

Copies	Smallfoot	slp	Asterix
1	0.01	0.11	0.17
2	0.07	0.06	0.19
3	1.03	0.08	0.23
4	9.53	0.13	0.26
5	55.85	0.38	0.31
6	245.69	2.37	0.39
7	(64%)	20.83	0.54
8	(15%)	212.17	0.85
9	—	—	1.49
10	—	—	2.81

Acknowledgements. This research was supported in part by the ERC project 308125 VeriSynth.

References

1. Barrett, C., Tinelli, C.: CVC3. In: Damm, W., Hermanns, H. (eds.) CAV 2007. LNCS, vol. 4590, pp. 298–302. Springer, Heidelberg (2007)

2. Berdine, J., Calcagno, C., Cook, B., Distefano, D., O'Hearn, P.W., Wies, T., Yang, H.: Shape analysis for composite data structures. In: Damm, W., Hermanns, H. (eds.) CAV 2007. LNCS, vol. 4590, pp. 178–192. Springer, Heidelberg (2007)
3. Berdine, J., Calcagno, C., O'Hearn, P.W.: A decidable fragment of separation logic. In: Lodaya, K., Mahajan, M. (eds.) FSTTCS 2004. LNCS, vol. 3328, pp. 97–109. Springer, Heidelberg (2004)
4. Berdine, J., Calcagno, C., O'Hearn, P.W.: Symbolic execution with separation logic. In: Yi, K. (ed.) APLAS 2005. LNCS, vol. 3780, pp. 52–68. Springer, Heidelberg (2005)
5. Berdine, J., Calcagno, C., O'Hearn, P.W.: Smallfoot: Modular automatic assertion checking with separation logic. In: de Boer, F.S., Bonsangue, M.M., Graf, S., de Roever, W.-P. (eds.) FMCO 2005. LNCS, vol. 4111, pp. 115–137. Springer, Heidelberg (2006)
6. Botincan, M., Parkinson, M.J., Schulte, W.: Separation logic verification of c programs with an SMT solver. Electr. Notes Theor. Comput. Sci. 254, 5–23 (2009)
7. Bruttomesso, R., Cimatti, A., Franzén, A., Griggio, A., Sebastiani, R.: The MATHSAT 4 SMT solver. In: Gupta, A., Malik, S. (eds.) CAV 2008. LNCS, vol. 5123, pp. 299–303. Springer, Heidelberg (2008)
8. Calcagno, C., Distefano, D., O'Hearn, P., Yang, H.: Compositional shape analysis by means of bi-abduction. In: POPL, pp. 289–300.
9. Chin, W.-N., David, C., Nguyen, H.H., Qin, S.: Automated verification of shape, size and bag properties via user-defined predicates in separation logic. Sci. Comput. Program. 77(9), 1006–1036 (2012)
10. Cook, B., Haase, C., Ouaknine, J., Parkinson, M., Worrell, J.: Tractable reasoning in a fragment of separation logic. In: Katoen, J.-P., König, B. (eds.) CONCUR 2011. LNCS, vol. 6901, pp. 235–249. Springer, Heidelberg (2011)
11. Cousot, P., Cousot, R.: Abstract interpretation: A unified lattice model for static analysis of programs by construction or approximation of fixpoints. In: POPL (1977)
12. Cousot, P., Cousot, R., Mauborgne, L.: The reduced product of abstract domains and the combination of decision procedures. In: Hofmann, M. (ed.) FOSSACS 2011. LNCS, vol. 6604, pp. 456–472. Springer, Heidelberg (2011)
13. de Moura, L., Bjørner, N.: Model-based theory combination. Electron. Notes Theor. Comput. Sci. 198(2) (2008)
14. de Moura, L., Bjørner, N.S.: Z3: An efficient SMT solver. In: Ramakrishnan, C.R., Rehof, J. (eds.) TACAS 2008. LNCS, vol. 4963, pp. 337–340. Springer, Heidelberg (2008)
15. Detlefs, D., Nelson, G., Saxe, J.B.: Simplify: a theorem prover for program checking. J. ACM 52(3) (2005)
16. Distefano, D., Parkinson, M.: jStar: Towards practical verification for Java. In: OOPSLA, pp. 213–226 (2008)
17. Dockins, R., Hobor, A., Appel, A.W.: A fresh look at separation algebras and share accounting. In: Hu, Z. (ed.) APLAS 2009. LNCS, vol. 5904, pp. 161–177. Springer, Heidelberg (2009)
18. Dutertre, B., Moura, L.D.: The Yices SMT solver. Technical report, Computer Science Laboratory, SRI International (2006)
19. Haase, C., Ishtiaq, S., Ouaknine, J., Parkinson, M.J.: SeLoger: A tool for graph-based reasoning in separation logic. In: Sharygina, N., Veith, H. (eds.) CAV 2013. LNCS, vol. 8044, pp. 790–795. Springer, Heidelberg (2013)

20. Iosif, R., Rogalewicz, A., Simacek, J.: The tree width of separation logic with recursive definitions. In: Bonacina, M.P. (ed.) CADE 2013. LNCS, vol. 7898, pp. 21–38. Springer, Heidelberg (2013)
21. Nanevski, A., Morrisett, G., Shinnar, A., Govereau, P., Birkedal, L.: Ynot: Dependent types for imperative programs. In: ICFP, pp. 229–240 (2008)
22. Navarro Pérez, J.A., Rybalchenko, A.: Separation Logic + Superposition Calculus = Heap Theorem Prover. In: PLDI, pp. 556–566 (2011)
23. Nieuwenhuis, R., Rubio, A.: Paramodulation-based theorem proving. In: Robinson, J.A., Voronkov, A. (eds.) Handbook of Automated Reasoning, vol. I, ch. 7, pp. 371–443. Elsevier (2001)
24. Piskac, R., Wies, T., Zufferey, D.: Automating separation logic using SMT. In: Sharygina, N., Veith, H. (eds.) CAV 2013. LNCS, vol. 8044, pp. 773–789. Springer, Heidelberg (2013)
25. Reynolds, J.C.: Separation logic: A logic for shared mutable data structures. In: LICS, pp. 55–74 (2002)

Bi-Abduction with Pure Properties for Specification Inference

Minh-Thai Trinh[1], Quang Loc Le[1], Cristina David[2], and Wei-Ngan Chin[1]

[1] National University of Singapore
{trinhmt,locle,chinwn}@comp.nus.edu.sg
[2] University of Oxford
cristina.david@gmail.com

Abstract. Separation logic is a state-of-the-art logic for dealing with the program heap. Using its frame rule, initial works have strived towards automated modular verification for heap-manipulating programs against user-supplied specifications. Since manually writing specifications is a tedious and error-prone engineering process, the so-called bi-abduction (a combination of the frame rule and abductive inference) is proposed to automatically infer pre/post specifications on data structure shapes. However, it has omitted the inference of pure properties of data structures such as their size, sum, height, content and minimum/maximum value, which are needed to express a higher level of program correctness.

In this paper, we propose a novel approach, called *pure bi-abduction*, for inferring pure information for pre/post specifications, using the result from a prior shape analysis step. The power of our new bi-abductive entailment procedure is significantly enhanced by its collection of proof obligations over *uninterpreted relations (functions)*. Additionally, we design a *predicate extension* mechanism to systematically extend shape predicates with pure properties. We have implemented our inference mechanism and evaluated its utility on a benchmark of programs. We show that pure properties are prerequisite to allow the correctness of about 20% of analyzed procedures to be captured and verified.

Keywords: Specification Inference, Pure Bi-Abduction, Separation Logic, Program Verification, Memory Safety, Functional Correctness.

1 Introduction

One of the challenging areas for software verification concerns programs using heap-based data structures. To prove the correctness of such programs, in the last decade, research methodologies based on separation logic have offered good solutions [1,13,3].

Separation logic [20,14], an extension of Hoare logic, is a state-of-the-art logic for dealing with the program heap. Its assertion language can succinctly describe how data structures are laid out in memory, by providing the separating conjunction operator that splits the heap into disjoint regions: reasoning about each such region is independent of the others. This local reasoning is captured by the frame rule of separation logic, a proof rule that enables compositional verification of heap-manipulating programs.

Initial works [1,13] based on separation logic have strived towards automated modular verification against user-supplied specifications. However, manually writing specifications is a tedious and error-prone engineering process. Thus, more recent separation

C.-c. Shan (Ed.): APLAS 2013, LNCS 8301, pp. 107–123, 2013.

logic-based shape analyses endeavor to automatically construct such specifications in order to prove that programs do not commit pointer-safety errors (dereferencing a null or dangling pointer, or leaking memory). One such leading shape analysis [3] proposes bi-abduction to be able to scale up to millions lines of codes. Bi-abduction, a combination of the frame rule and abductive inference, is able to infer "frames" describing extra, unneeded portions of state (via the frame rule) as well as the needed, missing portions (via abductive inference). Consequently, it would automatically infer both preconditions and postconditions on the shape of the data structures used by program codes, enabling a compositional and scalable shape analysis.

However, bi-abduction in [3] presently suffers from an inability to analyze for pure (i.e., heap-independent) properties of data structures, which are needed to express a higher-level of program correctness. For illustration, consider a simple C-style recursive function in Ex. 1 that zips two lists of integers into a single one. To reduce the performance overhead of redundant null-checking, in the `zip` method there is no null-checking for `y`. As a result, the field access `y.next` at line 7 may not be memory-safe. In fact, it triggers a null-dereferencing error whenever the list pointed by x is longer than the list pointed by y. Naturally, to ensure memory safety, the method's precondition needs to capture the size of each list.

Ex. 1. A method where pure properties of its data structure are critical for proving its memory safety.

```
1  data node {
2    int val; node next;}
3  node zip(node x,node y){
4    if (x==null) return y;
5    else {
6      node tmp =
7        zip(x.next,y.next);
8      x.next = y;
9      y.next = tmp;
10     return x;}}
```

A direct solution to such limitation is to rely on numerical analyses. However, since numerical static analyses are often unaware of the shape of a program's heap, it becomes difficult for them to capture pure properties of heap-based data structures.

In this paper, we propose a systematic methodology for inferring pure information for pre/post specifications in the separation logic domain, using the result from a prior shape analysis step. This pure information is not only critical for proving memory safety but also helpful to express a higher-level of program correctness. We call our inference methodology *pure bi-abduction*, and employ it for inferring pure properties of data structures such as their size, height, sum, content and minimum/maximum value. Like bi-abduction, pure bi-abduction is meant to combine the frame rule and abductive inference, but focused on the problem of inferring specifications with both heap and pure information. To achieve this, we have designed a new bi-abductive entailment procedure. Its power will be significantly enhanced by the collection of proof obligations over uninterpreted relations (functions).

Though the main novelty of our current work is a systematic inference of pure information for specifications of heap-manipulating programs, we have also devised a *predicate extension* mechanism that can systematically transform shape predicates in order to incorporate new pure properties. This technique is crucial for enhancing inductive shape predicates with relevant pure properties.

Contributions. Our contributions include the following:

- We design a new bi-abductive entailment procedure for inferring pure information for specifications of heap-manipulating programs. We design a set of fundamental mechanisms for pure bi-abduction to help ensure succinct and precise specifications. Our mechanisms include the inference of obligations and definitions for *uninterpreted relations*, prior to their synthesis via fixpoint analyses (Sections 4, 5, 6).

- We propose an extension mechanism for systematically enhancing inductive shape predicates with a variety of pure properties (Section 7).
- We have implemented our approach and evaluated it on a benchmark of programs (Section 8). We show that pure properties are prerequisite to allow the correctness of about 20% of analyzed procedures to be captured and verified.

2 Overview and Motivation

Memory Safety. For the `zip` method, by using shape analysis techniques [3,6], we could only obtain the following shape specification:

$$\texttt{requires}\ \texttt{ll}\langle\texttt{x}\rangle * \texttt{ll}\langle\texttt{y}\rangle$$
$$\texttt{ensures}\ \texttt{ll}\langle\texttt{res}\rangle;$$

where $\texttt{pred}\ \texttt{ll}\langle\texttt{root}\rangle \equiv (\texttt{root}{=}\texttt{null}) \vee \exists\, \texttt{q}\cdot(\texttt{root}{\mapsto}\texttt{node}\langle\_,\texttt{q}\rangle * \texttt{ll}\langle\texttt{q}\rangle)$.

Although this specification cannot ensure memory safety for the `y.next` field access (at lines 7 and 9), it still illustrates two important characteristics of separation logic. First, by using separation logic, the assertion language can provide inductive spatial predicates that describe the shape of unbounded linked data structures such as lists, trees, etc. For instance, the `ll` predicate describes the shape of an acyclic singly-linked list pointed by `root`. In its definition, the first disjunct corresponds to the case of an empty list, while the second one separates the list into two parts: the head $\texttt{root}{\mapsto}\texttt{node}\langle\_,\texttt{q}\rangle$, where $\mapsto$ is points-to operator, and the tail $\texttt{ll}\langle\texttt{q}\rangle$. Second, the use of $*$ (separating conjunction) operator guarantees that these two parts reside in disjoint memory regions. In short, for the `zip` method, its precondition requires `x` and `y` point to linked lists (using `ll`) that reside in disjoint memory regions (using $*$), while its postcondition ensures the result also points to a linked list.

Generally speaking, we cannot obtain any valid pre/post specification (valid Hoare triple) for the `zip` method by using only the shape domain. To prove memory safety, the specification must also capture the size of each list.

Using predicate extension mechanism, we first inject the size property (captured by `n`) into the `ll` predicate in order to derive the `llN` predicate as follows:

$$\texttt{pred}\ \texttt{llN}\langle\texttt{root},\texttt{n}\rangle \equiv (\texttt{root}{=}\texttt{null} \wedge \texttt{n}{=}0)$$
$$\vee\ \exists\, \texttt{q},\texttt{m}\cdot(\texttt{root}{\mapsto}\texttt{node}\langle\_,\texttt{q}\rangle * \texttt{llN}\langle\texttt{q},\texttt{m}\rangle \wedge \texttt{n}{=}\texttt{m}{+}1).$$

With the new `llN` predicate, we could then strengthen the specification to include uninterpreted relations: $\texttt{P}(\texttt{a},\texttt{b})$ in the precondition and $\texttt{Q}(\texttt{r},\texttt{a},\texttt{b})$ in the postcondition. Their purpose is to capture the relationship between newly-introduced variables $(\texttt{a},\texttt{b},\texttt{r})$ denoting size properties of linked lists. Uninterpreted relations in the precondition should be as weak as possible, while ones in the postcondition should be as strong as possible.

$$\texttt{infer}\ [\texttt{P},\texttt{Q}]$$
$$\texttt{requires}\ \texttt{llN}\langle\texttt{x},\texttt{a}\rangle * \texttt{llN}\langle\texttt{y},\texttt{b}\rangle \wedge \texttt{P}(\texttt{a},\texttt{b})$$
$$\texttt{ensures}\ \texttt{llN}\langle\texttt{res},\texttt{r}\rangle \wedge \texttt{Q}(\texttt{r},\texttt{a},\texttt{b});$$

Intuitively, it is meant to incorporate the inference capability (via `infer`) into a pair of pre/post-condition (via `requires/ensures`). And the inference will be applied to specified second-order variables `P, Q`.

By forward reasoning on the `zip` code, our bi-abductive entailment procedure would finally gather the following proof obligations on the two uninterpreted relations:

$$\begin{array}{l} \mathtt{P(a,b)} \Longrightarrow \mathtt{b}\neq 0 \vee \mathtt{a}\leq 0, \\ \mathtt{P(a,b)} \wedge \mathtt{a=ar+1} \wedge \mathtt{b=br+1} \wedge 0\leq \mathtt{ar} \wedge 0\leq \mathtt{br} \Longrightarrow \mathtt{P(ar,br)}, \\ \mathtt{P(a,b)} \wedge \mathtt{r=b} \wedge \mathtt{a=0} \wedge 0\leq \mathtt{b} \Longrightarrow \mathtt{Q(r,a,b)}, \\ \mathtt{P(a,b)} \wedge \mathtt{rn=r-2} \wedge \mathtt{bn=b-1} \wedge \mathtt{an=a-1} \wedge 0\leq \mathtt{bn,an,rn} \wedge \mathtt{Q(rn,an,bn)} \Longrightarrow \mathtt{Q(r,a,b)}. \end{array}$$

Using suitable fix-point analysis techniques, we can synthesize the approximations for these unknowns, which would add a pre-condition $\mathtt{a}\leq\mathtt{b}$ to guarantee memory safety. Specifically, we have $\mathtt{P(a,b)} \equiv \mathtt{a}\leq\mathtt{b}$, $\mathtt{Q(r,a,b)} \equiv \mathtt{r=a+b}$ and a new specification:

$$\begin{array}{l} \mathtt{requires\ llN\langle x,a\rangle * llN\langle y,b\rangle} \wedge \mathtt{a}\leq\mathtt{b} \\ \mathtt{ensures\ \ llN\langle res,r\rangle} \wedge \mathtt{r=a+b}; \end{array}$$

Program Termination. With inference of pure properties for specifications, we can go beyond memory safety towards functional correctness and even total correctness. Total correctness requires programs to be proven to terminate.

Program termination is typically proven with a well-founded decreasing measure. Our inference mechanism can help discover suitable well-founded ranking functions [16] to support termination proofs. For this task, we would introduce an uninterpreted function `F(a, b)`, as a possible measure, via the following termination-based specification that is synthesized right after size inference. Note that size inference is crucial for proving not only program safety but also program termination.

$$\begin{array}{l} \mathtt{infer\ [F]} \\ \mathtt{requires\ llN\langle x,a\rangle * llN\langle y,b\rangle} \wedge \mathtt{a}\leq\mathtt{b} \wedge \mathtt{Term[F(a,b)]} \\ \mathtt{ensures\ \ llN\langle res,r\rangle} \wedge \mathtt{r=a+b}; \end{array}$$

Similarly, applying our pure bi-abduction technique, we can derive the following proof obligations whose satisfaction would guarantee program termination.

$$\begin{array}{l} \mathtt{a}\geq 0 \wedge \mathtt{b}\geq 0 \wedge \mathtt{a}\leq\mathtt{b} \Longrightarrow \mathtt{F(a,b)}\geq 0 \\ \mathtt{an=a-1} \wedge \mathtt{bn=b-1} \wedge \mathtt{a}\leq\mathtt{b} \wedge \mathtt{an}\geq 0 \Longrightarrow \mathtt{F(a,b)>F(an,bn)} \end{array}$$

Using suitable fixpoint analyses, we can synthesize $\mathtt{F(a,b)} \equiv \mathtt{a-1}$, thus capturing a well-founded decreasing measure for our method. Though termination analysis of programs has been extensively investigated before, we find it refreshing to re-consider it in the context of pure property inference for pre/post specifications. For space reasons, we shall not consider this aspect that uses uninterpreted functions in the rest of the paper.

3 Specification Language

In this section, we introduce the specification language used in pure bi-abduction (Figure 1). The language supports data type declarations *datat* (e.g. `node`), inductive shape predicate definitions *spred* (e.g. `ll`) and method specifications *spec*. Each iterative loop is converted to an equivalent tail-recursive method, where mutations on parameters are made visible to the caller via pass-by-reference.

Regarding each method's specification, it is made up of a set of inferable variables $[v^*, v^*_{rel}]$, a precondition Φ_{pr} and a postcondition Φ_{po}. The intended meaning is whenever the method is called in a state satisfying precondition Φ_{pr} and the method terminates, the resulting state will satisfy the corresponding postcondition Φ_{po}. The specification inference process can be enabled by providing a specification with inferable variables. If $[v^*]$ is specified, suitable preconditions on these variables will be inferred while if $[v^*_{rel}]$ is specified, suitable approximations for these uninterpreted relations will be inferred.

Program	$prog ::= tdecl^*\ meth^*$	$tdecl ::= datat \mid spred \mid spec$
Data declaration	$datat ::= \texttt{data}\ c\ \{\ (t\ v)^*\ \}$	
Shape predicate	$spred ::= \texttt{pred}\ p\langle v^*\rangle \equiv \Phi$	
Method spec	$spec ::= \texttt{infer}\ [\ v^*, v^*_{rel}\ ]\ \texttt{requires}\ \Phi_{pr}\ \texttt{ensures}\ \Phi_{po};$	
Formula	$\Phi ::= \bigvee(\exists v^*\cdot\kappa\wedge\pi)^*$	
Heap formula	$\kappa ::= \kappa_1 * \kappa_2 \mid p\langle v^*\rangle \mid v\mapsto c\langle u^*\rangle \mid \texttt{emp}$	
Pure formula	$\pi ::= \pi\wedge\iota \mid \iota$	$\iota ::= v_{rel}(v^*) \mid \alpha$
	$\alpha ::= \gamma \mid i \mid b \mid \varphi \mid \alpha_1\vee\alpha_2 \mid \alpha_1\wedge\alpha_2 \mid \neg\alpha \mid \exists v\cdot\alpha \mid \forall v\cdot\alpha$	
Linear arithmetic	$i ::= a_1{=}a_2 \mid a_1{\leq}a_2$	
	$a ::= k^{\text{int}} \mid v \mid k^{\text{int}}\times a \mid a_1{+}a_2 \mid -a \mid \texttt{max}(a_1,a_2) \mid \texttt{min}(a_1,a_2)$	
Boolean formula	$b ::= \texttt{true} \mid \texttt{false} \mid v \mid b_1{=}b_2$	
Bag constraint	$\varphi ::= v{\in}\texttt{B} \mid \texttt{B}_1{=}\texttt{B}_2 \mid \texttt{B}_1{\sqsubset}\texttt{B}_2 \mid \forall v{\in}\texttt{B}{\cdot}\alpha \mid \exists v{\in}\texttt{B}{\cdot}\alpha$	
	$\texttt{B} ::= \texttt{B}_1{\sqcup}\texttt{B}_2 \mid \texttt{B}_1{\sqcap}\texttt{B}_2 \mid \texttt{B}_1{-}\texttt{B}_2 \mid \{\} \mid \{v\}$	
Ptr. (dis)equality	$\gamma ::= v_1{=}v_2 \mid v{=}\texttt{null} \mid v_1{\neq}v_2 \mid v{\neq}\texttt{null}$	
	$\beta ::= v_{rel}(v^*){\to}\alpha \mid \pi{\to}v_{rel}(v^*)$	
	$\Delta ::= \Delta_1{\vee}\Delta_2 \mid \Delta_1{*}\Delta_2 \mid \exists v{\cdot}\Delta \mid \kappa{\wedge}\pi$	$\phi ::= \pi$

Fig. 1. The Specification Language used in Pure Bi-Abduction

The Φ constraint is in disjunctive normal form. Each disjunct consists of a $*$-separated heap constraint κ, referred to as *heap part*, and a heap free constraint π, referred to as *pure part*. The pure part does not contain any heap nodes and is presently restricted to uninterpreted relations $v_{rel}(v^*)$, pointer (dis)equality γ, linear arithmetic i, boolean constraints b and bag constraints φ. Internally, each uninterpreted relation is annotated with @pr or @po, depending on whether it comes from the precondition or postcondition resp. This information will be later used to synthesize the approximation for each uninterpreted relation in Sec. 6. The relational definitions and obligations defined in Sec. 4.4 are denoted as $\pi{\to}v_{rel}(v^*)$ and $v_{rel}(v^*){\to}\alpha$ resp. Lastly, Δ denotes a composite formula that can be normalized into the Φ form, while ϕ represents a pure formula.

4 Principles of Pure Bi-Abduction

Initial works [1,13] are typically based on an entailment system of the form $\Delta_1 \vdash \Delta_2 \leadsto \Delta_r$, which attempts to prove that the current state Δ_1 entails an expected state Δ_2 with Δ_r as its frame (or residual) not required for proving Δ_2.

To support shape analysis, bi-abduction [3] would allow both preconditions and postconditions on shape specification to be automatically inferred. Bi-abduction is based on a more general entailment of the form $\Delta_1 \vdash \Delta_2 \leadsto (\Delta_p, \Delta_r)$, whereby a precondition Δ_p, the condition for the entailment proving to succeed, may be inferred.

In this paper, we propose pure bi-abduction technique to infer pure information for pre/post specifications. To better exploit the expressiveness of separation logic, we integrate inference mechanisms directly into it and propose to use an entailment system of the following form $[v_1, .., v_n]\ \Delta_1 \vdash \Delta_2 \leadsto (\phi_p, \Delta_r, \beta_c)$. Three new features are added here to support inference on pure properties:

- We may specify a set of variables $\{v_1, .., v_n\}$ for which inference is selectively applied. As a special case, when no variables are specified, the entailment system reduces to forward verification without inference capability.
- We allow second-order variables, in the form of *uninterpreted relations*, to support inference of pure properties for pre/post specifications.
- We then collect a set of constraints β_c of the form $\phi_1 \Longrightarrow \phi_2$, to provide interpretations for these second-order variables. This approach is critical for capturing inductive definitions that can be refined via fix-point analyses.

We first highlight key principles employed by pure bi-abduction with examples. Later in Sec. 5, we shall present the formalization for our proposed technique.

4.1 Selective Inference

Our first principle is based on the notion that pure bi-abduction is best done selectively. Consider three entailments below with $\mathtt{x}{\mapsto}\mathtt{node}\langle\_, \mathtt{q}\rangle$ as a consequent:

$$[\mathtt{n}]\ \mathtt{llN}\langle\mathtt{x}, \mathtt{n}\rangle \vdash \mathtt{x}{\mapsto}\mathtt{node}\langle\_, \mathtt{q}\rangle \leadsto (\mathtt{n}{>}0, \mathtt{llN}\langle\mathtt{q}, \mathtt{n}{-}1\rangle, \emptyset)$$
$$[\mathtt{x}]\ \mathtt{llN}\langle\mathtt{x}, \mathtt{n}\rangle \vdash \mathtt{x}{\mapsto}\mathtt{node}\langle\_, \mathtt{q}\rangle \leadsto (\mathtt{x}{\neq}\mathtt{null}, \mathtt{llN}\langle\mathtt{q}, \mathtt{n}{-}1\rangle, \emptyset)$$
$$[\mathtt{n}, \mathtt{x}]\ \mathtt{llN}\langle\mathtt{x}, \mathtt{n}\rangle \vdash \mathtt{x}{\mapsto}\mathtt{node}\langle\_, \mathtt{q}\rangle \leadsto (\mathtt{n}{>}0{\vee}\mathtt{x}{\neq}\mathtt{null}, \mathtt{llN}\langle\mathtt{q}, \mathtt{n}{-}1\rangle, \emptyset)$$

Predicate $\mathtt{llN}\langle\mathtt{x}, \mathtt{n}\rangle$ by itself does not entail a non-empty node. For the entailment proving to succeed, the current state would have to be strengthened with either $\mathtt{x}{\neq}\mathtt{null}$ or $\mathtt{n}{>}0$. Our procedure can decide on which pre-condition to return, depending on the set of variables for which pre-conditions are built from. The selectivity is important since we only consider a subset of variables (e.g. $\mathtt{a}, \mathtt{b}, \mathtt{r}$), which are introduced to capture pure properties of data structures. Note that this selectivity does not affect the automation of pure bi-abduction technique, since the variables of interest can be generated automatically right after applying predicate extension mechanism in Sec. 7.

4.2 Never Inferring `false`

Another principle that we strive in our selective inference is that we never infer any cumulative precondition that is equivalent to `false`, since such a precondition would not be provable for any satisfiable program state. As an example, consider $[\mathtt{x}]\ \mathtt{true} \vdash \mathtt{x}{>}\mathtt{x}$. Though we could have inferred $\mathtt{x}{>}\mathtt{x}$, we refrain from doing so, since it is only provable under dead code scenarios.

4.3 Antecedent Contradiction

The problem of traditional abduction is to find an explanatory hypothesis such that it is satisfiable with the antecedent. Our purpose here is different in the sense that we aim to find a sufficient precondition that would allow an entailment to succeed. Considering $[v^*]\ \Delta_1 \vdash \Delta_2$, if a contradiction is detected between Δ_1 and Δ_2, the only precondition (over variables v^*) that would allow such an entailment to succeed is one that contradicts the antecedent Δ_1. Although we disallow `false` to be inferred, we allow above precondition if it is not equivalent to `false`. For example, with [n] $x{=}null \wedge n{=}0 \vdash x{\neq}null$, we have a contradiction between $x{=}null \wedge n{=}0$ and $x{\neq}null$. To allow this entailment to succeed, we infer $n{\neq}0$ as its precondition over just the selected variable [n].

4.4 Uninterpreted Relations

Our inference deals with uninterpreted relations that may appear in either preconditions or postconditions. We refer to the former as pre-relations and the latter as post-relations. Pre-relations should be as weak as possible, while post-relations should be as strong as possible. Our inference mechanism respects this principle, and would use it to derive the weakest pre-relations and strongest post-relations, where possible.

To provide definitions for these uninterpreted relations, such as $R(v^*)$, we infer two kinds of relational constraints. The first kind, called relational obligation, is of the form $\pi \wedge R(v^*) \rightarrow c$, where the consequent c is a *known* constraint and *unknown* $R(v^*)$ is present in the antecedent. The second kind, called relational definition, is of the form $\pi \rightarrow R(v^*)$, where the unknown relation is in the consequent instead.

Relational Obligations. They are useful in two ways. For pre-relations, they act as initial preconditions for (recursive) methods. For post-relations, they denote proof obligations that post-relations must also satisfy. We will check these obligations after we have synthesized post-relations.

As an example, consider the entailment extracted from the motivating example: [P] $a{\geq}1 \wedge b{=}0 \wedge P(a,b) \vdash b{\neq}0$. We infer $P(a,b) \rightarrow a{\leq}0 \vee b{\neq}0$, which will denote an initial precondition for P. More generally, with [P] $\alpha_1 \wedge P(v^*) \vdash \alpha_2$ where α_1 and α_2 denote *known* constraints, we first selectively infer precondition ϕ over selected variables v^* and then collect $P(v^*) \rightarrow \phi$ as our relational obligation. To obtain succinct pre-conditions, we filter out constraints that contradict the current program state.

Relational Definitions. They are typically used to form definitions for fixpoint analyses. For post-relations, we should infer the strongest definitions. After gathering the relational definitions (both base and inductive cases), we would apply a least fixpoint procedure [17] to discover suitable closed-form definitions for post-relations. For pre-relations, while it may be possible to compute a greatest fixpoint to discover the weakest pre-relations that can satisfy all relational constraints, we have designed two simpler techniques for inferring pre-relations. After finding the interpretations for post-relations, we attempt to extract conditions on input variables from them. If the extracted conditions can satisfy all relational constraints for pre-relations, we simply use them as the approximations for our pre-relations. If not, we proceed with a second technique to first construct a recursive invariant which relates the parameters of an arbitrary call (e.g. REC_a, REC_b) to those of the first one (e.g. a, b) using top-down fixpoint [18]. For example, a recursive invariant `rec_inv` for `zip` method is $REC_a{\geq}0 \wedge a{\geq}1{+}REC_a \wedge REC_a{+}b{=}REC_b{+}a$. Next, since parameters of an arbitrary call must also satisfy relevant relational obligations, the precondition `pre_rec` is then $\forall REC_a, REC_b \cdot rec\_inv \rightarrow pre\_fst(REC_a, REC_b)$, where $pre\_fst(a,b){=}a{\leq}0 \vee b{\neq}0$ is the initial condition. Finally, the precondition for all method invocations is $pre\_fst \wedge pre\_rec \wedge a{\geq}0 \wedge b{\geq}0{=}0{\leq}a{\leq}b$. This approach allows us to avoid greatest fix-point analyses, whose important operators (i.e. narrowing) are supported in restricted domains, and is sufficient for all practical examples evaluated.

5 Formalization of Pure Bi-Abduction

Recall that our bi-abductive entailment proving procedure has the following form:

$$[v^*]\ \Delta_1 \vdash \Delta_2 \leadsto (\phi_3, \Delta_3, \beta_3).$$

This new entailment procedure serves two key roles:
• For our forward verification, its goal is to reduce the entailment between separation formulas to the entailment between pure formulas by successively matching up aliased heap nodes between the antecedent and the consequent through folding, unfolding and matching [13]. When this happens, the heap formula in the antecedent is soundly approximated by returning a pure approximation of the form $\bigvee(\exists v^* \cdot \pi)^*$ for each given heap formula κ (using *XPure* function as in [13]).
• For our inference, its goal is to infer a precondition ϕ_3 and gather a set of constraints β_3 over specified uninterpreted relations. Along with the inferred frame Δ_3, we should be able to finally construct relevant preconditions and postconditions for each method.

The focus of the current work is on the second category. From this perspective, the scenario of interest is when both the antecedent and the consequent are heap free, and the rules in Figure 2 can in turn apply. Take note that these rules are applied in a *top-down* and *left-to-right* order.

$$\frac{[v^*]\ \pi_1 \vdash \pi_2 \leadsto (\phi_2, \Delta_2, \beta_2) \qquad [v^*]\ \pi_1 \vdash \pi_3 \leadsto (\phi_3, \Delta_3, \beta_3)}{[v^*]\ \pi_1 \vdash \pi_2 \wedge \pi_3 \leadsto (\phi_2 \wedge \phi_3, \Delta_2 \wedge \Delta_3, \beta_2 \cup \beta_3)}\ [\textbf{INF-[AND]}]$$

$$\frac{\textbf{UNSAT}(\alpha_1)}{[v^*]\ \alpha_1 \vdash \alpha_2 \leadsto (\texttt{true}, \texttt{false}, \emptyset)}\ [\textbf{INF-[UNSAT]}] \qquad \frac{\alpha_1 \Rightarrow \alpha_2}{[v^*]\ \alpha_1 \vdash \alpha_2 \leadsto (\texttt{true}, \alpha_1, \emptyset)}\ [\textbf{INF-[VALID]}]$$

$$\frac{\phi = \forall(FV(\alpha_1) - v^*) \cdot \neg\alpha_1 \quad \textbf{UNSAT}(\alpha_1 \wedge \alpha_2) \quad \phi \neq \texttt{false}}{[v^*]\ \alpha_1 \vdash \alpha_2 \leadsto (\phi, \texttt{false}, \emptyset)}\ [\textbf{INF-[LHS-CONTRA]}]$$

$$\frac{\phi = \forall(FV(\alpha_1, \alpha_2) - v^*) \cdot (\neg\alpha_1 \vee \alpha_2) \quad \phi \neq \texttt{false}}{[v^*]\ \alpha_1 \vdash \alpha_2 \leadsto (\phi, \alpha_1 \wedge \phi, \emptyset)}\ [\textbf{INF-[PRE-DERIVE]}]$$

$$[\textbf{INF-[REL-DEFN]}] \quad [v^*, v_{rel}]\ \pi \vdash v_{rel}(u^*) \leadsto (\texttt{true}, \texttt{true}, \{\pi \rightarrow v_{rel}(u^*)\})$$

$$\frac{[u^*]\ \alpha_1 \vdash \alpha_2 \leadsto (\phi_1, \Delta_1, \emptyset) \qquad [v^*]\ \alpha_1 \vdash \alpha_2 \leadsto (\phi_2, \Delta_2, \emptyset)}{[v^*, v_{rel}]\ \alpha_1 \wedge v_{rel}(u^*) \vdash \alpha_2 \leadsto (\phi_2, \Delta_1 \wedge \Delta_2, \{v_{rel}(u^*) \rightarrow \phi_1\})}\ [\textbf{INF-[REL-OBLG]}]$$

Fig. 2. Pure Bi-Abduction Rules

- Rule [INF−[AND]] breaks the conjunctive consequent into smaller components.
- Rules [INF−[UNSAT]] and [INF−[VALID]] infer `true` precondition whenever the

entailment already succeeds. Specifically, rule [INF−[UNSAT]] applies when the antecedent α_1 of the entailment is unsatisfiable, whereas rule [INF−[VALID]] is used if [INF−[UNSAT]] cannot be applied, meaning that the antecedent is satisfiable.

• The pure precondition inference is captured by two rules [INF−[LHS−CONTRA]] and [INF−[PRE−DERIVE]]. While the first rule handles antecedent contradiction, the second one infers the missing information from the antecedent required for proving the consequent. Specifically, whenever a contradiction is detected between the antecedent α_1 and the consequent α_2, then rule [INF−[LHS−CONTRA]] applies and the precondition $\forall(FV(\alpha_1)-v^*) \cdot \neg\alpha_1$ contradicting the antecedent is being inferred. Note that $FV(\cdot)$ returns the set of free variables from its argument(s), while v^* is a shorthand notation for $v_1, .., v_n$[1]. On the other hand, if no contradiction is detected, then rule [INF−[PRE−DERIVE]] infers a sufficient precondition to prove the consequent. In order to not contradict the principle stated in Sec. 4.2, both aforementioned rules check that the inferred precondition is not equivalent to `false`.

• The last two rules [INF−[REL−DEFN]] and [INF−[REL−OBLG]] are used to gather definitions and obligations respectively, for the uninterpreted relation $v_{rel}(u^*)$. For simplicity, in rule [INF−[REL−OBLG]], we just formalize the case when there is only one uninterpreted relation in the antecedent.

6 Inference via Hoare-Style Rules

Code verification is typically formulated as a Hoare triple of the form: $\vdash \{\Delta_1\}\ c\ \{\Delta_2\}$, with a precondition Δ_1 and a postcondition Δ_2. This verification could either be conducted *forwards* or *backwards* for the specified properties to be successfully verified, in accordance with the rules of Hoare logic. In separation logic, the predominant mode of verification is forward. Specifically, given an initial state Δ_1 and a program code c, such a Hoare-style verification rule is expected to compute a best possible postcondition Δ_2 satisfying the inference rules of Hoare logic. If the best possible postcondition cannot be calculated, it is always sound and often sufficient to compute a suitable approximation.

To support pure bi-abduction, we extend this Hoare-style forward rule to the form: $[v^*] \vdash \{\Delta_1\}\ c\ \{\phi_2, \Delta_2, \beta_2\}$ with three additional features (i) a set of variables $[v^*]$ (ii) an extra precondition ϕ_2 that must be added (iii) a set of definitions and obligations β_2 on the specified uninterpreted relations. The selectivity criterion will help ensure that ϕ_2 and β_2 come from only the specified set of variables, namely $\{v^*\}$. If this set is empty, our new rule is simply the case that performs verification, without any inference.

Figure 3 captures a set of our Hoare rules with pure bi-abduction. Rule [INF−[SEQ]] shows how sequential composition $e_1; e_2$ is handled. The two inferred preconditions are conjunctively combined as $\phi_2 \wedge \phi_3$. Rule [INF−[IF]] deals with conditional expression. Our core language allows only boolean variables (e.g. w) in each conditional test. We use a primed notation whereby w denotes the old value, and w' denotes the latest value of each variable w. The conditions w' and $\neg w'$ are asserted for each of the two conditional branches. Since the two preconditions ϕ_2, ϕ_3 come from two branches, both of them must hold for soundness; thus they are combined conjunctively in a conservative manner. Rule [INF−[ASSIGN]] handles assignment statement. We first define a

[1] If there is no ambiguity, we can use v^* instead of $\{v^*\}$.

composition with update operator. Given a state Δ_1, a state change Δ_2, and a set of variables to be updated $X=\{x_1,\ldots,x_n\}$, the composition operator $\texttt{op}_X$ is defined as: $\Delta_1 \ \texttt{op}_X \ \Delta_2 \stackrel{def}{=} \exists\, r_1..r_n \cdot (\rho_1\Delta_1) \ \texttt{op} \ (\rho_2\Delta_2)$, where $r_1,\ldots,r_n$ are fresh variables and $\rho_1 = [r_i/x_i']_{i=1}^n$, $\rho_2 = [r_i/x_i]_{i=1}^n$. Note that ρ_1 and ρ_2 are substitutions that link each latest value of x_i' in Δ_1 with the corresponding initial value x_i in Δ_2 via a fresh variable r_i. The binary operator $\texttt{op}$ is either $\wedge$ or $*$. Instances of this operator will be used in the inference rules $\underline{[\textbf{INF-[ASSIGN]}]}$ and $\underline{[\textbf{INF-[CALL]}]}$. As illustrated in $\underline{[\textbf{INF-[CALL]}]}$, for each method call, we must ensure that its precondition is satisfied, and then add the expected postcondition into its residual state. Here, $(t_i\ v_i)_{i=1}^{m-1}$ are pass-by-reference parameters, that are marked with `ref`, while the pass-by-value parameters V are equated to their initial values through the *nochange* function, as their updated values are not visible to the method's callers. Note that inference may occur during the entailment proving for the method's precondition.

$$\underline{[\textbf{INF-[SEQ]}]}$$
$$\frac{[v^*] \vdash \{\Delta\}\ e_1\ \{\phi_2, \Delta_2, \beta_2\} \qquad [v^*] \vdash \{\Delta_2\}\ e_2\ \{\phi_3, \Delta_3, \beta_3\}}{[v^*] \vdash \{\Delta\}\ e_1; e_2\ \{\phi_2 \wedge \phi_3, \Delta_3, \beta_2 \cup \beta_3\}}$$

$$\underline{[\textbf{INF-[IF]}]}$$
$$\frac{[v^*] \vdash \{\Delta \wedge w'\}\ e_1\ \{\phi_2, \Delta_2, \beta_2\} \qquad [v^*] \vdash \{\Delta \wedge \neg w'\}\ e_2\ \{\phi_3, \Delta_3, \beta_3\}}{[v^*] \vdash \{\Delta\}\ \textbf{if}\ w\ \textbf{then}\ e_1\ \textbf{else}\ e_2\ \{\phi_2 \wedge \phi_3, \Delta_2 \vee \Delta_3, \beta_2 \cup \beta_3\}}$$

$$\underline{[\textbf{INF-[ASSIGN]}]}$$
$$\frac{[v^*] \vdash \{\Delta\}\ e\ \{\phi_2, \Delta_2, \beta_2\} \qquad \Delta_3 {=} \exists \textbf{res} \cdot (\Delta_2 \wedge_u u' {=} \textbf{res})}{[v^*] \vdash \{\Delta\}\ u{:=}e\ \{\phi_2, \Delta_3, \beta_2\}}$$

$$\underline{[\textbf{INF-[CALL]}]}$$
$$\frac{\begin{array}{c} t_0\ mn\ (\textbf{ref}\ (t_i\ v_i)_{i=1}^{m-1}, (t_j\ v_j)_{j=m}^{n})\ \Phi_{pr}\ \Phi_{po}\ \{c\} \in Prog \\ \rho{=}[v_k'/v_k]_{k=1}^n \quad \Phi_{pr}' = \rho(\Phi_{pr}) \quad W{=}\{v_1,\ldots,v_{m-1}\} \quad V{=}\{v_m,\ldots,v_n\} \\ [v^*]\ \Delta \vdash \Phi_{pr}' \leadsto (\phi_2, \Delta_2, \beta_2) \qquad \Delta_3{=}(\Delta_2 \wedge nochange(V))\ *_{V\cup W}\ \Phi_{po} \end{array}}{[v^*] \vdash \{\Delta\}\ mn(v_1,\ldots,v_{m-1}, v_m, \ldots v_n)\ \{\phi_2, \Delta_3, \beta_2\}}$$

$$\underline{[\textbf{INF-[METH]}]}$$
$$\frac{\begin{array}{c} [v^*, v_{rel}^*] \vdash \{\Phi_{pr} \wedge \bigwedge(u'{=}u)^*\}\ c\ \{\phi_2, \Delta_2, \beta_2\} \qquad [v^*, v_{rel}^*]\ \Delta_2 \vdash \Phi_{po} \leadsto (\phi_3, \Delta_3, \beta_3) \\ \rho_1 = infer\_pre(\beta_2 \cup \beta_3) \qquad \rho_2 = infer\_post(\beta_2 \cup \beta_3) \\ \Phi_{pr}^n = \rho_1(\Phi_{pr} \wedge \phi_2 \wedge \phi_3) \qquad \Phi_{po}^n = \rho_2(\Phi_{po} * \Delta_3) \end{array}}{\vdash t_0\ mn\ ((t\ u)^*)\ \textbf{infer}\ [v^*, v_{rel}^*]\ \Phi_{pr}\ \Phi_{po}\ \{c\} \leadsto \Phi_{pr}^n\ \Phi_{po}^n}$$

Fig. 3. Hoare Rules with Pure Bi-Abduction

Lastly, we discuss the rule $\underline{[\textbf{INF-[METH]}]}$ for handling each method declaration. At the program level, our inference rules will be applied to each set of mutually recursive methods in a bottom-up order in accordance with the call hierarchy. This allows us to gather the entire set β of definitions and obligations for each uninterpreted relation. From this set β we infer the pre- and post-relations via two techniques described below.

$$\begin{aligned}
\mathtt{def}_{\mathtt{po}}(\beta) &= \{\pi_i^k \rightarrow v_{rel_i}(v_i^*) \mid (\pi_i^k \rightarrow v_{rel_i}@\mathtt{po}(v_i^*)) \in \beta\} \\
\mathtt{obl}_{\mathtt{po}}(\beta) &= \{v_{rel_i}(v_i^*) \rightarrow \alpha_j \mid (v_{rel_i}@\mathtt{po}(v_i^*) \rightarrow \alpha_j) \in \beta\} \\
\mathtt{def}_{\mathtt{pr}}(\beta) &= \{\pi_i^k \rightarrow v_{rel_i}(v_i^*) \mid (\pi_i^k \rightarrow v_{rel_i}@\mathtt{pr}(v_i^*)) \in \beta\} \\
\mathtt{obl}_{\mathtt{pr}}(\beta) &= \{v_{rel_i}(v_i^*) \rightarrow \alpha_j \mid (v_{rel_i}@\mathtt{pr}(v_i^*) \rightarrow \alpha_j) \in \beta\}
\end{aligned}$$

Take note that, given the entire set β, we retrieve the set of definitions and obligations for post-relations through functions $\mathtt{def}_{\mathtt{po}}$ and $\mathtt{obl}_{\mathtt{po}}$ respectively, while we use functions $\mathtt{def}_{\mathtt{pr}}$ and $\mathtt{obl}_{\mathtt{pr}}$ for pre-relations.

• For post-relations, function *infer_post* applies a least fixed point analysis to the set of collected relational definitions $\mathtt{def}_{\mathtt{po}}(\beta)$. To compute the least fixed point over two domains used to instantiate the current framework, namely the numerical domain and the set/bag domain, we utilize FIXCALC [17] and FIXBAG [15], respectively. The call to the fixed point analysis is denoted as $\mathtt{LFP}(\mathtt{def}_{\mathtt{po}}(\beta))$. It takes as inputs the set of relational definitions, while returning a set of closed form constraints of the form $\alpha_i \rightarrow v_{rel_i}(v_i^*)$, where each constraint corresponds to uninterpreted relation $v_{rel_i}(v_i^*)$. Given that our aim is to infer the strongest post-relations, we further consider each post-relation $v_{rel_i}(v_i^*)$ to be equal to α_i. Finally, *infer_post* returns a set of substitutions, whereby each unknown relation is substituted by the inferred formula, provided that this formula satisfies all the corresponding relational obligations from $\mathtt{obl}_{\mathtt{po}}(\beta)$.

$$\begin{aligned}
\mathit{infer_post}(\beta) = \{\alpha_i / v_{rel_i}(v_i^*) \mid\ & (\alpha_i \rightarrow v_{rel_i}(v_i^*)) \in \mathtt{LFP}(\mathtt{def}_{\mathtt{po}}(\beta)) \\
& \wedge \forall (v_{rel_i}(v_i^*) \rightarrow \alpha_j) \in \mathtt{obl}_{\mathtt{po}}(\beta) \cdot \alpha_i \Rightarrow \alpha_j\}
\end{aligned}$$

• For pre-relations, we initially infer two kinds of precondition: one for base cases, the other for recursive calls. For base cases, we calculate the conjunction of all its obligations from $\mathtt{obl}_{\mathtt{pr}}(\beta)$ to obtain sufficient precondition $\mathtt{pre\_base_i}$ for each uninterpreted relation $v_{rel_i}(v_i^*)$. For recursive calls, we first derive the *recursive invariant* $\mathtt{rec\_inv_i}$ to relate the parameters of an arbitrary call to those of the first one. This can be achieved via a top-down fixed point analysis [18]. Because the parameters of an arbitrary call must also satisfy relevant relational obligations (e.g. $\mathtt{pre\_base_i}$), we will then be able to construct a precondition $\mathtt{pre\_rec_i}$ for each relation. An acceptable approximation α_i for each relation $v_{rel_i}(v_i^*)$ must satisfy simultaneously the precondition for base calls ($\mathtt{pre\_base_i}$), for an arbitrary recursive call ($\mathtt{pre\_rec_i}$) and the invariant $\mathtt{INV}$ (e.g. $\mathtt{a}\geq 0 \wedge \mathtt{b}\geq 0$ as in Sec. 4.4). The last step is to check the quality of candidate substitutions to keep the ones that satisfy not only the obligations but also definitions of each relation.

$$\frac{\begin{aligned}
\mathtt{pre_base_i} &= \{\wedge_j \alpha_j \mid (v_{rel_i}(v_i^*) \rightarrow \alpha_j) \in \mathtt{obl}_{\mathtt{pr}}(\beta)\} \\
\mathtt{rec_inv_i} &= \mathtt{TDFP}(\mathtt{def}_{\mathtt{pr}}(\beta)) \\
\mathtt{pre_rec_i} &= \forall (\mathit{FV}(\mathtt{rec_inv_i}) - v_i^*) \cdot (\neg \mathtt{rec_inv_i} \vee \mathtt{pre_base_i}) \\
\alpha_i &= \mathtt{pre_base_i} \wedge \mathtt{pre_rec_i} \wedge \mathtt{INV}
\end{aligned}}{\mathit{infer_pre}(\beta)\ =\ \mathtt{sanity_checking}(\{\alpha_i / v_{rel_i}(v_i^*)\}, \mathtt{obl}_{\mathtt{pr}}(\beta), \mathtt{def}_{\mathtt{pr}}(\beta))}$$

With the help of functions *infer_pre* and *infer_post*, we can finally define the rule for deriving the pre- and postconditions, Φ_{pr}^n and Φ_{po}^n, of a method *mn*. Note that v_{rel}^* denotes the set of uninterpreted relations to be inferred, while ρ_1 and ρ_2 represent the substitutions obtained for pre- and post-relations, respectively.

Soundness. Soundness of inference is given in the extended version of this paper [22].

7 Enhancing Predicates with Pure Properties

Since the user may encounter various kinds of inductive spatial predicates (from a shape analysis step), such as linked lists, doubly-linked lists, trees, etc. and there may be different pure properties to enrich shape predicates such as size, height, sum, head, min/max, set of values/addresses (and their combinations), we need to use a predicate extension mechanism to systematically incorporate pure properties into heap predicates.

Our mechanism is generic in the sense that each specified property can be applied to a broad range of recursive data structures, whose underlying structures can be quite different (see [22]). We can define these pure properties of data structures in the form of parameterized inductive definitions such as:

$$
\begin{array}{ll}
\texttt{prop\_defn HEAD[@V]}\langle\texttt{v}\rangle & \equiv \texttt{v=V} \\
\texttt{prop\_defn SIZE[@R]}\langle\texttt{n}\rangle & \equiv \texttt{n=0} \vee \texttt{SIZE}\langle\texttt{R,m}\rangle\wedge\texttt{n=1+m} \\
\texttt{prop\_defn HEIGHT[@R]}\langle\texttt{n}\rangle & \equiv \texttt{n=0} \vee \texttt{HEIGHT}\langle\texttt{R,m}\rangle\wedge\texttt{n=1+max(m)} \\
\texttt{prop\_defn SUM[@V,@R]}\langle\texttt{s}\rangle & \equiv \texttt{s=0} \vee \texttt{SUM}\langle\texttt{R,r}\rangle\wedge\texttt{s=V+r} \\
\texttt{prop\_defn SET[@V,@R]}\langle\texttt{S}\rangle & \equiv \texttt{S=\{\}} \vee \texttt{SET}\langle\texttt{R,S}_2\rangle\wedge\texttt{S=\{V\}}\sqcup\texttt{S}_2 \\
\texttt{prop\_defn SETADDR[@R]}\langle\texttt{S}\rangle & \equiv \texttt{S=\{\}} \vee \texttt{SETADDR}\langle\texttt{R,S}_2\rangle\wedge\texttt{S=\{root\}}\sqcup\texttt{S}_2 \\
\texttt{prop\_defn MINP[@V,@R]}\langle\texttt{mi}\rangle & \equiv \texttt{mi=min(V)} \vee \texttt{MINP}\langle\texttt{R,mi}_2\rangle\wedge\texttt{mi=min(V,mi}_2\texttt{)} \\
\texttt{prop\_defn MAXP[@V,@R]}\langle\texttt{mx}\rangle & \equiv \texttt{mx=max(V)} \vee \texttt{MAXP}\langle\texttt{R,mx}_2\rangle\wedge\texttt{mx=max(V,mx}_2\texttt{)},
\end{array}
$$

where `V`, `R` are values extracted from parameters `@V`, `@R` resp. For example, to determine if `n` is the size of some data structure whose recursive pointer is annotated as `@REC`, `SIZE[@REC]⟨n⟩` would check the satisfiability of the base case (e.g. `n=0`) and the inductive case (via recursive pointer `REC`).

Using such definition, one can use the following command to incorporate size property directly to a linked-list predicate definition. Below, the annotations `@VAL`, `@REC` are hardwired to two fields of the underlying heap structure `node`:

```
pred llN⟨root, n⟩ = extend ll⟨root⟩ with SIZE[@REC]⟨n⟩
data node {int val@VAL; node next@REC; }
```

Based on these commands and the definitions of pure properties, our system first constructs an entry (in a dictionary) for each targeting predicate. For example, there is one entry (`llN⟨root,n⟩`, (`F1`, `F2`, `BC`, `IC`)), where list of all value field annotations `F1=[]`, list of all recursive pointer annotations `F2=[@REC]`, base case `BC=\[_]` → `n=0` and inductive case `IC=\[`$\mathtt{m_{REC}}$`]` → `n=`$\mathtt{m_{REC}}$`+1` ($\mathtt{m_{REC}}$ is the size property of corresponding recursive pointer `REC` of the linked-list). Using the dictionary, we can transform the base case and inductive case of original spatial predicate `ll` as follows:

$$\texttt{root=null \#Dict}\leadsto\texttt{root=null}\wedge\texttt{n=0}$$
$$\exists\texttt{q}\cdot(\texttt{root}\mapsto\texttt{node}\langle\_,\texttt{q}\rangle*\texttt{ll}\langle\texttt{q}\rangle)\ \texttt{\#Dict}\leadsto\exists\texttt{q,m}\cdot(\texttt{root}\mapsto\texttt{node}\langle\_,\texttt{q}\rangle*\texttt{llN}\langle\texttt{q,m}\rangle\wedge\texttt{n=m+1})$$

Finally, we can synthesize `llN` predicate as previously shown in Sec. 2.

In short, the technique we present in this section aims at a systematic way to enrich spatial predicates with interesting pure properties. For space reasons, more complicated cases (i.e. when handling data structures with multiple links such as tree) can be found in [22]. While property extensions are user customizable, their use within our pure inference sub-system can be completely automated, as we can automatically construct predicate derivation commands and systematically apply them after shape analysis. We then replace each heap predicate with its derived counterpart, followed by the introduction of uninterpreted pre- and post-relations before applying Hoare-style verification rules with pure bi-abductive inference.

8 Experimental Results

We have implemented our pure bi-abduction technique into an automated program verification system for separation logic, giving us a new version with inference capability, called SPECINFER. We then have conducted three case studies in order to examine (i) the quality of inferred specifications, (ii) the feasibility of our technique in dealing with a variety of data structures and pure properties to be inferred, and (iii) the applicability of our tool in real programs.

Small Examples. To highlight the quality of inferred specifications, we summarize *sufficient specifications* that our tool can infer for some well-known recursive examples. Details can be found in the extended version of this paper [22]. Though codes for these examples are not too complicated, they illustrate the treatment of recursion (thus, the inter-procedural aspect). Therefore, the preconditions and postconditions derived can be quite intricate and would require considerable human efforts if they were constructed manually.[2]

Ex. 2. A method where the content of its data structure is helpful to ensure its functional correctness

```
node del_val(node x,int a)
  {
   if (x == null) return x;
   else if (x.val == a) {
       node tmp = x.next;
       free(x);
       return tmp; }
   else {
     x.next =
       del_val(x.next, a);
       return x; } }
```

One interesting thing to note is that each example may require different pure properties for its correctness to be captured and verified. Using our pure bi-abduction technique, we can derive more expressive specifications, which can help ensure a higher-level correctness of programs. For instance, the size property is not enough to capture the functional correctness of `del_val` method, whose source code is given in Ex. 2. Method `del_val` deletes the first node with value `a` from the linked-list pointed by `x`. Since the behavior of this method depends on the content of its list, SPECINFER needs to derive `llNB` predicate that also captures a bag `B` of values stored in the list:

$$\begin{array}{l}\texttt{pred llNB}\langle\texttt{root},\texttt{n},\texttt{B}\rangle \equiv (\texttt{root}{=}\texttt{null} \wedge \texttt{n}{=}0 \wedge \texttt{B}{=}\{\}) \vee \\ \exists\, \texttt{s},\texttt{q},\texttt{m},\texttt{B}_0 \cdot (\texttt{root}{\mapsto}\texttt{node}\langle\texttt{s},\texttt{q}\rangle * \texttt{llNB}\langle\texttt{q},\texttt{m},\texttt{B}_0\rangle \wedge \texttt{n}{=}\texttt{m}{+}1 \wedge \texttt{B}{=}\texttt{B}_0{\sqcup}\{\texttt{s}\}).\end{array}$$

Finally, our tool infers the following specification that guarantees the functional correctness of `del_val` method:

$$\begin{array}{l}\texttt{requires llNB}\langle\texttt{x},\texttt{n},\texttt{B}_1\rangle \\ \texttt{ensures llNB}\langle\texttt{res},\texttt{m},\texttt{B}_2\rangle \wedge ((\texttt{a}{\notin}\texttt{B}_1 \wedge \texttt{B}_2{=}\texttt{B}_1) \vee \texttt{B}_1{=}\texttt{B}_2{\sqcup}\{\texttt{a}\});\end{array}$$

where `res` denotes the method's result.

[2] The source code of all examples can be found in our website [22].

Medium Examples. We tested our tool on a set of challenging programs that use a variety of data structures. The results are shown in Table 1 (the first eight rows), where the first column contains tested program sets: `LList` (singly-linked list), `SoLList` (sorted singly-linked list), `DLList` (doubly-linked list), `CBTree` (complete binary tree), `Heaps` (priority queue), `AVLTree` (AVL tree), `BSTree` (binary search tree) and `RBTree` (red-black tree). The second and third columns denote the number of lines of code (LOC) and the number of procedures (P#) respectively.

For each test, we start with shape specifications that are obtained from the prior shape analysis step. The number of procedures with valid specifications (valid Hoare triples) is reported in the `V#` column while the percentage of these over all analyzed procedures is in the % column. In the next two phases, we incrementally add new pure properties (to be inferred) to the existing specifications. These additional properties are listed in the `Add.Properties` columns. While phase 2 only focuses on quantitative properties such as size (number of nodes) and height (for trees), phase 3 aims at other functional properties. We also measure the time (in seconds) taken for verification with inference, in the `Time` column.

In addition to illustrating the applicability of SPECINFER in dealing with different data structures and pure properties, Table 1 reaffirms the need of pure properties for capturing program correctness. Specifically, for procedures that SPECINFER cannot infer any valid specifications, we do construct the specifications manually. However due to the restriction of properties the resulting specification can capture, we fail to do so for these procedures. For illustration, we cannot construct any valid specification for about 18% of procedures in phase 1 (using shape domain only). Even in phase 2, there is still one example, `delete_max` method in `Heaps` test, for which we cannot obtain any valid specification. This method is used to delete the root of a heap tree, thus it requires the information of the maximum element.

Table 1. Specification Inference with Pure Properties for a Variety of Data Structures

			Shape		Shape + Quan				Shape + Quan + Func			
Program	LOC	P#	V#	%	Add.Properties	V#	%	Time	Add.Properties	V#	%	Time
`LList`	287	29	23	79	Size	29	100	1.53	Bag of values	29	100	3.09
`SoLList`	237	28	22	79	Size	28	100	0.93	Sortedness	28	100	1.62
`DLList`	313	29	23	79	Size	29	100	1.69	Bag of values	29	100	4.19
`Heaps`	179	5	2	40	Size	4	80	2.14	Max. element	5	100	6.63
`CBTree`	115	7	7	100	Size & Height	7	100	2.76	Bag of values	7	100	98.81
`AVLTree`	313	11	9	82	Size & Height	11	100	8.85	Balance factor	11	100	10.66
`BSTree`	177	9	9	100	Size & Height	9	100	1.76	Sortedness	9	100	2.75
`RBTree`	407	19	18	95	Size & Height	19	100	5.97	Color	19	100	6.01
`schedule`	512	18	13	72	Size	18	100	6.86				
`schedule2`	474	16	5	31	Size	16	100	10.58				
`pcidriver`	1036	29	29	100	Size	29	100	17.72				

Larger Examples. The last three rows from Table 1 demonstrate the applicability of SPECINFER on larger programs. The first two programs used to perform process scheduling are adopted from the Siemens test suite [8] while the last one is `pci_driver.c`

file from Linux Device Driver. Note that for this case study we enrich shape specifications with size property only. For Linux file, although it is sufficient to use only shape property to prove memory safety, size property is still useful for proving termination.

9 Related Works

Specification inference makes program verification more practical by minimizing on the need for manual provision of specifications. It can also be used to support formal software documentation.

One research direction in the area of specification inference is concerned with inferring shapes of data structures. SLAyer [2] is an automatic program analysis tool designed to prove the absence of memory safety errors such as dangling pointer dereferences, double frees, and memory leaks. The footprint analysis described in [4] infers descriptions of data structures without requiring a given precondition. Furthermore, in [3], Calcagno et al. propose a compositional shape analysis. Both aforementioned analyses use an abstract domain based on a limited fragment of separation logic, centered on some common heap predicates. Abductor [3] is a tool implementing a compositional shape analysis based on bi-abduction, which was used to check memory safety of large open source codebases [5]. A recent work [23] attempts to infer partial annotations required in a separation-logic based verifier, called Verifast. It can infer annotations related to unfold/fold steps, and also shape analysis when pre-condition is given. Our current proposal is complementary to the aforesaid works, as it is focused on inferring the more varied pure properties. We support it with a set of fundamental pure bi-abduction techniques, together with a general predicate extension mechanism. Our aim is to provide systematic machinery for deriving formal specifications with more precise correctness properties.

A closely related research direction to ours concerns the inference of both shape and numerical properties. In [11], the authors combine shape analysis based on separation logic with an external numeric-based program analysis in order to verify properties such as memory safety and absence of memory leaks. Their method was tested on a number of programs where memory safety depends on relationships between the lengths of the lists involved. In the same category, Thor [12] is a tool for reasoning about a combination of list reasoning and arithmetic by using two separate analyses. The arithmetic support added by Thor includes stack-based integers, integers in the heap and lengths of lists. However, these current works are limited to handling list segments together with its length as property, and does not cover other pure properties, such as min/max or set. In addition, they require two separate analysis, as opposed to our integrated analysis (or entailment procedure) that can handle both heap and pure properties simultaneously. A recent work [19] focuses on refining partial specifications, using a semi-automatic approach whereby predicate definitions are manually provided. This work did not take advantage of prior shape analysis, nor did it focus on the fundamental mechanisms for bi-abduction with pure properties. Our paper addresses these issues by designing a new pure bi-abduction entailment procedure, together with the handling of uninterpreted functions and relations. To utilize shape analyses' results, we also propose a predicate extension mechanism for systematically enhancing predicates with new pure properties.

Another recent work [7] aims to automatically construct verification tools that implement various input proof rules for reachability and termination properties in the form of Horn(-like) clauses. Also, on the type system side, the authors of [21,9,10] require templates in order to infer dependent types precise enough to prove a variety of safety properties such as the safety of array accesses. However, in both of these works, mutable data structures are not supported. Compared to above works, our proposal can be considered fundamental, as we seek to incorporate pure property inference directly into the entailment proving process for the underlying logics, as opposed to building more complex analyses techniques.

Acknowledgements. We would like to thank Duc-Hiep Chu for his useful comments.

References

1. Berdine, J., Calcagno, C., O'Hearn, P.W.: Smallfoot: Modular automatic assertion checking with separation logic. In: de Boer, F.S., Bonsangue, M.M., Graf, S., de Roever, W.-P. (eds.) FMCO 2005. LNCS, vol. 4111, pp. 115–137. Springer, Heidelberg (2006)
2. Berdine, J., Cook, B., Ishtiaq, S.: SLAYER: Memory safety for systems-level code. In: Gopalakrishnan, G., Qadeer, S. (eds.) CAV 2011. LNCS, vol. 6806, pp. 178–183. Springer, Heidelberg (2011)
3. Calcagno, C., Distefano, D., O'Hearn, P., Yang, H.: Compositional shape analysis by means of bi-abduction. In: POPL, pp. 289–300. ACM, New York (2009)
4. Calcagno, C., Distefano, D., O'Hearn, P.W., Yang, H.: Footprint analysis: A shape analysis that discovers preconditions. In: Riis Nielson, H., Filé, G. (eds.) SAS 2007. LNCS, vol. 4634, pp. 402–418. Springer, Heidelberg (2007)
5. Distefano, D.: Attacking large industrial code with bi-abductive inference. In: Alpuente, M., Cook, B., Joubert, C. (eds.) FMICS 2009. LNCS, vol. 5825, pp. 1–8. Springer, Heidelberg (2009)
6. Dudka, K., Peringer, P., Vojnar, T.: Predator: A practical tool for checking manipulation of dynamic data structures using separation logic. In: Gopalakrishnan, G., Qadeer, S. (eds.) CAV 2011. LNCS, vol. 6806, pp. 372–378. Springer, Heidelberg (2011)
7. Grebenshchikov, S., Lopes, N.P., Popeea, C., Rybalchenko, A.: Synthesizing software verifiers from proof rules. In: PLDI, pp. 405–416 (2012)
8. Hutchins, M., Foster, H., Goradia, T., Ostrand, T.: Experiments of the effectiveness of dataflow- and controlflow-based test adequacy criteria. In: ICSE, pp. 191–200 (1994)
9. Kawaguchi, M., Rondon, P.M., Jhala, R.: Type-based data structure verification. In: PLDI, pp. 304–315 (2009)
10. Kawaguchi, M., Rondon, P.M., Jhala, R.: Dsolve: Safety verification via liquid types. In: Touili, T., Cook, B., Jackson, P. (eds.) CAV 2010. LNCS, vol. 6174, pp. 123–126. Springer, Heidelberg (2010)
11. Magill, S., Berdine, J., Clarke, E., Cook, B.: Arithmetic strengthening for shape analysis. In: Riis Nielson, H., Filé, G. (eds.) SAS 2007. LNCS, vol. 4634, pp. 419–436. Springer, Heidelberg (2007)
12. Magill, S., Tsai, M.-H., Lee, P., Tsay, Y.-K.: THOR: A tool for reasoning about shape and arithmetic. In: Gupta, A., Malik, S. (eds.) CAV 2008. LNCS, vol. 5123, pp. 428–432. Springer, Heidelberg (2008)
13. Nguyen, H.H., David, C., Qin, S.C., Chin, W.-N.: Automated verification of shape and size properties via separation logic. In: Cook, B., Podelski, A. (eds.) VMCAI 2007. LNCS, vol. 4349, pp. 251–266. Springer, Heidelberg (2007)

14. O'Hearn, P.W., Reynolds, J.C., Yang, H.: Local Reasoning about Programs that Alter Data Structures. In: Fribourg, L. (ed.) CSL 2001 and EACSL 2001. LNCS, vol. 2142, pp. 1–19. Springer, Heidelberg (2001)
15. Pham, T.-H., Trinh, M.-T., Truong, A.-H., Chin, W.-N.: FIXBAG: A fixpoint calculator for quantified bag constraints. In: Gopalakrishnan, G., Qadeer, S. (eds.) CAV 2011. LNCS, vol. 6806, pp. 656–662. Springer, Heidelberg (2011)
16. Podelski, A., Rybalchenko, A.: A complete method for the synthesis of linear ranking functions. In: Steffen, B., Levi, G. (eds.) VMCAI 2004. LNCS, vol. 2937, pp. 239–251. Springer, Heidelberg (2004)
17. Popeea, C., Chin, W.-N.: Inferring disjunctive postconditions. In: Okada, M., Satoh, I. (eds.) ASIAN 2006. LNCS, vol. 4435, pp. 331–345. Springer, Heidelberg (2008)
18. Popeea, C., Xu, D.N., Chin, W.-N.: A practical and precise inference and specializer for array bound checks elimination. In: PEPM, pp. 177–187 (2008)
19. Qin, S., Luo, C., Chin, W.-N., He, G.: Automatically refining partial specifications for program verification. In: Butler, M., Schulte, W. (eds.) FM 2011. LNCS, vol. 6664, pp. 369–385. Springer, Heidelberg (2011)
20. Reynolds, J.: Separation Logic: A Logic for Shared Mutable Data Structures. In: IEEE LICS, pp. 55–74.
21. Rondon, P.M., Kawaguchi, M., Jhala, R.: Liquid types. In: PLDI, pp. 159–169 (2008)
22. Trinh, M.-T., Le, Q.L., David, C., Chin, W.-N.: Bi-Abduction with Pure Properties for Specification Inference (extended version) (2013) `loris-7.ddns.comp.nus.edu.sg/~project/SpecInfer/`
23. Vogels, F., Jacobs, B., Piessens, F., Smans, J.: Annotation inference for separation logic based verifiers. In: Bruni, R., Dingel, J. (eds.) FMOODS/FORTE 2011. LNCS, vol. 6722, pp. 319–333. Springer, Heidelberg (2011)

Laws of Programming for References

Giovanny Lucero[1], David Naumann[2], and Augusto Sampaio[1,*]

[1] Centro de Informática, Universidade Federal de Pernambuco
{gflp,acas}@cin.ufpe.br
[2] Dept of Computer Science, Stevens Inst of Technology
naumann@cs.stevens.edu

Abstract. We propose a set of algebraic laws for reasoning with sequential imperative programs that use object references like in Java. The theory is based on previous work by adding laws to cope with object references. The incrementality of the algebraic method is fundamental; with a few exceptions, existing laws for copy semantics are entirely reused, as they are not affected by the proposed laws for reference semantics. As an evidence of relative completeness, we show that any program can be transformed, through the use of our laws, to a normal form which simulates it using an explicit heap with copy semantics.

1 Introduction

The inherent difficulty of reasoning with pointers has been successfully addressed using different techniques for describing spatial separation of pointers, see for example [19,7,13,3]. However, there have been few initiatives using algebraic approaches [12,20], despite its well known advantages. Transformations are used in compilers, but these rely on context conditions presented algorithmically or by means of logic (as discussed in [4]); in many cases they apply only to intermediate representations. No comprehensive set of algebraic laws has been proposed to support transformations of source programs involving references.

In [10], Hoare and Staden highlight, among other advantages, the incrementality of the algebraic method. When a new programming language concept or design pattern is added, new axioms can be introduced, keeping intact at least some axioms and theorems of the existing theory of the language. Even when the new language features have an impact on the original ones, this tends to be controllable, affecting only a few laws. On the other hand, a pure algebraic presentation is based on postulating algebraic laws, which raises the questions of consistency and completeness of the proposed set of laws.

In this paper, we explore the incrementality of algebra to extend with object references a simple non-deterministic imperative language similar to that given in the seminal "Laws of Programming" by Hoare et al [9] (*LoP* for short). Our

* Authors from [1] are partially supported by the National Institute of Science and Technology for Software Engineering (INES), funded by Brazil CNPq, grant 573964/2008-4. The second author is partially supported by US NSF award CNS 1228930.

C.-c. Shan (Ed.): APLAS 2013, LNCS 8301, pp. 124–139, 2013.

language deals with references in the same way as in Java, i.e., aliasing (sharing) may only occur for fields of objects since the only operations with references are field access to read and write. There is no arithmetic on references nor operations returning addresses of variables.

Based on LoP, we generalize some laws to deal with references, in particular those related to assignments to object fields. The main difficulties are due to aliasing. We tackle them using techniques inspired in works of Morris [17] and Bornat [7] on program logic. We also propose new laws to deal with object creation and manipulation of assertions. Dynamic allocation poses challenges in semantic modeling, and thus in semantic notions of completeness [21]. As in LoP, we address the completeness of the laws by showing that any program can be transformed, by using the laws, to a normal form. Soundness of the laws is tackled in an extended report [15] by proving the validity of the laws with respect to a naive denotational semantics (which suffices because we only consider first order programs).

Our work is in a wider context of defining algebraic theories for reasoning about object-oriented programs. Previous work [6,8] defines theories for object-orientation useful to prove transformations of programs such as refactorings. However, the language used in these works has copy semantics, lacking the concept of reference and, thus, restricting the refactorings that can be characterized. By "copy semantics" we mean that it is only simple variables that are mutable; objects are immutable records (i.e., functional maps with update by copy) so aliasing cannot occur.

Our laws are intended to support program transformation and verification. They can be used, for instance, in the design of correct compilers and optimizers. Together with laws of object-orientation established in previous works, which are also valid in the context of references, they can be applied to a wider collection of refactorings and patterns which depend on the concept of reference.

In the next Section we show the abstract syntax of the language and briefly explain its constructions. Section 3 discusses how aliasing complicates the algebraic reasoning with programs and describes a substitution mechanism that deals with it. The laws are given in Section 4 and a notion of relative completeness for the proposed set of laws is shown in Section 5. Section 6 presents final considerations, including other notions of completeness, and discusses related and future works. Proofs and further details appear in the long version of this paper [15].

2 The Language

The programming language we consider is sequential and imperative. It extends that in LoP by including object references as values and assignments to object fields. The language is statically typed, thus each variable and field has a statically declared type. Formalization of types is routine and omitted.

The abstract syntax is in Figure 1. In this grammar x, X, f, and K range over given sets representing names for variables, recursive commands, fields of

c	$::=$	$x \leftarrow \mathbf{new}\, K \mid \overline{le} := \overline{e} \mid$	new instance, simultaneous assignment
		$\bot \mid [e] \mid \mathbf{skip} \mid c\,;\; c \mid$	abort, assertion, skip, sequence
		$c \lhd e \rhd c \mid c \cup c \mid e * c \mid$	conditional, non-determinism, while
		$\mu X \bullet c \mid X$	recursion, recursive call
le	$::=$	$x \mid \mathbf{null}.f \mid le.f \mid le \lhd e \rhd le$	variable, field, conditional
e	$::=$	$e\ op\ e \mid e \lhd e \rhd e \mid$	binary operator (e.g. ==), conditional
		$x \mid e.f \mid \mathbf{null} \mid \mathbf{false} \mid 0 \mid 1 \mid \ldots$	variable, field access, constants, others
cd	$::=$	$\mathbf{class}\ K\ \{\overline{f : T}\}$	class declaration
T	$::=$	$K \mid \mathbf{bool} \mid \mathbf{int}$	types
$prog$	$::=$	$\overline{cd} \bullet c$	program

Fig. 1. The Syntax of the Language

objects, and classes, respectively. The non terminal symbols cd, T, c, le and e are used for class declarations, types, commands, left expressions and expressions, respectively. As a convention, a line above syntactic elements denotes a list of them. Thus, for example, we use $\overline{e}$ to abbreviate a list $e_1, e_2, \ldots e_n$ of expressions, for some n. But the identifier $\overline{e}$ has no relation with the identifier e which represents any single expression not necessarily in $\overline{e}$. The empty list is written as "()".

A class declaration defines a named record type, i.e., $\mathbf{class}\ K\ \{\overline{f : T}\}$ declares a class with name K and fields $\overline{f : T}$. There are no methods and all the fields in the class are public. In our laws of commands, we assume there is a fixed set of class declarations which may be mutually recursive.

Like in Java, variables or fields of primitive types, **bool** and **int**, store values of the corresponding types. On the other hand, any variable or field having some K as its declared type does not store an object instance of K but a reference to it. This is the main difference of our language with respect to [6,8] where a copy semantics is adopted and variables/fields hold full objects.

The expression $\mathbf{null}.f$ is allowed, though it always aborts, because it may arise from the application of laws.

The language has all the programming commands given in LoP, extended with commands for creation of objects, assertions and richer left expressions for assignments to fields. We omit specification constructs like angelical choice. We use the same syntax as in LoP, e.g., $b \lhd e \rhd c$ and $e * c$ are conditional and iteration commands corresponding to the **if** and **while** of Java, respectively. In both cases e is the guard condition. For recursion we use the notation $\mu X \bullet c$, which binds X and defines a command where recursive calls can happen within c. The while command can be defined in terms of the μ construct: $e * c \ \widehat{=}\ \mu X \bullet c;\ X \lhd e \rhd \mathbf{skip}$.

The non-deterministic command $b \cup c$ denotes the demonic choice between b and c. The command $\bot$, also known as abort, represents the behaviour of a failing program. It is the most non-deterministic program since its execution may result in any state or may even fail to terminate.

The simultaneous assignment $\overline{le} := \overline{e}$ requires the same size for both lists, and, of course, the same type for each corresponding left and right expression. The assignment is executed by evaluating all the expressions in $\overline{e}$ and then assigning each resulting value to the corresponding left expression in $\overline{le}$. The assignment command in our language differs from that of LoP in some important aspects. First, it is allowed to have empty lists at each side of ":=". Indeed, we can define **skip** as $() := ()$, whose execution always ends successfully without performing any change. Second, left expressions are richer than those in LoP where only variables are allowed. Here, left expressions can also be fields of objects or even conditional left expressions.

Notably, it is allowed to have repeated left expressions on the left-hand side list of ":=". When this happens, the execution is non-deterministic. For example, the execution of $x, x := 1, 2$ assigns either 1 or 2 to x. This kind of non-determinism can happen even with syntactically distinct left expressions when the left-hand side list includes aliased fields, so we may as well allow it for variables as well.

The command $x \leftarrow$ **new** K creates in the heap a new instance of the class K and assigns its reference to x. The fields of the new instance are initialized by default with 0 for **int**, false for **bool** and **null** for objects.

Assertions are denoted by $[e]$, where e is a boolean expression. $[e]$ is a command that behaves like **skip** when e evaluates to **true** and like $\bot$ otherwise. Our assertions use only program expressions and can be defined in terms of more basic operators: $[e] \hat{=} \mathbf{skip} \triangleleft e \triangleright \bot$. However, assertions may refer to a distinguished variable, **alloc**, which in any state holds the set of currently allocated references. This device has been used in some program logics (e.g., [3]).

As usual we model input and output by the global variables of the main program. These global variables are assumed to have implicit type declarations.

We use a, b, c to stand for commands, d, e for expressions, f, g, k for field names, m for case lists (defined in Subsection 3.2), p, q, r stand for left expressions, x, y, z stand for variables, K stands for class names and T stands for type names, i.e. primitive types and classes.

3 Aliasing and Substitution

A fundamental idea behind algebra of programs [9,16,1], as well as in Hoare Logic and many other formalisms, is that variable substitution can capture the effects that assignments produce on expressions. However, when the language has references, several obstacles emerge. The main difficulty resides in the possibility of aliasing, which happens when two or more expressions or left expressions point to a single object field.

3.1 The Problem of Aliasing

Consider the following law, as originally presented in LoP, where aliasing is not possible. It combines two sequential assignments into a single one. The notation $d^{\overline{x}}_{\overline{e}}$ denotes a simultaneous substitution on d where each variable in the list $\overline{x}$ is replaced by the corresponding expression in $\overline{e}$. This law captures the behavior of the first assignment in the sequence through syntactic substitution.

$$(\overline{x} := \overline{e}\,;\ \overline{x} := \overline{d}) \quad = \quad \overline{x} := \overline{d^{\overline{x}}_{\overline{e}}} \triangleleft \mathfrak{D}\overline{e} \triangleright \bot \qquad (*)$$

Just like in LoP, we assume that for every expression e there is an expression $\mathfrak{D}e$ for checking if e is defined. We assume that $\mathfrak{D}e$ is always defined. For example, $\mathfrak{D}(x/y)$ is given by $y \neq 0$. Considering the left-hand side of the equation (*) above, if $\overline{e}$ is undefined it will behave as $\perp$. This justifies the checking for definedness on the right-hand side.

Under the conditions given in LoP, where the left-hand side $\overline{x}$ is a list of variables without duplicates, the law is valid. But our language allows duplicates on left-hand sides. Obviously, in this case the law does not make sense since the substitution $\overline{d}^{\overline{x}}_{\overline{e}}$ will not be well defined.

Moreover, because of the possibility of aliasing, we get in trouble if we apply the law to assignments with fields as left expressions. Note that a variable always denotes the same memory cell both in the first and in the second assignment on the left-hand side of the law. This is not true with fields. For example, in the command $x, x.f := a, b;\ x, x.f := x, x.f + 1$, the left expression $x.f$ in the second assignment may be referring to a different cell from that in the first since x may have changed to reference an object referenced by a.

It is well known that, with pointers or array, such a law is not valid if naive substitution is used for left expressions. For example, for the command $p.f := p.f + 1;\ p.f := p.f + q.f$, a naive substitution $(p.f + q.f)^{p.f}_{p.f+1}$ will give always $(p.f + 1) + q.f$, ignoring the possibility of aliasing between $p.f$ and $q.f$.

In order to generalize law (*) above for our language, we prefix a guard asserting that the left expressions of the first assignment are pairwise disjoint and, furthermore, that the left expressions of both assignments refer to the same cells. Also, we need to use a substitution mechanism that deals with aliasing and simultaneous assignments. In the following subsection we give a precise definition of substitution. We give the generalization of law (*) in Section 4 – see law (33).

Like in Java, aliasing may only occur for fields of objects. More precisely, field accesses as $p.f$ and $p.g$, where f and g are different field names, can never have the same *lvalues*, i.e, will never be aliased. On the other hand, $p.f$ and $q.f$ are aliased if and only if $p == q$, meaning that p and q hold the same value (object address). For simplicity we consider field names to be globally unique, i.e., distinct classes use distinct field names.

We define a state predicate $alias[p, q]$ that is true if and only if p and q are aliased. For convenience, we consider that any left expression is aliased with itself. We are using square brackets to stress that the arguments of *alias* are not semantic values but syntactic elements. Note however that the aliasing checking is state dependent. By recursion on structure we define

$$
\begin{array}{rlrl}
alias[x, x] & \hat{=}\ \mathbf{true} & alias[p.f, q.g] & \hat{=}\ \mathbf{false} \\
alias[x, y] & \hat{=}\ \mathbf{false} & alias[p \triangleleft e \triangleright q, r] & \hat{=}\ alias[p, r] \triangleleft e \triangleright alias[q, r] \\
alias[x, p.f] & \hat{=}\ \mathbf{false} & alias[p, q] & \hat{=}\ alias[q, p], \quad \textit{otherwise} \\
alias[p.f, q.f] & \hat{=}\ p == q & &
\end{array}
$$

where $x \not\equiv y$ and $f \not\equiv g$. We write $\equiv$ to mean syntactically the same.

3.2 Substitution

For substitution we borrow ideas from Bornat [7] who defines a field substitution operator for languages that treat references like in Java, as our language does. Like we do in this paper, he also assumes that distinct types of objects use distinct field names, which is useful to simplify the definition. We write $e^{f}_{\{f:p\mapsto d\}}$ to denote the expression obtained by syntactically replacing occurrences of the field name f by the *conditional field* $\{f : p \mapsto d\}$. A conditional field access $e_1.\{f : p \mapsto d\}$ is interpreted as being $d \lhd e_1 == p \rhd e_1.f$.

As an illustrative example, consider the effect caused by the assignment $x.f := e$ on the expression $x.f + y.g + z.f$. This effect is given by the following field substitution

$$\begin{array}{ll}
(x.f + y.g + z.f)^{f}_{\{f:x\mapsto e\}} = & \text{(def. of substitution)} \\
\quad x.\{f : x \mapsto e\} + y.g + z.\{f : x \mapsto e\} = & \text{(desugaring)} \\
\quad (e \lhd x == x \rhd x.f) + y.g + (e \lhd x == z \rhd z.f) = & (x == x \text{ is true}) \\
\quad e + y.g + (e \lhd x == z \rhd z.f) &
\end{array}$$

As expected, observe that, contrasting to the initial expression, in the resulting expression $x.f$ was replaced by e and $z.f$ by a conditional indicating that if $x.f$ and $z.f$ are aliased, $z.f$ also will be replaced by e, but if there is no such aliasing $z.f$ will be kept intact.

Field substitution also works for expressions containing nested accesses to fields. For example, it is easy to see that

$$(x.f.f)^{f}_{\{f:y\mapsto e\}} \;=\; e \lhd (e \lhd x == y \rhd x.f) == y \rhd (e \lhd x == y \rhd x.f).f$$

Because our language has simultaneous assignments, we need to extend Bornat's operator to work with simultaneous substitutions of fields and variables. We start by defining a syntax sugar. A *case expression* is defined by

$$\begin{array}{l}
\textbf{case } e \textbf{ of } e_1 \to d_1, \ldots, e_n \to d_n \textbf{ else } d_{n+1} \;\widehat{=} \\
\qquad\qquad\qquad d_1 \lhd e == e_1 \rhd (\ldots (d_n \lhd e == e_n \rhd d_{n+1}) \ldots)
\end{array}$$

Note that the order of the items in the case list is important, since it is chosen the first ith branch such that $e == e_i$.

We use m to represent case list like $e_1 \to d_1, \ldots, e_n \to d_n$. We then extend the notion of conditional field by allowing case lists and define

$$e.\{f : m\} \;\widehat{=}\; \textbf{case } e \textbf{ of } m \textbf{ else } e.f$$

Consider a list $\overline{xf}$ containing variable names and field names, and a corresponding list $\overline{em}$ containing expressions and conditional fields. Suppose the list $\overline{xf}$ has no repeated variable or field names, each variable in $\overline{xf}$ corresponds positionally to an expression in $\overline{em}$, and each field f in $\overline{xf}$ corresponds to a conditional field $\{f : m\}$ in $\overline{em}$. We denote with $e^{\overline{xf}}_{\overline{em}}$ the simultaneous substitution on e of each element in $\overline{xf}$ by the corresponding element in $\overline{em}$. For example, $e^{x,f,y}_{d_1,\{f:m\},d_2}$ represents the simultaneous substitution on e of x by d_1, f by $\{f : m\}$ and y by d_2.

We relax the notation to allow duplication of fields, but not variables, in $\overline{xf}$. In this case we interpret that the corresponding conditional fields are concatenated into a single one. For example, $e^{x,f,y,f,g}_{d_1,\{f:m_1\},d_2,\{f:m_2\},\{g:m_3\}}$ (with $f \not\equiv g$) can be written as $e^{x,f,y,g}_{d_1,\{f:m_1,m_2\},d_2,\{g:m_3\}}$. Note that in the conditional field $\{f : m_1, m_2\}$ the cases on m_1 have priority over those in m_2, since the order in a case list is relevant. Our simultaneous substitution prioritizes the first listed field substitutions, which may appear arbitrary. However, in our laws all uses of simultaneous substitutions will be for *disjoint assignments*, i.e., guarded by assertions that ensures that the left expressions reference distinct locations.

Field substitution can also be applied to left expressions. However, we need a slightly different notion because left values and right values need to be treated differently. We use $le^{/f}_{\{f:m\}}$ to denote a field substitution on the left expression. The idea is that a field substitution applied on a left expression like $x.f_1.f_2 \ldots f_n$ always ignores the last field, keeping it in the result, i.e.,

$$(le.g)^{/f}_{\{f:m\}} \;\widehat{=}\; le^{f}_{\{f:m\}}.g$$

even when f and g are the same name field. The field substitution on the right side of the equation is that described above for expressions.

4 The Laws

In this section we give an algebraic presentation for our imperative language. In general, our laws are either the same or generalizations of those in LoP. Furthermore, as one might expect, the only laws to be generalized are those related to assignment. Also, we establish a few orthogonal laws only related to references, for example one that allows to exchange a left expression by another aliased with it.

Our laws can be proved sound in a simple denotational model like that described in LoP. The main difference is that our program states include the heap as well as valuation of the variables in scope. A command denotes a relation from initial states to outcomes, where an outcome is an ordinary state or the fictitious state $\perp$ that represents both divergence and runtime error. For any initial state s, if the related outcomes include $\perp$ then s must also relate to all states; otherwise, the image of s is finite and non-empty. In this semantics, refinement is simply inclusion of relations, and equations mean equality of denotations. The semantics is parameterized on an arbitrary allocator that, for any state, returns a finite non-empty set of unused references (so **new** is boundedly non-deterministic).

A shortcoming of this simple semantics is that it does not validate laws like $x \leftarrow$ **new** $K = x \leftarrow$ **new** K; $x \leftarrow$ **new** K for which equality of heaps is too strong. An appropriate notion of program equality considers heaps up to bijective renaming of references (as in [2]). In this paper, we do not need such laws because the normal form reduction preserves allocation order.

$$\overline{p}, \overline{q}, \overline{r} := \overline{e_1}, \overline{e_2}, \overline{e_3} = \overline{q}, \overline{p}, \overline{r} := \overline{e_2}, \overline{e_1}, \overline{e_3} \quad (1)$$

$$\overline{p} := (\overline{e_1} \lhd d \rhd \overline{e_2}) = (\overline{p} := \overline{e_1}) \lhd d \rhd (\overline{p} := \overline{e_2}) \quad (2)$$

$$\mu X \bullet F(X) = F(\mu X \bullet F(X)) \quad (3)$$

$$F(Y) \sqsubseteq Y \Rightarrow \mu X \bullet F(X) \sqsubseteq Y \quad (4)$$

$$b \lhd \textbf{false} \rhd c = c = c \lhd \textbf{true} \rhd b \quad (5)$$

$$b \lhd d \Rightarrow e \rhd c = (b \lhd e \rhd c) \lhd d \rhd b \quad (6)$$

$$c \lhd e \rhd c = c \lhd \mathfrak{D} e \rhd \bot \quad (7)$$

$$(b \lhd e \rhd c) \lhd \mathfrak{D} e \rhd \bot = b \lhd e \rhd c \quad (8)$$

$$(a \lhd e \rhd b);\ c = (a;\ c) \lhd e \rhd (b;\ c) \quad (9)$$

Fig. 2. Selected laws kept intact from LoP [9]

Figure 2 lists some laws given in LoP that do not depend on references and therefore remain intact. For lack of space, we do not explain in detail these laws here. Readers not familiar with them are referred to [9].

The refinement relation, $\sqsubseteq$, is defined by $b \sqsubseteq c \mathrel{\widehat{=}} (b \cup c) = b$. The set of programs with $\sqsubseteq$ is a semi-lattice, where $\cup$ is the meet and $\bot$ the bottom, and all the command constructions are monotonic (indeed, continuous). Law (3) on recursion says that $\mu X.F(X)$ is a fixed point and law (4) that it is the least fixed point.

4.1 Laws for Assertions

We will be especially concerned with assertions that enable reasoning about aliasing. In Figure 3 we provide a set of laws that allow to decorate commands with assertions. Some of these laws add information brought from the conditions of conditional and while commands. Others spread assertions forward in the commands deducing them from some already known assertions at the beginning. Assertions are defined as syntax sugar, and all these laws are derived except for law (22) which is proved directly in the semantics using the definition of *alias*.

Laws (10)–(21) for assertions should be familiar. Law (22) enables to replace one alias by another. The hypothesis for laws (23) and (24) may be better understood if we interpret it through partial correctness assertions (triples) from Hoare logic. Observe that when an equation $[e_1];\ c = [e_1];\ c;\ [e_2]$ holds, if and when the execution of $[e_1];\ c$ finishes, $[e_2]$ must be equivalent to **skip**, which is the same as saying that e_2 must hold. That is exactly the same meaning intended for a triple $\{e_1\}c\{e_2\}$ from Hoare logic (cf. [14]). Laws (23) and (24) state that any invariant is satisfied at the beginning of each iteration and at the end of the loop.

We give an additional law for assertions that expresses the axiom for assignment in Hoare logic. For this we need some definitions. A *path* is a left expression that does not use conditionals, i.e., a path is a variable x, or a sequence of field accesses using the dot notation like $e.f.g$, for example. Given an assignment on paths $\overline{p} := \overline{e}$, we define functions *vf* and *em* to build a corresponding substitution. Define $vf[x] = x$ if x is a variable, $vf[p.f] = f$ and $vf[\overline{p}]$ is obtained applying *vf* to every element of $\overline{p}$. Also, for each e_i in $\overline{e}$, we define $em[e_i] = e_i$,

$$[e];\ c = c \lhd e \rhd \bot \quad (10)$$

$$[d \wedge e] = [d];\ [e] \quad (11)$$

$$b \lhd e \rhd c = ([\mathfrak{D}e];\ b) \lhd e \rhd c \quad (12)$$

$$b \lhd e \rhd c = b \lhd e \rhd ([\mathfrak{D}e];\ c) \quad (13)$$

$$b \lhd e \rhd c = ([e];\ b) \lhd e \rhd c \quad (14)$$

$$b \lhd e \rhd c = b \lhd e \rhd ([\mathbf{not}\ e];\ c) \quad (15)$$

$$[e];\ (b \lhd d \rhd c) = ([e];\ b) \lhd d \rhd ([e];\ c) \quad (16)$$

$$[e];\ (b \cup c) = ([e];\ b) \cup ([e];\ c) \quad (17)$$

$$e * c = e * ([\mathfrak{D}e];\ c) \quad (18)$$

$$e * c = (e * c);\ [\mathfrak{D}e] \quad (19)$$

$$e * c = e * ([e];\ c) \quad (20)$$

$$e * c = (e * c);\ [\mathbf{not}\ e] \quad (21)$$

$$[alias[q,r]];\ \overline{p}, q := \overline{e}, d = [alias[q,r]];\ \overline{p}, r := \overline{e}, d \quad (22)$$

If $[d \wedge e];\ c = [d \wedge e];\ c;\ [d]$ then

$$[d];\ e * c = [d];\ e * ([d];\ c) \quad (23)$$

$$[d];\ e * c = [d];\ (e * c);\ [d] \quad (24)$$

Fig. 3. Laws for assertions

if the corresponding $vf[p_i]$ is a variable, and $em[e_i] = \{f : p_i \mapsto e_i\}$ if $vf[p_i] = f$. Finally, $em[\overline{e}]$ is obtained applying em to each element of $\overline{e}$.

Let $\overline{p}$ be a list of paths $(p_1, p_2, \ldots, p_n)$. Define the disjointness state predicate

$$disj[\overline{p}] \mathrel{\widehat{=}} \forall i,j \bullet i \neq j \Rightarrow \mathbf{not}\ alias[p_i, p_j]$$

using "∀" as shorthand for conjunction. We have the law

$$[disj[\overline{p}]];\ [d^{vf[\overline{p}]}_{em[\overline{e}]}];\ \overline{p} := \overline{e} \quad = \quad [disj[\overline{p}]];\ \overline{p} := \overline{e};\ [d] \quad (25)$$

The assertion at the beginning of both sides of the equation ensures that the substitution $d^{vf[\overline{p}]}_{em[\overline{e}]}$ is well defined. The law states that if d is a post-condition of the assignment $\overline{p} := \overline{e}$ then $d^{vf[\overline{p}]}_{em[\overline{e}]}$ must be a precondition.

4.2 Laws for Assignment

Many of the laws for assignment (Figure 4) are guarded by assertions that say the assigned locations are disjoint.

Law (26) stipulates that attempting to evaluate the right-hand side outside its domain has a behaviour wholly arbitrary. We express that by prefixing the assertion $[\mathfrak{D}\overline{e}]$ on the assignment. Because left expressions also may be undefined, we also have law (27). The definition of $\mathfrak{D}p$ is straightforward if, for this purpose, we consider left expressions as being expressions. In Section 4.3 we determine when a field access $e.f$ is defined.

Law (28) characterizes the behaviour of simultaneous assignments to repeated left expressions as being non-deterministic. In a simultaneous assignment, if the same left expression q receives simultaneously the values of expressions d_1 and

$$\overline{p} := \overline{e} \;=\; [\mathfrak{D}\overline{e}];\ \overline{p} := \overline{e} \tag{26}$$

$$\overline{p} := \overline{e} \;=\; [\mathfrak{D}\overline{p}];\ \overline{p} := \overline{e} \tag{27}$$

$$\overline{p}, q, q := \overline{e}, d_1, d_2 \;=\; \overline{p}, q := \overline{e}, d_1 \,\cup\, \overline{p}, q := \overline{e}, d_2 \tag{28}$$

$$[\forall\, i \bullet \textbf{not}\ alias[p_i, q]];\ \overline{p}, q := \overline{e}, q \;=\; [\mathfrak{D}q \wedge \forall\, i \bullet \textbf{not}\ alias[p_i, q]];\ \overline{p} := \overline{e} \tag{29}$$

$$\textbf{skip} \;=\; () := () \tag{30}$$

$$\overline{p}, (q \lhd d \rhd r) := \overline{e}, e \;=\; (\overline{p}, q := \overline{e}, e) \lhd d \rhd (\overline{p}, r := \overline{e}, e) \tag{31}$$

Let $\overline{p}$ be a list of paths $(p_1, p_2, \ldots, p_n)$, then we have

$$[disj[\overline{p}]];\ \overline{p} := \overline{e};\ (b \lhd d \rhd c) = [disj[\overline{p}]];\ (\ \overline{p} := \overline{e};\ b \lhd d^{vf[\overline{p}]}_{em[\overline{e}]} \rhd \overline{p} := \overline{e};\ c\ ) \tag{32}$$

$$\begin{pmatrix} [disj[\overline{p}] \wedge alias[\overline{p}, \overline{q}^{/vf[\overline{p}]}_{em[\overline{e}]}]]; \\ \overline{p} := \overline{e};\quad \overline{q} := \overline{d} \end{pmatrix} = \begin{pmatrix} [disj[\overline{p}] \wedge alias[\overline{p}, \overline{q}^{/vf[\overline{p}]}_{em[\overline{e}]}] \wedge \mathfrak{D}\overline{e}\ ]; \\ \overline{p} := \overline{d}^{vf[\overline{p}]}_{em[\overline{e}]} \end{pmatrix} \tag{33}$$

Fig. 4. Laws for Assignment

d_2, there will occur a non-deterministic choice between both values and one of them will be assigned to q.

Law (29) is a generalization of a similar one given in LoP, but it is conceived to deal with non-determinism. It establishes that a simple assignment of the value of a left expression back to itself has no effect, when the expression is defined. We can add (or eliminate) such a dummy assignment to a simultaneous assignment whenever no non-determinism is introduced (eliminated). Note that if $\overline{p}, q$ is composed only by non-repeated variables then the assertion will be trivially true, and thus law (29) becomes the same established in LoP.

Law (31), when used from left to right, eliminates conditionals in left expressions. If we have a conditional left expression, we can pass the responsibility for checking the condition to a conditional command. This law resembles assignment law (2) in Figure 2 in that it behaves the same but for expressions on the right-hand side of assignments.

Law (34) below can be used together with (31) for transforming any assignment in an equivalent one where left expressions have no conditional. This transformation can be useful to enable the use of law (25).

$$(p \lhd e \rhd q).f \;=\; p.k \lhd e \rhd q.f \tag{34}$$

Law (32) states that when we have a disjoint assignment to paths followed by a conditional command, the assignment can be distributed rightward through the conditional, but changing occurrences of the assigned paths in the condition to reflect the effects of the assignment. Note that the assertion ensures that the assignment is disjoint, and therefore the substitution applied on the condition d is well defined.

$$x \leftarrow \mathbf{new}\, K \;=\; x \leftarrow \mathbf{new}\, K;\; x.f := \mathit{default}(f) \tag{35}$$

$$[y == \mathbf{alloc}];\; x \leftarrow \mathbf{new}\, K \;=\; [y == \mathbf{alloc}];\; x \leftarrow \mathbf{new}\, K;\; [x \neq \mathbf{null} \wedge x \notin y \wedge \mathbf{alloc} == y \cup \{x\}] \tag{36}$$

if x does not occur in $\overline{p}, \overline{e}$, then

$$x \leftarrow \mathbf{new}\, K;\; \overline{p} := \overline{e} \;=\; \overline{p} := \overline{e};\; x \leftarrow \mathbf{new}\, K \tag{37}$$

if x does not occur in d, then

$$x \leftarrow \mathbf{new}\, K;\; (b \triangleleft d \triangleright c) \;=\; (x \leftarrow \mathbf{new}\, K;\; b) \triangleleft d \triangleright (x \leftarrow \mathbf{new}\, K;\; c) \tag{38}$$

Fig. 5. Laws for **new**

Law (33) is our version for the law (*) already discussed in Subsection 3.1. This law permits merging two successive assignments to the same locations (variables or fields). The first conjunct in the assertion guarantees that the first assignment is disjoint, thus the substitutions $\overline{q}^{/vf[\overline{p}]}_{em[\overline{e}]}$ and $\overline{d}^{vf[\overline{p}]}_{em[\overline{e}]}$ will be well defined. In particular, note that $\overline{q}^{/vf[\overline{p}]}_{em[\overline{e}]}$ and $\overline{d}^{vf[\overline{p}]}_{em[\overline{e}]}$ denote the left value of $\overline{q}$ and the value of $\overline{d}$, respectively, after the execution of the assignment $\overline{p} := \overline{e}$. The second conjunct in the assertion states that the left expressions $\overline{p}$ and $\overline{q}$ are referring to same locations, and thus the assignments can be combined into a single one.

4.3 Laws for the new Command

The **new** construction in our language is a command. It cannot be handled as an expression because it alters the state of the program and our approach assumes side-effect-free expressions. The laws for **new** are given in Figure 5. Recall that there is a distinguished variable **alloc** which does not occur in commands except in assertions; its value is always the set of allocated references. Any attempt to access a field of a non allocated reference will be undefined. Thus, we have as definition that $\mathfrak{D} e.f \;\widehat{=}\; \mathfrak{D} e \wedge e \in \mathbf{alloc} \wedge f \in \mathit{fields}(e)$, where $\mathit{fields}(e) = \mathit{fields}(\mathit{type}(e))$ and $\mathit{type}(e)$ returns the class name of e. Recall that our laws are in an implicit context $\overline{cd}$ of class declarations and context Γ for types of variables; so the type of e is statically determined.

Law (35) determines that any field of a new object will be initialized with the default value. The value of $\mathit{default}(f)$ is 0, **false** or **null** depending on the type of f declared in K. Law (36) establishes that $x \leftarrow \mathbf{new}\, K$ assigns to x a fresh reference of type K and adds it to **alloc**. Law (37) allows to exchange the order of a **new** followed by an assignment, if the assignment does not depends on the created new object. Finally, law (38) distributes a **new** command to the right, inside a conditional, if the condition does not depend on the created new object.

5 Completeness

Our main result says that any command can be reduced to an equivalent one that simulates the original command by using a temporary variable representing explicitly the heap through copy semantics. The simulating program never accesses fields in the heap, neither for writing nor for reading. Instead, it just uses the explicit heap where any update is done by means of copy semantics. Reduction of a program to this form is used as a measure of the comprehensiveness of the proposed set of laws.

The explicit representation of the heap is given by a mapping from references to explicit objects and, in turn, every explicit object is represented by a mapping from field names to values. We assume there is a type, *Object*, of all object references, and a type, *Value*, of all primitive values (including **null**) and elements of *Object*. We also assume the existence of a type *Heap* whose values are mappings with the signature $Object \rightarrow (FieldName \rightarrow Value)$. *FieldName* is another primitive type whose values are names of fields. We assume the expression language includes functional updates of finite maps; we use Z notation so $h \oplus \{x \mapsto e\}$ denotes the map like h but with x mapped to the value of e.

The reduction is made in two stages. In the first stage, an arbitrary command is transformed (using the laws) into an equivalent one whose assignments are all disjoint and with paths as left expressions.

Theorem 1. *For any command c there is a provably equivalent one such that each assignment in it is prefixed by an assertion and follows the form* $[dis];\ \overline{p} := \overline{e}$ *where* $\overline{p}$ *is a list of paths and dis ensures that there is no pair of aliased paths in* $\overline{p}$.

The proof uses the following ideas. In order to have just paths on left expressions, we can use systematically assignment laws (34) and (31) for eliminating conditionals. For example, it is easy to prove

$$x.f, (y \triangleleft e_1 \triangleright y.g).f := e_2, e_3 \;=\; x.f, y.f := e_2, e_3 \triangleleft e_1 \triangleright x.f, y.g.f := e_2, e_3 \quad (\dagger)$$

After the elimination of conditionals, we can use systematically the derived law stated below to transform all the assignments to disjoint ones.

$$\begin{aligned}\overline{p}, q, r := \overline{d}, e_1, e_2 = \quad & \overline{p}, q := \overline{d}, e_1 \cup \overline{p}, q := \overline{d}, e_2 \\ & \triangleleft alias[q, r] \triangleright \\ & [\mathbf{not}\ alias[q, r]];\ \overline{p}, q, r := \overline{d}, e_1, e_2\end{aligned} \quad (\ddagger)$$

To illustrate the use of our laws, we give the proof of this derived law.

$$
\begin{aligned}
&(\ \overline{p}, q := \overline{d}, e_1 \cup\ \overline{p}, q := \overline{d}, e_2\ ) \ \lhd\, alias[q,r] \rhd\ [\textbf{not}\ alias[q,r]];\ \overline{p}, q, r := \overline{d}, e_1, e_2 \\
&= \text{by assert. (15)} \\
&\quad (\ \overline{p}, q := \overline{d}, e_1 \cup \overline{p}, q := \overline{d}, e_2\ ) \ \lhd\, alias[q,r] \rhd\ \overline{p}, q, r := \overline{d}, e_1, e_2 \\
&= \text{by assign. (28)} \\
&\quad \overline{p}, q, q := \overline{d}, e_1, e_2 \ \lhd\, alias[q,r] \rhd\ \overline{p}, q, r := \overline{d}, e_1, e_2 \\
&= \text{by assert. (14)} \\
&\quad\quad [alias[q,r]];\ \overline{p}, q, q := \overline{d}, e_1, e_2 \ \lhd\, alias[q,r] \rhd\ \overline{p}, q, r := \overline{d}, e_1, e_2 \\
&= \text{by assert. (22)} \\
&\quad\quad [alias[q,r]];\ \overline{p}, q, r := \overline{d}, e_1, e_2 \ \lhd\, alias[q,r] \rhd\ \overline{p}, q, r := \overline{d}, e_1, e_2 \\
&= \text{by assert (14) \& LoP (7)} \\
&\quad \overline{p}, q, r := \overline{d}, e_1, e_2 \ \lhd\, \mathfrak{D} alias[q,r] \rhd \bot \\
&= \text{by } \mathfrak{D}(\overline{p}, q, r) \Rightarrow \mathfrak{D} alias[q,r] \text{ \& LoP (6,8)} \\
&\overline{p}, q, r := \overline{d}, e_1, e_2.
\end{aligned}
$$

Continuing the example (†), using repeatedly law (‡), we obtain the following program where all assignments are disjoint.

$$
= \left(\begin{array}{rc}
 & x.f := e_2 \cup x.f := e_3 \\
 & \lhd x == y \rhd\ \ [x \neq y];\ x.f, y.f := e_2, e_3 \\
\lhd e_1 \rhd & x.f := e_2 \cup x.f := e_3 \\
 & \lhd x == y.g \rhd\ \ [x \neq y.g];\ x.f, y.g.f := e_2, e_3
\end{array} \right)
$$

Roughly speaking, the second stage of the reduction is to transform the command in the intermediate form (obtained from the first stage, with disjoint assignments) to an equivalent one that first loads the implicit heap into an explicit heap h : *Heap*, then simulates the original command always using h instead of object fields and finally, when it finishes, restores back the contents of h to the implicit heap, i.e, updates all the object fields accordingly as they are represented in h. The domain of h will be the entire set of allocated references, i.e. **alloc**. To keep this domain we use variables mirroring **alloc** before and after the transformed command.

Following our example, suppose that e_2 is $z + x.f$. The assignment $x.f := e_2$ will be simulated using the explicit heap h by

$$
h := h \oplus \{x \mapsto \{h(x) \oplus \{f \mapsto z + h(x)(f)\}\}
$$

where h is updated by copying a new mapping equal to the original except for the value of $h(x)$, which is updated accordingly. Note that $h(x)$ represents the object referenced by x, $h(x)(f)$ represents the value of the field f of this object.

For any c, we will define a command $S[c][h, al]$ that simulates c using the explicit heap h and the **alloc** mirror al. We will also define command $load[h, al]$

that loads the contents of the objects into the explicit heap h, and $store[h, al]$ that restores back h into the objects. In these terms we can state our main result.

Theorem 2. *For any command c in the intermediate form and where h, al_0 and al_1 do not occur free we have that*

$$[al_0 == \mathbf{alloc}];\ c;\ [al_1 == \mathbf{alloc}];\ load[h, al_1];\ al_0 := al_1 = \\ [al_0 == \mathbf{alloc}];\ load[h, al_0];\ S[c][h, al_0];\ [al_1 == \mathbf{alloc}];\ store[h, al_1]$$

Because the variable h is free on the right-hand side, we need the $load[h, al_1]$ after c on the left-hand side. That is according to the standard interpretation that free variables are the input and output of commands. al_0 and al_1 can be interpreted as variables that bring the value of **alloc** at the points of the assertions. An alternative would be to introduce h, al_0 and al_1 on the right-hand side as local variables; then the assertions could be removed from both sides. But, for brevity in this paper, we omit local variable blocks.

The formal definitions of *load* and *store* are given by

$$load[h, al] \mathrel{\hat{=}} h := \{r \mapsto \{f \mapsto r.f \mid f \in fields(r)\} \mid r \in al\}$$
$$store[h, al] \mathrel{\hat{=}} r.f \underset{(r,f) \in al \times fields(r)}{:=} h(r)(f)$$

Here, $fields(r) = fields(type(r))$ where $type(r)$ returns the class name of r.

We use an indexed multiple assignment $r.f \underset{(r,f) \in al \times fields(r)}{:=} h(r)(f)$. This is an abuse of notation since the index set $al \times fields(r)$ depends on the value of al which is determined at runtime (but is finite). This, and similar constructions in the definition of *load* and in (43) and (44), could be avoided using loops; but that would complicate the normal form proof with little benefit.

The definition for the simulation $S[c][h, al]$ for commands is sketched in Figure 6. The operator $\boxplus$ used in (43) is similar to map overriding ($\oplus$) with the difference that the right operand is an uncurried map. We also define the simulation $R[e][h]$ for expressions. The proof of theorem 2 is by induction on c.

6 Conclusions and Related Work

We established a comprehensive algebraic presentation for programs that deal with references in the way Java does. Taking as a basis the classical work in LoP [9], we explored the incrementality of algebra by generalizing laws of assignment and formulating others. Our normal form theorem gives a sense in which the laws are complete. Perhaps a more standard notion of completeness is whether every semantically true equation is provable. What we know is that our denotational model is not fully abstract with respect to contextual equivalence, owing to the missing laws about **new** mentioned in Section 4. For our first order language those laws can be validated by quotienting modulo renaming, e.g., by using FM-sets, though for higher order programs that would be unsatisfactory [21].

$$R[x][h] \mathrel{\widehat{=}} x \tag{39}$$

$$R[p.f][h] \mathrel{\widehat{=}} h(R[p][h])(f) \tag{40}$$

$$R[e_1 \lhd d \rhd e_2][h] \mathrel{\widehat{=}} R[e_1][h] \lhd R[d][h] \rhd R[e_2][h] \tag{41}$$

$$S[\bot][h, a] \mathrel{\widehat{=}} \bot \tag{42}$$

$$S[\overline{x}, \overline{p} := \overline{e}, \overline{d}][h, al] \mathrel{\widehat{=}} \\ \overline{x},\ h := R[\overline{e}][h],\ h \boxplus \{(R[p_i][h], f_i) \mapsto R[d_i][h]\} \mid p_i.f_i \in \overline{p} \wedge d_i \in \overline{d}\} \tag{43}$$

$$S[x \leftarrow \mathbf{new}\ K][h, al] \mathrel{\widehat{=}} x \leftarrow \mathbf{new}\ K;\ al := al \cup \{x\}; \\ h := h \oplus \{x \mapsto \{f \mapsto \mathit{default}(f) \mid f \in \mathit{fields}(K)\}\} \tag{44}$$

$$S[c_1 \lhd d \rhd c_2][h, al] \mathrel{\widehat{=}} S[c_1][h, al] \lhd R[d][h] \rhd S[c_2][h, al] \tag{45}$$

Fig. 6. The simulations R and S using explicit heap (selected cases)

In [20] some laws are presented as an initial attempt to characterize references. However, they are not comprehensive; the law for combining assignments does not consider the possibility of aliasing on left expressions. Furthermore, the laws depend on provisos that are hard to verify statically. Other initiatives like abstract separation algebras [11] do not deal with a concrete notation for manipulation of fields. Transformations used in compilers are conditioned on alias analyses that are not expressed algebraically. Staton proves Hilbert-Post completeness for a equational theory of ML-style references. The language lacks field update and null (and includes higher order functions and an unusual operator ref^n). The laws capture commutativity of allocations and aspects of locality, but the step from this work to handling refactorings in object-oriented programs is big.

A fundamental notion for our laws is field substitution. Inspired by the works of Bornat [7] and Morris [17] on program correctness, we adapt Bornat's definition for our language by extending it to deal with simultaneous assignments.

The problem approached in this paper is related with the difficulties for defining algebraic theories like those in [9,16,1] for a language with references. Like in [7], we only tackle the problem of pointer aliasing. Other kinds of aliasing, like parameter aliasing or aliasing through higher order references, are out of the scope of our work. For higher order programs, more complicated machinery is needed, e.g., content quantification as proposed in [5].

Another difficulty not addressed in this paper is caused by aliasing in combination with recursive data structures. This usually requires dealing with assertions with inductive formulas, and reasoning with substitution and aliasing can explode into numerous conditionals [7]. Note, however, that assertions in our laws use no inductive predicates, only boolean expressions involving pointer equalities. We intend to provide mechanisms for local reasoning as those proposed in [19,7,13,3] in an extension of our theory when dealing with a more expressive object-oriented language. In particular, we would like to connect the present work with that of Silva et al [18] where denotational semantics is used to prove refactoring laws from which others are derived. The goal is algebraic proof of refactoring laws based ultimately on basic laws like our extension of LoP, just as the works [6,8] do for object-oriented progams with copy semantics. In future work we will explore other laws for **new**, seeking to avoid the use of the implicit variable **alloc** in assertions.

References

1. Back, R.J.R., van Wright, J.: Refinement calculus: a systematic introduction. Springer (1998)
2. Banerjee, A., Naumann, D.: Ownership confinement ensures representation independence for object-oriented programs. J. ACM 52, 894–960 (2005)
3. Banerjee, A., Naumann, D.A., Rosenberg, S.: Local reasoning for global invariants, part I: Region logic. Journal of the ACM 60, 18:1–18:56 (2013)
4. Benton, N.: Simple relational correctness proofs for static analyses and program transformations. In: POPL, pp. 14–25 (2004)
5. Berger, M., Honda, K., Yoshida, N.: A logical analysis of aliasing in imperative higher-order functions. SIGPLAN Not. 40(9), 280–293 (2005)
6. Borba, P., Sampaio, A., Cavalcanti, A., Cornélio, M.: Algebraic reasoning for object-oriented programming. Science of Computer Programming (2004)
7. Bornat, R.: Proving pointer programs in Hoare logic. In: Backhouse, R., Oliveira, J.N. (eds.) MPC 2000. LNCS, vol. 1837, pp. 102–126. Springer, Heidelberg (2000)
8. Cornélio, M., Cavalcanti, A., Sampaio, A.: Sound refactorings. Science of Computer Programming (2010)
9. Hoare, C.A.R., et al.: Laws of programming. Communications of the ACM 30(8) (1987)
10. Hoare, C.A.R., Staden, S.: In praise of algebra. Formal Aspects of Computing, 423–431 (2012)
11. Hoare, T., Möller, B., Struth, G., Wehrman, I.: Concurrent Kleene algebra and its foundations. J. Log. Algebr. Program. 80(6), 266–296 (2011)
12. Jifeng, H., Li, X., Liu, Z.: rCOS: A refinement calculus of object systems. Theoretical Computer Science 365(1-2), 109–142 (2006)
13. Kassios, I.T.: The dynamic frames theory. Formal Aspects of Computing 23, 267–288 (2011)
14. Kozen, D.: On Hoare logic and Kleene algebra with tests. In: ACM Trans. Comput. Logic. (July 2000)
15. Lucero, G., Naumann, D., Sampaio, A.: Laws of programming for references, long version (2013), `http://www.cs.stevens.edu/~naumann/pub/LuceroNSfull.pdf`
16. Morgan, C.: Programming from specifications. Prentice-Hall, Inc. (1990)
17. Morris, J.: A general axiom of assignment. In: Broy, M., Schmidt, G. (eds.) Theoretical Foundations of Programming Methodology (1982)
18. Naumann, D.A., Sampaio, A., Silva, L.: Refactoring and representation independence for class hierarchies. Theoretical Computer Science 433, 60–97 (2012)
19. O'Hearn, P., Reynolds, J., Yang, H.: Local reasoning about programs that alter data structures. In: Computer Science Logic (2001)
20. Silva, L., A., Sampaio, Z.L.: Laws of object-orientation with reference semantics. In: IEEE Software Engineering and Formal Methods (2008)
21. Staton, S.: Completeness for algebraic theories of local state. In: Ong, L. (ed.) FOSSACS 2010. LNCS, vol. 6014, pp. 48–63. Springer, Heidelberg (2010)

Dynamic Alias Protection with Aliasing Contracts

Janina Voigt and Alan Mycroft

Computer Laboratory, University of Cambridge
JJ Thomson Avenue, Cambridge CB3 0FD, UK
Firstname.Lastname@cl.cam.ac.uk

Abstract. Object-oriented languages allow any object to point to any other object, limited only by type. The resultant possible aliasing makes programs hard to verify and maintain.

Much research has been done on *alias protection schemes* to restrict aliasing. However, existing schemes are either informal (design-pattern-like) or static type-like systems. The former are hard to verify, while the latter tend to be inflexible (e.g. shared ownership is problematic).

We introduce *aliasing contracts*: a novel, dynamic alias protection scheme which is highly flexible. We present JACON, a prototype implementation of aliasing contracts for Java, and use it to quantify their runtime performance overheads. Results show that aliasing contracts perform comparably to existing debugging tools, demonstrating practical feasibility.

1 Introduction

In typical object-oriented (OO) programming languages, object variables do not contain objects directly, but references to (addresses of) other objects. Multiple variables can contain the same address and thus point to the same object at the same time; this is known as *aliasing*.

Aliasing is an important feature of OO because it allows sharing of objects between different parts of a program; this is essential for the efficient implementation of important programming idioms, including iterators over collections. However, aliasing reduces modularity and encapsulation; an aliased object can be accessed and modified through any of the references pointing to it, without the knowledge of the others; this can create bugs which are difficult to trace.

Many modern OO programming languages provide *access modifiers* such as `private`, `protected` and `public`. These modifiers limit the scope of the variable, but do not protect the *object* to which the variable points.

For example, consider the program in Listing 1. Class `Person` provides a getter method `getName` for its `myName` field, which returns a reference to the object in `myName`. Although `myName` is declared to be `private`, any client can call `getName`, obtain an alias for the object in `myName` and modify it without the knowledge of the `Person`, for example by calling `setLastName`.

C.-c. Shan (Ed.): APLAS 2013, LNCS 8301, pp. 140–155, 2013.

```
public class Person {
  private Name myName;
  public Name getName() {
    return myName;
  }
}
```

```
Person p = new Person();
Name n = p.getName();
n.setLastName("Smith");
```

Listing 1. Access modifiers protect only the variable, not the object

A number of *alias protection schemes* have been proposed to avoid situations like this and protect the *object* rather than just the variable from unwanted accesses. However, they tend to be too inflexible and restrictive in practice and have not yet been widely adopted by the programming community.

The contributions of this paper are two-fold: firstly, in Section 3 we introduce a novel, dynamic alias protection scheme called *aliasing contracts* which aims to be flexible and expressive, while at the same time remaining conceptually simple. Secondly, in Section 4 we present JaCon, a prototype implementation of aliasing contracts in Java; measurements of the runtime overhead caused by the dynamic checks of aliasing contracts demonstrate their practical feasibility.

The name *contract* comes from work on software contracts [11] which allow the specification of preconditions and postconditions for methods. Aliasing contracts allow developers to annotate a variable with assumptions about which parts of the system should be able to access the object to which the variable points; these assumptions are checked at runtime. In this way, aliasing contracts prevent the use of unintentionally leaked references, as the reference in the example above, making them particularly valuable during the testing phase of a project.

Aliasing contracts also provide a unifying model of alias protection; aliasing contracts can model existing alias protection schemes, giving us a framework for expressing and comparing many different aliasing policies.

Our dynamic approach to alias control has similar advantages and disadvantages as dynamic type checking. It is more flexible and can cover conditions which cannot be checked statically; for example, static alias protection schemes struggle with design patterns like iterators and observers, which require sharing of objects, but they can easily be implemented with aliasing contracts. Dynamic schemes also tend to be conceptually simpler; static schemes often require more artifacts to compensate for the restrictions os static checking. On the other hand, the runtime checks required by dynamic schemes cause performance overheads. In addition, problems will only be discovered when (and if) the affected code is executed.

The timing of validity checks is also different in static and dynamic checking. Like dynamic type checking, we check the validity of an object access directly before the access is made at runtime. Static alias protection schemes instead restrict assignments so that references cannot be leaked in the first place.

2 Background

The literature on aliasing and its control is huge; see [5] for a detailed description. Here, we summarise the main strands of research for completeness.

The overall idea of alias control is to construct software engineering "design patterns"—or more formal programming language structures—to discipline programmer use of aliasing; a key concept is *encapsulation* whereby usage of some objects ("rep" objects) is restricted to certain other objects (the "owners"). Early conceptual designs include Hogg's islands [9] and Almeida's balloons [1]. They implement *full encapsulation*: each object is either encapsulated within another object or shared; any object reachable through an encapsulated object is also encapsulated. To increase flexibility (though at the cost of soundness) Hogg and Almeida restrict only pointers from fields of other objects ("static aliasing") but allow pointers from local variables and method parameters ("dynamic aliasing")—the latter being more transient and easier to track.

Clarke-style ownership types [6] added significantly to the subject area by showing a type-like system could capture aliasing restrictions (later known as *owners-as-dominators*) and that these could be checked statically.

Clarke-style ownership types require each object to have a *single* owner and also do not allow ownership of an object to be transferred at runtime; this makes them too inflexible to deal with common idioms such as iterators. Follow-up work partially addressed these shortcomings, introducing multiple ownership types [10], ownership with inner classes [2], gradual ownership types [15], and Universe types (*owners-as-modifiers*) [12].

There has also been some work on dynamic ownership. Gordon et al. [7] propose a system where ownership information is checked at runtime. Like our dynamic aliasing contracts, dynamic ownership types do not directly restrict aliasing itself, but allow any references to exist; instead, they limit how these references can be used. Gorden-style dynamic ownership types differ from our work since they support only one particular aliasing policy (owners-as-dominators), while aliasing contracts support many different ones.

Another approach to alias protection is that of capabilities [4,8] and permissions [3,19]. Capabilities and permissions associate access rights with each object reference, specifying whether the reference is allowed to, for example, read, write or check the identity of an object. This can be used to model various aliasing conditions, such as uniqueness and borrowing.

Throughout the vast literature on alias protection schemes, there is no unifying framework which can be used to embed and compare them. Boyland et al.'s [4] capabilities do this to some extent, but at a relatively low level where there is a large semantic gap to be bridged between them and high-level constructs like owners-as-dominators. Aliasing contracts provide a unifying, language-level framework which can be used to express and compare existing alias protection schemes.

3 Aliasing Contracts

This work proposes aliasing contracts which express and enforce restrictions about the circumstances under which an object can be accessed. Here, we give a basic overview of aliasing contracts; [18] presents aliasing contracts in more detail and proposes a syntax operational semantics. More detail also appears in the first author's forthcoming PhD thesis.

An aliasing contract consists of two boolean expressions, e^{r} and e^{w}, attached to a variable declaration. (Note that in this paper we use the term *variable* to refer to fields, local variables and method parameters.) An access to an object is permitted only if the contracts of *all* variables currently pointing to the object are satisfied; contracts thus essentially specify dynamically determined, conjunctive *preconditions* for object accesses. The expression e^{r} specifies preconditions for *read* accesses, while e^{w} concerns write accesses. Where the read and write contract expressions are the same, one can be omitted for convenience; we call such a contract a *rw-contract* (read-write-contract).

The distinction between read and write accesses requires a similar distinction between *pure* and *impure* methods: pure methods do not modify any state and may be called with read access permissions, while impure methods require both read and write access permissions.

For each contract, we call the nearest enclosing object the contract's *declaring* object. When the contract is evaluated, evaluation takes place in the context of its declaring object; that is `this` points to the declaring object. We can regard a contract as a `boolean` method of the class which declares it (and this is how we implement it in Section 4).

A contract may be any valid, *side-effect-free* boolean condition. Contracts have access to two special variables, in addition to `this`: `accessed` points to the object being accessed and `accessor` points to the object whose method is making the access. The value of `accessor` is determined immediately prior to contract evaluation; for a single contract, `accessor` varies between evaluations. Thus, an alternative view of a contract is a method which takes an object parameter (`accessor`) and returns a boolean value.

Listing 1 gave a program which leaks a reference from the `private` variable `myName`, thus making the object accessible and modifiable by any client. To address this problem, we instead annotate `myName` with the rw-contract "`accessor == this || accessor == accessed`" to enforce encapsulation:

```
Name myName {accessor == this || accessor == accessed};
```

This contract signifies that only the enclosing `Person` object and the `Name` object itself will be able to access the object in `myName`. The contract is evaluated in the context of the declaring object, the enclosing `Person` object; it will only evaluate to `true` if `accessor` is equal to `this` or if `accessor` and `accessed` are the same object; that is, if the access comes from the `Person` or from the `Name` itself. If a client now obtains a reference to the object in `myName` by calling `getName`, it will not be allowed to use it to read or write the object.

Alternatively, we could loosen the contract slightly to "`true, accessor == this || accessor == accessed`". This contract corresponds to an *owners-as-modifiers* approach [12]; it would allow any client to read the `Name` object (the read contract is "`true`") but would continue to prohibit write accesses.

Aliasing contracts are very flexible since their evaluation depends on the current state and aliasing structure of the program. If a client in the example above obtains a reference to a `Name` object by calling `getName` in a `Person` object, it cannot initially access it due to the contract on `myName`. Aliasing contracts do not restrict aliasing itself, but object accesses: obtaining the reference in this situation is legal but using it is not. If the `myName` field in the `Person` object is then pointed to a new `Name` object, the `Name` object referenced by the client will become accessible; the `myName` field's contract no longer applies to it.

Since aliasing contracts depend on the dynamic aliasing structure of a program at the time an access to an object is made, they cannot in general be verified statically. Instead, they need to be checked at runtime; when a contract violation is detected, an error is reported (cf. static and dynamic type checking).

Contract checks need to be performed for each object access, including field accesses, field updates and method calls. Reads and writes to local variables and parameters do not trigger contract evaluations; they represent accesses and modifications to the unaliased *stack*. Similarly, constructor calls do not change existing heap objects of themselves and thus do not require contract checks.

For each object access, we first retrieve all contracts which currently apply to the accessed object and evaluate them. Thus we track, for each object, which variables currently point to it. The conjunctive nature of contract evaluation means that if any contract evaluates to `false`, the entire evaluation fails.

Note that if there are multiple contracts to evaluate, the order in which they are evaluated is irrelevant. Expressions in contracts may not have side-effects; this means that a contract can change neither the state of the program nor its aliasing structure and therefore cannot affect other contract evaluations.

Although similar to assertions in spirit, aliasing contracts are significantly more expressive; the contracts which are evaluated depend on the aliasing structure of the program. An implementation must track references to determine exactly which contracts apply to an object. Alising contracts also have advanced features (briefly discussed in Section 6) which allow the expression of complex conditions that cannot be described using standard Java boolean expressions.

Extensions for Real-life OO Languages. Our theory of aliasing contracts is clean and simple—every object access causes a contract check—but real programming languages have more complex features that we need to address.

In particular, `static` methods do not fit well with our object-based approach. In accesses from `static` methods, there is no `accessor` object; in calls to `static` methods, there is no `accessed` object.

We address this problem by always allowing calls *to* `static` methods, since no `accessed` object means that there are no contracts to consider. In accesses *from* `static` methods, we set `accessor` to `null`; this causes contracts such as "`accessor == this`" to fail, while contracts which do not use `accessor` (such as "`true`" or "`false`") behave as expected.

Many modern OO languages include variables of primitive types, which store values instead of references to objects; values cannot be aliased and therefore accessessing them does not require contract checks.

Other language features, on the other hand, do not require special treatment due to the dynamic nature of aliasing contracts. Inheritance, for example, fits naturally and objects of inner classes can be treated just like other objects. Fields are inherited by subclasses, along with their contracts, but cannot be overridden; to fit with existing inheritance semantics, we similarly disallow the overriding of contracts in subclasses.

4 JaCon: Practical Aliasing Contracts for Java

We have implemented a prototype, JaCon, which supports the definition of aliasing contracts in Java programs and performs contract evaluations at runtime. The prototype consists of a modified Java compiler and a runtime library (which we call the *contract library* below). The compiler injects calls to the contract library into the source code, allowing it to monitor contracts at runtime. The code for our contract library is avaliable at `www.cl.cam.ac.uk/~jv323/contractlibrary`.

We chose Java as our base programming language since it is the most popular object-oriented programming language [17] and is used in a large number of open-source systems. However, Java is a relatively complex language with many different features, making the prototype implementation non-trivial. For example, Java's non-linear execution flow, caused by exceptions and `break` and `continue` statements, complicates the tracking of contracts.

For our prototype implementation, we modified the compiler *javac* of the OpenJDK 6 [14] to inject calls to the contract library.

Contracts are parsed and converted into anonymous inner classes extending our abstract `Contract` class; one such `Contract` class is created for each syntactically distinct contract expression in a class. Each of these `Contract` classes overrides the method `checkContract`, which can be called by the contract library to evaluate the contract. The `checkContract` method takes two parameters, `accessor` and `accessed`, both of type `Object`; the contract expression becomes the method's return statement. For example, the contract "`accessor == this || accessor == accessed`" of the `myName` field of `Person` from our example in Section 3 is transformed into

```
public Contract _contractPerson42 = new Contract() {
  public boolean checkContract(Object accessor, Object accessed) {
    return accessor == Person.this || accessor == accessed;
  }
};
```

We note that any references to `this` in the contract expression must be transformed to `OuterClass.this` in order to refer not to the `Contract` object but to the contract's enclosing object; in the example above, `this` becomes `Person.this`.

The contract library tracks the `Contracts` which apply to each object and invokes their `checkContract` methods when they need to be evaluated.

Contracts are registered and de-registered when an assignment occurs; `myName = newName` points `myName` away from the object it currently points to and to the object currently also pointed to by `newName`. This change of aliasing requires modification of the set of contracts associated with these two objects; to this end, JaCon inserts two calls to the contract library, one to de-register the contract of variable `myName` before the assignment and one to register the contract after the assignment. The assignment `myName = newName` becomes

```
ContractLibrary.removeContract(myName, _contractPerson42);
myName = newName;
ContractLibrary.addContract(myName, _contractPerson42);
```

Registration and de-registration of contracts is complicated by Java's non-linear flow of execution caused by, for example, exceptions. Contracts of local variables have to be removed at the end of the block in which they are declared; after this the variables are no longer available and their contracts should not persist. Exceptions are problematic because an exception causes execution to leave a block prematurely. We therefore wrap each block in a `try-finally` statement and remove local variable contracts in the `finally` block to ensure correct contract de-registration even when an exception is thrown.

Contract de-registration also takes place when an object is garbage collected; at this point, finalisation causes all of its `Contracts` to be deallocated and thus removed from the objects to which they applied. We discuss the implications of garbage collection in more detail in Section 6.

Registration and de-registration as explained above allow us to track which contracts apply to each object at any point in the program's execution. This tracking of contracts is equivalent to tracking of references for each object, which in itself is potentially useful; it means that JaCon could also be used to investigate the topology of the heap, independent of aliasing contracts.

Calls to the contract library to check contracts are inserted before any accesses and updates to fields. As explained above, accesses and updates to local variables do not require contract checks. For example, the assignment `x.f = y.g` contains a write access to `x` and a read access to `y`; it becomes

```
ContractLibrary.checkWriteContracts(x);
ContractLibrary.checkReadContracts(y);
x.f = y.g;
```

Methods may be declared `pure` or `impure`; if no method purity is given, JaCon automatically determines its purity. Calls to `pure` methods require read contract checks to be performed, while calls to `impure` methods need to trigger both read and write contract checks. Appropriate contract checks are inserted at the entry to the method bodies (rather than in the caller).

Finally, the contract library needs to keep track of which object is currently executing a method; this gives the value of `accessor` for contract evaluations. For this purpose, it maintains a call stack of the objects; calls to notify the contract library of context changes are inserted around each method body:

```
public void foo() {
  ContractLibrary.enterContext(this);
  ...
  ContractLibrary.leaveContext();
}
```

Our contract library implementation tracks and evaluates contracts correctly in the presence of concurrency. For example, accesses to the contract stores are synchronised and separate call stacks are maintained for each thread.

Optimisations. A naive implementation of aliasing contracts, as described above, performs many unnecessary contract checks; we have implemented optimisations to avoid such checks and improve the performance of JaCon.

A common contract is "`true`", meaning that there are no restrictions on object access. Since this contract obviously always evaluates to `true`, there is no need to store or evaluate it.

Evaluating all contracts every time an object is accessed is inefficient. JaCon includes an optimisation which allows it to skip many contract evaluations; it divides contracts into three categories.

- Contracts whose result does not change for different `accessor` objects and is not affected by changes to variables. Such contracts, for example, include the contracts "`true`" and "`false`". They need to be evaluated only *once*.
- Contracts whose result changes for different `accessor` objects but which are not affected by changes to fields. This includes the contract "`accessor == accessed`". These contracts need to be evaluated only *once for each distinct* `accessor` object. The contract "`accessor == this`" also falls into this category, as the value of `this` never changes for a given object.
- Contracts which depend on values of fields or call methods, for example "`accessor == this.f`" or "`accessor == getFoo()`". These contracts need to be evaluated every time an access is made, since the value of fields and return value of methods may have changed since the previous evaluation.

JaCon's contract library classifies contracts as above and uses this information to track which contracts need to be evaluated when an object is accessed and which contracts can be skipped.

5 Performance Evaluation

One of the main problems with aliasing contracts is the runtime performance overhead they cause; each assignment causes contracts to be added and removed, every object access triggers a contract check.

```
class SimpleExample {
  public void run()
    Bar b = new Bar();
    Foo[] foos = new Foo[NUM_OBJ];
    for(int i = 0; i < NUM_OBJ; i++){
      Foo f = new Foo();
      foos[i] = f;
      f.bar = b;
      b.num = i; // †[here]
    }
  }
}
```

```
class Foo {
  public Bar bar {<contract>};
}

class Bar {
  // Primitive types do not
  // have contracts.
  public int num;
}
```

Listing 2. A simple program measuring object access time at †`[here]`

Using JACON, we try to quantify this performance overhead. First, we investigate how the number of contracts for an object impacts the time taken to perform a single object access with contract checks. We also estimate the performance of real-world software using four open-source programs.

Performance measurements were made on a Windows laptop with 8GB of RAM and a 2.5GHz Intel Core i5 processor. All values stated below are averages of at least five separate measurements.

Performance for a Single Object Access. Whenever an object access is made, all contracts associated with the object must be checked. The time required for the object access thus increases with the number of contracts, assuming that all contracts need to be evaluated. If we assume that each contract is a simple boolean condition which can be evaluated in constant time, contract checking time increases linearly with the number of contracts of the object.

To measure object-access time, we construct a simple test program, shown in Listing 2. The program executes a loop, adding one reference (and hence contract) to an object `b` of type `Bar` per iteration. The assignment `b.num = i` performs a write access to the `Bar` object in `b`, causing all contracts associated with it to be checked. By measuring the time taken for this access on every iteration, we can measure how the object access time varies with the number of contracts.

We also vary the expressions of the contracts (marked as `<contract>` in Listing 2) to see how different contract expressions influence object access time.

Table 1 presents the results of our measurements; it shows the number of milliseconds required *for a single object access* depending on the number of contracts associated with the accessed object. The table shows results for three different contracts, highlighting the huge difference in performance they cause.

The contracts `alwaysTrue()` and `alwaysFalse()` call a method which always returns `true` or `false` respectively. JACON cannot optimise evaluation, since the contracts involve a method call; they needs to be re-evaluated for each object access. For the contract `alwaysTrue()`, contract checking time thus increases

Table 1. Time in milliseconds per object access for varying number n of contracts associated with the accessed object and varying contract expressions

n	`alwaysTrue()` (always succeeds)	`alwaysFalse()` (always fails)	`accessor==this||accessor==accessed` (always succeeds in this example)
0	0	0	0
5,000	0.84	0.0099	0.011
15,000	3.93	0.0038	0.0032
25,000	6.82	0.00084	0.00074
35,000	8.93	0.00060	0.00038
65,000	15.11	0.00040	0.00068
95,000	19.37	0.00054	0.00056

with the number of contracts, adding around two milliseconds for every 10,000 contracts. However, for the contract `alwaysFalse()` the very first contract evaluates to `false`, making it unnecessary to check the remaining contracts. Thus, the time required for each object access is very low and does not change as the number of contracts for the object increases.

The contract `accessor == this || accessor == accessed` always evaluates to `true` in the example given (but not in the general case). The contract depends on the value of `accessor` but is not affected by changes to fields; thus, it needs to be evaluated only once per `accessor`. Since `accessor` is always the same (the `SimpleExample` object running the loop), each contract needs to be evaluated exactly once; this means that for every iteration, only one contract is evaluated—the newly added contract. Time taken to access the object therefore matches the `alwaysFalse()` case and does not change as the number of contracts for the object increases.

Our measurements for the above example show that the time taken to access an object increases linearly with the number of contracts, for contracts whose evaluation is not optimised. Nevertheless, contract evaluation continues to appear feasible in this case, as long as the number of contracts remains low; we believe it is unlikely to have more than 10,000 references pointing to the same object at once, even in a large program.

We further suggest that even if there are many references to a single object, the performance presented above is unlikely to occur. In practice, it is difficult to construct a case where all contracts evaluate to `true` but none of them can be optimised. All of the contracts which we expect to be most commonly used, including "`true`", "`false`", "`accessor == this`", "`accessor == accessed`" and "`accessor instanceof Foo`" can be optimised by JaCon as outlined above and only need to be evaluated either once or once for each distinct `accessor`. This significantly cuts the number of required contract evaluations, making evaluation efficient even when many contracts are associated with a single object.

Case Studies. To study the performance of real-world software using aliasing contracts, we selected four open-source programs written in Java: JGraphT (`http://jgrapht.org`), JUnit (`http://junit.org/`), NekoHTML (`http://nekohtml.sourceforge.net`) and Trove (`http://trove.starlight-systems.`

Table 2. Version, size measurements and number of test cases of the test programs

Program	Version	Date	Source Files	Classes	Lines of Code	Test Cases
JGraphT	0.8.3	19/01/2012	188	270	34,266	152
JUnit	4.10	29/09/2011	168	281	13,276	524
NekoHTML	1.9.18	27/02/2013	32	60	13,262	222
Trove	3.0.3	15/02/2013	697	1,603	240,555	548

Table 3. Compilation Performance

Program	Compilation time (javac0)	Bytecode size (javac0)	Compilation time (javac1)	Bytecode size (javac1)
JGraphT	4.3 s	667 kB	7.3 s	1,182 kB
JUnit	2.3 s	524 kB	4.2 s	886 kB
NekoHTML	17.5 s	264 kB	29.7 s	444 kB
Trove	18.8 s	5,153 kB	31.2 s	8,797 kB

Table 4. Runtime Performance

Program	Time (javac0)	Time (javac1)	Ratio (javac1)	Time (ref tracking only)	Ratio (ref tracking only)
JGraphT	4.7 s	99.2 s	20.8	53.4 s	11.2
JUnit	13.1 s	21.0 s	1.6	16.4 s	1.4
NekoHTML	1.9 s	3.5 s	1.8	2.6 s	1.4
Trove	5.6 s	62.5 s	11.3	21.2 s	3.7

com). Table 2 shows version, size measurements and number of test cases for these programs.

We selected four programs from different domains. JGraphT is a graph library which implements various graph data structures and associated graph algorithms. It involves complex data structures likely to lead to interesting aliasing properties and runs algorithms with high asymptotic complexities; this means that its performance with aliasing contracts is likely to be particularly bad.

The Trove library provides high performance collections for Java. Again, the data structures it builds are likely to lead to interesting aliasing properties.

NekoHTML is an HTML scanner and tag balancer. As parsing involves a lot of comparatively slow input and output, we expect the performance of NekoHTML to be less strongly influenced by the presence of aliasing contracts.

JUnit is a well-known program to support unit testing for Java. It does not involve large data structures and complex algorithms and we therefore expect JUnit's performance to degrade only slightly when using aliasing contracts.

All four programs have been updated in the last two years. They include extensive unit test suites, making them suitable for performance evaluation.

Our test programs include thousands of lines of code, making it impossible for us to manually annotate them with contracts. Instead, we use default contracts for all variables. To get realistic results, we selected the contracts which we believe would be most common in practice: "`true`" for local variables and method parameters, as well as public fields, and "true, accessor == this || accessor == accessed" for non-public fields. These contracts are based on the assumption that objects stored in non-public fields are intended to be encapsulated and should be readable but not be modifiable from the outside. This corresponds to an owners-as-modifiers [12] approach.

These default contracts caused relatively few contract violations, indicating that they give a good approximation of the encapsulation used in the programs (and therefore of any manually added aliasing contracts). In Trove, we recorded the lowest rate of contract violation, at 9.3 percent (783,351 of 8,453,603 contract evaluations). NekoHTML had a highest rate of contract violation at 22.2 percent (17,612 of 79,295), while in JUnit and JGraphT the violation rates were 13.3 and 18.0 percent respectively.

We compiled each of the programs twice, first using the standard compiler (called javac0 below) and then using our the modified compiler (javac1 below). For both compilations, we noted the time taken by the compiler as well as the size of the generated Java byte code in bytes.

Table 3 shows the results of these measurements; they show that compiling a program with javac1 takes between 1.6 and 2.0 times longer than using the standard compiler; this closely corresponds to the amount of byte-code generated, which is around 1.6 to 1.8 times larger using javac1.

We also measured the time taken to execute the test suites when compiled with both of the compilers. In addition, we measured performance when contracts were only tracked by the contract library but not evaluated; this is equivalent to tracking of references for each object, for example for investigating the topology of the heap. Table 4 shows the measurement results.

The runtime measurements show that JGraphT runs 21 times more slowly with aliasing contracts than usual. While this is a significant decrease in performance, it is caused by a small number of test cases; 44 of 51 test suites run less than 10 times more slowly with contracts; the remaining 7 execute between 14 and 91 times more slowly. The situation is similar in Trove: only 5 of 26 test suites are slowed down by more than a factor of 10 in the presence of contracts.

For example, the worst-performing test suite in JGraphT is called FibonacciHeapTest, running 91 times more slowly with than without contracts. It builds up a fibonacci heap, performing 20,000 insertions followed by 10,000 removals. Building such a large and complex data structure requires numerous object accesses and assignments (leading to a lot of contract checks, additions and removals), explaining the observed performance overhead.

Trove runs around 11 times more slowly with aliasing contracts than normally. NekoHTML, as expected, is less affected by the presence of aliasing contracts due to the amount of input and output involved in its test cases; it runs 1.8 times more slowly with aliasing contracts. JUnit's performance is also only slightly affected by contracts, slowing down by a factor of 1.6.

Merely tracking contracts but not evaluating them roughly halved the performance overhead; this effect was particularly marked in Trove, which ran almost 4 times faster when only tracking references. This shows that the contract library spends roughly half of the time evaluating contracts and the other half tracking them. These results also show the feasibility of using JACON as a tool for tracking references to objects independently of aliasing contracts.

Java's garbage collection statistics indicate the impact of aliasing contracts on memory usage. We observed a significant increase in heap size for JGraphT and Trove, the two programs whose performance was most strongly affected by aliasing contracts. For JGraphT, the maximum heap size recorded in the presence of aliasing contracts was 722 kB, compared to 53 kB without contracts. This result is consistent with both the large increase in execution time for JGraphT, as well as the number of contract additions performed by JGraphT, more than 200 million. Similarly, Trove triggered around 12 million contract additions and showed an increase in maximum heap size of around 200 kB. For the remaining programs, maximum heap size increased by less than 35 kB, reflecting significantly lower number of contract additions they perform (around 210,000 for NekoHTML and 430,000 for JUnit).

6 Discussion

Aliasing contracts are a novel approach to alias protection. They gain much of their flexibility by using dynamic rather than static checking; this allows the definition of complex encapsulation policies. Below, we highlight and discuss some important considerations about aliasing contracts.

Runtime Performance. The case studies we conducted using four open-source Java programs show that aliasing contracts can cause significant performance overheads. However, we observed a wide range of behaviour; some programs, including JUnit and NekoHTML, were barely affected by aliasing contracts and would remain fully usable in the presence of contracts; others, including JGraphT, experienced severe decrease in performance, rendering the programs difficult to use in practice.

We argue that the effects of aliasing contracts vary depending on certain program attributes. The main performance issue occurs when many variables refer to the same object and re-assignment of variables is frequent. These conditions occur, for example, in programs building complex data structures, involving many assignments to build the data structure and many object accesses to visit it. We can see this effect in the performance of JGraphT's unit tests and in the example program in Listing 2.

Although unacceptable in release versions of a program, the performance overhead we measured is not a significant issue during the testing phase of a project. Executing the unit tests of our test programs in the presence of aliasing contracts is feasible, given the performance we recorded. This demonstrates that it is indeed possible to use aliasing contracts as a testing and debugging tool. Our results show that the performance of aliasing contracts is comparable to existing debugging tools such as Valgrind [13]; for Valgrind, some programs run up to 58 times more slowly using Valgrind, although the slow-down factor is below 20 for most programs.

Our case studies have also demonstrated JACON's robustness and ability to handle real-world software; we used it to generate more than 400,000 lines of code and execute multiple large test cases. This demonstrates its robustness and ability to handle real-world software.

Contract registration and de-registration (via hash tables) and contract evaluation are 'sensible' implementations which have only been optimised in terms of whether repeated evaluation is necessary. JACON was built as proof-of-concept; we suspect more attention to low-level implementation would expose further performance improvement of 2–5 times in contract tracking and evaluation.

Garbage Collection. In Java, objects persist until there are no more references to them and they are eventually garbage collected (at an unspecified time). This inherent uncertainty about how long objects exist significantly influences the semantics of aliasing contracts and indeed Java finalisation itself.

An object's fields (and the references they store) persist in memory until finalisation. But when should the associated contracts be removed? This is connected to the somewhat philosophical question about how long an object exists; does the object "die" when it becomes unreachable or when it is garbage collected?

We could remove the contracts of an object's fields when it is no longer reachable. However, this is complex to implement, requiring sophisticated tracking of references beyond simple reference counting. Alternatively, the contracts could persist (along with the object's references) until the object is garbage collected.

We take the second approach in our implementation for practical reasons and because it fits better with Java's approach to references; an object's fields and the references they store remain in memory until garbage collection, and so do their contracts. This means that the contract of an object waiting to be garbage collected can cause contract violation; garbage collection can remove contract violations but never introduce them.

Advanced Features of Aliasing Contracts. We have presented only the basic aspects of aliasing contracts; more detail is available in [18]. Two powerful features which were not discussed here are *encapsulation groups* and *contract parameters*. Encapsulation groups allow objects to be grouped, making it possible to refer to a whole group in a contract rather than just single objects. Encapsulation groups can also be specified recursively, enabling deep and transitive contract specifications. The power of encapsulation groups lies in the fact that they can contain an unlimited of objects, which may vary at runtime. This, for example, makes it possible to group all nodes in a linked list, without knowing exactly how many nodes will be in the list at runtime:

```
class LinkedList {
  Node head;
  group allNodes = {head,
    head.nextNodes};
}
```

```
class Node {
  Node next;
  group nextNodes = {next,
      next.nextNodes};
}
```

The encapsulation group `nextNodes` in `Node` contains all subsequent nodes in the list: `next` and all nodes following it (`next.nextNodes`). The group `allNodes` in `LinkedList` contains all nodes in the list, `head` and all nodes following it (`head.nextNodes`). At runtime, JACON evaluates these groups by resolving all paths in the group definitions to objects.

Groups can be referenced in contracts using the `in` operator; for example, the contract "`accessor in list.allNodes`" checks if `accessor` is in the set of objects described by `list.allNodes`, that is if it is a node of `list`. Using this contract, we can, for example, express the condition that all nodes in a linked list should have mutual access to each other. This example demonstrates how encapsulation groups can be used to specify transitive aliasing conditions.

Contract parameters make it possible for different instances of the same class to exhibit different aliasing behaviour. A class can take contract parameters which must be instantiated when an object of the class is created; the parameters can be used as contracts in the class, changing aliasing behaviour of objects of the class depending on the contract instantiations provided.

With encapsulation groups and contract parameters aliasing contracts can directly express the aliasing policies enforced by existing static alias protection schemes, including Clarke-style ownership types [6] and universe types [12]. They can also express many aliasing conditions not expressible with existing schemes.

7 Conclusions and Further Work

We have presented a novel, dynamic approach to alias protection called aliasing contracts. They are a general and flexible scheme, able to model a wide variety of different aliasing policies, including those already enforced by static schemes.

We have developed a prototype implementation for aliasing contracts in Java, JACON; by running JACON on open-source programs, we have demonstrated the practical feasibility of aliasing contracts, for example during the testing phase of a project. Our tests have shown that JACON can handle significant programs and that its performance is comparable to existing debugging tools like Valgrind.

We are currently developing a static checker to check many common aliasing contracts at compile-time. This would allow us to eliminate some contracts during the compilation process, leaving only the more complex ones to be checked at runtime; combining the static verifier with JACON will significantly improve performance. Combining static and dynamic checking of contracts is analogous to gradual typing [16], which combines static and dynamic type checking to gain the advantages of both.

We are also working on allowing temporary suspension of contracts; this can be used to model borrowing [4], where access to an object is granted *temporarily*, for example for the duration of a method call.

Acknowledgements. The authors thank the Rutherford Foundation of the Royal Society of New Zealand for the scholarship which supported this work, and the anonymous referees for their helpful suggestions.

References

1. Almeida, P.: Balloon types: Controlling sharing of state in data types. In: Akşit, M., Matsuoka, S. (eds.) ECOOP 1997. LNCS, vol. 1241, pp. 32–59. Springer, Heidelberg (1997)
2. Boyapati, C., Liskov, B., Shrira, L.: Ownership types for object encapsulation. In: POPL, pp. 213–223. ACM (2003)
3. Boyland, J.: Checking interference with fractional permissions. In: Cousot, R. (ed.) SAS 2003. LNCS, vol. 2694, pp. 55–72. Springer, Heidelberg (2003)
4. Boyland, J., Noble, J., Retert, W.: Capabilities for sharing: A generalisation of uniqueness and read-only. In: Lindskov Knudsen, J. (ed.) ECOOP 2001. LNCS, vol. 2072, pp. 2–7. Springer, Heidelberg (2001)
5. Clarke, D., Östlund, J., Sergey, I., Wrigstad, T.: Ownership types: A survey. In: Clarke, D., Noble, J., Wrigstad, T. (eds.) Aliasing in Object-Oriented Programming. LNCS, vol. 7850, pp. 15–58. Springer, Heidelberg (2013)
6. Clarke, D., Potter, J.M., Noble, J.: Ownership types for flexible alias protection. ACM SIGPLAN Notices 33, 48–64 (1998)
7. Gordon, D., Noble, J.: Dynamic ownership in a dynamic language. In: DLS: Dynamic Languages Symposium, pp. 41–52. ACM (2007)
8. Haller, P., Odersky, M.: Capabilities for uniqueness and borrowing. In: D'Hondt, T. (ed.) ECOOP 2010. LNCS, vol. 6183, pp. 354–378. Springer, Heidelberg (2010)
9. Hogg, J.: Islands: aliasing protection in object-oriented languages. In: OOPSLA, pp. 271–285. ACM (1991)
10. Li, P., Cameron, N., Noble, J.: Mojojojo - more ownership for multiple owners. In: FOOL (2010)
11. Meyer, B.: Writing correct software with Eiffel. Dr. Dobb's Journal 14(12), 48–60 (1989)
12. Müller, P., Poetzsch-Heffter, A.: Universes: A type system for controlling representation exposure. In: Poetzsch-Heffter, A., Meyer, J. (eds.) Programming Languages and Fundamentals of Programming (1999)
13. Nethercote, N., Seward, J.: Valgrind: a framework for heavyweight dynamic binary instrumentation. In: PLDI, pp. 89–100 (2007)
14. Oracle Corporation: OpenJDK (2013), `http://openjdk.java.net`
15. Sergey, I., Clarke, D.: Gradual ownership types. In: Seidl, H. (ed.) Programming Languages and Systems. LNCS, vol. 7211, pp. 579–599. Springer, Heidelberg (2012)
16. Siek, J., Taha, W.: Gradual typing for functional languages. In: Scheme and Functional Programming Workshop (September 2006)
17. TIOBE software: TIOBE programming community index for (May 2013), `http://www.tiobe.com/index.php/content/paperinfo/tpci/index.html`
18. Voigt, J., Mycroft, A.: Aliasing contracts: a dynamic approach to alias protection. Technical Report UCAM-CL-TR-836, University of Cambridge, Computer Laboratory (June 2013)
19. Westbrook, E., Zhao, J., Budimlić, Z., Sarkar, V.: Practical permissions for race-free parallelism. In: Noble, J. (ed.) ECOOP 2012. LNCS, vol. 7313, pp. 614–639. Springer, Heidelberg (2012)

Fine-Grained Function Visibility for Multiple Dispatch with Multiple Inheritance

Jieung Kim[1], Sukyoung Ryu[2], Victor Luchangco[3], and Guy L. Steele Jr.[3]

[1] Department of Computer Science, Yale University
[2] Department of Computer Science, KAIST
[3] Oracle Labs

Abstract. Object-oriented languages with multiple dispatch and multiple inheritance provide rich expressiveness but statically and modularly checking programs in such languages to guarantee that no ambiguous calls can occur at run time has been a difficult problem. We present a core calculus for Fortress, which provides various language features—notably *functional methods* and *components*—and solves the problem. Functional methods are declared within traits and may be inherited but are invoked by ordinary function calls, and therefore compete in overloading resolution with ordinary function declarations. A novel component system governs "visibility" of types and functions, and allows fine-grained control over the import of overloaded functions. We formally define the type system of Fortress with a set of static rules to guarantee no ambiguous calls at run time, and mechanize the calculus and its type safety proof in COQ.

1 Introduction

A longstanding problem for systems that support multiple inheritance is what to do when a method is invoked on an object that inherits that method from multiple parents: which inherited method should be executed? More generally, when a method or a function (collectively called *functional*) is *overloaded*—that is, there are multiple declarations of the same name—which declaration should be used when the functional is invoked? Intuitively, we want to use the most specific declaration that is applicable to the call. But there might not be a unique most-specific declaration: There may be two (or more) applicable declarations that are more specific than any of the other declarations but incomparable with each other. In this case, we say the invocation is *ambiguous*. Guaranteeing that there will be no ambiguous calls at run time is difficult in object-oriented languages because some declarations that are applicable at run time might not be applicable statically.

Castagna *et al.* [4] address this problem by requiring that the signatures (i.e., the parameter types) of overloaded functional declarations form a meet-bounded lattice. This approach has been taken by several languages that support multiple dispatch and multiple inheritance, such as MultiJava [7], Cecil [5], and Dubious [14]. We have followed this approach in the Fortress programming language [1], in which this requirement is called the *Meet Rule*, and our experience is that it feels natural in practice, and that checking it statically helps expose programming errors.

C.-c. Shan (Ed.): APLAS 2013, LNCS 8301, pp. 156–171, 2013.

However, checking this condition statically is complicated by modularity: Fortress programs are partitioned into modules, each of which must import functionality from other modules that it wants to use. Fortress allows fine-grained control over the import of not only type declarations but also overloaded functional declarations, so that different modules may see different sets of declarations for a given functional. Thus, calls with the exact same arguments but from different components to dispatch to different functionals. In contrast, prior languages avoid this complication by sacrificing fine-control over importing functional declarations: in these languages, either all or none of the overloaded declarations of a functional is visible in any given program scope [2,3,5,7,11].

Fortress provides a novel solution to the "operator method problem": *functional methods* [2]. A functional method may designate any argument, not just the textually leftmost, to be treated as the "dispatch target" or "receiver" so that it can enjoy a function call syntax. Functional methods are inherited like conventional dotted methods but have the visibility of top-level functions (i.e., they are in the top-level scope of a module). Thus, they can (and must) be imported to be used in a different module, giving programmers the same fine-grained control for functional methods as for top-level functions. (For this reason, we often find ourselves preferring functional methods to dotted methods in Fortress.) However, the expressive power of functional methods does not come for free. Allowing a functional method to designate any argument as the receiver enlarges the set of overloaded declarations among which the most specific one is chosen. Selectively importing operator (functional method) declarations requires that functional methods be overloaded with top level functions, which adds complexity to the static checks to guarantee the existence of the single most specific one among them.

In this paper, we extend the state of the art in statically typed object-oriented languages with symmetric multiple dispatch and multiple inheritance by allowing each set of overloaded functional declarations to have its own visibility via fine-grained imports. We present a core calculus of Fortress in which a program can be divided into components that can be modularly type-checked, *such that the components provide complete namespace control over <u>all</u> top-level names*; names of not only types, but also overloaded functions and functional methods, may be selectively imported. The Meet Rule makes possible a modular static checking of multimethod dispatch that enables separate compilation. We used COQ [8] to mechanize the calculus to prove the soundness of its type system, guaranteeing that there are no ambiguous calls at run time. Our COQ mechanization of the calculus and type soundness proof is publicly available [10].

2 Fortress Language Features

In this section, we describe the language features of Fortress relevant to overloading, dispatch and fine-grained namespace control, and the rules that enable modular type checking.

2.1 Traits and Objects for Multiple Inheritance

Fortress organizes objects into a multiple-inheritance hierarchy based on *traits* [19]. It may be helpful to think of a Fortress trait as a Java interface that can also contain concrete method declarations, and to think of a Fortress object declaration as a Java final class. Fortress objects inherit only from traits, not other objects, and fields are not inherited. Both traits and objects may contain method declarations, and may inherit method declarations from multiple supertraits (traits that they *extend*). Thus all traits and objects form a multiple inheritance hierarchy, a partial order defined by the `extends` relationship, in which all objects are at the leaves as in Sather [22]. By separating types into traits and objects, Fortress supports multiple inheritance without suffering from conflicts between inherited fields. As in Java and similar statically typed object-oriented languages, the name of a trait or object serves as the name of a type, which is the set of all objects at or below the named position in the trait hierarchy.

2.2 Three Kinds of Functionals for Multiple Dispatch

We consider three kinds of *functionals* in Fortress: *i)* traditional dotted methods associated with objects, *ii)* top-level functions not associated with any objects as in C++ [21], and *iii)* functional methods. As in Java, dotted methods are invoked with a *dotted method call* of the form "$e.m(e_1, \ldots, e_n)$" while top-level functions and functional methods are invoked with a *functional call* of the form "$m(e_1, \ldots, e_n)$" without any dot. Dotted methods and functional methods are collectively called *methods*; top-level functions and functional methods are collectively called *functions*.

Functionals may be *overloaded*; that is, several methods within an object, and several functions declared in the same scope, may have the same name. This raises the issue of overload resolution: at run time, we must resolve the overloading to determine what code to execute for each functional call. Typically, overloading is resolved by *dispatching* to the *most specific* functional declaration from among those declarations that are accessible and applicable, where declarations are compared by their parameter types. With *symmetric multiple dispatch*, the types of all the parameters of a functional declaration are considered equally in this comparison.

In an early report [2], we considered a restriction of Fortress in which top-level functions and functional methods could not be overloaded. Removing this restriction introduced some new issues, which we address in this paper. (Fortress does not allow dotted methods to be overloaded with functional methods or top-level functions, so we do not consider this case in this paper. However, if, within the body of a trait or object, dotted methods could be invoked by functional calls and overloaded with top-level functions and/or functional methods, we can handle this case by considering every dotted method declaration to also declare a function whose parameters do not include the receiver, and include this function in the set of candidates that must satisfy the overloading rules described in Section 2.4.)

2.3 Components and Selective Imports for Modularity

A program can be divided into *modules* that can be compiled separately, and provide a form of namespace control. In Fortress, these modules are called *components*, which can contain declarations of top-level functions, traits, and objects; trait and object declarations may contain dotted methods and functional methods. A component may selectively import type names and function names from other components. One of the main

```
component IntegerToString

  trait Int
    asString() = "-" || (− self).asString()
  end

  trait Nat extends Int
    asString() =
      if self < 10
      then "0123456789"[self : self]
      else
        q = self ÷ 10
        r = self − 10 q
        q.asString() || r.asString()
      end
  end

end IntegerToString
```

```
component IntegerToStringFunction

  trait Int end

  trait Nat extends Int end

  asString(x: Int) =
    "-" || asString(−x)

  asString(x: Nat) =
    if x < 10
    then "0123456789"[x : x]
    else
      q = x ÷ 10
      r = x − 10 q
      asString(q) || asString(r)
    end

end IntegerToStringFunction
```

Fig. 1. Overloaded dotted methods (left) and top-level functions (right)

contributions of this paper is to explain how the overloading checks and the overloading resolution safely interact with the namespace control imposed by components.

Let Int and Nat name the types whose members consist of the integers and natural numbers (i.e., nonnegative integers) respectively. Thus, Nat is a subtype of Int. Then they may be implemented in the component IntegerToString as illustrated in the left side of Figure 1 (shown only in part; they might define other methods) where || denotes string concatenation, `self` denotes the receiver object (like `this` in Java), and "0123456789"[`self` : `self`] denotes indexing of the string, a linear sequence of characters, with a range of size 1. Note the members of Int are the members of Nat plus all the negative integers. The method *asString* is implemented as an overloaded method: if the receiver object is nonnegative, then the declaration in Nat is used because it is more specific, but if the receiver object is negative, then the declaration in Int is used because the one in Nat is not applicable. Both declarations are part of the intended algorithm for converting a value of type Int to a string.

Now consider the same example using top-level functions rather than dotted methods as in the right side of Figure 1. When another component M imports the component, every function declaration and every method declaration is, in effect, required to defer (that is, possibly dispatch) to other functions or methods that are accessible within component M, applicable to the arguments received, and more specific than the function or method declaration.

Finally, the example in Figure 2 uses functional methods rather than dotted methods or top-level functions. Functional methods are inherited like dotted methods—most importantly, *abstract* functional methods, carrying the obligation to provide concrete implementations, are inherited like abstract dotted methods. But they are overloaded

```
component IntegerToStringFunctionalMethod
  trait Int
    asString(self) = "-" || asString(− self)
  end

  trait Nat extends Int
    asString(self) =
      if self < 10 then "0123456789"[self : self]
      else
        q = self ÷ 10
        r = self − 10 q
        asString(q) || asString(r)
      end
  end
end IntegerToStringFunctionalMethod
```

Fig. 2. Overloaded functional methods

```
component MyProgram
  import IntegerToStringFunctionalMethod.{ asString }
  asString(x : Boolean): String = if x then "true" else "false" end
  run() = println (asString (42))
end MyProgram
```

Fig. 3. Main component importing overloaded functional methods

in the same per-component namespace as top-level functions, and the dispatch model that works for top-level functions while preserving component modularity also works for functional methods. Thus, we often find ourselves preferring functional methods to other functionals in Fortress.

We might then have another component that can be run as a "main program", which imports only the *asString* functional method from IntegerToStringFunctionalMethod as shown in Figure 3. Note that the imported *asString* functional method is overloaded with the top-level *asString* function in the importing component. As the example shows, fine-grained imports of functionals affect which functional to invoke at run time.

2.4 Static Overloading Rules

To guarantee type safety in the presence of all the features described so far, we place static restrictions on overloaded functional declarations. We require every pair of overloaded functional declarations to satisfy the following two properties:

1. **The Subtype Rule**
   Whenever the parameter type of one is a subtype of the parameter type of the other, the return type of the first must also be a subtype of the return type of the second.
2. **The Meet Rule**
   Whenever the parameter types of the two declarations have a common lower bound (i.e., a common subtype), there is a unique declaration for the same functional whose parameter type is the greatest lower bound of the parameter types of the two declarations.

The flip side of the Meet Rule is this:

3. **The Exclusion Rule**
   Whenever the parameter types of two declarations are disjoint, the pair is a valid overloading.

Based on our experience with Fortress, these rules are not difficult to obey, especially because the compiler gives useful feedback.

While the Subtype Rule and the Meet Rule are necessary for type soundness, the Exclusion Rule enlarges a set of valid overloading. Fortress allows programmers to declare that two traits *exclude* each other (that is, no object can belong to both traits) and it also provides structural exclusion relationships. Each object type implicitly excludes every other object type because no object can extend them; an object type implicitly excludes types that are not its ancestors in the trait hierarchy. Also, a type of one parameter list excludes a type of another parameter list, if the sizes of the parameter lists are different, or any of their constituent types at the same position exclude each other. For simplicity, we consider only structural exclusion relationships rather than declared exclusion relationships in this paper. For details of a type system that handles declared exclusion relationships, see [3].

Checking the overloading rules consists of two parts: the overloaded methods in a trait are checked for validity, and overloaded top-level functions and functional methods in a component are checked for validity. In earlier work, we proposed an informal description of such overloading rules only for top-level functions and functional methods where top-level functions and functional methods may not be overloaded [2], and we proved that the overloading rules guarantee no ambiguous calls at run time [11]. In this paper, we present a system which allows overloading between top-level functions and functional methods, and fine-grained namespace control via modules and selective imports in Section 3, and we mechanize the system and the proof of its type soundness property in COQ in Section 4.

3 Calculus: MFFMM

We now define MFFMM (Modular Featherweight Fortress with Multiple dispatch and Multiple inheritance), a core calculus for Fortress. Due to space limitations, we describe only its central parts in prose in this section. The full syntax and semantics of MFFMM are available in our companion report [12].

$$\begin{array}{lcl}
p & ::= & \overline{comp}\ \texttt{import}\ \overline{M.\{\overline{i}\}}\ \overline{d}\ e \\
comp & ::= & \texttt{component}\ M\ \overline{\texttt{import}\ M.\{\overline{i}\}}\ \overline{d}\ \texttt{end} \\
i & ::= & C \mid m \\
d & ::= & td \mid od \mid fd \\
td & ::= & \texttt{trait}\ T\ \texttt{extends}\ \{\overline{T}\}\ \overline{md}\ \texttt{end} \\
od & ::= & \texttt{object}\ O(\overline{f\colon C})\ \texttt{extends}\ \{\overline{T}\}\ \overline{md}\ \texttt{end} \\
fd & ::= & m(\overline{x\colon C})\colon C = e \\
md & ::= & m(\overline{x\colon C}\ \texttt{self}^{?}\ \overline{x\colon C})\colon C = e \\
e & ::= & x \mid \texttt{self} \mid O^{M}(\overline{e}) \mid e.f \mid e.m(\overline{e}) \mid m^{M}(\overline{e})
\end{array}$$

Fig. 4. Syntax of MFFMM

3.1 Syntax and Adjustments for Components

The syntax of MFFMM is shown in Figure 4. The metavariables M ranges over component names; T ranges over trait names; O ranges over object names; C ranges over trait and object names; m ranges over function and method names; f ranges over field names; and x ranges over method and function parameter names. We write $\overline{x}$ as shorthand for a possibly empty sequence $x_1, \cdots, x_n$.

A program p is a sequence of component declarations followed by a designated "main" component. A component declaration consists of its name M, a sequence of import statements, and a sequence of top-level declarations. The main component is different from the other components in that it does not specify a name and it has a top-level expression denoting the "*run*" function of the program. For simplicity, we assume that the name of the main component is Mc, and it must not be the name of any other component. An import statement may import a set of imported items; an imported item is either a type name C or a (possibly overloaded) function name m. A top-level declaration may be a trait declaration, an object declaration, or a function declaration.

A trait or object declaration may extend multiple supertraits; it inherits the methods provided by its extended traits. It may include method declarations; a method declaration is either a dotted method declaration or a functional method declaration depending on the absence or presence of `self` in its parameter list. An object declaration may include field declarations as its value parameters. Traits and objects are collectively called types. While dotted methods in a type may be overloaded with only other dotted methods in the same type, functional methods in a type may be overloaded with not only other functional methods in the same type but also other functional methods and top-level functions in the component textually enclosing the type. Note that a dotted method may not be overloaded with a functional method nor with a top-level function.

An expression is either a variable reference, an object construction, a field access, a method invocation, or a function call. A variable reference is either a parameter name x or `self`. Note that the object name in an object construction and the function name in a function call are annotated by a component name M. As we discuss below, evaluation of a program consists of evaluation of expressions in various components, and evaluating an expression requires the component name textually enclosing the expression.

```
component MatrixLibrary
  trait Matrix extends {Object} end
  object UnitMatrix() extends {Matrix} end
end
component MyMatrixLibrary
  import MatrixLibrary.{Matrix}
  object UnitMatrix() extends {Matrix} end
  object GenUnitMatrix() extends {Object}
    gen(): UnitMatrix = UnitMatrix()
  end
end
import MatrixLibrary.{Matrix, UnitMatrix}
import MyMatrixLibrary.{GenUnitMatrix}
asString(x: Matrix): String = "Matrix"
asString(x: UnitMatrix): String = "UnitMatrix"
asString(GenUnitMatrix().gen())
```

Fig. 5. MFFMM program before the annotation phase

To support the component system with selective imports, MFFMM uses: *i)* annotations of enclosing component names on function calls and object constructions and *ii)* $actualTy_p(M, C)$, a pair of the type C appearing in M and its defining component, rather than C to take into account the component M in which the type C is defined. When a program consists of multiple components, evaluation of the program may require evaluation of the expressions in other components than the main component. Consider the example in Figure 5 where the object UnitMatrix in the component MatrixLibrary and the object UnitMatrix in the component MyMatrixLibrary are distinct types. The main component includes *asString*(GenUnitMatrix().*gen*()) which evaluates to *asString*(UnitMatrix()). Note that UnitMatrix here is the object defined in MyMatrixLibrary rather than in MatrixLibrary while the imported type UnitMatrix is imported from MatrixLibrary rather than from MyMatrixLibrary.

In order to evaluate the function call correctly, we need two pieces of information. First, we need to know in which component the function call of *asString* textually appears to collect a set of accessible (or visible) function declarations for the function call to decide which function to call. Secondly, we need to know in which component the object construction GenUnitMatrix() textually appears to know the argument type of the function call to decide which function to call. Such information is syntactically available and a simple preprocessing phase can annotate each function call and object construction with its textually enclosing component name. The annotated component names on function calls and object constructions denote the actual use sites of the functions and objects. For example, the preprocessing phase rewrites the *gen* method declaration in the object GenUnitMatrix as follows:

$$gen(): \mathrm{UnitMatrix} = \mathrm{UnitMatrix}^{\mathrm{MyMatrixLibrary}}()$$

and the function call in the main component as follows:

$$asString^{\mathrm{Mc}}(\mathrm{GenUnitMatrix}^{\mathrm{Mc}}().gen())$$

At run time, one step evaluation of the call would lead to the following:

$$asString^{\mathrm{Mc}}(\mathrm{UnitMatrix}^{\mathrm{MyMatrixLibrary}}())$$

which allows to select the correct function declaration to call:

$$asString(x\colon \mathrm{Matrix})\colon \mathrm{String} = \text{“}\texttt{Matrix}\text{”}$$

and evaluates to "`Matrix`" as desired.

As the example shows, MFFMM allows programmers to define types with the same name if they are in different components. While they do not produce any name conflicts syntactically, they may lead to name conflicts during type checking; types that are not defined nor imported by a component may not be explicitly used by the programmer but they may be implicitly available during type checking. For example, even though UnitMatrix in MyMatrixLibrary is not explicitly imported by the main component, it is available for type checking $\mathrm{GenUnitMatrix}^{\mathrm{Mc}}().gen()$. Thus, type names are not enough for identifying types but a pair of a type name and its defining component name can serve as a true identity for a type.

3.2 Static Semantics and Overloading Rules

In this section, we describe only the key rules of the static semantics especially for checking valid overloading; the full semantics is available in our companion report [12]. Type checking a program consists of checking its constituent component declarations and checking import statements, top-level declarations, overloaded functions, and the top-level expression of the main component. Checking function declarations consists of three parts: checking every pair of distinct declarations between top-level functions, between top-level functions and functional methods, and between functional methods.

Two top-level function declarations are valid if they satisfy any of the overloading rules: if their parameter types are disjoint, if one parameter type is more specific than the other, or if there exists a tie-breaking declaration between them.

A top-level function declaration and a functional method declaration in the same component may be a valid overloading if their parameter types are disjoint or the functional method declaration is more specific than the top-level function declaration. In other words, there must not be any top-level function whose signature is more specific than that of an overloaded functional method. The reason for this additional restriction is that for functional methods (unlike for top-level functions), we cannot statically determine all the declarations that are dynamically applicable. (Indeed, this is the reason the overloading rules are defined as they are, rejecting some sets of overloaded declarations even though there is no static ambiguity.)

For example:

```
component MoreSpecificTopLevel
  trait Matrix extends {Object}
```

```
    multiply(self, z: Object) = "In Matrix"
  end
  object SparseMatrix() extends {Matrix}
    multiply(self, z: ℤ) = "In SparseMatrix"
  end
  multiply(m: Matrix, z: ℤ) = "At Top-Level"
  double(m: Matrix) = multiply (m, 2)
  run() = double (SparseMatrix())
end MoreSpecificTopLevel
```

the signatures of the functional declarations above are as follows:

```
multiply(m: Matrix, z: Object)       // functional method from Matrix
multiply(m: SparseMatrix, z: ℤ)      // functional method from SparseMatrix
multiply(m: Matrix, z: ℤ)            // top-level function
```

Because the static type of the first argument m of the function call *multiply* $(m, 2)$ is Matrix, the functional method declared in SparseMatrix is not statically applicable to the call. Among the other two applicable declarations, the top-level function is the most specific statically applicable one. However, at run time, because m is SparseMatrix, the functional method declared in SparseMatrix is also applicable to the call and it is even the most specific one. Therefore, if we allow top-level functions to be more specific than their overloaded functional methods, we need to consider not only the top-level functions but also the functional methods and more specific functional methods overriding them at run time, which burdens the performance of dynamic dispatch.

Instead, if we require functional method declarations be more specific than the overloaded top-level function declarations, the overloaded declarations in the above example are invalid. Let us consider the slightly revised example:

```
component LessSpecificTopLevel
  trait Matrix extends {Object}
    multiply(self, z: ℤ) = "In Matrix"
  end
  object SparseMatrix() extends {Matrix}
    multiply(self, z: ℤ) = "In SparseMatrix"
  end
  multiply(m: Matrix, z: Object) = "At Top-Level"
  double(m: Matrix) = multiply (m, 2)
  run() = double (SparseMatrix())
end LessSpecificTopLevel
```

Now the signatures of the overloaded declarations are as follows:

```
multiply(m: Matrix, z: ℤ)            // functional method from Matrix
multiply(m: SparseMatrix, z: ℤ)      // functional method from SparseMatrix
multiply(m: Matrix, z: Object)       // top-level function
```

Among the applicable declarations to the call $multiply\,(m, 2)$, the functional method declared in Matrix is the most specific statically applicable one. Because we restrict top-level functions from being more specific than any overloaded functional method, for any call to which both a top-level function and a functional method are applicable (statically or dynamically), the top-level function will never be the most specific dynamically applicable declaration: there will always be some dynamically applicable functional method declaration that is more specific (because of the Meet Rule). Thus, at run time, we need to consider only the functional method and the more specific functional methods overriding it without considering any top-level functions, which largely reduces the set of the candidate methods to investigate.

Finally, two functional methods in a component which may be defined in different types are valid if the parameter types of them are disjoint or they have `self` in the same position of their parameter lists. When types A and B provide a functional method with the same name and `self` in the same position, and another type C extends both A and B inheriting both functional methods, then C itself should provide a disambiguating definition, and this is checked by the overloading rules when compiling C, because at that point, the declarations in both A and B are visible (since C extends both A and B).

To see why we need this requirement for the `self` position, consider the following Matrix and Vector example:

```
trait Matrix extends {Object}
  multiply(self, y: Vector) = "In Matrix"
end
trait Vector extends {Object}
  multiply(x: Matrix, self) = "In Vector"
end
```

Since both functional method declarations have the same signature, any call to *multiply* with two arguments of types Matrix and Vector is ambiguous. For example:

```
object MatrixVector extends {Matrix, Vector} end
```

because MatrixVector is both Matrix and Vector, the following call is ambiguous:

multiply(MatrixVector, MatrixVector)

because both functional method declarations from Matrix and Vector are accessible, applicable, and equally specific. With the restriction of the same position for `self`, all the functional method declarations in a valid overloading set whose parameter types are not disjoint have the `self` parameter in the same position and the type of `self` is its enclosing trait. Therefore, we can guarantee that a functional method declaration chosen with more specific argument types is defined in a subtype of the owner of a functional method declaration chosen with less specific argument types.

3.3 Dynamic Semantics and Functional Dispatch

Evaluation of a method invocation $O^M(\overline{v}).m(\overline{v'})$ is conventional except that we first find the component M' that defines O by $actualTy_p(M, O)$, which effectively computes visibility from M. Among a set of visible dotted methods in O defined in M', we collect a set of applicable methods to the call using the dynamic types of the arguments, and select the most specific one from the set.

Due to the unique characteristic of functional methods, evaluation of a function call $m^M(\overline{v})$ requires an additional step to find the most specific functional declaration. Among a set of visible functionals in M, we first collect a set of applicable functionals to the call using the dynamic types of the arguments, just like for the method invocation case. Then, if the candidate set consists of only top-level functions, we simply select the most specific one from the set. However, if the candidate set includes any functional method declaration, we collect yet another set of visible functional method declarations from the enclosing trait of the functional method declaration. We then perform the second dispatch by collecting a set of applicable functional method declarations from the set and selecting the most specific one from the set.

Let us revisit the *multiply* example in Section 3.2 one more time. For the function call $multiply(m, 2)$, the static types of the arguments are $(\text{Matrix}, \mathbb{Z})$ and the dynamic types of the arguments are $(\text{SparseMatrix}, \mathbb{Z})$. While the signatures of the statically applicable declarations are as follows:

$multiply(m\colon \text{Matrix}, z\colon \mathbb{Z})$ // functional method from Matrix
$multiply(m\colon \text{Matrix}, z\colon \text{Object})$ // top-level function

the signatures of the dynamically applicable declarations include the following as well:

$multiply(m\colon \text{SparseMatrix}, z\colon \mathbb{Z})$ // functional method from SparseMatrix

Because the dynamically applicable declarations include functional method declarations, we collect a set of visible functional method declarations from Matrix and SparseMatrix so that we do not miss any functional method declarations that are not visible at compile time but are visible at run time. Because we collect visible functional method declarations from static types at compile time and from dynamic types at run time, and because run-time types are more specific than compile-time types, more functional method declarations may be visible at run time. Then, we perform the second dispatch by collecting a set of applicable functional method declarations from the set and selecting the most specific one from the set.

This dispatch mechanism always selects the unique most specific function to each call. First, if the applicable functional set for a function call has no functional methods, all the candidates in the set are top-level functions, and the validity of top-level function overloading guarantees that there always exists the most specific function for the call. Secondly, if the applicable functional set for a function call has more than one functional methods, the functional methods are more specific than any of the top-level functions in the set and the most specific one from the set is a functional method. Note that because the static semantics guarantees that the overloaded top-level functions are less specific than the overloaded functional methods, we do not need to consider top-level functions here, which makes this second dispatch more efficient. Finally, because all the functional methods in the visible functional set have `self` in the same position in their parameter declarations unless their parameter types are disjoint, and the type of `self` is the owner type of each functional method, the dynamic type of the argument corresponding to `self` provides all the applicable functional methods to the call including the ones in a supertype of the dynamic type. Given all these conditions, the dispatch mechanism always selects the unique dynamically most specific function to a call.

4 Properties and Coq Mechanization

We fully mechanized MFFMM and its type safety proof in Coq. Our mechanization is based on the `metatheory` library developed by De Fraine *et al.* [9]. The Coq mechanization is very close to MFFMM so that one can easily find the corresponding declarations and rules between them. The few differences between them are mostly Coq-specific implementation details, which we omit in this paper.

We proved two traditional theorems for type safety of MFFMM:

Theorem 1 (Progress). *Suppose that* p *is well typed. If an expression* e *in* p *has type* (M, C)*, then* e *is a value or there exists some* e' *such that* e *evaluates to* e'.

Theorem 2 (Preservation). *Suppose that* p *is well typed. If an expression* e *in* p *has type* (M, C) *and* e *evaluates to* e'*, then* e' *has type* (M', C') *where* (M', C') *is a subtype of* (M, C).

To prove the type safety of MFFMM, we also proved that every functional call in a well-typed program is uniquely dispatched. Due to space limitations, we refer the interested readers to our companion report [12].

While Fortress provides separate compilation by components and *APIs* where interfaces between components are described by APIs, we omit APIs for simplicity in this paper. Note that our formalization captures separate compilation even without APIs because components must import declarations from other components to make them visible, and validity judgments are applied only to visible declarations. This is unlike Java, for example, in which importing only enables the use of unqualified names. Thus, each component can be checked separately with references only to those declarations from components that it explicitly imports.

As we discussed in Section 3.1, the key aspects of MFFMM to support components, which are essential in proving the type safety, are to annotate textually enclosing component names to function calls and object constructions and to use $actualTy_p(M, C)$ to denote a type C defined in a component M. Because evaluating an expression in a component may require evaluation of other expressions in different components, evaluation rules may keep track of the component where the current evaluation occurs and the component that the control goes back to when the current evaluation normally finishes. Because small-step operational semantics such as our dynamic semantics are not well suited for keeping track of such surrounding information, we use the annotations of textually enclosing component names to represent such information. Also, $actualTy_p(M, C)$ explicitly denotes the true identities of types that are necessary to distinguish between types of the same name from different components.

The Coq mechanization of MFFMM is based on our previous work [11] on FFMM, but we did not reuse much of the FFMM Coq code mainly because the design of FFMM lacks extensibility. We organized the syntax and semantics of MFFMM in a modular way so that the new features such as functional methods and components are represented seamlessly and possible future changes in the calculus can be integrated smoothly. The COQ mechanization is approximately 9,000 lines and it is available online [10].

5 Related Work

Millstein and Chambers introduce the *Dubious* language [14], which provides symmetric dynamic multimethod dispatch while allowing a program to be divided into modules that can be separately type-checked statically. Our work differs from Dubious in these respects: Dubious is a classless (prototype-oriented) object system, whereas Fortress traits are classes in this sense; Dubious has only explicitly declared objects, whereas our work supports dynamically created objects and state; Dubious does not provide disjoint relations between types and it requires every multimethod to have a principal type[1], thus it cannot support multimethods that take different numbers of arguments or otherwise do not have a principal type, nor can it allow the position of the owner to vary, whereas Fortress enlarges a set of valid overloadings thanks to disjoint type relations; and importing a Dubious module is an all-or-nothing proposition, (though the cited paper does sketch a possible way to introduce a `private` keyword to shield some objects in a module), whereas Fortress import statements allow fine-grained selective import of any parts of a component—in particular, it is possible to import only selected functional methods of a trait, rather than all methods. Other languages from the same research group that are similarly closely related to the present work are Cecil [5], EML [13], MultiJava [7], and Relaxed MultiJava [15]. A block-structured variant of Cecil, BeCecil [6], supports multimethod declarations in a nested scope, limiting their visibility to the scope. However, BeCecil does not support a module system, thus it does not support modular type checking.

Odersky, Wadler and Wehr's System O [17] supports overloaded declarations with completely different type signatures, and is modular in the sense that it has the Hindley/Milner type system. The system ensures no ambiguities by putting a simple restriction on type classes, but it requires that overloaded functions should be dispatched on the first parameter while Fortress allows multiple dispatch.

Scala provides a way to omit some arguments at a method call if they are bound to *implicit* parameters [18]. Selecting the most specific implicit parameter that applies in the method call is similar to overloading resolution in Fortress. While Fortress prohibits any possibilities of ambiguous calls at functional declaration sites, Scala statically rejects ambiguous calls at method use sites.

In Haskell typeclasses [23], overloaded functions must be contained in some type class, and their signatures must vary in exactly the same structural position. Typeclasses are ill-suited for functions lacking uniform variance in the domain and range, for example. Such behavior is consistent with the static, type-based dispatch of Haskell, but it would lead to irreconcilable ambiguity in the dynamic, value-based dispatch of Fortress. While Fortress supports fine-grained imports of overloaded declarations, all instance

[1] The parameter and return types of any declaration for a multimethod must be subtypes of their corresponding types in the principal type.

declarations in Haskell are globally visible, and each declaration should check that it does not overlap with any of the others.

Type safety proofs for several programming languages are mechanized in various proof assistant tools. Our previous work [11] mechanizes type safety proofs of core calculi for Fortress in COQ, and the present work is an extension of them especially with a component system, top-level functions, functional methods, and overloading between top-level functions and functional methods. Strniša *et al.* [20] introduce a formal calculus for Java with a module system, and mechanize its type safety proof using Isabelle/HOL [16]. The calculus does not provide overloading, and references across module boundaries use fully qualified names, which amounts to requiring programmers to use actual types. None of the calculi supports a module system, and the technique requires a calculus to have placeholders for future extension.

6 Conclusion

Namespace control in object-oriented languages is tricky: On one hand, we want to inherit method declarations implicitly and be able to override and overload them. On the other hand, we want to control access to specific methods by controlling where their names are in scope. Functional methods provide an effective solution: they are inherited like conventional dotted methods, but their visibility is controlled by components with selective imports that allow fine-grained namespace control, like top-level functions, with which they can be overloaded.

Functional methods are an effective approach to solving the operator method problem. The advantage over dotted methods is that any argument position may serve as the receiver; the advantage over ordinary functions is that a trait may declare a set of overloaded operators with disjoint parameter types. Ensuring the existence of the unique most specific functional declaration for a call in the presence of overloading between three kinds of functional declarations with symmetric multiple dispatch is tricky. A component system with selective imports introduces yet another problem that we should consider the *hidden* functional methods in traits when we select the most specific top-level function or functional method for a function call. We have shown how these features work in a manner that interacts well with namespace control. To guarantee that such features do not cause any undefined or ambiguous calls at run time, we present a core calculus for Fortress and fully mechanize its type safety proof in COQ.

In the future, we plan to extend this framework to parametrically polymorphic types, and more type relations such as explicit type exclusion and comprises relations [3].

Acknowledgments. This work is supported in part by Korea Ministry of Education, Science and Technology(MEST) / National Research Foundation of Korea(NRF) (Grants NRF-2011-0016139 and NRF-2008-0062609).

References

1. Allen, E., Chase, D., Hallett, J.J., Luchangco, V., Maessen, J.-W., Ryu, S., Steele Jr., G.L., Tobin-Hochstadt, S.: The Fortress Language Specification Version 1.0 (March 2008)

2. Allen, E., Hallett, J.J., Luchangco, V., Ryu, S., Steele, G.: Modular multiple dispatch with multiple inheritance. In: Proc. ACM Symposium on Applied Computing (2007)
3. Allen, E., Hilburn, J., Kilpatrick, S., Luchangco, V., Ryu, S., Chase, D., Steele Jr., G.L.: Type-checking Modular Multiple Dispatch with Parametric Polymorphism and Multiple Inheritance. In: OOPSLA (2011)
4. Castagna, G., Ghelli, G., Longo, G.: A calculus for overloaded functions with subtyping. In: LFP (1992)
5. Chambers, C.: Object-oriented multi-methods in Cecil. In: Madsen, O.L. (ed.) ECOOP 1992. LNCS, vol. 615, pp. 33–56. Springer, Heidelberg (1992)
6. Chambers, C., Leavens, G.T.: Bececil, a core object-oriented language with block structure and multimethods: Semantics and typing. In: Proceedings of the 4th International Workshop on Foundations of Object Oriented Languages (1997)
7. Clifton, C., Millstein, T., Leavens, G.T., Chambers, C.: MultiJava: Design rationale, compiler implementation, and applications. ACM TOPLAS 28(3), 517–575 (2006)
8. The COQ Development Team. The COQ Proof Assistant, `http://coq.inria.fr/`
9. De Fraine, B., Ernst, E., Südholt, M.: Cast-Free Featherweight Java (2008), `http://soft.vub.ac.be/~bdefrain/featherj`
10. Kim, J.: MFFMM in COQ (2012), `http://plrg.kaist.ac.kr/_media/research/software/mffmm_in_coq.tar.gz`
11. Kim, J., Ryu, S.: COQ mechanization of Featherweight Fortress with multiple dispatch and multiple inheritance. In: Proceedings of the First International Conference on Certified Programs and Proofs (2011)
12. Kim, J., Ryu, S.: MFFMM : Modular Featherweight Fortress with Multiple Dispatch and Multiple Inheritance (June 2013), `http://plrg.kaist.ac.kr/_media/research/publications/mffmm_calculus.pdf`
13. Millstein, T., Bleckner, C., Chambers, C.: Modular typechecking for hierarchically extensible datatypes and functions. ACM TOPLAS 26(5), 836–889 (2004)
14. Millstein, T., Chambers, C.: Modular statically typed multimethods. Information and Computation 175(1), 76–118 (2002)
15. Millstein, T.D., Reay, M., Chambers, C.: Relaxed MultiJava: balancing extensibility and modular typechecking. In: OOPSLA (2003)
16. Nipkow, T., Paulson, L.C., Wenzel, M.T.: Isabelle/HOL. LNCS, vol. 2283. Springer, Heidelberg (2002)
17. Odersky, M., Wadler, P., Wehr, M.: A second look at overloading. In: FPCA, pp. 135–146 (1995)
18. Oliveira, B.C.D.S., Moors, A., Odersky, M.: Type classes as objects and implicits. In: OOPSLA (2010)
19. Schärli, N., Ducasse, S., Nierstrasz, O., Black, A.P.: Traits: Composable Units of Behaviour. In: Cardelli, L. (ed.) ECOOP 2003. LNCS, vol. 2743, pp. 248–274. Springer, Heidelberg (2003)
20. Strniša, R., Sewell, P., Parkinson, M.: The Java module system: Core design and semantic definition. In: OOPSLA (2007)
21. Stroustrup, B.: The C++ Programming Language. Addison-Wesley, Reading (1986)
22. Szypersky, C., Omohundro, S., Murer, S.: Engineering a programming language: The type and class system of Sather. In: Gutknecht, J. (ed.) Programming Languages and System Architectures. LNCS, vol. 782, pp. 208–227. Springer, Heidelberg (1994)
23. Wadler, P., Blott, S.: How to make ad-hoc polymorphism less ad hoc. In: POPL (1989)

Internal Deployment of the Parfait Static Code Analysis Tool at Oracle (Invited Talk)

Cristina Cifuentes[1] and Nathan Keynes[2]

[1] Oracle Labs Australia, Oracle
[2] Parfait, Oracle
{cristina.cifuentes,nathan.keynes}@oracle.com

Abstract. The term static code analysis is used these days to refer to tools that find bugs and/or security vulnerabilities in source or executable code by performing static analysis of the code. In the past years, several static code analysis tools have transitioned from a research environment onto production mode; examples include Coverity [1], SLAM [2] and Goanna [3].

Parfait was developed as a research project at Sun Microsystems Laboratories with the aim to look into precision and scalability of static bug-detection analyses over millions of lines of source code (MLOC). The Oracle acquisition of Sun brought Parfait into a new playground where, in the course of one year, a small team of researchers and students showed "value for money" against codebases from "legacy" Oracle. Key to this value proposition was not only showing that the tool reported real bugs of interest to developers, but also that there was a high hit rate of reports and that it scaled well, allowing for not only nightly integration but also incremental, commit-time integration.

In this talk we summarise our experiences in the transitioning of Parfait from a research prototype at Oracle Labs, onto production mode at Oracle, as well as its deployment throughout the company, where it is used on a day-to-day basis by thousands of developers. We also elaborate on our recent experiences on extending Parfait to support the Java^{TM}language, for the purposes of detecting vulnerabilities in the Java Platform.

1 Introduction

The Parfait project started in 2007 with the aim of developing a static code analysis tool for C that was precise yet scalable to millions of lines of source code (MLOC). We were interested in checking systems code and used the core of the Oracle^{TM} Solaris operating system, known as the "ON" (operating system and networking) consolidation. ON had close to 6 MLOC of non-commented code. In formulating our research goals, we focused on development organisations at Sun Microsystems and their developers' needs, as they related to static code analysis tools. Key in their minds was the need for a low false positive rate, fast runtime so that the tool could be run over their MLOC overnight as part of their nightly

C.-c. Shan (Ed.): APLAS 2013, LNCS 8301, pp. 172–175, 2013.

build, and ease in build integration. By 2010 the ON codebase was reaching 10 MLOC.

The 2010 acquisition of Sun by Oracle brought new challenges in terms of sizes of codebases, as well as pleasant results when specialising our analyses to bugs that were of interest by the new developers we met. In the course of one year we were able to not only show proof-of-concept over the Oracle™ Database, the Oracle™ TimesTen In-Memory Database, the Oracle™ Essbase Analytics Link for Hyperion Financial Management, and the Oracle™ Linux operating system, we were also able to get management commitment for funding of Parfait as an internal product in 2012, in effect, transitioning the tool from our research laboratories onto product development. The year in between was used to lift the level of the research prototype into production code quality, as well as implement enhancement requests and bug fixes.

2 Design and Research Contributions

The design of Parfait was focused around the drawbacks that developers were seeing in the existing static analysis tools back in 2006/07, namely, long running times over millions of lines of code, as well as high numbers of spurious reports that were not true bugs in the user's code. This led to a design that was highly scalable while still providing good precision.

The research contributions of Parfait include

- its layered design [4],
- a scalable taint analysis algorithm [5],
- a demand-driven symbolic analysis for buffer overflow detection [6], that is also used for integer overflow detection,
- a new formulation of points-to analysis that is an order of magnitude faster than the state-of-the-art [7,8],
- an unpublished analysis we call "model-based analysis" that makes use of a model checker in an unsound yet scalable fashion [9], and
- a framework and benchmarks for the benchmarking of static code analysis tools [10].

The initial choice of bug types analysed in Parfait was driven by what we perceived were the most common and useful bug types to address across different organisations, namely, memory-related issues: buffer overflows, null pointer dereference, use after free, etc.

Scalability was achieved by developing demand-driven algorithms for most of the bug detection algorithms. Analyses such as points-to are used as a pre-pass prior to an individual bug detection algorithm, and as such are implemented in a global fashion.

At the core of Parfait there is a backwards flow, data flow framework, from which a variety of different bug types can be instantiated. A symbolic analyser, and a value flow data structure are also commonly used in other analyses. Other abstractions and analyses that the research team is working on may, in due course, become available in Parfait.

3 Development and Deployment

Parfait consists of a translator and the analysis tool proper. Parfait proper is built on top of the LLVM [11] infrastructure and makes use of the LLVM intermediate representation in the form of bitcode files. The Parfait translator makes use of a heavily-modified Clang [12] to be able to parse C and C++ source code traditionally compiled with compilers such as Intel's ICC, Oracle™ Solaris Studio, and GCC, into the LLVM bitcode representation.

For usability, Parfait was coupled with a graphical, web-based interface to more easily illustrate to developers why the tool reported a particular bug report. Integration into popular editors such as emacs was also provided.

For deployment, Parfait was coupled with a Server and a more extensive web-based interface. The Server keeps track of historical nightly run results, marked false positives or "won't fix" results, and status of the report, as well as integrates with the revision control and bug tracking systems used by the organisation.

Some of our experiences are summarised in [13]; we highlight the deployment options used by different organisations:

- Nightly: most of the organisations perform a nightly integration, adding the Parfait run as another test to be conducted in the nigthly regression. New bug reports are pushed onto the Server and either triaged the next morning, or, more commonly, pushed directly by the Server onto the relevant code owners.
- Commit-time: a large percentage of the organisations that have performed a nightly integration also integrate at commit-time. This allows for more timely feedback to the developer. Parfait is run over the developer's changeset (as well as any dependencies on other code) and be Parfait-clean prior to the commit being approved. This allows for bugs from being introduced into the codebase.
- Ad-hoc: some organisations integrate Parfait on an ad-hoc schedule, e.g., run it once a month or run it prior to certain milestone or releases. These runs are normally conducted by a QA team rather than being driven by the developers themselves.

4 Extending Parfait with Java Support

The recent increase of new Java vulnerabilities led to interest into extending Parfait to support the Java language, with an initial goal at detecting these new types of vulnerabilities: unguarded caller sensitive methods, unsafe use of doPrivileged, invalid serialisation of security-sensitive classes, trusted method chaining, invalid deserialisation of classes, etc.

The Jaffa translator for Java code translates to the LLVM bitcode file representation, including in it additional metadata to keep track of some Java language specific semantics. Jaffa translates for analysis, rather than for execution purposes. Based on the existing Parfait analysis infrastructure, new bug passes have been and are being developed for the abovementioned vulnerabilities. Although static analysis cannot resolve all dynamic dependencies in a language like Java, the analyses do find, nevertheless, a lot of useful results.

Acknowledgments. Many researchers, developers and interns have worked on Parfait throughout the years, contributing to different aspects of the research and the tool. Special thanks go to Curt Elsbernd, who is the champion for deployment of Parfait within the Database Systems Technology organisation.

References

1. Bessey, A., Block, K., Chelf, B., Chou, A., Fulton, B., Hallem, S., Henri-Gros, C., Kamsky, A., McPeak, S., Engler, D.: A few billion lines of code later – using static analysis to find bugs in the real world. Communications of the ACM 53, 66–75 (2010)
2. Ball, T., Levin, V., Rajamani, S.K.: A decade of software model checking with slam. Communications of the ACM 54, 68–76 (2011)
3. Huuck, R.: Formal verification, engineering and business value. In: Proceedings of the First International Workshop on Formal Techniques for Safety-Critical Systems, Electronic Proceedings in Theoretical Computer Science, pp. 1–4 (2012)
4. Cifuentes, C., Scholz, B.: Parfait – designing a scalable bug checker. In: Proceedings of the ACM SIGPLAN Static Analysis Workshop, June 12, pp. 4–11 (2008)
5. Scholz, B., Zhang, C., Cifuentes, C.: User-input dependence analysis via graph reachability. In: Proceedings of the Eighth IEEE Working Conference on Source Code Analysis and Manipulation, September 28-29, pp. 25–34 (2008)
6. Li, L., Cifuentes, C., Keynes, N.: Practical and effective symbolic analysis for buffer overflow detection. In: roceedings of the ACM SIGSOFT International Symposium on Foundations of Software Engineering, pp. 317–326. ACM, New York (2010)
7. Li, L., Cifuentes, C., Keynes, N.: Boosting the performance of flow-sensitive points-to analysis using value flow. In: Proceedings of the 19th ACM SIGSOFT Symposium and the 13th European Conference on Foundations of Software Engineering, pp. 343–353. ACM (2011)
8. Li, L., Cifuentes, C., Keynes, N.: Precise and scalable context-sensitive pointer analysis via value flow graph. In: Proceedings of the 2013 International Symposium on Memory Management (ISMM), pp. 85–96. ACM (2013)
9. Valdiviezo, M., Cifuentes, C., Krishnan, P.: A method for scalable and precise bug finding using program analysis and model checking techniques (2012) (unpublished manuscript)
10. Cifuentes, C., Hoermann, C., Keynes, N., Li, L., Long, S., Mealy, E., Mounteney, M., Scholz, B.: BegBunch: Benchmarking for C bug detection tools. In: Proceedings of the 2009 International Workshop on Defects in Large Software Systems (July 2009)
11. Lattner, C., Adve, V.: LLVM: A compilation framework for lifelong program analysis & transformation. In: Proceedings of the International Symposium on Code Generation and Optimization. IEEE Computer Society, Washington, DC (2004)
12. Clang: a C language family frontend for LLVM, `http://clang.llvm.org`
13. Cifuentes, C., Keynes, N., Li, L., Hawes, N., Valdiviezo, M.: Transitioning Parfait into a development tool. IEEE Security and Practice (May/June 2012)

Secure Compilation of Object-Oriented Components to Protected Module Architectures*

Marco Patrignani, Dave Clarke, and Frank Piessens

iMinds-DistriNet, Dept. Computer Science, KU Leuven
{first.last}@cs.kuleuven.be

Abstract. A fully abstract compilation scheme prevents the security features of the high-level language from being bypassed by an attacker operating at a particular lower level. This paper presents a fully abstract compilation scheme from a realistic object-oriented language with dynamic memory allocation, cross-package inheritance, exceptions and inner classes to untyped machine code. Full abstraction of the compilation scheme relies on enhancing the low-level machine model with a fine-grained, program counter-based memory access control mechanism. This paper contains the outline of a formal proof of full abstraction of the compilation scheme. Measurements of the overhead introduced by the compilation scheme indicate that it is negligible.

1 Introduction

Modern high-level languages such as ML, Java or Scala offer security features to programmers in the form of type systems, module systems, or encapsulation primitives. These mechanisms can be used as security building blocks to withstand the threat of attackers acting at the high level. For the software to be secure, attackers acting at lower levels need to be considered as well. Thus it is important that high-level security properties are preserved after the high-level code is compiled to machine code. Such a security-preserving compilation scheme is called *fully abstract* [1]. An implication of such a compilation scheme is that the power of a low-level attacker is reduced to that of a high-level one. The notion of fully abstract compilation is well suited for expressing the preservation of security policies through compilation, as it preserves and reflects contextual equivalence. Two programs are contextually equivalent if they cannot be distinguished by a third one. Contextual equivalence models security policies as follows: saying that variable f of program C is confidential is equivalent to saying that C is contextually equivalent to any program C' that differs from C in

* This work has been supported in part by the Intel Lab'sUniversity Research Office. This research is also partially funded by the Research Fund KU Leuven, and by the EU FP7 project NESSoS. With the financial support from the Prevention of and Fight against Crime Programme of the European Union (B-CCENTRE). Marco Patrignani holds a Ph.D. fellowship from the Research Foundation Flanders (FWO).

C.-c. Shan (Ed.): APLAS 2013, LNCS 8301, pp. 176–191, 2013.

its value for f. A fully abstract compilation scheme does not eliminate high-level security flaws. It is, in a sense, conservative, introducing no more vulnerabilities at the low level than the ones already exploitable at the high level.

Fully abstract compilation of modern high-level languages is hard to achieve. Compilation of Java to JVM or of C# to the .NET framework [12] are some of the examples where compilation is not fully abstract. Recent techniques that achieve fully abstract compilation rely on address space layout randomisation [2,9], type-based invariants [4,7], and enhancing the low-level machine model with a fine-grained program counter-based memory access control mechanism [3].

The threat model considered in this paper is that of an attacker with low-level code execution privileges. Such an attacker can inject and execute malicious code at machine level and violate the security properties of the machine code generated by the compiler. In order to withstand such a low-level attacker, high-level security features must be preserved in the code generated during compilation. Agten *et al.* [3] were the first to show that fully abstract compilation of a safe high-level programming language to untyped machine code is possible. They achieved this by enhancing the low-level machine model with a fine-grained program counter-based memory access control mechanism inspired by existing systems [14,15,17,21,22] and recent industrial prototypes [16]. One limitation of the work of Agten *et al.* is that it only considers a toy high-level language. The main contribution of this paper is showing how essential programming language features can be securely compiled to the same low-level machine model of Agten *et al.* The adopted low-level model is similar to a modern processor, so the compilation scheme handles subtleties such as flags and registers that an implementation would have to face. More precisely, this paper makes the following contributions:

- a secure compilation scheme from a model object-oriented language with dynamic memory allocation, cross-package inheritance, exceptions and inner classes to low-level, untyped machine code;
- the outline of a formal proof of full abstraction for this compilation scheme;
- measurements of the run-time overhead introduced by the compilation scheme.

The paper is organised as follows. Section 2 introduces background notions. Section 3 presents a secure compilation scheme for a language with dynamic memory allocation, cross-package inheritance, exceptions and inner classes. Section 4 outlines the proof of full abstraction of the compilation scheme. Section 5 presents benchmarks of the overhead introduced by the compilation scheme. Section 6 discusses limitations of the compilation scheme. Section 7 presents related work. Section 8 discusses future work and concludes.

2 Background

This section describes the low-level protection mechanism and the secure compilation scheme of Agten *et al.* [3], which is the starting point of this paper. Then the high-level language targeted by the compilation scheme is presented.

2.1 Low-Level Model

To model a realistic compilation scheme, the targeted low-level language should be close to what is used by modern processors. For this reason this paper adopts a low-level language that models a standard Von Neumann machine consisting of a program counter, a registers file, a flags register and memory space [3].

In order to support full abstraction of the compilation scheme, the low-level language is enhanced with a protection mechanism: a fine-grained, program counter-based memory access control mechanism inspired by existing systems [14,15,17,21,22] and recent industrial prototypes [16]. We review this addition from the work of Agten *et al.* [3] and Strackx and Piessens [22]. This mechanism assumes that the memory is logically divided into a protected and an unprotected section. The protected section is further divided into a code and a data section. The code section contains a variable number of entry points: the only addresses to which instructions in unprotected memory can jump and execute. The data section is accessible only from the protected section. The size and location of each memory section are specified in a memory descriptor. The table below summarises the access control model enforced by the protection mechanism.

From\ To	Protected			Unprotected
	Entry Point	Code	Data	
Protected	r x	r x	r w	r w x
Unprotected	x			r w x

This protection mechanism provides a secure environment for code that needs to be protected from a potentially malicious surrounding environment. It is appealing in the context of embedded systems, where kernel-level protection mechanisms are often lacking.

2.2 A Secure Compiler for a Simple Language

Agten *et al.* [3] presented a secure (fully abstract) compilation scheme for a simple object based language. In an effort to be self-contained, this paper summarises their key points.

General Notions. In the work of Agten *et al.*, programs consist of a single object with fields and methods declarations which are compiled to the protected memory partition. Compiled programs must be indistinguishable from the size point of view, thus a constant amount of space is reserved for each program, independent of its implementation. All methods and fields are sorted alphabetically. Thus equivalent compiled programs cannot be distinguished based on the ordering of low-level method calls. Methods and fields are given a unique index, starting from 0, based on their order of occurrence. Those indexes serve as the offset used to access methods and fields. Parameters and local variables are also given method-local indexes to be used as above.

Registers $\mathtt{r}_0$ to $\mathtt{r}_3$ are used as working registers for low-level instructions and registers $\mathtt{r}_4$ to $\mathtt{r}_{11}$ are used for parameters. The call stack is split into a protected and an unprotected part, the former is allocated in the protected memory partition. A shadow stack pointer that points to the base of the protected stack is introduced to implement stack switches. When entering the protected memory, the protected stack is set as the active one; when leaving it, the unprotected stack is set to be the active one. To prevent tampering with the control flow, the base of the protected stack points to a procedure that writes 0 in $\mathtt{r}_0$ and `halts`. For each method, a prologue and an epilogue are appended to the method body. They allocate and deallocate activation records on the secure stack, The program counter is initialised to a given address in unprotected memory.

Entry Points. For each method, an entry point in protected memory is created. Additionally, in order to enable returnbacks (returns from callbacks, which are calls to external code), a returnback entry point is created. Entry points act as proxies to the actual method implementations and are extended with security routines and checks.

These security routines reset unused registers and flags when leaving the protected memory to prevent them conveying unwanted information. For example, a callback to a function with two arguments resets all registers but $\mathtt{r}_4$ and $\mathtt{r}_5$ since they are the only ones that carry desired information. Checks are made to ensure that primitive-typed parameters have the right byte representation, e.g. `Unit`-typed parameters must have value 0, the chosen value of `Unit` type.

2.3 High-Level Language

The high-level language targeted by this paper is Jeffrey and Rathke's Java Jr. [11]. Java Jr. is a strongly-typed, single-threaded, component-based, object-oriented language that enforces `private` fields and `public` methods. Java Jr. supports all the basic constructs one expects from a modern programming language, including dynamic memory allocation. A program in Java Jr., called a component, is a collection of sealed packages that communicate via interfaces and public objects. Java Jr. enforces a partition of packages into *import* and *export* ones. Import packages are analogous to the `.h` header file of a C program; they define *interfaces* and *externs*, which are references to externally defined objects. Export packages define *classes* and *objects*; they provide an implementation of an import package. Listing 1.1 illustrates the package system of Java Jr.

Listing 1.1 contains two package declarations: `PI` is an import package and `PE` is an export package implementing `PI`. Object `extAccount` allocated in `PE` provides an implementation for the `extern` with the same name defined in `PI`.

In Java Jr., primitive values, types and operations on them are assumed to be provided by a `System` package, whose name is omitted for the sake of brevity. The only primitive type is `Unit`, inhabited by `unit`. Since the focus of this paper is security, we write access modifiers for methods and fields even though the syntax of Java Jr. does not require them.

The security mechanism of Java Jr. is given by `private` fields. In Java Jr., classes are private to the package that contains their declarations. Objects are allocated in the same package as the class they instantiate. Due to this package system, for a package to be compiled it only needs the import packages of any

```
package PI;
  interface Account {
    public createAccount() : Foo;
    public getBalance() : Int;
  }
  extern extAccount : Account;

package PE;
  class AccountClass implements PI.Account {
    AccountClass() { counter = 0; }
    public createAccount() : Account { return new PE.AccountClass(); }
    public getBalance() : Int { return counter; }
    private counter : Int;
  }
  object extAccount : AccountClass;
```

Listing 1.1. Example of the package system of Java Jr.

package it depends on. As a result, formal parameters in methods have interface types, since classes that implement those interfaces are unknown. Additionally, since constructors are not exposed in interfaces, cross-package object allocation must be through factory methods. For example, the name of class `AccountClass` from Listing 1.1 is not visible from outside package `PE`, thus expressions of the form `new PE.AccountClass()` cannot be written outside `PE`.

Java Jr. was chosen since it provides a clear notion of encapsulation for a high-level component, which makes for simpler reasoning about the secure compilation scheme. This allows us to pinpoint what the key insights are to achieve secure (fully abstract) compilation, so that they can be used when the language is extended with cross-package inheritance, exceptions and inner classes.

3 Secure Compilation of Java Jr.

After a series of examples describing possible attacks on a naïve compilation scheme, this section describes what is needed in order to provide a secure compiler for Java Jr., starting from the secure compiler described in Section 2.2, and extend it to support cross-package inheritance, exceptions and inner classes.

The following examples use some standard assumptions about how objects are compiled [6]. When an object is allocated, a word is reserved to indicate its class, which is used to dynamically dispatch methods. Fields are accessed via offsets and methods are dispatched based on offsets.

Example 1 (Type of the current object). *Suppose the compiled program includes two classes:* `Pair` *and* `Caesar`*. Class* `Pair` *implements pairs of* `Integer` *values with two fields* `first` *and* `second`*, with getters and setters for them, method* `getFirst()` *returns the value of field* `first`*. Class* `Caesar` *implements a caesar cypher. It has a single* `Integer` *field* `key` *and a method* `encrypt(v:Int)` *that returns value* `v` *encrypted with* `key`*. The* `key` *of the* `Caesar` *cypher is not accessible outside the class (i.e. it is private).*

The `key` *cannot be leaked at the high level, since high-level programs are strongly typed, but it can be leaked to low-level programs. A low-level, external program can perform a call to method* `getFirst()` *on an object of type* `Caesar`*; this will return the* `key` *field, since fields are accessed by offset. As low-level code is untyped, nothing prevents this attack from happening.*

Example 2 (Type of the arguments). *Similarly to Example 1, arguments of methods can be exploited in order to mount a low-level attack. Extend the program of Example 1 with another class* `ProxyPair` *with a method* `takeFirst(v:Pair)` *that returns* `getFirst()` *on the* `Pair` *object* `v`*. At the high level, this code gives rise to no attacks. At the low level, this code can be used to mount the following attack: if an object of type* `Caesar` *is passed as argument to method* `takeFirst( )`*, the code will leak the* `key`*.*

Example 3 (Leakage of object references). *Object references at the low-level are the address where objects are allocated. The attacker can call methods on objects it does not know of by guessing the address where an object is allocated. Passing object addresses from a secure program to an external one can also give away the allocation strategy of the compiler, as well as the size of allocated objects. An attacker that learns this information can then use it to mount attacks such as those presented in Example 1 and 2. From a technical point of view this means that leaking object addresses and accepting guessed addresses breaks full abstraction of the compilation scheme.*

3.1 A Secure Compiler for Java Jr.

Before proposing countermeasures to the attacks just listed, this section lists the modifications to the scheme of Section 2.2 that are needed in order to support compilation of Java Jr. and, more generally, of object-oriented programs.

Compilation of OO Languages. Fig. 1 shows a graphical representation of the protected memory section which is generated when securely compiling a Java Jr. component. Only a single protected memory section is needed, and all classes, objects and methods defined in the component are placed there. The protected code section contains entry points, described below, method body implementations, the procedure for object allocation and the dynamic dispatch.

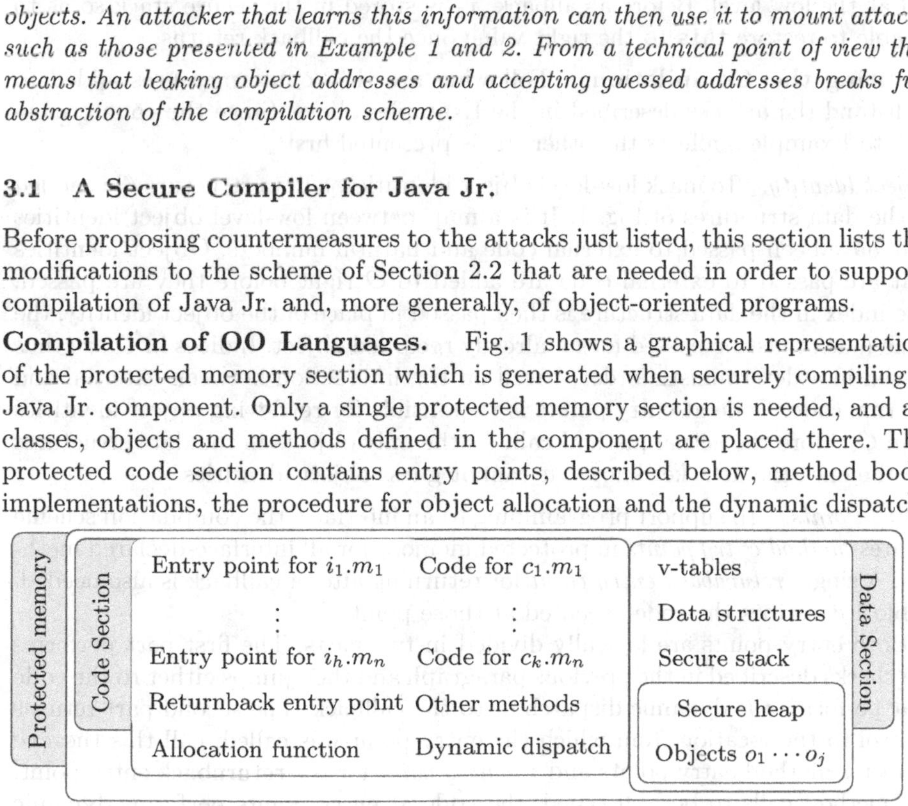

Fig. 1. Graphical representation of a compiled program

The protected data section contains the v-tables, support data structures, a secure stack and a secure heap. The v-tables are data structures used to perform the dynamic dispatch of method calls; they associate the address of the method to be executed on an object based on its type and the method name. Data structures are defined in the remainder of this section and in Section 3.3.

In order to specify how the component interacts with external code, assume the component being compiled provides one import package without a corresponding export one. Refer to this package as *the distinguished import package (DIP)*. The DIP contains interface and extern definitions, thus callbacks are calls on methods defined in the DIP. Component code is assumed not to implement interfaces defined in the DIP, while external code which provides an implementation for the DIP can also implement interfaces defined in the component. Assuming the calling convention with the outer world is known, dynamic dispatch can easily take care of external objects whose classes implement interfaces defined in the component. Method call implementation adopted by external code is more complex since function calls must jump to the correct entry point, but it still can be achieved for example using object wrappers.

Finally, register r_4 is used to identify the current object (`this`) in a method call at the low level. Before a callback, r_4 is stored in the secure stack so as to be able to restore `this` to the right value once the callback returns.

Securing the Compilation. Following are the countermeasures added to withstand the attacks described in the Examples above. Since the countermeasure to Example 3 affects the others, it is presented first.

Object Identity. To mask low-level object identities, a data structure $\mathcal{O}$ is added to the data structures of Fig. 1. It is a map between low-level object identities that have been passed to external code and natural numbers. Object identities that are passed to external code are added to $\mathcal{O}$ right before they are passed. The index in the data structure is then passed in place of the object identity, the same index must be passed for an already recorded object. Indices in $\mathcal{O}$ are thus passed in a deterministic order, based on the interaction between external and internal code. Code at entry points is responsible for retrieving object identities from $\mathcal{O}$ before the actual method call. As the only objects in the data structures are the ones the attacker knows, it cannot guess object identities.

Entry Points. To support programming to an interface, the compilation scheme creates *method entry points* in protected memory for all interface-declared methods. A single *returnback entry point* for returning after a callback is also needed. Table 1 describes the code executed at those points.

Both entry points are logically divided in two parts. The first part performs the checks described in the previous paragraph and then jumps either to the code that performs the dynamic dispatch or to the callback. The second part returns control to the location from which the entry point was called; call this the *exit point* for method entry points and *re-entry point* for the returnback entry point. For method calls to be well-typed, the code at entry points performs dynamic typechecks. This checks that a method is invoked on objects of the right type (line 2), with parameters of the right type (line 4). Similar checks are executed when

Table 1. Pseudo code executed at entry points. Loading means that a value is retrieved from the memory, push and pop are operations on the secure stack.

	Method p entry point		Returnback entry point
1	Load current object $v = \mathcal{O}(\mathsf{R}_4)$	a	Push current object $v = \mathsf{R}_4$, return address a and return type m
2	Check that v's class defines method p		
3	Load parameters $\overline{v}$ from $\mathcal{O}$	b	Reset flags and unused registers
4	Dynamic typecheck	c	Replace object identities with index in $\mathcal{O}$
5	Perform dynamic dispatch	d	Jump to callback address
	Exit point (*run method code*)		Re-entry point (*run external code*)
6	Reset flags and unused registers	e	Pop return type m and check it
7	Replace object identities with index in $\mathcal{O}$	f	Dynamic typecheck
		g	Pop return address a, current object v and resume execution

returning from a callback, in the returnback entry point (line f). These checks are performed only on objects whose class is defined in the compiled component, as they are allocated in protected memory; no control over externally allocated objects can be assumed. If any check fails, all registers and flags are cleared and the execution `halts`. Resetting flags and registers and `Unit`-typed value checks are as in Section 2.2. Dynamic typecheck involves checking primitive-typed values. These are needed for all primitive types inhabited by a finite number of values, such as `Unit` and `Bool`. For example, `bool`-typed parameters must have either value 1 or 0, which correspond to the high-level values `true` or `false` [7].

Insights. Following are the insights gained from developing a secure compilation scheme for Java Jr.; they will be useful in the following sections.

- Internal objects that are passed to external code must be remembered; their address must be masked.
- Strong typing of methods must be enforced with additional runtime checks.
- The low-level code must not introduce additional functionality (low-level functions in entry points) that is not available at the high level.

3.2 Secure Compilation of Cross-Package Inheritance

Cross-package inheritance arises whenever class `D` from an export package `PSUB` **`extends`** class `C` from a different export package `PSUP`, as in Listing 1.2. Cross-package inheritance is not provided by Java Jr., as it would break the main result proven in the Java Jr. paper [11]. In order to allow cross-package inheritance, classes that can be extended must appear in import packages. Thus, given an import package, entry points are created not only for interface-defined methods, but also for class-defined ones and for constructors. Class `D` can optionally override methods of the super class `C`, as is the case with method `m()`. Within those methods, calls to `super` can be used in order to call method `m()` of the super class `C`. Alternatively, if a method is not overridden, such as method `z()`, calling d.`z()` on an object d of type `D` executes method `z()` defined in the super class `C`.

```
package PSUP;
   class C { // called the super class
      public m():Int { ··· }
      public z(): Int { ··· }
   }
package PSUB;
   class D extends PSUP.C { // called the sub class
      public m():Int{ super.m(); ··· }
   }
```

Listing 1.2. Example of cross-package inheritance

If the normal compilation scheme were followed, at the low-level d is allocated to a single memory area where fields from subobjects C and D are both allocated. Example 4 highlights the problems that arise in this setting.

Example 4 (Allocation of d). *Consider the case when* C *is protected and* D *is not. If d is allocated outside the protected memory partition, private fields of the* C *subobject become accessible to external code. If d is allocated inside the protected memory partition, two options arise. The first one is placing untrusted methods of* D *in the protected memory partition, violating the security of the compilation scheme. Otherwise, if methods of* D *are placed in the unprotected memory partition, they cannot access* D*'s fields via offset. Getters and setters for fields of* D *could be exposed through entry points, but this would violate full abstraction, as those methods are not available at the high level.*

The problems just presented above also arise when C *is not protected but* D *is, thus compilation of cross-package inheritance cannot be achieved normally.*

To allocate d securely, it is split in two sub-objects: dc, with fields of class C, and dd, with fields of class D; the object identity of d is dd [23].

Consider firstly the case when C is protected and D is not. External code needs to compile the expression d = `new D()` so that it calls `new C()` to create object dc in the protected memory section. External code must then save the resulting identifier for dc to perform `super` calls, since they are translated as method calls. The additional checks inserted at entry points presented in Section 3.1 ensure that `super` calls are always well-typed.

Consider then the case when C is not protected and D is. The secure compiler needs to call `new D()` and save the returned object identity for dd in a memory location, since `super` calls in this case are compiled as callbacks. When expression d = `new D()` is compiled, the unprotected address dc is stored at the low-level, right after the type of dd. The expression `super.m()` is compiled as dc.`m()`.

The creation of two separate objects may seem to break full abstraction of the compilation scheme in a way similar to what Abadi found out for inner classes [1]. In fact, low level external code is given the functionality to call dc.`m()`, which is not explicitly possible in the high-level language. However, d.`super.m()` is an implicit call to the `m()` method of C, functionality that the high-level language already has. Handling of cross-package inheritance does not add functionality at the low level, so it does not break full abstraction of the compilation scheme.

3.3 Exceptions

Secure compilation of languages supporting exceptions must handle the difficulties that result from the modification of the flow of execution of a program.

```
package P1;
   class G {
      public m():Void{
         try{ new P2.H().e(); } catch (e : P3.MyException){ // handle e
               } }
   }
package P2;
   class H {
      public e():Void throws P3.MyException { throw new P3.MyException();
            }
   }
package P3;
   class MyException implements Throwable {···}
```

Listing 1.3. Example of exceptions usage

Exception handling can be securely implemented by modifying the runtime of the language so that it knows where to dispatch a thrown exception. Activation records are responsible for pointing to the exception handlers in order to propagate a thrown exception to the right handler. In Listing 1.3, the `catch` block of method `m()` in class `G` defines a handler for exceptions of type `MyException`. When the activation record for `m()` is allocated, the handler is registered. When an exception of type `MyException` is thrown, the stack is traversed to find the closest handler for exceptions of type `MyException`. As activation records are traversed and a handler is not found, those records are popped from the stack.

In the context of secure compilation, exception handlers are compiled in the usual manner. In order to implement throwing an exception in secure code that is caught in insecure code (or vice versa), throwing is compiled as callbacks (or calls). Thus two additional entry points are created: the *throw entry point* and the *throwback entry point*. These entry points forward calls to the secure and insecure exception dispatchers, respectively. The secure exception dispatcher traverses the secure stack looking for handlers for the thrown exception. After an activation record has been inspected and deallocated, the exception is forwarded to the external code through the throwback entry point. In order to prevent exploits similar to those of Example 2, the throwback entry point must remember internally allocated exceptions that are thrown to external code. So, a data structure $\mathcal{E}$, similar to $\mathcal{O}$, is created to register leaked exceptions. This prevents external code from passing a fake object identity to the secure exception handler in place of the object identity of an exception, effectively throwing a non-existent exception. External code can implement a wrapper around the exception object identity in order to be able to associate it to its type and then be able to recognise the type of the exception in the handler.

Fig. 2 presents a graphical overview of how exceptions are handled normally (on the left) and in the presented compilation scheme (on the right). Lower case letters indicate the allocation record for the corresponding function. A subscript s indicates a secure function; the stack grows downward. The order in which

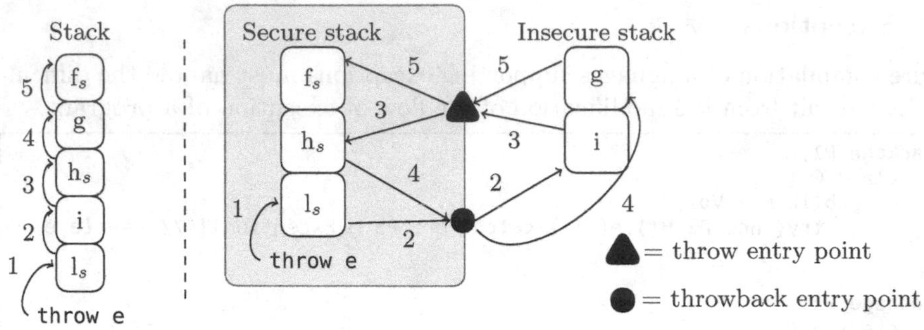

Fig. 2. Comparison of ways to handle exceptions

exception handlers are searched is indicated on arrows. The throw and throwback entry point split the same call in two parts.

Full abstraction of the compilation scheme is preserved since the low-level is not extended with functionality that the high-level lacks. Only exceptions of existing types can be thrown and handling exceptions follows the normal course of the stack. The external code could replace an exception with a fake one, but this is equivalent to the high-level language functionality to catching an exception and throwing another one. Thus the low-level is not granted additional functionality.

3.4 Secure Compilation of Inner Classes

Inner classes are classes that are defined inside another class, as in Listing 1.4. Inner classes have access to private fields of the class they are defined within.

```
class AccountClass implements PI.Account {
  AccountClass() { counter = 0; }
  private counter : Int;

  class Inner { // Inner has access to counter }
}
```

Listing 1.4. Example of an inner class

Inner classes of the secure component are compiled as normal classes in the protected memory partition, in the usual fashion. To implement access from the inner class to the private fields of the surrounding class, a getter and a setter for each of its private fields are created. In the case of Listing 1.4, class `AccountClass` is extended with getters and setters for the `counter` field when compiled. Access from `Inner` to `counter` is compiled as method calls via the getter and setter.

This approach is inspired by Abadi [1], who shows that it breaks full abstraction of compilation in an early version of the JVM. In that setting, the additional low-level methods are not available at the high level, thus other low-level code other than the inner classes can call those methods, achieving something that was not possible at the high level. In our secure compilation scheme, the additional methods are available in the surrounding class. However the additional methods are not made available through entry points, thus the external code cannot invoke them. This means that the addition of inner classes to the secure compilation scheme preserves the full abstraction property.

4 Full Abstraction of the Compilation Scheme

This section presents an outline of the proof of full abstraction of the compilation scheme of Section 3. As mentioned in Section 1, a fully abstract compilation scheme preserves and reflects contextual equivalence of high- and low-level programs. This paper does not argue about the choice of contextual equivalence for modelling security properties [1,2,3,4,7,9,12].

Informally speaking, two programs C_1 and C_2 are contextually equivalent if they behave the same for all possible evaluation contexts they interact with. An evaluation context $\mathbb{C}$ can be thought of as a larger program with a hole. If the hole is filled either with C_1 or C_2, the behaviour of the whole program does not vary. Formally, contextual equivalence is defined as: $C_1 \simeq C_2 \triangleq \forall \mathbb{C}.\ \mathbb{C}[C_1]\Uparrow \iff \mathbb{C}[C_2]\Uparrow$, where $\Uparrow$ denotes divergence [20].

Denote the result of compiling a component C as $C^{\downarrow}$. Full abstraction of the compilation scheme is formally expressed as: $C_1 \simeq C_2 \iff C_1^{\downarrow} \simeq C_2^{\downarrow}$. The co-implication is split in two cases. The direction $C_1^{\downarrow} \simeq C_2^{\downarrow} \Rightarrow C_1 \simeq C_2$ states that the compiler outputs low-level programs that behave as the corresponding source programs. This is what most compilers achieve, at times even certifying the result [5,13]; we are not interested in this direction. This is thus assumed, the consequences of this assumption are made explicit (Assumption 1 below). The direction $C_1 \simeq C_2 \Rightarrow C_1^{\downarrow} \simeq C_2^{\downarrow}$ states that high-level properties are preserved through compilation to the low level. Proving this direction requires reasoning about contexts, which is notoriously difficult [4]. This is even more so in this setting, where low-level contexts are memories lacking any inductive structure. To avoid working with contexts, we equip the low-level language with a trace semantics that is equivalent to its operational semantics [18] (Proposition 1 below) and prove the contrapositive: $\mathsf{Traces_L}(C_1^{\downarrow}) \neq \mathsf{Traces_L}(C_2^{\downarrow}) \Rightarrow C_1 \not\simeq C_2$. This proof is based on an algorithm that creates a high-level component, a "witness" that differentiates C_1 from C_2, given that they have different low-level traces $\overline{\alpha_1}$ and $\overline{\alpha_2}$. This proof strategy is known [3,10], its complexity resides in handling features of the high-level language such as typing or dynamic memory allocation.

This proof, as well as the formalisation of Java Jr. and the assembly language, can be found in the companion report [19]. To further support the validity of this proof, the algorithm has been implemented in Scala, and it outputs Java components that adhere to the Java Jr. formalisation.[1]

Assumption 1 (Compiler preserves behaviour). *The compiler is assumed to output low-level programs that behave as the corresponding input program.*

[1] Available at `http://people.cs.kuleuven.be/~marco.patrignani/Publications.html`

Thus a high-level expression is translated into a list of low-level instructions that preserve the behaviour. By this, we mean that the following properties hold:

- $C_1^{\downarrow} \simeq C_2^{\downarrow} \Rightarrow C_1 \simeq C_2$.
- *There exists an equivalence relation between high-level states and low-level states, such that:*
  - *The initial high- and low-level states are equivalent.*
  - *Given two equivalent states and two corresponding internal transitions, the states these transitions lead to are equivalent. Moreover, given two equivalent states and two equivalent actions, the states these transitions lead to are equivalent.*

Proposition 1 (Trace semantics is equivalent to operational semantics [18]). *For any two low-level components $C_1^{\downarrow}$ and $C_2^{\downarrow}$ obtained from compiling Java Jr. components C_1 and C_2 with the secure compilation scheme, we have that:* $\mathsf{Traces_L}(C_1^{\downarrow}) = \mathsf{Traces_L}(C_2^{\downarrow}) \iff C_1^{\downarrow} \simeq C_2^{\downarrow}$.

Theorem 1 (Differentiation of components). *Any two high-level components C_1 and C_2 that exhibit two different low-level trace semantics are not contextually equivalent. Formally:* $\mathsf{Traces_L}(C_1^{\downarrow}) \neq \mathsf{Traces_L}(C_2^{\downarrow}) \Rightarrow C_1 \not\simeq C_2$.

Theorem 2 (Full abstraction of the compilation scheme). *For any two high-level components C_1 and C_2, we have (assuming there is no overflow of the secure stack or of the secure heap): $C_1 \simeq C_2 \iff C_1^{\downarrow} \simeq C_2^{\downarrow}$.*

5 Benchmarks

This section presents benchmarking of the overhead of the secure compiler, which is proportional to the amount of boundaries crossing.

As a target low-level architecture we chose Fides [3,22]. The Fides architecture implements precisely the protection mechanism described in Section 2.1 in a very reduced TCB: ~7000 lines of code. Fides consists of a hypervisor that runs two virtual machines: one handles the secure memory partition and one handles the other [22]. One consequence is that switching between the two virtual machines of Fides (performing calls and callbacks) is a costly operation.

For the benchmarks, we implemented a secure runtime in C. The secure runtime adds the checks presented in Section 3 to calls, callbacks (both with different number of parameters, ranging from one to eight), returns and returnbacks. These operations are executed on stub objects. A stub objects is a data structure that models the low-level representation of objects; it has an `integer` field that indicates the class of the object followed by the fields of the object. The secure runtime also contains the data structure $\mathcal{O}$ and functions that mask object references through it. Each operation was tested 1000 times on a MacBook Pro with a 2.3 GHz Intel Core i5 processor and 4GB 1333MHz DDR3 RAM. The overhead introduced for each operation ranged from 0.09% to 7.89%, averaging a 3.25% overhead. Details of the measurements can be found in the companion report [19].

6 Limitations

This section presents limitations of the compilation scheme of Section 3 and discusses garbage collection when part of the program is compiled securely.

Like many model languages [2,9], Java Jr. lacks features that real-world programming languages have, such as multithreading, foreign-function interfaces and garbage collection. A thorough investigation of the changes needed in order to support secure compilation of languages with those features is left for future work. Let us now informally discuss how garbage collection can be achieved in concert with a secure compiler.

Garbage collection is a runtime addition that handles whole programs. Firstly, assume that the external code is well-behaved and it does not disrupt the garbage collector, such as by introducing fake pointers. To perform garbage collection when part of the whole program is securely compiled, a part of the garbage collector must be trusted and allocated in the protected memory partition so that it can access $\mathcal{O}$. In this way the garbage collector can traverse the whole object graph and identify the location of a reference that is an index of $\mathcal{O}$.

Assume now that external code can disrupt the functionality of the garbage collector. The classical notion of garbage collection becomes void. In this setting the securely compiled component can be extended with a secure memory manager in charge of the secure memory partition. Here, an arguable safe methodology is to not deallocate a reference that is passed from the secure component to external code, a fact that creates problems when the allocated object is large or when many objects are passed out. In order to provide a solution to part of the problem, the compiler can introduce leasing [8]; this gives objects that are leaked a lifetime duration which, upon expiration, causes object deallocation. Alternatively, the caretaker pattern can be introduced. Instead of leaking an object reference o, the reference is wrapped in a proxy p (the caretaker) and the reference to p is leaked. In addition to method proxies for methods of o, p has a method to set the reference to o to `null`, allowing the secure memory manager to free o's memory. The problem that arises now is a breach in full abstraction: the caretaker pattern must be lifted to the high level to preserve full abstraction.

7 Related Work

This paper extends the work of Agten *et al.* [3], where the same result is achieved, but for a simpler, object-based, high-level language. This work adopts an object-oriented language with dynamic object allocation, cross-package inheritance, exceptions and inner classes, which makes the result significantly harder to achieve.

Secure compilation through full abstraction was pioneered by Abadi [1], where, alongside a result in the π-calculus setting, Java bytecode compilation in the early JVM is shown to expose methods used to access private fields by private inner classes. Kennedy [12] listed six full abstraction failures in the compilation to .NET, half of which have been fixed in modern $C^{\#}$ implementations.

Address space layout randomisation has been adopted by Abadi and Plotkin [2] and subsequently by Jagadeesan *et al.* [9] to guarantee probabilistic full abstraction of a compilation scheme. In both works the low-level language is more high-level than ours and the protection mechanism is different. Compilation does not necessarily need to target machine code, as Fournet *et al.* [7] show by providing a fully abstract compilation scheme from an ML dialect named F* to JavaScript that relies on type-based invariants. Similarly, Ahmed and Blume [4] prove full abstraction of a continuation-passing style translation from simply-typed λ-calculus to System F. In both works, the low-level language is typed and more high-level than ours. The checks introduced by our compilation scheme seem simpler than the checks of Fournet *et al.*

A large amount of work on secure compilation applies to unsafe languages such as C, as surveyed by Younan *et al.* [24]. That research is devoted to strengthening the run-time of C and not on fully abstract compilation.

A different area of research provides security architectures with fine-grained low-level protection mechanisms. Different security architectures with access control mechanisms comparable to ours have been developed in recent years: TrustVisor [14], Flicker [15], Nizza [21], SPMs [17,22][2] and the Intel SGX [16]. The existence of industrial prototypes underlines the feasibility of this approach to bringing efficient, secure, low-level memory access control in commodity hardware. No results comparable to ours were proven for these systems.

8 Conclusion and Future Work

This paper presented a fully abstract compilation scheme for a strongly-typed, single-threaded, component-based, object-oriented programming language with dynamic memory allocation, exceptions, cross-package inheritance and inner classes to untyped machine code enhanced with a low-level protection mechanism. Full abstraction of the compilation scheme is proven correct, guaranteeing preservation and reflection of contextual equivalence between high-level components and their compiled counterparts. From the security perspective this ensures that low-level attackers are restricted to the same capabilities high-level attackers have. To the best of our knowledge, this is the first result of its kind for such an expressive high-level language and such a powerful low-level one.

Future work includes extending the results to a language with more real-world programming language features such as concurrency and distribution.

References

1. Abadi, M.: Protection in programming-language translations. In: Vitek, J. (ed.) Secure Internet Programming. LNCS, vol. 1603, pp. 19–34. Springer, Heidelberg (1999)
2. Abadi, M., Plotkin, G.: On protection by layout randomization. In: CSF 2010, pp. 337–351. IEEE (2010)
3. Agten, P., Strackx, R., Jacobs, B., Piessens, F.: Secure compilation to modern processors. In: CSF 2012, pp. 171–185. IEEE (2012)
4. Ahmed, A., Blume, M.: An equivalence-preserving CPS translation via multi-language semantics. SIGPLAN Not. 46(9), 431–444 (2011)

[2] More thoroughly described at: `https://distrinet.cs.kuleuven.be/software/pcbac`

5. Chlipala, A.: A certified type-preserving compiler from lambda calculus to assembly language. SIGPLAN Not. 42(6), 54–65 (2007)
6. Ducournau, R.: Implementing statically typed object-oriented programming languages. ACM Comput. Surv. 43(3), 18:1–18:48 (2011)
7. Fournet, C., Swamy, N., Chen, J., Dagand, P.-E., Strub, P.-Y., Livshits, B.: Fully abstract compilation to JavaScript. In: POPL 2013, pp. 371–384. ACM, New York (2013)
8. Gray, C., Cheriton, D.: Leases: an efficient fault-tolerant mechanism for distributed file cache consistency. SIGOPS Oper. Syst. Rev. 23(5), 202–210 (1989)
9. Jagadeesan, R., Pitcher, C., Rathke, J., Riely, J.: Local memory via layout randomization. In: CSF 2011, pp. 161–174. IEEE (2011)
10. Jeffrey, A., Rathke, J.: A fully abstract testing semantics for concurrent objects. Theor. Comput. Sci. 338(1-3), 17–63 (2005)
11. Jeffrey, A., Rathke, J.: Java JR: Fully Abstract Trace Semantics for a Core Java Language. In: Sagiv, M. (ed.) ESOP 2005. LNCS, vol. 3444, pp. 423–438. Springer, Heidelberg (2005)
12. Kennedy, A.: Securing the.NET programming model. Theor. Comput. Sci. 364(3), 311–317 (2006)
13. Leroy, X.: A formally verified compiler back-end. J. Autom. Reason. 43(4), 363–446 (2009)
14. McCune, J.M., Li, Y., Qu, N., Zhou, Z., Datta, A., Gligor, V., Perrig, A.: Trustvisor: Efficient TCB reduction and attestation. In: SP 2010, pp. 143–158. IEEE (2010)
15. McCune, J.M., Parno, B.J., Perrig, A., Reiter, M.K., Isozaki, H.: Flicker: an execution infrastructure for TCB minimization. SIGOPS Oper. Syst. Rev. 42(4), 315–328 (2008)
16. McKeen, F., Alexandrovich, I., Berenzon, A., Rozas, C.V., Shafi, H., Shanbhogue, V., Savagaonkar, U.R.: Innovative instructions and software model for isolated execution. In: HASP 2013, pp. 10:1–10:1. ACM (2013)
17. Noorman, J., Agten, P., Daniels, W., Strackx, R., Van Herrewege, A., Huygens, C., Preneel, B., Verbauwhede, I., Piessens, F.: Sancus: Low-cost trustworthy extensible networked devices with a zero-software Trusted Computing Base. In: Proceedings of the 22nd USENIX Conference on Security Symposium. USENIX Association (2013)
18. Patrignani, M., Clarke, D.: Fully abstract trace semantics for low-level isolation mechanisms (under submission, 2013)
19. Patrignani, M., Clarke, D., Piessens, F.: Secure Compilation of Object-Oriented Components to Protected Module Architectures – Extended Version. CW Reports CW646, Dept. of Computer Science, K.U.Leuven (2013)
20. Plotkin, G.D.: LCF considered as a programming language. Theoretical Computer Science 5, 223–255 (1977)
21. Singaravelu, L., Pu, C., Härtig, H., Helmuth, C.: Reducing TCB complexity for security-sensitive applications: three case studies. SIGOPS Oper. Syst. Rev. 40(4), 161–174 (2006)
22. Strackx, R., Piessens, F.: Fides: Selectively hardening software application components against kernel-level or process-level malware. In: CCS 2012, pp. 2–13. ACM Press (October 2012)
23. van Dooren, M., Clarke, D., Jacobs, B.: Subobject-oriented programming. In: Formal Methods for Objects and Components (to appear, 2013)
24. Younan, Y., Joosen, W., Piessens, F.: Runtime countermeasures for code injection attacks against C and C++ programs. ACM Computing Surveys 44(3), 17:1–17:28 (2012)

Generalized Quantitative Analysis of Metric Transition Systems

Uli Fahrenberg and Axel Legay

Irisa / INRIA Rennes, France

Abstract. The formalism of metric transition systems, as introduced by de Alfaro, Faella and Stoelinga, is convenient for modeling systems and properties with quantitative information, such as probabilities or time. For a number of applications however, one needs other distances than the point-wise (and possibly discounted) linear and branching distances introduced by de Alfaro *et.al.* for analyzing quantitative behavior.

In this paper, we show a vast generalization of the setting of de Alfaro *et.al.*, to a framework where any of a large number of other useful distances can be applied. Concrete instantiations of our framework hence give *e.g.* limit-average, discounted-sum, or maximum-lead linear and branching distances; in each instantiation, properties similar to the ones of de Alfaro *et.al.* hold.

In the end, we achieve a framework which is not only suitable for modeling different kinds of quantitative systems and properties, but also for analyzing these by using different application-determined ways of measuring quantitative behavior.

1 Introduction

During the last decade, formal verification has seen a trend towards modeling and analyzing systems which contain quantitative information. This is motivated by applications in real-time systems, hybrid systems, embedded systems and others. Quantitative information can thus be a variety of things: probabilities, time, tank pressure, energy intake, *etc.*

A number of quantitative models have hence been developed: probabilistic automata [39], stochastic process algebras [30], timed automata [2], hybrid automata [1], continuous-time Markov chains [40], *etc.* Similarly, there is a number of specification formalisms for expressing quantitative properties: timed computation tree logic [29], probabilistic computation tree logic [26], metric temporal logic [31], stochastic continuous logic [3], *etc.*

Quantitative model checking, the verification of quantitative properties for quantitative systems, has also seen rapid development: for probabilistic systems in PRISM [32] and PEPA [23], for real-time systems in UPPAAL [35] and RED [46], and for hybrid systems in HyTech [27] and SpaceEx [22], to name but a few.

Quantitative model checking has, however, a problem of *robustness*. When the answers to model checking problems are Boolean—either a system meets its

C.-c. Shan (Ed.): APLAS 2013, LNCS 8301, pp. 192–208, 2013.

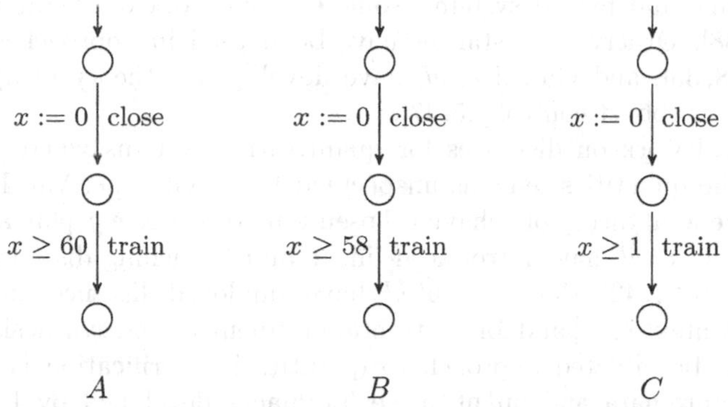

Fig. 1. Three timed automata modeling a train crossing

specification or it does not—then small perturbations in the system's parameters may invalidate the result. This means that, from a model checking point of view, small, perhaps unimportant, deviations in quantities are indistinguishable from larger ones which may be critical.

As an example, Fig. 1 shows three simple timed-automata models of a train crossing, each modeling that once the gates are closed, some time will pass before the train arrives. Now if the specification of the system is "The gates have to be closed 60 seconds before the train arrives", then model A does satisfy the specification, and models B and C do not. What this does not tell us, however, is that model C is dangerously far away from the specification, whereas model B only violates it slightly (and may be acceptable from a practical point of view).

In order to address the robustness problem, one approach is to replace the Boolean yes-no answers of standard verification with distances. That is, the Boolean co-domain of model checking is replaced by the non-negative real numbers. In this setting, the Boolean `true` corresponds to a distance of zero and `false` to the non-zero numbers, so that quantitative model checking can now tell us not only that a specification is violated, but also *how much* it is violated, or *how far* the system is from corresponding to its specification.

In our example, and depending on precisely how one wishes to measure distances, the distance from A to our specification is 0, whereas the distances from B and C to the specification may be 2 and 59, respectively. Note that the precise interpretation of distance values will be application-dependent; but in any case, it is clear that C is much further away from the specification than B is.

The distance-based approach to quantitative verification has been developed the furthest for probabilistic and stochastic systems, perhaps akin to the fact that for these systems, the need for a truly quantitative verification is felt the most urgent. Panangaden and Desharnais *et.al.* have worked with distances for Markov processes *e.g.* in [4, 16, 34, 37], and van Breugel and Worrell *et.al.* have developed distances for probabilistic transition systems *e.g.* in [44, 45]. De Alfaro and Stoelinga *et.al.* have worked on distances between probabilistic systems and specifications in [13, 14] and other papers.

For real-time and hybrid systems, some explicit work on distances is available in [28, 38]. Otherwise, distances have been used in approaches to robust verification [8, 33], and Girard *et.al.* have developed a theory of approximate bisimulation for robust control [25, 47].

Also general work on distances for quantitative systems where the precise meaning of the quantities remains unspecified has been done. Van Breugel has developed a general theory of behavioral pseudometrics, see *e.g.* [43], and Fahrenberg and Legay *et.al.* have introduced linear and branching distances for such systems in [5, 6, 21, 42]. Henzinger *et.al.* have employed distances in a software engineering context in [9] and for abstraction refinement and synthesis in [10, 11].

A different but related approach to quantitative verification is the theory of weighted automata and quantitative languages developed by Droste *et.al.* in [17–19] and by Henzinger and Chatterjee *et.al.* in [7, 12].

Common to all the above distance-based approaches is that they introduce distances between systems, or between systems and specifications, and then employ these for approximate or quantitative verification. However, depending on the application context, a plethora of different distances are being used. Consequently, there is a need for a general theory of quantitative verification which depends as little as possible on the concrete distances being used. This is a point of view which is argued in [6, 10, 11, 21], and a number of the above papers [7, 17, 19, 37, 43] attempt to develop the theory at this general level.

To be more specific, most of the above approaches can be classified according to the way they measure distances between *executions*, or system traces. The perhaps easiest such way is the *point-wise* distance, which measures the greatest individual distance between corresponding points in the traces. Theory for this specific distance has been developed *e.g.* in [8, 13–15, 42]. Sometimes *discounting* is applied to diminish the influence of individual distances far in the future, *e.g.* in [13–15].

Another distance which has been used is the *accumulating* one, which sums individual distances along executions. Two major types have been considered here: the *discounted* accumulating distance *e.g.* in [5, 9, 42] and the *limit-average* accumulating distance *e.g.* in [9]. For real-time systems, a useful distance is the *maximum-lead* one of [28, 42] which measures the maximum difference between accumulated time delays along traces. For hybrid systems, things are more complicated, as distances between hybrid traces have to take into account both spatial and timing differences, see *e.g.* [24, 25, 38, 47].

It is our point of view that the differences between measuring distances between system traces are fundamental, in the sense that specifying one concrete way of measuring such trace distances fixes the quantitative semantics to a concrete application. Any general theory of quantitative verification should, then, be independent of the way one measures distances between traces.

In this paper we show how such a distance-independent theory of quantitative verification may be attempted. Taking as our model of quantitative systems the *metric transition systems* of [15] and starting out with an abstract distance on traces, we define linear and branching distances and show that they have the expected properties. Our linear distances generalize trace inclusion and equivalence to the general quantitative setting, and the branching distances generalize simulation and bisimulation.

As a central technical tool in our developments, we assume that the trace distance factors through a complete lattice, and that this lifted trace distance has a recursive characterization. We show that this assumption holds for most of the trace distances considered in the above-mentioned papers; specifically, our theory can be instantiated with the point-wise (and possibly discounted) distance, the accumulating distance (both discounted and limit-average), and the maximum-lead distance.

This paper follows up on work in [21], where we develop a general quantitative theory for weighted transition systems, using the theory of quantitative games. Compared to this work, the present paper uses a different model for quantitative systems (namely, the one from [15]), hence the linear and branching distances have to be defined differently; also, no game theory is necessary for us here.

2 Metric Transition Systems

We recapitulate the setting and terminology of [15], adapting it slightly to our needs.

A *hemimetric* on a set X is a function $d : X \times X \to \mathbb{R}_{\geq 0} \cup \{\infty\}$ which satisfies $d(x, x) = 0$ and $d(x, y) + d(y, z) \geq d(x, z)$ (the *triangle inequality*) for all $x, y, z \in X$. The hemimetric is said to be *symmetric* if also $d(x, y) = d(y, x)$ for all $x, y \in X$; it is said to be *separating* if $d(x, y) = 0$ implies $x = y$. The terms "pseudometric" for a symmetric hemimetric, "quasimetric" for a separating hemimetric, and "metric" for a hemimetric which is both symmetric and separating are also in use, but we will not use them here. The tuple (X, d) is called a *hemimetric space*.

In [15], hemimetrics are called "directed metrics", "undirected" is used instead of "symmetric", and "proper" instead of "separating". Our choice of jargon is driven by a wish to follow more-or-less established terminology; specifically, the term "metric" has a standard meaning in mathematics, so that we find the term "directed metric" for what should better be called a "directed *quasi*metric" (or, "pseudometric") unfortunate. Similarly, our use of "separating" instead of "proper" is motivated by the use of this term in topology: the topology induced by a (separating) metric has the T_2 Hausdorff separation property, whereas the one induced by a pseudometric does not.

Note that our hemimetrics are *extended* in that they can take the value ∞. This is convenient for several reasons, *cf.* [36], one of them being that it allows for a disjoint union, or coproduct, of hemimetric spaces: the disjoint union of (X_1, d_1) and (X_2, d_2) is the hemimetric space $(X_1, d_1) \uplus (X_1, d_2) = (X_1 \uplus X_2, d)$ where points from different components are infinitely far away from each other, *i.e.* with d defined by

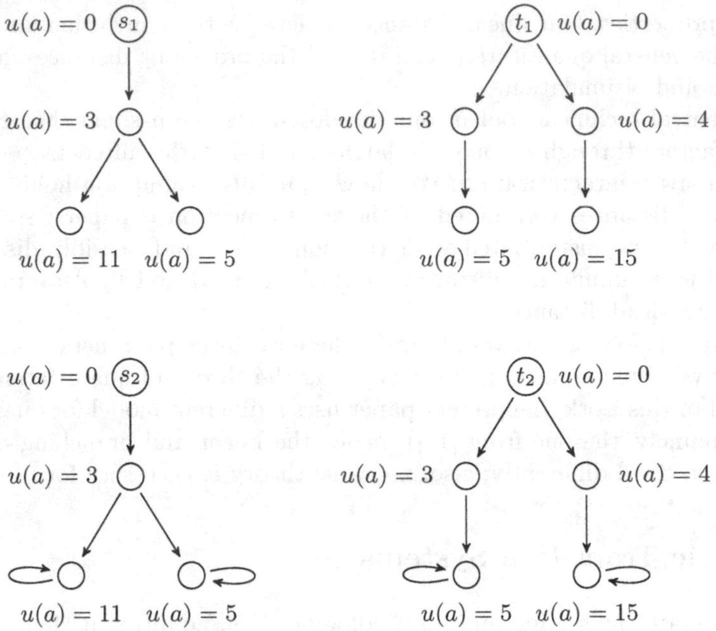

Fig. 2. Example of a metric transition system

$$d(x,y) = \begin{cases} d_1(x,y) & \text{if } x, y \in X_1, \\ d_2(x,y) & \text{if } x, y \in X_2, \\ \infty & \text{otherwise.} \end{cases}$$

We will need to generalize hemimetrics to codomains other than $\mathbb{R}_{\geq 0} \cup \{\infty\}$. For a partially ordered monoid $(M, \sqsubseteq, \oplus, \not\vdash)$, an *M-hemimetric* on X is a function $d : X \times X \to M$ which satisfies $d(x,x) = \not\vdash$ and $d(x,y) \oplus d(y,z) \sqsupseteq d(x,z)$ for all $x, y, z \in X$; symmetry and separation are generalized in similar ways.

Let Σ be a set of atomic propositions and (X, d) a hemimetric space; these will be fixed throughout this paper. A *valuation* on Σ is a mapping $u : \Sigma \to X$; the set of all valuations on Σ is denoted $\mathcal{U}[\Sigma]$. Note that in the setting of [15], each proposition a takes values in a separate hemimetric space X_a. Using extended hemimetrics allows us to unite all these spaces into one. The *propositional distance* [15] is the mapping $pd : \mathcal{U}[\Sigma] \times \mathcal{U}[\Sigma] \to \mathbb{R}_{\geq 0}$ defined by $pd(u, v) = \sup_{a \in \Sigma} d(u(a), v(a))$.

A *metric transition system* (MTS) $\mathcal{S} = (S, T, [\cdot])$ consists of sets S of states and $T \subseteq S \times S$ of transitions, together with a state valuation mapping $[\cdot] : S \to \mathcal{U}[\Sigma]$. For $s, t \in S$, we write $s \to t$ iff $(s,t) \in T$. Fig. 2 shows a simple example of a MTS over $\Sigma = \{a\}$ which we will use later.

A *path* in $\mathcal{S}$ is a (finite or infinite) sequence $\pi = (\pi_0, \pi_1, \dots)$ of states $\pi_i \in S$ in which $\pi_i \to \pi_{i+1}$ for all i. Note that, extending [15], we also handle finite paths instead of only infinite ones.

A *trace* in Σ is a (finite or infinite) sequence $\sigma = (\sigma_0, \sigma_1, \dots)$ of valuations $\sigma_i \in \mathcal{U}[\Sigma]$. The set of such traces is denoted $\mathcal{U}[\Sigma]^\infty$. For a path π in S, its *induced trace* is $[\pi] = ([\pi_0], [\pi_1], \dots)$. For a state $s \in S$, we let $\text{Tr}(s) = \{[\pi] \mid \pi_0 = s\}$ denote the set of traces emanating from s. We introduce some convenient notation for traces: ϵ denotes the empty trace, $u.\sigma$ the concatenation of $u \in \mathcal{U}[\Sigma]$ with $\sigma \in \mathcal{U}[\Sigma]^\infty$, and $\mathsf{len}(\sigma)$ the length (finite or ∞) of σ.

As usual, a relation $R \subseteq S \times S$ is called a *simulation* (on S) if it holds that $[s] = [t]$ for all $(s,t) \in S$ and

- for all $s \to s'$ there is $t \to t'$ such that $(s', t') \in R$.

R is called a *bisimulation* if, additionally,

- for all $t \to t'$ there is $s \to s'$ such that $(s', t') \in R$.

We write $s \preceq t$ if there is a simulation R with $(s,t) \in R$, and $s \approx t$ if there is a bisimulation R with $(s,t) \in R$.

3 Examples of Trace Distances

We can now give concrete examples of trace distances which have been used in the literature.

The *point-wise* trace distance is $td_{\mathsf{pw}} : \mathcal{U}[\Sigma]^\infty \times \mathcal{U}[\Sigma]^\infty \to \mathbb{R}_{\geq 0} \cup \{\infty\}$ defined by

$$td_{\mathsf{pw}}(\sigma,\tau) = \begin{cases} \infty & \text{if } \mathsf{len}(\sigma) \neq \mathsf{len}(\tau), \\ \sup_i pd(\sigma_i, \tau_i) & \text{otherwise.} \end{cases}$$

This distance has been employed in [8, 13–15, 42].

Using a *discount factor* $\lambda \in \mathbb{R}_{\geq 0}$ with $\lambda < 1$, one may discount the influence of individual distances which occur further along the traces. The *discounted point-wise* trace distance, which has been used in [13–15], is thus $td_{\mathsf{pw},\lambda} : \mathcal{U}[\Sigma]^\infty \times \mathcal{U}[\Sigma]^\infty \to \mathbb{R}_{\geq 0} \cup \{\infty\}$ defined by

$$td_{\mathsf{pw},\lambda}(\sigma,\tau) = \begin{cases} \infty & \text{if } \mathsf{len}(\sigma) \neq \mathsf{len}(\tau), \\ \sup_i \lambda^i pd(\sigma_i, \tau_i) & \text{otherwise.} \end{cases}$$

The *accumulating* trace distance is $td_{\mathsf{acc}} : \mathcal{U}[\Sigma]^\infty \times \mathcal{U}[\Sigma]^\infty \to \mathbb{R}_{\geq 0} \cup \{\infty\}$ defined by

$$td_{\mathsf{acc}}(\sigma,\tau) = \begin{cases} \infty & \text{if } \mathsf{len}(\sigma) \neq \mathsf{len}(\tau), \\ \sum_i pd(\sigma_i, \tau_i) & \text{otherwise.} \end{cases}$$

This distance is typically used with discounting or limit-averaging:

Using again a discount factor $\lambda \in \mathbb{R}_{\geq 0}$ with $\lambda < 1$, the *discounted accumulating* trace distance is $td_{\mathsf{acc},\lambda} : \mathcal{U}[\Sigma]^\infty \times \mathcal{U}[\Sigma]^\infty \to \mathbb{R}_{\geq 0} \cup \{\infty\}$ defined by

$$td_{\mathsf{acc},\lambda}(\sigma,\tau) = \begin{cases} \infty & \text{if } \mathsf{len}(\sigma) \neq \mathsf{len}(\tau), \\ \sum_i \lambda^i pd(\sigma_i, \tau_i) & \text{otherwise.} \end{cases}$$

This distance has been used in [5,9,42].

The *limit-average* trace distance, which has been used in [9], is $td_{\mathsf{limavg}} : \mathcal{U}[\Sigma]^\infty \times \mathcal{U}[\Sigma]^\infty \to \mathbb{R}_{\geq 0} \cup \{\infty\}$ defined by

$$td_{\mathsf{limavg}}(\sigma, \tau) = \begin{cases} \infty & \text{if } \mathsf{len}(\sigma) \neq \mathsf{len}(\tau), \\ \liminf_j \frac{1}{j+1} \sum_{i=0}^{j} pd(\sigma_i, \tau_i) & \text{otherwise.} \end{cases}$$

This is generally defined only for infinite traces. If one wants it defined also for finite traces σ, τ (of equal length N), one can patch σ and τ so that $pd(\sigma_i, \tau_i) = 0$ for $i > N$; then $td_{\mathsf{limavg}}(\sigma, \tau) = 0$ in this case.

Both the discounted accumulating and limit-average trace distances are well-known from the theory of discounted and mean-payoff games [20,48].

The *maximum-lead* trace distance $td_{\mathsf{maxlead}} : \mathcal{U}[\Sigma]^\infty \times \mathcal{U}[\Sigma]^\infty \to \mathbb{R}_{\geq 0} \cup \{\infty\}$ from [28,42] is only defined for the case where the valuation space is $X = \mathbb{R}$. It is given by

$$td_{\mathsf{maxlead}}(\sigma, \tau) = \begin{cases} \infty & \text{if } \mathsf{len}(\sigma) \neq \mathsf{len}(\tau), \\ \sup_j \sup_{a \in \Sigma} \left| \sum_{i=0}^{j} \sigma_i(a) - \sum_{i=0}^{j} \tau_i(a) \right| & \text{otherwise.} \end{cases}$$

4 Linear Distances

To generalize the examples of the previous section, we define a trace distance to be a general hemimetric on traces which specializes to the propositional distance on individual valuations and is finite only for traces of equal length:

Definition 1. *A* trace distance *is a hemimetric* $td : \mathcal{U}[\Sigma]^\infty \times \mathcal{U}[\Sigma]^\infty \to \mathbb{R}_{\geq 0} \cup \{\infty\}$ *for which* $td(u, v) = pd(u, v)$ *for all* $u, v \in \mathcal{U}[\Sigma]$ *and* $td(\sigma, \tau) = \infty$ *whenever* $\mathsf{len}(\sigma) \neq \mathsf{len}(\tau)$.

We note that in case pd is separating, then also all example trace distances from Section 3 are separating, except for the limit-average distance. For the latter, $td_{\mathsf{limavg}}(\sigma, \tau) = 0$ iff either $\sigma = \tau$ are finite traces, or there exists an index k such that $\sigma_i = \tau_i$ for all $i \geq k$. Also, the maximum-lead trace distance is symmetric; the others are symmetric iff pd is symmetric.

For any given trace distance, we can define the linear distance between states in S as the (asymmetric) *Hausdorff distance* between the corresponding sets of traces:

Definition 2. *For a given trace distance td, the* linear distance *induced by td is* $ld : S \times S \to \mathbb{R}_{\geq 0} \cup \{\infty\}$ *given by*

$$ld(s, t) = \sup_{\sigma \in \mathrm{Tr}(s)} \inf_{\tau \in \mathrm{Tr}(t)} td(\sigma, \tau).$$

The symmetric linear distance *induced by td is* $\overline{ld} : S \times S \to \mathbb{R}_{\geq 0} \cup \{\infty\}$ *given by* $\overline{ld}(s, t) = \max(ld(s, t), ld(t, s))$.

Continuing the example from Fig. 2, we compute the linear distances $ld(s_1, t_1)$ and $ld(s_2, t_2)$ induced by all our example trace distances, using the usual metric on $\mathbb{R}$ for valuations and a discount factor of $\lambda = .9$ where applicable:

$$\begin{aligned} ld_{\mathsf{pw}}(s_1, t_1) &= 4 & ld_{\mathsf{pw}}(s_2, t_2) &= 4 \\ ld_{\mathsf{pw},\lambda}(s_1, t_1) &= 3.24 & ld_{\mathsf{pw}}(s_2, t_2) &= 3.24 \\ ld_{\mathsf{acc}}(s_1, t_1) &= 5 & ld_{\mathsf{acc}}(s_2, t_2) &= \infty \\ ld_{\mathsf{acc},\lambda}(s_1, t_1) &= 4.14 & ld_{\mathsf{acc},\lambda}(s_2, t_2) &= 33.3 \\ ld_{\mathsf{limavg}}(s_1, t_2) &= 0 & ld_{\mathsf{limavg}}(s_2, t_2) &= 4 \\ ld_{\mathsf{maxlead}}(s_1, t_1) &= 5 & ld_{\mathsf{maxlead}}(s_2, t_2) &= \infty \end{aligned}$$

Our first theorem shows that for separating trace distances on finite transition systems, trace inclusion is the kernel of ld and trace equivalence the kernel of $\overline{ld}$:

Theorem 1. *Let S be finite and td separating. For all $s, t \in S$, $\mathrm{Tr}(s) \subseteq \mathrm{Tr}(t)$ iff $ld(s,t) = 0$ and $\mathrm{Tr}(s) = \mathrm{Tr}(t)$ iff $\overline{ld}(s,t) = 0$.*

Proof. It is clear that $\mathrm{Tr}(s) \subseteq \mathrm{Tr}(t)$ implies $ld(s,t) = 0$. For the opposite direction, assume $ld(s,t) = 0$ and let $\sigma \in \mathrm{Tr}(s)$. For every $i \in \mathbb{N}_+$, there exists $\tau_i \in \mathrm{Tr}(t)$ for which $td(\sigma, \tau_i) < \frac{1}{i}$. Because S is finite, there is an index N such that $\tau_i = \tau_N$ for all $i \geq N$. Then $td(\sigma, \tau_N) = 0$ and thus, as td is separating, $\sigma = \tau_N$. The second bi-implication is now clear. □

Note that we have also shown the statement that, whether td is separating or not, $ld(s,t) = 0$ implies that for every $\sigma \in \mathrm{Tr}(s)$, there exists $\tau \in \mathrm{Tr}(t)$ with $td(\sigma, \tau) = 0$. An example in [15] shows that precisely this statement may fail in case S is not finite.

5 Branching Distances

We have seen in Theorem 1 that the linear distances of the previous section are generalizations of trace inclusion and trace equivalence. In order to generalize simulation and bisimulation in a similar manner, we define branching distances.

To be able to introduce these branching distances, we need to assume that our trace distance td factors through a complete lattice, and that the lifted trace distance has a recursive characterization as given below. We will see in Section 6 that this is the case for all the example trace distances of Section 3.

For any set M, let $\mathbb{L}M = (\mathbb{R}_{\geq 0} \cup \{\infty\})^M$ be the set of functions from M to $\mathbb{R}_{\geq 0} \cup \{\infty\}$. Then $\mathbb{L}M$ is a complete lattice with partial order $\sqsubseteq$ given by $\alpha \sqsubseteq \beta$ iff $\alpha(x) \leq \beta(x)$ for all $x \in M$, and with an addition $\oplus$ given by $(\alpha \oplus \beta)(x) = \alpha(x) + \beta(x)$. The bottom element of $\mathbb{L}M$ is also the zero of $\oplus$ and given by $\bot(x) = 0$, and the top element is $\top(x) = \infty$.

Definition 3. *A* recursive specification *of a trace distance td consists of a set M, a lattice homomorphism* $\mathsf{eval} : \mathbb{L}M \to \mathbb{R}_{\geq 0} \cup \{\infty\}$ *and an $\mathbb{L}M$-hemimetric*

$td^{\mathbb{L}} : \mathcal{U}[\Sigma]^\infty \times \mathcal{U}[\Sigma]^\infty \to \mathbb{L}M$ which together satisfy $td = \mathsf{eval} \circ td^{\mathbb{L}}$, and a function $F : \mathcal{U}[\Sigma] \times \mathcal{U}[\Sigma] \times \mathbb{L}M \to \mathbb{L}M$. F must be monotone in the third coordinate, i.e. $F(u, v, \cdot) : \mathbb{L}M \to \mathbb{L}M$ is monotone for all $u, v \in \mathcal{U}[\Sigma]$, have $F(u, u, \bot) = \bot$ for all $u \in \mathcal{U}[\Sigma]$, and satisfy, for all $u, v \in \mathcal{U}[\Sigma]$ and $\sigma, \tau \in \mathcal{U}[\Sigma]^\infty$, that $td^{\mathbb{L}}(u.\sigma, v.\tau) = F(u, v, td^{\mathbb{L}}(\sigma, \tau))$.

Now if *td* is recursively specified as above, then we can use the recursion to introduce branching distances *sd* and *bd* which generalize simulation and bisimulation:

Definition 4. *For a recursively specified trace distance td, let $sd^{\mathbb{L}}, bd^{\mathbb{L}} : S \times S \to \mathbb{L}M$ be the respective least fixed points to the equations*

$$sd^{\mathbb{L}}(s,t) = \sup_{s \to s'} \inf_{t \to t'} F([s], [t], sd^{\mathbb{L}}(s', t')), \tag{1}$$

$$bd^{\mathbb{L}}(s,t) = \max \begin{cases} \sup_{s \to s'} \inf_{t \to t'} F([s], [t], bd^{\mathbb{L}}(s', t')), \\ \sup_{t \to t'} \inf_{s \to s'} F([s], [t], bd^{\mathbb{L}}(s', t')). \end{cases} \tag{2}$$

The simulation distance *induced by td is $sd : S \times S \to \mathbb{R}_{\geq 0} \cup \{\infty\}$ given by $sd = \mathsf{eval} \circ sd^{\mathbb{L}}$; the* bisimulation distance *induced by td is $bd : S \times S \to \mathbb{R}_{\geq 0} \cup \{\infty\}$ given by $bd = \mathsf{eval} \circ bd^{\mathbb{L}}$.*

Note that we define the distances using *least* fixed points, as opposed to the *greatest* fixed point definition of standard (bi)simulation. Informally, this is because our order is reversed: we are not interested in maximizing (bi)simulation relations, but in *minimizing* (bi)simulation distance.

Lemma 1. *The mappings sd and bd are well-defined hemimetrics on S.*

Proof. We show the proof for *sd*; for *bd* it is similar. Let $\mathbb{F}S = \mathbb{L}M^{S \times S}$ be the lattice of functions from $S \times S$ to $\mathbb{L}M$, then $\mathbb{F}S$ is complete because $\mathbb{L}M$ is. Let $I : \mathbb{F}S \to \mathbb{F}S$ be defined by

$$I(f)(s,t) = \sup_{s \to s'} \inf_{t \to t'} F([s], [t], f(s', t')),$$

similarly to (1). Because $F([s], [t], \cdot) : \mathbb{L}M \to \mathbb{L}M$ is monotone for all $s, t \in S$, I is monotone. Using Tarski's fixed-point theorem, we can hence conclude that I has a unique minimal fixed point, which is $sd^{\mathbb{L}}$. Clearly $sd^{\mathbb{L}}(s, s) = \bot$ for all $s \in S$, and by induction one can show that $sd^{\mathbb{L}}(s,t) \oplus sd^{\mathbb{L}}(t,u) \sqsupseteq sd^{\mathbb{L}}(s,u)$ for all $s, t, u \in S$. Hence $sd^{\mathbb{L}}$ is an $\mathbb{L}M$-hemimetric and *sd* is a hemimetric. □

In order to show, similarly to Theorem 1, that simulation is the kernel of simulation distance, we need a condition on the recursive F which mimics the separation condition for hemimetrics. We say that a recursively specified trace distance *td* is *recursively separating* if $F : \mathcal{U}[\Sigma] \times \mathcal{U}[\Sigma] \times \mathbb{L}M \to \mathbb{L}M$ satisfies the condition that whenever $F(u, v, x) = \bot$, then $u = v$ and $x = \bot$. Note that this condition implies that $td^{\mathbb{L}}$ is separating.

Theorem 2. *Let S be finite and td recursively specified and recursively separating. For all $s, t \in S$, $s \preceq t$ iff $sd^{\mathbb{L}}(s,t) = \bot$ and $s \approx t$ iff $bd^{\mathbb{L}}(s,t) = \bot$.*

Proof. It is clear that $s \preceq t$ implies $sd^{\mathbb{L}}(s,t) = \bot$. For the other direction, let $R = \{(s',t') \mid sd^{\mathbb{L}}(s',t') = \bot\} \subseteq S \times S$. Then $(s,t) \in R$. Let $(s',t') \in R$, then $\sup_{s' \to s''} \inf_{t' \to t''} F([s'],[t'], sd^{\mathbb{L}}(s'',t'')) = \bot$. As S is finite, this implies that for all $s' \to s''$, there exists $t' \to t''$ with $F([s'],[t'], sd^{\mathbb{L}}(s'',t'')) = \bot$. By recursive separation, we hence have $[s'] = [t']$ and $sd^{\mathbb{L}}(s'',t'') = \bot$. We have shown that R is a simulation on S. The proof that $s \approx t$ iff $bd^{\mathbb{L}}(s,t) = \bot$ is similar. □

The next theorem gives the relations between the different distances we have introduced. Also these relations generalize the situation in the Boolean setting: in light of Theorems 1 and 2, they are quantitative analogues to the facts that simulation implies trace inclusion and that bisimulation implies simulation and trace equivalence.

Theorem 3. *Let td be recursively specified. For all $s, t \in S$, $ld(s,t) \le sd(s,t) \le bd(s,t)$ and $\overline{ld}(s,t) \le bd(s,t)$.*

Proof. The proof is best understood in a setting of *quantitative games, cf.* [21]. In this setting, the standard simulation and bisimulation games [41] are generalized to games with quantitative objectives. One can then see that the linear distances can be computed by similar games, and that the only differences between these games are given by certain restrictions on the strategies available to the first player. The result follows from inclusions on these sets of restricted strategies.

We can, however, also give a direct proof of the fact that $ld(s,t) \le sd(s,t)$ without resorting to games (and similar proofs may be given for the other inequalities). To do so, we need to lift ld to the lattice $\mathbb{L}M$: for $s, t \in S$, define

$$ld^{\mathbb{L}}(s,t) = \sup_{\sigma \in \mathrm{Tr}(s)} \inf_{\tau \in \mathrm{Tr}(t)} td^{\mathbb{L}}(\sigma, \tau),$$

then $ld = \mathsf{eval} \circ ld^{\mathbb{L}}$ because eval is monotone. We show that $ld^{\mathbb{L}}(s,t) \sqsubseteq sd^{\mathbb{L}}(s,t)$ for all $s, t \in S$, which will imply the result.

Let $s, t \in S$. We have

$$\begin{aligned}
ld^{\mathbb{L}}(s,t) &= \sup_{\sigma \in \mathrm{Tr}(s)} \inf_{\tau \in \mathrm{Tr}(t)} td^{\mathbb{L}}(\sigma, \tau) \\
&= \sup_{s \to s'} \sup_{\sigma' \in \mathrm{Tr}(s')} \inf_{t \to t'} \inf_{\tau' \in \mathrm{Tr}(t')} td^{\mathbb{L}}([s].\sigma', [t].\tau') \\
&= \sup_{s \to s'} \sup_{\sigma' \in \mathrm{Tr}(s')} \inf_{t \to t'} \inf_{\tau' \in \mathrm{Tr}(t')} F([s],[t], td^{\mathbb{L}}(\sigma', \tau')) \\
&\sqsubseteq \sup_{s \to s'} \inf_{t \to t'} \sup_{\sigma' \in \mathrm{Tr}(s')} \inf_{\tau' \in \mathrm{Tr}(t')} F([s],[t], td^{\mathbb{L}}(\sigma', \tau')) \\
&= \sup_{s \to s'} \inf_{t \to t'} F([s],[t], \sup_{\sigma' \in \mathrm{Tr}(s')} \inf_{\tau' \in \mathrm{Tr}(t')} td^{\mathbb{L}}(\sigma', \tau')) \\
&= \sup_{s \to s'} \inf_{t \to t'} F([s],[t], ld^{\mathbb{L}}(s',t')),
\end{aligned}$$

and the statement now follows by induction. □

6 Examples Revisited

We can now apply the constructions of Section 5 to the example trace distances from Section 3. We give recursive specifications for all distances and deduce the corresponding branching distances. For ease of exposition, we will only consider ourselves with the simulation distances here, but similar things can be said about the bisimulation distances.

For the *point-wise* trace distance td_{pw}, a recursive specification is given as follows (where $\{*\}$ denotes the one-point set; hence $\mathbb{L}M$ is isomorphic to $\mathbb{R}_{\geq 0} \cup \{\infty\}$):

$$M = \{*\} \qquad \mathsf{eval}(x) = x$$
$$td^{\mathbb{L}}(\sigma, \tau) = \sup_i pd(\sigma_i, \tau_i)$$
$$F(u, v, x) = \max(pd(u, v), x)$$

Using Definition 4, the corresponding simulation distance $sd_{\mathsf{pw}} = sd^{\mathbb{L}}_{\mathsf{pw}}$ is the least fixed point to the equations

$$sd_{\mathsf{pw}}(s, t) = \sup_{s \to s'} \inf_{t \to t'} \max(pd([s], [t]), sd_{\mathsf{pw}}(s', t')).$$

This is similar to the formulation given in [14, 15]. Note that if pd is separating, then F is recursively separating, hence Theorem 2 applies.

For the *discounted point-wise* trace distance $td_{\mathsf{pw},\lambda}$ the recursive specification is similar:

$$M = \{*\} \qquad \mathsf{eval}(x) = x$$
$$td^{\mathbb{L}}(\sigma, \tau) = \sup_i \lambda^i pd(\sigma_i, \tau_i)$$
$$F(u, v, x) = \max(pd(u, v), \lambda x)$$

The corresponding simulation distance is hence the least fixed point to the equations

$$sd_{\mathsf{pw},\lambda}(s, t) = \sup_{s \to s'} \inf_{t \to t'} \max(pd([s], [t]), \lambda sd_{\mathsf{pw},\lambda}(s', t')),$$

which is similar to what is in [14, 15]. Note again that if pd is separating, then F is recursively separating, hence also here Theorem 2 applies.

Also the *accumulating* trace distance td_{acc} has a simple recursive specification with $\mathbb{L}M$ isomorphic to $\mathbb{R}_{\geq 0} \cup \{\infty\}$:

$$M = \{*\} \qquad \mathsf{eval}(x) = x$$
$$td^{\mathbb{L}}(\sigma, \tau) = \sum_i pd(\sigma_i, \tau_i)$$
$$F(u, v, x) = pd(u, v) + x$$

The corresponding simulation distance is hence the least fixed point to the equations

$$sd_{\mathsf{acc}}(s, t) = \sup_{s \to s'} \inf_{t \to t'} (pd([s], [t]) + sd_{\mathsf{acc}}(s', t')).$$

Again, if *pd* is separating, then F is recursively separating, hence Theorem 2 applies.

A recursive specification for the *discounted accumulating* trace distance is given as follows:

$$M = \{*\} \qquad \mathsf{eval}(x) = x$$
$$td^{\mathbb{L}}(\sigma, \tau) = \textstyle\sum_i \lambda^i pd(\sigma_i, \tau_i)$$
$$F(u, v, x) = pd(u, v) + \lambda x$$

The corresponding simulation distance is then the least fixed point to the equations

$$sd_{\mathsf{acc},\lambda}(s,t) = \sup_{s \to s'} \inf_{t \to t'} pd([s],[t]) + \lambda sd_{\mathsf{acc},\lambda}(s',t'),$$

similarly to what is in [9]. If *pd* is separating, then F is recursively separating, hence Theorem 2 applies also in this case.

To obtain a recursive specification of the *limit-average* trace distance, we need a richer lattice:

$$M = \mathbb{N} \qquad \mathsf{eval}(x) = \liminf_j x(j)$$
$$td^{\mathbb{L}}(\sigma, \tau)(j) = \tfrac{1}{j+1} \textstyle\sum_{i=0}^{j} pd(\sigma_i, \tau_i)$$
$$F(u, v, x)(j) = \tfrac{1}{j+1} pd(u, v) + \tfrac{j}{j+1} x(j-1)$$

Using Definition 4, we obtain the corresponding lifted simulation distance as the least fixed point to the equations

$$sd^{\mathbb{L}}_{\mathsf{limavg}}(s,t)(j) = \sup_{s \to s'} \inf_{t \to t'} \Big(\tfrac{1}{j+1} pd([s],[t]) + \tfrac{j}{j+1} sd^{\mathbb{L}}_{\mathsf{limavg}}(s',t')(j-1) \Big).$$

The limit-average simulation distance is then

$$sd_{\mathsf{limavg}}(s,t) = \liminf_j sd^{\mathbb{L}}_{\mathsf{limavg}}(s,t)(j).$$

To the best of our knowledge, this formulation of limit-average simulation distance is new. We again remark that if *pd* is separating, then F is recursively separating, hence Theorem 2 applies.

For the *maximum-lead* trace distance, we need a lattice which maps leads to maximum leads. A recursive specification is as follows:

$$M = \mathbb{R} \qquad \mathsf{eval}(x) = x(0)$$
$$td^{\mathbb{L}}(\sigma, \tau)(\delta) = \max(|\delta|, \sup_j \sup_{a \in \Sigma} |\delta + \textstyle\sum_{i=0}^{j} \sigma_i(a) - \sum_{i=0}^{j} \tau_i(a)|)$$
$$F(u, v, x)(\delta) = \sup_{a \in \Sigma} \max(|\delta + u(a) - v(a)|, x(\delta + u(a) - v(a)))$$

The lifted simulation distance is then the least fixed point to the equations

$$sd^{\mathbb{L}}_{\mathsf{maxlead}}(s,t)(\delta) = \sup_{s \to s'} \inf_{t \to t'} \sup_{a \in \Sigma} \max \begin{cases} |\delta + [s](a) - [t](a)|, \\ sd^{\mathbb{L}}_{\mathsf{maxlead}}(s',t')(\delta + [s](a) - [t](a)), \end{cases}$$

cf. [28], and maximum-lead simulation distance is

$$sd_{\mathsf{maxlead}}(s,t) = sd^{\mathbb{L}}_{\mathsf{maxlead}}(s,t)(0).$$

Also here it holds that if *pd* is separating, then F is recursively separating, hence Theorem 2 applies.

Finishing the example from Fig. 2, we compute the simulation distances $sd(s_1,t_1)$ and $sd(s_2,t_2)$ induced by all our example trace distances, using the usual metric on $\mathbb{R}$ for valuations and a discount factor of $\lambda = .9$ where applicable:

$$\begin{aligned} sd_{\mathsf{pw}}(s_1,t_1) &= 6 & sd_{\mathsf{pw}}(s_2,t_2) &= 6 \\ sd_{\mathsf{pw},\lambda}(s_1,t_1) &= 5.46 & sd_{\mathsf{pw},\lambda}(s_2,t_2) &= 5.46 \\ sd_{\mathsf{acc}}(s_1,t_1) &= 6 & sd_{\mathsf{acc}}(s_2,t_2) &= \infty \\ sd_{\mathsf{acc},\lambda}(s_1,t_1) &= 5.46 & sd_{\mathsf{acc},\lambda}(s_2,t_2) &= 54 \\ sd_{\mathsf{limavg}}(s_1,t_2) &= 0 & sd_{\mathsf{limavg}}(s_2,t_2) &= 6 \\ sd_{\mathsf{maxlead}}(s_1,t_1) &= 6 & sd_{\mathsf{maxlead}}(s_2,t_2) &= \infty \end{aligned}$$

7 A Note on Robustness

In [15] it is shown that with respect to the *point-wise* linear and branching distances, metric transition systems are *robust* to perturbations in the state valuations. To be precise, let $[\cdot]_1, [\cdot]_2 : S \to \mathcal{U}[\Sigma]$ be two different state valuations on a MTS S and define their *valuation distance* by $vd([\cdot]_1,[\cdot]_2) = \sup_{s\in S} pd([s]_1,[s]_2)$. This measures how close the state valuations are to each other.

Now write ld^i_{pw} and sd^i_{pw} (with $i \in \{1,2\}$) for the point-wise linear and simulation distances with respect to the valuation $[\cdot]_i$. It is shown in [15] that for all $s,t \in S$,

$$\begin{aligned} |ld^1_{\mathsf{pw}}(s,t) - ld^2_{\mathsf{pw}}(s,t)| &\le vd([\cdot]_1,[\cdot]_2) + vd([\cdot]_2,[\cdot]_1), \\ |sd^1_{\mathsf{pw}}(s,t) - sd^2_{\mathsf{pw}}(s,t)| &\le vd([\cdot]_1,[\cdot]_2) + vd([\cdot]_2,[\cdot]_1). \end{aligned}$$

This is, hence, a *robustness* result: given that the two valuations are close to each other, also the linear and branching distances will be.

Similar results can easily be seen to hold also for the symmetric linear and the bisimulation distances, and also for the *discounted point-wise* versions of these distances. A result similar in spirit, also for the point-wise distance, is reported for robustness of timed automata in [8].

Using almost the same arguments as in [15], one can show that for the *discounted accumulating* distances,

$$\begin{aligned} |ld^1_{\mathsf{acc},\lambda}(s,t) - ld^2_{\mathsf{acc},\lambda}(s,t)| &\le \tfrac{1}{1-\lambda}(vd([\cdot]_1,[\cdot]_2) + vd([\cdot]_2,[\cdot]_1)), \\ |sd^1_{\mathsf{acc},\lambda}(s,t) - sd^2_{\mathsf{acc},\lambda}(s,t)| &\le \tfrac{1}{1-\lambda}(vd([\cdot]_1,[\cdot]_2) + vd([\cdot]_2,[\cdot]_1)). \end{aligned}$$

Hence MTS are also robust with respect to the discounted accumulating distances. In the proof, one uses the convergence of the geometric series: after the ith

Fig. 3. Example of a MTS with two different state valuations

step, distances are discounted by λ^i, so no more than $\lambda^i(vd([\cdot]_1, [\cdot]_2)+vd([\cdot]_2, [\cdot]_1))$ can be added to the total distance. Hence the distance is bounded above by $(vd([\cdot]_1, [\cdot]_2) + vd([\cdot]_2, [\cdot]_1)) \sum_{i=0}^{\infty} \lambda^i = \frac{1}{1-\lambda}(vd([\cdot]_1, [\cdot]_2) + vd([\cdot]_2, [\cdot]_1))$.

Unfortunately, no general robustness results are available, and our other example distances do not have similar properties. This is shown by the example in Fig. 3. Here, $vd([\cdot]_1, [\cdot]_2) = vd([\cdot]_2, [\cdot]_1) = 1$, and the linear distances are as follows, with the usual metric on $\mathbb{R}$ and $\lambda = .9$ where applicable:

$$\begin{array}{llll}
ld^1_{\mathsf{pw}}(s,t) = 0 & ld^2_{\mathsf{pw}}(s,t) = 1 & ld^1_{\mathsf{pw}}(t,s) = 0 & ld^2_{\mathsf{pw}}(t,s) = 1 \\
ld^1_{\mathsf{pw},\lambda}(s,t) = 0 & ld^2_{\mathsf{pw},\lambda}(s,t) = 1 & ld^1_{\mathsf{pw},\lambda}(t,s) = 0 & ld^2_{\mathsf{pw},\lambda}(t,s) = 1 \\
ld^1_{\mathsf{acc}}(s,t) = 0 & ld^2_{\mathsf{acc}}(s,t) = \infty & ld^1_{\mathsf{acc}}(t,s) = 0 & ld^2_{\mathsf{acc}}(t,s) = \infty \\
ld^1_{\mathsf{acc},\lambda}(s,t) = 0 & ld^2_{\mathsf{acc},\lambda}(s,t) = 10 & ld^1_{\mathsf{acc},\lambda}(t,s) = 0 & ld^2_{\mathsf{acc},\lambda}(t,s) = 10 \\
ld^1_{\mathsf{limavg}}(s,t) = 0 & ld^2_{\mathsf{limavg}}(s,t) = \infty & ld^1_{\mathsf{limavg}}(t,s) = 0 & ld^2_{\mathsf{limavg}}(t,s) = \infty \\
ld^1_{\mathsf{maxlead}}(s,t) = 0 & ld^2_{\mathsf{maxlead}}(s,t) = \infty & ld^1_{\mathsf{maxlead}}(t,s) = 0 & ld^2_{\mathsf{maxlead}}(t,s) = \infty
\end{array}$$

(The branching distances are equal to the linear distances in all cases.)

8 Conclusion

We have shown how the model of metric transition systems from [15] can be embedded in a general quantitative framework which allows quantitative verification using a large number of different system distances. As these distances are an essential part of quantitative verification and, at the same time, typically depend on what precise application one has in mind, it is important to develop a general quantitative theory of systems which is independent of the employed distances. This is what we have done here.

Assuming an abstract trace distance as input, we have developed corresponding linear and branching distances. What we have not done, however, is to compare linear and branching distances which arise from *different* trace distances. One important question is, for example, whether the linear and branching distances one obtains from two Lipschitz equivalent, or topologically equivalent, trace distances will again be Lipschitz or topologically equivalent. This would be a crucial step in a *classification* of system distances and is part of our ongoing research.

Another issue which we have not treated here is the *logical* side of quantitative verification. In [15], the authors introduce a quantitative variant of LTL which characterizes the point-wise linear distance, and a quantitative μ-calculus which characterizes the point-wise simulation and bisimulation distances. We plan to work on similar logics for our general setting.

References

1. Alur, R., Courcoubetis, C., Halbwachs, N., Henzinger, T.A., Ho, P.-H., Nicollin, X., Olivero, A., Sifakis, J., Yovine, S.: The algorithmic analysis of hybrid systems. TCS 138(1), 3–34 (1995)
2. Alur, R., Dill, D.L.: A theory of timed automata. TCS 126(2), 183–235 (1994)
3. Aziz, A., Sanwal, K., Singhal, V., Brayton, R.K.: Model-checking continous-time Markov chains. ACM Trans. Comput. Log. 1(1), 162–170 (2000)
4. Bacci, G., Bacci, G., Larsen, K.G., Mardare, R.: On-the-fly exact computation of bisimilarity distances. In: Piterman, N., Smolka, S.A. (eds.) TACAS 2013. LNCS, vol. 7795, pp. 1–15. Springer, Heidelberg (2013)
5. Bauer, S.S., Fahrenberg, U., Juhl, L., Larsen, K.G., Legay, A., Thrane, C.: Weighted modal transition systems. Form. Meth. Syst. Design (2013) (online first)
6. Bauer, S.S., Fahrenberg, U., Legay, A., Thrane, C.: General quantitative specification theories with modalities. In: Hirsch, E.A., Karhumäki, J., Lepistö, A., Prilutskii, M. (eds.) CSR 2012. LNCS, vol. 7353, pp. 18–30. Springer, Heidelberg (2012)
7. Boker, U., Henzinger, T.A.: Approximate determinization of quantitative automata. In: FSTTCS, pp. 362–373 (2012)
8. Bouyer, P., Larsen, K.G., Markey, N., Sankur, O., Thrane, C.: Timed automata can always be made implementable. In: Katoen, J.-P., König, B. (eds.) CONCUR 2011. LNCS, vol. 6901, pp. 76–91. Springer, Heidelberg (2011)
9. Černý, P., Henzinger, T.A., Radhakrishna, A.: Simulation distances. In: Gastin, P., Laroussinie, F. (eds.) CONCUR 2010. LNCS, vol. 6269, pp. 253–268. Springer, Heidelberg (2010)
10. Černý, P., Henzinger, T.A., Radhakrishna, A.: Quantitative abstraction refinement. In: POPL, pp. 115–128 (2013)
11. Chatterjee, K., de Alfaro, L., Faella, M., Henzinger, T.A., Majumdar, R., Stoelinga, M.: Compositional quantitative reasoning. In: QEST, pp. 179–188 (2006)
12. Chatterjee, K., Doyen, L., Henzinger, T.A.: Quantitative languages. ACM Trans. Comput. Log. 11(4) (2010)
13. de Alfaro, L., Faella, M., Henzinger, T.A., Majumdar, R., Stoelinga, M.: Model checking discounted temporal properties. TCS 345(1), 139–170 (2005)
14. de Alfaro, L., Faella, M., Stoelinga, M.: Linear and branching metrics for quantitative transition systems. In: Díaz, J., Karhumäki, J., Lepistö, A., Sannella, D. (eds.) ICALP 2004. LNCS, vol. 3142, pp. 97–109. Springer, Heidelberg (2004)
15. de Alfaro, L., Faella, M., Stoelinga, M.: Linear and branching system metrics. IEEE Trans. Softw. Eng. 35(2), 258–273 (2009)
16. Desharnais, J., Gupta, V., Jagadeesan, R., Panangaden, P.: Metrics for labelled Markov processes. TCS 318(3), 323–354 (2004)
17. Droste, M., Gastin, P.: Weighted automata and weighted logics. TCS 380(1-2), 69–86 (2007)
18. Droste, M., Meinecke, I.: Weighted automata and weighted MSO logics for average and long-time behaviors. Inf. Comp. 220, 44–59 (2012)
19. Droste, M., Rahonis, G.: Weighted automata and weighted logics with discounting. TCS 410(37), 3481–3494 (2009)
20. Ehrenfeucht, A., Mycielski, J.: Positional strategies for mean payoff games. International Journal of Game Theory 8, 109–113 (1979)
21. Fahrenberg, U., Legay, A., Thrane, C.: The quantitative linear-time–branching-time spectrum. In: FSTTCS, pp. 103–114 (2011)

22. Frehse, G., et al.: SpaceEx: Scalable verification of hybrid systems. In: Gopalakrishnan, G., Qadeer, S. (eds.) CAV 2011. LNCS, vol. 6806, pp. 379–395. Springer, Heidelberg (2011)
23. Gilmore, S., Hillston, J.: The PEPA workbench: A tool to support a process algebra-based approach to performance modelling. In: CPE, pp. 353–368 (1994)
24. Girard, A.: Synthesis using approximately bisimilar abstractions: Time-optimal control problems. In: CDC, pp. 5893–5898 (2010)
25. Girard, A., Pappas, G.J.: Approximation metrics for discrete and continuous systems. IEEE Trans. Automat. Contr. 52(5), 782–798 (2007)
26. Hansson, H., Jonsson, B.: A logic for reasoning about time and reliability. Formal Asp. Comput. 6(5), 512–535 (1994)
27. Henzinger, T.A., Ho, P.-H., Wong-Toi, H.: Hytech: A model checker for hybrid systems. Int. J. Softw. Tools Techn. Trans. 1(1-2), 110–122 (1997)
28. Henzinger, T.A., Majumdar, R., Prabhu, V.S.: Quantifying similarities between timed systems. In: Pettersson, P., Yi, W. (eds.) FORMATS 2005. LNCS, vol. 3829, pp. 226–241. Springer, Heidelberg (2005)
29. Henzinger, T.A., Nicollin, X., Sifakis, J., Yovine, S.: Symbolic model checking for real-time systems. Inf. Comp. 111(2), 193–244 (1994)
30. Hillston, J.: A Compositional Approach to Performance Modelling. Cambridge University Press (1996)
31. Koymans, R.: Specifying real-time properties with metric temporal logic. Real-Time Systems 2(4), 255–299 (1990)
32. Kwiatkowska, M., Norman, G., Parker, D.: Probabilistic symbolic model checking with PRISM: A hybrid approach. In: Katoen, J.-P., Stevens, P. (eds.) TACAS 2002. LNCS, vol. 2280, pp. 52–66. Springer, Heidelberg (2002)
33. Larsen, K.G., Legay, A., Traonouez, L.-M., Wąsowski, A.: Robust specification of real time components. In: Fahrenberg, U., Tripakis, S. (eds.) FORMATS 2011. LNCS, vol. 6919, pp. 129–144. Springer, Heidelberg (2011)
34. Larsen, K.G., Mardare, R., Panangaden, P.: Taking it to the limit: Approximate reasoning for markov processes. In: Rovan, B., Sassone, V., Widmayer, P. (eds.) MFCS 2012. LNCS, vol. 7464, pp. 681–692. Springer, Heidelberg (2012)
35. Larsen, K.G., Pettersson, P., Yi, W.: UPPAAL in a nutshell. Int. J. Softw. Tools Techn. Trans. 1(1-2), 134–152 (1997)
36. Lawvere, F.W.: Metric spaces, generalized logic, and closed categories. In: Rendiconti del seminario matématico e fisico di Milano, vol. XLIII, pp. 135–166 (1973)
37. Panangaden, P.: Labelled Markov Processes. Imperial College Press (2009)
38. Quesel, J.-D., Fränzle, M., Damm, W.: Crossing the bridge between similar games. In: Fahrenberg, U., Tripakis, S. (eds.) FORMATS 2011. LNCS, vol. 6919, pp. 160–176. Springer, Heidelberg (2011)
39. Segala, R., Lynch, N.A.: Probabilistic simulations for probabilistic processes. In: Jonsson, B., Parrow, J. (eds.) CONCUR 1994. LNCS, vol. 836, pp. 481–496. Springer, Heidelberg (1994)
40. Stewart, W.J.: Introduction to the Numerical Solution of Markov Chains. Princeton University Press (1994)
41. Stirling, C.: Modal and temporal logics for processes. In: Moller, F., Birtwistle, G. (eds.) Logics for Concurrency. LNCS, vol. 1043, pp. 149–237. Springer, Heidelberg (1996)
42. Thrane, C., Fahrenberg, U., Larsen, K.G.: Quantitative analysis of weighted transition systems. J. Log. Alg. Prog. 79(7), 689–703 (2010)
43. van Breugel, F.: An introduction to metric semantics: operational and denotational models for programming and specification languages. TCS 258(1-2), 1–98 (2001)

44. van Breugel, F., Worrell, J.: A behavioural pseudometric for probabilistic transition systems. TCS 331(1), 115–142 (2005)
45. van Breugel, F., Worrell, J.: Approximating and computing behavioural distances in probabilistic transition systems. TCS 360(1-3), 373–385 (2006)
46. Wang, F., Mok, A.K., Emerson, E.A.: Symbolic model checking for distributed real-time systems. In: Larsen, P.G., Wing, J.M. (eds.) FME 1993. LNCS, vol. 670, pp. 632–651. Springer, Heidelberg (1993)
47. Zheng, G., Girard, A.: Bounded and unbounded safety verification using bisimulation metrics. In: Majumdar, R., Tabuada, P. (eds.) HSCC 2009. LNCS, vol. 5469, pp. 426–440. Springer, Heidelberg (2009)
48. Zwick, U., Paterson, M.: The complexity of mean payoff games. In: Li, M., Du, D.-Z. (eds.) COCOON 1995. LNCS, vol. 959, pp. 1–10. Springer, Heidelberg (1995)

GDSL: A Universal Toolkit for Giving Semantics to Machine Language

Julian Kranz, Alexander Sepp, and Axel Simon

Technische Universität München, Institut für Informatik II, Garching, Germany
firstname.lastname@in.tum.de

Abstract. The static analysis of executable programs has gained importance due to the need to audit larger and larger programs for security vulnerabilities or safety violations. The basis for analyzing executables is the decoding of byte sequences into assembler instructions and giving a semantics to them. We illustrate how our domain specific language GDSL facilitates this task by specifying Intel x86 semantics. In particular, we show how simple optimizations of the generated code can drastically reduce its size. Since these optimizations are also written in GDSL they can be re-used with other processor front-ends. Hence, analyses based on our toolkit can be adapted to several architectures with little change.

1 Introduction

The static analysis of executable programs has gained increasing importance in the last decade. Reasons are the need to audit larger and larger programs for security vulnerabilities, the online detection of malware in virus scanners, and the need to verify software in the presence of binary third-party libraries, inline assembler, and compiler-induced semantics. The basis for analyzing executables is the decoding of byte sequences into assembler instructions and giving a semantics to them. The challenge here is one of scalability: a single line in a high-level language is translated into several assembler (or "native") instructions. Each native instruction, in turn, is translated into several semantic primitives. These semantic primitives are usually given as an *intermediate representation* (IR) and are later evaluated over an abstract domain [3] tracking intervals, value sets, taints, etc. In order to make the evaluation of the semantic primitives more efficient, a *transformer-specification language* (TSL) was recently proposed that compiles the specification of each native instruction directly into operations (transformers) over the abstract domain [6], thus skipping the generation of an IR. These tailored transformers are then optimized by a standard compiler. Our toolkit follows the more traditional approach of generating an IR that an analysis later interprets over the abstract domains. In contrast to the TSL approach, we perform optimizations on the IR program that represents a complete basic block rather than on a single native instruction. We show that the semantics of instructions can be simplified considerably when taking the surrounding instructions into account which highlights the optimization potential of using an IR.

[1] This work was supported by DFG Emmy Noether programme SI 1579/1.

C.-c. Shan (Ed.): APLAS 2013, LNCS 8301, pp. 209–216, 2013.

```
stmts ::= ε | stmt ; stmts                          var    ::= id | id . int
stmt  ::= var =:int expr                            addr   ::= linear :int
        | var =:int [ addr ]                        linear ::= int · var + linear | int
        | [ addr ] =:int expr                       sexpr  ::= linear | arbitrary
        | if (sexpr) {stmts} else {stmts}                    | linear cmp :int linear
        | while ( sexpr ) { stmts }                 expr   ::= sexpr
        | cbranch sexpr ? addr : addr                        | linear bin linear
        | branch(jump | call | ret) addr                     | sign-extend linear :int
        | (var :int)* = " id "(linear :int)*                 | zero-extend linear :int
cmp   ::= ≤s | ≤u | <s | <u | = | ≠                 bin    ::= and | or | xor | shr | ...
```

Fig. 1. The syntax of our RReil (Relational Reverse Engineering Language) IR. The construct "*: int*" denotes the size in bits whereas "*. int*" in the **var** rule denotes a bit offset. The statements are: assignment, read from address, write to address, conditional, loop (both only used to express the semantics within a native instruction), conditional branch, unconditional branch with a hint of where it originated, and a primitive *"id"*.

2 RReil Intermediate Representation

Many intermediate representations for giving semantics to assembler instructions exist, each having its own design goals such as minimality [1,4], mechanical verifiability [5], reversibility [7], or expressivity [1,9]. Our own RReil IR [9], presented in Fig. 1, was designed to allow for a precise numeric interpretation. For instance, comparisons are implemented with special tests rather than expressed at the level of bits which is common in other IRs [4,5,6].

3 The Generic Decoder Specification Language (GDSL)

We developed a domain specific language called GDSL [8] that is best described as a functional language with ML-like syntax. It features bespoke pattern matching syntax for specifying instruction decoders. Dependability of GDSL programs is increased by a sophisticated type inference [10] that eliminates the need of specifying any types. The algebraic data types and a special infix syntax facilitates the specification of instruction semantics and program optimizations.

The GDSL toolkit contains a compiler for GDSL as well as decoders, semantic translations and optimizations written in GDSL. The benefit of specifying optimizations in GDSL is that they can be re-used for any input architecture since they operate only on RReil. Besides a few instruction decoders for 8-bit processors, the toolkit provides an Intel x86 decoder for 32- and 64-bit mode that handles all 897 Intel instructions. In terms of translations into RReil, we provide semantics for 457 instructions. Of the 440 undefined instructions, 228 are floating point instructions that we currently do not handle since our own analyzer cannot handle floating point computations. Many of the remaining undefined instructions would have to be treated as primitives as they modify or query the internal CPU state or because they perform computations whose RReil semantics is too cumbersome to be useful (e.g. encryption instructions).

a)
```
val sem-cmovcc insn cond = do
  size <- sizeof insn.opnd1;
  dst <- lval size insn.opnd1;
  dst-old <- rval size insn.opnd1;
  src <- rval size insn.opnd2;

  temp <- mktemp;
  mov size temp dst-old;

  _if cond _then
   mov size temp src;

  write size dst (var temp)
end
```

b)
```
t0 =:32 B
if (ZF) {
  t0 =:32 A
} else {
}
B =:32 t0
B.32 =:32 0
```

Fig. 2. The translator function a) and a translation result b)

4 Writing Semantics Using GDSL

As a pure, functional language with algebraic data types and a state monad, GDSL lends itself for writing translators in a concise way as illustrated next.

4.1 An Example Intel Instruction

The following GDSL example shows the translation of the Intel instruction cmov. The instruction copies the contents of its source operand to its destination operand if a given condition is met. The instruction contains a condition (which is part of the opcode) and two operands, one of which can be a memory location. The translation of the instruction instance `cmovz ebx, eax` (using the Intel x86 architecture with the 64 bit extension) into RReil is shown in Fig. 2b). In order to illustrate the translation, we first detail the output of the GDSL decoder which is a value of the algebraic data type `insn` that is defined as follows:

```
type insn =                                          # an x86 instruction
   CMOVZ of {opnd1: opnd, opnd2: opnd}
 | ...        # other instruction definitions omitted
```

Thus, the `CMOVZ` constructor carries a record with two fields as payload. Both fields are of type `opnd` which, for instance, carry a register or a memory location:

```
type opnd =                                          # an x86 operand
   REG of register
 | MEM of memory
 | ...        # immediates, scaled operands and operands with offsets omitted
```

Note that all variants (here `REG` and `MEM`) implicitly contain information about the access size. In the example above, the instruction `cmovz ebx, eax` is represented by `CMOVZ {opnd1 = REG EBX, opnd2 = REG EAX}` where `EAX` is 32-bits. The following section details helper functions that operate on `opnd` values.

4.2 Generating RReil Statements Using GDSL Monadic Functions

Each semantic translator function generates a sequence of RReil statements. The sequence is stored inside the state of a monad. An RReil statement is added to the sequence by calling a GDSL monadic function which builds the abstract syntax tree of the statement. In order to explain the example in Fig. 2 we detail the GDSL functions for assignment, called `mov`, and conditional:

- `mov sz dst src`
  The `mov` function generates the RReil assignment statement `dst =:sz src` that copies the RReil expression `src` to the RReil variable `dst`.
- `_if cond _then stmts`
  This function generates the RReil statement `if (cond) { stmts } else {}`. The special mix-fix notation `_if cond _then stmts` is a call to a mix-fix function whose name `_if _then` is a sequence of identifiers that each commence with an underscore. It is defined as follows:

```
val _if c _then a = do
  ...           # add if ( c ) { a } else { } to statement list
end
```

We further require the following functions that operate on x86 operands of type `opnd`. They are necessary to translate x86 registers, memory locations, or immediate values, that are encoded in the x86 operand, into RReil:

- `sizeof x86-operand`
  Returns the size of an x86 operand in bits; here, `sizeof (REG EBX) = 32`.
- `lval size x86-operand`
  The `lval` function turns an x86 operand into an RReil left hand side expression, that is, either *var* or *[addr]*. Here, `lval 32 (REG EBX)` yields the RReil register B that contains the 32 bits of the Intel `EBX` register.
- `rval size x86-operand`
  The `rval` function turns an x86 operand into an RReil **expr**. In the example, `rval 32 (REG EAX)` yields the RReil register A.
- `write size destination source`
  The `write` function emits all statements necessary to write to an x86 operand. The operand is specified using the *destination* parameter; it is the return value of an associated call to `lval`. In Fig. 2b) lines 6 through 7 originate from the call to `write`.

Finally, the `mktemp` function is used to allocate a temporary variable.

4.3 The Translator

The translator function for `cmovz ebx, eax` is shown in Fig. 2a). The **do ... end** notation surrounding the function body is used to execute each of the enclosed

```
t0 =:32 A - B
CF =:1 A <u:32 B
CForZF =:1 A ≤u:32 B
SFxorOF =:1 A <s:32 B
SFxorOFforZF =:1 A ≤s:32 B
ZF =:1 A =:32 B
SF =:1 t0 <s:32 0
OF =:1  SFxorOF xor SF
cbranch  SFxorOF ? nxt : tgt
```

⟹ dead-code elimination

```
SFxorOF =:1 A <s:32 B
cbranch  SFxorOF ? nxt : tgt
```

⇓ forward expression substitution

```
cbranch  A <s:32 B ? nxt : tgt
```

Fig. 3. Translation of the native Intel instructions `cmp eax, ebx; jl tgt` into RReil and applying optimizations. Here, `CForZF`, `SFxorOF`, `SFxorOFforZF` are *virtual flags*, that is, translation-specific variables whose value reflect what their names suggest [9]. Note that this example is idealized since the removed flags may not actually be dead.

monadic functions in turn. The decoded Intel instruction is passed-in using the *insn* parameter; the condition is determined by the caller depending on the actual mnemonic. The condition is an one-bit RReil expression. In the `cmovz ebx, eax` example, it is `ZF` which corresponds to the zero-flag.

The translation itself starts with a code block that is very common in instruction semantics: The operation's size is determined by looking at the size of one operand (line 2) and the respective operands are prepared for reading (using the `rval` monadic function) and writing (using the `lval` monadic function). Next, a new temporary RReil register is allocated and initialized to the current value of the destination operand (lines 7 and 8). This completes all preparations; the actual semantics of the instruction is implemented by the code lines 10 through 11. The condition is tested and, if it evaluates to *true*, the source operand is copied to the destination operand. It is important to note that the conditional is not evaluated at translation time, but that it is part of the emitted code. Finally, the (possibly) updated value of the temporary RReil register is written to the corresponding Intel register by code line 13.

One might think that the instruction pointlessly reads the source operand and writes the destination operand in case the condition evaluates to *false*. It is, however, necessary since the writeback can also cause further side effects that still need to occur, even if no data is copied. This is exemplified in Fig. 2b): since the instruction uses a 32 bit register in 64 bit mode, the upper 32 bits of the register are zeroed even if the lower 32 bits are unchanged (see line 7). The additional code is emitted by the `write` function.

5 Optimizing the RReil Code

The design of RReil also allows for an effective optimization of the IR [9] which is illustrated in Fig. 3. The example shows the typical code bloat when translating two native instructions where the first sets many flags of which the second only evaluates one. Implementing these optimizations in GDSL is not only concise but also avoids the need to re-implement them in the individual analyses. The next sections consider two optimizations, one of which is currently implemented.

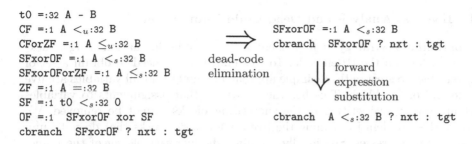

5.1 Liveness Analysis and Dead Code Elimination

The optimization strategy we implement is a dead-code elimination using a backwards analysis on the RReil code. To this end, we first need to obtain a set of live variables to start with. A simple approach assumes that all variables are live at the end of the block. This has the drawback that assignments to variables that are always overwritten in the succeeding blocks cannot be removed. We address this problem by refining the live-set for basic blocks that do not jump to computed addresses: Specifically, we infer the live variable set of the immediately succeeding blocks and use this live set as start set, thereby removing many more assignments to dead variables. We perform a true liveness analysis, that is, we refrain from marking a variable as live if it is used in the right-hand side of an assignment to a dead variable. For the body of while loops, however, this approach would require the calculation of a fixpoint. Since `while` loops are used rarely by our translator and since their bodies show little potential for optimization, a more conservative notion of liveness is used that does not require a fixpoint computation. This approach marks a variable as live even if it used in an assignment to a dead variable. With this strategy, the dead code elimination takes linear time in the size of the basic block.

5.2 Forward Expression Substitution

In the future, we plan to also perform forward substitution and simplification. These optimizations become important for architectures like ARM where most instructions may be executed conditionally, depending on a processor flag. Compilers use this feature to translate small bodies of conditionals without jumps. Consider a conditional whose body translates to two native instructions i_1; i_2 that are executed if f holds. These are translated into the RReil statements $\underline{if}\, f\, \underline{then}\, [\![i_1]\!]\, \underline{else}\,;$; $\underline{if}\, f\, \underline{then}\, [\![i_2]\!]\, \underline{else}\,;$ which ideally should be simplified to $\underline{if}\, f\, \underline{then}\, [\![i_1]\!]; [\![i_2]\!]\, \underline{else}\,;$. Without this optimization, a static analysis will compute a join of the unrelated states of the $\underline{then}$- and $\underline{else}$-branches of the first $\underline{if}$-statement. The thereby incurred loss of precision is particularly problematic for the TSL approach since each instruction is executed on a single domain that, in general, will not be able to join two states without loss of precision.

6 Empirical Evaluation

We measured the impact of our dead-code elimination on a linear-sweep disassembly of standard Unix programs. Each basic block, that is, a sequence of Intel instructions up to the next jump, is translated into semantics. Figure 4 presents our experimental results where the 'fac' column denotes the size of the RReil code (in 1000 lines of code, 'kloc') in relation to the native x86 disassembly ('nat. kloc'). Here, column 'translation' shows that, without optimizations, about six RReil instructions are generated for each Intel instruction. The colums 'single', 'intra', and 'inter' show how the size of the RReil code reduces due to

prog.	nat.	translation			single				intra				inter			
	kloc	kloc	time	fac	kloc	time	red	fac	kloc	time	red	fac	kloc	time	red	fac
bash	144	907	1.0s	6.3	778	5.1s	14%	5.4	640	3.7s	30%	4.4	454	9.1s	50%	3.2
cat	7	39	0.0s	5.9	34	0.2s	15%	5.0	28	0.2s	30%	4.1	21	0.4s	46%	3.2
echo	3	15	0.0s	5.6	13	0.1s	14%	4.8	11	0.1s	29%	4.0	8	0.1s	46%	3.0
less	21	152	0.1s	7.3	131	0.7s	14%	6.3	105	0.6s	31%	5.1	61	1.4s	60%	2.9
ls	15	106	0.1s	6.9	90	0.5s	16%	5.8	66	0.4s	38%	4.3	49	1.0s	54%	3.2
mkdir	7	45	0.0s	6.5	37	0.2s	16%	5.4	29	0.2s	35%	4.2	21	0.4s	53%	3.1
netstat	15	86	0.1s	5.6	75	0.4s	12%	4.9	63	0.3s	26%	4.2	53	0.7s	39%	3.5
ps	13	68	0.1s	5.3	57	0.4s	16%	4.5	45	0.3s	33%	3.5	40	0.6s	41%	3.1
pwd	3	19	0.0s	5.6	16	0.1s	14%	4.8	14	0.1s	27%	4.1	11	0.2s	43%	3.2
rm	8	47	0.0s	6.0	41	0.2s	14%	5.2	33	0.2s	30%	4.2	25	0.4s	47%	3.2
sed	9	54	0.1s	6.3	45	0.3s	16%	5.3	37	0.2s	31%	4.3	28	0.5s	49%	3.2
tar	50	317	0.3s	6.4	270	1.6s	15%	5.4	215	1.3s	32%	4.3	161	3.1s	49%	3.2
touch	8	47	0.0s	6.3	41	0.2s	14%	5.4	31	0.2s	34%	4.1	23	0.5s	51%	3.1
uname	3	15	0.0s	5.6	13	0.1s	14%	4.8	11	0.1s	28%	4.1	8	0.1s	45%	3.1
Xorg	346	2080	2.3s	6.0	1803	10.6s	13%	5.2	1408	8.4s	32%	4.1	1067	20.9s	49%	3.1

Fig. 4. Evaluating the reduction of the RReil code size due to dead-code optimization. The overall running time is the sum of the translation time plus the time for one of the optimizations. All measurements were obtained on an Intel Core i7 running at 3.40Ghz.

our optimizations and the time required to do so. Performing liveness analysis and dead code elimination on the semantics of a single instruction reduces the size by about 14% (column 'single'). Applying these optimizations on basic blocks reduces the size by about one third (column 'intra'). The 'inter' column shows the result of the optimizations as per Sect. 5.1: for basic blocks ending in a direct jump, the (one or two) blocks that are branched-to are translated and their set of live variables is computed. Using this refined liveness set, the dead code elimination removes between 40% and 60% of the RReil code relative to the non-optimized translation. Thus, with the information of the neighboring basic blocks, our RReil semantics is roughly 3 times larger than the x86 disassembly.

In order to compare our translation into RReil with the TSL approach [6] where a bespoke abstract transformer is generated for each native instruction, again consider column 'single' of Fig. 4. Since this column shows the reduction when considering the semantics of a single instruction, it provides an estimate of how many abstract transformers in a TSL translation a standard compiler can remove due to dead code elimination. While the TSL translations are optimized in other ways, it is questionable if this can rival the effect of removing not 14%, but around 50% of instructions, as our inter-basic block analysis does.

The GDSL compiler emits C code that closely resembles handwritten C programs. As a consequence, the resulting C code is easy to debug and allows the GDSL compiler to rely on the optimizations implemented by off-the-shelf C compilers. Indeed, the optimizations should be fast enough to re-apply them on-the-fly each time a basic block is analyzed. Even then, future work will address the elimination of bottlenecks in both, the GDSL compiler and optimizations written in GDSL.

Given these benefits, we hope that our open-source[1] GDSL toolkit becomes an attractive front-end for any analysis targeting executable programs.

7 Future Work

Future work will extend our toolkit with decoders and translations for other architectures. In particular, it would be interesting to mechanically translate the verified bit-level ARM semantics [5] into RReil. Moreover, given that an analysis that features a GDSL front-end can handle any architecture specified in GDSL, we hope for contributions from the community to further extend the range of architectures that GDSL offers. GDSL would also lend itself for defining semantics besides the RReil value semantics, namely energy or timing semantics.

In the long run, we hope that the GDSL toolkit will become the preferred choice for analyzing machine code, thereby replacing proprietary decoders (such as the popular xed2 decoder from Intel's PIN toolkit [2]) that are often equipped with a minimal, application-specific semantics covering only a few instructions.

References

1. Bardin, S., Herrmann, P., Leroux, J., Ly, O., Tabary, R., Vincent, A.: The BINCOA framework for binary code analysis. In: Gopalakrishnan, G., Qadeer, S. (eds.) CAV 2011. LNCS, vol. 6806, pp. 165–170. Springer, Heidelberg (2011)
2. Intel Corp. xed2 (2012), `http://www.pintool.org`
3. Cousot, P., Cousot, R.: Static Determination of Dynamic Properties of Programs. In: Robinet, B. (ed.) International Symposium on Programming, Paris, France, pp. 106–130 (April 1976)
4. Dullien, T., Porst, S.: REIL: A platform-independent intermediate representation of disassembled code for static code analysis. CanSecWest, Canada (2009)
5. Fox, A., Myreen, M.O.: A Trustworthy Monadic Formalization of the ARMv7 Instruction Set Architecture. In: Kaufmann, M., Paulson, L.C. (eds.) ITP 2010. LNCS, vol. 6172, pp. 243–258. Springer, Heidelberg (2010)
6. Lim, J., Reps, T.: A System for Generating Static Analyzers for Machine Instructions. In: Hendren, L. (ed.) CC 2008. LNCS, vol. 4959, pp. 36–52. Springer, Heidelberg (2008)
7. Ramsey, N., Fernández, M.F.: Specifying Representations of Machine Instructions. Trans. of Programming Languages and Systems 19(3), 492–524 (1997)
8. Sepp, A., Kranz, J., Simon, A.: GDSL: A Generic Decoder Specification Language for Interpreting Machine Language. In: Tools for Automatic Program Analysis, Deauville, France. ENTCS. Springer (September 2012)
9. Sepp, A., Mihaila, B., Simon, A.: Precise Static Analysis of Binaries by Extracting Relational Information. In: Pinzger, M., Poshyvanyk, D. (eds.) Working Conference on Reverse Engineering, Limerick, Ireland. IEEE Computer Society (October 2011)
10. Simon, A.: Deriving a Complete Type Inference for Hindley-Milner and Vector Sizes using Expansion. In: Partial Evaluation and Program Manipulation, SIGPLAN, Rome, Italy. ACM (January 2013)

[1] The toolkit is available at `http://code.google.com/p/gdsl-toolkit`

Paragon for Practical Programming with Information-Flow Control

Niklas Broberg, Bart van Delft, and David Sands

Chalmers University of Technology, Sweden

Abstract. Conventional security policies for software applications are adequate for managing concerns on the level of access control. But standard abstraction mechanisms of mainstream programming languages are not sufficient to express how information is allowed to flow between resources once access to them has been obtained. In practice we believe that such control - information flow control - is needed to manage the end-to-end security properties of applications.

In this paper we present Paragon, a Java-based language with first-class support for static checking of information flow control policies. Paragon policies are specified in a logic-based policy language. By virtue of their explicitly stateful nature, these policies appear to be more expressive and flexible than those used in previous languages with information-flow support.

Our contribution is to present the design and implementation of Paragon, which smoothly integrates the policy language with Java's object-oriented setting, and reaps the benefits of the marriage with a fully fledged programming language.

Keywords: information flow, static enforcement.

1 Introduction

The general goal of this work is to construct innovative design methods for the construction of secure systems that put security requirements at the heart of the construction process, namely *security by design*. To do this we must (i) understand how we can unambiguously formulate the policy aims for secure systems, and (ii) develop technology to integrate these goals into design mechanisms and technologies that enable an efficient construction or verification of systems with respect to those policies.

We address this challenge using a programming language-centric approach, presenting a full-fledged security-typed programming language that allows the programmer to specify how data may be used in the system. These security policies are then enforced by compile-time type checking, thus requiring little run-time overhead. Through this we can guarantee that well-typed programs are secure by construction.

But which security policies might we want for our data, and why do we need special support to express them? Certain security policies, for example access control, are relatively easy to express in many modern programming languages. This is because limiting access to resources is something that good programming language abstraction mechanisms are designed to handle. However, access control mechanisms are often a poor tool to express the intended end-to-end security properties that we wish to impose on our applications.

C.-c. Shan (Ed.): APLAS 2013, LNCS 8301, pp. 217–232, 2013.

Consider a travel planner "app" which permits you to plan a bus journey, and even add your planned trip to your calendar[1]. In order to function, the app must have access to the network to fetch the latest bus times, and must have access to your calendar in order to add or remove schedules. But an app with these permissions can, for example, send your whole calendar to anywhere on the net.

What we want is to grant necessary access, but limit the *information flows*. In this case we want to at least limit the information flows from the calendar to the network while retaining the app's ability to read and write to both.

Research on controlling these information flows has progressed over the last decades. In this paper we identify three generations of security properties and control mechanisms for information-flow:

Information-Flow Control. In the 70's, Denning & Denning pioneered the idea of certifying programs for compliance with information flow policies based on military-style secrecy classifications [7,8]. They used program analysis to validate that information labelled with a given clearance level could never influence output at any levels lower in the hierarchy – so for example a certified program could never leak top-secret information over a channel labelled as public.

The language FlowCAML [24], a variant of ML with information-flow types and type inference, represents the state-of-the-art in support for static Denning-style confidentiality policies.

Beyond Mandatory Information Flow Control. Although a rigid, static hierarchy of security levels may be appropriate in a military message-passing scenario, it became quickly apparent that such a strict and static information flow policy is too rigid for modern software requirements. In practice we need a finer-grained and more dynamic view of information flow.

The concept of *declassification* – the act of deliberately releasing (or leaking) sensitive information – is an important example of such a requirement. Without a possibility to leak secrets, some systems would be of no practical use.

For example an information purchase protocol reveals the secret information once a condition (such as "payment transferred") has been fulfilled. Yet another example is a password checking program that inevitably leaks some information: even when a login attempt fails the attacker learns that the guess is *not* the password.

With this in mind, the *Jif* programming language [17,20] can be seen as the next milestone after the pure Denning-style approach. Jif is a subset of Java extended with information flow labels.

As well as implementing an important distributed view of data ownership, the so-called *Decentralised label model* [18,19], Jif included the possibility of *declassification*, which provides a liberal information flow escape hatch for programs which would otherwise be rejected.

[1] The example is based on a family of actual Android apps (e.g. de.hafas.android.vasttrafik).

Paragon, a Third-Generation IF Language. Declassification, in many shapes and forms, has been widely studied in the research community in recent years [23]. The large variety of declassification concepts is testament to the fact that there is simply no single right way to control the flow of information that goes against the grain. Moreover, it is not always natural to view information flow policies as consisting of "good flows plus exceptional cases" at all; in some situations there is no obvious base-line policy, and the flows which are deemed acceptable may depend on the state of the system at any given moment.

In earlier work [5] we introduced a new highly versatile policy language, *Paralocks*, based around the idea of *Flow Locks*. We demonstrated its ability to model a wide variety of policy paradigms, from classical Denning-style policies to Jif's decentralised label model, as well as the capability to model *stateful* information flow policies. But the idea of using Paralocks as types in a statically-checked programming language was only demonstrated for a toy language. The question whether a Flow Locks-based policy language could feasibly scale to inclusion in a full-fledged programming language, to allow practical programming with information flow control, was left open.

The main contribution of this paper is to answer that question with an emphatic yes. We present the new programming language Paragon, which extends the Java programming language with information flow policy specifications based on an object-oriented generalisation of Paralocks. Not only does it turn out to be feasible, but the marriage of our stateful policy mechanism and Java's encapsulation facilities yields a whole that is greater than the sum of its parts: it allows for the creation of complex policy mechanisms as libraries, giving even stronger control over flows and declassification than the policy language alone.

The remainder of the paper is structured as follows. Section 2 presents the language Paragon: its policy language and integration in Java; followed by a simple showcase of Paragon in Section 3. In Section 4 we give an overview of the enforcement mechanism and details of our implementation. Section 5 discusses our experience from two larger case studies. Related work in Section 6 and conclusions in Section 7 round out the paper.

2 The Language Paragon

Paragon is largely an extension to the Java language and type system. Our choice for Java is motivated by its relatively clear semantics and the wide adoption of Java in both commercial and academical settings. In addition, it allows us to reuse existing ideas from, and simultaneously compare Paragon with, Jif [17,20], the only (other) java-based full-fledged security-typed programming language to date. We discuss Paragon's relation to Jif in more detail in § 6. We do not, however, rely on any particular features of Java for the integration of our policy language to work, and posit that it would be equally feasible to do this for other statically typed languages with safe memory management, e.g. ML or Scala.

In this section we give a high-level overview of Paragon and its various components, leaving more technical features, such as extending Java Generics, to the technical report version of this paper [1].

2.1 The Paragon Policy Language

The subjects of Paragon policies are the information-flow relevant entities, which we refer to as *actors*. An actor could be a user, a resource, a system component, an information source or sink, etc.; any entity that has an information-flow concern.

In Paragon, these entities are represented by *object references*. For instance, the code fragment below creates regular instances of the `User` and `File` class, where `alice` and `f1` can play a dual role; both as program variables, and as actors in Paragon policies.

```
User alice = new User();
User bob   = new User();
File f1 = new File();
File f2 = new File();
```

A *paragon policy* is used to label information containers in the program (fields, local variables), and specifies to which actors the information in that container is allowed to flow. A policy consists of a set of *clauses*, each specifying one particular actor, or one group of actors of a particular type.

For example, the policy `p1` states that information may flow to the specific users Alice and Bob, while the policy `p2` states that information may flow to any file:

```
policy p1 = { alice: ; bob: };
policy p2 = { File f: };
```

This makes the policy `{ Object o: }` the most permissive, and the policy with no clauses (denoted `{:}`) the most restrictive paragon policy.

A clause may have a *body* that constrains the states in which the information may flow to the actors specified in the head. These constraints come in the form of *locks*; typed predicates representing the policy-relevant state of the system.

A lock can be opened or closed for given actor arguments. Viewing a lock as a predicate, opening a lock corresponds to assigning it the value true. Below we define two locks, one for modelling the ownership of files, and another for the organisational hierarchy among users.

```
lock Owns(File, User);
lock ActsFor(User, User);
policy p3 = { File f: Owns(f, alice) } ;
policy p4 = { (User u) File f: Owns(f, u), ActsFor(u, alice) };
```

The policy `p3` expresses that information can flow to any file owned by Alice, while the policy `p4` states that `u` ranges over users, and that information having this policy may flow to any file `f` for which `f` is owned by some `u` such that `u` acts for `alice`. Note that variables that are mentioned in the head of a clause are universally quantified, whereas those only appearing in the body are existentially quantified.

A lock can be declared to have *properties*. A property specifies conditions under which some locks are *implicitly* open. For example, we might want to express that the acts-for relation is transitive and reflexive.

This requirement can be stated at the point of declaration by replacing line 2 in the above with:

```
lock ActsFor(User, User)
  { (User x)       ActsFor(x,x) :
  ; (User x y z) ActsFor(x,y): ActsFor(x,z), ActsFor(z,y) }
```

Transitivity and reflexivity properties (as well as symmetry) are a common pattern, so Paragon provides syntactic sugar for these:

```
reflexive transitive lock ActsFor(User, User);
```

The Paragon Policy Language is an object-based generalisation of Paralocks [5,29], and is described in more detail in the technical report [1].

2.2 Information-Flow Policies in Paragon

The various flows of information that need to be controlled in Paragon are essentially the same as the ones occurring in Java. As is common in information-flow analysis we make a distinction between *direct* and *indirect* information flows.

Direct Flows. The typical direct flow is an assignment, where information flows directly from one location to another. Direct flows also happen at method calls (arguments flow to parameters), returns (the return value flows to the caller) and exception throws (an exception value flows to its enclosing catch clause).

Continuing in the style of the examples from the previous section, let x be a variable with the policy `{File f:Owns(f, alice)}` and y a variable with the policy `{f1:}` in the assignment `y = x;`. Whether or not the assignment will be flagged as an error by the Paragon compiler depends on the lock state in which the direct flow occurs.

If the `Owns(f1,alice)` lock is statically determined to be closed the compiler raises an error, since the information stored in `x`, according to its policy, should only flow into file `f1` when the file is owned by Alice, whereas the information in `y` can always flow to `f1`. In other words, the assignment has insecure information flow because it moves information to a place where it becomes visible to more actors than its policy declares. If, however, the lock is determined to be open, i.e. declaring that `alice` owns `f1`, the assignment occurs in a state where `f1` can already read the information in `x`, and so the program compiles successfully.

Indirect Flows. An indirect flow is one where the effect of evaluating one term reveals information about a completely different term that was evaluated previously. The typical indirect flow is a side-effect happening in a branch that reveals which branch was chosen, which in turn reveals the value of the conditional expression that was branched on. Indirect flows also arise from other control flow constructions (including loops and exceptions), and field updates or instance method-calls (possibly revealing the object they belonged to).

Due to the delayed nature of these information flows, the lock state in effect at the time of the indirect flow might be different to that in effect at the point at which it is revealed. Therefore, indirect flows are handled conservatively, by not allowing the lock state to affect which of these flows are considered secure.

2.3 Policy Annotations

When integrating the policy language into Java, the two core design issues are (i) how policies are to be associated to data, and (ii) how the lock state is specified, updated, and queried.

Policies as Modifiers. In Paragon every information container (field, variable, parameter, lock) has a policy detailing how the information contained therein may be used. Every expression has an effective policy which is (an upper bound on) the conjunction of all policies on all containers whose contents affect its resulting value – we refer to this as the expression's *read effect*.

Paragon separates policies from base (Java) types syntactically by having all policy annotations as modifiers. A modifier `?pol` denotes a policy on an information container, and the read effect of accessing that container. When used on a method we refer to it as the *return policy*, as it is the read effect on the value returned by the method. Using modifiers for policies allows for a clean separation of concerns, allowing us to analyse base types and policies separately.

Similarly, every expression (and statement) has a *write effect*, which is (a lower bound on) the disjunction of all policies on all containers whose contents are modified by the expression. Write effects allow us to control implicit information flows, by limiting the contexts in which expressions with side-effects may occur. A modifier `!pol` denotes a write effect, and is used to annotate methods.

Policy modifiers are also placed on exceptions declared to be thrown by a method. A read effect modifier on an exception denotes the read effect of inspecting the thrown and caught exception object. More interesting is the write effect modifier, which serves two purposes in relation to indirect flows. First, it restricts the contexts in which the exception may be thrown within the method. Second, it imposes a restriction of its own on all subsequent side-effects until the point where the exception has been caught and handled. Together, these two restrictions ensure that no information leaks can occur by observing whether or not an exception has been thrown.

All exceptions in Paragon must be *checked*, i.e. declared to be thrown by methods that may terminate with such exceptions. This implies the need for analyses that can rule out the possibility of exceptions, in particular for null pointers, to avoid a massive blow-up in the number of potential exceptions that must be declared. Paragon adds the modifier **`notnull`** for fields, variables and method parameters that may never be null, to aid the null-pointer analysis.

To reduce the burden on the programmer to put in policy annotations, Paragon attempts either to infer, or to supply clever defaults for, policies on variables, fields and methods. We omit the details of policy defaulting, and discuss the inference mechanism in § 4.

Lock State Analysis. Manipulation of the lock state is done programmatically through the use of the Paragon-specific statements **`open`** and **`close`**. The compiler performs a *lock state analysis* which conservatively approximates the set of locks guaranteed to be open at any given program point.

In cases where we cannot know statically that a lock is open, we allow runtime *lock queries* to guide the analysis: A lock can be used syntactically as an expression of type

boolean, with the value **true** if the lock is currently open. If a lock query appears as the condition to e.g. an **if** statement, the analysis can include the knowledge of the lock's status when checking the respective branches.

To facilitate modularity, Paragon introduces three modifiers, used on methods and constructors, to specify their interaction with the lock state:

- `+locks` says that the annotated method *will* open the specified lock(s), for every execution in which the method returns normally. We call this the *opens* modifier.
- `-locks`, dubbed the *closes* modifier, says that the method *may* close the specified lock(s), for *some* execution.
- `~locks`, the *expects* modifier, says that the specified lock(s) must be open whenever the method is called.

The *opens* and *closes* modifiers are also used to annotate each exception type thrown by a method, to signal to the analysis what changes to the lock state can be assumed if the method terminates by throwing an exception of that type.

As a middleground between private and public locks, Paragon introduces the modifier **readonly** for locks, indicating that outside the class the lock can be queried, but not opened or closed.

3 Brief Example

To illustrate the language features of Paragon we present the scenario of a simple social network. In the network, users can befriend each other and share messages in the form of posts that can be read by their friends. The scenario contains two information flow policies that we want Paragon to enforce.

First, posts can only be read by a direct friend of the poster or, if the poster so indicates, by friends of friends of the poster. A user can decide, per post, whether it should be shared with friends-of-friends or not. Paragon should thus enforce that the network properly checks the friendship relations before allowing a user to read a post.

Second, to prevent injection or scripting attacks, a message should be properly *sanitised* before it is stored in the network. That is, we want to enforce the policy that all posted messages first pass through a sanitising function.

The Paragon implementation of this network is shown in Figure 1. Some policy annotations are omitted in the implementation, since Paragon provides default policies in these cases. For example, all fields that do not specify a read effect automatically get the least restrictive policy `{Object x:}`.

To establish the first policy we define the `Friend` lock to model friendships. Similarly we create a lock `FoFriend` to model friend-of-friend relations. Since the `User` class does not explicitly open or close this lock and exports it as **readonly** we know that it models a purely derived property of the `Friend` lock, and thus one that will evolve correctly as the friendship status changes over time.

With the locks in place we can now create the desired policy as `messagePol`, which we use for the read-effect on a post's content. We assume that the correct `Friend` instances are opened elsewhere in the program. Turning sharing with friends-of-friends on per post is handled in the `post` method by opening the `ShareFoF` lock for that post.

```
public class User {
  public reflexive symmetric lock Friend(User, User);
  public readonly lock FoFriend(User, User)
    { (User x y z) FoFriend(x,y) : Friend(x,z), Friend(z,y) };
  public void receive(?{this:} String data) {
    ... // User receives provided data
  }
}


public class Post {
  public lock ShareFoF(Post);
  public final User poster;
  public static final policy messagePol =
    { User x : User.Friend(x, poster)
    ; User x : User.FoFriend(x, poster), ShareFoF(this) };
  public final ?messagePol String message;
  public Post(?{Object x:} User p, ?messagePol String m) {
    this.poster = p;
    this.message = m;
  }
}


public class Sanitiser {
  private lock Sanitised;
  public static final policy unsanitised = {Object x : Sanitised};
  public static ?{Object x:} String sanitise (?unsanitised String s) {
    open Sanitised {
      return /* Sanitised string */ ;
    }
  }
}


public class Network {
  private static Post[] posts = new Post[10]; // Shifting list of posts
  private static int index = 0;               // Where to place the next post

  !{Object x:} static void post( ?{Object x:}               User    user
                               , ?Sanitiser.unsanitised String  message
                               , ?{Object x:}               boolean shareFoF ) {
    String sM = Sanitiser.sanitise(message);
    Post p = new Post(user, sM);
    if (shareFoF)
      open Post.ShareFoF(p);
    posts[index] = p;
    index = (index + 1) % posts.length;  // Next time overwrite oldest post
  }

  static void read(?{Object x:} User user, ?{Object x:} int i) {
    ?{user:} String res = null;
    Post p = posts[i];
    if (p != null) {
      if (User.Friend(user, p.poster))
        res = p.message;
      if (Post.ShareFoF(p))
        if (User.FoFriend(user, p.poster))
          res = p.message;
    }
    user.receive(res);
  }
}
```

Fig. 1. A simple social network application written in Paragon

As an effect of calling this method the array `posts` is changed (among others). Any observer that may notice this change (i.e. of level `{Object x:}` and above) may thus notice that this method has been called. To prevent this method from being called in a context where these side-effects result in implicit flows, we are required to annotate the method with the corresponding write effect.

The user's `receive` method lets the user read the provided information, therefore arguments to this method should be allowed to flow to that user. All combined, we get Paragon's enforcement ensuring that the policy-relevant state is properly checked before sharing a post with another user.

Leveraging on Java's encapsulation mechanism we are able to provide the ingredients for the sanitisation policy entirely as a separate library. The lock `Sanitised` is private to the class, meaning that no code outside the class is able to open, close or even mention the lock. Therefore, any data labelled with the `unsanitised` policy cannot lose its `Sanitised` constraint, other than by actually sanitising the data by calling the exported `sanitise` method. With this library we can thus easily enforce our second policy by labelling each newly incoming message as `unsanitised`.

The example demonstrates the three different generations of information-flow control policies and how Paragon models them.

As per traditional non-interference, some flows are never allowed in the network. For example, Paragon enforces that a posted message can only flow to users in the network, and not to any other channel. We see an example of the exceptional information declassification pattern in the sanitiser library: the `sanitise` function serves as a declassifier, deliberately allowing the provided argument to flow to more actors. Finally, the locks used to model friendships exemplify third-generation information-flow policies. There is no explicit declassification of information, rather flows are allowed or not depending on the state of the system – in this case the state of the social network.

4 Enforcement of Paragon Policies

Enforcement of information flow policies in Paragon is no small task, and presenting the information flow type system in its entirety is beyond the scope of this paper. Instead, we sketch a high-level overview of the most important analyses involved, presented as a sequence of *phases*, and focus on the last phase in which information flows are tracked.

Phase 1: Type Checking. The first phase roughly corresponds to ordinary Java type checking, albeit with some additions for Paragon-specific constructs. Particularly, we must assure that arguments to locks are type correct, and that policy expressions used in modifiers are indeed of type **`policy`**. This phase also checks that potential (runtime) exceptions are properly handled.

Phase 2: Policy Type Evaluation. Locks, policies, and object references all play a dual role, both as type-level and value-level entities. In this phase the values of each of these entities are statically approximated. For *locks* we ensure that, whenever a lock is queried, the information in the query is propagated to the respective branch (or loop body).

For fields and variables holding *actors*, i.e. object references, approximating their runtime values means performing an alias analysis. Our present analysis is simple but has performed well enough in practice. However, work is in progress to improve its precision by adapting the work by Whaley and Rinard [30].

Since policies can be used as values at runtime, and dynamically hoisted to the type level, our analysis needs to approximate policies as *singleton types*, similar to the analysis of actors. For each field or variable storing a *policy*, and for each policy expression appearing in a modifier, we thus calculate upper and lower bounds on the policy held by that variable at runtime.

Further, we need ways to relate policies that are not known statically to other (static or dynamic) policies, to improve precision. Similar to runtime lock queries, we thus let our policy analysis be guided by inequality constraints between policies appearing as the condition in `if` statements and conditional `?:` expressions. This problem has been studied by Zheng and Myers in the context of Jif [32], and our solution closely follows theirs.

Phase 3: Lock State Evaluation. The next sub-phase approximates the *lock state*, i.e. it calculates the set of locks which we can statically know to be open, at each program point. This amounts to a dataflow analysis over the control flow graph, to properly capture the influence of method calls and exceptions, and to handle loops. Each program point where a direct flow takes place is annotated with the lock state in effect at that point.

Phase 4: Policy Constraint Generation. The constraint generation phase will result in a set of constraints on the form $p \sqsubseteq_{LS} q$ where p and q are policy expressions and LS is the lock state (calculated in Phase 3) at the program point where the constraint was generated (omitted if empty). As argued in §2.2 the lock state is only taken into account for direct flows. Policy expressions possibly contain meta-variables, for which the constraint solving phase then solves.

Phase 5: Policy Constraint Solving. The last phase solves the generated constraints, on a per-method basis. A solution to a set of constraints is an assignment of policies to constraint variables that satisfies all the policy comparison constraints. The algorithm needs only determine whether there exists a solution, and does not need to actually produce one. The constraint solver is based on the algorithm presented by Rehof and Mogensen [21].

4.1 Paragon Implementation

We have implemented Paragon in a compiler that performs type checking for policies, and compiles policy-compliant programs into vanilla Java code. Once we know that a given program satisfies the intended information flow properties, we can safely remove all Paragon-specific type-level aspects of policies, locks and actors.

We must still retain the runtime aspects, such as querying the lock state and performing inequality comparisons between policies. The Paragon runtime library provides Java implementations for locks and properties, including operations for opening, closing and querying locks to which the Paragon **`open`**, **`close`** and query statements are compiled. Similarly, the library provides Java implementations for policies and operations for performing runtime inequality comparisons between them.

Compiler Statistics. Our Paragon compiler is written in Haskell and comprises roughly 16k lines of code, including comments. Approximately half of that code is due to our policy type checker, and only a small fraction, just over 600 lines of code, deals with generation of Java code and the Paragon interface files needed for modular compilation. On top of that, some 1500 lines of Java code are written for our runtime representations of Paragon entites. The compiler can be downloaded from our Paragon website [1], or from the central Haskell "hackage" repository using the command `cabal install paragon`.

Runtime Overhead. Supporting lock queries and policy comparisons at runtime yields a negligible overhead on Paragon programs. Most of the additional generated code handles the initalisation of policies and locks upon class or object instantiation, as well as the opening and closing of locks, which should not give any significant performance penalty. More involved are the lock queries and policy comparisons themselves since they resemble essentialy Datalog program evaluation and respectively containment [29]. However, our experience shows that clause bodies consist of just a few atoms, and have yet to find an example involving locks with arity higher than two, so in practice we posit that this overhead is negligible as well.

5 Case Studies

We put the compiler to the test with two case studies, both based on applications written in the Jif programming language, to which we further relate in §6.

Mental Poker. In [3], a non-trivial cryptographic protocol for playing online poker without a trusted third party is implemented in Jif. During the distribution of the cards, players communicate cards encrypted with a per-player, per-game symmetric key. That is, the receiving player cannot decrypt the received card. At the end of the game the players reveal their symmetric key such that the other player may verify the outcome of the card distribution. For the purpose of non-repudiation each player signs outgoing messages with her private key.

From an information-flow perspective we desire an implementation of this protocol to satisfy various policies. The public key of a player is visible to everyone, as it is used to verify the player's signatures, but the private key should never leave the player's client. The cards to be communicated should not be sent before they are encypted with the symmetric key and then signed. The symmetric key should remain confidential to the player until the end of the game.

The value of the symmetric key leaks partially when performing encryption. In our Paragon implementation (6.5k lines) this leak is controlled by a lock private to the class performing the encryption, similar to the approach taken in the sanitiser class from the example in §3. That is, the class ensures that only the result of the operation is released and not the value of the key involved. The symmetric key is protected with a policy guarded by this private lock. A similar approach is used to protect the private key, to only reveal the outcome of the signing operation in which it was involved. The cards to be encrypted are protected with both the private locks of the encryption and the signing operation, indicating that they have to go through both declassifiers before they can be sent to the other player. The symmetric key is also allowed to be released when the `EndGame` lock is open. That is, this lock is used to represent a policy-relevant state of the application.

By constrast, Jif uses owner-based policies. The Jif policies here can simply state whether the data is owned by a given player or not, and cannot, in an obvious way, express anything beyond that. The fact that a Jif program has access to exactly one declassification mechanism prevents it from distinguishing or controlling different forms of declassification. In this case study it cannot make a distinction between declassifications that are allowed due to encryption, and those due to signing. In addition, Jif does not provide a means to write temporal policies and needs to rely on programming patterns to prevent declassifications occuring in a state where they are not supposed to be allowed.

JPMail. The second case study implements a functional e-mail client based on JPMail [11]. In JPMail the user can specify a mail-policy file, partly dictating the information-flow policies that the mail client has to enforce.

JPMail ensures that an e-mail is only sent if its body has been encrypted under an algorithm that is trusted by the receiver of the e-mail. Which encryption algorithms are trusted by what JPMail users is specified in the mail-policy file. In addition JPMail needs to enforce more static policies, e.g. preventing the login credentials from flowing anywhere else than to the e-mail server.

In the Paragon implementation (2.6k lines) these latter, static policies are easily modelled as specifying only the e-mail server as a receiving actor. The partly dynamic policy on the e-mail body is represented by a set of clauses of the form:

```
(User u) server: Receiver(mail, u), AESEncrypted(mail), TrustsAES(u)
```

That is, the e-mail can be sent to the mail server only if it has been encrypted under AES and the receiver of that e-mail trusts AES encryption. The `TrustsAES` and similar locks representing the user-specific policies are opened after parsing the mail-policy file, during initialisation of the client. The `Receiver` lock is opened based on the To-field information, and the `AESEncrypted` lock is encapsulated analogous to the encryption / signing locks of the previous case study.

The issues for the Jif implementation in the mental poker case study show up in the JPMail example [11] as well. Moreover, stateful policies are central to this example and are challenging to model in Jif; Hicks *et al*'s solution involves generating the policy part of the Jif source code from the mail-policy file, hardcoding the user-specific policies in the client. This implies that if a mail-policy file changes, the only way for the Jif solution to handle it is by recompilation of the code. By contrast, Paragon handles policy change mechanisms naturally (by opening and closing locks) without stopping the code or recompiling.

6 Related Work

In this section we consider the related work on languages and language support for expressive information flow policies. We focus on actual systems rather than theoretical studies on policy mechanisms and formalisms. We note, however, that there are several policy languages in the access control and authorisation area which have some superficial similarity with the Paragon Policy Language, since they are based on datalog-like clauses to express properties like delegation and roles, see e.g. [4,9,13,14]. Key differences are (i) the information flow semantics that lies at the heart of Paragon, and (ii) the fact that the principal operation in Paragon is comparison and combination of policies, whereas in the aforementioned works the only operation of interest is querying of rules.

Languages with Explicit Information-Flow Tracking. Two "real-sized" languages stand out as providing information-flow primitives as types, namely FlowCAML and Jif – as discussed in the introduction.

Comparing Paragon to Jif is inevitable, being at the same time a competitor and a source of inspiration. Due to the unique position Jif has enjoyed in the domain of information flow research over many years, much research has been done using Jif for context and examples. It is thus natural to ask how research done on or with Jif can carry over to Paragon.

The main advantage of Paragon over Jif is undoubtedly the flexibility of the concept of locks, including their stateful nature. Where Jif has a single declassify construct, Paragon can provide different declassifying methods to work on different data, as needed by the domain at hand, and relate that declassification to the state of the program. Jif rigidly builds in some stateful aspects in the form of authority and delegations, which in Paragon would just be special cases of working with locks.

In many aspects, our work on Paragon has greatly benefitted from Jif's trailblazing, as well as research done in the context of Jif. Policy defaulting mechanisms, handling of runtime policies, and having all exceptions checked, are all features where we have been able to adopt Jif's solution directly.

In separate work, as of yet unpublished, we have conducted a complete and in-depth comparison between the two languages and all their features, including a Paragon library that gives a complete implementation of Jif, but the full details of that comparison are out of scope for this paper.

Compilers Performing IF Tracking. Information flow tracking can be performed in a language which has no inherent security policies, lattice-based or otherwise. In such a setting one tracks the way that information flows from e.g. method parameters to outputs. Examples of tools performing such analysis are the Spark Examiner operating over a safety-critical subset of Ada [6], and Hammer and Snelting [10] explain how state-of-the-art program slicing methods can support a more accurate analysis of such information flows in Java (e.g. both flow sensitive and object sensitive).

Dynamic Information Flow Tracking with Expressive Policies. Runtime information flow tracking systems have experienced a recent surge of interest. The most relevant examples from the perspective of the present paper are those which perform full information flow tracking (rather than the semantically incomplete "taint analysis"), and employ expressive policies. The first example is Stefan *et al*'s embedding of information flow in Haskell [25]. In principle one could also use Paralocks in a dynamic context, and we are currently investigating a stateful extension of their LIO framework which could be instantiated with the generalised Paralocks described in this work.

Yang *et al*'s *Jeeves* language [31] focusses on confidentiality properties of data expressed as context-dependent data visibility policies. The Jeeves approach is noteworthy in it's novel implementation techniques and greater emphasis on the separation of policy and code.

Encoding Information Flow Policies with Existing Type Systems. With suitably expressive type systems and abstraction mechanisms, static information flow constraints can be expressed via a library [15,16,22].

A number of recent expressive languages are aimed at expressing a variety of rich security policies, but do not have information flow control as a primitive notion (as Paragon or Jif) [12,28]. F* [27], a full-fledged implementation of a dependently typed programming ML-stye programming language, is perhaps the most successful in this class, with a large number of examples showing how security properties can be encoded and verified by typing.

Typestate. The way that Paragon tracks locks is related to the concept of *typestate* [26]. Typestate acknowledges that the runtime state of e.g. an object often determines which methods are safe to call. For example, for a Java `File` object, the method `read()` can only be called if the file has first been opened with the `open()` method. Systems with typestate, such as *Plaid* [2], support formal specification of typestate properties, and enforce that programs correctly follow the specifications. In Paragon, typestate properties can be specified through the use of lock state modifiers. Paragon cannot express features that depend on Plaid's first-class states, e.g. "an array of open files", but can otherwise express solutions to their motivating examples.

7 Conclusions and Further Work

It is our expectation that one day programming languages with built-in support for expressing and enforcing information-flow concerns become widely deployed. Paragon's strong integration with Java and its relatively natural yet expressive policy specification language lowers the threshold for adopting information-flow aware programming outside the research community. Still, much work is left to be done before Paragon can become a serious competitor to existing programming.

One notable direction for future work in the Paragon language is concurrency support. This direction requires both theoretical and practical work, in particular if declassification mechanisms are shared among threads. Another planned direction is to present a more substantial formalisation of Paragon's type system, including a proof of soundness with respect to information flow security.

Acknowledgments. Thanks to the reviewers and all members of the ProSec group at Chalmers for improving this paper with every iteration. We thank our colleagues Wolfgang Ahrendt, Pablo Buiras, Filippo Del Tedesco, Willard Rafnsson and Alejandro Russo for their valuable comments and feedback. Furthermore we would like to thank Jens Lidestrõm, Shayan Najd Javadipour, Javed Nazir and Yannick Zakowski for assisting in the implementation of the Paragon compiler. This work is partly funded by the Swedish agencies SSF and VR, and Websand EC FP7-ICT-STREP.

References

1. Paragon website (July 2013), `http://www.cse.chalmers.se/research/group/paragon`
2. Aldrich, J., Sunshine, J., Saini, D., Sparks, Z.: Typestate-oriented programming. In: OOPSLA Companion, pp. 1015–1022 (2009)
3. Askarov, A., Sabelfeld, A.: Security-typed languages for implementation of cryptographic protocols: A case study. In: di Vimercati, S.d.C., Syverson, P.F., Gollmann, D. (eds.) ESORICS 2005. LNCS, vol. 3679, pp. 197–221. Springer, Heidelberg (2005)
4. Becker, M.Y., Fournet, C., Gordon, A.D.: Design and semantics of a decentralized authorization language. In: Proc. IEEE Computer Security Foundations Symposium, pp. 3–15. IEEE Computer Society (2007)
5. Broberg, N., Sands, D.: Paralocks – role-based information flow control and beyond. In: POPL 2010, Proceedings of the 37th Annual ACM SIGACT-SIGPLAN Symposium on Principles of Programming Languages (2010)
6. Chapman, R., Hilton, A.: Enforcing security and safety models with an information flow analysis tool. ACM SIGAda Ada Letters 24(4), 39–46 (2004)
7. Denning, D.E.: A lattice model of secure information flow. Comm. of the ACM 19(5), 236–243 (1976)
8. Denning, D.E., Denning, P.J.: Certification of programs for secure information flow. Comm. of the ACM 20(7), 504–513 (1977)
9. Dougherty, D.J., Fisler, K., Adsul, B.: Specifying and reasoning about dynamic access-control policies. In: Furbach, U., Shankar, N. (eds.) IJCAR 2006. LNCS (LNAI), vol. 4130, pp. 632–646. Springer, Heidelberg (2006)
10. Hammer, C., Snelting, G.: Flow-sensitive, context-sensitive, and object-sensitive information flow control based on program dependence graphs. International Journal of Information Security 8(6), 399–422 (2009)
11. Hicks, B., Ahmadizadeh, K., McDaniel, P.D.: From languages to systems: Understanding practical application development in security-typed languages. In: ACSAC. IEEE Computer Society (2006)
12. Jia, L., Zdancewic, S.: Encoding information flow in aura. In: Proceedings of the ACM SIGPLAN Fourth Workshop on Programming Languages and Analysis for Security (2009)
13. Jim, T.: SD3: A trust management system with certified evaluation. In: Proc. IEEE Symp. on Security and Privacy (2001)
14. Li, N., Mitchell, J.C., Winsborough, W.H.: Design of a role-based trust-management framework. In: IEEE Symposium on Security and Privacy, pp. 114–130 (2002)
15. Li, P., Zdancewic, S.: Arrows for secure information flow. Theor. Comput. Sci. 411(19) (2010)
16. Morgenstern, J., Licata, D.R.: Security-typed programming within dependently-typed programming. In: Proceedings of the 15th ACM SIGPLAN International Conference on Functional Programming (2010)

17. Myers, A.C.: JFlow: Practical mostly-static information flow control. In: Proc. ACM Symp. on Principles of Programming Languages, pp. 228–241 (January 1999)
18. Myers, A.C., Liskov, B.: A decentralized model for information flow control. In: Proc. ACM Symp. on Operating System Principles, pp. 129–142 (October 1997)
19. Myers, A.C., Liskov, B.: Protecting privacy using the decentralized label model. ACM Transactions on Software Engineering and Methodology 9(4), 410–442 (2000)
20. Myers, A.C., Zheng, L., Zdancewic, S., Chong, S., Nystrom, N.: Jif: Java information flow. Software release (2001–2013), `http://www.cs.cornell.edu/jif`
21. Rehof, J., Mogensen, T.: Tractable constraints in finite semilattices. In: Cousot, R., Schmidt, D.A. (eds.) SAS 1996. LNCS, vol. 1145, pp. 285–300. Springer, Heidelberg (1996)
22. Russo, A., Claessen, K., Hughes, J.: A library for light-weight information-flow security in haskell. In: Proceedings of the 1st ACM SIGPLAN Symposium on Haskell (2008)
23. Sabelfeld, A., Sands, D.: Declassification: Dimensions and principles. Journal of Computer Security 15(5), 517–548 (2009)
24. Simonet, V.: The Flow Caml system. Software release (July 2003), `http://cristal.inria.fr/~simonet/soft/flowcaml`
25. Stefan, D., Russo, A., Mitchell, J.C., Mazières, D.: Flexible dynamic information flow control in Haskell. In: Proceedings of the 4th ACM Symposium on Haskell (2011)
26. Strom, R.E., Yemini, S.: Typestate: A programming language concept for enhancing software reliability. IEEE Trans. Software Eng. 12(1), 157–171 (1986)
27. Swamy, N., Chen, J., Fournet, C., Strub, P., Bharagavan, K., Yang, J.: Secure distributed programming with value-dependent types. In: The 16th ACM SIGPLAN International Conference on Functional Programming (2011)
28. Swamy, N., Corcoran, B.J., Hicks, M.: Fable: A language for enforcing user-defined security policies. In: Proc. IEEE Symp. on Security and Privacy, pp. 369–383 (2008)
29. van Delft, B., Broberg, N., Sands, D.: A datalog semantics for paralocks. In: Jøsang, A., Samarati, P., Petrocchi, M. (eds.) STM 2012. LNCS, vol. 7783, pp. 305–320. Springer, Heidelberg (2013)
30. Whaley, J., Rinard, M.: Compositional pointer and escape analysis for Java programs. In: Proceedings of the 14th ACM SIGPLAN Conference on Object-oriented Programming, Systems, Languages, and Applications, OOPSLA 1999, pp. 187–206. ACM (1999)
31. Yang, J., Yessenov, K., Solar-Lezama, A.: A language for automatically enforcing privacy policies. In: Proceedings of the 39th ACM SIGPLAN-SIGACT Symposium on Principles of Programming Languages. ACM (2012)
32. Zheng, L., Myers, A.C.: Dynamic security labels and static information flow control. International Journal of Information Security 6 (2007)

`ThisJava`: An Extension of Java with Exact Types

Hyunik Na[1] and Sukyoung Ryu[2]

[1] S-Core., Ltd.
hina@kaist.ac.kr

[2] Department of Computer Science, KAIST
sryu.cs@kaist.ac.kr

Abstract. We propose `ThisJava`, an extension of Java-like programming languages with exact class types and `This` types, to support more useful methods with more precise types. To realize the proposed approach, we provide an open-source prototype implementation of the language and show its practicality and backward compatibility. We believe that our system elucidates the long pursuit of an object-oriented language with "`This` types."

1 Introduction

Objects in object-oriented programming often provide methods whose signatures include the object types themselves. The type of a receiver e of a method invocation "$e.m(e')$" is always the enclosing object type that defines or inherits the method m, which we call the method's *owner type*. In addition, many useful methods have their owner types in their parameter types or return types. In this paper, we call such methods with their owner types in their signatures *This-typed methods*.

Researchers have proposed various approaches to support `This`-typed methods. While the traditional `This` type denotes the "declared" type of a receiver, the `This` type in this paper denotes the "run-time" type of a receiver. Because run-time types of method receivers are mostly not available at compile time due to subtyping, the existing `This` types denote inexact compile-time types. To precisely capture the exact run-time type at compile time, our type system generates fresh type variables for the unknown run-time types at type checking time. This new notion of `This` types serves an essential role in the safe coexistence of recursive types and subtyping-by-inheritance.

To realize the proposed approach in a programming language, we extend Java with exact class types and `This` types. To support more methods with `This`-typed formal parameters, we enhance the type system with named wildcards and exact type inference, and we also introduce exact class type matching. To support more methods with `This`-typed results, we provide virtual constructors. We implemented our extension of Java, `ThisJava`, using JastAddJ [5] and made it open to the public:

`http://plrg.kaist.ac.kr/research/software`

We describe how the new features are compiled to Java bytecode, and how the new features interact with the existing Java features.

C.-c. Shan (Ed.): APLAS 2013, LNCS 8301, pp. 233–240, 2013.

2 Main Features of ThisJava

We extend Java with new typing features and language constructs to support more uses of exact types by allowing more This-typed methods. Due to space limitations, we briefly summarize the main features here and refer the interested reader to our earlier work [10,9].

We introduce *exact class types* of the form #C (read as "exact C") for a class C to represent run-time exact types of objects, and a type variable implicitly declared in the definition of C, This. In ThisJava, a This type appearing in the definition of a class (or interface) C denotes the *run-time type* of the special variable this (whereas the traditional This types denote its *declared type*).

To describe the relationships between exact types, ThisJava provides a type annotation of the form </X/>, called *named wildcards*. Using named wildcards, programmers can state that two formal parameter types or the result type and a formal parameter type are the same run-time types. Also, ThisJava performs a type-flow analysis called *exact type inference* to collect more equality relationships between exact types. Exact type inference lessens the programmers' burden of using exact type annotations such as exact class types and named wildcards. Exact type inference traces the flows of run-time types through the chains of def-use pairs. In particular, it infers exact types in a flow-sensitive manner to make more precise judgements on the run-time type matches of expressions.

To enhance the expressive power taking advantage of This types, ThisJava provides *virtual constructors* to represent "generic factory methods," methods that have the This type as their return type, and generates and returns an object of the same run-time type as its receiver, even when it is inherited by a subclass. In addition to generic factory methods, virtual constructors are useful to reduce code duplication by implementing common tasks for object generation in a superclass and allowing subclasses to inherit or override them, unlike ordinary constructors. An invocation of a virtual constructor is dynamically dispatched based on the run-time type of the receiver and generates an object of the same run-time type as the receiver.

While the This type in this paper allows more This-typed methods than traditional This types because it denotes run-time exact types rather than compile-time inexact types, purely static approaches to typing invocations of This-typed methods may require more relaxation. To allow more This-typed methods, ThisJava provides a language construct, classesmatch, to compare run-time types:

```
classesmatch (x,y) { /* then-block */ ... }
else { /* else-block */ ... }
```

At run time, it checks whether the run-time types of two variables are identical or not. If they are, the execution continues to evaluate then-block, otherwise the execution continues to evaluate else-block. Because the semantics of classesmatch guarantees that the run-time types of two variables are the same in then-block, it allows This-typed method invocations on the variables in then-block. Because programmers use (inexact) class types in most cases to enjoy subtype polymorphism, checking exact class types by run-time tests with classesmatch would provide full flexibility in using This-typed methods.

3 Compilation of ThisJava

The ThisJava compiler generates class files that can run on JVMs [8]. In this section, we describe how the compiler translates new language features into Java bytecode.

Exact Types Because JVM does not support exact types, the ThisJava compiler converts exact types to class types that JVM can understand. We call this process *inexactization*, which is very similar to *type erasure* [7, Section 4.6] in Java. The inexactization process converts most of the exact types to class types as follows:

1. A This type in a class C definition is converted to C.
2. For a class D and a named wildcard X, types #D and D</X/> are converted to D.

The only exception to the rule 1 is to support overriding a method or a virtual constructor that has a This-typed formal parameter as follows:

1′. When the declared parameter type of a method or a virtual constructor is This, the This type is converted to Object and appropriate type casting is applied to the formal parameter so that the generated class files can pass the *verification process* [8, Section 4.9].

Virtual Constructors. The ThisJava compiler converts a virtual constructor definition into an ordinary constructor definition and two stub method definitions. The ordinary constructor definition has the same signature and body as the original virtual constructor except that any exact types are converted to class types as described above. The first stub method, vcStub0, has the same list of formal parameters as the original virtual constructor, packs the parameters into an array of Objects, and invokes the second stub method. Unless the class defining the virtual constructor is abstract, the second stub method, vcStub1, unpacks the packed parameters and invokes the ordinary constructor discussed above. Any virtual constructor invocation in the original source code is converted to the invocation of a vcStub0 method. For example, the following:

```
class C {
  int fi; Point fp;
  This(int i, Point p) { fi = i; fp = p; }
  This copy() { return new This(fi,fp); }
}
```

is converted to the following:

```
class C {
  int fi; Point fp;
  C(int i, Point p) { fi = i; fp = p; }
  C vcStub0(int i, Point p) {
    Object[] pack = new Object[] {Integer.valueOf(i), p};
    return vcStub1(pack);
  }
  C vcStub1(Object[] pack) {
    int i = ((Integer)pack[0]).intValue();
    Point p = (Point)pack[1];
    return new C(i,p);
  }
  C copy() { return vcStub0(fi,fp); }
}
```

If the class defining a virtual constructor is abstract, the generated `vcStub1` method is also abstract. When a class inherits a virtual constructor, the code conversion adds to the class an ordinary constructor which has the same signature as the inherited constructor and just calls its super-constructor. If the class is not abstract, the code conversion also redefines (overrides) the `vcStub1` method so that it calls the added constructor. Under our compilation strategy for virtual constructors, the `vcStub1` methods always have the same signature `vcStub1(Object[])` to simulate overriding of virtual constructors by overriding the `vcStub1` methods. Packing and unpacking of parameters are necessary to keep the uniform signature of the `vcStub1` methods.

Compilation of virtual constructor definitions actually require more strategies than discussed above to properly handle *inner classes* [3, Chapter 5] in Java. When a class defining or inheriting a virtual constructor is an inner class or a subclass of an inner class, the code conversion has to take enclosing objects [3, Section 5.2] and variables in an enclosing scope [3, Section 5.3] into account so that they can be correctly passed to the generated constructor and stub methods at run time. We omit the details of such compilation, but our `ThisJava` compiler implementation is publicly available.

Type Testing and Casting with Exact Types. `ThisJava` supports type testing and casting with exact class types:

```
... (o instanceof #Point) ...       // (1)
... (#Point) o ...                  // (2)
```

Because `#Point` is an exact class type, when `o` has a `ColorPoint` object, a subclass of `Point`, at run time (1) should produce `false` and (2) should produce an exception. Thus, the bytecode generated for (1) is similar to the bytecode generated for the following:

```
... (o == null ? false : o.getClass() == Point.class) ...
```

and the bytecode generated for (2) is similar to the one generated for the following:[1]

```
... (o == null || o.getClass() == Point.class ? (Point) o
                                   : throw new ClassCastException()) ...
```

`ThisJava` does not support type testing and casting with `This` types and types with named wildcards because they can be expressed by the `classesmatch` construct. For example, the following example is illegal in `ThisJava`:

```
Object o; ...
if (o instanceof This) {
  This t = (This) o;  /* do something with t */ ...
}
```

but the following is legal and does what the above intends:

```
Object o; ...
classesmatch (o, this) { /* do it with o */ ... }
```

[1] Note that it is not legal Java code but pseudo code for explanation. The `throw` statement is syntactically illegal.

4 Interactions with Existing Features of Java

4.1 Overloading

Java supports *overloading* [3, Section 2.8], which allows two or more methods visible in a scope to have the same name if they have different signatures. For an invocation of overloaded methods, the types of the actual arguments to the invocation may be compatible with two or more signatures of the overloaded methods. In such cases, a Java compiler chooses the most specific method among the applicable ones, if any. Otherwise, it signals an ambiguous invocation error at compile time.

ThisJava extends the Java rule for selecting the most specific method because This types and types with named wildcards may put additional run-time type match constraints on some of the arguments to a method invocation. The ThisJava compiler selects the most specific method for a method invocation as follows:

1. For every occurrence of This type, if any, in the signatures of applicable methods, replace it as follows:
   - if the declared type of the receiver is This, replace the This type with the class enclosing the method invocation;
   - if the declared type of the receiver is C</X/> for a class C and a named wildcard X, replace the This type with C; and
   - otherwise, replace the This type with the declared type of the receiver.
2. For every type with a named wildcard C</X/>, if any, in the signatures of applicable methods, replace it with C;
3. Among the applicable methods with the modified signatures by the above steps 1 and 2, select the most specific one by using the Java rule for selecting the most specific method [7, Section 15.12.2.5] extended with exact class types.
4. If the most specific method is determined, we are done. Otherwise, compare the run-time type match constraints of applicable methods as follows:
   - for two run-time type match constraints A and B, A is more specific than B if A is not equal to B and A includes every constraint in B.
5. If the most specific method is determined, we are done. Otherwise, the method invocation is ambiguous.

If a method has formal parameters declared with exact types, the ThisJava compiler *mangles* the method's name when it generates a class file to avoid possible conflicts between overloaded method signatures.

4.2 Arrays

ThisJava allows *exact array types* such as #C[], This[][], and C</X/>[], but with some limitations. Subtyping with exact array types is different from subtyping with Java array types. While Java array types are covariant in the sense that D[] is a subtype of C[] if D is a subtype of C, exact array types in ThisJava are not covariant; while the This type in the definition of C, C</X/>, and #C are subtypes of C, This[], C</X/>[], and #C[] are not subtypes of C[]. In general, covariant array types are unsound and JVM checks every assignment to an array at run time [13, Section 15.5].

ThisJava supports array creation of exact class types but not the other exact types, and it does not allow the root class Object to define a virtual constructor. While ThisJava supports 'new #C[10]', for example, and inexactizes it as discussed in Section 3, 'new This[10]' and 'new C</X/>[10]' are not allowed because they should produce arrays of different types depending on the run-time type of an object. Similarly, because any array type is a subtype of Object, if Object defines a virtual constructor then array types should inherit the virtual constructor, which should create arrays of different types depending on the run-time type of an object.

4.3 Generics and Wildcards

Since J2SE 5.0, Java supports type-parameterized classes and methods, known as *generics*, and it allows *type wildcards* (denoted by the question mark "?") to serve as type arguments for parameterized types [3, Chapter 11]. The new features of ThisJava work well with generics and wildcards of Java, but there are some restrictions on mixed uses of ThisJava's exact types and Java's generics and wildcards.

First, ThisJava does not allow an exact type as the declared upper bound of a type variable or a type wildcard. For example, all the following upper bounds are illegal:

```
class C<X extends #Point> { ...                    // illegal
  class I<Y extends This> {...}                    // illegal
  void m(Point</E/> p) {
    class L<Z extends Point</E/>> {...} ... // illegal
  }
}
```

Even if ThisJava allowed the above example, because no exact type has a proper subtype, the type variables X, Y and Z may be instantiated only by their respective upper bounds. Therefore, the above is nothing more than the following:

```
class C { /* #Point instead of X */ ...
  class I { /* C.This instead of Y */ ...}
  void m(Point</E/> p) {
    class L { /* Point</E/> instead of Z */ ...} ...
  }
}
```

Similarly, List<? extends #Point> denotes the same type as List<#Point>.

Unlike type variables, type wildcards may have lower bounds in Java. ThisJava allows This types and exact class types as lower bounds of type wildcards, but it does not allow types with named wildcards as lower bounds of type wildcards. For example, the following use of Point</X/> is not allowed:

```
class C { void mth(List<? super Point</X/>> l) {...} // illegal}
```

because there may exist multiple run-time types for the named wildcard. For example, if the above definition was allowed in ThisJava, in the following invocation of mth:

```
class C { void mth2(C c, List<Point> l) { ... c.mth(l); ... }}
```

Point</X/> may be #Point or #ColorPoint. Instead, the following definition:

```
class C { void mth2(C</X/> c, List<? super Point</X/>> l) {...}}
```

is legal because for any invocation of mth2, the named wildcard X is singly determined to the run-time type of the first argument of the invocation.

4.4 Type Checking Existing Java Programs

To see the backward compatibility of our ThisJava implementation, we compiled 7637 Java source files that comprise most of the standard class library from the Open-JDK 1.6 source code [12] using the ThisJava compiler. We found only one case that requires a user annotation to be compiled by the ThisJava compiler, but considering the diversity of the test files that we used, we believe that all valid Java programs (possibly with some annotations described below) are valid ThisJava programs.

The following example shows the exceptional case that needs a user annotation:

```
List<C> l = Arrays.asList(new C(...));
```

where the asList static method defined in the utility class java.util.Arrays takes a variable number of arguments of type T for a type variable T and returns a list of type List<T>. Because the invocation of asList does not explicitly provide a type to instantiate the type argument T, a compiler should infer it from the type of the actual argument new C(...), which is C. Then, the type of the right-hand side of the assignment is List<C> which is the declared type of the left-hand side, l. However, in ThisJava, the type of new C(...) is #C, which makes the type of the right-hand side List<#C>, which is not a subtype of the declared type of l. Thus, the assignment expression is not well typed in ThisJava. However, ThisJava can accept it with an explicit type instantiation rather than depending on the type inference as follows:

```
List<C> l = Arrays.<C>asList(new C(...));
```

5 Related Work

One may use *F-bounded polymorphism* [4] to define binary methods. In a class (or interface) definition of C<X>, the type variable X acts like a This type because it denotes a concrete class that extends C<X>. However, unlike This types, X is not the type of the special variable this; the type of this is C<X> which is not a subtype of X. Therefore, when programmers need an object of type X, they may need to declare an abstract method to use instead of this, as Altherr and Cremet [2] described.

An *abstract type* in Scala [1], which is a type member of a class (or trait) whose complete definition is deferred to its subclasses, may act like a This type. However, Scala still has the code duplication problem because it does not have virtual constructors, and the classes should declare and define the abstract type explicitly while the ThisJava classes do not declare or define a This type.

In Jx [11], a value-dependent type x.class denotes the exact type of an *immutable* variable x. Jx's this.class and x.class appear to be the same as our This and X, respectively, when x is declared with C</X/> for some C in our mechanism. Thus, Jx's type system and ours have comparable expressiveness in handling exact types. But Jx's constraint that the variable x in x.class should be immutable may be too restrictive.

In *Rupiah* [6], Foster introduced ThisClass constructors. However, while a subclass in ThisJava may inherit its superclass' virtual constructor, a subclass in Rupiah should always override its superclass' ThisClass constructor. Similarly, Saito and Igarashi [14] propose *nonheritable methods*, which may not be inherited but should always be overridden by subclasses. In the definition of a nonheritable method whose return type is `This`, the `This` type is considered as a supertype of the enclosing class so that the method can use an ordinary constructor to generate a return value. On the contrary, by allowing inheritance of a superclass' virtual constructor, `ThisJava` reduces code duplication of virtual constructors.

6 Conclusion

We have presented `ThisJava`, an extension of Java with exact types, virtual constructors, and run-time type matches, to support more useful methods with more precise types than the traditional object-oriented languages with `This` types. We describe the compilation strategies and the interaction between the new features and existing features such as overloading, covariant array types, and generics. We believe that `ThisJava` elucidates the long pursuit of an object-oriented language with `This` types by providing a flexible type system and language features and a practical open-source prototype implementation. Our future work includes rewriting of the standard class library using `This` types to experiment its practicality and usability.

Acknowledgments. This work is supported in part by Korea Ministry of Education, Science and Technology(MEST) / National Research Foundation of Korea(NRF) (Grants NRF-2011-0016139 and NRF-2008-0062609).

References

1. Scala home, http://www.scala-lang.org/
2. Altherr, P., Cremet, V.: Adding type constructor parameterization to Java. In: 9th Workshop on Formal Techniques for Java-like Programs (2007)
3. Arnold, K., Gosling, J., Holmes, D.: The Java™ Programming Language, 4th edn. Addison-Wesley (August 2005)
4. Canning, P., Cook, W., Hill, W., Olthoff, W., Mitchell, J.C.: F-bounded polymorphism for object-oriented programming. In: FPCA (1989)
5. Ekman, T., Hedin, G.: The JastAdd extensible Java compiler. In: Conference Proceedings on Object-Oriented Programming Systems, Languages and Applications, OOPSLA, pp. 1–18 (2007)
6. Foster, J.: Rupiah: Towards an expressive static type system for java. Williams College Senior Honors Thesis (2001)
7. Gosling, J., Joy, B., Jr., Steele, G.L., Bracha, G.: The Java™ Language Specification, 3rd edn. Addison-Wesley (June 2005)
8. Lindholm, T., Yellin, F.: The Java™ Virtual Machine Specification, 2nd edn. Addison-Wesley (April 1999)
9. Na, H., Ryu, S.: A new formalization of subtyping to match subclasses to subtypes (June 2013), http://plrg.kaist.ac.kr/_media/research/publications/resubtyping_report.pdf
10. Na, H., Ryu, S., Choe, K.: Exact type parameterization and this Type support. In: TLDI (2012)
11. Nystrom, N., Chong, S., Myers, A.C.: Scalable extensibility via nested inheritance. In: OOPSLA (2004)
12. Oracle. Openjdk 6 source, http://download.java.net/openjdk/jdk6/
13. Pierce, B.C.: Types and Programming Languages. The MIT Press (2002)
14. Saito, C., Igarashi, A.: Matching ThisType to subtyping. In: SAC (2009)

Semantics of Probabilistic Programs: A Weak Limit Approach

Alessandra Di Pierro[1] and Herbert Wiklicky[2]

[1] Dipartimento di Informatica, Università di Verona, Italy
[2] Department of Computing, Imperial College London, UK

Abstract. For a simple probabilistic language we present a semantics based on linear operators on infinite dimensional Hilbert spaces. We show the equivalence of this semantics with a standard operational one and we discuss its relationship with the well-known denotational semantics introduced by Kozen. For probabilistic programs, it is typical to use Banach spaces and their norm topology to model the properties to be analysed (observables). We discuss the advantages in considering instead Hilbert spaces as denotational domains, and we present a weak limit construction of the semantics of probabilistic programs which is based on the inner product structure of this space, i.e. the duality between states and observables.

1 Introduction

The formal analysis of probabilistic systems is gaining increasing importance for its recognised benefits in various areas such as distributed systems, where randomised schemes are used to enhance efficiency, and in general to the design of systems with unreliable and unpredictable behaviour, where probability provides a means to make predictions based on the evaluation of performance characteristics (see e.g. [1] and the references therein). A recent trend in system design is highlighting the need for formal analysis techniques that are able to provide quantitative estimates of a system property and mathematical tools for cost optimisation. Several of our own recent works have shown how probabilistic static analysis can serve this purpose (see e.g. [2, 3]).

In order to have a sound basis for such an analysis we need a formal semantics of probabilistic programs. A popular choice for this is the denotational semantics introduced by Kozen in [4]. Despite its mathematical simplicity and clarity this semantics presents some limitations when used for program analysis. One problem is that it is mainly concerned with I/O behaviours, i.e. it only takes into account the final results of a program execution. This implies the identification of a number of behaviours and consequently a loss of precision of any static analyses based on it. Another limitation is that it does not provide a good basis for a relational analysis as correlations between program variables and properties are not made explicit.

We will investigate in this paper an alternative approach to probabilistic semantics which we argue is better suited for probabilistic program analysis. It

C.-c. Shan (Ed.): APLAS 2013, LNCS 8301, pp. 241–256, 2013.

essentially constructs the generator of a Discrete Time Markov Chain (DTMC) in a syntax-driven way similarly to the collecting semantics in classical program analysis [5]. The topological aspects of the resulting so-called Linear Operator Semantics (LOS) stem from the theory of infinite-dimensional Hilbert spaces. The choice of Hilbert spaces instead of the Banach spaces used in [4] is mainly motivated by the presence of an inner product. More precisely, the notion of an observable as a functional in the dual space of the state space coincides here with the notion of a state (i.e. a probability distribution) as Hilbert spaces are self-dual. We will show that this allows us to define a semantics based on a notion of equivalence which is finer than I/O semantics.

An additional aspect of our construction is an explicit consideration of program labels which are used on one hand to identify particular intermediate execution points but which also allow us to investigate the control flow within a program explicitly. The importance of considering labels has been discussed recently, for example, in the context of program obfuscation [6]. The removal of label information makes it more difficult to de-obfuscate programs via static program analysis, even if one can develop ways to reconstruct such information later. We compare in Section 4 the LOS semantics with Kozen's approach which does not consider program labels.

The main drawback of the construction of semantical operators on infinite-dimensional Hilbert spaces is the fact that even for simple programs, e.g. a constant assignment, it leads to unbounded operators, making it problematic the construction of a well-defined semantics for the program. Ideally, for semantical purposes one would like to consider only operators which are bounded as this requirement is equivalent to continuity of set-theoretical structures.

In order to overcome this problem we replace the notion of norm limit used in [4] by a weaker one, namely the *weak limit*, where convergence is defined directly in terms of inner product. Using weak limit constructions we can approximate the object we are interested in (i.e. the semantics $\mathbf{T}(P)$ of a program P) even though it is not in the semantical domain by considering the effects of its finite dimensional (and thus bounded) approximations on the state space. The classical concept which this approach resembles is the theory of generalised function (developed by Schwartz, Sobolev, et.al.), in particular Dirac's δ "function" which is not a function and yet can be modelled as the weak, more precisely weak$-^*$, limit of functions [7, 8].

As already mentioned, the weak limit semantics we introduce in this paper is intended to provide a sound mathematical basis for program analysis and in particular for probabilistic abstract interpretation [9–11]. This technique allows us to obtain a simplified semantics via an abstraction $\mathbf{A}$ and its corresponding concretisation $\mathbf{A}^\dagger$ defined by the so-called *Moore-Penrose pseudo-inverse.* The abstract semantics for a program P is then obtained as $\mathbf{T}^\#(P) = \mathbf{A}^\dagger\mathbf{T}(P)\mathbf{A}$ and can be constructed compositionally thanks to the properties of the tensor product operation and of the particular notion of generalised inverse we use for the abstraction on infinite-dimensional Hilbert space. In fact, these properties allow us to construct both concrete and abstract semantics by combining (via the tensor product) the effects of individual statements and their local effects.

Mathematical Background and Notation. For the mathematical notions and notation used in this paper we refer to the standard literature and, in particular, to the recent monograph by Kubrusly [12] for the functional analytical and operator algebraic concepts and to the presentation in [13] for the measure theoretic notions.

2 The Language

We will discuss our approach by referring to a probabilistic language which is a simplified version of the language in [10] and essentially the same as the one used [4]. In this section we introduce both the syntax and the operational semantics for this language, which we call **pWhile**.

Syntax. In a style typical of static analysis [5], we introduce labels in the syntax of the language. Labels are used to identify the programs points and are crucial for defining a formal semantics that is suitable for static analysis.

$$S ::= [\texttt{skip}]^\ell \mid [x \texttt{ := } e]^\ell \mid [x \texttt{ ?= } \rho]^\ell \mid S_1 \texttt{;}\ S_2$$
$$\mid \texttt{if}\ [b]^\ell\ \texttt{then}\ S_1\ \texttt{else}\ S_2\ \texttt{fi} \mid \texttt{while}\ [b]^\ell\ \texttt{do}\ S\ \texttt{od}$$

We denote by **Stmt** the set of all **pWhile** statements S and assume a unique labelling (by numbers $\ell \in$ **Lab**).

The statement `skip` does not have any operational effect but can be used, for example, as a placeholder in conditional statements. We have the usual (deterministic) assignment x `:=` e, sometimes also in the form x `:=` $f(x_1, \ldots, x_n)$.

In the random assignment x `?=` ρ, the value of a variable x is set to a value according to some random distribution ρ. In [4] it is left open how to define or specify distributions ρ in detail. We will use occasionally an ad-hoc notation as sets of tuples $\{(v_i, p_i)\}$ expressing the fact that value v_i will be selected with probability p_i; or just as a set $\{v_i\}$ assuming a uniform distribution on the values v_i. It might be useful to assume that the random number generator or scheduler which implements this construct can only implement choices over finite ranges, but in principle we can also use distributions with infinite support.

For the rest we have the usual sequential composition, conditional statement and loop. We leave the detailed syntax of functions f or expressions e open as well as for boolean expressions or test b in conditionals and loop statements.

SOS Semantics. The operational semantics of **pWhile** is defined in the SOS style [14] by means of a probabilistic transition system on the set **Conf** of configurations $\langle S, s\rangle$, where S is a **pWhile** program and s a classical state s : **Var** $\to$ **Value**. The transition rules are given in Table 1. We assume an evaluation function $\mathcal{E}$: **Expr** $\to$ (**State** $\to$ **Value**) for expressions defined in the usual way (assuming that **Value** contains e.g. integers as well as booleans `true` and `false`).

Table 1. The rules of the SOS semantics of **pWhile**

$$\textbf{R0}\ \langle \texttt{stop}, s\rangle \longrightarrow_1 \langle \texttt{stop}, s\rangle \qquad \textbf{R4}_1\ \frac{\langle S_1, s\rangle \longrightarrow_p \langle S_1', s'\rangle}{\langle S_1; S_2, s\rangle \longrightarrow_p \langle S_1'; S_2, s'\rangle}$$

$$\textbf{R1}\ \langle \texttt{skip}, s\rangle \longrightarrow_1 \langle \texttt{stop}, s\rangle$$

$$\textbf{R2}\ \langle v := e, s\rangle \longrightarrow_1 \langle \texttt{stop}, s[v \mapsto \mathcal{E}(e)s]\rangle \qquad \textbf{R4}_2\ \frac{\langle S_1, s\rangle \longrightarrow_p \langle \texttt{stop}, s'\rangle}{\langle S_1; S_2, s\rangle \longrightarrow_p \langle S_2, s'\rangle}$$

$$\textbf{R3}\ \langle v\ \texttt{?=}\ \rho, s\rangle \longrightarrow_{\rho(r)} \langle \texttt{stop}, s[v \mapsto r]\rangle$$

$$\textbf{R5}_1\ \langle \texttt{if}\ b\ \texttt{then}\ S_1\ \texttt{else}\ S_2\ \texttt{fi}, s\rangle \longrightarrow_1 \langle S_1, s\rangle \quad \text{if } \mathcal{E}(b)s = \texttt{true}$$

$$\textbf{R5}_2\ \langle \texttt{if}\ b\ \texttt{then}\ S_1\ \texttt{else}\ S_2\ \texttt{fi}, s\rangle \longrightarrow_1 \langle S_2, s\rangle \quad \text{if } \mathcal{E}(b)s = \texttt{false}$$

$$\textbf{R6}_1\ \langle \texttt{while}\ b\ \texttt{do}\ S\ \texttt{od}, s\rangle \longrightarrow_1 \langle S;\ \texttt{while}\ b\ \texttt{do}\ S\ \texttt{od}, s\rangle \quad \text{if } \mathcal{E}(b)s = \texttt{true}$$

$$\textbf{R6}_2\ \langle \texttt{while}\ b\ \texttt{do}\ S\ \texttt{od}, s\rangle \longrightarrow_1 \langle \texttt{stop}, s\rangle \quad \text{if } \mathcal{E}(b)s = \texttt{false}$$

Our aim is to identify the execution (process) of a program P according to the SOS rules as the realisation of a Discrete Time Markov Chain (DTMC) [15]. Markov chains are essentially transition systems where the successor state of a state is chosen according to a probability distribution. This probability distribution only depends on the current state, so that the system evolution is independent of the history. This is known as the memoryless property. The name Discrete Time Markov Chain refers to the fact that Markov chains are used as a time-abstract model (like transition systems): each transition is assumed to take a single time unit.

DTMC are non-terminating processes: it is assumed that there is always a next state and the process goes on forever. In order to reflect this property in our semantics, we introduce a terminal statement `stop` which indicates successful termination. Then the termination with a state s in the classical setting is represented here by reaching the final configuration $\langle \texttt{stop}, s\rangle$ which then 'loops' forever after. This means that we implicitly extend a statement S to construct full programs of the form $P \equiv S;\ [\texttt{stop}]^{\ell^*}$.

The probabilistic transition system defined in Table 1 is indeed describing a DTMC, as we obviously have a memoryless process: the transitions in Rules **R0** to **R6** depend only on the current configuration and not on the sequence of the configurations that preceded it. It is well-known that the matrix of transition probabilities of a DTMC on a countable state space is a stochastic matrix, i.e. a square (possibly infinite) matrix $\mathbf{P} = (p_{ij})$ whose elements are real numbers in the closed interval $[0, 1]$, for which $\sum_j p_{ij} = 1$ for all i [15, 16]. We can therefore represent the SOS semantics for a **pWhile** program P by the stochastic matrix on the vector space over the set **Conf** of all configurations of a program P defined by the rules in Table 1.

3 Linear Operator Semantics

The SOS semantics introduced in Section 2 specifies effectively the generator of a DTMC representing all executions of the program. However, the representation of this operator as a single unstructured matrix is not a convenient one for a denotational approach as it is not *compositional* (it stems from the SOS).

The labelled version of the syntax introduced in Section 2 allows us to use labels as a kind of program counter. Labels in **Lab** can therefore be used as delimiters of those relevant parts of the program that effectively correspond to the application of each language constructor. Moreover, they allow us to track the computational progress through the program execution, so yielding a semantics which is not only concerned with the I/O behaviour of the program but can also capture some finer notions of observables.

In the following we will present a semantics that we call Linear Operator Semantics (LOS), as it is the composition of different linear operators on the Hilbert space $\ell_2(\mathbf{Conf})$ over configurations, each expressing a particular operation, and contributing to the overall behaviour of the program. More precisely, the LOS is constructed compositionally by means of the operators representing each block of the program. The resulting operator $\mathbf{T}(P)$ is represented by an infinite matrix which we will show to be equivalent to the SOS matrix from Section 2. Moreover, we will show how this can be constructed as the weak limit of a sequence of finite approximations.

States and Observables. We assume that variables occurring in a **pWhile** program can take values in some countable set $\mathbb{X}$ that might be finite (e.g. Booleans) or infinite (typically $\mathbb{Z}$ or $\mathbb{N}$). We will refer to an implicitly given enumeration $\xi : \mathbb{X} \rightarrow \mathbb{N}$ of $\mathbb{X}$ (e.g. $\xi = \text{id}$ for $\mathbb{X} = \mathbb{N}$). For high-order languages or languages with e.g. real-valued variables one might need to work with uncountable sets (e.g. $\mathbb{X} = \mathbb{Z} \rightarrow \mathbb{Z}$ or $\mathbb{X} = \mathbb{R}$). However, for imperative languages like the one we consider in this paper a finite or countable infinite value space will do. We can nevertheless extend our framework also to deal with the uncountable case.

The *classical state* is defined as a map $s : \mathbf{Var} \rightarrow \mathbb{X}$. For a set of v variables $\mathbf{Var} = \{x_1, \ldots, x_v\}$ we can identify the classical state space with the v-fold cartesian product $\mathbb{X}^v = \mathbb{X} \times \ldots \times \mathbb{X}$. Concretely, the classical state $[x_1 \mapsto v_1, x_2 \mapsto v_2, \ldots x_v \mapsto v_v]$ corresponds to the v-tuple $(v_1, v_2, \ldots, v_v)$.

In our model *probabilistic states* σ are vectors of a *Hilbert space*, i.e. an inner product space that is complete under the metric induced by the inner product, [17, 12]. We recall that an inner product space $\mathcal{H}$ (over the reals $\mathbb{R}$) is a vector space $\mathcal{H}$ together with an inner product $\langle \cdot, \cdot \rangle : \mathcal{H} \times \mathcal{H} \rightarrow \mathbb{R}$, that is a function that is linear and continuous in both its arguments. An inner product induces a norm on $\mathcal{H}$ defined by $\|x\| = \sqrt{\langle x, x \rangle}$.

The concrete Hilbert space we will consider is $\ell_2(\mathbb{X})$, i.e. the space of all sequences $x = (x_i)_{i \in \mathbb{X}}$ for which $\sum_i |x_i|^2 < \infty$ holds [18, Def 1.14]. In fact, all Hilbert spaces with a countable infinite base are isomorphic to $\ell_2(\mathbb{N}) = \ell_2$ [17, Thm 2.2.12]. With the 2-norm $\|x\|_2 = \|(x_i)\|_2 = \left(\sum_{i \in \mathbb{X}} |x_i|^2\right)^{\frac{1}{2}}$ this is a Hilbert space as its norm $\|x\|_2 = \sqrt{\langle x, x \rangle}$ is induced by the inner product $\langle (x_i), (y_i) \rangle = \sum_i x_i y_i$. It contains as a dense sub-space the Banach space $\ell_1(\mathbb{X})$ which is equipped with the 1-norm $\|x\|_1 = \|(x_i)\|_1 = \sum_{i \in \mathbb{X}} |x_i| < \infty$ [18, Exercise 1.14]. We can represent the state of several variables $x_1, \ldots, x_v$ by a vector in the tensor product $\ell_2(\mathbb{X}) \otimes \ldots \otimes \ell_2(\mathbb{X}) = \ell_2(\mathbb{X}^v)$.

Table 2. The control flow

$$\mathit{flow}([\texttt{skip}]^\ell) = \mathit{flow}([v \texttt{ := } e]^\ell) = \mathit{flow}([v \texttt{ ?= } e]^\ell) = \emptyset$$
$$\mathit{flow}(S_1; S_2) = \mathit{flow}(S_1) \cup \mathit{flow}(S_2) \cup \{(\ell, \mathit{init}(S_2)) \mid \ell \in \mathit{final}(S_1)\}$$
$$\mathit{flow}(\texttt{if } [b]^\ell \texttt{ then } S_1 \texttt{ else } S_2 \texttt{ fi}) = \mathit{flow}(S_1) \cup \mathit{flow}(S_2) \cup \{(\ell, \underline{\mathit{init}(S_1)}), (\ell, \mathit{init}(S_2))\}$$
$$\mathit{flow}(\texttt{while } [b]^\ell \texttt{ do } S \texttt{ od}) = \mathit{flow}(S) \cup \{(\ell, \underline{\mathit{init}(S)})\} \cup \{(\ell', \ell) \mid \ell' \in \mathit{final}(S)\}$$

The tensor product is an essential element of the description of probabilistic states. This tensor product – more precisely, the Kronecker product, i.e. the coordinate based version of the abstract concept of a tensor product – of two vectors $(x_1, \ldots, x_n)$ and $(y_1, \ldots, y_m)$ is given by $(x_1y_1, \ldots, x_1y_m, \ldots, x_ny_1, \ldots, x_ny_m)$ an nm dimensional vector. For an $n \times m$ matrix $\mathbf{A} = (\mathbf{A}_{ij})$ and an $n' \times m'$ matrix $\mathbf{B} = (\mathbf{B}_{kl})$ we construct similarly an $nn' \times mm'$ matrix $\mathbf{A} \otimes \mathbf{B} = (\mathbf{A}_{ij}\mathbf{B})$, i.e. each entry $\mathbf{A}_{ij}$ in $\mathbf{A}$ is multiplied with a copy of the matrix or block $\mathbf{B}$. The tensor product of two vector spaces $\mathcal{V} \otimes \mathcal{W}$ can be defined as the formal linear combinations of the tensor products $v_i \otimes w_j$ with v_i and w_j base vectors in $\mathcal{V}$ and $\mathcal{W}$, respectively. For further details we refer e.g to [19, Chap. 14] and for a detailed discussion of tensor products of Hilbert spaces to [17, Sect.2.6].

The notions of semantic states and observables – which are typically both identified with the subsets of some appropriate cpo in the standard approach to nondeterministic semantics – are in the probabilistic case two distinct geometrical aspects that are *dual* to each other in the sense that they belong to *dual spaces*. The dual space of a normed space $\mathcal{X}$, denoted $\mathcal{X}^*$, is the normed space of all continuous linear functionals on $\mathcal{X}$. If $\mathcal{X}$ is a Hilbert spaces then its dual is again a Hilbert space. Thus, as $\ell_2(\mathbb{X})^* = \ell_2(\mathbb{X})$, we have for states $y \in \ell_2(\mathbb{X})$ that observables x are also in $\ell_2(\mathbb{X})$. They are related to each other by the notion of expected value, $\mathbf{E}(x, y)$, which represents the probability that we will observe a certain property x when the state of the system is described by y. In $\ell_2(\mathbb{X})$ we can take $\mathbf{E}(x, y) = \langle x, y \rangle$. Duality is more involved for general Banach spaces, where for example the dual, $\ell_1(\mathbb{X})^*$, of the space $\ell_1(\mathbb{X})$ is $\ell_\infty(\mathbb{X})$, i.e. the space of all sequences with $\|(x_i)\|_\infty = \sup(x_i) < \infty$.

The Control Flow. For the definition of the control flow of a program we follow the presentation in [5]. It is based on two auxiliary operations $\mathit{init} : \mathbf{Stmt} \to \mathbf{Lab}$ and $\mathit{final} : \mathbf{Stmt} \to \mathcal{P}(\mathbf{Lab})$ which return the initial and the final labels of a statement. The control flow in a statement S is then defined by the function $\mathit{flow} : \mathbf{Stmt} \to \mathcal{P}(\mathbf{Lab} \times \mathbf{Lab})$ which maps statements to sets of pairs which represent the control flow graph. It is defined in Table 2. This only records that a certain control flow step is possible. For tests b in conditionals and loops we indicate the branch corresponding to the case when the test succeeds by underlining it. As our semantics is ultimately modelling the semantics of a program via the generator of a DTMC we are also confronted with the fact that such processes never terminate. This can be fixed by adding an additional label ℓ^* to the set of labels and define the flow of a program P as $\mathcal{F}(P) = \mathit{flow}(P) \cup \{(\ell, \ell^*) \mid \ell \in \mathit{final}(P)\} \cup \{(\ell^*, \ell^*)\}$.

Infinite Generator Matrix. Given a program P, our aim is to define compositionally an infinite matrix representing the program behaviour as a DTMC. The domain of the associated linear operator $\mathbf{T}(P)$ is the space of *probabilistic configurations*, that is distributions over classical configurations, defined by $\mathbf{Dist}(\mathbf{Conf}) = \mathbf{Dist}(\mathbb{X}^v \times \mathbf{Lab}) \subseteq \ell_2(\mathbb{X}^v \times \mathbf{Lab})$, where we identify a statement with its label or, more precisely, an SOS configuration $\langle S, s\rangle \in \mathbf{Conf}$ with the pair $\langle s, init(S)\rangle \in \mathbb{X}^v \times \mathbf{Lab}$.

Among the building blocks of the construction of $\mathbf{T}(P)$ are the *identity matrix* $\mathbf{I}$ and the *matrix units* $\mathbf{E}_{ij}$ containing only a single non zero entry $(\mathbf{E}_{ij})_{ij} = 1$ and zero otherwise. We denote by e_i the unit vector with $(e_i)_i = 1$ and zero otherwise. As we represent distributions by row vectors we use post-multiplication, i.e. $\mathbf{T}(x) = x \cdot \mathbf{T}$.

A basic operator is the *update matrix* $\mathbf{U}(c)$ which implements state changes. The intention is that from an initial probabilistic state σ, e.g. a distribution over classical states, we get a new probabilistic state σ' by the product $\sigma' = \sigma \cdot \mathbf{U}$. The matrix $\mathbf{U}(c)$ implements the deterministic update of a variable to a constant c via $(\mathbf{U}(c))_{ij} = 1$ if $\xi(c) = j$ and 0 otherwise, with $\xi : \mathbb{X} \to \mathbb{N}$ the underlying enumeration of values in $\mathbb{X}$. In other words, this is a (possibly infinite) matrix which has only one column (corresponding to c) containing 1s while all other entries are 0. Whatever the value of a variable is, after applying $\mathbf{U}(c)$ to the state vector describing the current situation we get a *point* distribution expressing the fact that the value of our variable is now c.

We also define for any Boolean expression b on $\mathbb{X}$ a diagonal *projection matrix* $\mathbf{P}$ with $(\mathbf{P}(b))_{ii} = 1$ if $b(c)$ holds and $\xi(c) = i$ and 0 otherwise. The purpose of this diagonal matrix is to "filter out" only those states which fulfil the condition b. If we want to apply an operator with matrix representation $\mathbf{T}$ only if a certain condition b is fulfilled then pre-multiplying this $\mathbf{P}(b) \cdot \mathbf{T}$ achieves this effect.

In Table 3 we first define a multi-variable versions of the test matrices and the update matrices via the tensor product '$\otimes$'. We define with $\mathbf{P}(s)$ an operator which tests if the current state is the same as the (classical) state s: Given the state $s = [\mathtt{x}_i \mapsto s(\mathtt{x}_i)]$ we test for each variable $\mathtt{x}_i$ with $i = 1, \ldots, v$ if it has the same value as specified in s by applying $\mathbf{P}(s)$ in each factor of the tensor product, i.e. $\mathbf{P}(s(\mathtt{x}_i)) = \mathbf{P}(\mathtt{x}_i = s(\mathtt{x}_i))$. If we apply $\mathbf{P}(s)$ to a probabilistic state σ then $\mathbf{P}(s)$ filters out the probabilities that each variable has exactly the value specified by the state s. The operator $\mathbf{P}(e = c)$ tests in a similar way if the current state is such that the expression e evaluates to the constant c. In order to accommodate for general expressions e (not just constants) we collect (sum up) the matrices for which $\mathcal{E}(e)s = e$. The update operator $\mathbf{U}(\mathtt{x}_k \leftarrow c)$ assigns a definitive constant value c to variable $\mathtt{x}_k$, all other variables remain unchanged (which is expressed by the fact that the factors corresponding to the other variables in the tensor product are all the identity $\mathbf{I}$). Finally, the operator $\mathbf{U}(\mathtt{x}_k \leftarrow e)$ assigns the value of an expression e to $\mathtt{x}_k$. This is achieved by testing whether in the current state e evaluates to any of the possible constants c, and if so to assign c to $\mathtt{x}_k$.

With the help of the auxiliary matrices we can now define for every program P the matrix $\mathbf{T}(P)$ of the DTMC representing the program executions as the sum

Table 3. Elementary Operators

$$\mathbf{P}(s) = \bigotimes_{i=1}^{v} \mathbf{P}(s(\mathtt{x}_i)) \qquad \mathbf{U}(\mathtt{x}_k \leftarrow c) = \bigotimes_{i=1}^{k-1} \mathbf{I} \otimes \mathbf{U}(c) \otimes \bigotimes_{i=k+1}^{v} \mathbf{I}$$

$$\mathbf{P}(e = c) = \sum_{\mathcal{E}(e)s=c} \mathbf{P}(s) \qquad \mathbf{U}(\mathtt{x}_k \leftarrow e) = \sum_{c} \mathbf{P}(e = c)\mathbf{U}(\mathtt{x}_k \leftarrow c)$$

Table 4. Elements of the LOS

$$[\![[x \texttt{ := } e]^{\ell}]\!] = \mathbf{U}(x \leftarrow e) \qquad [\![[v \texttt{ ?= } \rho]^{\ell}]\!] = \textstyle\sum_{c \in \mathbf{X}} \rho(c)\mathbf{U}(x \leftarrow c)$$

$$[\![[b]^{\ell}]\!] = \mathbf{P}(b = \texttt{false}) \qquad \underline{[\![[b]^{\ell}]\!]} = \mathbf{P}(b = \texttt{true})$$

$$[\![[\texttt{skip}]^{\ell}]\!] = \underline{[\![[\texttt{skip}]^{\ell}]\!]} = \underline{[\![[x \texttt{ := } e]^{\ell}]\!]} = \underline{[\![[v \texttt{ ?= } \rho]^{\ell}]\!]} = \mathbf{I}$$

of the effects of the individual control flow steps. For each individual control flow step it is of the form $[\![[B]^{\ell}]\!] \otimes \mathbf{E}_{\ell,\ell'}$ or $\underline{[\![[B]^{\ell}]\!]} \otimes \mathbf{E}_{\ell,\ell'}$, where (ℓ, ℓ') or $(\ell, \underline{\ell'}) \in \mathcal{F}(P)$ and $[\![[B]^{\ell}]\!]$ represents the semantics of the block B labelled by ℓ. The matrix $\mathbf{E}_{\ell,\ell'}$ represents the control flow from label ℓ to ℓ'; it is a finite $l \times l$ matrix, where l is the number of (unique) distinct labels in P.

The definitions of $[\![[B]^{\ell}]\!]$ and $\underline{[\![[B]^{\ell}]\!]}$ are given in Table 4. The semantics of an assignment block is obviously given by $\mathbf{U}(\mathtt{x} \leftarrow e)$. For the random assignment we simply take the linear combination of assignments to all possible values, weighted by the corresponding probability given by the distribution ρ. The semantics of a test block $[b]^{\ell}$ is given by its positive and its negative part, both are test operators $\mathbf{P}(b = \texttt{true})$ and $\mathbf{P}(b = \texttt{false})$ as described before. The meaning of $\underline{[\![[B]^{\ell}]\!]}$ is non-trivial only for tests b while it is the identity for all the other blocks. The positive and negative semantics of all blocks is independent of the context and can be studied and analysed in isolation from the rest of the program P.

Based on the local (forward) semantics of each labelled block, i.e. $[\![[B]^{\ell}]\!]$ and $\underline{[\![[B]^{\ell}]\!]}$, in P we can define the LOS semantics of P as:

$$\mathbf{T}(P) = \sum_{(\ell,\ell') \in \mathcal{F}(P)} [\![[B]^{\ell}]\!] \otimes \mathbf{E}_{\ell,\ell'} + \sum_{(\ell,\underline{\ell'}) \in \mathcal{F}(P)} \underline{[\![[B]^{\ell}]\!]} \otimes \mathbf{E}_{\ell,\ell'}$$

A minor adjustment is required to make our semantics conform to the DTMC model. As paths in a DTMC are *maximal* (i.e. infinite) in the underlying directed graph, we will add a single final loop via a virtual label ℓ^* as discussed in Section 2. This corresponds to adding to $\mathbf{T}(P)$ the factor $\mathbf{I} \otimes \mathbf{E}_{\ell^*,\ell^*}$.

Correspondence between SOS and LOS. As $\mathbf{T}(P)$ operates on $\mathbf{Dist}(\mathbf{Conf})$, we can index the entries in its matrix representation by pairs of classical states s and program labels ℓ. We can show that these entries are in a one-to-one correspondence with the generator matrix of the operational semantics in Table 1.

Proposition 1. *Let P be a* **pWhile** *program and* $\mathbf{T}(P)$ *its LOS operator. We have that if init(P) $= \ell$ and init(P') $= \ell'$ and s, s' are classical states, then* $\langle P, s\rangle \longrightarrow_p \langle P', s'\rangle$ *if and only if* $(\mathbf{T}(P))_{(s,\ell)(s',\ell')} = p$.

The Weak Limit of $\mathbf{T}(P)$. In the standard denotational approach to the semantics of programming languages continuity is an essential requirement for the semantical functions: it guarantees the existence of fixpoints and therefore that the semantics is well-defined. For linear operators the concept of continuity is equivalent to the concept of *boundedness.* This is a basic result in functional analysis and operator theory (see, e.g. [12, Thm. 4.14]). We recall that a linear operator $\mathbf{T} : \mathcal{X} \rightarrow \mathcal{Y}$ between two normed vector spaces $\mathcal{X}$ and $\mathcal{Y}$ is bounded if $\|\mathbf{T}\| = \sup \|\mathbf{T}(x)\|/\|x\| < \infty$.

One feature of Markov chains is that, due to their memoryless property, we can obtain the future of an initial situation $x = x(0)$ (a given distribution) by iterating the generator matrix. The distribution at time t is simply $x(t) = x(0)\mathbf{T}^t$.This can be extended to infinity, i.e. we can compute the limit state distribution as $x(\infty) = \lim_{t\rightarrow\infty} x(0)\mathbf{T}^t$. The question is therefore: does this limit exist for $\mathbf{T}(P)$ for all P and input $x(0) \in \ell_2(\mathbb{X})$? The answer obviously depends on the notion of limit we have in mind. If we refer to the norm limit then the question boils down to whether $\mathbf{T}(P)$ is a bounded operator on $\ell_2(\mathbb{X})$ and the answer is negative as the following example shows.

Example 1. The operator represented by the matrix $\mathbf{U}(x \leftarrow e)$ is in general not bounded on $\ell_2(\mathbb{X})$. To see this, consider $x = (x_i)_{i=0}^{\infty} = (1, \frac{1}{2}, \frac{1}{3}, \ldots)$. Then calculating the 2-norm, $\|x\|_2$, gives rise to a well-known convergent series[1], whereas $\|\mathbf{U}(x \leftarrow 1)\|_2 = \|x\|_1$ corresponds to the harmonic series which is a well-known divergent infinite series.

However, in our setting it makes sense to consider a particular notion of limit, namely the *weak limit*, which allows us to look at the computation as the physical process of *measuring* an observable by means of successive approximations each constructed as the inner product between the observable and an approximation of its dual state.

Definition 1 (Weak Limit [12, Sect 5.11]). *A sequence of vectors $\{x_n\}_n$ in a Hilbert space $\mathcal{H}$* converges weakly *to $x \in \mathcal{H}$, denoted by $x_n \stackrel{w}{\rightarrow} x$ or $w\text{-}\lim_n x_n = x$, iff for all $y \in \mathcal{H}$ we have $\lim_{n\rightarrow\infty} \langle x_n, y\rangle = \langle x, y\rangle$.*

With respect to this notion of limit we can show that the LOS operator $\mathbf{T}(P)$ converges weakly for any initial state and any observable (specified as vector distributions in $\ell_2(\mathbf{Conf})$).

Definition 2 (Weak Limit of Operators[12, Sect 5.11]). *A sequence of linear operators $\mathbf{A}_n$ on a Hilbert space $\mathcal{H}$ is said to* converge weakly *to a linear operator $\mathbf{A}$, denoted by $\mathbf{A}_n \stackrel{w}{\rightarrow} \mathbf{A}$ iff for all $x \in \mathcal{H}$ we have $\mathbf{A}_n(x) \stackrel{w}{\rightarrow} \mathbf{A}(x)$.*

[1] The problem of finding the closed form of the infinite series $1 + \frac{1}{2^2} + \frac{1}{3^2} + \frac{1}{4^2} + \ldots$, aka the Basel problem, was solved by Euler who showed that the series is approximately equal to 1.644934.

We first need to introduce the following definition of finite approximations (or sections) of a matrix. Let $\mathbf{P}_n$ be the orthogonal projection onto the spaces spanned by the first n base vectors; then its matrix representation is given by $\mathbf{P}_n = \text{diag}(1, \ldots, 1, 0, 0, \ldots)$, i.e. a diagonal matrix with only the first n diagonal entries being one and the rest all zero. For any infinite matrix $\mathbf{T}$ representing a bounded or unbounded operator, we can define its finite approximations as $\mathbf{T}_n = \mathbf{P}_n\mathbf{T}\mathbf{P}_n$, that is the effect of $\mathbf{T}$ only on the sub-space spanned by the the first n dimensions.

We will show that the numerical series obtained by calculating the inner products between the n-th approximation vector $x \cdot (\mathbf{T}(P))_n$ and an observable y always converges in $\mathbb{R}$, and we will take this limit to define $\langle x \cdot \mathbf{T}(P), y\rangle$.

Proposition 2. *Given a program P and its LOS operator $\mathbf{T}(P)$, we have that for all $x, y \in \mathbf{Dist}(\mathbf{Conf}) \subset \ell_2(\mathbf{Conf})$ converges, $\lim_{n\to\infty} \langle x \cdot \mathbf{T}(P)_n, y\rangle < \infty$.*

Proof. Let $x_n = x \cdot \mathbf{T}(P)_n$ and $y \in \mathbf{Dist}(\mathbf{Conf}) \subset \ell_1(\mathbf{Conf}) \subset \ell_2(\mathbf{Conf})$. We need to show that $\langle x_n, y\rangle = \sum_{k=1}^{\infty}(x_n)_k \cdot y_k$ converges in $\mathbb{R}$. Since the $\mathbf{T}(P)_n$ are (sub-)stochastic matrices and x is a distribution with $\|x\|_1 = 1$, we have that $\|x_n\|_1 \leq 1$ and $\langle x_n, y\rangle \leq \langle x_{n+1}, y\rangle$, i.e. monotone. Moreover, by the Cauchy-Schwarz inequality (e.g. [17, Prop. 2.1.1]) we have $\langle x_n, y\rangle \leq \|x_n\|_2\|y\|_2$, Thus, as in general $\|v\|_2 \leq \|v\|_1$ holds for all v(cf. [18, Exercise 1.14]), we have $\langle x_n, y\rangle \leq \|x_n\|_2\|y\|_2 \leq \|x_n\|_1\|y\|_1 \leq 1$, i.e. $\langle x_n, y\rangle$ is a bounded, monotone sequence of real numbers. □

Example 2. Consider $\mathbf{T} = \mathbf{U}(x \leftarrow 1)$, a distribution $s = (s_i)$ as input and observables represented by the base vectors e_i. Then we have

$$\lim_{n\to\infty} \langle s \cdot \mathbf{T}_n, e_i\rangle = \begin{cases} 1 \text{ for } i = 1 \\ 0 \text{ otherwise} \end{cases}$$

In fact, we have that $\lim_{n\to\infty} \langle s \cdot \mathbf{T}_n, e_1\rangle = \lim_{n\to\infty} \sum_{i=1}^{n} s_i = 1$, while for e_i with $i \neq 1$ it is either always zero or converges towards zero. The probability of observing $[x \mapsto 1]$ after executing `x := 1` is 1 and 0 for all other possible values.

Based on the weak limit we can also assert the adequacy of the LOS.

Proposition 3. *Given programs P and P' with init$(P) = \ell$ and init$(P') = \ell'$, if $\langle P, s\rangle \longrightarrow_p \langle P', s'\rangle$ then $\lim_{n\to\infty} \langle (s \otimes e_\ell) \cdot \mathbf{T}_n, (s' \otimes e_{\ell'})\rangle = p$.*

The weak limit construction also allows us to work with measures on $\mathbb{X}$ which are not representable by distributions. This is important as it is a well known problem that not all semantically interesting probabilistic behaviours (even on countable infinite spaces) can be described by distributions.

Example 3. Consider the program fragment $P \equiv$ `x := 2x`. Its LOS operator is given by a bounded operator $\mathbf{T}(P) = \mathbf{U}(x \leftarrow 2x)$. If we are interested in the probability of obtaining any even number as the result of executing P on an initial distribution x then we can test it on an elementary observable, i.e.

Table 5. Kozen's semantics

$[\![\mathtt{skip}]\!]$	$= \mathbf{I}$
$[\![x\ \mathtt{:=}\ f(x_1,\ldots,x_n)]\!]$	$= \mathbf{U}(x \leftarrow f(x_1,\ldots,x_n))$
$[\![x\ \mathtt{?=}\ \rho]\!]$	$= (\sum_c \rho(c)\mathbf{U}(x \leftarrow c))$
$[\![S_1\,\mathtt{;}\,S_2]\!]$	$= ([\![S_1]\!][\![S_2]\!])$
$[\![\mathtt{if}\ b\ \mathtt{then}\ S_1\ \mathtt{else}\ S_2\ \mathtt{fi}]\!]$	$= (\mathbf{P}(b)[\![S_1]\!] + \mathbf{P}(\neg b)[\![S_2]\!])$
$[\![\mathtt{while}\ b\ \mathtt{do}\ S\ \mathtt{od}]\!]$	$= (\mathbf{P}(b)[\![S]\!][\![\mathtt{while}\ b\ \mathtt{do}\ S\ \mathtt{od}]\!] + \mathbf{P}(\neg b))$

a test which can return only 'yes' or 'no'. This implements a kind of *uniform measure* over all even numbers. Strictly speaking, no measure can exists on $\mathbb{Z}$ which would give equal probability to each even number and $\frac{1}{2}$ to the set of all evens. Such a *uniform measure* μ_{ev} cannot be represented by a distribution. However, we can approximate it by considering the distributions ev_n over the first n even numbers, i.e. $ev_1 = (1,0,0,\ldots), ev_2 = (\frac{1}{2},0,\frac{1}{2},0,\ldots),\ldots$ Then we get $\lim_{n\to\infty} \langle x \cdot \mathbf{T}(P), ev_n\rangle = 1$ for any initial distribution x – as expected. In other words, $\mu_{ev} = w\text{-}\lim ev_n$.

By measure on $\mathbb{Z}$ we usually mean a measure based on the σ-algebra $\mathcal{P}(\mathbb{Z})$ of all subsets of $\mathbb{Z}$. On this σ-algebra it is obviously impossible to define an atomic measure – i.e. one which is generated by the point measures $\mu(\{n\})$ of singletons $n \in \mathbb{Z}$ – which reflects the fact that half of all numbers are even and half are odd. However, it is possible to define such a measure on the (non-standard) σ-algebra $\{\emptyset, E, O, \mathbb{Z}\}$ with E and O the set of all even and odd numbers, respectively. In fact, on this σ-algebra we can introduce the measure $\mu(E) = \mu(O) = \frac{1}{2}$. Thus, the weak limit construction can simulate this measure. This appears to be consistent with classical results in measure theory like the Portemanteau theorem, e.g. [13, Thm 13.16], which allows the representation of certain measures as weak limits.

4 Comparison with Kozen's Semantics

In this section we develop a comparison with the well-known probabilistic semantics defined in [4]. We consider here the formulation which in the original paper is referred to as Semantics 2 and which is based on an iterative construction of the fixed point in the style of Knaster-Tarski [20]. Contrary to the LOS we introduced before, which describes the stepwise behaviour of a program, Kozen's semantics captures the I/O behaviour of a program by means of the probability measure reached after termination (possibly after an infinite number of steps).

Kozen's semantics 2 is defined as the fixed point of a bounded operator on a Banach space which fulfils the recursive equations in Table 5.

There are several features of Kozen's semantics which are in striking contrast with LOS. The first one consists in the fact that all probabilistic choices are assumed to be made before the program execution starts rather than during the execution as in the LOS. This seems to prevent any (non-terminating) program with infinitely many probabilistic assignments (e.g. `while true do` x `?=` $\{0,1\}$ `od`) from ever starting. A second issue is the fact that it treats all execution paths which do not terminate in the same way, namely as the zero operator Not least in the context of program analysis this seems to be rather imprecise as it might well be interesting what happens during an infinite execution path, e.g. if a non-terminating program such as an operating system will cause a variable overflow or not, c.f. `while true do` x `:=` $x+1$ `od`. Another difference is related to the fact that Kozen's semantics does not explicitly refer to relational aspects, e.g. the fact that the values of two variables might be correlated. The LOS semantics on the other hand is essentially constructed using a tensor product which models conditional probabilities in a compositional way.

It might be worth noting that in later work [21] Kozen also presents a backward semantics [21, p165] which is concerned with how measurable functions, which represent observables, need to be transformed in order to define the semantics of a program S. This is intuitively the reverse of the measure transformer semantics in [4]. This backward semantics also appears to be strongly related to the weakest pre-condition calculus. In our self-dual setting the backward semantics is easily identified as the *adjoint* operator of $[\![S]\!]$ via the conditions

$$\langle x \cdot [\![S]\!], f\rangle = \langle x, f \cdot [\![S]\!]^*\rangle$$

for a state x and an observable f in $\ell_2(\mathbf{Conf})$.

Recovering Kozen's Semantics. We can use the LOS to reconstruct the semantics of Kozen by simply taking the limit of $\mathbf{T}(S)^n(s_0)$ for $n \to \infty$ for all initial states s_0. The limit state $\mathbf{T}(S)^n(s_0)$ still contains too much information in relation to Kozen's semantics; in fact we only need the probability distributions on the possible values of the variables at the final label.

In order to extract information about the probability that variables have certain values at a certain label, i.e. program point ℓ, we can use the operator $\mathbf{I}\otimes\ldots\otimes\mathbf{I}\otimes\mathbf{E}_{\ell,\ell}$. In particular, for extracting the information about a probabilistic state we will use $\mathbf{S}_\ell = \mathbf{I}\otimes\ldots\otimes\mathbf{I}\otimes e_\ell$ which forgets about all distributions at other labels than ℓ. In particular we use $\mathbf{S}_f = \mathbf{S}_{\ell^*}$ for the final looping `stop` statement and $\mathbf{S}_i$ for the initial label *init*(P) of the program. We denote by e_0 the base vector in $\mathbb{R}^l$ which expresses the fact that we are in the initial label, i.e. $e_0 = e_{init(P)}$.

Proposition 4. *Given a program P and an initial state s_0 as a distribution over the program variables, then $(s_0\otimes e_0)\mathbf{T}(P)^n\mathbf{S}_f$ corresponds to the distribution over all states on which P terminates in n or less computational steps.*

We can now show that the effect of the operator we obtain as solution to Kozen's fixed-point equations agrees with the "output" $\lim_{n\to\infty}(s_0 \otimes e_0)\mathbf{T}^n\mathbf{S}_f$ we get via the LOS. Essentially, both semantics define the same I/O operator, provided we supply them with the appropriate input. However, the LOS also provides information about internal labels and reflects the relation between different variables via the tensor product representation. It is therefore not possible to reconstruct the LOS from Kozen's semantics.

Proposition 5. *Given a program P and an initial probabilistic state s_0 as a distribution over the program variables, let $[\![P]\!]$ be Kozen's semantics of P and $\mathbf{T}(P)$ the LOS. Then $(s_0 \otimes e_0)(\lim_{n\to\infty} \mathbf{T}^n)\mathbf{S}_f = s_0[\![P]\!]$.*

The proof follows by induction.

5 Semantics-Based Analysis

Although the LOS semantics we presented here is of interest in itself its main motivation is to provide a basis for a semantics based program analysis. Classically the correctness of a program analysis is asserted with respect to the semantics in terms of a correctness relation. The theory of Abstract Interpretation allows for constructing analyses that are automatically correct without having to prove it a posteriori [22, 23]. The main applications of this theory are for the analysis of safety-critical systems as it guarantees correct answers at the cost of precision. For probabilistic systems or the probabilistic analysis of (non-)deterministic ones, the theory of Probabilistic Abstract Interpretation (PAI) allows for the construction of analyses that are possibly unsafe but maximally precise [9, 11]. Its main applications are therefore in fields like speculative optimisation and the analysis of trade-offs. PAI has been used for the definition of various analyses based on the LOS (see e.g. [3, 24, 25] and all involving finite-dimensional spaces.

PAI relies on the notion of generalised (or pseudo-)inverse. This notion is well established in mathematics where it is used for finding approximate, so-called least square solutions (cf. e.g. [26]).

Definition 3. *Let $\mathcal{H}_1$ and $\mathcal{H}_2$ be two Hilbert spaces and $\mathbf{A} : \mathcal{H}_1 \mapsto \mathcal{H}_2$ a linear map between them. A linear map $\mathbf{A}^\dagger = \mathbf{G} : \mathcal{H}_2 \mapsto \mathcal{H}_1$ is the* Moore-Penrose pseudo-inverse *of $\mathbf{A}$ iff $\mathbf{A} \circ \mathbf{G} = \mathbf{P_A}$ and $\mathbf{G} \circ \mathbf{A} = \mathbf{P_G}$, where $\mathbf{P_A}$ and $\mathbf{P_G}$ denote orthogonal projections onto the ranges of $\mathbf{A}$ and $\mathbf{G}$.*

A linear operator $\mathbf{P} : \mathcal{H} \to \mathcal{H}$ is an *orthogonal projection* if $\mathbf{P}^* = \mathbf{P}^2 = \mathbf{P}$, where $(.)^*$ denotes the *adjoint*. The adjoint is defined implicitly via the condition $\langle x \cdot \mathbf{P}, y\rangle = \langle x, y \cdot \mathbf{P}^*\rangle$ for all $x, y \in \mathcal{H}$. For real matrices the adjoint correspond simply to the transpose matrix $\mathbf{P}^* = \mathbf{P}^t$ [19, Ch 10].

If $\mathcal{C}$ an $\mathcal{D}$ are two Hilbert spaces, and $\mathbf{A} : \mathcal{C} \to \mathcal{D}$ and $\mathbf{G} : \mathcal{D} \to \mathcal{C}$ are linear operators between $\mathcal{C}$ and $\mathcal{D}$, such that $\mathbf{G}$ is the Moore-Penrose pseudo-inverse of $\mathbf{A}$, then we say that $(\mathcal{C}, \mathbf{A}, \mathcal{D}, \mathbf{G})$ forms a *probabilistic abstract interpretation*, with $\mathcal{C}$ the concrete domain and $\mathcal{D}$ the abstract one.

Important for the applicability of PAI is the fact that it possesses some nice compositionality properties. These allow us to construct the abstract semantics $\mathbf{T}(P)^\#$ by abstracting the single blocks of the concrete semantics $\mathbf{T}(P)$ as follows:

$$\mathbf{T}(P)^\# = \mathbf{A}^\dagger \mathbf{T}(P)\mathbf{A} = \mathbf{A}^\dagger \Big(\sum_{(\ell,\underline{\ell}')\in\mathcal{F}(P)} [\![[B]^\ell]\!] \otimes \mathbf{E}_{\ell\ell'} \Big)\mathbf{A} =$$

$$= \sum_{(\ell,\underline{\ell}')\in\mathcal{F}(P)} (\mathbf{A}^\dagger [\![[B]^\ell]\!] \mathbf{A}) \otimes \mathbf{E}_{\ell\ell'} = \sum_{(\ell,\underline{\ell}')\in\mathcal{F}(P)} [\![[B]^\ell]\!]^\# \otimes \mathbf{E}_{\ell\ell'},$$

where, for simplicity, we do not distinguish between the positive and negative semantics of blocks, and we assume that $\mathbf{A}$ does not abstract $\mathbf{E}_{\ell\ell'}$. The fact that we can work with the abstract semantics of individual blocks instead of the full operator obviously reduces the complexity of the analysis substantially.

Another important fact is that the Moore-Penrose pseudo-inverse of a tensor product can be computed as $(\mathbf{A}_1 \otimes \mathbf{A}_2 \otimes \ldots \otimes \mathbf{A}_v)^\dagger = \mathbf{A}_1^\dagger \otimes \mathbf{A}_2^\dagger \otimes \ldots \otimes \mathbf{A}_v^\dagger$ [26, 2.1,Ex 3]. We can therefore abstract properties of individual variables and then combine them in the global abstraction. This is also made possible by the definition of the concrete LOS semantics which is heavily based on the use of tensor product. Typically we have $[\![[B]^\ell]\!] = (\bigotimes_{i=1}^{v} \mathbf{T}_{i\ell}) \otimes \mathbf{E}_{\ell\ell'}$ or a sum of a few of such terms. The $\mathbf{T}_{i\ell}$ represents the effect of $\mathbf{T}(S)$, and in particular of $[\![[B]^\ell]\!]$, on variable i at label ℓ (both labels and variables only form a finite set). For example, we can define an abstraction $\mathbf{A}$ for one variable and apply it individually to all variables (e.g. extracting their even/odd property), or use different abstractions for different variables (maybe even forgetting about some of them by using $\mathbf{A}_f = (1, 1, \ldots)^t$) and define $\mathbf{A} = \bigotimes_{i=1}^{v} \mathbf{A}_i$ such that $\mathbf{A}^\dagger = \bigotimes_{i=1}^{v} \mathbf{A}_i^\dagger$ in order to get an analysis on the full state space.

Clearly, for (countably) infinite value spaces $\mathbb{X}$ the abstraction maps which we use in the construction of Probabilistic Abstract Interpretations are often also represented by unbounded operators (similar to the $\mathbf{U}(c)$ of Example 1). The use of weak limits will again help us in order to construct the Moore-Penrose pseudo-inverse $\mathbf{A}^\dagger$. Fortunately, the approximations by finite dimensional abstractions $\mathbf{A}_n$ and $\mathbf{A}_n^\dagger$ converge weakly for closed operators and in particular if the range of the abstraction is finite dimensional, i.e. if $\mathbf{A} : \ell_2(\mathbb{X}) \rightarrow \mathbb{R}^n$. Various general results of operator theory and linear algebra as found, for example in [27–29] offer a rigorous support for extending PAI to infinite-dimensional Hilbert spaces. We have dedicated a companion paper to a full treatment of this infinite case [30].

6 Conclusions

We have introduced a linear operator semantics (LOS) for probabilistic programs based on infinite-dimensional Hilbert space. We have shown how weak limits can be used to guarantee the existence of observable program properties, even for unbounded operators. In contrast with the norm limit on Banach spaces used in the work by Kozen, we are able to capture properties of the intermediate states of a program execution. This is important for program analysis. In fact, the aim of the work presented here is to provide a mathematically sound framework for probabilistic program analysis. The two main elements for this are (i) a compositionally defined semantics, i.e. LOS, and (ii) a way to reduce the concrete semantics in order to obtain a more manageable abstract one via PAI. The concepts of a linear operator semantics and probabilistic abstract interpretation have been used before in the setting of *finite* domains in [3, 24, 31, 25] for the analysis of programs and security properties. This paper extends LOS to infinite (concrete and abstract) domains and informally shows how PAI can be extended accordingly.

The LOS is closely related to various models used in Performance Analysis, like Stochastic Automata Networks (SAN) [32, 33]. As performance models are often based on Continuous Time Markov Chains (CTMC) it would be interesting to develop a continuous time version of the LOS which might help to establish a bridge between performance and program analysis.

From a semantical point of view one important feature of LOS is the notion of duality between states and observables and a weak limit construction to overcome problems with unboundedness. For a more direct approach it would be interesting to investigate which programs lead directly to bounded operators in the LOS approach. It seems that this issue is related to reversibility and finite branching of the reverse computation: for infinite (un-oriented) graphs it is known that the adjacency operator represents a bounded operator on ℓ_2 if and only if it is finitely branching [34, Thm. 3.1]. Similarly, it is also possible to model reversible Markov Chains, e.g. [16], via bounded Hilbert space operators. We aim to explore these aspects further in future work.

References

1. Baier, C., Haverkort, B.R., Hermanns, H., Katoen, J.P.: Performance evaluation and model checking join forces. Commun. ACM 53(9), 76–85 (2010)
2. Di Pierro, A., Hankin, C., Wiklicky, H.: Probabilistic timing covert channels: To close or not to close? Int. J. of Inf. Security 10(2), 83–106 (2011)
3. Di Pierro, A., Sotin, P., Wiklicky, H.: Relational analysis and precision via probabilistic abstract interpretation. In: QAPL 2008. ENTCS, vol. 220(3), pp. 23–42. Elsevier (2008)
4. Kozen, D.: Semantics of probabilistic programs. J. Comp. Sys. Sci. 22(3), 328–350 (1981)
5. Nielson, F., Nielson, H.R., Hankin, C.: Principles of Program Analysis. Springer (1999)
6. Kinder, J.: Towards static analysis of virtualization-obfuscated binaries. In: IEEE 19th Working Conference on Reverse Engineering, WCRE 2012, pp. 61–70 (2012)
7. Lighthill, M.: Introduction to Fourier Analysis and Generalised Functions. Cambridge University Press (1958)
8. Lax, P.D.: Functional Analysis. John Wiley & Sons (2002)
9. Di Pierro, A., Wiklicky, H.: Concurrent Constraint Programming: Towards Probabilistic Abstract Interpretation. In: PPDP 2000, pp. 127–138. ACM (2000)
10. Di Pierro, A., Hankin, C., Wiklicky, H.: Probabilistic semantics and program analysis. In: Aldini, A., Bernardo, M., Di Pierro, A., Wiklicky, H. (eds.) SFM 2010. LNCS, vol. 6154, pp. 1–42. Springer, Heidelberg (2010)
11. Di Pierro, A., Wiklicky, H.: Measuring the precision of abstract interpretations. In: Lau, K.-K. (ed.) LOPSTR 2000. LNCS, vol. 2042, pp. 147–164. Springer, Heidelberg (2001)
12. Kubrusly, C.S.: The Elements of Operator Theory, 2nd edn. Birkhäuser (2011)
13. Klenke, A.: Probability Theory - A Comprehensive Course. Springer (2006)
14. Plotkin, G.: A structured approach to operational semantics. Technical Report DAIMI FN-19, Computer Science Department, Aarhus University (1981)
15. Seneta, E.: Non-negative Matrices and Markov Chains. Springer (1981)
16. Woess, W.: Denumerable Markov Chains. EMS (2009)

17. Kadison, R., Ringrose, J.: Fundamentals of the Theory of Operator Algebras: Elementary Theory. AMS (1997); reprint from Academic Press edition 1983
18. Fabian, M., Habala, P., Hájek, P., Montesinos, V., Zizler, V.: Banach Space Theory – The Basis for Linear and Nonlinear Analysis. Springer (2011)
19. Roman, S.: Advanced Linear Algebra, 2nd edn. Springer (2005)
20. Davey, B., Priestley, H.: Introduction to Lattices and Order. Cambridge University Press, Cambridge (1990)
21. Kozen, D.: A probabilistic PDL. J. Comp. Sys. Sci. 30(2), 162–178 (1985)
22. Cousot, P., Cousot, R.: Abstract Interpretation: A Unified Lattice Model for Static Analysis of Programs by Construction or Approximation of Fixpoints. In: POPL 1977, pp. 238–252 (1977)
23. Cousot, P., Cousot, R.: Systematic Design of Program Analysis Frameworks. In: POPL 1979, pp. 269–282 (1979)
24. Di Pierro, A., Hankin, C., Wiklicky, H.: A systematic approach to probabilistic pointer analysis. In: Shao, Z. (ed.) APLAS 2007. LNCS, vol. 4807, pp. 335–350. Springer, Heidelberg (2007)
25. Di Pierro, A., Hankin, C., Wiklicky, H.: Probabilistic timing covert channels: to close or not to close? Int. Journal of Inform. Security 10(2), 83–106 (2011)
26. Ben-Israel, A., Greville, T.N.E.: Gereralized Inverses – Theory and Applications, 2nd edn. CMS Books in Mathematics. Springer, New York (2003)
27. Groetsch, C.W.: Stable Approximate Evaluation of Unbounded Operators. Lecture Notes in Mathematics, vol. 1894. Springer (2007)
28. Du, N.: Finite-dimensional approximation settings for infinite-dimensional Moore-Penrose inverses. SIAM Journal of Numerical Analysis 46(3), 1454–1482 (2008)
29. Kulkarni, S., Ramesh, G.: Projection methods for computing Moore-Penrose inverses of unbounded operators. Indian Journal of Pure and Applied Mathematics 41(5), 647–662 (2010)
30. Di Pierro, A., Wiklicky, H.: Probabilistic analysis of programs: A weak limit approach (2013), `http://fopara2013.cs.unibo.it/Proceedings.pdf` [Online Informal Pre-proceedings]
31. Di Pierro, A., Hankin, C., Wiklicky, H.: Measuring the confinement of probabilistic systems. Theoretical Computer Science 340(1), 3–56 (2005)
32. Plateau, B., Atif, K.: Stochastic automata network of modeling parallel systems. IEEE Trans. Softw. Eng. 17(10), 1093–1108 (1991)
33. Fourneau, J.M., Plateau, B., Stewart, W.: Product form for stochastic automata networks. In: Proceedings of ValueTools 2007, pp. 32:1–32:10. ICST (2007)
34. Mohar, B., Woess, W.: A survey on spectra of infinite graphs. Bulletin of the London Mathematical Society 21 (1988)

Ambivalent Types for Principal Type Inference with GADTs

Jacques Garrigue[1] and Didier Rémy[2]

[1] Nagoya University, Graduate School of Mathematics
[2] INRIA, Rocquencourt*

Abstract. GADTs, short for *Generalized Algebraic DataTypes*, which allow constructors of algebraic datatypes to be non-surjective, have many useful applications. However, pattern matching on GADTs introduces local type equality assumptions, which are a source of ambiguities that may destroy principal types—and must be resolved by type annotations. We introduce *ambivalent types* to tighten the definition of ambiguities and better confine them, so that type inference has principal types, remains monotonic, and requires fewer type annotations.

1 Introduction

GADTs, short for *Generalized Algebraic DataTypes*, extend usual algebraic datatypes with a form of dependent typing by enabling type refinements in pattern-matching branches [2,16,1]. They can express many useful invariants of data-structures, provide safer typing, and allow for more polymorphism [13]. They have already been available in some Haskell implementations (in particular GHC) for many years and now appear as a natural addition to strongly typed functional programming languages.

However, this addition is by no means trivial. In their presence, full type inference seems undecidable in general, even in the restricted setting of ML-style polymorphism [12]. Moreover, many well-typed programs lack a most general type. Using explicit type annotations solves both problems. Unfortunately, while it is relatively easy to design a sound typing algorithm for a language with GADTs, it is surprisingly difficult to keep principal types without requesting full type annotations on every case analysis.

Repeatedly writing full type annotations being cumbersome, a first approach to a stronger type inference algorithm is to *propagate* annotations. This comes from the basic remark that, in many cases, the type of a function contains enough information to determine the type of its inner case analyses. A simple way to do this is to use program transformations, pushing type annotations inside the body of expressions.

Stratified type inference for GADTs [11] goes further in that direction, converting from an external language where type annotations are optional to an internal language where the scrutinee of case analysis and all coercions between equivalent types must be annotated. This conversion is an elaboration phase that collects all *typing information* —not only type annotations— and propagates it where it is needed. The internal language allows for straightforward type inference and it has the principal type property.

* Part of this work has been done at IRILL.

C.-c. Shan (Ed.): APLAS 2013, LNCS 8301, pp. 257–272, 2013.

It also enjoys *monotonicity*: strengthening the type of a free variable by making it more general preserves well-typedness. As expected, principality does not hold in general in the external type system (a program may be typable but have no principal type), but it does hold if we restrict ourselves to those programs whose elaboration in the internal language is typable. However, since elaboration extracts information from the typing context, monotonicity is lost: strengthening the type of a free variable by making it more general before elaboration can reduce the amount of type information available on the elaborated program and make it ill-typed. Monotonicity is a property that has often been underestimated, because it usually (but not always) holds in languages with principal types. However, losing monotonicity can be worse for the programmer than losing principal types. It reveals a lack of modularity in the language, since some simple program transformations such as simplifying the body of a function may end up inferring more general types, which may subsequently break type inference. Propagating only type annotations would preserve monotonicity, but it is much weaker.

GHC 7 follows a similar strategy, called *OutsideIn* [15], using constraint solving rather than elaboration to extract all typing information from the *outer context*. As a result, propagation and inference are interleaved. That is, the typing information obtained by solving constraints on the outer context enclosing a GADT case analysis is directly used to determine the types of both the scrutinee and the result in this case analysis. Type inference can then be performed in the body of the case analysis. By allowing information to flow only from the outside to the inside, principality is preserved when inference succeeds. Yet, as for stratified type inference [11], it lacks monotonicity.

While previous approaches have mostly attempted to propagate types to GADT case analyses, we aim in the opposite direction at reducing the need for type information in case analysis. This aspect is orthogonal to propagation and improving either one improves type inference as a whole. Actually, OutsideIn already goes one step in that direction, by allowing type information to flow out of a pattern-matching case when no type equation was added. But it stops there, because if type equations were added, they could have been used and consequently the type of the branch is flagged *ambiguous*.

This led us to focus our attention on the definition of ambiguity. Type equations are introduced inside a pattern-matching branch, but with a *local scope*: the equation is not valid outside of the branch. This becomes a source of ambiguities. Indeed, a type equation allows implicit type conversions, *i.e.* there are several inter-convertible forms for types that we need not distinguish while in the scope of the equation, but they become nonconvertible—hence ambiguous—when leaving its scope, as the equation can no longer be used. Ambiguity depends both on the equations available, and on the types that leak outside of the branch: if removing the equation does not impair convertibility for a type, either because it was not convertible to start with, or because other equations are available, it need not be seen as ambiguous.

Since ambiguities must generally be solved by adding type annotations, a more precise definition and better detection of ambiguities become essential to reduce the need for explicit type information. By defining ambiguity inside the type system, we are able to restrict the set of valid typings. In this paper we present a type system such that among the valid typings there is always a principal one (*i.e.* subsuming all of them) and we provide a type inference algorithm that returns the principal solution when it exists.

Moreover, our type system keeps the usual properties of ML, including monotonicity. This detection of ambiguity is now part of OCaml [8].

Since propagating type information and reducing the amount of type information needed by case analysis are orthogonal issues, our handling of ambiguity could be combined with existing type inference algorithms to further reduce the need for type annotations. As less type information is needed, it becomes possible to use a weaker propagation algorithm that preserves monotonicity. This is achieved in OCaml by relying on the approach previously developed for first-class polymorphism [5].

The rest of this paper is organized as follows. We give an overview of our solution in §2. We present our system formally and state its soundness in §3. We state principality and monotonicity in §4; by lack of space, we leave out some technical developments, all proofs, and the description of the type inference algorithm, which can all be found in the accompanying technical report [6]. Finally, we compare with related works in §5.

2 An Overview of Our Solution

The standard notion of ambiguity is so general that it may just encompass too many cases. Consider the following program.[1]

```
type (_,_) eq = Eq : (α,α) eq
let f (type a) (x : (a,int) eq) = match x with Eq -> 1
```

Type `eq` is the classical equality witness. It is a GADT with two index parameters, denoted by the two underscores, and a single case Eq, for which the indices are the same type variable α. Thus, a value of type (a,b) `eq` can be seen as a witness of the equality between types a and b.

In the definition of `f`, we first introduce an explicit universal variable a, called a *rigid* variable, treated in a special way in OCaml as it can be refined by GADT pattern matching. By constraining the type of `x` to be $(a,$`int`$)$ `eq`, we are able to refine a when pattern-matching `x` against the constructor `Eq`: the equation $a = \texttt{int}$ becomes available in the corresponding branch, *i.e.* when typechecking the expression `1`, which can be assigned either type a or `int`. As a result, `f` can be given either type $(\alpha, \texttt{int})\ \texttt{eq} \to \texttt{int}$ or $(\alpha, \texttt{int})\ \texttt{eq} \to \alpha$. This fulfills the standard definition of ambiguity and so should be rejected. But should we really reject it? Consider these two slight variations in the definition of `f`:

```
let f₁ (type a) (x : (a,int) eq) = match x with Eq -> true
let f₂ (type a) (x : (a,int) eq) (y : a) = match x with Eq -> (y > 0)
```

In $\texttt{f}_1$, we just return `true`, which has the type `bool`, unrelated to the equation. In $\texttt{f}_2$, we actually use the equation to turn `y` into an `int` but eventually return a boolean. These variants are not ambiguous. How do they differ from the original `f`? The only reason we have deemed `f` to be ambiguous is that `1` could potentially have type a by using the equation. However, nothing forces us to use this equation, and, if we do not use it, the only possible type is `int`. It looks even more innocuous than $\texttt{f}_2$, where we indirectly need the equation to infer the type of the body.

So, what would be a truly ambiguous type? We obtain one by mixing a's and `int`'s in the returned value (the left-margin vertical rules indicate failure):

[1] Examples in this section use OCaml syntax [8]. Letter α stands for a flexible variable as usual while letter a stands for a rigid variable that cannot be instantiated. This will be detailed later.

```
let g (type a) (x : (a,int) eq) (y : a) =
  match x with Eq -> if y > 0 then y else 0
```

Here, the `then` branch has type a while the `else` branch has type `int`, so choosing either one would be ambiguous.

How can we capture this refined notion of ambiguity? The idea is to track whether such mixed types are escaping from their scope. Intuitively, we may do so by disallowing the expression to have either type and instead viewing it with an ambivalent type $a \approx \texttt{int}$, which we just see syntactically as a set of types.

An ambivalent type must still be *coherent*, *i.e.* all the types it contains must be provably equal under the equations available in the current scope. Hence, although $a \approx \texttt{int}$ can be interpreted as an intersection type, it is not more expressive than choosing either representation (since by equations this would be convertible to the other type), but more precise: it retains the information that the equivalence of a and `int` has been assumed to give the expression the type a or `int`.

Since coherence depends on the typing context, a coherent ambivalent type may suddenly become incoherent when leaving the scope of an equation. This is where *ambiguity* appears. Hence, while an ambivalent type is a set of types that have been assumed interchangeable, an ambiguity arises only when an ambivalent type becomes incoherent by escaping the scope of an equation it depends on.

Ambiguous programs are to be rejected. Fortunately, ambiguities can be eliminated by using type annotations. Intuitively, in an expression $(e : \tau)$, the expressions e and $(e : \tau)$ have sets of types ψ_1 and ψ_2 that may differ, but such that τ is included in both, ensuring soundness of the change of view. In particular, while the inner view, *e.g.* ψ_1, may be large and a potential source of ambiguities, the outer view, *e.g.* ψ_2, may contain fewer types and remain coherent; this way the ambivalence of the inner view does not leak outside and does not create ambiguities. Consider, for example the program:

```
let g1 (type a) (x : (a,int) eq) y =
  match x with Eq -> (if (y : a) > 0 then (y : a) else 0 : a)
```

Type annotations on y and the conditional let them have unique outer types, which are thus unambiguous when leaving the scope of the equation. More precisely, `(y : a)` and `0` can be both assigned type $a \approx \texttt{int}$, which is also that of the conditional `if ... else 0`, while the annotation `(if ... else 0 : a)` and variable y both have the singleton type a. (Note that the type of the annotated expression is the inner view for y but the outer view for the conditional.)

Of course, it would be quite verbose to write annotations everywhere, so in a real language we shall let annotations on parameters propagate to their uses and annotations on results propagate inside pattern-matching branches. The function $\texttt{g}_1$ may be written more concisely as follows—but we will ignore this aspect in this work:

```
let g2 (type a) (x : (a,int) eq) (y : a) : a =
  match x with Eq -> if y > 0 then y else 0
```

A natural question at this point is why not just require that the type of the result of pattern-matching a GADT be fully known from annotations? This would avoid the need for this new notion of ambiguity. This is perhaps good enough if we only consider small functions: as shown for $\texttt{g}_2$, we may write the function type in one piece and still get the full type information. However, the situation degrades with local `let` bindings:

```
let p (type a) (x : (a,int) eq) : int =
```

```
let y = (match x with Eq -> 1) in y * 2
```

The return type `int` only applies to `y*2`, so we cannot propagate it automatically as an annotation for the definition of `y`. Basically, one would have to explicitly annotate all `let` bindings whose definitions use pattern-matching on GADTs. This may easily become a burden, especially when the type is completely unrelated to the GADTs (or accidentally related as in the definition of `f`, above).

We believe that our notion of ambiguity is simple enough to be understood easily by users, avoids an important number of seemingly redundant type annotations, and provides an interesting alternative to non-monotonic approaches (see §5 for comparison).

3 Formal Presentation

Since our interest is type inference, we may assume without loss of generality that there is a unique predefined (binary) GADT $\mathsf{eq}(\cdot,\cdot)$ with a unique constructor Eq of type $\forall(\alpha)\ \mathsf{eq}(\alpha,\alpha)$. The type $\mathsf{eq}(\tau_1,\tau_2)$ denotes a witness of the equality of τ_1 and τ_2 and Eq is the unique value of type $\mathsf{eq}(\tau_1,\tau_2)$. For conciseness, we specialize pattern matching to this unique constructor and just write $\mathsf{use}\ M_1 : \tau\ \mathsf{in}\ M_2$ for $\mathtt{match}\ M_1 : \tau\ \mathtt{with\ Eq\ ->}\ M_2$.

Types occurring in the source program are simple types:

$$\tau ::= \alpha \mid a \mid \tau \to \tau \mid \mathsf{eq}(\tau,\tau) \mid \mathtt{int}$$

Type variables are split into two different syntactic classes: flexible type variables, written α, and rigid type variables, written a. As usual, flexible type variable are meant to be instantiated by any type—either during type inference or after their generalization. Conversely, rigid variables stand for some unknown type and thus are not meant to be instantiated by an arbitrary type. They behave like skolem constants. We write $\mathscr{V}$, $\mathscr{V}_f$, and $\mathscr{V}_r$ for the set of variables, flexible variables, and rigid variables.

Terms are expressions of the λ-calculus with constants (written c), the datatype Eq, pattern matching $\mathsf{use}\ M_1 : \tau\ \mathsf{in}\ M_2$, the introduction of a rigid variable $\nu(a)\,M$ or a type annotation (τ), *i.e.* the usual annotation $(M : \tau)$ is seen as the application $(\tau)\ M$:

$$\begin{aligned} M ::=\ & x \mid c \mid M_1\, M_2 \mid \lambda(x)M \mid \mathsf{let}\ x = M_1\ \mathsf{in}\ M_2 \\ \mid\ & \mathsf{Eq} \mid \mathsf{use}\ M_1 : \tau\ \mathsf{in}\ M_2 \mid \nu(a)\,M \mid (\tau) \end{aligned}$$

Although type annotations in source programs are simple types, their flexible type variables are interpreted as universally quantified in the type of the annotation (see §3.5).

Besides, we use—and infer—*ambivalent types* internally to keep track of the use of typing equations and detect ambiguities more accurately.

3.1 Ambivalent Types

Intuitively, ambivalent types are sets of types. Technically, they refine simple types to express certain type equivalences within the structure of types. Every node becomes a set of type expressions instead of a single type expression and is labeled with a flexible type variable. More precisely, ambivalent types, written ζ, are recursively defined as:

$$\rho ::= a \mid \zeta \to \zeta \mid \mathsf{eq}(\zeta,\zeta) \mid \mathtt{int} \qquad \psi ::= \varepsilon \mid \rho \approx \psi \qquad \zeta ::= \psi^{\alpha} \qquad \sigma ::= \forall(\bar{\alpha})\ \zeta$$

A raw type ρ is a rigid type variable a, an arrow type $\zeta \to \zeta$, an equality type $\mathsf{eq}(\zeta, \zeta)$, or the base type `int`. A *proper* raw type is one that is not a rigid type variable. An *(ambivalent) type* ζ is a pair ψ^α of a *set* ψ of *raw types* ρ labeled with a *flexible type variable* α. We use $\approx$ to separate the elements of sets of raw types: it is associative commutative, has the empty set ε for neutral element, and satisfies the idempotence axiom $(\psi \approx \psi) = \psi$. An ambivalent type ζ is always of the form ψ^α and we write $\lfloor \zeta \rfloor$ for ψ. When ψ is empty ζ is a leaf of the form ε^α, which corresponds to a type variable in simple types, hence we may just write α instead of ε^α, as in the examples above.

Type schemes σ are defined as usual, by generalizing zero or more flexible type variables. Rigid type variables may only be used free and cannot be quantified over. We introduce them in the typing environment but turn them into flexible type variables before quantifying over them, so they never appear as bound variables in type schemes.

In our representation, every node is labeled by a flexible type variable. This is essential to make type inference modular, as it is needed for incremental instantiation.

To see this, consider a context that contains a rigid type variable a, an equation $a \doteq \mathtt{int}$, and a variable x of type a, under which we apply a function `choice` of type $\alpha \to \alpha \to \alpha$ to x and 1. We first reason in the absence of labels on inner nodes. The partial application `choice` x has type $a \to a$. To further apply it to 1, we must use the equation to convert both 1 of type `int` and the domain of the partial application to the ambivalent type $\mathtt{int} \approx a$. The type of the full application is then a. However, if we inverted the order of arguments, it would be `int`. Something must be wrong. In fact, if we notice in advance that both types a and `int` will eventually have to be converted to $\mathtt{int} \approx a$, we may see both x and 1 with type $\mathtt{int} \approx a$ before performing the applications. In this case, we get yet another result $\mathtt{int} \approx a$, which happens to be the right one.

What is still wrong is that as soon as we instantiate α, we lose the information that all occurrences of α must be synchronized. The role of labels on inner nodes is to preserve this information. Revisiting the example, the partial application now has type $a^\alpha \to a^\alpha$ (we still temporarily omit the annotation on arrow types, as they do not play a role in this example). This is saying that the type is currently $a \to a$ but remembering that the domain and codomain must be kept synchronized. Then, the integer 1 of type $\mathtt{int}^\gamma$ can also be seen with type $(\mathtt{int} \approx a)^\gamma$ and unified with the domain of the function a^α, with the effect of replacing all occurrences of a^α and of $\mathtt{int}^\gamma$ by $(\mathtt{int} \approx a)^\alpha$. Thus, the function has type $(\mathtt{int} \approx a)^\alpha \to (\mathtt{int} \approx a)^\alpha$ and the result of the application has type $(\mathtt{int} \approx a)^\alpha$—the correct one. We now obtain the same result whatever the scenario.

This result type may still be unified with some other rigid variable a', as long as this is allowed by having some equation $a' \doteq \mathtt{int}$ or $a' \doteq a$ in the context, and refine its type to $(\mathtt{int} \approx a \approx a')^\alpha$. Since we cannot tell in advance which type constructors will eventually be mixed with other ones, all nodes must keep their label when substituted.

Replaying the example with full label annotations, `choice` has type $\forall(\alpha, \gamma, \gamma')\ (\alpha \to (\alpha \to \alpha)^\gamma)^{\gamma'}$ and its partial application to x has type $\forall(\alpha, \gamma)\ (a^\alpha \to a^\alpha)^\gamma$ after generalization. Observe that this is less general than $\forall(\alpha, \alpha', \gamma)\ (a^\alpha \to a^{\alpha'})^\gamma$ but more general than $\forall(\alpha, \gamma)\ ((\mathtt{int} \approx a)^\alpha \to (\mathtt{int} \approx a)^\alpha)^\gamma$.

Type Variables. Type variables are either rigid variables a or flexible variables α. We write $\mathsf{frv}(\zeta)$ for the set of rigid variables that are free in ζ and $\mathsf{ffv}(\zeta)$ for the set of flexible variables that are free in ζ. These definitions are standard. For example, free flexible variables are defined as:

$$\begin{aligned} \mathsf{ffv}(\psi^\alpha) &= \{\alpha\} \cup \mathsf{ffv}(\psi) & \mathsf{ffv}(a) &= \emptyset \\ \mathsf{ffv}(\varepsilon) &= \emptyset & \mathsf{ffv}(\mathtt{int}) &= \emptyset \\ \mathsf{ffv}(\rho \approx \psi) &= \mathsf{ffv}(\rho) \cup \mathsf{ffv}(\psi) & \mathsf{ffv}(\zeta_1 \to \zeta_2) &= \mathsf{ffv}(\zeta_1) \cup \mathsf{ffv}(\zeta_2) \\ \mathsf{ffv}(\forall(\alpha)\ \sigma) &= \mathsf{ffv}(\sigma) \setminus \{\alpha\} & \mathsf{ffv}(\mathsf{eq}(\zeta_1, \zeta_2)) &= \mathsf{ffv}(\zeta_1) \cup \mathsf{ffv}(\zeta_2) \end{aligned}$$

The definition is analogous for free rigid variables, except that $\mathsf{frv}(\psi^\alpha)$ is equal to $\mathsf{frv}(\psi)$ and $\mathsf{frv}(a)$ is equal to $\{a\}$. We write $\mathsf{ftv}(\zeta)$ the subset of $\mathsf{ffv}(\zeta)$ of variables that appear as leaves, *i.e.* labeling empty nodes and $\mathsf{fnv}(\zeta)$ the subset of $\mathsf{ffv}(\zeta)$ that are labeling nonempty nodes. In well-formed types these two sets are disjoint, *i.e.* $\mathsf{ffv}(\zeta)$ is the disjoint union of $\mathsf{ftv}(\zeta)$ and $\mathsf{fnv}(\zeta)$.

Rigid type variables lie between flexible type variables and type constructors. A rigid variable a stands for explicit polymorphism: it behaves like a nullary type constructor and clashes, by default, with any type constructor and any other rigid variable but itself. However, pattern matching a GADT may introduce type equations in the typing context while type checking the body of the corresponding branch, which may allow a rigid type variable to be compatible with another type. Type equations are used to verify that all ambivalent types occurring in the type derivation are well-formed, which requires in particular that all types of a same node can be proved equal.

Interpretation of Types. Ambivalent types may be interpreted as sets of simple types by unfolding ambivalent nodes as follows:

$$\begin{aligned} [\![\varepsilon^\alpha]\!] &= \{\alpha\} & [\![\mathtt{int}]\!] &= \mathtt{int} \\ [\![(\rho_1 \approx \psi)^\alpha]\!] &= \textstyle\bigcup_{\rho \in \rho_1 \approx \psi} [\![\rho]\!] & [\![\zeta_1 \to \zeta_2]\!] &= \{\tau_1 \to \tau_2 \mid \tau_1 \in [\![\zeta_1]\!], \tau_2 \in [\![\zeta_2]\!]\} \\ [\![a]\!] &= a & [\![\mathsf{eq}(\zeta_1, \zeta_2)]\!] &= \{\mathsf{eq}(\tau_1, \tau_2) \mid \tau_1 \in [\![\zeta_1]\!], \tau_2 \in [\![\zeta_2]\!]\} \end{aligned}$$

The interpretation ignores labels of inner nodes. It is used below for checking coherence of ambivalent types, which is a semantic issue and does not care about sharing of inner nodes. For example, types $(\mathtt{int} \approx a)^\alpha \to (\mathtt{int} \approx a)^\alpha$ and $(\mathtt{int} \approx a)^{\alpha_1} \to (\mathtt{int} \approx a)^{\alpha_2}$ are interpreted in the same way, namely as $\{\mathtt{int} \to \mathtt{int}, a \to a, a \to \mathtt{int}, \mathtt{int} \to a\}$.

A type ζ is said *truly ambivalent* if its interpretation is not a singleton. Notice that ψ may be a singleton ρ even though ψ^α is truly ambivalent, since ambivalence may be buried deeper inside ρ, as in $((\mathtt{int} \approx a)^\alpha \to (\mathtt{int} \approx a)^\alpha)^{\alpha_0}$.

Converting a Simple Type to an Ambivalent Type. Given a simple type τ, we may build a (not truly) ambivalent type ζ such that $[\![\zeta]\!] = \{\tau\}$. This introduces new variables $\bar{\gamma}$ that are in $\mathsf{fnv}(\zeta)$, while the variables of $\mathsf{ftv}(\zeta)$ come from τ. We write $\wr\tau\int$ for the most general type scheme of the form $\forall(\bar{\gamma})\ \zeta$, which is obtained by labeling all inner nodes of τ with different labels and quantifying over these fresh labels. For example, $\wr\mathtt{int} \to \mathtt{int}\int$ is $\forall(\gamma_0, \gamma_1, \gamma_2)\ (\mathtt{int}^{\gamma_1} \to \mathtt{int}^{\gamma_2})^{\gamma_0}$ and $\wr\alpha \to \alpha\int$ is $\forall(\gamma_0)\ (\varepsilon^\alpha \to \varepsilon^\alpha)^{\gamma_0}$. Notice that free type variables of τ remain free in $\wr\tau\int$.

3.2 Typing Contexts

Typing contexts Γ bind program variables to types, and introduce rigid type variables a, type equations $\tau_1 \doteq \tau_2$, and *node descriptions* $\alpha :: \psi$:

$$\Gamma ::= \emptyset \mid \Gamma, x : \sigma \mid \Gamma, a \mid \Gamma, \tau_1 \doteq \tau_2 \mid \Gamma, \alpha :: \psi$$

$$\frac{\text{WF-CTX-EQUAL}\quad \vdash \Gamma \quad \Gamma \vdash \tau_1 \doteq \tau_2}{\vdash \Gamma, \tau_1 \doteq \tau_2} \qquad \frac{\text{WF-TYPE-EQUAL}\quad \Gamma \vdash \tau_1 \quad \Gamma \vdash \tau_2 \quad \mathsf{ftv}(\tau_1) = \mathsf{ftv}(\tau_2) = \emptyset}{\Gamma \vdash \tau_1 \doteq \tau_2} \qquad \frac{\text{WF-TYPE-FLEX}\quad \vdash \Gamma \quad \alpha :: \psi \in \Gamma}{\Gamma \vdash \psi^\alpha}$$

$$\frac{\text{WF-CTX-FLEX}\quad \vdash \Gamma \quad \Gamma \vdash \psi \quad \alpha \notin \mathsf{dom}(\Gamma)}{\vdash \Gamma, \alpha :: \psi} \qquad \frac{\text{WF-TYPE-AMBIVALENT}\quad (\Gamma \vdash \rho)^{\rho \in \psi} \quad \Gamma \Vdash \psi \quad |\psi \setminus \mathcal{V}_r| \leq 1}{\Gamma \vdash \psi}$$

Fig. 1. Well-formedness of contexts and types (excerpt)

Both flexible and rigid type variables are explicitly introduced in typing contexts. Hence, well-formedness of types is defined relatively to some typing context.

In addition to routine checks, well-formedness judgments also ensure soundness of ambivalent types and coherent use of type variables.

Well-formedness of contexts $\vdash \Gamma$ is recursively defined with the well-formedness of types $\Gamma \vdash \rho$ and type schemes $\Gamma \vdash \sigma$. Characteristic rules are in Figure 1. It also uses the entailment judgment $\Gamma \Vdash \psi$, which means, intuitively, that all raw types appearing in the set ψ can be proved equal from the equations in Γ (see §3.3). The last premise of Rule WF-TYPE-AMBIVALENT ensures that ambivalent types contain at most one raw-type that is not a rigid variable. As usual well-formedness of contexts ensures that type variables are introduced before being used and that types are well-formed. It also ensures coherent use of type variables: alias constraints $\alpha :: \psi$ in the context Γ define a mapping that provides evidence that α is used coherently in the type σ. This is an essential feature of our system so that refining ambivalence earlier or later commutes, as explained above.

3.3 Entailment

Typing contexts may contain type equations. Type equations are used to express equalities between types that are known to hold when the evaluation of a program has reached a given program point. Type equations are added to the typing context while typechecking the expression at the current program point.

The set of equations in the context defines an equivalence between types. Rule WF-TYPE-AMBIVALENT shows that ambivalent types can only be formed between equivalent types: the well-formedness of the judgment $\Gamma \vdash \psi$ requires $\Gamma \Vdash \psi$, *i.e.* that all types in ψ are provably equal under the equations in Γ, which is critical for type soundness; the rightmost premise requires that at most one type in ψ is not a rigid variable. For example, the ambivalent types $\mathsf{int} \approx (\mathsf{int}^\gamma \to \mathsf{int}^\gamma)$ and $(\mathsf{int}^\gamma \to \mathsf{int}^\gamma) \approx (a^\gamma \to a^\gamma)$ are ill-formed. This is however not restrictive as the former would be unsound in any consistent context while the later could instead be written $(\mathtt{int} \approx a)^\gamma \to (\mathtt{int} \approx a)^\gamma$.

Well-formedness of a type environment requires that its equations do not contain free type variables. Equalities in Γ may thus be seen as unification problems where rigid variables are the unknowns. If they admit a principal solution, it is a substitution of the form $(a_i \mapsto \tau_i)^{i \in I}$; then, the set of equations $(a_i \doteq \tau'_i)^{i \in I}$ is equivalent to the equations in Γ. If the unification problem fails, then the equations are inconsistent—in the standard model where type constructors cannot be equated[2]. This is acceptable and it just means

[2] This is not always true for ML abstract types, as type constructors may be compatible in another context, but we do not address this problem here.

$$(\psi^{\alpha_i})\theta = \zeta_i \qquad (a)\theta = a$$
$$(\psi^{\gamma})\theta = (\psi\theta)^{\gamma} \qquad (\mathtt{int})\theta = \mathtt{int}$$
$$(\rho_i^{i\in I})\theta = (\rho_i\theta)^{i\in I} \qquad (\zeta_1 \to \zeta_2)\theta = \zeta_1\theta \to \zeta_2\theta$$
$$(\forall(\alpha)\,\zeta)\theta = \forall(\alpha)\,\zeta(\theta \setminus \{\alpha\}) \qquad (\mathsf{eq}(\zeta_1,\zeta_2))\theta = \mathsf{eq}(\zeta_1\theta,\zeta_2\theta)$$

Fig. 2. Application of substitution θ equal to $[\alpha_i \leftarrow \zeta_i]^{i\in I}$

that the current program point cannot be reached. Therefore, any ambivalent type is admissible in an inconsistent context.

The semantic judgment $\Gamma \Vdash \psi$ means by definition that any ground instance of Γ that satisfies the equations in Γ makes all types in the semantics of ψ equal. Formally:

Definition 1 (Entailment). *Let Γ be a typing environment. A ground substitution θ from rigid variables to simple types* models Γ *if $\theta(\tau_1)$ and $\theta(\tau_2)$ are equal for each equation $\tau_1 \doteq \tau_2$ in Γ. We say that Γ entails ψ and write $\Gamma \Vdash \psi$ if $\theta([\![\psi]\!])$ is a singleton for any ground substitution θ that models Γ.*

This gives a simple algorithm to check for entailment: compute the most general unifier θ of Γ; then $\Gamma \Vdash \psi$ holds if and only if $\theta([\![\psi]\!])$ is a singleton or θ does not exist.

3.4 Substitution

In our setting, substitutions operate on ambivalent types where type variables are used to label inner nodes of types and not just their leaves. They allow the replacement of an ambivalent node ψ^{α} by a "more ambivalent" one $\psi \approx \psi'^{\alpha}$, using the substitution $[\alpha \leftarrow (\psi \approx \psi')^{\alpha}]$; or merging two ambivalent nodes $\psi_1^{\alpha_1}$ and $\psi_2^{\alpha_2}$ using the substitution $[\alpha_1, \alpha_2 \leftarrow \psi_1 \approx \psi_2{}^{\alpha_1}]$. To capture all these cases with the same operation, we define in Figure 2 a general form of substitution $[\alpha_i \leftarrow \zeta_i]^{i\in I}$ that may graft arbitrary nodes ζ_i at every occurrence of a label α_i, written $[\alpha \leftarrow \zeta]$;

As a result of this generality, substitutions are purely syntactic and may replace an ambivalent node with a less ambivalent one—or even prune types replacing a whole subtree by a leaf. Of course, we should only apply substitutions to types when they preserve (or increase) ambivalence.

Definition 2. *A substitution θ* preserves ambivalence in a type *ζ if and only if, for any α in* $\mathsf{dom}(\theta)$ *and any node ψ^{α} in ζ, we have $\psi\theta \subseteq \lfloor(\psi^{\alpha})\theta\rfloor$.*

As a particular case, an atomic substitution $[\alpha \leftarrow \zeta_0]$ preserves ambivalence in ζ if for any node ψ^{α} in ζ, we have $\psi \subseteq \lfloor\zeta_0\rfloor$—since well-formedness of ψ^{α} implies that α may not occur free in ψ, hence $\psi\theta$ is just ψ.

3.5 Typing Rules

Typing judgments are of the form $\Gamma \vdash M : \sigma$ as in ML. However, typing rules, defined in Figure 3, differ from the traditional presentation of ML typing rules in two ways. On the one hand, we use a constraint framework where Γ carries node descriptions $\alpha :: \psi$ to enforce their sharing within different types. On the other hand, typing rules

$$\frac{\vdash \Gamma \quad x:\sigma \in \Gamma}{\Gamma \vdash x:\sigma}\ \text{M-VAR} \qquad \frac{\Gamma \vdash M : \forall(\alpha)\ (\sigma[\alpha \leftarrow \psi_0^\alpha]) \quad \psi_0 \subseteq \psi \quad \Gamma \vdash \psi^\gamma}{\Gamma \vdash M : \sigma[\alpha \leftarrow \psi^\gamma]}\ \text{M-INST}$$

$$\frac{\Gamma, \alpha :: \psi \vdash M : \sigma}{\Gamma \vdash M : \forall(\alpha)\ \sigma}\ \text{M-GEN} \qquad \frac{\Gamma, a, \alpha :: a \vdash M : \sigma \quad \Gamma \vdash \forall(\alpha)\ \sigma[\alpha \leftarrow \varepsilon^\alpha]}{\Gamma \vdash \nu(a) M : \forall(\alpha)\ \sigma[\alpha \leftarrow \varepsilon^\alpha]}\ \text{M-NEW}$$

$$\frac{\Gamma, x : \zeta_0 \vdash M : \zeta}{\Gamma \vdash \lambda(x) M : \forall(\gamma)\ (\zeta_0 \to \zeta)^\gamma}\ \text{M-FUN} \qquad \frac{\Gamma \vdash M_1 : ((\zeta_2 \to \zeta) \approx \psi)^\alpha \quad \Gamma \vdash M_2 : \zeta_2}{\Gamma \vdash M_1\, M_2 : \zeta}\ \text{M-APP}$$

$$\frac{\Gamma \vdash M_1 : \sigma_1 \quad \Gamma, x : \sigma_1 \vdash M_2 : \zeta_2}{\Gamma \vdash \mathsf{let}\ x = M_1\ \mathsf{in}\ M_2 : \zeta_2}\ \text{M-LET} \qquad \frac{\Gamma \vdash \forall(\mathsf{ftv}(\tau))\ \tau}{\Gamma \vdash (\tau) : \forall(\mathsf{ftv}(\tau))\ \wr \tau \to \tau \int}\ \text{M-ANN}$$

$$\frac{\vdash \Gamma}{\Gamma \vdash \mathsf{Eq} : \forall(\alpha, \gamma)\ \mathsf{eq}(\alpha, \alpha)^\gamma}\ \text{M-WITNESS} \qquad \frac{\Gamma \vdash (\mathsf{eq}(\tau_1, \tau_2))\, M_1 : \zeta_1 \quad \Gamma, \tau_1 \doteq \tau_2 \vdash M_2 : \zeta_2}{\Gamma \vdash \mathsf{use}\ M_1 : \mathsf{eq}(\tau_1, \tau_2)\ \mathsf{in}\ M_2 : \zeta_2}\ \text{M-USE}$$

Fig. 3. Typing rules

also carry type equations $\tau_1 \doteq \tau_2$ in typing contexts that are used to show the coherence of ambivalent types via direct or indirect uses of well-formedness judgments.

All axioms require well-formedness of Γ so that whenever a judgment $\Gamma \vdash M : \sigma$ holds, we have $\vdash \Gamma$. Rule M-INST instantiates the outermost variable of a type scheme. It is unusual in two ways. First, we write $\sigma[\alpha \leftarrow \psi_0^\alpha]$ rather than just σ in the quantified type. This trick ensures that all nodes labeled with α were indeed ψ_0^α and overcomes the absence of ψ_0 in the binder. Intuitively, the instantiated type should be $\sigma[\alpha \leftarrow \psi_0^\alpha][\alpha \leftarrow \psi^\gamma]$, but this happens to be equal to $\sigma[\alpha \leftarrow \psi^\gamma]$. Second, we require $\psi_0 \subseteq \psi$ to ensure preservation of ambivalence, as explained in the previous subsection. Finally, the premise $\Gamma \vdash \psi^\gamma$ ensures that the resulting type is well-formed.

Rule M-GEN introduces polymorphism implicitly, as in ML: variables that do not appear in the context can be generalized. The following rule is derivable from M-GEN and M-INST, and can be used as a shortcut when variable α does not appear in ψ^γ:

$$\frac{\Gamma, \alpha :: \psi_1 \vdash M : \psi^\gamma \qquad \alpha \neq \gamma}{\Gamma \vdash M : \psi^\gamma}\ \text{M-BIND}$$

Rule M-NEW enables explicit polymorphism (and explicit type equations using witnesses). For that purpose, it introduces a rigid type variable a in the typing context that may be used inside M—typically for introducing type annotations. However, polymorphism becomes implicit in the conclusion by turning the rigid type variable a into a quantified flexible type variable α when exiting the scope of the ν-form. Polymorphism can then be eliminated implicitly[3] as regular polymorphism in ML. The second premise ensures that the rigid type variable a does not appear anywhere else but in a^α.

Our version of Rule M-FUN generalizes the type γ introduced for annotating the arrow type, which avoids introducing $\gamma :: \zeta_0 \to \zeta$ in the premise. Rule M-APP differs from the standard application rule in two ways: a minor difference is that the arrow type has a

[3] This is why we write this $\nu(a) M$ rather than $\Lambda a M$.

label as in Rule M-FUN; a major difference is that the type of M_1 may be ambivalent—as long as it contains an arrow (raw) type of the form $\zeta_2 \to \zeta$. In particular, the premise $\Gamma \vdash M_1 : ((\zeta_2 \to \zeta) \approx \psi)^\alpha$ does not, in general, imply $\Gamma \vdash M_1 : (\zeta_2 \to \zeta)^\alpha$, as this could lose sharing. Hence, we have to read the arrow structure directly from the ambivalent type. Rule M-LET is as usual.

Rule M-ANN allows explicit loss of sharing via type annotations. It is presented as a retyping function of type scheme (τ), *i.e.* a function that changes the labeling of the type of its argument without changing its behavior. The types of the argument and the result need not be exactly τ but consistent instances of τ—see the definition of $\wr\tau\int$, above. Annotations are typically meant to be used in expressions such as $(\tau)\ M$, which forces M to have a type that is an instance of τ. While this is the only effect it would have in ML, here it also duplicates the polymorphic skeleton of M, which allows different labeling of *inner nodes* in the type of M passed to the annotation and its type after the annotation. By contrast, free type variables of τ remain shared between both types. The example below illustrates how type annotations can be used to remove ambivalence.

Rule M-WITNESS says that the Eq type constructor can be used to witness an equality between equal types as $\mathsf{eq}(\zeta,\zeta)^\gamma$, for any type ζ. Conversely, an equality type $\mathsf{eq}(\zeta_1,\zeta_2)^\gamma$, can only have been built from the Eq type constructor.

Rule M-USE uses this fact to learn and add the equation $\tau_1 \doteq \tau_2$ in the typing context while typechecking the body of M_2; the witness M_1 must be typable as an instance of the type $\mathsf{eq}(\tau_1,\tau_2)$ up to sharing of inner nodes. Since the equation is only available while typechecking M_2, it is not present in the typing context of the conclusion. Hence, the type ζ_2 must be well-formed in Γ. But this is a direct consequence of the second premise: it implies $\Gamma, \tau_1 \doteq \tau_2 \vdash \zeta_2$, which in turn requires that all labels of ζ_2 (which contain no quantifiers) have node descriptions in Γ, so that they cannot depend on $\tau_1 \doteq \tau_2$. Typically, ambivalent types needed for the typing of M_2 are introduced using rule M-BIND, which means that they cannot remain inside ζ_2, so that there is no way to keep an ambiguous type. Notice that the well-formedness of $\Gamma, \tau_1 \doteq \tau_2$ implies that τ_1 and τ_2 contain no flexible type variables (rules WF-TYPE-EQUAL and WF-CTX-EQUAL).

We now illustrate the typing rules on an example. Assume that (if _ then _ else _) is given as a primitive with type scheme $\forall(\gamma_b,\gamma_2,\gamma_1,\gamma_0)\ \forall(\alpha)\ (\mathtt{bool}^{\gamma_b} \to (\alpha \to (\alpha \to \alpha)^{\gamma_2})^{\gamma_1})^{\gamma_0}$. Let Γ be $\Gamma_a, \Delta, \Delta', y : (\mathtt{int} \approx a)^\alpha$ where Γ_a is $a, a \doteq \mathtt{int}$ and Δ is $\alpha :: \mathtt{int}, \gamma_2 :: \alpha \to \alpha, \gamma_1 :: \alpha \to (\alpha \to \alpha)^{\gamma_2}$ and Δ' is $\gamma_b :: \mathtt{bool}, \gamma_0 :: \gamma_b \to (\alpha \to (\alpha \to \alpha)^{\gamma_2})^{\gamma_1}$. Using M-VAR for premises, we have:

$$\text{M-APP}\ \frac{\Gamma \vdash \mathsf{if\ \_\ then\ \_\ else\ \_} : (\mathtt{bool}^{\gamma_b} \to (\alpha \to (\alpha \to \alpha)^{\gamma_2})^{\gamma_1})^{\gamma_0} \qquad \Gamma \vdash \mathsf{true} : \gamma_b}{\Gamma \vdash \mathsf{if\ true\ then\ \_\ else\ \_} : (\alpha \to (\alpha \to \alpha)^{\gamma_2})^{\gamma_1}}$$

We also have $\Gamma \vdash 1 : (\mathtt{int} \approx a)^\alpha$ and $\Gamma \vdash y : (\mathtt{int} \approx a)^\alpha$ by M-INST and M-VAR. Hence, we have $\Gamma \vdash \mathsf{if\ true\ then\ 1\ else}\ y : (\mathtt{int} \approx a)^\alpha$ by M-APP. This leads to:

$$\text{M-GEN}\ \frac{\text{M-BIND}\ \dfrac{\text{M-INST}\ \dfrac{\text{M-FUN}\ \dfrac{\Gamma \vdash \mathsf{if\ true\ then\ 1\ else}\ y : (\mathtt{int} \approx a)^\alpha}{\Gamma_a, \Delta, \Delta' \vdash \lambda(y)\ \mathsf{if\ true\ then\ 1\ else}\ y : \forall(\gamma)\ ((\mathtt{int} \approx a)^\alpha \to (\mathtt{int} \approx a)^\alpha)^\gamma}}{\Gamma_a, \Delta, \Delta' \vdash M : ((\mathtt{int} \approx a)^\alpha \to (\mathtt{int} \approx a)^\alpha)^{\gamma_2}}}{\Gamma_a, \Delta \vdash M : ((\mathtt{int} \approx a)^\alpha \to (\mathtt{int} \approx a)^\alpha)^{\gamma_2}}}{\Gamma_a \vdash M : \forall(\alpha,\gamma)\ ((\mathtt{int} \approx a)^\alpha \to (\mathtt{int} \approx a)^\alpha)^\gamma}$$

where M is $\lambda(y)$ if true then 1 else y. Rule M-BIND is used for variables γ_b and γ_0 in Δ' that are no longer used (we omitted the other premises), while Rule M-GEN is used for variables α and γ_2 in Δ. Notice that neither $\Gamma_a \vdash M : \forall(\alpha,\alpha',\gamma)\ ((\mathtt{int} \approx a)^{\alpha} \to \mathtt{int} \approx a^{\alpha'})^{\gamma}$ nor $\Gamma_a \vdash M : \forall(\alpha,\gamma)\ (\mathtt{int}^{\alpha} \to \mathtt{int}^{\alpha})^{\gamma}$ are derivable. It is a key feature of our system that sharing and ambivalence can only be increased *implicitly*. Still, it is sound to decrease them *explicitly*, using a type annotation, as in $\Gamma_a \vdash (a \to \mathtt{int})\,M : \forall(\alpha,\alpha',\gamma)\ (a^{\alpha} \to \mathtt{int}^{\alpha'})^{\gamma}$. This is obtained by applying the coercion $(a \to \mathtt{int})$ of type $\wr(a \to \mathtt{int}) \to (a \to \mathtt{int})\int$, *i.e.*

$$\forall(\alpha_1,\alpha_2,\alpha_1',\alpha_2',\gamma,\gamma',\gamma_0)\ ((a^{\alpha_1} \to \mathtt{int}^{\alpha_2})^{\gamma} \to (a^{\alpha_1'} \to \mathtt{int}^{\alpha_2'})^{\gamma'})^{\gamma_0}$$

to M. The expression M_0 equal to use $x : \mathsf{eq}(a,\mathtt{int})$ in $(a \to \mathtt{int})\,M$ is not ambiguous thanks to the annotation around M. Hence, we have:

$$\text{M-APP*}\ \dfrac{\text{M-NEW}\ \dfrac{\text{M-FUN*}\ \dfrac{\text{M-USE*}\ \dfrac{\Gamma' \vdash (\mathsf{eq}(a,\mathtt{int}))\,x : \zeta_1 \qquad \Gamma', a \doteq \mathtt{int} \vdash (a \to \mathsf{int})\,M : \wr a \to \mathtt{int}\int}{\Delta'', a, \Delta''', x : \mathsf{eq}(a^{\gamma_1}, \mathtt{int}^{\gamma_2})^{\gamma} \vdash M_0 : \wr a \to \mathtt{int}\int}}{\Delta'', a, \alpha :: a \vdash \lambda(x)\,M_0 : \wr \mathsf{eq}(a,\mathtt{int}) \to a \to \mathtt{int}\int}}{\Delta'' \vdash \nu(a)\,\lambda(x)\,M_0 : \forall(\alpha)\ \wr \mathsf{eq}(\alpha,\mathtt{int}) \to \alpha \to \mathtt{int}\int} \qquad \Delta'' \vdash \mathsf{Eq} : \ldots}{\vdash (\nu(a)\,\lambda(x)\,M_0)\ \mathsf{Eq} : \wr \mathtt{int} \to \mathtt{int}\int}$$

for some well-chosen Δ'', Δ''' and Γ', where $R*$ means R preceded and followed by a sequence of M-INST, M-BIND, and M-GEN. The rigid variable a is turned into the polymorphic variable α which is then instantiated to $\mathtt{int}^{\alpha}$ before the application to Eq.

4 Properties

By lack of space, we omit formal statements and their proofs, as well as a description of type inference, and we refer the reader to the accompanying technical report [6].

Type Soundness. Type soundness is established by seeing our system as a subset of HMG(X) [14]. Formally, we exhibit a translation from our language to HMG(X) that preserves typing judgments. The key is that well-formed ambivalent types are such that all simple types in their interpretation are provably equal in the current context, *i.e.* under the equations introduced by use expressions. Ambivalent types are only used for type inference and are dropped during the translation.

Monotonicity. Let $\Gamma \vdash \sigma' \prec \sigma$ be the instantiation relation, which says that any monomorphic instance of σ well-formed in Γ is also a monomorphic instance of σ'. This relation is extended point-wise to typing contexts: $\Gamma' \prec \Gamma$ if for any term variable x in $\mathsf{dom}(\Gamma)$, $\Gamma \vdash \Gamma'(x) \prec \Gamma(x)$, all other components of Γ and Γ' being identical. We may now state monotonicity: in our system, if $\Gamma \vdash M : \zeta$ and $\Gamma' \prec \Gamma$, then $\Gamma' \vdash M : \zeta$.

Existence of Principal Solutions to Type Inference Problems. This is our main result. A typing problem is a typing judgment skeleton $\Gamma \triangleright M : \zeta$, where Γ omits all node descriptions $\alpha :: \psi$ (hence, Γ is usually not well-formed, but can be extended into a well-formed environment by interleaving the appropriate node descriptions with bindings in Γ). A solution to a typing problem is a pair of a substitution θ that preserves ambivalence for the types in Γ and ζ, together with a context Δ that contains only node descriptions, such that $\Gamma\theta$ and Δ can be interleaved to produce a well-formed typing context, written $\Gamma\theta \mid \Delta$, and the judgment $\Gamma\theta \mid \Delta \vdash M : \zeta\theta$ holds.

For any typing problem, the set of solutions is stable by substitution and is either empty or has a principal solution (Δ, θ), *i.e.* one such that any other solution (Δ', θ') is of the form $\theta' = \theta'' \circ \theta$ for some substitution θ'' that preserves well-formedness in $\Gamma\theta \mid \Delta$, *i.e.* for any type ζ' such that $\Gamma\theta \mid \Delta \vdash \zeta'$, we have $\Gamma\theta' \mid \Delta' \vdash \zeta'\theta''$.

Sound and Complete Type Inference. Principality of type inference is proved as usual by exhibiting a concrete type inference algorithm. This algorithm (presented in the extended version) relies on a variant of the standard unification algorithm that works on ambivalent types and preserves their sharing. It uses a typing constraint approach, which converts typing problems to unification problems, while also ensuring that inferred types are well-formed, *i.e.* coherent, properly scoped, and acyclic. The use of constraints here is however just a convenience: since the ambivalence information is contained in types themselves, constraints can always be solved prior to type generalization so that we do not need constrained type schemes. That is, constraints are just a way to describe the algorithmic steps without getting into implementation details: OCaml itself uses a variant of Milner's algorithm $\mathscr{J}$ [10].

5 Related Works

While GADTs have been an active research area for about 10 years, early works usually focused on their type checking and expressiveness, ignoring ML-style type inference. Typically, they rely on an explicitly typed core language and use local type inference techniques to leave some type information implicit. Other recent works with rich dependent type systems also fit in this category and are only loosely related to ours.

Relatively few papers are dedicated to *principal* type inference for GADTs. The tension between ambiguity and principality is so strong that it has been assumed that the only way to reach principality is to know exactly the external type of each GADT match case. As a result, research has not been so much focused on finding a type system with principal types, but rather on clever propagation of type information so that programs have enough type annotations after propagation to admit principal types—or are rejected otherwise. Hence, some existing approaches always return principal solutions, but do not have a clear specification of when they will succeed, because this depends on the propagation algorithm (or some idealized version of it) which does not have a compositional specification.

OutsideIn improves on this by using uses constraint solving in place of directional annotation propagation, which greatly reduces the need for annotations. Stratified type inference [11] is another interesting approach to type inference for GADTs that uses several sophisticated passes to propagate local typing constraints (and not just type annotations) progressively to the rest of the program.

The following table summarizes the typability of the programs given in the overview, for our approach (including simple syntactic propagation of type annotations), OutsideIn[4], and stratified type inference [11].

Program	f	f_1	f_2	g	g_1	g_2	p	p_1
Ambivalent	√	√	√	–	√	√	√	–
OutsideIn	–	–	–	–	–	√	√	√
Stratified	–	√	√	–	–	√	–	–

The results for `f` are unsurprising: this example is not even principal in the naive type system: without an internal notion of ambivalence, a type system is unable to tell that the equality between two types is only accidental and should not be considered as a source of ambiguity. The results for $\texttt{f}_1$ and $\texttt{f}_2$ are more interesting. While OutsideIn requires an external type annotation in both cases, stratified type inference accepts to infer the type of the branch from its body. More precisely, the propagation algorithm operates in a bi-directional way and is able to extract non-ambiguous information from GADT pattern-matching branches. The exported information is pruned so that it remains compatible with any interpretation of the internal information, even in a context with fewer type equations. Thus, the type of the result is pruned in function `f`, but it can be propagated for $\texttt{f}_1$ and $\texttt{f}_2$. This corresponds exactly to the naive notion of ambiguity.

Typing of g fails in all three systems, as it is fundamentally ambiguous, whichever definition is chosen. The results for g_1 may look surprising: while it contains many type annotations, both OutsideIn and stratified type inference still fail on it. The reason is that type annotations are inside the branch: in both systems, only type annotations outside of a branch can disambiguate types for which an equation has been introduced. We find this behavior counter-intuitive. The freedom of where to add type annotations stands as a clear advantage of ambivalent types. By contrast, g_2 provides full type annotations in a standard style, so that all systems succeed—although ambivalent types need some (simple) propagation mechanism to push annotations inside.

Programs p and p_1 demonstrate the power of OutsideIn. The program p_1 is the following variant of p, which we deem ambiguous:

```
let p1 (type a) (x : (a,int) eq) (y : a) =
  let z = (match x with Eq -> if y>0 then y else 0) in z + 1
```

Indeed, the match expression in p_1 would have to be given the ambivalent type $a \approx \texttt{int}$, which is not allowed outside the scope of the equation $a = \texttt{int}$. Both p and p_1 are accepted by OutsideIn, since type information can be propagated upward, even for local let definitions. This comes at a cost, though: local let-definitions are monomorphic by default (but can be made polymorphic by adding a type annotation). While local polymorphic definitions are relatively rare, so that this change of behavior appears as a good compromise for Haskell, they are still frequent enough, and their corresponding type annotations large enough, so that we prefer to keep local polymorphism in OCaml [4]. Moreover, local polymorphism is critical to the annotation propagation mechanism used by OCaml, originally for polymorphic methods, and now for GADTs too.

[4] Results differ for GHC 7.6, as it slightly departs from OutsideIn allowing some biased choices, but next versions of GHC should strictly comply with OutsideIn.

All examples above are specifically chosen to illustrate the mechanisms underlying ambivalence and do not cover all uses of GADTs. Thus, they do not mean that our approach always outperforms other ones, but they emphasize the relevance of ambivalence. The question is not whichever approach taken alone performs better, but rather how ambivalence can be used to improve type inference with GADTs. Indeed, ambivalence could be added to other existing approaches to improve them as well.

Besides this comparison on examples, the main advantage of ambivalent types is to preserve principal type inference and monotonicity, so that type inference and program refactoring are less surprising.

An interesting proposal by Lin and Sheard [9], called point-wise type inference, is also tackling type inference *à la* ML, but restricting the expressiveness of the system—some uses of GADT will be rejected—so that more aggressive type propagation can be done in a principal way. Point-wise type inference is hard to compare to our approach, as many programs have to be modified. For instance, it rejects all our examples, because equality witnesses can only be matched on if they relate two rigid type variables. To be accepted, we could replace `eq` by a specialized version, `type _ t = Int : int t`.

Ambivalent types borrow ideas from earlier works. The use of sharing to track known type information was already present in our work on semi-explicit first-class polymorphism [5]. There, we only tracked sharing on a special category of nodes containing explicitly polymorphic types. Here, we need to track sharing on all nodes, as any type can become ambivalent. In our type inference algorithm, we also reuse the same definition style, describing type inference as a constraint resolution process, but introducing some points where constraints have to be solved before continuing.

The formalization itself borrows a lot from previous work on *structural polymorphism* for polymorphic variant and record types [3]. In particular, unification of ambivalent types, which merges sets of rigid variables and requires checking coherence constraints, can be seen as an instance of the unification of structurally polymorphic nodes. The difference is again that all nodes are potentially ambivalent in our case, while structural polymorphism only cares about variant and record types.

6 Conclusion

Ambivalent types are a refinement of ML types, which represents within types themselves ambiguities resulting from the use of local equations. They permit a more accurate definition of ambiguity, which in turn reduces the need for type annotations while preserving both the principal type property and monotonicity.

This approach has been implemented in OCaml. We have not addressed propagation of type information in this work, although this is quite useful in practice. A simple propagation mechanism based on polymorphism, similar to that used for semi-explicit first-class polymorphism, as already in use in OCaml, seems sufficient to alleviate the need for most local type annotations, while preserving principality of type inference.

The notion of ambivalence is orthogonal to previous techniques used for GADT type inference. Therefore, it should also benefit other approaches such as OutsideIn or stratified type inference. Hopefully, ambivalent types might be transferable to MLF [7], as the techniques underlying both ambivalent types and semi-explicit first-class polymorphism have many similarities.

Acknowledgments. We thank Gabriel Scherer and the anonymous reviewers for detailed comments on this paper.

References

1. Baars, A.I., Swierstra, S.D.: Typing dynamic typing. In: ICFP 2002: Proceedings of the 7th ACM SIGPLAN International Conference on Functional Programming, pp. 157–166. ACM Press (2002)
2. Cheney, J., Hinze, R.: First-class phantom types. Computer and Information Science Technical Report TR2003-1901, Cornell University (2003)
3. Garrigue, J.: A certified implementation of ML with structural polymorphism. In: Ueda, K. (ed.) APLAS 2010. LNCS, vol. 6461, pp. 360–375. Springer, Heidelberg (2010)
4. Garrigue, J.: Monomophic let in OCaml? (September 2013), Blog article at: `http://gallium.inria.fr/blog/monomorphic_let/`
5. Garrigue, J., Rémy, D.: Semi-explicit first-class polymorphism for ML. Information and Computation 155, 134–171 (1999)
6. Garrigue, J., Rémy, D.: Ambivalent types for principal type inference with GADTs (June 2013), Available electronically at `http://gallium.inria.fr/~remy/gadts/`
7. Le Botlan, D., Rémy, D.: Recasting MLF. Information and Computation 207(6), 726–785 (2009)
8. Leroy, X., Doligez, D., Frisch, A., Garrigue, J., Rémy, D., Vouillon, J.: The OCaml system release 4.00, Documentation and user's manual. Projet Gallium, INRIA (July 2012)
9. Lin, C.-K., Sheard, T.: Pointwise generalized algebraic data types. In: Proceedings of the 5th ACM SIGPLAN Workshop on Types in Language Design and Implementation, TLDI 2010, pp. 51–62. ACM, New York (2010)
10. Milner, R.: A theory of type polymorphism in programming. Journal of Computer and System Sciences 17, 348–375 (1978)
11. Pottier, F., Régis-Gianas, Y.: Stratified type inference for generalized algebraic data types. In: Proceedings of the 33rd ACM Symposium on Principles of Programming Languages (POPL 2006), Charleston, South Carolina, pp. 232–244 (January 2006)
12. Schrijvers, T., Peyton Jones, S., Sulzmann, M., Vytiniotis, D.: Complete and decidable type inference for gadts. In: Proceedings of the 14th ACM SIGPLAN International Conference on Functional Programming, ICFP 2009, pp. 341–352. ACM, New York (2009)
13. Sheard, T., Linger, N.: Programming in Omega. In: Horváth, Z., Plasmeijer, R., Soós, A., Zsók, V. (eds.) CEFP 2007. LNCS, vol. 5161, pp. 158–227. Springer, Heidelberg (2008)
14. Simonet, V., Pottier, F.: A constraint-based approach to guarded algebraic data types. ACM Transactions on Programming Languages and Systems 29(1) (January 2007)
15. Vytiniotis, D., Peyton Jones, S., Schrijvers, T., Sulzmann, M.: OutsideIn(X) Modular type inference with local assumptions. Journal of Functional Programming 21(4-5), 333–412 (2011)
16. Xi, H., Chen, C., Chen, G.: Guarded recursive datatype constructors. In: Proceedings of the 30th ACM SIGPLAN-SIGACT Symposium on Principles of Programming Languages, POPL 2003, pp. 224–235. ACM, New York (2003)

Temporal Specification Mining for Anomaly Analysis

Farn Wang, Jung-Hsuan Wu, Chung-Hao Huang, Cheng-Chieh Chang, and Chung-Cheng Li

Dept. of Electrical Engineering & Graduate Institute of Electronic Engineering
National Taiwan University
Nr.1, Sec. 4, Roosevelt Rd. Taipei, Taiwan 106, ROC
`http://cc.ee.ntu.edu.tw/~farn/`

Abstract. [1] We investigate how to use specification mining techniques for program anomaly analysis. We assume the input of positive traces (with- out execution anomalies) and negative traces (with execution anomalies). We then partition the traces into the following clusters: a positive cluster that contains all positive traces and some negative clusters according to the characteristics of trace anomalies. We present techniques for learn- ing temporal properties in Linear Temporal Logic with finite trace se- mantics (FLTL). We propose to mine FLTL properties that distinguish the negative clusters from the positive cluster. We experiment with 5 Android applications from Google Code and Google Play with traces of GUI events and crashes as the target anomaly. The report of FLTL properties with high support or confidence reveal the temporal patterns in GUI traces that cause the crashes. The performance data also shows that the clustering of negative traces indeed enhances the accuracy in mining meaningful temporal properties for test verdict prediction.

Keywords: Specification mining, FLTL, Clustering, Program trace, Android.

1 Introduction

Nowadays, many software programs are developed with rapid life-cycles. For example, various applications running on mobile devices emerge with billion times of monthly downloads. Most of these applications keep frequent bug fixing, performance improvement, and feature enhancement during their life cycles. As a result, to keep a correct and up-to-date specification of such an application of a non-trivial size has become a daunting challenge. One promising technology to address this problem is *specification mining* [2,11,20] that extracts specifications from program execution *traces* collected via program code instrumentation. In this work, we investigate how to mine temporal specifications for the diagnosis of anomalies in traces.

[1] The work is partially supported by NSC, IIS and Academia Sinica.

C.-c. Shan (Ed.): APLAS 2013, LNCS 8301, pp. 273–289, 2013.

Our work assumes a test oracle that issues verdicts to execution traces. A trace is *positive* if it is labeled with the verdict of no anomaly; otherwise, it is *negative.* A specification property is *positive* if it is expected of a correct implementation; otherwise, it is *negative.* Previous work in specification mining focuses on mining positive properties from all traces. To help in diagnosis, we need consider the following issues.

- There are usually more than one anomaly with different root causes exhibited in the traces. Thus the behavior patterns of an anomaly may not be shared by all the negative traces and could be mined with low support. To counter this problem, we propose to partition the negative traces to clus- ters according to trace characteristics related to anomalies. Our experiment shows that mining the individual clusters of the negative traces indeed helped us in mining useful and meaningful negative specification properties.
- To help in diagnosis, we need to consider what patterns can be typical of anomalies in traces. Since most bugs are reported as program traces, we adopt *linear temporal logic* with finite trace semantics (FLTL) as our specification language for behavior patterns of traces. Moreover, we identified five types of FLTL formulas that are typical of trace anomalies. In our experiment, the five types helped in mining FLTL properties for recognizing trace anomalies.
- Finally, we want to avoid mining effective FLTL properties shared by both negative and positive traces. This is easily done by subtracting the mined properties of the positive traces from those of the negative ones.

We have implemented our ideas and experimented with 5 Android applications from Google Code and Google Play. The preliminary experiment data shows the promise of our techniques.

The organization of this paper is structured as follows. Section 2 compares this work with related work in the literature. Section 3 reviews the background knowledge. Section 4 respectively present our diagnosis property mining framework and the five types of FLTL properties that we target to mine. Section 6 explains our mining algorithms for the five types of FLTL properties. In Section 7, we explain our implementation on the Android platform. Section 8 reports our experiment with five benchmarks. Section 9 is the conclusion.

2 Related Work

Several approaches about specification mining have been proposed in the literatures. Ernst et al. developed a tool, Daikon, for automatic deduction of likely invariants involving program variables from dynamic traces [4]. Specifically, Daikon mines arithmetic relationships, such as $x \geq y$, that hold at specific statements. Our work is for mining FLTL properties that relate several program states.

Ammons et al. introduced an automata learning framework to learn *nondeterministic finite-state automata* (*NFSA*) from program traces [2]. The programs traces are collected from an instrumented program that is well-debugged to reveal strong hints of correct behaviors. In our work, we do not assume such a golden program.

Dallmeier et al. proposed an incremental approach to mine normal program behaviors [3]. Starting with a set of program traces, they construct an initial automata and generate more test cases based on this automata to explore more execution space. These test cases either end in a legal state or raise an exception. The test case execution leads to repetitive enrichment to the automata. This procedure repeats until no further test cases can be generated.

Lorenzoli et al. presented a technique to automatically generate extended finite-state machines from program traces [14]. By labelling transitions with conditions on data values, an extended finite-state machine can model the interplay between data values and component interactions.

In contrast to the work on mining automata, we focus on mining FLTL properties which are more appropriate in expressing behavior patterns relating events far apart and in expressing liveness properties than automata.

Yang et al. developed a tool, Perracotta, to discover temporal properties between only two events in traces about application program interface [20].

Lo et al. proposed several approaches to mine program specifications from execution traces [13,12]. In [13], they mined universal Live Sequence Chart which captures the inter-object behaviors of multiple events in arbitrary length. In [9], they mined recurrent rules in the form of "whenever a series of precedent events occurs, eventually a series of consequent event occurs". These are similar to one type of FLTL properties that we target to mine. In our experiment, we found that other types of properties are also important in anomaly diagnosis. In [12], they mined past-time temporal rules while our TLTL templates express future time temporal properties.

Since the target SUT may suffer from different anomalies, mining directly from the collected program negative traces may be ineffective due to the interference of different anomalies. Lo et al. clustered program traces by their similarity between pairs of data item [10]. Our works cluster negative traces by the program subroutines of topmost exception call stack frame.

3 Preliminaries

3.1 Model of Finite Program Execution Traces

A *trace* is intuitively a finite linear sequence of events. For convenience, we use $|\theta|$ to denote the length of a trace θ. Rigorously, a trace θ is a function from $[0, |\theta| - 1]$ to a set of events. For any integer i and j with $0 \leq i \leq j \leq |\theta|$, we let $\theta[i...j] = \theta(i)\theta(i+1)\theta(i+2)...\theta(j)$. We also use θ_i to denote the ith suffix of θ, i.e., $\theta_i = \theta(i)\theta(i+1)\theta(i+2)...\theta(|\theta| - 1)$.

3.2 Linear Temporal Logic with Semantics on Finite Trace

In 1977, Pnueli proposed linear temporal logic (LTL) as a formal language for expressing and reasoning about the behavioral properties of parallel programs and reactive systems[15]. In this work, we focus on the analysis of finite-length program traces. Therefore we adopt FLTL [6,18,7]. FLTL formulae (ranged over by $\varphi, \psi, ...$) on a finite set P of events are of the following syntax.

$$\varphi ::= true \mid e \mid \neg\varphi \mid \varphi \wedge \psi \mid X\varphi \mid \varphi U \psi$$

Here $e \in P$ is an event in a program trace. Operators $\neg$ and $\wedge$ are Boolean negation and conjunction respectively. X and U are temporal operators next and until respectively.

Boolean connectives such as $\vee$, $\rightarrow$ and $\leftrightarrow$ are derived operators from $\neg$ and $\wedge$. Other useful shorthands include $false \equiv \neg true$, $F\varphi \equiv trueU\varphi$ (the *eventually* operator), and $G\varphi \equiv \neg(trueU\neg\varphi)$ (the *always* operator).

The satisfaction of an FLTL formula φ by a finite program trace θ, written $\theta \models \varphi$, is defined inductively as follows.

$$\begin{array}{lll}
\theta \models true & \text{iff} & true \\
\theta \models e & \text{iff} & |\theta| > 0 \wedge \theta(0) = e \\
\theta \models \neg\varphi & \text{iff} & \theta \not\models \varphi \\
\theta \models \varphi \wedge \psi & \text{iff} & \theta \models \varphi \wedge \theta \models \psi \\
\theta \models X\varphi & \text{iff} & |\theta| > 0 \wedge \theta_1 \models \varphi \\
\theta \models \varphi U \psi & \text{iff} & \exists k \leq |\theta|, (\theta_k \models \psi \wedge \forall j \in [0, k-1], \theta_j \models \varphi)
\end{array}$$

Intuitively, $X\varphi$ says that φ is true in the next position. A formula $\varphi U \psi$ means that ψ is true either now or in the future and φ holds since now until that moment.

Example 1. A program trace $\theta = s_0e_0s_1e_1s_0e_2s_2e_3s_0$ would satisfy property $\varphi = G((s_0 \wedge Xe_2) \rightarrow XXs_2)$. This property can be interpreted as that state s_0 with input e_2 will always transit to state s_2. □

3.3 Association Rule Mining

In the field of data mining, association rule mining is one of the most important and well researched techniques[8,21]. It was first introduced by Agrawal [1] and aims to extract interesting correlations, associations, frequent patterns among sets of items in a dataset. Since then, it has been widely used in various areas, such as telecommunication networks, market and risk management, inventory control etc. Given a set I of items of a record, an *association rule* is of the form $X \mapsto Y$, where $X, Y \subset I$ and $X \cap Y = \emptyset$, that specifies that the occurrences of all items in X implies that the occurrences of all items in Y is also likely to occur.

Example 2. In daily supermarket transactions, a transaction could consist of buying tomatoes, cheeses, noodles, eggs, etc. The rule {tomatoes, noodles} $\mapsto$ {eggs} mined from transactions would indicate that if a customer buys tomatoes and noodles together, he is likely to also buy eggs. □

There are two important basic measures to evaluate how likely an association rule is. They are *support* and *confidence*. Support is the statistical significance of an association rule. It is defined as the percentage/fraction of records that contain all items in $X \cup Y$ to the total number of records in the dataset, i.e.,

$$support(X \mapsto Y) = \frac{\text{Number of records in dataset with all items in } X \cup Y}{\text{Total number of records in dataset}}$$

Intuitively, a high support value is an evidence that the related rule is significant. Users can specify a support value as a threshold for mining significant rules. Only association rules with supports higher than the threshold are then reported.

However, sometimes an association rule with low supports could also be interesting. For example, in the supermarket case mentioned above, transactions with high price items could be rare. But association rules related to these expensive items are also important to the retailer. Therefore, another measure, confidence, has also been used to deal with this situation. Confidence is a measure of strength of the association rules. It is defined as the percentage/fraction of the number of records that contain $X \cup Y$ to the total number of records that contain X. Formally, confidence is calculated by the following formula:

$$confidence(X \mapsto Y) = \frac{\text{Number of records in dataset with all items in } X \cup Y}{\text{Number of records in dataset with all items in X}}$$

If the confidence of the association rule $X \mapsto Y$ is 80%, it means that 80% of the records that contain X also contain Y. Similarly, users can also prescribe a confidence threshold to ensure that only interesting rules are reported.

4 Anomaly Specification Mining Framework

In order to mine FLTL properties from the negative traces, we propose the framework showed in Figure 1. At the top-left corner, we accept program execution traces. After normalization, we may change the traces to a format suitable for efficient and accurate processing. Specifically, we only keep the last state event in a sequence of consecutive state events so that all normalized traces are strict alternations of state and input events.

We assume that there is a test oracle (module verdict) that issues verdicts to the normalized traces. The test oracle can be a human engineer or can be a program that checks the traces against a formal specification. Traces without anomalies are labeled 'pass' and treated as positive traces. The other traces are labeled 'fail' and treated as negative traces. For example, in our experiment, we target system exceptions as anomalies. If there is a system exception during the trace execution, the trace will be labelled as a fail trace.

Since we use data mining technic to extract FLTL properties from fail traces, we want to make sure that the bug-trigger behaviors come into the miner's notice. For this reason, we try to class the fail traces into different clusters according to the bugs they triggered, automatically. After that, the cause of a bug should appear overwhelmingly in the cluster it belongs. In this work, the fail (negative) traces are partitioned (by module cluster) into clusters, say C_1 through C_k, according to trace characteristics related to anomalies. For example,

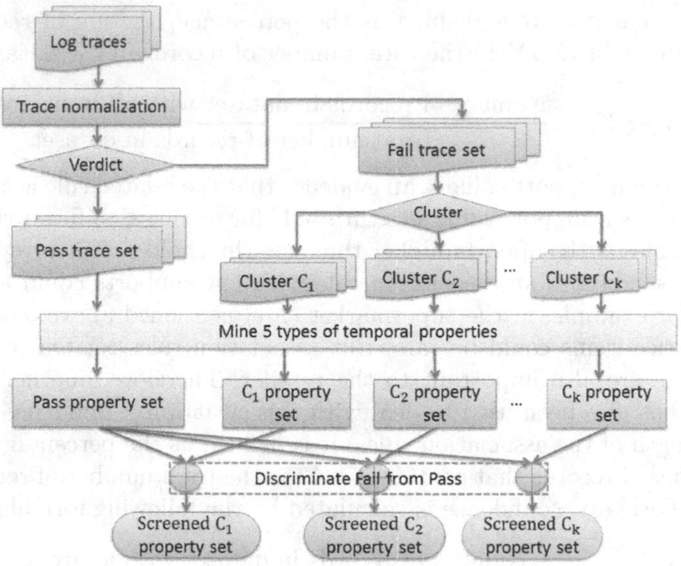

Fig. 1. The anomaly specification mining framework

in our experiment, since we view system exceptions as evidences of trace anomalies, we use the contents of the exception call stack to partition the negative traces. That is negative traces are partitioned into the same cluster, if the top-most stack frames issued by the SUT are with the same subroutine. Ideally, each cluster should contain negative traces with anomalies of the same root cause.

For convenience, we assume that the set of positive traces is in cluster C_0. Then we apply our FLTL property mining algorithm to cluster C_0 through C_k and get FLTL property sets R_0 through R_k respectively. If the mining algorithm works well, then for each $i \in [1, k]$, R_i should contain FLTL properties that sufficiently recognize the anomalies of the root cause for C_i.

Finally, to avoid producing diagnosis properties also satisfied by the positive traces, we only output $R_1 \backslash R_0$ (screened C_1 property set) through $R_k \backslash R_0$ (screened C_k property set), i.e., the set subtraction of R_1 through R_k by R_0.

5 Target FLTL Templates

For this work, we applied our techniques to the *graphical user-interface* (*GUI*) event traces of Android applications. There are 2 types of events in the execution traces we collected from Android applications. The first type, called *state* events, consists of durational events representing values of screen attributes. The second type, called *input* events, consists of instantaneous user input via the GUI components on the screen. For example, the display of a button on the screen is a state event. A finger stroke on the screen is an input event. We use E to denote the set of input events while S to denote the set of state events.

Traditional mining techniques are usually bottom-up and deduce complex properties from simple formulas. Such an approach is not guided and is usually drowned in the sea of small properties without any hope for mining larger and complex properties. For example, we may mine property ϕ_A as a positive evidence and ϕ_B as a negative evidence of a cluster respectively. Then together, this cluster may satisfy $\neg(\phi_A \rightarrow \phi_B)$ with high confidence. If ϕ_A and ϕ_B are already complex FLTL properties, then it is not likely that we can mine $\neg(\phi_A \rightarrow \phi_B)$ in a bottom-up style without proper guidance. In this work, we propose to guide the mining procedure via property templates whose logical combinations can capture some complex and maybe interesting properties. Considering most bugs in Android applications can be triggered by a series of screen touch behaviors or by a screen touch under certain system conditions, we defined five target FLTL templates that, we believe, have good opportunity to find the root cause of bugs.

In the following, we explain the detail of the five types of FLTL properties. Please be reminded that these five types have been used effectively in our experiment for our purpose. It is certainly possible that in the future, more types are designed for other experiments.

5.1 Γ_1: Nested Eventuality Properties

In previous work, temporal properties with very restricted syntax are mined to contain the search space for mined properties [4,11,20]. Such approaches usually can deduce piecewise behavior patterns of the positive traces. In contrast, a negative trace in a bug report may contain a long sequence of events leading to the exhibition of an anomaly. Specifically, for GUI event traces, a trace anomaly usually is triggered by an interleaved sequence of state events and input events. Thus, intuitively, a sequence of interleaved events naturally matches nested FLTL eventually properties. For example, the following FLTL property specifies the anomaly of the tapping of the "next" button at screen $Page_1$ followed by the tapping of "yes" button at screen $Page_2$ that leads to screen $Page_3$.

$$F(Page_1 \wedge X(next \wedge XF(Page_2 \wedge X(yes \wedge XF(Page_3)))))$$

In general, a trace anomaly of this type can extend to any depth of nesting. Specifically, we can use the following syntax to define this type.

$$\varphi ::= F(s) \mid F(s \wedge X(e \wedge X\varphi))$$

Here $s \in S$ and $e \in E$. We let Γ_1 be the set of FLTL properties of this type.

5.2 Γ_2: Nested Conditional Next Properties

Sometimes, a strict sequence of events must happen for the setup of certain procedures. In such a procedure, if one step is wrong, an anomaly may occur. For example, we may want to say that after the query for password, if the user taps either button 'cancel' or button 'prev' (for previous page), the login should not be successful. This can be expressed with the following two properties.

$$G(login\_display \to X(cancel \to X(login\_succ)))$$
$$G(login\_display \to X(prev \to X(login\_succ)))$$

Here *login_display* is a state event for the screen of the login page that queries an account name and a password. State event *login_succ* flags the success of the login procedure. As can be seen, several properties of this type together may be used to express the 'or' concept in detecting events. For example, the following two traces both satisfy the two properties.

login_display cancel login_succ logout login_display prev login_succ
login_display prev login_succ logout login_display cancel login_succ

Here we use *logout* to denote the input event for logging out.

In general, a trace anomaly of this type can extend to any depth of nesting. Specifically, a property φ of this type is of the following syntax.

$$\varphi ::= G(s \to X(e \to X(\psi)))$$
$$\psi ::= s \mid s \to X(e \to X(\psi))$$

Here $s \in S$ and $e \in E$. We let Γ_2 be the set of FLTL properties of this type.

5.3 Γ_3: Nested Conditional Eventuality Properties

In Γ_2, the strict sequence is in lock-steps and one event in the sequence must be followed by another in the sequence. Sometimes, especially for multi-thread or distributed programs, there could be some irrelevant events from other threads or applications in the traces. Thus, by replacing the 'X' operators before the state events with the XF operators (eventuality), we can rewrite properties in Γ_2 for more flexibility in the sequence. In general, a trace anomaly of this type can extend to any depth of nesting. Specifically, a property φ of this type is of the following syntax.

$$\varphi ::= G(s \to X(e \to XF(\psi)))$$
$$\psi ::= s \mid s \to X(e \to XF(\psi))$$

Here $s \in S$ and $e \in E$. We let Γ_3 be the set of FLTL properties of this type.

5.4 Γ_4: For Uninitialization Anomaly

We also considered the anomalies with improper initializations. For example, program may access an object before it is instantiated. Such an anomaly can be specified as: $(\neg new)U\,read$. The syntax of such properties is the following.

$$\varphi ::= (\neg s_0)U(s_1 \wedge Xe_1) \mid (\neg e_0)U(s_1 \wedge Xe_1)$$

Here $s_0, s_1 \in S$ and $e_0, e_1 \in E$. We use Γ_4 to denote the set of all such properties. There is no expansion to such properties in this work.

Algorithm 1. Expand(φ, d)

if d is greater than the prescribed expansion depth **then**
    Return.
end if
for each $e \in E$ *and* $s \in S$ **do**
    if $\frac{|\{\theta|\theta\in C,\theta\models\varphi+e+s\}|}{|C|} \geq t$ **then**
        Report $\varphi + e + s$ and call Expand($\varphi + e + s$, $d + 1$)
    end if
end for

5.5 Γ_5: For Nested Starvation Anomaly

Some anomalies exhibit the denial of services after some event sequences have been observed. For example, an anomaly that two consecutive reads to a page make the page no longer readable can be specified with the following property.

$$G(page\_loaded \rightarrow X(read \rightarrow X(page\_loaded \rightarrow X(read \rightarrow X(G\neg page\_loaded)))))$$

The syntax of such a property φ is of the following.

$$\varphi ::= G(s \rightarrow X(e \rightarrow X(\psi)))$$
$$\psi ::= G\neg s \mid G\neg e \mid s \rightarrow X(e \rightarrow X(\psi))$$

Here $s \in S$ and $e \in E$. We let Γ_5 be the set of FLTL properties of this type.

6 Mining Algorithms

In the following, we first define how to expand properties of a type and then use the expansion operator to explore the space of FLTL properties up to a limit of nesting of the templates prescribed by the users. We assume that the users have prescribed a threshold t of both support and confidence. Only properties with support (or confidence) no less than t will be reported and used for further expansion. In the following, we assume that we are given a trace cluster C.

6.1 Mining Algorithm for Γ_1 Properties

Given a $\varphi \in \Gamma_1$ of the form $\varphi = F(s_1 \wedge X(e_1 \wedge XF(\ldots XF(s_n)\ldots)))$, we let $\varphi + e + s$ denote the expansion of φ with one more nesting of the eventuality of an input e followed by a state s. Specifically, $\varphi + e + s$ represents

$$F(s_1 \wedge X(e_1 \wedge XF(\ldots XF(s_n \wedge X(e \wedge XF(s)))\ldots))).$$

Given a state event s and an input event e, we only use the support of $\varphi+e+s$, defined as $\frac{|\{\theta|\theta\in C,\theta\models\varphi+e+s\}|}{|C|}$, to evaluate the property. Then we use algorithm 1 to recursively expand the properties of a type. The mining algorithm starts by calling Expand($F(s \wedge X(e \wedge XF(s')))$, 0) for all $s, s' \in S$ and $e \in E$.

6.2 Mining Algorithm for Γ_2 Properties

Given a $\varphi \in \Gamma_2$ of the form: $\varphi = G(s_1 \rightarrow X(e_1 \rightarrow X(\ldots X(s_n)\ldots)))$, we let $\varphi + e + s$ denote the expansion of φ with one more nesting of the eventuality of an input e followed by a state s. Specifically, $\varphi + e + s$ represents

$$G(s_1 \rightarrow X(e_1 \rightarrow X(\ldots X(s_n \rightarrow X(e \rightarrow X(s)))\ldots))).$$

According to the literature, there can be many different granularities in defining the confidence of such properties. Here we want to use a granularity smaller than traces. That is, we want to count how many times a property in Γ_2 is honored in a trace. For this purpose, we need to define the following concepts. Given a property $\varphi \in \Gamma_2$, we let $\boxplus(\varphi)$ be the sequence of events in φ listed in the order that they appear in φ. For example, $\boxplus(G(a \rightarrow X(b \rightarrow X(c)))) = abc$.

Given a property $\varphi \in \Gamma_2$, a state event s, and an input event e, we only use the confidence of properties of this type to evaluate them. The confidence of $\varphi+e+s$ is defined as $\frac{|\{(\theta,i,j)|\theta \in C, 0 \leq i \leq j < |\theta|, \theta[i \ldots j] = \boxplus(\varphi)es\}|}{|\{(\theta,i,j)|\theta \in C, 0 \leq i \leq j < |\theta|, \theta[i \ldots j] = \boxplus(\varphi)e\}|}$. The mining algorithm is basically Algorithm 1 except that line (5) is replaced with

$$\textbf{if } \frac{|\{(\theta,i)|\theta \in C, 0 \leq i \leq j < |\theta|, \theta[i \ldots j] = \boxplus(\varphi)es\}|}{|\{(\theta,i)|\theta \in C, 0 \leq i \leq j < |\theta|, \theta[i \ldots j] = \boxplus(\varphi))e\}|} \geq t$$

The mining algorithm starts by calling Expand$(G(s \rightarrow X(e \rightarrow X(s'))), 0)$ for all $s, s' \in S$ and $e \in E$.

6.3 Mining Algorithm for Γ_3 Properties

Given a $\varphi \in \Gamma_3$ of the form: $\varphi = G(s_1 \rightarrow X(e_1 \rightarrow XF(\ldots XF(s_n)\ldots)))$, we also let $\varphi + e + s$ denote the expansion of φ with one more nesting of the eventuality of an input e followed by a state s. Specifically, $\varphi + e + s$ represents

$$G(s_1 \rightarrow X(e_1 \rightarrow XF(\ldots XF(s_n \rightarrow X(e \rightarrow XF(s)))\ldots))).$$

We also let $\boxtimes(\varphi)$ be the regular language:

$$s_1 e_2 (S \cup E)^* s_2 e_2 (S \cup E)^* \ldots (S \cup E)^* s_{n-1} e_{n-1} (S \cup E)^* s_n.$$

Here $(S \cup E)^*$ represents the set of sequences with only zero or more events in $S \cup E$. That is, $\boxtimes(\varphi)$ is obtained from $\boxplus(\varphi)$ by inserting $(S \cup E)^*$ before every state event except the first one. For example,

$$\boxtimes(G(a \rightarrow X(b \rightarrow XF(c)))) = ab(S \cup E)^* c$$

We use $\langle L \rangle$ to denote the set of strings in a regular language L.

Given a property $\varphi \in \Gamma_3$, a state event s, and an input event e, we only use the confidence of properties of this type to evaluate them. The confidence of $\varphi + e + s$ is defined as $\frac{|\{(\theta,i,j)|\theta \in C, 0 \leq i \leq j < |\theta|, \theta[i \ldots j] \in \langle \boxtimes(\varphi)e(S \cup E)^* s \rangle\}|}{|\{(\theta,i,j)|\theta \in C, 0 \leq i \leq j < |\theta|, \theta[i \ldots j] \in \langle \boxtimes(\varphi)e \rangle\}|}$. The mining algorithm is basically Algorithm 1 except that line (5) is replaced with

$$\textbf{if } \frac{|\{(\theta,i,j)|\theta \in C, 0 \leq i \leq j < |\theta|, \theta[i \ldots j] \in \langle \boxtimes(\varphi)e(S \cup E)^* s \rangle\}|}{|\{(\theta,i,j)|\theta \in C, 0 \leq i \leq j < |\theta|, \theta[i \ldots j] \in \langle \boxtimes(\varphi)e \rangle\}|} \geq t$$

The mining algorithm starts by calling Expand$(G(s \rightarrow X(e \rightarrow XF(s'))), 0)$ for all $s, s' \in S$ and $e \in E$.

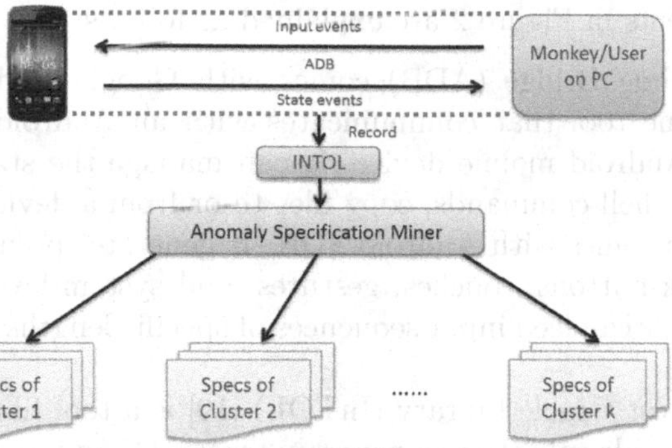

Fig. 2. The implmentation

6.4 Mining Algorithm for Γ_4 Properties

This mining algorithm is pretty much Algorithm 1. We also use the support to evaluate such properties as in line (5) of algorithm 1. Due to the straightforwardness, we omit the explanation.

6.5 Mining Algorithm for Γ_5 Properties

Given a $\varphi \in \Gamma_5$ of the form: $\varphi = G(s_1 \rightarrow X(e_1 \rightarrow X(\ldots X(s_n \rightarrow X(e_n \rightarrow X(G\neg s)))\ldots)))$, we let $\varphi + s_{n+1} + e_{n+1}$ denote the expansion of φ as

$$G(s_1 \rightarrow X(e_1 \rightarrow X(\ldots X(s_n \rightarrow X(e_n \rightarrow X(s_{n+1} \rightarrow X(e_{n+1} \rightarrow X(G\neg s)))))\ldots))).$$

We also let $\boxdot(\varphi)$ be the sequence of events $s_0e_0 \ldots s_ne_n$ and $\boxminus(\varphi)$ be the regular language $s_0e_0 \cdots s_ne_n(S \cup E \backslash s)^*$. Given a property $\varphi \in \Gamma_5$, a state s and an event e, we define the confidence of $\varphi + e + s$ as $\frac{|\{(\theta,i)|\theta \in C, 0 \leq i < |\theta|, \theta[i \ldots |\theta|] \in \langle \boxminus(\varphi+s+e) \rangle\}|}{|\{(\theta,i,j)|\theta \in C, 0 \leq i \leq j < |\theta|, \theta[i \ldots j] = \boxdot(\varphi+s+e)\}|}$. The mining algorithm is basically Algorithm 1 except that line (5) is replaced with

$$\textbf{if } \frac{|\{(\theta,i)|\theta \in C, 0 \leq i < |\theta|, \theta[i \ldots |\theta|] \in \langle \boxminus(\varphi+s+e) \rangle\}|}{|\{(\theta,i,j)|\theta \in C, 0 \leq i \leq j < |\theta|, \theta[i \ldots j] = \boxdot(\varphi+s+e)\}|} \geq t$$

The mining algorithm starts by calling Expand($G(\neg s)$,0) for all $s \in S$.

7 Implementation

We have implemented our mining tool for Android applications. As showed in Figure 2, we first instrumented Android source code of Ice Cream Sandwich 4.0.3 version with Intelligent Test Oracle Library (InTOL) [19] to intercept GUI state events and input events, such as *onTouch*, *onKeyDown*, *onKeyUp*, etc. Then we use Monkey, a pseudo-random stream of user events generator, from Android SDK to automatically exercise an android application under test to collect the execution traces. Then through the framework proposed in Section 4, the temporal properties for each cluster are mined from the normalized traces.

The components in Figure 2 are explained as follows:

- Android Debug Bridge (ADB) comes with Google Android SDK. It is a command-line tool that communicates with an Android virtual device or connected Android mobile device. It can manage the state of the Android system, run shell commands, copy files to or from a device, and etc.
- Monkey also comes with Android SDK. It generates pseudo-random events, such as click-buttons, touches, gestures, and system-level events. Through ADB, Monkey can feed input sequences of specific lengths to the applications under test.
- Intelligent Test Oracle Library (InTOL) [19] is a tool library for the convenient and flexible collection of program traces. It can record the input events and system GUI states in traces. In addition, when the system crashes, InTOL can also log the crash event and mark the trace with 'fail.'

We also implemented a procedure that normalizes identifiers of the events and UI components in the traces. For trace-specific identifiers, we normalize them according to their order of occurrence. For process and platform-specific identifiers, we change them to constants according to our knowledge of Android.

8 Experiment

The experiment is deployed on a Samsung Galaxy Nexus i9025 running Android Ice-cream Sandwich 4.0.3 and a PC running ubuntu 10.04. Program traces are collected on the Galaxy Nexus and analyzed on the PC. In collecting the traces, we use Monkey to exercise each benchmark 3000 times with 300 input stimulus per exercising. To simulate a normal user's pace in operating an Android application, Monkey injects 10 events per second. If an application crashes in an exercising, the trace will be ended immediately with a fail verdict. Each benchmark takes approximately 20 hours on average to collect 3000 traces.

We use expansion depth of 6 in all mining processes. In the following, we first introduce our benchmarks. Then we report the performance of our techniques when used for test verdict prediction. Finally we examine an example property mined via our tool and argue for their values.

8.1 Benchmarks

We have five Android applications from Google Code and Google Play as our benchmarks. The five benchmarks are chosen because the provided services are common in modern smartphones and suffer from anomalies exhibited by Monkey. Each benchmark has several versions and we arbitrarily selected one. Brief descriptions of these benchmarks are listed below:

- AtPak (version 1.1.0) is a social-platform photo browser, which allows users to manage local photo galleries and upload photos to QQ.com.
- SMS Bomber (version 1.1) is an SMS text editor. Users can bomb a receiver by sending lots of messages in a short time.

- AnkiDroid (version 2.0 beta18) is a flashcard learning application. It helps users to manage vocabulary cards on the cloud and reminds them to review vocabulary in a desirable period. It also supports multiple languages and speech synthesis from texts.
- Surround (version 1.2) is a music player that allows for music sharing among nearby mobile devices.
- Taskcatapp (version 2011090101) is a memoir application which helps users to easily create, navigate, and search through memoirs.

8.2 Evaluation of Mined Temporal Properties

To measure the preciseness of the mined temporal properties, we also collect another 500 traces for each benchmark as the testing trace set to verify the accuracy of our miners. We designed a predicting mechanism to label these 500 traces as pass or fail according to the mined FLTL properties. If the prediction is with high accuracy, we can imply these mined properties are representive. Similar idea can be found in [9] which mined a classifier from execution traces to classify software behaviors.

The most difficult part of the predicting mechanism is to decide the importance of each property. In this work, for each cluster, we decide a set of weights(each one for a template) and a threshold by applying *cross-validation*[5] technique on the original 3000 traces. *Cross-validation* is a common technique in data mining for assessing how the result of statistical analysis will generalize to an independent data set.

By giving a new trace θ and the weights and the threshold of each cluster, the predicting mechanism works in the following procedures:

1. For each cluster, we sum up all the weights of properties which can be satisfied by θ(properties from the same template won't be count repeatedly). If the summation is higher than the threshold, then label θ as a potential member of the cluster.
2. If θ is not a potential member of any cluster, then θ is predicted as pass. Otherwise it is predicted as fail.

To measure the quality of our predicting mechanism, we compare the predicting result to the real execution result of these 500 traces and use 4 measures *accuracy*, *precision*, *recall* and *F-score* [16,17] to quantify the effectiveness of our implementation in test verdict prediction. To proceed, we first need the following concepts.

- A trace is a *true positive* if it is a 'fail' trace with test verdict correctly issued by our tool. Let *TP* be the number of true positives in the given trace set.
- A trace is a *true negative* if it is a 'pass' trace with test verdict correctly issued by our tool. labelled as fail. We let *TN* be the number of true negatives.
- A trace is a *false positive* (false alarm) if it is a 'pass' trace to which our tool issues a 'fail' verdict. We let *FP* be the number of false positives.
- A trace is a *false negative* if it is a 'fail' trace to which our tool issues a 'pass' verdict. Let *FN* be the number of false negatives.

Table 1. Accuracy of Clustered and no Clustered Mined Properties

	#Pass Traces	#Fail Traces	#Cluster Fail	TP	TN	FP	FN	Acc.	Prec.	Rec.	F-score
ATPak	458	42	1	5	433	25	37	87.6%	0.16	0.11	0.126
ATPak (Clustered)			2	38	424	34	4	92.4%	0.52	0.90	0.791
SMSBomber	473	27	1	22	401	72	5	84.6%	0.23	0.81	0.544
SMSBomber (Clustered)			2	27	418	55	0	89%	0.32	1	0.71
Taskcatapp	481	19	1	11	374	107	8	77%	0.09	0.57	0.283
Taskcatapp (Clustered)			2	13	453	28	6	93.2%	0.31	0.68	0.555
Surround	475	25	1	21	411	64	4	86.4%	0.24	0.84	0.567
Surround (Clustered)			3	20	451	24	5	94.2%	0.45	0.8	0.694
AnkiDroid	461	39	1	39	333	128	0	74.4%	0.23	1	0.603
AnkiDroid (Clustered)			3	33	461	0	6	98.8%	1	0.84	0.873

Table 2. Weights and Threshold Learned by Cross Validation

	Cluster Index	W1	W2	W3	W4	W5	Threshold
ATPak	1	1	1	1	1	6	8
	2	1	1	3	0	5	7
SMSBomber	1	1	0	0	1	8	1
	2	6	1	1	1	1	8
Taskcatapp	1	2	2	1	1	4	6
	2	3	0	1	5	1	7
Surround	1	3	1	4	1	1	8
	2	3	1	1	1	4	8
	3	3	2	2	1	2	8
AnkiDroid	1	1	2	2	1	4	7
	2	2	2	2	1	3	5
	3	3	2	2	1	2	8

Note that $Fscore_\beta$ is the harmonic mean of *Precision* and *Recall*, in our work we let $\beta = 2$ which means we weight *Recall* higher than *Precision*. We show the definitions of these metrics as follows:

$$Accuracy = \frac{TP+TN}{TP+TN+FP+FN} \qquad Precision = \frac{TP}{TP+FP}$$

$$Recall = \frac{TP}{TP+FN} \qquad Fscore_\beta = (1+\beta\cdot\beta)\cdot\frac{Precision\cdot Recall}{\beta\cdot\beta\cdot Precision+Recall}$$

The performance of our mining algorithms is measured on these five benchmarks with clustered and unclustered fail traces. Table 1 shows the result while Table 2 shows the weights and the threshold learned by cross validation(and used in the prediction). The result shows that properties mined via clustered traces can predict with higher accuracy and precision to the new 500 traces than those via unclustered. This might show clustering can effectively reduce the interference among the behavior patterns of different negative clusters. Note that the weight in Table 2 shows that each template has been the most representitive one in some bugs(if we view each cluster represents an individual bug). This denotes the trigger behaviors of bugs are different and require different property templates to describe. When user want to find the root cause of a bug, he can start by viewing the properties with highest weight.

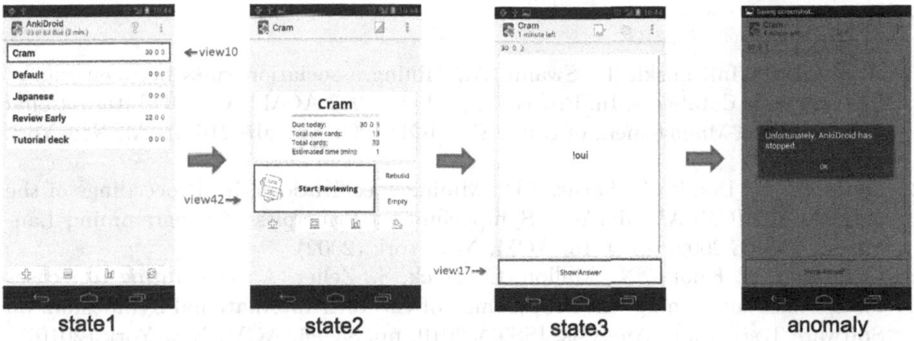

Fig. 3. State transition on AnkiDroid

8.3 Example of Mined Properties and Anomaly Analysis

We use one FLTL property mined via our tool to argue why our techniques can also be useful in diagnosis of anomalies exhibited in traces. The screen shots in Figure 3 demonstrate an anomaly existed in AnkiDroid. One Γ_2 property mined by our implementation is $G(state1 \to X(onTouch\_view10 \to X(state2 \to X(onTouch\_view42 \to X(state3 \to X(onTouch\_view17))))))$. This property shows an operation sequence leading to the exception with high confidence. Without this property, developers may only be aware of the existence of the anomaly but unaware of its reason. For example, bug reports from Google to an Android application developer only show the call stacks when a crash or freeze happens. Such a temporal property with high confidence could serve as a starting clue for root-causing the anomaly.

9 Conclusion and Future Works

In this work, we present an automated mining approach for detecting and diagnosing software defects. We have implemented our mining tool for Android applications. We chose five actively developing applications from Google Code and Google Play as benchmarks to test our approach. For diagnosis, we propose more types of temporal properties as mining target than previous approach did. To enhance the performance, we also propose to cluster the fail traces. By subtracting the mined temporal properties of pass traces from negative traces, the outcome temporal properties can effectively issue correct verdicts for each benchmark. The experiment data shows the effectiveness of our techniques.

In the future, we plan to mine more target types of temporal properties. Also, we expect to extend the framework from diagnosis to run-time monitoring and deploy our implementation on scalable industrial projects.

References

1. Agrawal, R., Imieliński, T., Swami, A.: Mining association rules between sets of items in large databases. In: Proceedings of the 1993 ACM SIGMOD International Conference on Management of Data, SIGMOD 1993, pp. 207–216. ACM, New York (1993)
2. Ammons, G., Bodík, R., Larus, J.R.: Mining specifications. In: Proceedings of the 29th ACM SIGPLAN-SIGACT Symposium on Principles of Programming Languages, POPL 2002, pp. 4–16. ACM, New York (2002)
3. Dallmeier, V., Knopp, N., Mallon, C., Hack, S., Zeller, A.: Generating test cases for specification mining. In: Proceedings of the 19th International Symposium on Software Testing and Analysis, ISSTA 2010, pp. 85–96. ACM, New York (2010)
4. Ernst, M.D., Cockrell, J., Griswold, W.G., Notkin, D.: Dynamically discovering likely program invariants to support program evolution. In: Proceedings of the 21st International Conference on Software Engineering, ICSE 1999, pp. 213–224. ACM, New York (1999)
5. Geisser, S.: Predictive Inference: An Introduction. Monographs on Statistics and Applied Probability. Chapman & Hall (1993)
6. Havelund, K., Rosu, G.: Testing linear temporal logic formulae on finite execution traces. Technical report (2001)
7. Kamp, H.W.: Tense Logic and the Theory of Linear Order. Phd thesis, Computer Science Department, University of California at Los Angeles, USA (1968)
8. Kotsiantis, S., Kanellopoulos, D.: Association rules mining: A recent overview. GESTS International Transactions on Computer Science and Engineering 32(1), 71–82 (2006)
9. Lo, D., Cheng, H., Han, J., Khoo, S.-C., Sun, C.: Classification of software behaviors for failure detection: a discriminative pattern mining approach. In: Proceedings of the 15th ACM SIGKDD International Conference on Knowledge Discovery and Data Mining, KDD 2009, pp. 557–566. ACM, New York (2009)
10. Lo, D., Khoo, S.-C.: Smartic: towards building an accurate, robust and scalable specification miner. In: Proceedings of the 14th ACM SIGSOFT International Symposium on Foundations of Software Engineering, SIGSOFT 2006/FSE-14, pp. 265–275. ACM, New York (2006)
11. Lo, D., Khoo, S.-C., Liu, C.: Efficient mining of recurrent rules from a sequence database. In: Haritsa, J.R., Kotagiri, R., Pudi, V. (eds.) DASFAA 2008. LNCS, vol. 4947, pp. 67–83. Springer, Heidelberg (2008)
12. Lo, D., Khoo, S.-C., Liu, C.: Mining past-time temporal rules from execution traces. In: Proceedings of the 2008 International Workshop on Dynamic Analysis: Held in Conjunction with the ACM SIGSOFT International Symposium on Software Testing and Analysis (ISSTA 2008), WODA 2008, pp. 50–56. ACM, New York (2008)
13. Lo, D., Maoz, S., Khoo, S.-C.: Mining modal scenario-based specifications from execution traces of reactive systems. In: Proceedings of the Twenty-Second IEEE/ACM International Conference on Automated Software Engineering, ASE 2007, pp. 465–468. ACM, New York (2007)
14. Lorenzoli, D., Mariani, L., Pezzè, M.: Automatic generation of software behavioral models. In: Proceedings of the 30th International Conference on Software Engineering, ICSE 2008, pp. 501–510. ACM, New York (2008)
15. Pnueli, A.: The temporal logic of programs. In: Proceedings of the 18th Annual Symposium on Foundations of Computer Science, SFCS 1977, pp. 46–57. IEEE Computer Society, Washington, DC (1977)

16. Powers, D.M.W.: Evaluation: From precision, recall and f-measure to roc, informedness, markedness & correlation. Journal of Machine Learning Technologies 2(1), 37–63 (2011)
17. Rijsbergen, C.J.V.: Information Retrieval, 2nd edn. Butterworth-Heinemann, Newton (1979)
18. Strejček, J.: Linear Temporal Logic: Expressiveness and Model Checking. PhD thesis, Faculty of Informatics, Masaryk University, Brno, Czech Republic (2004)
19. Wang, F., Yao, L.-W., Wu, J.-H.: Intelligent test oracle construction for reactive systems without explicit specifications. In: Proceedings of the 2011 IEEE Ninth International Conference on Dependable, Autonomic and Secure Computing, DASC 2011.IEEE Computer Society, Washington, DC (2011)
20. Yang, J., Evans, D.: Perracotta: mining temporal api rules from imperfect traces. In: Proceedings of the 28th International Conference on Software Engineering, ICSE 2006, pp. 282–291. ACM Press (2006)
21. Zhao, Q., Bhowmick, S.S.: Association Rule Mining: A Survey

Automated Inference of Library Specifications for Source-Sink Property Verification*

Haiyan Zhu[1], Thomas Dillig[2], and Isil Dillig[3]

[1] College of William & Mary
[2] University College London
[3] Microsoft Research Cambridge

Abstract. Many safety properties in program analysis, such as many memory safety and information flow problems, can be formulated as *source-sink* problems. While there are many existing techniques for checking source-sink properties, the soundness of these techniques relies on all relevant source code being available for analysis. Unfortunately, many programs make use of libraries whose source code is either not available or not amenable to precise static analysis. This paper addresses this limitation of source-sink verifiers through a technique for inferring exactly those library specifications that are needed for verifying the client program. We have applied the proposed technique for tracking explicit information flow in Android applications, and we show that our method effectively identifies the needed specifications of the Android SDK.

1 Introduction

Many safety properties of interest in program analysis can be formulated in terms of verifying the absence of *source-sink* errors. Such an error arises if a value constructed at a location designated as a *source* reaches a location designated as a *sink*. Examples of source-sink problems include the following:

– Confidential information (source) cannot be sent to an untrusted party (sink).
– A pointer assigned to null (source) should not reach a dereference (sink).
– A closed file f (source) should not be read or written (sink).

Over the last decade, there has been much progress in verifying the absence of source-sink errors [1–3]. Given a value v constructed at source location l_1, and a value w consumed at sink location l_2, source-sink checkers determine if there exists a feasible execution path from l_1 to l_2 on which v and w are equal. As an example, consider the following Java-like code:

```
Data d = new Data();
Location x = null;
if(R) x = getGPSLocation();
d.loc = x ;
if(R) send(d.loc, "http://xue.com/stealmyloc.php");
```

* This work is supported in part by DARPA #FA8750-12-2-0020.

C.-c. Shan (Ed.): APLAS 2013, LNCS 8301, pp. 290–306, 2013.

Here, we want to determine whether confidential data can be sent over the network. The method `getGPSLocation` is a source since it returns the user's confidential GPS location. In contrast, the method `send(x,y)` called at line 5 is a sink because it sends data `x` to URL `y`. Assuming predicate `R` can be true, the above code snippet has a source-sink error because there is a feasible execution path from the source to the sink in which `x` and `d.loc` are aliases.

While automated source-sink checkers have improved substantially in terms of precision and scalability over the last decade, they typically make two assumptions to guarantee soundness: First, they require sources and sinks to be specified by the user. Second, they require all relevant source code to be available for analysis. The first requirement is often not too cumbersome because there are typically few kinds of sources and sinks, and there has been recent progress on automating source and sink inference [4]. On the other hand, the second assumption is more problematic because modern software uses of many layers of complex libraries. While calls to library methods can –and often do– affect source-to-sink flows, it is often impractical to analyze library code together with the client, for example, because library code may be unavailable or may be written in a different language. Furthermore, even when library code is available, its implementation is typically much larger and much lower-level than the client, making it undesirable to analyze the library's implementation for verifying the client. Existing source-sink checkers deal with this difficulty in one of three ways:

1. Assume an *angelic* environment by treating library calls as no-ops. Unfortunately, this amounts to the optimistic but unsound assumption that library methods do not introduce flows from sources to sinks.
2. Assume a *demonic* environment by making worst-case assumptions about library methods, which means that a library method m may introduce a flow between any pair of locations reachable in m.
3. Require the user to write *flow specifications* of library methods, which describe whether input x may transitively reach output y.

Unfortunately, all of these options have serious drawbacks. The first option is unsound and yields many false negatives. The second option is sound but grossly imprecise, yielding many false positives. Finally, the third alternative is extremely cumbersome for users: In modern software, there are typically *many* calls to library functions, each of which could require several flow annotations. In principle, not all of these flow specifications are relevant for verifying the absence of source-sink errors, but it is very difficult for humans to reliably identify which specifications are needed to guarantee soundness of the analysis.

In this paper, we address this limitation of source-sink checkers by automating the inference of library specifications that are needed for soundness. Given a client program A, our technique infers a *smallest* set of *must-not-flow* requirements on library functions that are sufficient to ensure that A is free of source-sink errors. Since our technique only analyzes implementations of clients but not libraries, specifications inferred by our technique must be checked against either the documentation or the implementation of the library. However, as we show

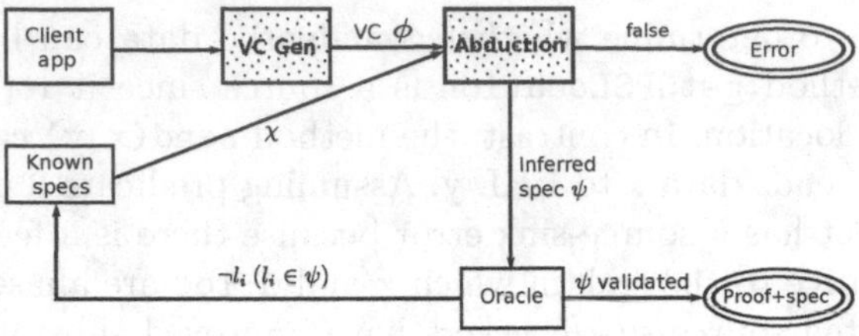

Fig. 1. A schematic illustration of our approach

experimentally, the number of must-not-flow requirements inferred by our technique are only a small fraction of the possible flow relations that are possible; hence, our technique minimizes the effort required to guarantee soundness.

1.1 Overview

The high-level architecture of our approach is shown in Figure 1. Given a client application A, our technique first analyzes A to generate a verification condition (VC) ϕ. This VC is parametrized over the possible flows that can be introduced due to library calls and its validity guarantees the absence of source-sink errors in A. Given such a VC ϕ and a formula χ encoding known partial specifications of library methods, our technique enters a refinement loop with the "Abduction" component at its core. The formula χ is initially just true, meaning there are no known specifications of library methods, but becomes logically stronger as the refinement process continues.

At every step of the refinement loop, we use an inference technique known as *abduction* to speculate a candidate specification ψ, which asserts a minimal set of must-not-flow requirements on library methods that are sufficient to guarantee program A's correctness. Since our technique does not analyze library implementations, each must-not-flow requirement in ψ must be externally validated by an oracle. This oracle can be a user who can consult the documentation of the library or a different technique for analyzing the library's source code or binary. In either case, since we want to minimize the amount of work to be performed by the oracle, our inferred candidate specification ψ should be as small as possible.

Given the candidate specification ψ, we then ask the oracle to confirm or refute each must-not-flow requirement l_i in ψ. If the oracle can confirm each $l_i \in \psi$, we have found a correct and minimal specification sufficient to verify A. In this case, the refinement loop terminates with $\psi \Rightarrow \phi$ as a proof of correctness of A. On the other hand, if the oracle cannot certify some must-not-flow relation l_i from α to β in ψ, this means there is a may-flow relation from α to β. Therefore, the negation of l_i is added to the set of known specifications χ, and abduction is used again to infer a different candidate specification ψ'. This process continues until either we find a correct specification sufficient to verify A or until we prove that there is no correct must-not-flow specification of the library sufficient to discharge the VC ϕ. We now give a brief overview of the two key components underlying our technique, illustrated as "VC Gen" and "Abduction" in Figure 1.

VC Generation. Our approach to generating VCs is based on the following insight: Rather than making purely angelic or purely demonic assumptions, we introduce *constraints* describing the possible effects of library methods. These constraints are composed of boolean *flow variables* $f_{l_1 \mapsto l_2}$, which describe whether the value in location l_1 *may* flow to location l_2 in library function f. As an example, consider the statement x = f(y) where f is a library method. Here, if y was tainted before the call, our analysis will taint x under the constraint $f_{a_1 \mapsto \text{ret}}$, where the boolean variable $f_{a_1 \mapsto \text{ret}}$ represents whether f's first argument may (transitively) flow to its return value.

Now, when we encounter a sink, we generate a VC that is parametric over these flow variables. Specifically, if a variable x used at a sink has value v under constraint φ, then the generated VC asserts that φ implies that v is not tainted. Since the value constraints φ are parametrized over possible flow relations, the validity of the VC therefore depends on the truth assignment to flow variables.

The advantage of this strategy is that the generated VC captures the full range of possible assumptions on the library in between the angelic and demonic ones. On one extreme, if the VC is valid, the client application can be verified even under demonic assumptions. On the other hand, if the VC is unsatisfiable, the client application cannot be verified even with angelic assumptions about library calls. However, if the formula is contingent, the VC still contains useful information about flow specifications needed to discharge the source-sink flow.

Abductive Inference. The second insight underlying our technique is that *logical abduction* can be used to infer a minimal set of must-not-flow requirements that are needed to guarantee the absence of source-sink errors in the client application. Specifically, given two formulas ϕ and χ, logical abduction is the problem of finding an explanatory hypothesis ψ such that:

$$(1)\ \chi \wedge \psi \models \phi \quad \text{and} \quad (2)\ \text{SAT}(\chi \wedge \psi)$$

In our setting, ϕ corresponds to the VC generated for the client, and χ corresponds to the known assumptions on library methods. Therefore, the first condition says that, together with known specifications χ, the solution ψ to the inference problem should imply the verification condition ϕ. The second condition says that the abductive solution ψ should not contradict known specifications χ.

In addition to these two requirements, we want our solution ψ to be the smallest conjunction of flow literals satisfying the above conditions. This requirement is important since we want to minimize the number of assumptions to be externally validated by an oracle. For this purpose, our technique uses *minimum-size prime implicants* of boolean formulas to compute the desired abductive solutions.

1.2 Organization and Contributions

The rest of this paper is organized as follows: Section 2 gives the syntax and semantics of a small language used for our formalization. Section 3 describes a sound static analysis for generating VCs parametric over flow variables, and

Program P	$:= m\ f^*$
Client m	$:= \text{def } m = \{\kappa\}$
Library function f	$:= \text{def } f(\alpha_1, \ldots, \alpha_n) = \{\varsigma;\ \chi_f \leftarrow v\}$
Client stmt κ	$:= v \leftarrow \mathcal{S} \mid \text{check}(v) \mid a \mid \kappa_1; \kappa_2 \mid \text{if}(\star) \text{ then } \kappa_1 \text{ else } \kappa_2 \mid v \leftarrow^{\rho} f(v_1, \ldots, v_n)$
Library stmt ς	$:= a \mid \varsigma_1; \varsigma_2 \mid \text{if}(\star) \text{ then } \varsigma_1 \text{ else } \varsigma_2$
Assignment a	$:= v \leftarrow c \mid v_1 \leftarrow v_2$
Constant c	$:= \mathcal{C}_1 \mid \ldots \mid \mathcal{C}_k$

Fig. 2. Language used for formal development

Section 4 describes our inference algorithm based on minimum-size prime implicants. Sections 5 and 6 describe important extensions and our implementation. Finally, Sections 7, 8, 9 describe experimental results, related work, and future directions. To summarize, this paper makes the following key contributions:

- We present a novel technique for inferring flow specifications of libraries for source-sink property verification.
- We show how to generate verification conditions that are parametric over the unknown behavior of library methods.
- We formulate the minimum flow specification inference problem as an instance of logical abduction and give an algorithm based on minimum-size prime implicants for solving the generated inference problems.
- We apply the proposed technique for verifying confidentiality of Android applications that heavily use unanalyzed library methods. Experimentally, we show that our method is effective at identifying a small set of relevant flow specifications that are needed for analyzing the client.

2 Language and Concrete Semantics

Figure 2 defines an imperative call-by-value language used for our formalization. In this language, a program consists of one client application m and zero or more library functions f. The client m has body κ, and our goal is to verify m without analyzing libraries called by m. While our technique will not analyze library functions f, we give their syntax and semantics in order to precisely define what we mean by their flow specifications.

In this language, the special constant $\mathcal{S}$ denotes a *source*; hence, the assignment $v \leftarrow \mathcal{S}$ *taints* variable v. The statement check(v) is a *sink*: It evaluates to false if v is tainted (i.e., value of v is $\mathcal{S}$); otherwise, it evaluates to true. If the check statement check(v) evaluates to false, we say that the check *fails*.

In client m, statements are sources, sinks, assignments, sequencing, conditionals, and calls to library functions, which are annotated with a unique *label* ρ. Library functions f can take any number of arguments $\alpha_1, \ldots, \alpha_n$ and consist of a body ς and a statement $\chi_f \leftarrow v$, where χ_f denotes the return value of f. Statements ς used in library functions are the same as those used in the client except that they cannot be sources or sinks, since we assume library methods

$$(1)\frac{\Gamma' = \Gamma[v \mapsto c]}{\Pi, \Gamma \vdash v \leftarrow c : \Gamma', \text{true}} \quad (2)\frac{\Gamma(v_2) = c \quad \Gamma' = \Gamma[v_1 \mapsto c]}{\Pi, \Gamma \vdash v_1 \leftarrow v_2 : \Gamma', \text{true}} \quad (3)\frac{\Pi, \Gamma \vdash s_1 : \Gamma_1, b_1 \quad \Pi, \Gamma_1 \vdash s_2 : \Gamma_2, b_2}{\Pi, \Gamma \vdash s_1; s_2 : \Gamma_2, b_1 \wedge b_2}$$

$$(4a)\ \frac{\Gamma(v) = c \quad c \neq \mathcal{S}}{\Pi, \Gamma \vdash \text{check}(v) : \Gamma, \text{true}} \quad (4b)\ \frac{\Gamma(v) = c \quad c = \mathcal{S}}{\Pi, \Gamma \vdash \text{check}(v) : \Gamma, \text{false}}$$

$$(5a)\ \frac{(s_1 \oplus s_2) = s_1 \quad \Pi, \Gamma \vdash s_1 : \Gamma_1, b_1}{\Pi, \Gamma \vdash \text{if}(\star) \text{ then } s_1 \text{ else } s_2 : \Gamma_1, b_1} \quad (5b)\ \frac{(s_1 \oplus s_2) = s_2 \quad \Pi, \Gamma \vdash s_2 : \Gamma_2}{\Pi, \Gamma \vdash \text{if}(\star) \text{ then } s_1 \text{ else } s_2 : \Gamma_2, b_2}$$

$$(6)\ \frac{\begin{array}{c}\Pi(f) = \lambda\alpha_1, \ldots, \alpha_n.\{s; \chi_f \leftarrow v\} \\ \Gamma(v_1) = c_1 \ \ldots \Gamma(v_n) = c_n \\ \Pi, [\alpha_1 \mapsto c_1, \ldots, \alpha_n \mapsto c_n] \vdash \{s; \chi_f \leftarrow v\} : \Gamma' \\ \Gamma'(\chi_f) = c\end{array}}{\Pi, \Gamma \vdash v \leftarrow^{\rho} f(v_1, \ldots, v_n) : \Gamma[v \mapsto c, \pi_\rho \mapsto c], \text{true}}$$

Fig. 3. Operational semantics

corresponding to sources and sinks are annotated. Hence, while library functions can propagate taint, they neither generate nor leak tainted values.

To focus on the novel ideas underlying our technique, our formal development intentionally omits pointers. Section 5 will explain how the proposed technique can reason about flows between objects in the heap.

2.1 Operational Semantics

To allow providing a soundness proof of our approach, Figure 3 presents a large-step operational semantics of the language from Figure 2. The operational semantics are described using judgments of the form $\Pi, \Gamma \vdash s : \Gamma', b$. Here, Π maps each function name to its definition, and the store Γ maps each variable to its value at run-time. A new store Γ' is obtained by executing statement s starting with store Γ, and the boolean value b indicates whether there is a failing check statement in s. Therefore, rules (4a) and (4b) for check(v) statements produce true or false depending on whether v is $\mathcal{S}$. In rules (5a) and (5b) for if statements, the notation $s_1 \oplus s_2$ non-deterministically chooses either s_1 or s_2.

Rule (6) in Figure 3 gives the semantics of calls to library methods. Since this language has call-by-value semantics, only the value of variable v can change in the client code as a result of the call $v \leftarrow^{\rho} f(v_1, \ldots, v_n)$. Specifically, since χ_f denotes function f's return value, v is assigned to c whenever χ_f evaluates to c. The variable π_ρ used in rule (6) is an instrumentation variable and is only introduced to facilitate the soundness proof of our abstract semantics.

Definition 1. *A concrete execution of a program P has a* source-sink error *if and only if P evaluates to false.*

2.2 Flows in Concrete Executions

Since our technique will infer flow specifications of library functions, we first formally define what we mean by a *flow* in a concrete execution. In this section, we represent a concrete execution of a program by a *trace* $\sigma = s_1, s_2, \ldots, s_n$

consisting of the sequential execution of *instructions* s_1 through s_n. Instructions can be assignments, check statements, function invocations, or function returns. We write call$^\rho$ $f(v_1, \ldots, v_n)$ to denote the invocation of function f with actuals $v_1, \ldots, v_n$ at a call site $v \leftarrow^\rho f(v_1, \ldots, v_n)$, and we write return$^\rho$ $f \mapsto v$ to indicate f's return and the assignment of its return value to variable v.

Given a trace $\sigma = s_1, s_2, \ldots, s_n$, we write s_i^+ and s_i^- to represent the control points *right after* and *right before* the execution of instruction s_i respectively. Observe that this implies $s_i^+ = s_{i+1}^-$. We can now define a *one-step flow* relation $\rightsquigarrow$ between variables u, v on a concrete execution σ:

Definition 2. *Let $\sigma = s_1, s_2, \ldots, s_n$ be an execution trace. We define the one-step flow relation $\rightsquigarrow$ to be the smallest relation satisfying the following conditions:*

- $(u, s_i^-) \rightsquigarrow (u, s_i^+)$ *if* $s_i \neq (u \leftarrow \ldots)$
- $(u, s_i^-) \rightsquigarrow (v, s_i^+)$ *if* $s_i = (v \leftarrow u)$

The first condition here states that $(u, s_i^-) \rightsquigarrow (u, s_i^+)$ if s_i does not reassign u. The second condition says that $(u, s_i^-) \rightsquigarrow (v, s_i^+)$ if instruction s_i is an assignment from u to v. Thus, intuitively, the one-step flow relation $(u, s_i^-) \rightsquigarrow (v, s_i^+)$ encodes whether the value of variable u flows to variable v in instruction s_i. Using the relation $\rightsquigarrow$, we now define a *multi-step flow relation* $\rightsquigarrow^*$ as follows:

Definition 3. *The multi-step flow relation $\rightsquigarrow^*$ is the smallest relation satisfying the following conditions:*

- $(u, s_i^-) \rightsquigarrow^* (v, s_j^+)$ *if* $(u, s_i^-) \rightsquigarrow (v, s_j^+)$
- $(u, s_i^-) \rightsquigarrow^* (w, s_k^+)$ *if* $(u, s_i^-) \rightsquigarrow^* (v, s_j^+)$ *and* $(v, s_{j+1}^-) \rightsquigarrow^* (w, s_k^+)$
- $(v_k, s_i^-) \rightsquigarrow^* (v, s_j^+)$ *if* $s_i = \text{call}^\rho f(v_1, \ldots v_n)$ *and* $s_j = \text{return}^\rho f \mapsto v$ *and* $(\alpha_k, s_{i+1}^-) \rightsquigarrow^* (\chi_f, s_{j-1}^+)$

If $(u, s_i^-) \rightsquigarrow^* (v, s_j^+)$, we say that u at s_i *flows to* v at s_j. The first two conditions in Definition 3 state that $\rightsquigarrow^*$ includes the transitive closure of $\rightsquigarrow$. The third condition deals with flows that are introduced due to calls to library functions. Specifically, consider a pair (s_i, s_j) of matching function call/return instructions where $s_i = \text{call}^\rho\ f(v_1, \ldots, v_n)$ and $s_j = \text{return}^\rho f \mapsto v$. Observe that the sub-trace given by $s_{i+1}, s_{i+2}, \ldots, s_{j-1}$ corresponds to the execution of f's body. According to the third rule of Definition 3, if the k'th argument of f flows to the return value of f between s_{i+1} and s_{j-1}, then the value of the actual v_k before instruction s_i also flows to variable v after instruction s_j.

Example 1. Consider the following trace σ:

$s_1 : u \leftarrow \mathcal{S}$	$s_2 : v \leftarrow u$	$s_3 : \text{call}^\rho f(v)$	$s_4 : x \leftarrow \alpha_1$
$s_5 : \chi_f \leftarrow x$	$s_6 : \text{return}^\rho f \mapsto w$	$s_7 : z \leftarrow w$	$s_8 : \text{check}(z)$

Here, $(\alpha_1, s_4^-) \rightsquigarrow^* (\chi_f, s_5^+)$ because f's first argument is transitively assigned to its return value. Due to the call between s_3 and s_6, $(v, s_3^-) \rightsquigarrow^* (w, s_6^+)$. Finally, since $(u, s_1^+) \rightsquigarrow^* (v, s_3^-)$ and $(w, s_6^+) \rightsquigarrow^* (z, s_8^-)$, we have $(u, s_1^+) \rightsquigarrow^* (z, s_8^-)$.

Since we will use flow specifications of library functions to determine the absence of source-sink errors, it is helpful to give the following alternate characterization of source-sink errors in terms of flows:

Proposition 1. *Trace* $\sigma = s_1, s_2, \ldots, s_n$ *has a source-sink error iff there exists some* $s_i, s_j \in \sigma$ *such that* $s_i : (u \leftarrow \mathcal{S})$ *and* $s_j : \text{check}(v)$ *and* $(u, s_i^+) \rightsquigarrow^* (v, s_j^-)$.

Example 2. The trace from Example 1 has a source-sink error because $(u, s_1^+) \rightsquigarrow^* (z, s_8^-)$ and s_1 is $u \leftarrow \mathcal{S}$ and s_8 is check(z).

3 Analysis and VC Generation

This section describe a static analysis for generating *verification conditions* that, if valid, imply the absence of source-sink errors. As mentioned earlier, the VCs generated by our analysis are parametrized over boolean *flow variables*, which soundly model the unknown effects of calls to library functions.

The VC generation procedure is described as inference rules shown in Figure 4. These rules use an environment Ω, which is the abstract counterpart of the concrete store Γ from the operational semantics. The abstract store Ω maps each program variable to a *guarded value set* θ, consisting of value, constraint pairs. Values $\mathcal{A}$ in the analysis include sources $\mathcal{S}$, constants $\mathcal{C}_1, \ldots, \mathcal{C}_n$, and special variables π which are used to model the unknown return values of library functions. If $(\mathcal{A}_i, \phi_i) \in \Omega(v)$, this means v may be equal to $\mathcal{A}_i$ if constraint ϕ_i is satisfied. *Constraints* ϕ are formed according to the following grammar:

$$\phi := \text{true} \mid \text{false} \mid \mathcal{A} \neq \mathcal{S} \mid f_i \mid \phi_1 \wedge \phi_2 \mid \phi_1 \vee \phi_2 \mid \phi_1 \Rightarrow \phi_2$$

Hence, constraints are boolean combinations of flow variables f_i and disequality constraints $\mathcal{A} \neq \mathcal{S}$. As expected, $(\mathcal{S} \neq \mathcal{S}) \equiv$ false and $(\mathcal{C}_i \neq \mathcal{S}) \equiv$ true for any $\mathcal{C}_i$. Given an interpretation σ mapping each flow variable to a boolean constant and each π variable to a constant $\mathcal{C}_i$ or $\mathcal{S}$, $\sigma(\phi)$ evaluates to true or false.

Figure 4 presents the analysis using judgments of the form $\Omega \vdash s : \Omega', \phi$. The meaning of this judgment is that, given an abstract store Ω, the analysis of statement s yields a new abstract store Ω' and a verification condition ϕ.

Rules (1) and (2) in Figure 4 describe the analysis of assignments and are straightforward analogues of the concrete semantics. For example, rule (2) for assignments $(v_1 \leftarrow v_2)$ says that if v_2 has guarded value set θ in Ω, then Ω' also maps v_1 to θ. For both rules, the resulting VC is just true since these statements do not contain sinks. Rule (3) for sequencing also closely parallels the concrete semantics. The resulting VC is $\phi_1 \wedge \phi_2$ because the VCs of both s_1 and s_2 must hold to ensure that the program is error-free.

Rule (4) generates the VC for check statements. In this rule, we first retrieve the guarded value set θ of variable v. For each pair, $(\mathcal{A}_i, \phi_i) \in \theta$, we must check that $\mathcal{A}_i$ is not equal to $\mathcal{S}$ under constraint ϕ_i, which is a necessary condition for v to have value $\mathcal{A}_i$. Thus, the generated verification condition is the conjunction of constraints $\phi_i \Rightarrow (\mathcal{A}_i \neq \mathcal{S})$ for each $(\mathcal{A}_i, \phi_i) \in \theta$.

Rule (5) describes the analysis of conditionals. Since the analysis must account for the possibility that either branch may execute, the resulting store Ω' is obtained by taking the *join* of Ω_1 and Ω_2:

$$(1)\ \frac{\Omega' = \Omega[v \mapsto (c, \text{true})]}{\Omega \vdash v \leftarrow c : \Omega', \text{true}} \qquad (2)\ \frac{\Omega(v_2) = \theta \ \ \Omega' = \Omega[v_1 \mapsto \theta]}{\Omega \vdash v_1 \leftarrow v_2 : \Omega', \text{true}}$$

$$(3)\ \frac{\begin{array}{c}\Omega \vdash s_1 : \Omega_1, \phi_1 \\ \Omega_1 \vdash s_2 : \Omega_2, \phi_2\end{array}}{\Omega \vdash s_1 ;^{\rho} s_2 : \Omega_2, \phi_1 \wedge \phi_2} \qquad (4)\ \frac{\begin{array}{c}\Omega(v) = \theta \\ \phi = \bigwedge_{(\mathcal{A}_i, \phi_i) \in \theta} \phi_i \Rightarrow (\mathcal{A}_i \neq \mathcal{S})\end{array}}{\Omega \vdash \text{check}(v) : \Omega, \phi}$$

$$(5)\ \frac{\begin{array}{c}\Omega \vdash s_1 : \Omega_1, \phi_1 \\ \Omega \vdash s_2 : \Omega_2, \phi_2\end{array}}{\Omega \vdash \text{if}(\star) \text{ then } s_1 \text{ else } s_2 : \Omega_1 \sqcup \Omega_2, \phi_1 \wedge \phi_2}$$

$$(6)\ \frac{\begin{array}{c}\theta_i = \{(\mathcal{A}_{ij}, \phi_{ij} \wedge f_i) \mid (\mathcal{A}_{ij}, \phi_{ij}) \in \Omega(v_i)\} \\ \theta = (\bigcup_{1 \le i < n} \theta_i) \cup (\pi_\rho, \pi_\rho \neq \mathcal{S})\end{array}}{\Omega \vdash v \leftarrow^{\rho} f(v_1, \ldots, v_n) : \Omega[v \mapsto \theta, \pi_\rho \mapsto (\pi_\rho, \text{true})], \text{true}}$$

Fig. 4. VC Generation rules

Definition 4. *Given two abstract stores Ω_1 and Ω_2, $\Omega_1 \sqcup \Omega_2$ is defined as follows:*

$$(\mathcal{A}, \phi) \in \Omega_1(v) \wedge (\mathcal{A}, \phi') \in \Omega_2(v) \Rightarrow (\mathcal{A}, \phi \vee \phi') \in (\Omega_1 \sqcup \Omega_2)(v)$$
$$(\mathcal{A}, \phi) \in \Omega_i(v) \wedge (\mathcal{A}, \_) \notin \Omega_j(v) \Rightarrow (\mathcal{A}, \phi) \in (\Omega_1 \sqcup \Omega_2)(v)$$

The VC we generate in rule (5) is $\phi_1 \wedge \phi_2$ because the VCs of both branches must hold to guarantee that any execution of the program is error-free.

The last rule (6) describes the analysis of calls to library methods. Since library methods do not contain sinks, the VC here is just true. The more interesting part of this rule is the computation of the new guarded value set θ. To account for the possibility that f's i'th argument may flow to its return value, we introduce a propositional flow variable f_i representing whether or not there is such a flow. Specifically, if $(\mathcal{A}_{ij}, \phi_{ij}) \in \Omega(v_i)$, then $(\mathcal{A}_{ij}, \phi_{ij} \wedge f_i) \in \Omega'(v_i)$, where Ω' is the abstract store after analyzing the function call. Now, in addition, to account for the possibility that f may return a fresh value, v's value set in Ω' also contains a variable π_ρ, which represents an unknown value produced in f. However, since sources are disallowed in library methods, the guard $\pi_\rho \neq \mathcal{S}$ for v in θ stipulates that π_ρ is not a source.

Example 3. Consider the following code snippet:

1. $x \leftarrow \mathcal{S};\ y \leftarrow \mathcal{C}_2;\ \text{if}(\star) \text{ then } z \leftarrow x \text{ else } z \leftarrow y;$
2. $a \leftarrow^1 f(z);\ b \leftarrow^2 g(y);\ c \leftarrow^3 f(x);$
3. $\text{if}(\star) \text{ then } d \leftarrow^4 m(a) \text{ else } d \leftarrow^5 h(b, c);$
4. $\text{check}(d)$

Here, after line 2, we have:

$$\begin{array}{lll} \Omega(x) = \{(\mathcal{S}, \text{true})\} & & \Omega(y) = \{(\mathcal{C}_2, \text{true})\} \\ \Omega(z) = \{(\mathcal{S}, \text{true}), (\mathcal{C}_2, \text{true})\} & & \Omega(a) = \{(\mathcal{S}, f_1), (\mathcal{C}_2, f_1), (\pi_1, \pi_1 \neq \mathcal{S})\} \\ \Omega(b) = \{(\mathcal{C}_2, g_1), (\pi_2, \pi_2 \neq \mathcal{S})\} & & \Omega(c) = \{(\mathcal{S}, f_1), (\pi_3, \pi_3 \neq \mathcal{S})\} \end{array}$$

Here, f_1, g_1 are flow variables indicating whether f and g's first arguments may flow to their return value. After analyzing the if statement at line 3, we have:

$$(\mathcal{S}, (f_1 \wedge m_1) \vee (f_1 \wedge h_2)) \in \Omega(d)$$

This means that d is tainted at line 4 under constraint $(f_1 \wedge m_1) \vee (f_1 \wedge h_2)$. Here, the first disjunct $(f_1 \wedge m_1)$ comes from the then branch of the if statement, while the second disjunct, $(f_1 \wedge h_2)$ comes from the else branch. Specifically, in the then branch, d is tainted if a is tainted and m's first argument flows to its return value. Since a is tainted under guard f_1, d is tainted under guard $f_1 \wedge m_1$ where m_1 is a flow variable for function m. Similarly, in the else branch, d is tainted if either (i) b is tainted and h's first argument flows to its return value, or (ii) c is tainted and h's second argument flows to its return value. Since $\mathcal{S}$ is not in the value set for b, it is not tainted, and the first condition is false. Since c is tainted under constraint f_1, the second condition is $f_1 \wedge h_2$. Thus, in the else branch, d is tainted under constraint $f_1 \wedge h_2$. Finally, when we take the join of the two value sets for d, we obtain that d is tainted under the guard $(f_1 \wedge m_1) \vee (f_1 \wedge h_2)$ after line 4. Finally, after analyzing the check statement at line 5, the (simplified) VC is given by $((f_1 \wedge m_1) \vee (f_1 \wedge h_2)) \Rightarrow \text{false}$.

4 Inference of Flow Specifications

Given a program P and its VC ϕ, our goal is now to infer a smallest set candidate flow specifications ψ such that ψ is sufficient to prove the validity of ϕ. At a technical level, we define flow specifications as follows:

Definition 5. *A flow specification for a library function f is an assignment from a flow variable f_i to a boolean constant.*

A flow specification for a function f is said to be *correct* if it assigns f_i to false only if there is no possible execution $\sigma = \{s_1, \ldots, s_n\}$ of f where $(\alpha_i, s_1^-) \rightsquigarrow^* (\chi_f, s_n^+)$. In the rest of this section, we assume there is an oracle which can confirm or refute the correctness of a candidate flow specification. This oracle may be a human who can consult the documentation of the library or some other sound analysis capable of analyzing the library code or binary. Since our goal is to minimize the number of queries to the oracle, we are interested in inferring a *minimal specification* sufficient for the verification task.

4.1 Computing Minimal Candidate Flow Specifications

We formulate the minimal specification inference problem in terms of abduction in logic. Specifically, given a VC ϕ for a source-sink problem, and a formula χ representing known flow specifications, we want to infer a formula ψ such that:

$$(1)\ \chi \wedge \psi \models \phi \quad (2)\ \text{SAT}(\chi \wedge \psi)$$

Here, (1) says the candidate specification ψ, together with known specifications χ, should be sufficient to discharge the VC ϕ, and (2) says the candidate specification ψ should not contradict known specifications χ, since such a solution

ψ cannot be correct. The inference of a formula ψ satisfying the above requirements is an abduction problem in logic. However, in addition to being a solution to the abduction problem, we require ψ to satisfy two additional requirements:

- First, since ψ represents a set of flow specifications, it should be a conjunction of literals, where each literal is either a flow variable f_i or its negation.
- Second, since we want a *minimal* specification, ψ should contain as few literals as possible. Since each literal in ψ corresponds to a query to the oracle, this minimizes the number of queries needed to verify the client.

Our insight is that we can compute a solution ψ satisfying these two requirements using *minimum-size prime implicants* (MPI) defined as follows:

Definition 6 (Minimum-size prime implicant). *A minimum-size prime implicant (MPI) of a boolean formula φ is a set S of literals such that $\bigwedge_{l_i \in S} l_i \models \varphi$ and for any other set S' such that $|S'| < |S|$, $\bigwedge_{l_i' \in S'} l_i' \not\models \varphi$.*

Practical algorithms for computing MPIs of boolean formulas have been studied, for example, in [5, 6]. To see how MPIs are useful for solving our abduction problem, observe that the first requirement $\chi \wedge \psi \models \phi$ can be written as $\psi \models \chi \Rightarrow \phi$. Since we want ψ to be a smallest conjunction of literals that implies $\chi \Rightarrow \phi$, a solution to the abduction problem is an MPI of $\chi \Rightarrow \phi$ that does not contradict χ. The algorithm given in [6] can be used to compute an MPI of $\chi \Rightarrow \phi$ consistent with χ, which yields the solution ψ to our abduction problem.

Example 4. Consider again the code from Example 3. Recall that we computed the VC for this program as $\phi : ((f_1 \wedge m_1) \vee (f_1 \wedge h_2)) \Rightarrow \text{false}$. Assuming $\chi = \text{true}$, an MPI for $\chi \Rightarrow \phi$ is $\neg f_1$. Hence, the program is free of source-sink errors if there is no flow from the first argument of f to its return value.

4.2 Computing Correct Minimal Flow Specifications

The solution ψ to the abduction problem from Section 4.1 yields a minimal candidate specification sufficient to verify the client. However, since ψ is effectively a speculation, it does not have to be correct. This section describes a refinement algorithm that interacts with the oracle until a correct specification is found. The FindSpec algorithm used for this purpose is shown in Figure 5. It takes as input the VC ϕ and returns a set of correct flow specifications that are sufficient to discharge the error. If no such specification exists, it returns false.

The idea behind FindSpec is the following: First, at line (3), it computes a set $I = \{l_1, \ldots, l_n\}$ of candidate flow specifications as discussed in Section 4.1 using minimum prime implicants. In the inner loop of FindSpec, we use an oracle to certify each flow specification $l_i \in I$. If the oracle can certify each $l_i \in I$, then we are done. However, if the oracle cannot validate some candidate specification $l_i \in I$, this means I may not be correct, and we therefore backtrack from this choice by breaking out of the inner loop (line 9). In each iteration of the outer while loop, we compute a new candidate specification I using abduction. To ensure that the current solution I is distinct from previous ones, we maintain a formula χ which represents previous answers given by the oracle. This formula

```
Procedure FindSpec
    input: verification condition φ
    output: inferred specification χ
    χ := true
    while true do
        I := MinPrimeImp(χ ⇒ φ, χ)
        if I = ∅ then return false
        proven := false
        for each l_i ∈ I
            proven := CertifiedByOracle(l_i)
            if proven then χ := χ ∧ l_i
            else (χ := χ ∧ ¬l_i; break)
        if proven then return χ
```

Fig. 5. Algorithm for finding correct flow specifications

χ is initially true, but becomes stronger after every query to the oracle: If the oracle certifies specification l_i, we conjoin l_i with χ; otherwise, we conjoin $\neg l_i$. This strategy ensures that we do not obtain inferences containing literal l_i in the future. This process continues until we either find a valid proof or conclude that the program cannot be verified relative to the oracle.

Theorem 1. *The FindSpec algorithm is guaranteed to terminate.*

Theorem 2. *If there exists a set of correct flow specifications sufficient to discharge ϕ, then FindSpec will not return false assuming completeness of the oracle.*

Example 5. Consider again the code from Example 3 and its corresponding VC $\phi : ((f_1 \wedge m_1) \vee (f_1 \wedge h_2)) \Rightarrow \text{false}$. FindSpec first computes an MPI of ϕ, which is $\neg f_1$ as discussed in Example 4. Thus, I starts out as $\{\neg f_1\}$. If the oracle certifies that f's first argument never flows to its return value, the program is verified. Otherwise, we conjoin f_1 with χ (true). In the next iteration, the solution to the abduction problem is $\{\neg m_1, \neg h_2\}$. Now, we ask the oracle to certify $\neg m_1$. If the oracle cannot do so, the algorithm terminates because m_1 is conjoined with χ, and there is no abductive solution consistent with $f_1 \wedge m_1$. If the oracle can certify m_1, the program can be verified iff the oracle can also certify $\neg h_2$.

5 Tracking Flows in the Heap

While the language used in the formalization did not allow pointers, our implementation targets Java, where method calls can introduce flows between any pair of heap objects reachable in the called method. Therefore, to soundly handle flows through the heap, we introduce one flow variable for any ordered pair of abstract memory locations (l_1, l_2) for which the value in l_2 may flow to l_1. That is, a flow variable f_{l_1,l_2} expresses that there is a flow in f from some concrete memory location represented by l_1 to a concrete location represented by l_2. Since

Java is type-safe, we consider a flow between two heap locations l_1 and l_2 feasible if the static type of l_1 is a subtype of that of l_2 or vice versa. If these types are class types and field declarations in the library are visible, we also consider their nested fields with their respective types. [1] As an example, consider the following Java code, where library definitions and client code are shown:

```
/* Library Definitions */
class Name { private String name; };
class Phone { private String phone; }
class Contact { private Name n; private Phone p; };

/* Client Code */
String str = TAINTED; Name n = new Name ("John Smith");
Phone p = new Phone(str); Contact c = new Contact(n, p);
Network.send(n);
```

Here, assume `TAINTED` is a secret value and `Network.send` is a sink. Since `p.phone` and `str` are type compatible, a boolean variable $Phone_{arg_0,ret.phone}$ expresses a possible flow from the first argument of the `Phone` constructor to the `phone` field of its return value. Similarly, since the `name` and `phone` fields of heap locations `p` and `n` are type compatible, the boolean variables $Contact_{arg_1.phone,arg_0.name}$ and $Contact_{arg_0.name,arg_1.phone}$ express potential flows from `p.phone` to `n.name` and vice versa. Therefore, for this example, our technique generates the VC: $\neg Contact_{arg_1.phone,arg_0.name} \vee \neg Phone_{arg_0,ret.phone}$.

6 Implementation

We have implemented a tool for tracking explicit information flow properties of Android smart phone applications. Android applications are developed in the Java programming language, but make extensive use of the Android software development kit (SDK). Since the Android SDK is many orders of magnitude larger than the typical client application and since it is written in a variety of languages besides Java, it is impractical to perform a precise static analysis of the framework code along with the application code. Therefore, our implementation uses the technique described in this paper to reason about calls to the Android framework when analyzing a given smart phone application.

While the language from Section 2 does not contain many of the standard features of Java, such as pointers and virtual method calls, our implementation handles the full Java language (except some uses of reflection). For reasoning about the heap, we use a flow- and context-sensitive pointer analysis that we introduced in our previous work (see [7]). Since our pointer analysis also does not analyze the Android framework code, we deal with calls to the Android framework methods as outlined in Section 5.

[1] If library declarations are not visible, we conservatively introduce a flow variable for any pair of locations (l_1, l_2) where l_2 is an instance of a library-defined class.

App	LOC	lib calls	possible flows	time	queries	$\frac{\text{queries}}{\text{possible}}$	SSF actual	SSF demonic
ContentProvider	342	26	27	0.9s	2	7.41%	1	3
ContactManager	1017	206	319	5.2s	2	0.63%	1	4
TUIOdroid	1612	437	646	16.4s	2	0.31%	1	24
eu.domob.angulo	1748	141	163	5.0s	1	0.61%	1	22
RemoteDroid	3781	505	680	33.9s	4	0.59%	3	48
tomdroid	10316	1515	2853	126.3s	4	0.14%	2	31
net.rocrail.android	13499	1940	3281	214.0s	4	0.12%	0	103
org.yaaic	18099	1517	2800	96.7s	9	0.32%	1	92
Average	6302	786	1346	62.3s	3.5	0.26%	1.25	40.9

Fig. 6. Experimental Results. The column labeled "SSF actual" shows the number of actual source-sink flows, while "SSF demonic" shows the number of source-sink flows reported when making conservative assumptions about library methods.

7 Experiments

We used the proposed technique for verifying confidentiality in Android applications. Specifically, we targeted explicit information flow properties where sources correspond to private user data and sinks are methods that send data. Since the proposed technique is not meant for inferring sources and sinks, we manually annotated a total of six different sources and sinks found in these applications. Sources include phone contacts, GPS location, call records, and IMEI number, while sinks include methods that send data over the network and methods for sending SMS messages.

In our experimental evaluation, we chose to focus on Android applications because they are programmed against the complex Android SDK library. While individual Android applications are typically a few thousand or ten thousand lines of code, the size of the entire Android library stack is several millions of lines of code, containing a mix of Java, C, and C++ code. Therefore, Android applications are good examples of software for which it is neither feasible nor desirable to analyze implementations of libraries in order to verify the client.

The eight applications we analyzed range from 342 to 18,099 lines of code and include an instant messaging client, a miniature train controller, an angle measurement software, two remote control programs, a note-taking software, and two small Android developer example applications. With the exception of the miniature train control (net.rocrail.android), all applications contain some source-sink flows. However, many of these flows are necessary for the application to perform its functionality and do not show malicious intent.

The first four columns in Figure 6 give details about the experimental benchmarks. As indicated by the column "lib calls", the number of calls to library methods range from 26 to 1940 calls per application. On average, there are 786 calls to unanalyzed library methods. The column labeled "possible flows" shows the total number of flows that could be introduced due to calls to library methods. On average, there are 1346 possible flows that could arise from library calls.

The next five columns in Figure 6 present analysis results. As shown in the column labeled "time", the analysis takes an average of 62.3 seconds for analyzing an average of 6302 lines of code. The next column labeled "queries" shows the number of queries made to the oracle. As shown in the "queries" column, the number of queries to the oracle range from one to nine, with an average of 3.5 queries across all benchmarks. In our experimental setup, all queries to the oracle were answered by one of the authors who consulted the documentation of the library methods in the Android SDK. Observe that the number of flow specifications that must be confirmed by the user is a very small percentage of the possible flows that could be introduced due to calls to library methods. The column labeled "queries/possible" shows the percentage of flow specifications that must be confirmed by the user relative to all possible flows that could be introduced due to library calls. As the table shows, this percentage is very small; on average, the user only needs to examine 0.26% of all the possible flows.

The next column labeled "SSF actual" in Figure 6 shows the number of source-sink flows identified by our analysis. On these benchmarks, our analysis identifies zero to three possible source-sink flows. We manually inspected all of these flows and found that none of them are spurious. We believe the absence of false positives indicates that the may-flow abstraction is sufficiently precise for summarizing the behavior of libraries for source-sink property verification.

Finally, the last column labeled "SSF demonic" shows the number of source-sink errors identified by the analysis when we make demonic (i.e., conservative) assumptions about flows that could be introduced due to library calls. As shown in Figure 6, there are an average of 40.9 source-sink flows identified by the analysis when we make conservative assumptions about library calls. On average, this is 33 times larger than the number of actual source-sink flows found in these applications and shows that making conservative assumptions about library method behavior results in a very high number of false alarms.

8 Related Work

Specification Inference. Existing work for specification inference [8–10, 4, 11–14] can be classified as static vs. dynamic and library-side vs. client-side. Our technique is client-side and static, but differs from previous work in several ways: First, our technique infers flow specifications for source-sink problems, which is not addressed by existing work. Second, our approach uses a novel form of VC generation and minimum prime implicants to identify the required specifications. Third, our goal is *not* to infer as many facts as possible about the library, but rather to identify exactly those specifications needed to verify a given client.

Specifications for Source-Sink Properties. Other work for specification inference, such as [4, 15], also target source-sink problems. In particular, Merlin [4] infers sources, sinks, and sanitizers for explicit information flow problems using probabilistic inference. We believe our proposed technique and [4] are complementary since we assume that sources and sinks are known, whereas [4] does not infer specifications of methods that propagate taint, but that are neither sources nor sinks. The recent work presented in [15] addresses taint analysis of framework-based web applications and gives a specification language for annotating taint-related framework behavior.

Other Source-Sink Checkers. Many techniques have been proposed for checking source-sink properties [16–19]. Many of these tools focus on taint analysis in the context of SQL injection attacks [20, 17, 16], where it is important to consider *sanitizers* in addition to sources and sinks. While we have not considered sanitizers in the technical development, our technique can be easily extended to infer flow specifications in the presence of sanitizers. However, we assume that sources, sinks, and sanitizers are known and infer specifications regarding *taint propagation* rather than taint introduction, removal, or consumption.

Use of Abduction in Static Analysis. Several other approaches have used abductive inference in the context of program verification [21–23]. Among these, [22] also uses abduction for inferring specifications of unknown procedures but differs from this work in several ways: First, here, our goal is to verify the absence of source-sink errors whereas [22] addresses verifying pointer safety. The second difference is that we consider an algorithmic approach to performing abduction in propositional logic whereas [22, 21] use a rule-based approach in separation logic. Third, while [22] generates a single abductive solution and fails if the candidate specification is wrong, our technique iteratively refines the candidate specification until the program is verified.

Our own previous work uses abductive inference for helping users diagnose warnings generated by static analysis [24]. However, that technique is not useful for inferring flow specifications because the generated constraints do not express possible input-output dependencies due to unknown method calls. Furthermore, the abduction algorithm used here is different: Here, we are interested in conjunctive propositional formulas over flow variables whereas [24] generates possibly disjunctive solutions of Presburger arithmetic formulas.

9 Conclusions and Future Work

We have presented a new technique for source-sink property verification of open programs that call unanalyzed library methods. We have applied the proposed technique to checking confidentiality in Android applications and show that our method can effectively identify the necessary specifications required for ruling out a large number of potential source-sink flows. A promising direction for future research is to combine the proposed technique with dynamic symbolic execution which can rule out many spurious must-not-flow assumptions inferred by our technique.

References

1. Henzinger, T.A., Jhala, R., Majumdar, R., Sutre, G.: Software verification with BLAST. In: Ball, T., Rajamani, S.K. (eds.) SPIN 2003. LNCS, vol. 2648, pp. 235–239. Springer, Heidelberg (2003)
2. Aiken, A., Bugrara, S., Dillig, I., Dillig, T., Hackett, B., Hawkins, P.: An overview of the saturn project. In: PASTE, pp. 43–48. ACM (2007)

3. Ball, T., Rajamani, S.: The SLAM project: debugging system software via static analysis. In: POPL, NY, USA, pp. 1–3 (2002)
4. Livshits, B., Nori, A.V., Rajamani, S.K., Banerjee, A.: Merlin: Specification inference for explicit information flow problems. In: PLDI (2009)
5. Silva, J.: On computing minimum size prime implicants. In: International Workshop on Logic Synthesis, Citeseer (1997)
6. Dillig, I., Dillig, T., McMillan, K.L., Aiken, A.: Minimum satisfying assignments for SMT. In: Madhusudan, P., Seshia, S.A. (eds.) CAV 2012. LNCS, vol. 7358, pp. 394–409. Springer, Heidelberg (2012)
7. Dillig, I., Dillig, T., Aiken, A., Sagiv, M.: Precise and compact modular procedure summaries for heap manipulating programs. In: PLDI 2011, pp. 567–577 (2011)
8. Nimmer, J.W., Ernst, M.D.: Automatic generation of program specifications. In: ISSTA, pp. 232–242 (2002)
9. Ammons, G., Bodík, R., Larus, J.R.: Mining specifications. In: POPL 2002, pp. 4–16 (2002)
10. Yang, J., Evans, D., Bhardwaj, D., Bhat, T., Das, M.: Perracotta: mining temporal api rules from imperfect traces. In: ICSE 2006, pp. 282–291 (2006)
11. Alur, R., Černý, P., Madhusudan, P., Nam, W.: Synthesis of interface specifications for java classes. In: POPL 2005, pp. 98–109 (2005)
12. Shoham, S., Yahav, E., Fink, S., Pistoia, M.: Static specification mining using automata-based abstractions. In: ISSTA 2007, pp. 174–184 (2007)
13. Beckman, N.E., Nori, A.V.: Probabilistic, modular and scalable inference of typestate specifications. In: PLDI, pp. 211–221. ACM (2011)
14. Ramanathan, M.K., Grama, A., Jagannathan, S.: Static specification inference using predicate mining. In: PLDI 2007, pp. 123–134 (2007)
15. Sridharan, M., Artzi, S., Pistoia, M., Guarnieri, S., Tripp, O., Berg, R.: F4F: taint analysis of framework-based web applications. In: OOPSLA 2011, pp. 1053–1068 (2011)
16. Tripp, O., Pistoia, M., Fink, S.J., Sridharan, M., Weisman, O.: Taj: effective taint analysis of web applications. In: PLDI 2009, pp. 87–97 (2009)
17. Livshits, V.B., Lam, M.S.: Finding security vulnerabilities in java applications with static analysis. In: USENIX Security Symposium, SSYM 2005, p. 18 (2005)
18. Enck, W., Gilbert, P., Chun, B.G., Cox, L.P., Jung, J., McDaniel, P., Sheth, A.N.: Taintdroid: an information-flow tracking system for realtime privacy monitoring on smartphones. In: OSDI 2010, pp. 1–6 (2010)
19. Clause, J., Li, W., Orso, A.: Dytan: a generic dynamic taint analysis framework. In: ISSTA 2007, pp. 196–206 (2007)
20. Wassermann, G., Su, Z.: Sound and precise analysis of web applications for injection vulnerabilities. In: PLDI, pp. 32–41. ACM (2007)
21. Calcagno, C., Distefano, D., O'Hearn, P., Yang, H.: Compositional shape analysis by means of bi-abduction. In: POPL, pp. 289–300 (2009)
22. Luo, C., Craciun, F., Qin, S., He, G., Chin, W.N.: Verifying pointer safety for programs with unknown calls. J. Symb. Comput. 45(11), 1163–1183 (2010)
23. Giacobazzi, R.: Abductive analysis of modular logic programs. In: International Symposium on Logic Programming, Citeseer, pp. 377–391 (1994)
24. Dillig, I., Dillig, T., Aiken, A.: Automated error diagnosis using abductive inference. In: PLDI (2012)

The Proof Assistant as an Integrated Development Environment

Nick Benton

Microsoft Research
nick@microsoft.com

Abstract. We discuss the potential of doing program development, code generation, application-specific modelling, and verification entirely within a proof assistant.

Managing the interaction between programming and proving creates challenging problems in the design of languages, logics and user interfaces. Almost independent from the deep research problems associated with designing reasoning methods for programs, it is not clear what a 'ideal' environment or tool-chain for producing verified software might even look like.

Many automated verification tools start with conventional languages, compilers and development environments, which are extended to allow Hoare-style assertions and invariants to be added as annotations, for example as structured comments. Assertions are verified behind the scenes, for example by an SMT solver, and failures reported by 'red squigglies' and textual error messages, just like conventional syntax and type errors. This comfortably familiar approach is minimally disruptive to development practices and can work very well, particularly for comparatively simple or specific properties. But there are limitations.

Firstly, when the automation fails (which is the common case), the programmer has to change the program, change the specification, or add further annotations as hints to the prover. Making such changes can be hard: the programmer is, at least morally, interacting with the prover to try to construct a proof, without any direct feedback of what the proof looks like and only one mechanism – stating new lemmas – to guide its construction. The alternative of generating verification conditions for residual obligations and shipping them to a proof assistant allows some interactivity, but often generates large, incomprehensible goals, with no clear link back to the original program. Accurately relating the annotation language, prover language, proof assistant language and, in the case of interesting properties, the semantics of the programming language is challenging. Even arranging to persist the VC proofs along with the program isn't entirely trival.

Secondly, the idea of just marking up a conventional program with a few well-chosen pre/postconditions and invariants and then pressing a magic button only gets one so far. There are simple syntactic limitations on what one can say if specification level constructs must align with programming language ones (e.g. insisting that each procedure has a single specification, or disallowing quantification scoped over more than one procedure). More fundamentally, to verify 'deep'

C.-c. Shan (Ed.): APLAS 2013, LNCS 8301, pp. 307–314, 2013.

functional correctness properties one needs a rich logic just to write the specifications. Really verifying a compiler, linear algebra library, crypto protocol or video decoder involves a model of the desired behaviour that can only be formally captured in a language that is powerful enough to express, essentially, arbitrary mathematics, especially if we want the specifications to be comprehensible and modular. The necessary reasoning about such models is not generally fully automatable, so some form of explicit representation of proofs seems unavoidable.[1] As the amount of text involved in defining the model, proving properties of it, writing specifications and establishing that they hold of the program (even with the help of some automation) can easily be at least as great as that associated with the actual program (and almost always takes at least as long to write), an environment's support for convenient proving is arguably more important than its support for programming.

An attractive alternative to Hoare-style verification is to write one's software in a dependently-typed language, such as Coq or Agda, in the first place. Dependent type theories do have the power to express the mathematically rich specifications one needs for full functional correctness (as well as a full range of simpler ones, of course). And dependently typed languages provide an elegant integration of programming and proving, such that programs can be said to be 'correct by construction' (even if achieving correctness requires a more elaborate construction). There are actually two slightly different styles of writing verified software in dependently-typed systems: one one can either use the full power of dependency to capture specifications directly in the types of functions, or write conventionally-typed programs about which one separately, though still all in the same system, proves correctness theorems. The latter style is common in Coq – e.g. for CompCert [12] – as there is good tactical support for proving, strongly-dependent programming is trickier than it should be, and because extraction of the computationally relevant parts of a program to OCaml for actual execution is thereby more straightforward.

Beautiful though it often is, programming directly in type theory comes with its own trade-offs. Firstly, one must program in a rather fundamentalist pure functional language, in which only provably total functions can be written. Such a language is not obviously the most natural choice for writing *all* the kinds of software component one might wish to verify. Secondly, compilation is typically via extraction/translation to a more conventional functional language, such as OCaml or Haskell. This is convenient both for reusing existing infrastructure (optimising compilation, runtime systems, etc.) and for interfacing verified and unverified code, for example to add impure IO and UI code to a verified algorithmic core. But if we insist on a very high level assurance (which we often don't), then we might have reservations about including a sophisticated

[1] For particular applications, such as cryptography, or forms of property, such as memory safety, one can usefully use an interactive prover to verify the metatheory associated with specialized automation, but in the general case it is impossible to insulate the developer of seriously verified software from thinking about proofs.

compiler, its runtime system and libraries in our trusted computing base.[2] And if the theorems we really want to prove make non-trivial statements about the IO behaviour of our program, that behaviour really needs to be brought within the scope of our formal reasoning.

An popular alternative approach is to use a proof assistant to reason about a program written in a conventional language, such as C or ML. Given a formalized semantics for the programming language and a representation of the program code as an object in the prover's internal language, one can prove program properties by many methods, including Hoare-style reasoning, with the soundness of the reasoning principles being formally justified in terms of the semantics of the specific language, which may be high or low level, pure or impure. Actual executable code is generated by running the textual version of the program through a conventional compiler. This approach is particularly appropriate for verifying low-level code and has been successfully used in many significant projects, such as the sel4 verification [9]. As with program extraction, an external compiler becomes part of the TCB, though in both cases that concern can be removed by a separate formal verification of the compiler itself.[3] The state of the art here is the Verified Software Toolchain [1], which builds provably sound separation logic reasoning (and other program analysis tools) for a version of C on top of the CompCert semantics and compiler.

As previously mentioned, interactive verification of programs written in standard programming languages has huge advantages. In many practical situations, it will, clearly, be the only kind of verification that is acceptable. And yet, as well as the potential weakening of the guarantees that are obtained if one does not also use a verified compiler, it is inherently a little clumsy. One's workflow involves tools to translate between the programming language syntax and that of whatever representation is chosen in the prover's language. Naive representation choices (of the sort that would mesh well with a compiler correctness proof and are much more acceptable in metatheoretic work) lead to theorems being proved about objects that are rather more unwieldy than the original source, such as abstract syntax trees with their own encoded representations of definitions, scope, etc. Even slightly more idiomatic translations (that, for example, map definitions in the language to definitions in the prover) make it trickier to verify formally the correctness of the workflow as a whole. There are numerous complexities, from differences in identifier naming rules, through dealing with preprocessors to linking, build scripts, code generation, and keeping the program and proof in sync.

Now, proof assistants are powerful tools, verification researchers are smart, and code is malleable stuff. Many ingenious strategies for reducing the pain

---

[2] And whilst the story about the relation between Coq semantics and OCaml semantics might be reasonably clear for whole programs, it seems less so for components, as the OCaml type system can't express the purity constraints assumed by Coq functions.

[3] Or alleviated by testing, though even that really ought to be strongly connected with the formalized semantics. One reason for verifying programs written in an existing language is to be able to use existing tools.

of impedence matching have been devised, including the circular verification of the F* typechecker [20] and Myreen et al.'s automatic extraction of HOL functions, together with correspondence proofs, from low-level programs [16,15]. But ultimately, a proof assistant like Coq is in many respects simply a better programming language than most conventional ones. Ideally, we'd like to keep the expressive structuring and integration between programming and proving that we get from programming in type theory and *also* have high assurance compilation down to the machine, the ability to do low-level programming, and effects, including general recursion.

Various projects have involved writing imperative (or other non-purely-functional) programs directly in a proof assistant. But this is often just to do examples for papers on metatheoretic work: a small program is coded up as a term in an AST type, or directly into some more semantic representation, and something interesting is proved about it, but it is not often suggested that this is a way of writing programs one would ever want to actually run. A notable exception is Ynot: an ML-like, higher-order, imperative language, with Hoare-style assertions in types [17]. Ynot is built as a library in Coq, from which it inherits structuring and proving mechanisms. The model of effectful programs is axiomatised rather than formally verified in Coq, and programs are run via extraction to OCaml, so Ynot may not quite achieve the highest level of assurance, but the programming model of 'type theory with effects' is an attractive one. Verified programs that have been written in Ynot include web services [21] and a simple database [13].

Over the last few years, Andrew Kennedy and I, together with a number of collaborators, have been investigating formally verified compilation and reasoning principles for low-level level languages. Like many others, we aim to verify systems-level code right down to the hardware and so, having done several bits of work involving very idealized assembly code and abstract machines, we embarked on constructing a Coq model of (a sequential subset of) x86 machine code. The model is foundational in style: starting from bits, bytes and words, on top of which we model the machine architecture, instruction encoding and decoding, and the operational semantics.

The scientifically 'deep' part of the project involves the design and semantics of a separation logic for unstructured machine code, supporting both first- and higher-order frame rules, a full range of intuitionistic connectives and a 'later' modality, all with good logical properties [7]. Along the way, however, we also discovered that Coq was not *such* a bad system for actually writing the programs we wanted to verify. Being based on type theory, Coq can do more than contemplate eternal verities: it can actually compute. We implemented an assembler in Coq which, thanks to user-defined notations (including custom binding forms), is syntactically compatible with existing assemblers. The assembler has been proved correct, but also actually runs inside Coq: we can extract a bootable binary image or a runnable .exe file from Coq, with no other external dependencies.[4]

[4] Well, apart from hex2bin and a small bootloader borrowed from Singularity.

Moreover, Coq's powerful abstraction mechanisms allow us to define conveniently parameterized higher-level programming constructs, including control structures and a variety of calling conventions, as macros. These macros also come with their own verified specifications, allowing one to move up the abstraction hierarchy in both programming and proving [8]. Chlipala's Bedrock system [5] takes a similar approach, allowing imperative programs to be written within Coq using very conventional-looking macro syntax that incorporates pre/post conditions and invariants and supports a very high degree of Coq automation for producing foundational proofs about the generated (machine-independent) low-level code.

One could keep going up until one had recreated most of the features of a general-purpose high-level language, but we are more excited about the prospect of producing verified code via much more explicit orchestration of staging and metaprogramming within the prover, combining general purpose programming abstractions with the use of embedded domain-specific languages; sharing pieces, but each with their own metatheory and code generation strategies. As a small example of the kind of thing we have in mind, we implemented a verified compiler for regular expressions that builds on an existing third-party formalization [4] of the theory of Kleene algebras – not merely at the specification level, but reusing a verified and computable function from regular languages to finite state machines as part of the compilation process.

Such an approach is not universally applicable, but for producing, say, a small, foundationally verified operating system kernel, the use of a conventional language seems eminently avoidable. Indeed, combining domain-specific compilers specialized to packet processing, scheduling, protocol definitions, event processing, policy checking, and so on, and able to describe those domains and their theory declaratively, using the full power of type theory, rather than indirectly through an implementation of some aspect of them in a general-purpose, low-level programming language, is very appealing. There is much talk about 'model-driven' software engineering, but it would be good to do it for real, using tools that can both actually build meaningful models and generate code that provably implements them. Mixing up different programming and specification paradigms might seem (or even be) a recipe for chaos, but the need to verify composed systems at least keeps us honest, and not only were we going to have to think carefully about the specifications of boundaries in any case, but those specifications provide guidance for designing the combination.

Even for unverified software, there is a trend towards integrating special purpose sub-languages into mainstream, general-purpose ones. $C\sharp$ has been extended with (amongst other things) asynchronous concurrency, reactive programming, database queries and parallelism. Trying to make such a range of features fit together into a single coherent language design is challenging, to say the least, and conventional type systems are often not up to the job of expressing domain-specific invariants (e.g. noninterference between parallel tasks). If we are going to verify multiparadigm programs, we do have to capture those invariants in our specification language, so perhaps that could take the place of, or augment, types at the programming stage too.

Furthermore, the potential performance advantages of metaprogramming and domain-specific code generation are considerable. Serious software (presumably the only kind on which one would spend the effort of verification) already often makes use of code generation techniques, from parser generators and template metaprogramming to the custom approach of, for example, FFTW. Composing code generators, rather than working with a monolithic compiler, would allow many optimizations (such as smoothly combining manual memory management and garbage collection), limited only by the effort one is willing to put into establishing their safety.

Of course, there are many obstacles, both large and enormous, to be overcome before the rather utopian vision of UNCOL-with-extra-maths [6] can be realized: Computation within Coq is comparatively slow, and naive definitions often don't compute at all. Despite much research, it is still hard to work comfortably with object languages with binding. Interfacing different styles of specification may prove impossibly hard. It's not really clear how to factor definitions to allow sharing of important optimizations like register allocation, or to get the right degree of machine-independence. We've given no thought to debugging or profiling. And so on. Nevertheless, for a restricted range of high-assurance verification tasks, multiparadigm code generation directly from a proof assistant is an exciting and promising research direction.

More broadly, programming languages have, in a sense, lost control of their environments. However good we are at compiling and verifying individual languages, modern software components increasingly live in a complex, heterogenous world, with rich interfaces to other components, libraries and services. Building genuinely trustworthy *systems* means that the scope of specification and verification has to extend beyond closed programs written in a single language. Modern proof assistants are simply the only tools we have in which *all* the artefacts in which we are interested (programs, languages, models, specifications, proofs, compilers . . .) can coexist and be formally related.

The research community is beginning to build up quite a collection of machine formalizations of important artefacts, including network protocols [3], machine architectures, languages, logics, and programming-related theory [2]. These are expensive to construct, and it is a shame that many are abandoned after a couple of papers. However, there are encouraging signs that reuse is not only possible, but is really happening: VST [1] builds on CompCert [12], Bedrock [5] on XCAP [18], and the CakeML compiler [11] on components also used in other projects, including a (tested) model of x86-64 [19,14] and (a translation of) a formalization of Parsing Expression Grammars [10]. As such formalizations mature, it should be possible to integrate them into the process of software development, rather than just post-hoc verification.

A mature high assurance development environment will probably look more like Visual Studio than an Emacs buffer with blue highlights. But the underlying technology that ties it all together should be logic and type theory.

Acknowledgements. My thanks go to Andrew Kennedy and to the other friends who've contributed and collaborated with us on many aspects of mechanized reasoning about software: Pierre-Evariste Dagand, Chris Hawblitzel, Chung-Kil Hur, Guilhem Jaber, Jonas Jensen, Neel Krishnaswami, Conor McBride, Georg Neis, Marco Paviotti, Valentin Robert, Nicolas Tabareau, Carsten Varming, Uri Zarfaty.

References

1. Appel, A.W., Dockins, R., Hobor, A., Beringer, L., Dodds, J., Stewart, G., Blazy, S., Leroy, X.: Program Logics for Certified Compilers. CUP (2014)
2. Benton, N., Kennedy, A., Varming, C.: Some domain theory and denotational semantics in Coq. In: Berghofer, S., Nipkow, T., Urban, C., Wenzel, M. (eds.) TPHOLs 2009. LNCS, vol. 5674, pp. 115–130. Springer, Heidelberg (2009)
3. Bishop, S., Fairbairn, M., Norrish, M., Sewell, P., Smith, M., Wansbrough, K.: TCP, UDP, and Sockets: Rigorous and experimentally-validated behavioural specification. volume 2: The specification. Technical Report 625, University of Cambridge Computer Laboratory (2005)
4. Braibant, T., Pous, D.: An efficient Coq tactic for deciding Kleene algebras. In: Kaufmann, M., Paulson, L.C. (eds.) ITP 2010. LNCS, vol. 6172, pp. 163–178. Springer, Heidelberg (2010)
5. Chlipala, A.: The Bedrock structured programming system: Combining generative metaprogramming and Hoare logic in an extensible program verifier. In: ACM International Conference on Functional Programming, ICFP (2013)
6. Conway, M.E.: Proposal for an UNCOL. Communications of the ACM 1(10), 5–8 (1958)
7. Jensen, J., Benton, N., Kennedy, A.: High-level separation logic for low-level code. In: ACM Symposium on Principles of Programming Languages, POPL (2013)
8. Kennedy, A., Benton, N., Jensen, J., Dagand, P.: Coq: The world's best macro assembler? In: International Symposium on Principles and Practice of Declarative Programming, PPDP (2013)
9. Klein, G., Elphinstone, K., Heiser, G., Andronick, J., Cock, D., Derrin, P., Elkaduwe, D., Engelhardt, K., Kolanski, R., Norrish, M., Sewell, T., Tuch, H., Winwood, S.: Sel4: Formal verification of an OS kernel. In: 22nd ACM Symposium on Operating Systems Principles, SOSP (2009)
10. Koprowski, A., Binsztok, H.: TRX: A formally verified parser interpreter. Logical Methods in Computer Science 7(2) (2011)
11. Kumar, R., Myreen, M.O., Owens, S.A., Norrish, M.: CakeML: A verified implementation of ML. In: ACM Symposium on Principles of Programming Languages, POPL (2014)
12. Leroy, X.: Formal verification of a realistic compiler. Communications of the ACM 52(7), 107–115 (2009)
13. Malecha, G., Morrisett, G., Shinnar, A., Wisnesky, R.: Toward a verified relational database management system. In: ACM Symposium on Principles of Programming Languages, POPL (2010)
14. Myreen, M.O.: Verified just-in-time compiler on x86. In: ACM Symposium on Principles of Programming Languages, POPL (2010)
15. Myreen, M.O., Gordon, M.J.C.: Function extraction. Science of Computer Programming (2010)

16. Myreen, M.O., Slind, K., Gordon, M.J.C.: Machine-code verification for multiple architectures - an application of decompilation into logic. In: Formal Methods in Computer-Aided Design, FMCAD (2008)
17. Nanevski, A., Morrisett, G., Shinnar, A., Govereau, P., Birkedal, L.: Ynot: Reasoning with the awkward squad. In: ACM International Conference on Functional Programming, ICFP (2008)
18. Ni, Z., Shao, Z.: Certified assembly programming with embedded code pointers. In: ACM Symposium on Principles of Programming Languages, POPL (2006)
19. Sarkar, S., Sewell, P., Zappa Nardelli, F., Owens, S., Ridge, T., Braibant, T., Myreen, M.O., Alglave, J.: The semantics of x86-cc multiprocessor machine code. In: ACM Symposium on Principles of Programming Languages, POPL (2009)
20. Strub, P.-Y., Swamy, N., Fournet, C., Chen, J.: Self-certification: Bootstrapping certified typecheckers in F* with Coq. In: ACM Symposium on Principles of Programming Languages, POPL (2012)
21. Wisnesky, R., Malecha, G., Morrisett, G.: Certified web services in Ynot. In: International Workshop on Automated Specification and Verification of Web Systems, WWV (2009)

Sorting and Searching by Distribution: From Generic Discrimination to Generic Tries

Fritz Henglein[1] and Ralf Hinze[2]

[1] Department of Computer Science, University of Copenhagen
henglein@diku.dk

[2] Department of Computer Science, University of Oxford
ralf.hinze@cs.ox.ac.uk

Abstract. A discriminator partitions values associated with keys into groups listed in ascending order. Discriminators can be defined generically by structural recursion on representations of ordering relations. Employing type-indexed families we demonstrate how tries with an optimal-time lookup function can be constructed generically in worst-case linear time. We provide generic implementations of comparison, sorting, discrimination and trie building functions and give equational proofs of correctness that highlight core relations between these algorithms.

1 Introduction

Sorting and searching are some of the most fundamental topics in computer science. In this paper we define *generic* functions for solving sorting and searching problems, based on *distributive*, that is "radix-sort-like", techniques rather than comparison-based techniques. The functions are indexed by representations of ordering relations on keys of type K. In each case the input is an association list of key-value pairs, and the values are treated as *satellite data*, that is, the functions are *parametric* in the value type V. Intuitively, this means values are pointers that are not dereferenced during execution of these functions [1]. We identify a hierarchy of operations:[1]

$$\begin{aligned} &sort :: Order\ k \to [k \times v] \to [v] \\ &discr :: Order\ k \to [k \times v] \to [[v]] \\ &trie :: Order\ k \to [k \times v] \to \mathsf{Trie}\ k\ [v] \end{aligned}$$

The *sorting function*, *sort*, outputs the value components according to the given order on K without, however, returning the key component. For example,

$\gg$ *sort* (*OList OChar*) [("ab", 1), ("ba", 2), ("abc", 3), ("ba", 4)]
[1, 3, 2, 4] ,

[1] Executable code is rendered in Haskell, which requires lower-case identifiers for type variables. We use the corresponding upper-case identifiers in the running text and in program calculations.

C.-c. Shan (Ed.): APLAS 2013, LNCS 8301, pp. 315–332, 2013.

where *OList OChar* denotes the standard lexicographic order on strings. We require that *sort* be stable in the sense that the relative order of values with equivalent keys is preserved. Discarding the keys may seem surprising and restrictive at first. Nothing is lost, however, since parametricity allows us to arrange it so that the keys are also returned. We simply associate the keys with themselves.

$\gg$ *sort* (*OList OChar*) [("ab", "ab"), ("ba", "ba"), ("abc", "abc"), ("ba", "ba")]
["ab", "abc", "ba", "ba"]

The *discriminator*, *discr*, outputs the value components grouped into runs of values associated with equivalent keys. For example,

$\gg$ *discr* (*OList OChar*) [("ab", 1), ("ba", 2), ("abc", 3), ("ba", 4)]
[[1], [3], [2, 4]] .

The *trie constructor*, *trie*, outputs a trie that can subsequently be efficiently searched for values associated to a particular key. The type of trie constructed depends on the type of the keys. For example,

$\gg$ **let** *t* = *trie* (*OList OChar*) [("ab", 1), ("ba", 2), ("abc", 3), ("ba", 4)]
$\gg$ *lookup t* "ba"
Just [2, 4] .

The function *discr* was introduced by Henglein [2,3] (originally called *sdisc*). It provides a framework for bootstrapping any base sorting algorithm for a *finite* type, such as bucket sort, to a large class of user-definable orders on first-order and recursive types. To this end it employs a strategy corresponding to most-significant-digit (MSD) in radix sorting.

The functions *sort* and *trie* are novel. Algorithmically, *sort* does the same as *discr*, but employing a least-significant-digit (LSD) strategy. Drawing on the informal correspondence of MSD radix sort with tries [4, p. 3], *trie* generalizes *discr* and generates the generalized tries introduced by Hinze [5]. It subsumes *discr* (which in turn subsumes *sort*) in the sense that it executes in the same time (usually linear in the size of the input keys), but additionally facilitates efficient search for values associated with any key.

In this paper we make the following novel contributions:

- We show that a function of type $[K \times V] \to [V]$ is a *stable sorting function* if and only if it is *strongly natural* in V, preserves singleton lists, and sorts lists of length 2 correctly. A function is strongly natural if it commutes with filtering, that is, the removal of elements from a list.
- We give new *generic* definitions of: *sort*, which generalizes least-significant-digit (LSD) radix sort to arbitrary types and orders definable by an expressive language of *order representations*; and *trie*, which generalizes *discr* to construct efficiently key-searchable tries. Both run in worst-case linear time for a large class of orders.
- We provide equational proofs for *sort o* being a stable sorting function and show that *sort o* = *concat* · *discr o* and *discr o* = *flatten* · *trie o* for all

inductively defined order representations *o*, where *concat* is list concatenation and *flatten* lists the values stored in a trie in ascending key order. The first equality is nontrivial as *discr* and *sort* have different underlying algorithmic strategies for product types: MSD versus LSD. The proof highlights the strong naturality properties of *sort* and *discr*.
- We offer preliminary benchmark results of our generic distributive sorting functions, which are surprisingly promising when compared to Haskell's built-in comparison-based sorting function.

The paper focuses on and highlights the core relations between these algorithms, notably the role of *strong naturality*. Here we limit ourselves to a restricted class of orders and leave asymptotic analysis, performance engineering, and a proper empirical performance analysis for future work. But certainly some benchmarks are not amiss to whet the appetite. The task is to sort the words of Project Gutenberg's The Bible, King James Version (5218802 characters, 824337 words). We compare Haskell's built-in *sortBy* called with Haskell's own *compare* and our generically defined comparison function *cmp o*, to generic sorting and generic discrimination, and to sorting via generic tries.

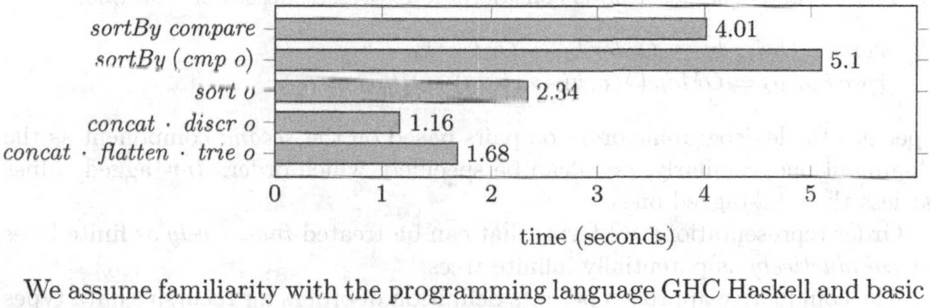

We assume familiarity with the programming language GHC Haskell and basic notions of category theory. Unless noted otherwise, we work in **Set**, the category of sets and total functions.

2 Order Representations

Comparison-based sorting and searching methods are attractive because they easily generalize to arbitrary orders: simply parameterize the program code for, say, Quicksort [6] over its comparison function, and apply it to a user-defined ordering $leq :: T \to T \to \mathbb{B}$. An analogous approach works for searching on T using, say, red-black trees [7,8]. While maximally expressive, specifying orders via such "black-box" binary comparisons, has two disadvantages:

1. Deliberately or erroneously, *leq* may not implement a total preorder.
2. Both sorting and searching are subject to lower bounds on their performance: sorting requires $\Omega(n \log n)$ comparisons, and searching for a key requires $\Omega(\log n)$, where n is the number of keys in the input.

However, theoretically and practically faster *distributive* methods are known for *certain* orders, notably radix sorting and tries.

As shown by Henglein [3], many orders can be denoted by *order representations*, constructors for building new orders from old:

$$
\begin{array}{l}
\textbf{data}\ \mathit{Order} :: * \to * \ \textbf{where} \\
\quad \mathit{OUnit} :: \mathit{Order}\,() \\
\quad \mathit{OSum} :: \mathit{Order}\ k_1 \to \mathit{Order}\ k_2 \to \mathit{Order}\,(k_1 + k_2) \\
\quad \mathit{OProd} :: \mathit{Order}\ k_1 \to \mathit{Order}\ k_2 \to \mathit{Order}\,(k_1 \times k_2) \\
\quad \mathit{OMap} :: (k_1 \to k_2) \to (\mathit{Order}\ k_2 \to \mathit{Order}\ k_1) \\
\quad \mathit{OChar} :: \mathit{Order}\ \mathit{Char} \quad \text{-- 7 bit ASCII}\ .
\end{array}
$$

Here *OUnit* denotes the trivial order on the unit type. *OSum* $o_1\ o_2$ represents the lexicographic order on tagged values such that *Inl*-tagged values are less than *Inr*-tagged values, and values with the same tag are ordered by o_1 or o_2, depending on the tag. *OProd* $o_1\ o_2$ denotes the lexicographic order on pairs, ordering pairs according to their first component, where pairs with equivalent first component are ordered according to their second component. *OMap f o* orders the domain of *f* according to the order *o* on its codomain. Note that *OMap* is contravariant. Finally, *OChar* denotes the standard order on 7-bit ASCII characters.

The *OMap*-constructor adds considerable expressiveness. For example,

$$
\begin{array}{l}
\mathit{rprod} :: \mathit{Order}\ k_1 \to \mathit{Order}\ k_2 \to \mathit{Order}\,(k_1 \times k_2) \\
\mathit{rprod}\ o_1\ o_2 = \mathit{OMap}\,(\lambda(a,b) \to (b,a))\,(\mathit{OProd}\ o_2\ o_1)
\end{array}
$$

specifies the lexicographic order on pairs based on the *second* component as the dominant one. Similarly, *rsum* can be specified, which orders *Inr*-tagged values as less than *Inl*-tagged ones.

Order representations are terms that can be treated *inductively* as finite trees or *coinductively* as potentially infinite trees.

The coinductive approach permits definition of orders for recursive data types by guarded recursion. For example,

$$
\begin{array}{l}
\mathit{olist} :: \mathit{Order}\ k \to \mathit{Order}\,[k] \\
\mathit{olist}\ o = \mathit{os}\ \textbf{where}\ \mathit{os} = \mathit{OMap}\ \mathit{out}\,(\mathit{OSum}\ \mathit{OUnit}\,(\mathit{OProd}\ o\ \mathit{os})) \\
\mathit{out} :: [a] \to () + a \times [a] \\
\mathit{out}\,[\,] \qquad\ = \mathit{Inl}\,() \\
\mathit{out}\,(a : \mathit{as}) = \mathit{Inr}\,(a, \mathit{as})
\end{array}
$$

defines the standard lexicographic order on lists, based on the element order *o*. Henglein [3] takes the coinductive approach with additional order constructors for inverse, multiset and set orders.

In the inductive approach we can add new constructors explicitly:

$$
\mathit{OList} :: \mathit{Order}\ k \to \mathit{Order}\,[k]
$$

or, more generally, employ an explicit fixed point operator [2].

The expressiveness of order representations is orthogonal to the aims of this paper. For simplicity we assume the inductive approach and concentrate on sums and products.

3 Generic Comparison

We require order representations to denote *total preorders.*

$$
\begin{array}{lll}
leq :: Order\ k \to (k \to k \to \mathbb{B}) & & \\
leq\ OUnit\ a\ b & = True & \\
leq\ (OSum\ o_1\ o_2)\ a\ b & = \mathbf{case}\ (a, b)\ \mathbf{of} & \\
 & \quad (Inl\ a_1, Inl\ a_2) \to leq\ o_1\ a_1\ a_2 & \\
 & \quad (Inl\ \_, \ Inr\ \_) \to True & \\
 & \quad (Inr\ \_, \ Inl\ \_) \to False & \\
 & \quad (Inr\ b_1, Inr\ b_2) \to leq\ o_2\ b_1\ b_2 & \\
leq\ (OProd\ o_1\ o_2)\ a\ b & = leq\ o_1\ (fst\ a)\ (fst\ b) \wedge & \\
 & \quad (leq\ o_1\ (fst\ b)\ (fst\ a) \Longrightarrow leq\ o_2\ (snd\ a)\ (snd\ b)) & \\
leq\ (OMap\ g\ o)\ a\ b & = leq\ o\ (g\ a)\ (g\ b) & \\
leq\ (OChar)\ a\ b & = a \leqslant b &
\end{array}
$$

leq o is indeed a total preorder; it is transitive and total, $leq\ o\ x\ y \vee leq\ o\ y\ x$. Because of totality the case for *OProd* can also be written as

$$
\begin{array}{l}
leq\ (OProd\ o_1\ o_2)\ a\ b = \mathbf{if}\ leq\ o_2\ (snd\ a)\ (snd\ b)\ \mathbf{then}\ leq\ o_1\ (fst\ a)\ (fst\ b) \\
\qquad\qquad\qquad\qquad\qquad\qquad\qquad\qquad\qquad \mathbf{else}\ \neg\,(leq\ o_1\ (fst\ b)\ (fst\ a))
\end{array}
$$

This variant is strict ($leq\ o_1$ and $leq\ o_2$ are called), but it calls $leq\ o_1$ only once. The first variant is lazy ($leq\ o_2$ is not necessarily called), but possibly calls $leq\ o_1$ twice.

The function *leq* implements a two-way comparison; a more useful function is $cmp :: Order\ k \to (k \to k \to Ordering)$, which implements a three-way comparison and avoids the double traversal in the product case.

4 Generic Distributive Sorting

Generic sorting takes a list of key-value pairs and returns the values in non-decreasing order of their associated keys. The keys are discarded in the course of this process. The idea is that, barring *OMap* in order representations, each component of each key is touched *exactly* once. Consequently, the running time of *sort* is proportional to the total size of the keys (again, ignoring *OMap*).

$$
\begin{array}{ll}
sort :: Order\ k \to [k \times v] \to [v] & \\
sort\ o & [\,] = [\,] \\
sort\ (OUnit) & rel = map\ val\ rel \\
sort\ (OSum\ o_1\ o_2) & rel = sort\ o_1\ (filter\ froml\ rel) +\!\!+ sort\ o_2\ (filter\ fromr\ rel) \\
sort\ (OProd\ o_1\ o_2) & rel = sort\ o_1\ (sort\ o_2\ (map\ curryr\ rel)) \\
sort\ (OMap\ g\ o) & rel = sort\ o\ (map\ (g \times id)\ rel) \\
sort\ (OChar) & rel = bucketSort\ (\texttt{'\textbackslash NUL'}, \texttt{'\textbackslash DEL'})\ rel
\end{array}
$$

Like generic comparison, *sort* is indexed by order representations. It is furthermore parametric in the type of values. Let us discuss each case in turn.

The first equation is vital for the coinductive approach to recursive types. It is necessary to ensure that for each recursive invocation of *sort* the total size of the keys is strictly decreasing.

For the unit type there is little to do: we simply discard the keys using *val* defined $val\,(k, v) = v$.

The case for sums takes an approach à la Quicksort: the input list is partitioned into a list whose keys are of the form $Inl\ k_1$ and a second list whose keys are of the form $Inr\ k_2$. The constructors are discarded, the sub-lists are sorted recursively using the appropriate orders, and the final results are concatenated. (As an aside, in the partitioning phase we touch the keys actually twice, but this is easily avoided by combining the two sweeps into a single one.) The function $filter :: (a \to \mathsf{Maybe}\ b) \to ([a] \to [b])$, called *mapMaybe* elsewhere, combines mapping and filtering: if the argument function returns a value of the form *Just b*, then *b* is included in the output list. If the result is *Nothing*, well, nothing is added. (Don't confuse our *filter* with Haskell's $filter :: (a \to \mathbb{B}) \to ([a] \to [a])$).

$$filter :: (a \to \mathsf{Maybe}\ b) \to ([a] \to [b])$$
$$filter\ p\ xs = [y \mid x \leftarrow xs, Just\ y \leftarrow [p\ x]]$$

The function $froml :: (k_1 + k_2 \times v) \to \mathsf{Maybe}\ (k_1 \times v)$ maps $(Inl\ k_1, v)$ to $Just\ (k_1, v)$, and $(Inr\ k_2, v)$ to *Nothing*. The function *fromr* is defined analogously.

The most interesting case is the one for products. The natural isomorphism $curryr : (K_1 \times K_2) \times V \cong K_2 \times (K_1 \times V)$ shifts the *more significant* part of the key into the value component. Then *sort* is called twice: the first invocation sorts according to o_2 discarding the K_2 part, the second sorts according to o_1 discarding the K_1 component. For this to be correct, $sort\ o_1$ had better be stable; we shall return to this point below. Furthermore, *sort* relies on *polymorphic recursion*: the first call to *sort* instantiates V to $K_1 \times V$.

For *OMap* we simply apply the key transformation using $map\ (g \times id)$ and then sort the transformed keys-value pairs.

Characters are sorted using bucket sort, which can be seen as a specialization of *sort* (actually of *discr* introduced in Section 5) for enumeration types.

$$bucketSort :: (Bounded\ i, Ix\ i) \Rightarrow (i, i) \to [(i, v)] \to [v]$$
$$bucketSort\ bs\ rel = concat\ (elems\ (accumArray\ (\lambda ws\ w \to ws +\!\!+ [w])\ [\,]\ bs\ rel))$$

(Here $+\!\!+$ is used for clarity; in our implementation it is replaced by a constant-time operation.) Any other algorithm for sorting characters or, for that matter, other primitive types could be used. The particular algorithm invoked can even be made *data dependent*; for small *rel* we might choose insertion sort instead of bucket sort to avoid sparse bucket table traversals. The key point is that *sort* reduces a sorting problem to basic sorting on finite domains. Conversely, it extends distributive sorting from their restricted domains such as small integers and character strings to arbitrary orders definable by order representations.

Let us now turn to the correctness of *sort*. Its implementation builds upon standard components, except perhaps the case for sums, which relies on the function *filter*. Note that *filter* takes a partial function as an argument, represented by a total function of type $A \to \mathsf{Maybe}\ B$, an arrow in the Kleisli category induced by the monad Maybe. For the proofs it will be convenient to actually work in this Kleisli category (but only for the arguments of *filter*). In the calculations, we signal these steps by the hint "Kleisli:". A few remarks are in order.

Working in the Kleisli category has the advantage that the notation is fairly light-weight: we write *id* rather than η, and we write $p \cdot q$ for the Kleisli composition of p and q rather than $\mu \cdot \mathsf{Maybe}\ p \cdot q$. We also silently embed total functions into the Kleisli category: *filter f* really means $\mathit{filter}\ (\eta \cdot f)$. In any case, there is little room for confusion since we let $f, g \ldots$ range over total functions and p, q over partial functions. The product $\times$ can be lifted to a binary functor $\otimes$ over the Kleisli category, which is, however, not a categorical product. Rather, $\otimes$ is a so-called tensor product, a binary functor which is coherently associative and commutative. We overload $\times$ to denote both the product in the underlying category and the tensor product.

A partial function that we will use time and again is inl°, the left-inverse of *inl*. The partial function *froml* can be neatly expressed in terms of inl°: we have $\mathit{froml} = \mathit{inl}^{\circ} \otimes \mathit{id}$, or just $\mathit{inl}^{\circ} \times \mathit{id}$. Likewise, $\mathit{fromr} = \mathit{inr}^{\circ} \otimes \mathit{id}$.

The function *filter* satisfies a variety of properties. First and foremost, it is a monoid homomorphism:

$$\mathit{filter}\ p\ [\,] = [\,] \ , \tag{4.1a}$$

$$\mathit{filter}\ p\ (\mathit{xs} \mathbin{+\!\!+} \mathit{ys}) = \mathit{filter}\ p\ \mathit{xs} \mathbin{+\!\!+} \mathit{filter}\ p\ \mathit{ys} \ . \tag{4.1b}$$

Furthermore, *filter* is functorial, taking Kleisli arrows to arrows in the underlying category. Formally, *filter* is the arrow part of the functor $\mathsf{Filter} : \mathbf{Kleisli} \to \mathbf{Set}$, whose object part is defined $\mathsf{Filter}\ A = \mathsf{List}\ A$. In other words, *filter* preserves identity and composition.

$$\mathit{filter}\ \mathit{id} = \mathit{id} \tag{4.2a}$$

$$\mathit{filter}\ (p \cdot q) = \mathit{filter}\ p \cdot \mathit{filter}\ q \tag{4.2b}$$

Moreover, if its first argument is a total function, then *filter f* is just List *f*.

Most of the following proofs will be conducted in a point-free style. For reference, here is a suitably reworked version of *sort*.

$$\begin{aligned}
&\mathit{sort}\ (\mathit{OUnit}) &&= \mathsf{List}\ \mathit{val}\\
&\mathit{sort}\ (\mathit{OSum}\ o_1\ o_2) &&= \mathit{sort}\ o_1 \cdot \mathit{filter}\ (\mathit{inl}^{\circ} \times \mathit{id}) \mathbin{+\!\!+} \mathit{sort}\ o_2 \cdot \mathit{filter}\ (\mathit{inr}^{\circ} \times \mathit{id})\\
&\mathit{sort}\ (\mathit{OProd}\ o_1\ o_2) &&= \mathit{sort}\ o_1 \cdot \mathit{sort}\ o_2 \cdot \mathsf{List}\ \mathit{curryr}
\end{aligned}$$

The sum case uses a lifted variant of append, $(f \mathbin{+\!\!+} g)\ x = f\ x \mathbin{+\!\!+} g\ x$, overloading the operator $\mathbin{+\!\!+}$ to denote both the lifted and the unlifted version.

4.1 Naturality

A vital property of *sort o* is that it is natural in the type of values, $\mathit{sort}\ o : \mathsf{List} \circ (K \times) \dot{\to} \mathsf{List}$, that is

$$\mathsf{List}\ f \cdot \mathit{sort}\ o = \mathit{sort}\ o \cdot \mathsf{List}\ (\mathit{id} \times f) \ , \tag{4.3}$$

for all $f : A \to B$.

Because of naturality it is sufficient to show that the instance $sort\ o : [K \times \mathbb{N}] \to [\mathbb{N}]$ works correctly. (Recall that values can be seen as pointers; natural numbers are like unique pointers.) Formally, $sort\ o$ is fully determined by this instance:

$$\begin{aligned} & sort\ o\ [(k_1, v_1), \ldots, (k_n, v_n)] \\ = \ & \{ \text{ let } ix : \mathbb{N} \to V \text{ be an indexing function so that } ix\ i = k_i \ \} \\ & sort\ o\ (\mathsf{List}\ (id \times ix)\ [(k_1, 1), \ldots, (k_n, n)]) \\ = \ & \{ \ sort \text{ is natural (4.3) } \} \\ & \mathsf{List}\ ix\ (sort\ o\ [(k_1, 1), \ldots, (k_n, n)]) \ . \end{aligned}$$

In the last equation $sort\ o$ is used at instance $\mathbb{N}$.

Of course, the statement that $sort\ o$ is natural requires proof. Actually, $sort$ satisfies a much stronger property, which we discuss next.

4.2 Strong Naturality

Property (4.3) remains valid if we replace List by *filter*:

$$filter\ p \cdot sort\ o = sort\ o \cdot filter\ (id \times p) \ , \qquad (4.4)$$

for all $p : A \to \mathsf{Maybe}\ B$. It does not matter whether we filter before or after an invocation of $sort\ o$, as long as *filter* only refers to the values, and not the keys.

Now, since *filter* is the arrow part of a functor between the Kleisli category of Maybe and the underlying category, (4.4) also amounts to a naturality property, $sort\ o : \mathsf{Filter} \circ (K \otimes\ ) \dot{\to} \mathsf{Filter}$. A simple consequence of what we call strong naturality (4.4) is that *sort* preserves the empty list.

Turning to the proof of (4.4), we proceed by induction over the structure of order representations.

Case $o = OUnit$:

$$\begin{aligned} & filter\ p \cdot sort\ OUnit \\ = \ & \{ \text{ definition of } sort \ \} \\ & filter\ p \cdot \mathsf{List}\ val \\ = \ & \{ \text{ Kleisli: } p \cdot val = val \cdot (id \times p) \ \} \\ & \mathsf{List}\ val \cdot filter\ (id \times p) \\ = \ & \{ \text{ definition of } sort \ \} \\ & sort\ OUnit \cdot filter\ (id \times p) \end{aligned}$$

Recall that $\times$ aka $\otimes$ is *not* a categorical product in the Kleisli category, we have $val \cdot (id \times p) = p \cdot val$, but *not* $key \cdot (id \times p) = id \cdot key$ where $key\ (k, v) = k$.

Case $o = OSum\ o_1\ o_2$: the central step is the fourth one, where we swap two filters, one that acts on the keys and a second that acts on the values.

$$\begin{aligned} & filter\ p \cdot sort\ (OSum\ o_1\ o_2) \\ = \ & \{ \text{ definition of } sort \ \} \\ & filter\ p \cdot (sort\ o_1 \cdot filter\ (inl^{\circ} \times id) +\!\!+ \ldots) \\ = \ & \{ \ filter \text{ is a monoid homomorphism (4.1b) } \} \\ & filter\ p \cdot sort\ o_1 \cdot filter\ (inl^{\circ} \times id) +\!\!+ \ldots \\ = \ & \{ \text{ ex hypothesi } \} \end{aligned}$$

$$\begin{aligned}
& \mathit{sort}\ o_1 \cdot \mathit{filter}\,((\mathit{id}+\mathit{id}) \times p) \cdot \mathit{filter}\,(\mathit{inl}^{\circ} \times \mathit{id}) +\!\!+ \ldots \\
=\; & \{\ \text{Kleisli: } \times \text{ is a binary functor}\ \} \\
& \mathit{sort}\ o_1 \cdot \mathit{filter}\,(\mathit{inl}^{\circ} \times \mathit{id}) \cdot \mathit{filter}\,((\mathit{id}+\mathit{id}) \times p) +\!\!+ \ldots \\
=\; & \{\ \text{fusion: } f \cdot h +\!\!+ g \cdot h = (f +\!\!+ g) \cdot h\ \} \\
& (\mathit{sort}\ o_1 \cdot \mathit{filter}\,(\mathit{inl}^{\circ} \times \mathit{id}) +\!\!+ \ldots) \cdot \mathit{filter}\,((\mathit{id}+\mathit{id}) \times p) \\
=\; & \{\ \text{definition of } \mathit{sort}\ \} \\
& \mathit{sort}\,(\mathit{OSum}\ o_1\ o_2) \cdot \mathit{filter}\,((\mathit{id}+\mathit{id}) \times p)
\end{aligned}$$

Note that the lifting of $+$ is a categorical coproduct in the Kleisli category.

Case $o = \mathit{OProd}\ o_1\ o_2$: note that Property (4.4) is universally quantified over all p. This is essential as *sort* relies on polymorphic recursion: the second use of the induction hypothesis $(*)$ instantiates p to $\mathit{id} \times p$.

$$\begin{aligned}
& \mathit{filter}\ p \cdot \mathit{sort}\,(\mathit{OProd}\ o_1\ o_2) \\
=\; & \{\ \text{definition of } \mathit{sort}\ \} \\
& \mathit{filter}\ p \cdot \mathit{sort}\ o_1 \cdot \mathit{sort}\ o_2 \cdot \mathsf{List}\ \mathit{curryr} \\
=\; & \{\ \text{ex hypothesi}\ \} \\
& \mathit{sort}\ o_1 \cdot \mathit{filter}\,(\mathit{id} \times p) \cdot \mathit{sort}\ o_2 \cdot \mathsf{List}\ \mathit{curryr} \\
=\; & \{\ \text{ex hypothesi } (*)\ \} \\
& \mathit{sort}\ o_1 \cdot \mathit{sort}\ o_2 \cdot \mathit{filter}\,(\mathit{id} \times (\mathit{id} \times p)) \cdot \mathsf{List}\ \mathit{curryr} \\
=\; & \{\ \text{Kleisli: } (q \times (p \times r)) \cdot \mathit{curryr} = \mathit{curryr} \cdot ((p \times q) \times r)\ \} \\
& \mathit{sort}\ o_1 \cdot \mathit{sort}\ o_2 \cdot \mathsf{List}\ \mathit{curryr} \cdot \mathit{filter}\,((\mathit{id} \times \mathit{id}) \times p) \\
=\; & \{\ \text{definition of } \mathit{sort}\ \} \\
& \mathit{sort}\,(\mathit{OProd}\ o_1\ o_2) \cdot \mathit{filter}\,((\mathit{id} \times \mathit{id}) \times p)
\end{aligned}$$

The natural isomorphisms $\mathit{val}{:}1 \times K \cong K$ and $\mathit{curryr}{:}(K_1 \times K_2) \times V \cong K_2 \times (K_1 \times V)$ are also natural isomorphisms in the Kleisli category.

4.3 Correctness: Permutation

Our first goal is to show that *sort o* produces a permutation of the input values. Perhaps surprisingly, it suffices to show that *sort o* permutes one-element lists! We already know that it is sufficient to show the correctness of a particular instance: $\mathit{sort}\ o\ [(k_1,1),\ldots,(k_n,n)]$. Now, let $\wr i \int$ be the partial function that maps i to i and is undefined otherwise. Let $1 \leqslant i \leqslant n$, then

$$\begin{aligned}
& \mathit{filter}\ \wr i \int\ (\mathit{sort}\ o\ [(k_1,1),\ldots,(k_n,n)]) \\
=\; & \{\ \mathit{sort} \text{ is strongly natural (4.4)}\ \} \\
& \mathit{sort}\ o\ (\mathit{filter}\,(\mathit{id} \times \wr i \int)\ [(k_1,1),\ldots,(k_n,n)]) \\
=\; & \{\ \mathit{filter}\,(\mathit{id} \times \wr i \int)\ [(k_1,1),\ldots,(k_n,n)] = [(k_i,i)]\ \} \\
& \mathit{sort}\ o\ [(k_i,i)] \\
=\; & \{\ \textit{proof obligation: sort} \text{ permutes 1-element lists (4.5)}\ \} \\
& [i]\ .
\end{aligned}$$

Thus, *sort o* outputs each index exactly once; in other words, it permutes the input list. The proof obligation (recall that $\mathit{return}\ a = [a]$)

$$\mathit{sort}\ o \cdot \mathit{return} = \mathit{return} \cdot \mathit{val} \tag{4.5}$$

is easy to discharge and left as an instructive exercise to the reader.

4.4 Correctness: Ordered

Our second task is to show that the values are output in non-decreasing order of their associated keys. We aim to show

$$sort\ o\ [\ldots,(k_i,i),\ldots,(k_j,j),\ldots] = [\ldots,i,\ldots,j,\ldots] \iff leq\ o\ k_i\ k_j\ .$$

Due to strong naturality, it suffices to show that *sort o* works correctly on two-element lists! Let $\wr i,j \int$ be the partial function that maps i to i and j to j and is undefined otherwise. Let $1 \leqslant i,j \leqslant n$, then

$$\begin{aligned}
& \mathit{filter}\ \wr i,j\int\ (\mathit{sort}\ o\ [(k_1,1),\ldots,(k_n,n)]) = [i,j] \\
\iff & \{\ \mathit{sort} \text{ is strongly natural (4.4)}\ \} \\
& \mathit{sort}\ o\ (\mathit{filter}\ (\mathit{id} \times \wr i,j\int)\ [(k_1,1),\ldots,(k_n,n)]) = [i,j] \\
\iff & \{\ \mathit{filter}\ (\mathit{id} \times \wr i,j\int)\ [(k_1,1),\ldots,(k_n,n)] = [(k_i,i),(k_j,j)]\ \} \\
& \mathit{sort}\ o\ [(k_i,i),(k_j,j)] = [i,j] \\
\iff & \{\ \textit{proof obligation: sort} \text{ sorts 2-element lists (4.6)}\ \} \\
& \mathit{leq}\ o\ k_i\ k_j\ .
\end{aligned}$$

Thus, *sort o* outputs i before j if and only if $leq\ o\ k_i\ k_j$. Since we already know that *sort o* permutes its input, this implies the correctness of *sort o*.

It remains to show that *sort* treats 2-element lists correctly: let $i \not\equiv j$, then

$$sort\ o\ [(a,i),(b,j)] = [i,j] \iff leq\ o\ a\ b\ . \tag{4.6}$$

Since only a small finite number of cases have to be considered, this is a simple exercise, which we relegate to Appendix A.

5 Generic Discrimination

A discriminator returns a list of non-empty lists of values, where the inner lists group values whose keys are equivalent. Again, the keys are discarded in the process, but, barring *OMap* in order representations, this time each component of each key is touched *at most* once.

```
discr :: Order k → [k × v] → [[v]]
discr o                  []       = []
discr o                  [(k, v)] = [[v]]
discr OUnit              rel      = [map val rel]
discr (OSum o1 o2)       rel      = discr o1 (filter froml rel) ++ discr o2 (filter fromr rel)
discr (OProd o1 o2)      rel      = concat (map (discr o2) (discr o1 (map curryl rel)))
discr (OMap g o)         rel      = discr o (map (g × id) rel)
discr (OChar)            rel      = bucketDiscr ('\NUL', '\DEL') rel
```

In the unit case we have identified a group of key-value pairs whose keys are equivalent, even identical. This group is returned as a singleton list. The sum case is the same as for *sort*. The most interesting case is again the one for products.

The natural isomorphism *curryl*: $(K_1 \times K_2) \times V \cong K_1 \times (K_2 \times V)$ also known as *assoc* shifts the *least significant* part of the key into the value component. The resulting list is discriminated according to o_1, each of the resulting groups is discriminated according to o_2, and finally the nested groups are flattened. The definition of *discr* has an additional base case for the singleton list. This may improve the performance dramatically since the key component in the argument need not be traversed. For lexicographic string sorting this specializes to the property of MSD radix sort, which only traverses the *minimum distinguishing prefixes* of the strings, which may be substantially fewer characters than their total number. Finally, characters are sorted using bucket sort—this time we simply return the list of *non-empty* buckets.

$$\begin{aligned}
&\mathit{bucketDiscr} :: (\mathit{Bounded}\ i, \mathit{Ix}\ i) \Rightarrow (i, i) \to [i \times v] \to [[v]] \\
&\mathit{bucketDiscr}\ \mathit{bs}\ \mathit{rel} \\
&\quad = [\mathit{xs} \mid \mathit{xs} \leftarrow \mathit{elems}\ (\mathit{accumArray}\ (\lambda \mathit{ws}\ w \to \mathit{ws} +\!\!+ [w])\ []\ \mathit{bs}\ \mathit{rel}), \neg\ (\mathit{null}\ \mathit{xs})]
\end{aligned}$$

As for *sort*, any other base type discriminator could be plugged in.

5.1 Correctness

If we concatenate the groups returned by a generic discriminator, we obtain generic sorting.

$$\mathit{concat} \cdot \mathit{discr}\ o = \mathit{sort}\ o \tag{5.1}$$

The proof is straightforward for units and sums, the interesting case is again the one for products. For products discrimination works from left to right, whereas sorting proceeds right to left. This means we have to be able to swap operations:

$$\begin{aligned}
&\mathit{concat} \cdot \mathit{discr}\ (\mathit{OProd}\ o_1\ o_2) \\
= &\quad \{\ \text{definition of } \mathit{discr}\ \} \\
&\mathit{concat} \cdot \mathit{concat} \cdot \mathsf{List}\ (\mathit{discr}\ o_2) \cdot \mathit{discr}\ o_1 \cdot \mathsf{List}\ \mathit{curryl} \\
= &\quad \{\ \text{monad law}\ \} \\
&\mathit{concat} \cdot \mathsf{List}\ \mathit{concat} \cdot \mathsf{List}\ (\mathit{discr}\ o_2) \cdot \mathit{discr}\ o_1 \cdot \mathsf{List}\ \mathit{curryl} \\
= &\quad \{\ \text{ex hypothesi}\ \} \\
&\mathit{concat} \cdot \mathsf{List}\ (\mathit{sort}\ o_2) \cdot \mathit{discr}\ o_1 \cdot \mathsf{List}\ \mathit{curryl} \\
= &\quad \{\ \textit{proof obligation:}\ \text{see below}\ \} \\
&\mathit{concat} \cdot \mathit{discr}\ o_1 \cdot \mathit{sort}\ o_2 \cdot \mathsf{List}\ \mathit{curryr} \\
= &\quad \{\ \text{ex hypothesi}\ \} \\
&\mathit{sort}\ o_1 \cdot \mathit{sort}\ o_2 \cdot \mathsf{List}\ \mathit{curryr} \\
= &\quad \{\ \text{definition of } \mathit{sort}\ \} \\
&\mathit{sort}\ (\mathit{OProd}\ o_1\ o_2)\ .
\end{aligned}$$

The property used in the central step, being able to swap *sort* o_2 and *discr* o_1, is actually not specific to *sort*. Our generic discriminators commute with *every strong* natural transformation. Let *discr* o: $[K \times V] \to [[V]]$ and π: $[A \times V] \to [V]$. If π is strongly natural, *filter* $p \cdot \pi = \pi \cdot$ *filter* $(id \times p)$, then

$$\mathsf{List}\ \pi \cdot \mathit{discr}\ o = \mathit{discr}\ o \cdot \pi \cdot \mathsf{List}\ \mathit{swap}\ , \tag{5.2}$$

where $swap : K_1 \times (K_2 \times V) \cong K_2 \times (K_1 \times V)$. Note that $swap \cdot curryl = curryr$.
Case $o = OUnit$:

$$\begin{aligned}
& \mathsf{List}\,\pi \cdot discr\ OUnit \ :\ [1 \times (A \times V)] \to [[V]] \\
= & \ \{ \text{definition of } discr \} \\
& \mathsf{List}\,\pi \cdot return \cdot \mathsf{List}\ val \\
= & \ \{ return \text{ is natural: } \mathsf{List}\,f \cdot return = return \cdot f \} \\
& return \cdot \pi \cdot \mathsf{List}\ val \\
= & \ \{ \text{Kleisli: } val = (id \times val) \cdot swap \} \\
& return \cdot \pi \cdot \mathsf{List}\,(id \times val) \cdot \mathsf{List}\ swap \\
= & \ \{ \textit{assumption: } \pi \text{ is (strongly) natural} \} \\
& return \cdot \mathsf{List}\ val \cdot \pi \cdot \mathsf{List}\ swap \\
= & \ \{ \text{definition of } discr \} \\
& discr\ OUnit \cdot \pi \cdot \mathsf{List}\ swap
\end{aligned}$$

Case $o = OSum\ o_1\ o_2$:

$$\begin{aligned}
& \mathsf{List}\,\pi \cdot discr\,(OSum\ o_1\ o_2) \ :\ [(K_1 + K_2) \times (A \times V)] \to [[V]] \\
= & \ \{ \text{definition of } discr \} \\
& \mathsf{List}\,\pi \cdot (discr\ o_1 \cdot filter\,(inl^{\circ} \times id) +\!\!+ \ldots) \\
= & \ \{ \mathsf{List}\,\pi \text{ is a monoid homomorphism} \} \\
& \mathsf{List}\,\pi \cdot discr\ o_1 \cdot filter\,(inl^{\circ} \times id) +\!\!+ \ldots \\
= & \ \{ \text{ex hypothesi} \} \\
& discr\ o_1 \cdot \pi \cdot \mathsf{List}\ swap \cdot filter\,(inl^{\circ} \times id) +\!\!+ \ldots \\
= & \ \{ \text{Kleisli: } swap \cdot (p \times (q \times r)) = (q \times (p \times r)) \cdot swap \} \\
& discr\ o_1 \cdot \pi \cdot filter\,(id \times (inl^{\circ} \times id)) \cdot \mathsf{List}\ swap +\!\!+ \ldots \\
= & \ \{ \textit{assumption: } \pi \text{ is strongly natural} \} \\
& discr\ o_1 \cdot filter\,(inl^{\circ} \times id) \cdot \pi \cdot \mathsf{List}\ swap +\!\!+ \ldots \\
= & \ \{ \text{fusion: } f \cdot h +\!\!+ g \cdot h = (f +\!\!+ g) \cdot h \} \\
& (discr\ o_1 \cdot filter\,(inl^{\circ} \times id) +\!\!+ \ldots) \cdot \pi \cdot \mathsf{List}\ swap \\
= & \ \{ \text{definition of } discr \} \\
& discr\,(OSum\ o_1\ o_2) \cdot \pi \cdot \mathsf{List}\ swap
\end{aligned}$$

Case $o = OProd\ o_1\ o_2$:

$$\begin{aligned}
& \mathsf{List}\,\pi \cdot discr\,(OProd\ o_1\ o_2) \ :\ [(K_1 \times K_2) \times (A \times V)] \to [[V]] \\
= & \ \{ \text{definition of } discr \} \\
& \mathsf{List}\,\pi \cdot concat \cdot \mathsf{List}\,(discr\ o_2) \cdot discr\ o_1 \cdot \mathsf{List}\ curryl \\
= & \ \{ concat \text{ is natural: } \mathsf{List}\,f \cdot concat = concat \cdot \mathsf{List}\,(\mathsf{List}\,f) \} \\
& concat \cdot \mathsf{List}\,(\mathsf{List}\,\pi \cdot discr\ o_2) \cdot discr\ o_1 \cdot \mathsf{List}\ curryl \\
= & \ \{ \text{ex hypothesi} \} \\
& concat \cdot \mathsf{List}\,(discr\ o_2 \cdot \pi \cdot \mathsf{List}\ swap) \cdot discr\ o_1 \cdot \mathsf{List}\ curryl \\
= & \ \{ discr\ o \text{ is natural: } \mathsf{List}\,(\mathsf{List}\,f) \cdot discr\ o = discr\ o_1 \cdot \mathsf{List}\,(id \times f) \} \\
& concat \cdot \mathsf{List}\,(discr\ o_2 \cdot \pi) \cdot discr\ o_1 \cdot \mathsf{List}\,((id \times swap) \cdot curryl) \\
= & \ \{ \text{ex hypothesi} \} \\
& concat \cdot \mathsf{List}\,(discr\ o_2) \cdot discr\ o_1 \cdot \pi \cdot \mathsf{List}\,(swap \cdot (id \times swap) \cdot curryl) \\
= & \ \{ \text{Kleisli: } swap \cdot (id \times swap) \cdot curryl = (id \times curryl) \cdot swap \}
\end{aligned}$$

$$
\begin{aligned}
& \mathit{concat} \cdot \mathsf{List}\,(\mathit{discr}\ o_2) \cdot \mathit{discr}\ o_1 \cdot \pi \cdot \mathsf{List}\,((\mathit{id} \times \mathit{curryl}) \cdot \mathit{swap}) \\
= \; & \{ \text{ \textit{assumption:} } \pi \text{ is (strongly) natural } \} \\
& \mathit{concat} \cdot \mathsf{List}\,(\mathit{discr}\ o_2) \cdot \mathit{discr}\ o_1 \cdot \mathsf{List}\ \mathit{curryl} \cdot \pi \cdot \mathsf{List}\ \mathit{swap} \\
= \; & \{ \text{ definition of } \mathit{discr} \ \} \\
& \mathit{discr}\,(\mathit{OProd}\ o_1\ o_2) \cdot \pi \cdot \mathsf{List}\ \mathit{swap}
\end{aligned}
$$

Of course, *discr o* itself is also strongly natural:

$$\mathsf{List}\,(\mathit{filter}\ p) \cdot \mathit{discr}\ o = \mathit{discr}\ o \cdot \mathit{filter}\,(\mathit{id} \times p) \ , \tag{5.3}$$

for all $p : A \to \mathsf{Maybe}\ B$. The proof is similar to the one for *sort*.

6 Generic Distributive Searching

Let us now turn to distributive searching using tries. In this paper we concentrate on bulk operations such as *trie* and *flatten*. One-at-a-time operations such as *lookup* and *insert* have been described elsewhere [5]. It turns out that *trie* is very similar to *discr*—we essentially replace ++ and *concat* by trie constructors. This move retains more of the original information, which is vital for supporting subsequent *efficient random* access to the values associated with a key. By storing the keys together with the values in the trie, we can even recreate all of the original keys. (If *OMap*'s key transformations are injective this can even be done without explicitly storing the keys.)

For every order representation there is a corresponding trie constructor. Additionally, we have an empty trie, which is important for efficiency reasons [5].

$$
\begin{array}{l}
\textbf{data}\ \mathsf{Trie} :: * \to * \to * \ \textbf{where} \\
\quad \begin{array}{ll}
\mathit{TEmpty} & :: \mathsf{Trie}\ k\ v \\
\mathit{TUnit} & :: v \to \mathsf{Trie}\ ()\ v \\
\mathit{TSum} & :: \mathsf{Trie}\ k_1\ v \to \mathsf{Trie}\ k_2\ v \to \mathsf{Trie}\ (k_1 + k_2)\ v \\
\mathit{TProd} & :: \mathsf{Trie}\ k_1\ (\mathsf{Trie}\ k_2\ v) \to \mathsf{Trie}\ (k_1, k_2)\ v \\
\mathit{TMap} & :: (k_1 \to k_2) \to (\mathsf{Trie}\ k_2\ v \to \mathsf{Trie}\ k_1\ v) \\
\mathit{TChar} & :: \mathit{Char}.\mathsf{Trie}\ v \to \mathsf{Trie}\ \mathit{Char}\ v
\end{array}
\end{array}
$$

A trie of type $\mathsf{Trie}\ K\ V$ represents a finite mapping from K to V, sometimes written V^K. The cases for unit, sums, and products are based on the law of exponentials: $V^1 \cong V$, $V^{K_1+K_2} \cong V^{K_1} \times V^{K_2}$, and $V^{K_1 \times K_2} \cong (V^{K_2})^{K_1}$. The second but last case is interesting: the counterpart of *OMap* is *TMap*, which retains the key transformation. This is necessary when searching for a key that is subject to an *OMap*-order. Finally, we assume the existence of a suitable library, *Char*, implementing finite maps with character keys; for instance, character-indexed arrays, simple lists, binary trees (the basis of ternary tries). Indeed, depending on the actual data encountered, multiple data structures may even be mixed.

A trie for a given key type is a functor.

$$
\begin{array}{l}
\textbf{instance}\ \mathit{Functor}\ (\mathsf{Trie}\ k)\ \textbf{where} \\
\quad \mathit{fmap}\ f\,(\mathit{TEmpty}) \quad\ = \mathit{TEmpty} \\
\quad \mathit{fmap}\ f\,(\mathit{TUnit}\ v) \quad = \mathit{TUnit}\ (f\ v)
\end{array}
$$

$$\begin{aligned}
&\mathit{fmap}\ f\ (\mathit{TSum}\ t_1\ t_2) = \mathit{TSum}\ (\mathit{fmap}\ f\ t_1)\ (\mathit{fmap}\ f\ t_2)\\
&\mathit{fmap}\ f\ (\mathit{TProd}\ t) \quad = \mathit{TProd}\ (\mathit{fmap}\ (\mathit{fmap}\ f)\ t)\\
&\mathit{fmap}\ f\ (\mathit{TMap}\ g\ t) \quad = \mathit{TMap}\ g\ (\mathit{fmap}\ f\ t)\\
&\mathit{fmap}\ f\ (\mathit{TChar}\ t) \quad = \mathit{TChar}\ (\mathit{fmap}\ f\ t)
\end{aligned}$$

The operation *flatten* lists the values stored in a trie.

$$\begin{aligned}
&\mathit{flatten} :: \mathsf{Trie}\ k\ v \to [v]\\
&\mathit{flatten}\ (\mathit{TEmpty}) \quad = [\,]\\
&\mathit{flatten}\ (\mathit{TUnit}\ v) \quad = [v]\\
&\mathit{flatten}\ (\mathit{TSum}\ t_1\ t_2) = \mathit{flatten}\ t_1 +\!\!+ \mathit{flatten}\ t_2\\
&\mathit{flatten}\ (\mathit{TProd}\ t) \quad = \mathit{concatMap}\ \mathit{flatten}\ (\mathit{flatten}\ t)\\
&\mathit{flatten}\ (\mathit{TMap}\ g\ t) \quad = \mathit{flatten}\ t\\
&\mathit{flatten}\ (\mathit{TChar}\ t) \quad = \mathit{Char.flatten}\ t
\end{aligned}$$

It is natural in V, that is, $\mathit{flatten} : \mathsf{Trie}\ K \dot{\to} \mathsf{List}$.

The operation *trie* turns a finite relation, represented by an association list of type $[K \times V]$, into a finite list-valued map, represented by a trie of type $\mathsf{Trie}\ K\,[V]$.

$$\begin{aligned}
&\mathit{trie} :: \mathit{Order}\ k \to [k \times v] \to \mathsf{Trie}\ k\ [v]\\
&\mathit{trie}\ o \qquad\qquad\quad [\,] = \mathit{TEmpty}\\
&\mathit{trie}\ \mathit{OUnit} \qquad\quad \mathit{rel} = \mathit{TUnit}\ (\mathit{map}\ \mathit{val}\ \mathit{rel})\\
&\mathit{trie}\ (\mathit{OSum}\ o_1\ o_2)\ \mathit{rel} = \mathit{TSum}\ (\mathit{trie}\ o_1\ (\mathit{filter}\ \mathit{froml}\ \mathit{rel}))\ (\mathit{trie}\ o_2\ (\mathit{filter}\ \mathit{fromr}\ \mathit{rel}))\\
&\mathit{trie}\ (\mathit{OProd}\ o_1\ o_2)\ \mathit{rel} = \mathit{TProd}\ (\mathit{fmap}\ (\mathit{trie}\ o_2)\ (\mathit{trie}\ o_1\ (\mathit{map}\ \mathit{curryl}\ \mathit{rel})))\\
&\mathit{trie}\ (\mathit{OMap}\ g\ o) \quad \mathit{rel} = \mathit{TMap}\ g\ (\mathit{trie}\ o\ (\mathit{map}\ (g \times \mathit{id})\ \mathit{rel}))\\
&\mathit{trie}\ (\mathit{OChar}) \qquad \mathit{rel} = \mathit{TChar}\ (\mathit{Char.trie}\ \mathit{rel})
\end{aligned}$$

As we have noted before, *trie* arises out of *discr* by replacing $+\!\!+$, *concat* etc by the appropriate trie constructors.

Indeed, if we 'undo' the transformation using *flatten*, we obtain the generic discriminator.

$$\mathit{discr}\ o = \mathit{flatten} \cdot \mathit{trie}\ o \tag{6.1}$$

The straightforward proof can be found in Appendix B.

7 Related Work

Drawing on the algorithmic techniques termed *multiset discrimination* developed by Paige and others [9], Henglein [2,3] has shown how to make MSD distributive sorting generic by introducing generic discriminators, which have linear-time performance over a rich class of orders.

Building on the work of Connelly and Morris [10], Hinze [5] pioneered the type-indexed tries we produce. Here they are extended to support orders defined with *OMap*. The generic LSD distributive sorting and trie building functions developed here are also new. In particular, *trie* constructs a trie in bulk without incurring the substantial update costs of one-by-one insertion.

Wadler [11] derives as a "free theorem" that any function parametric in binary comparison $\leqslant$ commutes with *map f* if the function *f* is an order embedding, $f\,x \leqslant' f\,y \Longleftrightarrow x \leqslant y$; this includes all comparison-based sorting algorithms. As shown by Day et al. [12], Knuth's *0-1 principle* for sorting networks [13] can also be seen as a free theorem for sorting networks formulated as comparator-parametrized functions. These properties correspond to naturality, respectively parametricity properties on the keys; they are *different* from our naturality property 4.3 since the latter applies to the value components and leaves the key components invariant.

Our strong naturality property 4.4, coupled with preserving singletons and correct sorting of two-element lists, corresponds to Henglein's *consistent permutativity*, which characterizes stable sorting functions [14]. It is, however, a more general and a more elegant formulation supporting equational reasoning. In particular, it highlights the semantic benefits of adopting a formulation for sorting based on key-value pairs rather than keys alone.

Gibbons [15] shows how an LSD radix sort for lists can be derived from a stable MSD radix sort that first builds an explicit trie and then flattens it into the result list. Since MSD radix sort, even with explicit tries, is sometimes preferable to LSD radix sort (to avoid sparse bucket table traversal [16] and for large data sets [17]), the derivation makes sense in both directions. Our development can be seen as a generalization of Gibbons' work: it works for arbitrary denotable orders over any type; we decompose MSD sorting into discrimination followed by concatenation, without the need for a trie (though it can be achieved by way of *trie*); and our commutativity property 5.2 holds for *any* strong natural transformation, not just for sorting functions.

8 Conclusion

Comparison-based sorting algorithms and search trees are easily made generic, that is, applicable to user-defined orders, by abstraction over the comparison function. This has arguably contributed to their popularity even though distributive (radix/trie) and hashing techniques often have superior performance for special types, such as machine integers and character strings.

We have shown how to construct generic comparison, sorting, discrimination and trie building operations by induction over a class of orders including standard orders on primitive types; lexicographic orders on sums, products and lists; and orders defined as the inverse image of a given order under an arbitrary function.

We have identified strong naturality—commutativity with filtering—as a powerful property of stable sorting functions, and shown discrimination to commute with any strongly natural transformation, including, but not limited to, stable sorting functions.

The trie building operation yields a data structure that is not only asymptotically as efficient as discrimination but also supports efficient key-based random access, without incurring a one-at-a-time insertion overhead during construction.

Future work consists of extending equational reasoning and calculational correctness proofs to coinductive order representations; investigating *data-dependent* variations of our generic functions and staged execution for our *data-independent* generic functions by compile-time specialization (partial evaluation) and exploiting parallelism at word, multicore, and manycore/GPU levels; and eventually providing architecture-independent frameworks encapsulating distributive sorting and searching methods as semantically (obeying representation independence) and computationally (exhibiting superior performance) well-behaved alternatives to comparison-based methods.

Acknowledgements. We would like to thank the anonymous referees of APLAS 2013 and Nicolas Wu for suggesting various presentational improvements. We owe a particular debt of gratitude to Richard Bird for carefully reading a draft version of this paper, pointing out typographical errors, glitches of language, and for suggesting pronounceable identifiers. This work has been funded by EPSRC grant number EP/J010995/1 and Danish Research Council grant 10-092299 for HIPERFIT.

References

1. Strachey, C.: Fundamental concepts in programming languages. Higher-order and Symbolic Computation 13(1), 11–49 (2000)
2. Henglein, F.: Generic discrimination: Sorting and partitioning unshared data in linear time. In: Hook, J., Thiemann, P. (eds.) Proc. 13th ACM SIGPLAN Int'l Conf. on Functional Programming (ICFP), pp. 91–102. ACM (September 2008)
3. Henglein, F.: Generic top-down discrimination for sorting and partitioning in linear time. Journal of Functional Programming (JFP) 22(3), 300–374 (2012)
4. Bentley, J.L., Sedgewick, R.: Fast algorithms for sorting and searching strings. In: SODA 1997: Proceedings of the Eighth Annual ACM-SIAM Symposium on Discrete Algorithms, pp. 360–369. Society for Industrial and Applied Mathematics, Philadelphia (1997)
5. Hinze, R.: Generalizing generalized tries. Journal of Functional Programming 10(4), 327–351 (2000)
6. Hoare, C.A.: Quicksort. The Computer Journal 5(1), 10–16 (1962)
7. Bayer, R.: Symmetric binary B-trees: Data structure and maintenance algorithms. Acta Informatica 1(4), 290–306 (1972)
8. Guibas, L.J., Sedgewick, R.: A dichromatic framework for balanced trees. In: Proc. 19th Annual Symposium on Foundations of Computer Science (FOCS), pp. 8–21. IEEE (1978)
9. Cai, J., Paige, R.: Using multiset discrimination to solve language processing problems without hashing. Theoretical Computer Science (TCS) 145(1-2), 189–228 (1995)
10. Connelly, R.H., Morris, F.L.: A generalization of the trie data structure. Mathematical Structures in Computer Science 5(3), 381–418 (1995)
11. Wadler, P.: Theorems for free! In: Proc. Functional Programming Languages and Computer Architecture (FPCA), pp. 347–359. ACM Press, London (1989)

12. Day, N.A., Launchbury, J., Lewis, J.: Logical abstractions in Haskell. In: Proc. Haskell Workshop. Number UU-CS-1999-28 in Technical Report, Utrecht, The Netherlands, Utrecht University (1999)
13. Knuth, D.: The Art of Computer Programming: Sorting and Searching, 2nd edn., vol. 3. Addison Wesley (1998)
14. Henglein, F.: What is a sorting function? J. Logic and Algebraic Programming (JLAP) 78(5), 381–401 (2009)
15. Gibbons, J.: A pointless derivation of radix sort. Journal of Functional Programming 9(3), 339–346 (1999)
16. Paige, R., Tarjan, R.E.: Three partition refinement algorithms. SIAM Journal of Computing 16(6), 973–989 (1987)
17. Sinha, R., Zobel, J.: Efficient trie-based sorting of large sets of strings. In: Proc. 26th Australasian Computer Science Conference (ACSC), pp. 11–18 (2003)

A Proof of Property (4.6)

The cases for unit and sums are straightforward. We only consider the product case, which is actually instructive.

Case $o = \mathit{OProd}\ o_1\ o_2$: again, we make use of naturality to be able to apply the induction assumption.

$$\begin{aligned}
& \mathit{sort}\ (\mathit{OProd}\ o_1\ o_2)\ [((a_1, a_2), i), ((b_1, b_2), j)] = [i, j] \\
\iff & \ \{ \text{ definition of } \mathit{sort} \ \} \\
& \mathit{sort}\ o_1\ (\mathit{sort}\ o_2\ (\mathsf{List}\ \mathit{curryr}\ [((a_1, a_2), i), ((b_1, b_2), j)])) = [i, j] \\
\iff & \ \{ \text{ definition of } \mathit{curryr} \ \} \\
& \mathit{sort}\ o_1\ (\mathit{sort}\ o_2\ [(a_2, (a_1, i)), (b_2, (b_1, j))]) = [i, j] \\
\iff & \ \{ \text{ let } \mathit{re}\ i = (a_1, i) \text{ and } \mathit{re}\ j = (b_1, j) \ \} \\
& \mathit{sort}\ o_1\ (\mathit{sort}\ o_2\ (\mathsf{List}\ (\mathit{id} \times \mathit{re})\ [(a_2, i), (b_2, j)]) = [i, j] \\
\iff & \ \{ \ \mathit{sort} \text{ is natural (4.3) } \} \\
& \mathit{sort}\ o_1\ (\mathsf{List}\ \mathit{re}\ (\mathit{sort}\ o_2\ [(a_2, i), (b_2, j)]) = [i, j]
\end{aligned}$$

The strict version of *leq* suggests to conduct a case analysis on $\mathit{leq}\ o_2\ a_2\ b_2$.

Case $\mathit{leq}\ o_2\ a_2\ b_2$:

$$\begin{aligned}
\iff & \ \{ \text{ ex hypothesi } \} \\
& \mathit{sort}\ o_1\ (\mathsf{List}\ \mathit{re}\ [i, j]) = [i, j] \\
\iff & \ \{ \text{ definition of } \mathit{re} \ \} \\
& \mathit{sort}\ o_1\ [(a_1, i), (b_1, j)] = [i, j] \\
\iff & \ \{ \text{ ex hypothesi } \} \\
& \mathit{leq}\ o_1\ a_1\ b_1 \\
\iff & \ \{ \text{ definition of } \mathit{leq} \ \} \\
& \mathit{leq}\ (\mathit{OProd}\ o_1\ o_2)\ (a_1, a_2)\ (b_1, b_2)
\end{aligned}$$

Case $\neg\ (\mathit{leq}\ o_2\ a_2\ b_2)$:

$$\begin{aligned}
\iff & \ \{ \text{ ex hypothesi } \} \\
& \mathit{sort}\ o_1\ (\mathsf{List}\ \mathit{re}\ [j, i]) = [i, j] \\
\iff & \ \{ \text{ definition of } \mathit{re} \ \} \\
& \mathit{sort}\ o_1\ [(b_1, j), (a_1, i)] = [i, j] \\
\iff & \ \{ \text{ ex hypothesi } \} \\
& \neg\ (\mathit{leq}\ o_1\ b_1\ a_1) \\
\iff & \ \{ \text{ definition of } \mathit{leq} \ \} \\
& \mathit{leq}\ (\mathit{OProd}\ o_1\ o_2)\ (a_1, a_2)\ (b_1, b_2)
\end{aligned}$$

B Proof of $discr\ o = flatten \cdot trie\ o$ (6.1)

Case $o = OUnit$:

$$
\begin{aligned}
& flatten \cdot trie\ OUnit \\
= \;& \{ \text{definition of } trie \} \\
& flatten \cdot TUnit \cdot map\ val \\
= \;& \{ \text{definition of } flatten \} \\
& return \cdot map\ val \\
= \;& \{ \text{definition of } discr \} \\
& discr\ OUnit
\end{aligned}
$$

Case $o = OSum\ o_1\ o_2$:

$$
\begin{aligned}
& flatten \cdot trie\,(OSum\ o_1\ o_2) \\
= \;& \{ \text{definition of } trie \} \\
& flatten \cdot TSum \cdot (trie\ o_1 \cdot filter\,(inl^{\circ} \times id) \vartriangle \ldots) \\
= \;& \{ \text{definition of } flatten \} \\
& (flatten \cdot outl + \!\! + \ldots) \cdot (trie\ o_1 \cdot filter\,(inl^{\circ} \times id) \vartriangle \ldots) \\
= \;& \{ \text{fusion and computation} \} \\
& flatten \cdot trie\ o_1 \cdot filter\,(inl^{\circ} \times id) + \!\! + \ldots \\
= \;& \{ \text{ex hypothesi} \} \\
& discr\ o_1 \cdot filter\,(inl^{\circ} \times id) + \!\! + \ldots \\
= \;& \{ \text{definition of } discr \} \\
& discr\,(OSum\ o_1\ o_2)
\end{aligned}
$$

Case $o = OProd\ o_1\ o_2$: here we make essential use of the fact that Trie K is a functor and that *flatten* is natural in V.

$$
\begin{aligned}
& flatten \cdot trie\,(OProd\ o_1\ o_2) \\
= \;& \{ \text{definition of } trie \} \\
& flatten \cdot TProd \cdot \mathsf{Trie}\ K_1\ (trie\ o_2) \cdot trie\ o_1 \cdot \mathsf{List}\ curryl \\
= \;& \{ \text{definition of } flatten \} \\
& concat \cdot \mathsf{List}\ flatten \cdot flatten \cdot \mathsf{Trie}\ K_1\ (trie\ o_2) \cdot trie\ o_1 \cdot \mathsf{List}\ curryl \\
= \;& \{ flatten \text{ is natural: } \mathsf{List}\ f \cdot flatten = flatten \cdot \mathsf{Trie}\ K\ f \} \\
& concat \cdot \mathsf{List}\ flatten \cdot \mathsf{List}\ (trie\ o_2) \cdot flatten \cdot trie\ o_1 \cdot \mathsf{List}\ curryl \\
= \;& \{ \text{ex hypothesi, twice} \} \\
& concat \cdot \mathsf{List}\ (discr\ o_2) \cdot discr\ o_1 \cdot \mathsf{List}\ curryl \\
= \;& \{ \text{definition of } discr \} \\
& discr\,(OProd\ o_1\ o_2)\ .
\end{aligned}
$$

Environmental Bisimulations for Delimited-Control Operators

Dariusz Biernacki[1] and Sergueï Lenglet[2]

[1] Institute of Computer Science, University of Wrocław
[2] LORIA, Université de Lorraine

Abstract. We present a theory of environmental bisimilarity for the delimited-control operators *shift* and *reset*. We consider two different notions of contextual equivalence: one that does not require the presence of a top-level control delimiter when executing tested terms, and another one, fully compatible with the original CPS semantics of shift and reset, that does. For each of them, we develop sound and complete environmental bisimilarities, and we discuss up-to techniques.

1 Introduction

Control operators for delimited continuations [8,10] provide elegant means for expressing advanced control mechanisms [8,12]. Moreover, they play a fundamental role in the semantics of computational effects [11], normalization by evaluation [2] and as a crucial refinement of abortive control operators such as *callcc* [10,21]. Of special interest are the control operators *shift* and *reset* [8] due to their origins in continuation-passing style (CPS) and their connection with computational monads – as demonstrated by Filinski [11], shift and reset can express in direct style arbitrary computational effects, such as mutable state, exceptions, etc. Operationally, the control delimiter reset delimits the current continuation and the control operator shift abstracts the current delimited continuation as a first class value that when resumed is composed with the then-current continuation.

Because of the complex nature of control effects, it can be difficult to determine if two programs that use shift and reset are equivalent (i.e., behave in the same way) or not. *Contextual equivalence* [17] is widely considered as the most natural equivalence on terms in languages similar to the λ-calculus. Roughly, two terms are contextually equivalent if we cannot tell them apart when they are executed within any context. The latter quantification over contexts makes this relation hard to use in practice, so we usually look for simpler characterizations of contextual equivalence, such as coinductively defined *bisimilarities*.

In our previous work, we defined *applicative* [4] and *normal form* [5] bisimilarities for shift and reset. Applicative bisimilarity characterizes contextual equivalence, but still quantifies over some contexts to relate terms (e.g., λ-abstractions are applied to the same arbitrary argument). As a result, some equivalences remain quite difficult to prove. In contrast, normal form bisimilarity does not contain any quantification over contexts or arguments in its definition: the tested

C.-c. Shan (Ed.): APLAS 2013, LNCS 8301, pp. 333–348, 2013.

terms are reduced to normal forms, which are then decomposed in bisimilar subterms. Consequently, proofs of equivalence are usually simpler than with applicative bisimilarity, and they can be simplified even further with *up-to techniques*. However, normal form bisimilarity is not *complete*, i.e., there exist contextually equivalent terms which are not normal form bisimilar.

Environmental bisimilarity [19] is a different kind of behavioral equivalence which in terms of strength and practicality can be situated in between applicative and normal form bisimilarities. It has originally been proposed in [23] and has been since defined in various higher-order languages (see, e.g., [20,22,18]). Like applicative bisimilarity, it uses some particular contexts to test terms, except that the testing contexts are built from an environment, which represents the knowledge built so far by an outside observer. Environmental bisimilarity usually characterizes contextual equivalence, but is harder to establish than applicative bisimilarity. Nonetheless, like with normal form bisimilarity, one can define powerful up-to techniques [19] to simplify the equivalence proofs. Besides, the authors of [15] argue that the additional complexity of environmental bisimilarity is necessary to handle more realistic features, like local state or exceptions.

In the quest for a powerful enough (i.e., as discriminative as contextual equivalence) yet easy-to-use equivalence for delimited control, we study in this paper the environmental theory of a calculus with shift and reset. More precisely, we consider two semantics for shift and reset: the original one [3], where terms are executed within a top-level reset, and a more relaxed semantics where this requirement is lifted. The latter is commonly used in implementations of shift and reset [9,11] as well as in some studies of these operators [1,13], including our previous work [4,5]. So far, the behavioral theory of shift and reset with the original semantics has not been studied. Firstly, we define environmental bisimilarity for the relaxed semantics and study its properties; especially we discuss the problems raised by delimited control for the definition of bisimulation up to context, one of the most powerful up-to techniques. Secondly, we propose the first behavioral theory for the original semantics, and we pinpoint the differences between the equivalences of the two semantics. In particular, we show that the environmental bisimilarity for the original semantics is complete w.r.t. the axiomatization of shift and reset of [14], which is not the case for the relaxed semantics, as already proved in [4] for applicative bisimilarity.

In summary, we make the following contributions in this paper.

- We show that environmental bisimilarity can be defined for a calculus with delimited control, for which we consider two different semantics. In each case, the defined bisimilarity equals contextual equivalence.
- For the relaxed semantics, we explain how to handle *stuck terms*, i.e., terms where a capture cannot go through because of the lack of an outermost reset.
- We discuss the limits of the usual up-to techniques in the case of delimited control.
- For the original semantics, we define a contextual equivalence, and a corresponding environmental bisimilarity. Proving soundness of the bisimilarity w.r.t. contextual equivalence requires significant changes from the usual

soundness proof scheme. We discuss how environmental bisimilarity is easier to adapt than applicative bisimilarity.
- We give examples illustrating the differences between the two semantics.

The rest of the paper is organized as follows: in Section 2, we present the calculus $\lambda_{\mathcal{S}}$ used in this paper, and recall some results, including the axiomatization of [14]. We develop an environmental theory for the relaxed semantics in Section 3, and for the original semantics in Section 4. We conclude in Section 5. An extended version of this article [6] contains most of the omitted proofs.

2 The Calculus $\lambda_{\mathcal{S}}$

2.1 Syntax

The language $\lambda_{\mathcal{S}}$ extends the call-by-value λ-calculus with the delimited-control operators *shift* and *reset* [8]. We assume we have a set of term variables, ranged over by x, y, z, and k. We use k for term variables representing a continuation (e.g., when bound with a shift), while x, y, and z stand for any values; we believe such distinction helps to understand examples and reduction rules. The syntax of terms is given by the following grammar:

$$\text{Terms: } t ::= x \mid \lambda x.t \mid t\,t \mid \mathcal{S}k.t \mid \langle t \rangle$$

Values, ranged over by v, are terms of the form $\lambda x.t$. The operator shift ($\mathcal{S}k.t$) is a capture operator, the extent of which is determined by the delimiter reset ($\langle\cdot\rangle$). A λ-abstraction $\lambda x.t$ binds x in t and a shift construct $\mathcal{S}k.t$ binds k in t; terms are equated up to α-conversion of their bound variables. The set of free variables of t is written $\mathsf{fv}(t)$; a term t is *closed* if $\mathsf{fv}(t) = \emptyset$.

We distinguish several kinds of contexts, represented outside-in, as follows:

$$\begin{array}{ll} \text{Pure contexts:} & E ::= \Box \mid v\,E \mid E\,t \\ \text{Evaluation contexts:} & F ::= \Box \mid v\,F \mid F\,t \mid \langle F \rangle \\ \text{Contexts:} & C ::= \Box \mid \lambda x.C \mid t\,C \mid C\,t \mid \mathcal{S}k.C \mid \langle C \rangle \end{array}$$

Regular contexts are ranged over by C. The pure evaluation contexts[1] (abbreviated as pure contexts), ranged over by E, represent delimited continuations and can be captured by shift. The call-by-value evaluation contexts, ranged over by F, represent arbitrary continuations and encode the chosen reduction strategy. Filling a context C (respectively E, F) with a term t produces a term, written $C[t]$ (respectively $E[t]$, $F[t]$); the free variables of t may be captured in the process. We extend the notion of free variables to contexts (with $\mathsf{fv}(\Box) = \emptyset$), and we say a context C (respectively E, F) is *closed* if $\mathsf{fv}(C) = \emptyset$ (respectively $\mathsf{fv}(E) = \emptyset$, $\mathsf{fv}(F) = \emptyset$).

[1] This terminology comes from Kameyama (e.g., in [14]).

2.2 Reduction Semantics

The call-by-value reduction semantics of $\lambda_{\mathcal{S}}$ is defined as follows, where $t\{v/x\}$ is the usual capture-avoiding substitution of v for x in t:

$$
\begin{array}{lrl}
(\beta_v) & F[(\lambda x.t)\; v] & \rightarrow_{\mathrm{v}} F[t\{v/x\}] \\
(\mathit{shift}) & F[\langle E[\mathcal{S}k.t]\rangle] & \rightarrow_{\mathrm{v}} F[\langle t\{\lambda x.\langle E[x]\rangle/k\}\rangle] \text{ with } x \notin \mathsf{fv}(E) \\
(\mathit{reset}) & F[\langle v\rangle] & \rightarrow_{\mathrm{v}} F[v]
\end{array}
$$

The term $(\lambda x.t)\; v$ is the usual call-by-value redex for β-reduction (rule (β_v)). The operator $\mathcal{S}k.t$ captures its surrounding context E up to the dynamically nearest enclosing reset, and substitutes $\lambda x.\langle E[x]\rangle$ for k in t (rule (shift)). If a reset is enclosing a value, then it has no purpose as a delimiter for a potential capture, and it can be safely removed (rule (reset)). All these reductions may occur within a metalevel context F, so the reduction rules specify both the notion of reduction and the chosen call-by-value evaluation strategy that is encoded in the grammar of the evaluation contexts. Furthermore, the reduction relation $\rightarrow_{\mathrm{v}}$ is compatible with evaluation contexts F, i.e., $F[t] \rightarrow_{\mathrm{v}} F[t']$ whenever $t \rightarrow_{\mathrm{v}} t'$.

There exist terms which are not values and which cannot be reduced any further; these are called *stuck terms.*

Definition 1. *A term t is stuck if t is not a value and $t \not\rightarrow_{\mathrm{v}}$.*

For example, the term $E[\mathcal{S}k.t]$ is stuck because there is no enclosing reset; the capture of E by the shift operator cannot be triggered.

Lemma 1. *A closed term t is stuck iff $t = E[\mathcal{S}k.t']$ for some E, k, and t'.*

Definition 2. *A term t is a normal form if t is a value or a stuck term.*

We call *redexes* (ranged over by r) terms of the form $(\lambda x.t)\; v$, $\langle E[\mathcal{S}k.t]\rangle$, and $\langle v\rangle$. Thanks to the following unique-decomposition property, the reduction relation $\rightarrow_{\mathrm{v}}$ is deterministic.

Lemma 2. *For all closed terms t, either t is a normal form, or there exist a unique redex r and a unique context F such that $t = F[r]$.*

Finally, we write $\rightarrow_{\mathrm{v}}^{*}$ for the transitive and reflexive closure of $\rightarrow_{\mathrm{v}}$, and we define the evaluation relation of $\lambda_{\mathcal{S}}$ as follows.

Definition 3. *We write $t \Downarrow_{\mathrm{v}} t'$ if $t \rightarrow_{\mathrm{v}}^{*} t'$ and $t' \not\rightarrow_{\mathrm{v}}$.*

The result of the evaluation of a closed term, if it exists, is a normal form. If a term t admits an infinite reduction sequence, we say it *diverges*, written $t \Uparrow_{\mathrm{v}}$. Henceforth, we use $\Omega = (\lambda x.x\; x)\; (\lambda x.x\; x)$ as an example of such a term.

2.3 CPS Equivalence

In [14], the authors propose an equational theory of shift and reset based on CPS [8]. The idea is to relate terms that have $\beta\eta$-convertible CPS translations.

Definition 4. *Terms t_0 and t_1 are CPS equivalent, written $t_0 \equiv t_1$, if their CPS translations are $\beta\eta$-convertible.*

Kameyama and Hasegawa propose eight axioms in [14] to characterize CPS equivalence: two terms are CPS equivalent iff one can derive their equality using the equations below. Note that the axioms are defined on open terms, and suppose variables as values.

$$(\lambda x.t)\, v =_{\text{KH}} t\{v/x\} \qquad (\lambda x.E[x])\, t =_{\text{KH}} E[t] \text{ if } x \notin \mathsf{fv}(E)$$

$$\langle E[\mathcal{S}k.t]\rangle =_{\text{KH}} \langle t\{\lambda x.\langle E[x]\rangle/k\}\rangle \qquad \langle(\lambda x.t_0)\,\langle t_1\rangle\rangle =_{\text{KH}} (\lambda x.\langle t_0\rangle)\,\langle t_1\rangle$$

$$\langle v\rangle =_{\text{KH}} v \qquad \mathcal{S}k.\langle t\rangle =_{\text{KH}} \mathcal{S}k.t$$

$$\lambda x.v\, x =_{\text{KH}} v \text{ if } x \notin \mathsf{fv}(v) \qquad \mathcal{S}k.k\, t =_{\text{KH}} t \text{ if } k \notin \mathsf{fv}(t)$$

We use the above relations as examples throughout the paper. Of particular interest is the axiom $(\lambda x.E[x])\, t =_{\text{KH}} E[t]$ (if $x \notin \mathsf{fv}(E)$), called β_Ω in [14], which can be difficult to prove with bisimilarities [4].

2.4 Context Closures

Given a relation $\mathcal{R}$ on terms, we define two context closures that generate respectively terms and evaluation contexts. The term generating closure $\widehat{\mathcal{R}}$ is defined inductively as the smallest relation satisfying the following rules:

$$\frac{t\,\mathcal{R}\,t'}{t\,\widehat{\mathcal{R}}\,t'} \qquad x\,\widehat{\mathcal{R}}\,x \qquad \frac{t\,\widehat{\mathcal{R}}\,t'}{\lambda x.t\,\widehat{\mathcal{R}}\,\lambda x.t'} \qquad \frac{t_0\,\widehat{\mathcal{R}}\,t_0' \quad t_1\,\widehat{\mathcal{R}}\,t_1'}{t_0\,t_1\,\widehat{\mathcal{R}}\,t_0'\,t_1'} \qquad \frac{t\,\widehat{\mathcal{R}}\,t'}{\mathcal{S}k.t\,\widehat{\mathcal{R}}\,\mathcal{S}k.t'} \qquad \frac{t\,\widehat{\mathcal{R}}\,t'}{\langle t\rangle\,\widehat{\mathcal{R}}\,\langle t'\rangle}$$

Even if $\mathcal{R}$ is defined only on closed terms, $\widehat{\mathcal{R}}$ is defined on open terms. In this paper, we consider the restriction of $\widehat{\mathcal{R}}$ to closed terms unless stated otherwise. The context generating closure $\widetilde{\mathcal{R}}$ of a relation $\mathcal{R}$ is defined inductively as the smallest relation satisfying the following rules:

$$\frac{}{\square\,\widetilde{\mathcal{R}}\,\square} \qquad \frac{F_0\,\widetilde{\mathcal{R}}\,F_1 \quad v_0\,\widehat{\mathcal{R}}\,v_1}{v_0\,F_0\,\widetilde{\mathcal{R}}\,v_1\,F_1} \qquad \frac{F_0\,\widetilde{\mathcal{R}}\,F_1 \quad t_0\,\widehat{\mathcal{R}}\,t_1}{F_0\,t_0\,\widetilde{\mathcal{R}}\,F_1\,t_1} \qquad \frac{F_0\,\widetilde{\mathcal{R}}\,F_1}{\langle F_0\rangle\,\widetilde{\mathcal{R}}\,\langle F_1\rangle}$$

Again, we consider only the restriction of $\widetilde{\mathcal{R}}$ to closed contexts.

3 Environmental Relations for the Relaxed Semantics

In this section, we define an environmental bisimilarity which characterizes the contextual equivalence of [4,5], where stuck terms can be observed.

3.1 Contextual Equivalence

We recall the definition of contextual equivalence $\approx_c$ for the relaxed semantics (given in [4]).

Definition 5. *For all t_0, t_1 be terms. We write $t_0 \approx_c t_1$ if for all C such that $C[t_0]$ and $C[t_1]$ are closed, the following hold:*

- *$C[t_0] \Downarrow_{\mathrm{v}} v_0$ implies $C[t_1] \Downarrow_{\mathrm{v}} v_1$;*
- *$C[t_0] \Downarrow_{\mathrm{v}} t'_0$, where t'_0 is stuck, implies $C[t_1] \Downarrow_{\mathrm{v}} t'_1$, with t'_1 stuck as well;*

and conversely for $C[t_1]$.

The definition is simpler when using the following context lemma [16] (for a proof see Section 3.4 in [4]). Instead of testing with general, closing contexts, we can close the terms with values and then put them in evaluation contexts.

Lemma 3 (Context Lemma). *We have $t_0 \approx_c t_1$ iff for all closed contexts F and for all substitutions σ (mapping variables to closed values) such that $t_0\sigma$ and $t_1\sigma$ are closed, the following hold:*

- *$F[t_0\sigma] \Downarrow_{\mathrm{v}} v_0$ implies $F[t_1\sigma] \Downarrow_{\mathrm{v}} v_1$;*
- *$F[t_0\sigma] \Downarrow_{\mathrm{v}} t'_0$, where t'_0 is stuck, implies $F[t_1\sigma] \Downarrow_{\mathrm{v}} t'_1$, with t'_1 stuck as well;*

and conversely for $F[t_1\sigma]$.

In [4], we prove that $\approx_c$ satisfies all the axioms of CPS equivalence except for $\mathcal{S}k.k\,t =_{\mathrm{KH}} t$ (provided $k \notin \mathsf{fv}(t)$): indeed, $\mathcal{S}k.k\,t$ is stuck, but t may evaluate to a value. Conversely, some contextually equivalent terms are not CPS equivalent, like Turing's and Church's call-by-value fixed point combinators. Similarly, two arbitrary diverging terms are related by $\approx_c$, but not necessarily by $\equiv$.

3.2 Definition of Environmental Bisimulation and Basic Properties

Environmental bisimulations use an environment $\mathcal{E}$ to accumulate knowledge about two tested terms. For the λ-calculus [19], $\mathcal{E}$ records the values (v_0, v_1) the tested terms reduce to, if they exist. We can then compare v_0 and v_1 at any time by passing them arguments built from $\mathcal{E}$. In $\lambda_{\mathcal{S}}$, we have to consider stuck terms as well; therefore, environments may also contain pairs of stuck terms, and we can test those by building pure contexts from $\mathcal{E}$.

Formally, an environment $\mathcal{E}$ is a relation on closed normal forms which relates values with values and stuck terms with stuck terms; e.g., the identity environment $\mathcal{I}$ is $\{(t,t) \mid t \text{ is a normal form}\}$. An environmental relation $\mathcal{X}$ is a set of environments $\mathcal{E}$, and triples $(\mathcal{E}, t_0, t_1)$, where t_0 and t_1 are closed. We write $t_0\ \mathcal{X}_{\mathcal{E}}\ t_1$ as a shorthand for $(\mathcal{E}, t_0, t_1) \in \mathcal{X}$; roughly, it means that we test t_0 and t_1 with the knowledge $\mathcal{E}$. The *open extension* of $\mathcal{X}$, written $\mathcal{X}^\circ$, is defined as follows: if $\overrightarrow{x} = \mathsf{fv}(t_0) \cup \mathsf{fv}(t_1)$[2], then we write $t_0\ \mathcal{X}_{\mathcal{E}}{}^\circ\ t_1$ if $\lambda\overrightarrow{x}.t_0\ \mathcal{X}_{\mathcal{E}}\ \lambda\overrightarrow{x}.t_1$.

[2] Given a metavariable m, we write $\overrightarrow{m}$ for a set of entities denoted by m.

Definition 6. *A relation $\mathcal{X}$ is an environmental bisimulation if*

1. $t_0\ \mathcal{X}_{\mathcal{E}}\ t_1$ *implies:*
   (a) *if* $t_0 \rightarrow_{\mathrm{v}} t_0'$, *then* $t_1 \rightarrow_{\mathrm{v}}^* t_1'$ *and* $t_0'\ \mathcal{X}_{\mathcal{E}}\ t_1'$;
   (b) *if* $t_0 = v_0$, *then* $t_1 \rightarrow_{\mathrm{v}}^* v_1$ *and* $\mathcal{E} \cup \{(v_0, v_1)\} \in \mathcal{X}$;
   (c) *if* t_0 *is stuck, then* $t_1 \rightarrow_{\mathrm{v}}^* t_1'$ *with* t_1' *stuck, and* $\mathcal{E} \cup \{(t_0, t_1')\} \in \mathcal{X}$;
   (d) *the converse of the above conditions on* t_1;
2. $\mathcal{E} \in \mathcal{X}$ *implies:*
   (a) *if* $\lambda x.t_0\ \mathcal{E}\ \lambda x.t_1$ *and* $v_0\ \widehat{\mathcal{E}}\ v_1$, *then* $t_0\{v_0/x\}\ \mathcal{X}_{\mathcal{E}}\ t_1\{v_1/x\}$;
   (b) *if* $E_0[\mathcal{S}k.t_0]\ \mathcal{E}\ E_1[\mathcal{S}k.t_1]$ *and* $E_0'\ \widetilde{\mathcal{E}}\ E_1'$, *then* $\langle t_0\{\lambda x.\langle E_0'[E_0[x]]\rangle/k\}\rangle\ \mathcal{X}_{\mathcal{E}}$ $\langle t_1\{\lambda x.\langle E_1'[E_1[x]]\rangle/k\}\rangle$ *for a fresh* x.

Environmental bisimilarity, written $\approx$, is the largest environmental bisimulation. To prove that two terms t_0 and t_1 are equivalent, we want to relate them without any predefined knowledge, i.e., we want to prove that $t_0 \approx_{\emptyset} t_1$ holds; we also write $\simeq$ for $\approx_{\emptyset}$.

The first part of the definition makes the bisimulation game explicit for t_0, t_1, while the second part focuses on environments $\mathcal{E}$. If t_0 is a normal form, then t_1 has to evaluate to a normal form of the same kind, and we extend the environment with the newly acquired knowledge. We then compare values in $\mathcal{E}$ (clause (2a)) by applying them to arguments built from $\mathcal{E}$, as in the λ-calculus [19]. Similarly, we test stuck terms in $\mathcal{E}$ by putting them within contexts $\langle E_0'\rangle$, $\langle E_1'\rangle$ built from $\mathcal{E}$ (clause (2b)) to trigger the capture. This reminds the way we test values and stuck terms with applicative bisimilarity [4], except that applicative bisimilarity tests both values or stuck terms with the same argument or context. Using different entities (as in Definition 6) makes bisimulation proofs harder, but it simplifies the proof of congruence of the environmental bisimilarity.

Example 1. We have $\langle(\lambda x.t_0)\ \langle t_1\rangle\rangle \simeq (\lambda x.\langle t_0\rangle)\ \langle t_1\rangle$, because the relation $\mathcal{X} = \{(\emptyset, \langle(\lambda x.t)\ \langle t'\rangle\rangle, (\lambda x.\langle t\rangle)\langle t'\rangle), (\emptyset, \langle(\lambda x.t)\ v\rangle, (\lambda x.\langle t\rangle) v)\} \cup \{(\mathcal{E}, t, t) \mid \mathcal{E} \subseteq \mathcal{I}\} \cup \{\mathcal{E} \mid \mathcal{E} \subseteq \mathcal{I}\}$ is a bisimulation. Indeed, if $\langle t'\rangle$ evaluates to v, then $\langle(\lambda x.t)\ \langle t'\rangle\rangle \rightarrow_{\mathrm{v}}^* \langle(\lambda x.t)\ v\rangle$ and $(\lambda x.\langle t\rangle)\ \langle t'\rangle \rightarrow_{\mathrm{v}}^* (\lambda x.\langle t\rangle)\ v$, which both reduce to $\langle t\{v/x\}\rangle$.

As usual with environmental relations, the candidate relation $\mathcal{X}$ in the above example could be made simpler with the help of up-to techniques.

Definition 6 is written in the small-step style, because each reduction step from t_0 has to be matched by t_1. In the big-step style, we are concerned only with evaluations to normal forms.

Definition 7. *A relation $\mathcal{X}$ is a big-step environmental bisimulation if* $t_0\ \mathcal{X}_{\mathcal{E}}\ t_1$ *implies:*

1. $t_0\ \mathcal{X}_{\mathcal{E}}\ t_1$ *implies:*
   (a) *if* $t_0 \rightarrow_{\mathrm{v}}^* v_0$, *then* $t_1 \rightarrow_{\mathrm{v}}^* v_1$ *and* $\mathcal{E} \cup \{(v_0, v_1)\} \in \mathcal{X}$;
   (b) *if* $t_0 \rightarrow_{\mathrm{v}}^* t_0'$ *with* t_0' *stuck, then* $t_1 \rightarrow_{\mathrm{v}}^* t_1'$, t_1' *stuck, and* $\mathcal{E} \cup \{(t_0', t_1')\} \in \mathcal{X}$;
   (c) *the converse of the above conditions on* t_1;
2. $\mathcal{E} \in \mathcal{X}$ *implies:*
   (a) *if* $\lambda x.t_0\ \mathcal{E}\ \lambda x.t_1$ *and* $v_0\ \widehat{\mathcal{E}}\ v_1$, *then* $t_0\{v_0/x\}\ \mathcal{X}_{\mathcal{E}}\ t_1\{v_1/x\}$;

(b) if $E_0[\mathcal{S}k.t_0]$ $\mathcal{E}$ $E_1[\mathcal{S}k.t_1]$ *and* E'_0 $\widetilde{\mathcal{E}}$ E'_1, *then* $\langle t_0\{\lambda x.\langle E'_0[E_0[x]]\rangle/k\}\rangle$ $\mathcal{X}_{\mathcal{E}}$ $\langle t_1\{\lambda x.\langle E'_1[E_1[x]]\rangle/k\}\rangle$ *for a fresh* x.

Lemma 4. *If* $\mathcal{X}$ *is a big-step environmental bisimulation, then* $\mathcal{X} \subseteq \approx$.

Big-step relations can be more convenient to use when we know the result of the evaluation, as in Example 1, or as in the following one.

Example 2. We have $\langle\langle t\rangle\rangle \simeq \langle t\rangle$. Indeed, we can show that $\langle\langle t\rangle\rangle \rightarrow_{\mathrm{v}}^{*} v$ iff $\langle t\rangle \rightarrow_{\mathrm{v}}^{*} v$, therefore $\{(\emptyset, \langle\langle t\rangle\rangle, \langle t\rangle)\} \cup \{(\mathcal{E}, t, t) \mid \mathcal{E} \subseteq \mathcal{I}\} \cup \{\mathcal{E} \mid \mathcal{E} \subseteq \mathcal{I}\}$ is a big-step environmental bisimulation.

We use the following results in the rest of the paper.

Lemma 5 (Weakening). *If* $t_0 \approx_{\mathcal{E}} t_1$ *and* $\mathcal{E}' \subseteq \mathcal{E}$ *then* $t_0 \approx_{\mathcal{E}'} t_1$.

A smaller environment is a weaker constraint, because we can build less arguments and contexts to test the normal forms in $\mathcal{E}$. The proof is as in [19]. Lemma 6 states that reduction (and therefore, evaluation) is included in $\simeq$.

Lemma 6. *If* $t_0 \rightarrow_{\mathrm{v}} t'_0$, *then* $t_0 \simeq t'_0$.

3.3 Soundness and Completeness

We now prove soundness and completeness of $\simeq$ w.r.t. contextual equivalence. Because the proofs follow the same steps as for the λ-calculus [19], we only give here the main lemmas and sketch their proofs. The complete proofs can be found in [6]. First, we need some basic up-to techniques, namely up-to environment (which allows bigger environments in the bisimulation clauses) and up-to bisimilarity (which allows for limited uses of $\simeq$ in the bisimulation clauses), whose definitions and proofs of soundness are classic [19].

With these tools, we can prove that $\simeq$ is sound and complete w.r.t. contextual equivalence. For a relation $\mathcal{R}$ on terms, we write $\mathcal{R}^{\mathrm{nf}}$ for its restriction to closed normal forms. The first step consists in proving congruence for normal forms, and also for any terms but only w.r.t. evaluation contexts.

Lemma 7. *Let* t_0, t_1 *be normal forms. If* $t_0 \approx_{\mathcal{E}} t_1$, *then* $C[t_0] \approx_{\mathcal{E}} C[t_1]$.

Lemma 8. *If* $t_0 \approx_{\mathcal{E}} t_1$, *then* $F[t_0] \approx_{\mathcal{E}} F[t_1]$.

Lemmas 7 and 8 are proved simultaneously by showing that, for any environmental bisimulation $\mathcal{Y}$, the relation

$$\mathcal{X} = \{(\widehat{\mathcal{E}}^{\mathrm{nf}}, F_0[t_0], F_1[t_1]) \mid t_0\ \mathcal{Y}_{\mathcal{E}}\ t_1, F_0\ \widetilde{\mathcal{E}}\ F_1\} \cup \{(\widehat{\mathcal{E}}^{\mathrm{nf}}, t_0, t_1) \mid \mathcal{E} \in \mathcal{Y}, t_0\ \widehat{\mathcal{E}}\ t_1\} \cup \{\widehat{\mathcal{E}}^{\mathrm{nf}} \mid \mathcal{E} \in \mathcal{Y}\}$$

is a bisimulation up-to environment. Informally, the elements of the first set of $\mathcal{X}$ reduce to elements of the second set of $\mathcal{X}$, and we then prove the bisimulation property for these elements by induction on $t_0\ \widehat{\mathcal{E}}\ t_1$. We can then prove the main congruence lemma.

Lemma 9. *$t_0 \simeq t_1$ implies $C[t_0] \approx_{\widehat{\simeq}^{\mathrm{nf}}} C[t_1]$.*

We show that $\{(\widehat{\simeq}^{\mathrm{nf}}, t_0, t_1) \mid t_0 \widehat{\simeq} t_1\} \cup \{\widehat{\simeq}^{\mathrm{nf}}\}$ is a bisimulation up-to bisimilarity by induction on $t_0 \widehat{\simeq} t_1$. By weakening (Lemma 5), we can deduce from Lemma 9 that $\simeq$ is a congruence, and therefore is sound w.r.t. $\approx_c$.

Corollary 1 (Soundness). *We have $\simeq \subseteq \approx_c$.*

The relation $\simeq$ is also complete w.r.t. contextual equivalence.

Theorem 1 (Completeness). *We have $\approx_c \subseteq \simeq$.*

The proof is by showing that $\{({\approx_c}^{\mathrm{nf}}, t_0, t_1) \mid t_0 \approx_c t_1\} \cup \{{\approx_c}^{\mathrm{nf}}\}$ is a big-step bisimulation, using Lemma 3 as an alternate definition for $\approx_c$.

3.4 Bisimulation Up to Context

Equivalence proofs based on environmental bisimilarity can be simplified by using up-to techniques, such as up to reduction, up to expansion, and up to context [19]. We only discuss the last, since the first two can be defined and proved sound in $\lambda_{\mathcal{S}}$ without issues. Bisimulations up to context may factor out a common context from the tested terms. Formally, we define the context closure of $\mathcal{X}$, written $\overline{\mathcal{X}}$, as follows: we have $t_0 \; \overline{\mathcal{X}_\mathcal{E}} \; t_1$ if

- either $t_0 = F_0[t_0']$, $t_1 = F_1[t_1']$, $t_0' \; \mathcal{X}_\mathcal{E} \; t_1'$, and $F_0 \; \widetilde{\mathcal{E}} \; F_1$;
- or $t_0 \; \widehat{\mathcal{E}} \; t_1$.

Note that terms t_0' and t_1' (related by $\mathcal{X}_\mathcal{E}$) can be put into evaluation contexts only, while normal forms (related by $\mathcal{E}$) can be put in any contexts. This restriction to evaluation contexts in the first case is usual in the definition of up-to context techniques for environmental relations [19,22,20,18].

Definition 8. *A relation $\mathcal{X}$ is an environmental bisimulation up to context if*

1. *$t_0 \; \mathcal{X}_\mathcal{E} \; t_1$ implies:*
   (a) *if $t_0 \rightarrow_{\mathrm{v}} t_0'$, then $t_1 \rightarrow_{\mathrm{v}}^* t_1'$ and $t_0' \; \overline{\mathcal{X}_\mathcal{E}} \; t_1'$;*
   (b) *if $t_0 = v_0$, then $t_1 \rightarrow_{\mathrm{v}}^* v_1$ and $\mathcal{E} \cup \{(v_0, v_1)\} \subseteq \widehat{\mathcal{E}'}^{\mathrm{nf}}$ for some $\mathcal{E}' \in \mathcal{X}$;*
   (c) *if t_0 is stuck, then $t_1 \rightarrow_{\mathrm{v}}^* t_1'$ with t_1' stuck, and $\mathcal{E} \cup \{(t_0, t_1')\} \subseteq \widehat{\mathcal{E}'}^{\mathrm{nf}}$ for some $\mathcal{E}' \in \mathcal{X}$;*
   (d) *the converse of the above conditions on t_1;*
2. *$\mathcal{E} \in \mathcal{X}$ implies:*
   (a) *if $\lambda x.t_0 \; \mathcal{E} \; \lambda x.t_1$ and $v_0 \; \widehat{\mathcal{E}} \; v_1$, then $t_0\{v_0/x\} \; \overline{\mathcal{X}_\mathcal{E}} \; t_1\{v_1/x\}$;*
   (b) *if $E_0[\mathcal{S}k.t_0] \; \mathcal{E} \; E_1[\mathcal{S}k.t_1]$ and $E_0' \; \widetilde{\mathcal{E}} \; E_1'$, then $\langle t_0\{\lambda x.\langle E_0'[E_0[x]]\rangle/k\}\rangle \; \overline{\mathcal{X}_\mathcal{E}} \; \langle t_1\{\lambda x.\langle E_1'[E_1[x]]\rangle/k\}\rangle$ for a fresh x.*

Lemma 10. *If $\mathcal{X}$ is an environmental bisimulation up to context, then $\mathcal{X} \subseteq \approx$.*

The soundness proof is the same as in [19]. While this definition is enough to simplify proofs in the λ-calculus case, it is not that helpful in $\lambda_{\mathcal{S}}$, because of the restriction to evaluation contexts (first item of the definition of $\overline{\mathcal{X}}$). In the λ-calculus, when a term t reduces within an evaluation context, the context is not affected, hence Definition 8 is enough to help proving interesting equivalences. It is not the case in $\lambda_{\mathcal{S}}$, as (a part of) the evaluation context can be captured.

Indeed, suppose we want to construct a candidate relation $\mathcal{X}$ to prove the β_Ω axiom, i.e., $E[t]$ is equivalent to $(\lambda x.E[x])\ t$, assuming $x \notin \mathsf{fv}(E)$. The problematic case is when t is a stuck term $E_0[\mathcal{S}k.t_0]$; we have to add the stuck terms $(\lambda x.E[x])\ E_0[\mathcal{S}k.t_0]$ and $E[E_0[\mathcal{S}k.t_0]]$ to an environment $\mathcal{E}$ of $\mathcal{X}$. For $\mathcal{X}$ to be a bisimulation, we then have to prove that for all $E_1\ \widetilde{\mathcal{E}}\ E_2$, we have $\langle t_0\{\lambda y.\langle E_1[(\lambda x.E[x])\ E_0[y]]\rangle/k\}\rangle\ \mathcal{X}_{\mathcal{E}}\ \langle t_0\{\lambda y.\langle E_2[E[E_0[y]]]\rangle/k\}\rangle$. At this point, we would like to use the up-to context technique, because the subterms $(\lambda x.E[x])\ E_0[y]$ and $E[E_0[y]]$ are similar to the terms we want to relate (they can be written $(\lambda x.E[x])\ t''$ and $E[t'']$ with $t'' = E_0[y]$). However, we have at best $\langle t_0\{\lambda y.\langle E_1[(\lambda x.E[x])\ E_0[y]]\rangle/k\}\rangle\ \widehat{\mathcal{X}_{\mathcal{E}}}^{\circ}\ \langle t_0\{\lambda y.\langle E_2[E[E_0[y]]]\rangle/k\}\rangle$ (and not $\overline{\mathcal{X}_{\mathcal{E}}}$), because (i) $(\lambda x.E[x])\ E_0[y]$ and $E[E_0[y]]$ are open terms, and (ii) t_0 can be any term, so $(\lambda x.E[x])\ E_0[y]$ and $E[E_0[y]]$ can be put in any context, not necessarily in an evaluation one. Therefore, Definition 8 cannot help there.

Problem (ii) could be somewhat dealt with in the particular case of the β_Ω axiom by changing clause (2b) of Definition 8 into

(b) if $E_0[\mathcal{S}k.t_0]\ \mathcal{E}\ E_1[\mathcal{S}k.t_1]$ and $E_0'\ \widetilde{\mathcal{X}_{\mathcal{E}}}\ E_1'$, then $\langle t_0\{\lambda x.\langle E_0'[E_0[x]]\rangle/k\}\rangle\ \widehat{\mathcal{X}_{\mathcal{E}}}$ $\langle t_1\{\lambda x.\langle E_1'[E_1[x]]\rangle/k\}\rangle$ for a fresh x.

and similarly for clause (2a). In plain text, we build the testing contexts E_0', E_1' from $\mathcal{X}_{\mathcal{E}}$ (instead of $\mathcal{E}$), and the resulting terms have to be in $\widehat{\mathcal{X}_{\mathcal{E}}}$ (without any evaluation context restriction). The resulting notion of bisimulation up to context is sound. The new clause would be more difficult to establish in general than the original one (of Definition 8), because it tests more pairs of contexts. However, for the β_Ω axiom, we would have to prove that for all $E_1\ \widehat{\mathcal{X}_{\mathcal{E}}}\ E_2$, $\langle t_0\{\lambda y.\langle E_1[(\lambda x.E[x])\ E_0[y]]\rangle/k\}\rangle\ \widehat{\mathcal{X}_{\mathcal{E}}}\ \langle t_0\{\lambda y.\langle E_2[E[E_0[y]]]\rangle/k\}\rangle$ holds; it would be easy, except $(\lambda x.E[x])\ E_0[y]$ and $E[E_0[y]]$ are open terms (problem (i)).

Problem (i) seems harder to fix, because for $(\lambda x.E[x])\ E_0[y]\ \mathcal{X}_{\mathcal{E}}{}^{\circ}\ E[E_0[y]]$ to hold, we must have $(\lambda x.E[x])\ E_0[v_0]\ \mathcal{X}_{\mathcal{E}}\ E[E_0[v_1]]$ for all $v_0\ \widehat{\mathcal{E}}\ v_1$. Because E_0 can be anything, it means that we must have $(\lambda x.E[x])\ t_0'\ \mathcal{X}_{\mathcal{E}}\ E[t_1']$ with $t_0'\ \widehat{\mathcal{E}}\ t_1'$; t_0' and t_1' are plugged in different contexts, therefore bisimulation up to context (which factors out only a common context) cannot help us there; a new kind of up-to technique is required.

The β_Ω axiom example suggests that we need more powerful up-to techniques for environmental bisimilarity for delimited control; we leave these potential improvements as a future work. Note that we do not have such issues with up-to techniques for normal form bisimilarity: it relates open terms without having to replace their free variables, and normal form bisimulation up to context is not restricted to evaluation contexts only. But even if environmental bisimulation up to context is not as helpful as wished, it still simplifies equivalence proofs, as we can see with the next example.

Example 3. In [7], a variant of Turing's call-by-value fixed point combinators using shift and reset has been proposed. Let $\theta = \lambda xy.y\ (\lambda z.x\ x\ y\ z)$. We prove that $t_0 = \theta\ \theta$ is bisimilar to its variant $t_1 = \langle \theta\ \mathcal{S}k.k\ k\rangle$. Let $\theta' = \lambda x.\langle \theta\ x\rangle$, $v_0 = \lambda y.y\ (\lambda z.\theta\ \theta\ y\ z)$, and $v_1 = \lambda y.y\ (\lambda z.\theta'\ \theta'\ y\ z)$. We define $\mathcal{E}$ inductively such that $v_0\ \mathcal{E}\ v_1$, and if $v_0'\ \widehat{\mathcal{E}}\ v_1'$, then $\lambda z.\theta\ \theta\ v_0'\ z\ \mathcal{E}\ \lambda z.\theta'\ \theta'\ v_1'\ z$. Then $\mathcal{X} = \{(\mathcal{E}, t_0, t_1), (\mathcal{E}, t_0, \theta'\ \theta'), \mathcal{E}\}$ is a (big-step) bisimulation up to context. Indeed, we have $t_0 \Downarrow_{\mathrm{v}} v_0$, $t_1 \Downarrow_{\mathrm{v}} v_1$, and $\theta'\ \theta' \Downarrow_{\mathrm{v}} v_1$, therefore clause (1b) of Definition 8 is checked for both pairs. We now check clause (2a), first for $v_0\ \mathcal{E}\ v_1$. For all $v_0'\ \widehat{\mathcal{E}}\ v_1'$, we have $v_0'\ (\lambda z.\theta\ \theta\ v_0'\ z)\ \widehat{\mathcal{E}}\ v_1'\ (\lambda z.\theta'\ \theta'\ v_1'\ z)$ (because $\lambda z.\theta\ \theta\ v_0'\ z\ \mathcal{E}\ \lambda z.\theta'\ \theta'\ v_1'\ z$), hence the result holds. Next, let $\lambda z.\theta\ \theta\ v_0'\ z\ \mathcal{E}\ \lambda z.\theta'\ \theta'\ v_1'\ z$ (with $v_0'\ \widehat{\mathcal{E}}\ v_1'$), and let $v_0''\ \widehat{\mathcal{E}}\ v_1''$. We have to check that $\theta\ \theta\ v_0'\ v_0''\ \overline{\mathcal{X}_{\mathcal{E}}}\ \theta'\ \theta'\ v_1'\ v_1''$, which is true, because $\theta\ \theta\ \mathcal{X}_{\mathcal{E}}\ \theta'\ \theta'$, and $\square\ v_0'\ v_0''\ \widehat{\mathcal{E}}\ \square\ v_1'\ v_1''$.

4 Environmental Relations for the Original Semantics

The original CPS semantics for shift and reset [8] as well as the corresponding reduction semantics [3] assume that terms can be considered as programs to be executed, only when surrounded by a top-level reset. In this section, we present a CPS-compatible bisimulation theory that takes such a requirement into account. Henceforth, we call *programs*, ranged over by p, terms of the form $\langle t\rangle$.

4.1 Contextual Equivalence

To reflect the fact that terms are executed within an enclosing reset, the contextual equivalence we consider in this section tests terms in contexts of the form $\langle C\rangle$ only. Because programs cannot reduce to stuck terms, the only possible observable action is evaluation to values. We therefore define contextual equivalence for programs as follows.

Definition 9. *Let t_0, t_1 be terms. We write $t_0 \dot{\approx}_c t_1$ if for all C such that $\langle C[t_0]\rangle$ and $\langle C[t_1]\rangle$ are closed, $\langle C[t_0]\rangle \Downarrow_{\mathrm{v}} v_0$ implies $\langle C[t_1]\rangle \Downarrow_{\mathrm{v}} v_1$, and conversely for $\langle C[t_1]\rangle$.*

Note that $\dot{\approx}_c$ is defined on all terms, not just programs. It is easy to check that $\approx_c$ is more discriminative than $\dot{\approx}_c$. We will see in Section 4.4 that this inclusion is in fact strict.

Lemma 11. *We have $\approx_c \subseteq \dot{\approx}_c$.*

4.2 Definition and Properties

We now propose a definition of environmental bisimulation adapted to programs (but defined on all terms, like $\dot{\approx}_c$). Because stuck terms are no longer observed, environments $\mathcal{E}$ henceforth relate only values. Similarly, we write $\mathcal{R}^{\mathrm{v}}$ for the restriction of a relation $\mathcal{R}$ on terms to pairs of closed values.

Definition 10. *A relation $\mathcal{X}$ is an environmental bisimulation for programs if*

1. *if $t_0 \mathcal{X}_\mathcal{E} t_1$ and t_0 and t_1 are not both programs, then for all $E_0 \widetilde{\mathcal{E}} E_1$, we have $\langle E_0[t_0]\rangle \mathcal{X}_\mathcal{E} \langle E_1[t_1]\rangle$;*
2. *if $p_0 \mathcal{X}_\mathcal{E} p_1$*
   (a) if $p_0 \rightarrow_\mathrm{v} p_0'$, then $p_1 \rightarrow_\mathrm{v}^* p_1'$ and $p_0' \mathcal{X}_\mathcal{E} p_1'$;
   (b) if $p_0 \rightarrow_\mathrm{v} v_0$, then $p_1 \rightarrow_\mathrm{v}^* v_1$, and $\{(v_0, v_1)\} \cup \mathcal{E} \in \mathcal{X}$;
   (c) the converse of the above conditions on p_1;
3. *for all $\mathcal{E} \in \mathcal{X}$, if $\lambda x.t_0 \; \mathcal{E} \; \lambda x.t_1$ and $v_0 \; \widehat{\mathcal{E}} \; v_1$, then $t_0\{v_0/x\} \mathcal{X}_\mathcal{E} t_1\{v_1/x\}$.*

Environmental bisimilarity for programs, written $\dot{\approx}$, is the largest environmental bisimulation for programs. As before, the relation $\dot{\approx}_\emptyset$, also written $\dot{\simeq}$, is candidate to characterize $\dot{\approx}_c$.

Clauses (2) and (3) of Definition 10 deal with programs and environment in a classical way (as in plain λ-calculus). The problematic case is when relating terms t_0 and t_1 that are not both programs (clause (1)). Indeed, one of them may be stuck, and therefore we have to test them within some contexts $\langle E_0\rangle$, $\langle E_1\rangle$ (built from $\mathcal{E}$) to potentially trigger a capture that otherwise would not happen. We cannot require both terms to be stuck, as in clause (2b) of Definition 6, because a stuck term can be equivalent to a term free from control effect. E.g., we will see that $v \dot{\simeq} \mathcal{S}k.k\; v$, provided that $k \notin \mathsf{fv}(v)$.

Example 4. Suppose we want to prove $\langle(\lambda x.t_0)\,\langle t_1\rangle\rangle \dot{\simeq} (\lambda x.\langle t_0\rangle)\,\langle t_1\rangle$ (as in Example 1). Because $(\lambda x.\langle t_0\rangle)\,\langle t_1\rangle$ is not a program, we have to put both terms into a context first: we have to change the candidate relation of Example 1 into $\mathcal{X} = \{(\emptyset, \langle(\lambda x.t_0)\,\langle t_1\rangle\rangle, (\lambda x.\langle t_0\rangle)\,\langle t_1\rangle)\} \cup \{(\emptyset, \langle E[\langle(\lambda x.t_0)\,\langle t_1\rangle\rangle]\rangle, \langle E[(\lambda x.\langle t_0\rangle)\,\langle t_1\rangle]\rangle)\} \cup \{(\emptyset, \langle E[\langle(\lambda x.t_0)\, v\rangle]\rangle, \langle E[(\lambda x.\langle t_0\rangle)\, v]\rangle)\} \cup \{(\mathcal{E}, t, t) \mid \mathcal{E} \subseteq \mathcal{I}\} \cup \{\mathcal{E} \mid \mathcal{E} \subseteq \mathcal{I}\}$. In contrast, to prove $\langle\langle t\rangle\rangle \dot{\simeq} \langle t\rangle$, we do not have to change the candidate relation of Example 2, since both terms are programs.

We can give a definition of big-step bisimulation by removing clause (2a) and changing $\rightarrow_\mathrm{v}$ into $\rightarrow_\mathrm{v}^*$ in clause (2b). Lemmas 5 and 6 can also be extended to $\dot{\approx}$ and $\dot{\simeq}$. The next lemma shows that $\simeq$ is more discriminative than $\dot{\simeq}$.

Lemma 12. *We have $\simeq \subseteq \dot{\simeq}$.*

A consequence of Lemma 12 is that we can use Definition 6 as a proof technique for $\dot{\simeq}$. E.g., we have directly $\langle(\lambda x.t_0)\,\langle t_1\rangle\rangle \dot{\simeq} (\lambda x.\langle t_0\rangle)\,\langle t_1\rangle$, because $\langle(\lambda x.t_0)\,\langle t_1\rangle\rangle \simeq (\lambda x.\langle t_0\rangle)\,\langle t_1\rangle$.

4.3 Soundness and Completeness

We sketch the proofs of soundness and completeness of $\dot{\simeq}$ w.r.t. $\dot{\approx}_c$; see [6] for the complete proofs. The soundness proof follows the same scheme as in Section 3.3, with some necessary adjustments. As before, we need up-to environment and up-to bisimilarity techniques to prove the following lemmas.

Lemma 13. *If $v_0 \dot{\approx}_\mathcal{E} v_1$, then $C[v_0] \dot{\approx}_\mathcal{E} C[v_1]$.*

Lemma 14. *If* $t_0 \approx_{\mathcal{E}} t_1$*, then* $F[t_0] \approx_{\mathcal{E}} F[t_1]$.

We prove Lemmas 13 and 14 by showing that a relation similar to the relation $\mathcal{X}$ defined in Section 3.3 is a bisimulation up to environment. We then want to prove the main congruence lemma, akin to Lemma 9, by showing that $\mathcal{Y} = \{(\widehat{\dot{\simeq}}^{\mathsf{v}}, t_0, t_1) \mid t_0 \,\widehat{\dot{\simeq}}\, t_1\} \cup \{\widehat{\dot{\simeq}}^{\mathsf{v}}\}$ is a bisimulation up to bisimilarity. However, we can no longer proceed by induction on $t_0 \,\widehat{\dot{\simeq}}\, t_1$, as for Lemma 9. Indeed, if $p_0 = \langle t_0 \rangle$, $p_1 = \langle t_1 \rangle$ with $t_0 \,\widehat{\dot{\simeq}}\, t_1$, and if t_0 is a stuck term, then p_0 reduces to some term, but the induction hypothesis does not tell us anything about t_1. To circumvent this, we decompose related programs into related subcomponents.

Lemma 15. *If* $p_0 \,\widehat{\dot{\simeq}}\, p_1$*, then either* $p_0 \dot{\simeq} p_1$*, or one of the following holds:*
- $p_0 = \langle v_0 \rangle$;
- $p_0 = F_0[\langle E_0[t_0] \rangle]$, $p_1 = F_1[\langle E_1[t_1] \rangle]$, $F_0 \,\widetilde{\dot{\simeq}}\, F_1$, $E_0 \,\widetilde{\dot{\simeq}}\, E_1$, $t_0 \dot{\simeq} t_1$ *and* $t_0 \rightarrow_{\mathsf{v}} t'_0$ *or* t_0 *is stuck;*
- $p_0 = F_0[\langle E_0[r_0] \rangle]$, $p_1 = F_1[\langle E_1[t_1] \rangle]$, $F_0 \,\widetilde{\dot{\simeq}}\, F_1$, $E_0 \,\widetilde{\dot{\simeq}}\, E_1$, $r_0 \,\widehat{\dot{\simeq}}\, t_1$ *but* $r_0 \not\dot{\simeq} t_1$.

Lemma 15 generalizes Lemma 2 to related programs: we know p_0 can be decomposed into contexts F, $\langle E \rangle$, and a redex r, and we relate these subterms to p_1. We can then prove that $\mathcal{Y}$ (defined above) is a bisimulation up to bisimilarity, by showing that, in each case described by Lemma 15, p_0 and p_1 reduce to terms related by $\mathcal{Y}$. From this, we deduce $\dot{\simeq}$ is a congruence, and is sound w.r.t. $\dot{\approx}_c$.

Lemma 16. $t_0 \dot{\simeq} t_1$ *implies* $C[t_0] \approx_{\dot{\simeq}^{\mathsf{v}}} C[t_1]$.

Corollary 2 (Soundness). *We have* $\dot{\simeq} \subseteq \dot{\approx}_c$.

Remark 1. Following the ideas behind Definition 10, one can define an applicative bisimilarity $\mathcal{B}$ for programs. However, proving that $\mathcal{B}$ is sound seems more complex than for $\dot{\simeq}$. We remind that the soundness proof of an applicative bisimilarity consists in showing that a relation called the *Howe's closure* $\mathcal{B}^{\bullet}$ is an applicative bisimulation. To this end, we need a version of Lemma 15 for $\mathcal{B}^{\bullet}$. However, $\mathcal{B}^{\bullet}$ is inductively defined as the smallest congruence which contains $\mathcal{B}$ and satisfies $\mathcal{B}^{\bullet}\mathcal{B} \subseteq \mathcal{B}^{\bullet}$ (1), and condition (1) makes it difficult to write a decomposition lemma for $\mathcal{B}^{\bullet}$ similar to Lemma 15.

We prove completeness of $\dot{\simeq}$ by showing that the relation $\ddot{\approx}_c$, defined below, coincides with $\dot{\approx}_c$ and $\dot{\simeq}$. By doing so, we also prove a context lemma for $\dot{\approx}_c$.

Definition 11. *Let* t_0, t_1 *be closed terms. We write* $t_0 \ddot{\approx}_c t_1$ *if for all closed* F, $\langle F[t_0] \rangle \Downarrow_{\mathsf{v}} v_0$ *implies* $\langle F[t_1] \rangle \Downarrow_{\mathsf{v}} v_1$*, and conversely for* $\langle F[t_1] \rangle$.

By definition, we have $\dot{\approx}_c \subseteq \ddot{\approx}_c$. With the same proof technique as in Section 3.3, we prove the following lemma.

Lemma 17 (Completeness). *We have* $\ddot{\approx}_c \subseteq \dot{\simeq}$.

With Lemma 17 and Corollary 2, we have $\dot{\approx}_c \subseteq \ddot{\approx}_c \subseteq \dot{\simeq} \subseteq \dot{\approx}_c$. Defining up-to context for programs is possible, with the same limitations as in Section 3.4.

4.4 Examples

We illustrate the differences between $\simeq$ and $\dot{\simeq}$, by giving some examples of terms related by $\dot{\simeq}$, but not by $\simeq$. First, note that $\dot{\simeq}$ relates non-terminating terms with stuck non-terminating terms.

Lemma 18. *We have* $\Omega \dot{\simeq} \mathcal{S}k.\Omega$.

The relation $\{(\emptyset, \Omega, \mathcal{S}k.\Omega), (\emptyset, \langle E[\Omega]\rangle, \langle E[\mathcal{S}k.\Omega]\rangle), (\emptyset, \langle E[\Omega]\rangle, \langle \Omega\rangle)\}$ is a bisimulation for programs. Lemma 18 does not hold with $\simeq$ because Ω is not stuck.

As wished, $\dot{\simeq}$ satisfies the only axiom of [14] not satisfied by $\simeq$.

Lemma 19. *If* $k \notin \mathsf{fv}(t)$, *then* $t \dot{\simeq}^{\circ} \mathcal{S}k.k\, t$.

We sketch the proof for t closed; for the general case, see [6]. We prove that $\{(\emptyset, t, \mathcal{S}k.k\, t), (\emptyset, \langle E[t]\rangle, \langle E[\mathcal{S}k.k\, t]\rangle)\} \cup \simeq$ is a bisimulation for programs. Indeed, we have $\langle E[\mathcal{S}k.k\, t]\rangle \rightarrow_{\mathrm{v}} \langle(\lambda x.\langle E[x]\rangle)\, t\rangle$, and because $\simeq$ verifies the β_Ω axiom ($\simeq$ is complete, and $\approx_c$ verifies the β_Ω axiom [4]), we know that $\langle(\lambda x.\langle E[x]\rangle)\, t\rangle \simeq \langle\langle E[t]\rangle\rangle$ holds. From Example 2, we have $\langle\langle E[t]\rangle\rangle \simeq \langle E[t]\rangle$, therefore we have $\langle E[\mathcal{S}k.k\, t]\rangle \simeq \langle E[t]\rangle$.

Consequently, $\dot{\simeq}^{\circ}$ is complete w.r.t. $\equiv$.

Corollary 3. *We have* $\equiv \subseteq \dot{\simeq}^{\circ}$.

As a result, we can use $\equiv$ (restricted to closed terms) as a proof technique for $\dot{\simeq}$. E.g., the following equivalence can be derived from the axioms [14].

Lemma 20. *If* $k \notin \mathsf{fv}(t_1)$, *then* $(\lambda x.\mathcal{S}k.t_0)\, t_1 \dot{\simeq} \mathcal{S}k.((\lambda x.t_0)\, t_1)$.

This equivalence does not hold with $\simeq$, because the term on the right is stuck, but the term on the left may not evaluate to a stuck term (if t_1 does not terminate). We can generalize this result as follows, again by using $\equiv$.

Lemma 21. *If* $k \notin \mathsf{fv}(t_1)$ *and* $x \notin \mathsf{fv}(E)$, *then we have* $(\lambda x.E[\mathcal{S}k.t_0])\, t_1 \dot{\simeq} E[\mathcal{S}k.((\lambda x.t_0)\, t_1)]$.

Proving Lemma 19 without the β_Ω axiom and Lemmas 20 and 21 without $\equiv$ requires complex candidate relations (see the proof of Lemma 20 in [6]), because of the lack of powerful enough up-to techniques.

5 Conclusion

We propose sound and complete environmental bisimilarities for two variants of the semantics of $\lambda_{\mathcal{S}}$. For the semantics of Section 3, we now have several bisimilarities, each with its own merit. Normal form bisimilarity [5] (and its up-to techniques) leads to minimal proof obligations, however it is not complete, and distinguishes very simple equivalent terms (see Proposition 1 in [5]). Applicative bisimilarity [4] is complete but sometimes requires complex bisimulation proofs (e.g., for the β_Ω axiom). Environmental bisimilarity $\simeq$ (Definition 6) is also complete, can be difficult to use, but this difficulty can be mitigated with up-to techniques. However, bisimulation up to context is not as helpful as we could hope (see Section 3.4), because we have to manipulate open terms (problem (i)), and the context closure of an environmental relation is restricted to evaluation contexts (problem (ii)). As a result, proving the β_Ω axiom is more difficult with environmental than with applicative bisimilarity. We believe dealing with problem (i) requires new up-to techniques to be developed, and lifting the evaluation context restriction (problem (ii)) would benefit not only for $\lambda_\mathcal{S}$, but also for process calculi with passivation [18]; we leave this as a future work.

In contrast, we do not have as many options when considering the semantics of Section 4 (where terms are evaluated within a top-level reset). The environmental bisimilarity of this paper $\dot{\simeq}$ (Definition 10) is the first to be sound and complete w.r.t. Definition 9. As argued in [5] (Section 3.2), normal form bisimilarity cannot be defined on programs without introducing extra quantifications (which defeats the purpose of normal form bisimilarity). Applicative bisimilarity could be defined for programs, but proving its soundness would require a new technique, since the usual one (Howe's method) does not seem to apply (see Remark 1). This confirms that environmental bisimilarity is more flexible than applicative bisimilarity [15]. However, we would like to simplify the quantification over contexts in clause (1) of Definition 10, so we look for sub-classes of terms where this quantification is not mandatory.

Other future works include the study of the behavioral theory of other delimited control operators, like the dynamic ones (e.g., *control* and *prompt* [10] or *shift*$_0$ and *reset*$_0$ [7]), but also of abortive control operators, such as *callcc*, for which no sound and complete bisimilarity has been defined so far.

Acknowledgments. We thank Małgorzata Biernacka and the anonymous referees for many helpful comments on the presentation of this work.

References

1. Asai, K., Kameyama, Y.: Polymorphic delimited continuations. In: Shao, Z. (ed.) APLAS 2007. LNCS, vol. 4807, pp. 239–254. Springer, Heidelberg (2007)
2. Balat, V., Cosmo, R.D., Fiore, M.P.: Extensional normalisation and type-directed partial evaluation for typed lambda calculus with sums. In: Leroy, X. (ed.) POPL 2004, Venice, Italy. SIGPLAN Notices, vol. 39(1), pp. 64–76. ACM Press (2004)
3. Biernacka, M., Biernacki, D., Danvy, O.: An operational foundation for delimited continuations in the CPS hierarchy. Logical Methods in Computer Science 1(2:5), 1–39 (2005)
4. Biernacki, D., Lenglet, S.: Applicative bisimulations for delimited-control operators. In: Birkedal, L. (ed.) FOSSACS 2012. LNCS, vol. 7213, pp. 119–134. Springer, Heidelberg (2012)
5. Biernacki, D., Lenglet, S.: Normal form bisimulations for delimited-control operators. In: Schrijvers, T., Thiemann, P. (eds.) FLOPS 2012. LNCS, vol. 7294, pp. 47–61. Springer, Heidelberg (2012)
6. Biernacki, D., Lenglet, S.: Environmental bisimulations for delimited-control operators (September 2013), `http://hal.inria.fr/hal-00862189`

7. Danvy, O., Filinski, A.: A functional abstraction of typed contexts. DIKU Rapport 89/12, DIKU, Computer Science Department, University of Copenhagen, Copenhagen, Denmark (July 1989)
8. Danvy, O., Filinski, A.: Abstracting control. In: Wand (ed.) [24], pp. 151–160
9. Dybvig, R.K., Peyton-Jones, S., Sabry, A.: A monadic framework for delimited continuations. Journal of Functional Programming 17(6), 687–730 (2007)
10. Felleisen, M.: The theory and practice of first-class prompts. In: Ferrante, J., Mager, P. (eds.) POPL 1988, pp. 180–190. ACM Press, San Diego (1988)
11. Filinski, A.: Representing monads. In: Boehm, H.-J. (ed.) POPL 1994, Portland, Oregon, pp. 446–457. ACM Press (January 1994)
12. Hieb, R., Dybvig, R.K., Anderson III, C.W.: Subcontinuations. Lisp and Symbolic Computation 5(4), 295–326 (1993)
13. Kameyama, Y.: Axioms for control operators in the CPS hierarchy. Higher-Order and Symbolic Computation 20(4), 339–369 (2007)
14. Kameyama, Y., Hasegawa, M.: A sound and complete axiomatization of delimited continuations. In: Shivers, O. (ed.) ICFP 2003, Uppsala, Sweden. SIGPLAN Notices, vol. 38(9), pp. 177–188. ACM Press (August 2003)
15. Koutavas, V., Levy, P.B., Sumii, E.: From applicative to environmental bisimulation. Electronic Notes in Theoretical Computer Science 276, 215–235 (2011)
16. Milner, R.: Fully abstract models of typed λ-calculi. Theoretical Computer Science 4(1), 1–22 (1977)
17. Morris, J.H.: Lambda Calculus Models of Programming Languages. PhD thesis, Massachusets Institute of Technology (1968)
18. Piérard, A., Sumii, E.: A higher-order distributed calculus with name creation. In: LICS 2012, Dubrovnik, Croatia, pp. 531–540. IEEE Computer Society Press (June 2012)
19. Sangiorgi, D., Kobayashi, N., Sumii, E.: Environmental bisimulations for higher-order languages. ACM Transactions on Programming Languages and Systems 33(1), 1–69 (2011)
20. Sato, N., Sumii, E.: The higher-order, call-by-value applied pi-calculus. In: Hu, Z. (ed.) APLAS 2009. LNCS, vol. 5904, pp. 311–326. Springer, Heidelberg (2009)
21. Sitaram, D., Felleisen, M.: Reasoning with continuations II: Full abstraction for models of control. In: Wand (ed.) [24], pp. 161–175
22. Sumii, E.: A bisimulation-like proof method for contextual properties in untyped lambda-calculus with references and deallocation. Theoretical Computer Science 411(51-52), 4358–4378 (2010)
23. Sumii, E., Pierce, B.C.: A bisimulation for dynamic sealing. Theoretical Computer Science 375(1-3), 169–192 (2007)
24. Wand, M. (ed.): Proceedings of the 1990 ACM Conference on Lisp and Functional Programming, Nice, France. ACM Press (June 1990)

On Bar Recursion and Choice in a Classical Setting

Valentin Blot and Colin Riba

ENS de Lyon, Université de Lyon, LIP*
{valentin.blot,colin.riba}@ens-lyon.fr
http://perso.ens-lyon.fr/valentin.blot/
http://perso.ens-lyon.fr/colin.riba/

Abstract. We show how Modified Bar-Recursion, a variant of Spector's Bar-Recursion due to Berger and Oliva can be used to realize the Axiom of Countable Choice in Parigot's Lambda-Mu-calculus, a direct-style language for the representation and evaluation of classical proofs.

We rely on Hyland-Ong innocent games. They provide a model for the instances of the axiom of choice usually used in the realization of classical choice with Bar-Recursion, and where, moreover, the standard datatype of natural numbers is in the image of a CPS-translation.

1 Introduction

Peano's Arithmetic in all finite types (PA^ω) is a multisorted version of first-order Peano's Arithmetic, with one sort for each simple type, together with the constants of Gödel's System T and their defining equations. When augmenting PA^ω with the Axiom of Countable Choice (CAC), we obtain a system known to contain large parts of classical analysis (see e.g. [9, 16]). A similar system can be obtained by extending Peano's Arithmetic to Second-Order Logic (see e.g. [16]).

We are interested here in the realizability interpretation of $\mathsf{PA}^\omega + \mathsf{CAC}$. Realizability is a mathematical tool, part of the Curry-Howard correspondence, used to extract computational content from formal proofs.

The usual route to get a computational interpretation of (some extension of) PA^ω is to apply a negative translation, yielding proofs in (some extension of) Heyting's Arithmetic in all finite types (HA^ω, the intuitionist variant of PA^ω, see e.g. [19]), followed by a computational interpretation of the translated proofs. Realizability for HA^ω can be obtained in simply-typed settings, typically using Gödel's System T. In this way, CAC is translated to a formula which can be realized by combining a realizer of the *Intuitionistic Axiom of Choice* (IAC) with a realizer of the *Double Negation Shift* (DNS, see Sect. 3). Intuitionistic choice is easily realizable, and realizers of DNS can be obtained by adapting Spector's *Bar-Recursion* to realizability [3, 4].

We are interested here in a computational interpretation of $\mathsf{PA}^\omega + \mathsf{CAC}$ based on a realizability interpretation directly for classical proofs. It has been noted by

* UMR 5668 CNRS ENS Lyon UCBL INRIA.

C.-c. Shan (Ed.): APLAS 2013, LNCS 8301, pp. 349–364, 2013.

Griffin [6] that the control operator `call/cc` of the functional language Scheme can be typed using *Peirce's Law*, which gives full Classical Logic when added to Intuitionistic Logic. Since then, there have been much work on calculi for Classical Logic, starting from Parigot's $\lambda\mu$-calculus [14]. Moreover, Krivine has developed a notion of Classical Realizability for Second-Order Peano's Arithmetic which relies on Girard's System F [10] (see also [13, 12]).

In this paper, we investigate a version of Spector's Bar-Recursion in a classical realizability setting for PA^ω, obtained by adapting Krivine's Realizability to a simply-typed extension of Parigot's $\lambda\mu$-calculus. Handling Bar-Recursion in realizability (typically to show that it realizes DNS) usualy involves some form of the axiom of choice (typically bar-induction). Suitable instances of bar-induction can be applied to some programming language extended with infinite terms, as in [3]. Another possibility, as done in [4], is to internalize realizability in the logic, reason within the logic on finite terms using bar-induction, and provide a suitable model (typically a model of PCF). Similarly to [3] and contrary to [4], our notion of realizability is not internalized in the logic. For extraction of programs from proofs, our approach is similar to [4]: we separate the programming language from the model in which the realizability argument is made.

Most non-degenerate models and operational semantics for the $\lambda\mu$-calculus rely on CPS translations (see e.g. [15]). We work here with the call-by-name translation of Lafont-Reus-Streicher (see e.g. [18, 15]). In the coproduct completion of the innocent unbracketed Hyland-Ong game model of PCF [8, 11], the usual flat game arena of natural numbers is in the image of such a CPS translation (this was observed in [11]).

We define a notion of classical realizability in this game model. Our main result is that the usual realizer of classical choice obtained by combining a realizer of IAC with Berger-Oliva's variant of Bar-Recursion [4], is indeed a realizer of classical countable choice in our framework. We then obtain an extraction result for the $\lambda\mu$-terms by a logical relation argument (see e.g. [2]), relating the operational semantics and the model.

The paper is organized as follows: We begin by presenting PA^ω in Sect. 2. We then briefly discuss the usual computational interpretation of CAC by negative translation in Sect. 3. In Sect. 4, we present the bare minimum we need on Hyland-Ong games. Parigot's $\lambda\mu$-calculus, as well as its game interpretation and its operational semantics are discussed in Sect. 5. We then devise our notion of realizability in Sect. 6 and discuss the realization of CAC in Sect. 7.

2 Peano's Arithmetic in All Finite Types

In this section, we briefly discuss the logical system on which we work in this paper, namely PA^ω (Peano's Arithmetic in all finite types), as well as its extension with the axiom of countable choice. We build on usual versions of HA^ω (see e.g. [19, 9]), with ideas of [14, 10] for classical logic.

Language. The language of PA^ω is multisorted, with one sort for each simple type. We use the following syntax of simple types, where ι is intended to be the base type of natural numbers:

$$\sigma, \tau \in \mathcal{T} \quad ::= \quad \iota \quad | \quad \sigma \to \tau \quad | \quad \sigma \times \tau$$

We assume given, for each simple type τ, a countable set $\mathcal{V}_\tau = \{x^\tau, y^\tau, \ldots\}$ of *individual variables of type* τ. Individuals are simply-typed terms

$$a, b \in \mathcal{I} \quad ::= \quad x^\tau \quad | \quad ab \quad | \quad \mathsf{c}$$

where $(ab)^\tau$ provided $a^{\sigma\to\tau}$, b^σ for some σ, and c ranges over the constants 0^ι, $\mathsf{S}^{\iota\to\iota}$, $\mathsf{Rec}^{\tau\to(\iota\to\tau\to\tau)\to\iota\to\tau}$, $\mathsf{Pair}^{\sigma\to\tau\to\sigma\times\tau}$, $\mathsf{P}_i^{\tau_1\times\tau_2\to\tau_i}$ $(i = 1, 2)$, $\mathsf{k}^{\sigma\to\tau\to\sigma}$ and $\mathsf{s}^{(\rho\to\sigma\to\tau)\to(\rho\to\sigma)\to\rho\to\tau}$. Let $\mathcal{I}_0$ be the set of closed individuals and $\mathcal{I}_0^\tau$ be the set of closed individuals of type τ.

Formulas are defined as follows:

$$A, B \in \mathcal{F} \quad ::= \quad (a^\tau \neq_\tau b^\tau) \quad | \quad \bot \quad | \quad A \Rightarrow B \quad | \quad A \wedge B \quad | \quad \forall x^\tau A$$

Note the atomic inequality $(\_ \neq_\tau \_)$. It is inspired from Krivine's work [10] and will greatly ease our realizability interpretation (see Sect. 6).

We use the following abbreviations:

$$\begin{array}{rclcrcl} \neg A & := & A \Rightarrow \bot & \quad & \exists x^\tau A & := & \neg\forall x^\tau \neg A \\ (a =_\tau b) & := & \neg(a \neq_\tau b) & & A \vee B & := & \neg(\neg A \wedge \neg B) \end{array}$$

Deduction. We consider the following deduction system (see e.g. [14]). It is parametrized by a set Ax of axioms (containing only closed formulas).

$$\frac{}{\Gamma, A \vdash A \mid \Delta} \qquad \frac{}{\Gamma \vdash A \mid \Delta}\,(A \in Ax) \qquad \frac{\Gamma \vdash \bot \mid \Delta}{\Gamma \vdash a^\tau \neq_\tau b^\tau \mid \Delta}$$

$$\frac{\Gamma, A \vdash B \mid \Delta}{\Gamma \vdash A \Rightarrow B \mid \Delta} \qquad \frac{\Gamma \vdash A \Rightarrow B \mid \Delta \qquad \Gamma \vdash A \mid \Delta}{\Gamma \vdash B \mid \Delta}$$

$$\frac{\Gamma \vdash A \mid \Delta \qquad \Gamma \vdash B \mid \Delta}{\Gamma \vdash A \wedge B \mid \Delta} \qquad \frac{\Gamma \vdash A_1 \wedge A_2 \mid \Delta}{\Gamma \vdash A_i \mid \Delta}\,(i = 1, 2)$$

$$\frac{\Gamma \vdash A \mid \Delta}{\Gamma \vdash \forall x^\tau A \mid \Delta}\,(x \notin \mathrm{FV}(\Gamma, \Delta)) \qquad \frac{\Gamma \vdash \forall x^\tau A \mid \Delta}{\Gamma \vdash A[a^\tau/x] \mid \Delta}$$

$$\frac{\Gamma \vdash A \mid \Delta, A}{(\Gamma \vdash \Delta, A)} \qquad \frac{(\Gamma \vdash \Delta, A)}{\Gamma \vdash A \mid \Delta}$$

This system is chosen so as to have a direct extraction of realizers in Parigot's $\lambda\mu$-calculus (see Sect. 5 and 6).

Note that the Ex Falso rule is restricted to atomic formulas. For each formula A one can easily derive $\Gamma \vdash A \mid \Delta$ from $\Gamma \vdash \bot \mid \Delta$. The introduction rules for existential quantification and disjunction are easy to derive:

$$\frac{\Gamma \vdash A \mid \Delta}{\Gamma \vdash A \vee B \mid \Delta} \qquad \frac{\Gamma \vdash A[a^\tau/x] \mid \Delta}{\Gamma \vdash \exists x^\tau A \mid \Delta}$$

One can also derive Peirce's Law and Double Negation Elimination (see e.g. [14]):

$$\overline{\Gamma \vdash ((A \Rightarrow B) \Rightarrow A) \Rightarrow A \mid \Delta} \qquad \overline{\Gamma \vdash ((A \Rightarrow \bot) \Rightarrow \bot) \Rightarrow A \mid \Delta}$$

as well as the elimination rules of disjunction and existential quantification: $\Gamma \vdash C \mid \Delta$ provided $\Gamma \vdash A \vee B \mid \Delta$, $\Gamma, A \vdash C \mid \Delta$ and $\Gamma, B \vdash C \mid \Delta$; and $\Gamma \vdash C \mid \Delta$ provided $\Gamma \vdash \exists x^\tau A \mid \Delta$ and $\Gamma, A \vdash C \mid \Delta$ with x not free in Γ, C, Δ.

Axioms for Equality and Arithmetic. The axioms of PA^ω are the universal closures of the following formulas:

- Equality axioms are *reflexivity* $\forall x^\tau (x =_\tau x)$ and *Leibniz's scheme*:

$$\text{for all formula } A, \qquad \forall x^\tau y^\tau (A[x/z] \;\Rightarrow\; \neg A[y/z] \;\Rightarrow\; x \neq_\tau y)$$

  Note that the usual version of Leibniz's scheme is derivable:

$$\forall x^\tau y^\tau (x =_\tau y \;\Rightarrow\; A[x/z] \;\Rightarrow\; A[y/z])$$

- Equational axioms (with variables of the appropriate types):

$$\mathsf{k}\,x\,y \;=_\tau\; x \qquad \mathsf{s}\,x\,y\,z \;=_\tau\; x\,z\,(y\,z) \qquad \mathsf{P}_i\,(\mathsf{Pair}\,x_1\,x_2) \;=_{\tau_i}\; x_i \quad (i = 1,2)$$
$$\mathsf{Rec}\,x\,y\,0 \;=_\tau\; x \qquad \mathsf{Rec}\,x\,y\,(\mathsf{S}\,z) \;=_\tau\; y\,z\,(\mathsf{Rec}\,x\,y\,z)$$

- Arithmetic axioms are $\forall x^\iota (\mathsf{S}\,x \neq_\iota 0)$ and the *Induction scheme*:

$$\text{for all formula } A, \qquad A[0/x] \;\Rightarrow\; \forall x^\iota (A \;\Rightarrow\; A[\mathsf{S}x/x]) \;\Rightarrow\; \forall x^\iota A$$

We write $\mathsf{PA}^\omega \vdash A$ if $\vdash A|$ is derivable using the axioms of PA^ω.

Axiom of Countable Choice. Given $\tau \in \mathcal{T}$, we write $\mathsf{CAC}^{\iota,\tau}$ for the following version of the axiom (scheme) of countable choice:

$$\text{for all formula } A, \qquad (\forall x^\iota \exists y^\tau A) \;\Rightarrow\; \exists f^{\iota\to\tau} \forall x^\iota A[fx/y]$$

Note that this unfolds to

$$\forall x^\iota (\forall y^\tau (A \Rightarrow \bot) \Rightarrow \bot) \;\Rightarrow\; \forall f^{\iota\to\tau} (\forall x^\iota A[fx/y] \Rightarrow \bot) \;\Rightarrow\; \bot$$

We write $\mathsf{PA}^\omega + \mathsf{CAC}^{\iota,-}$ for provability in PA^ω using any $\mathsf{CAC}^{\iota,\tau}$ for $\tau \in \mathcal{T}$.

3 Intuitionistic Modified Realizability and Bar-Recursion

In this section, we briefly and informally recall the realization of CAC via negative translation to $\mathsf{HA}^\omega + \mathsf{DNS}$, and discuss some aspects of our realization of CAC.

HA^ω can be obtained from our presentation of PA^ω by restricting deduction to *intuitionistic sequents*, *i.e.* sequents of the form $\Gamma \vdash A|$. One also has to take a primitive notion of equality (instead of our primitive $(\_ \neq_\tau \_)$), and primitive existential quantification (disjunction can be coded). Gödel's negative translation maps PA^ω to HA^ω: let $(\_)^\neg$ commute over the connectives of PA^ω (remember that there is no $\vee$, $\exists$ in $\mathcal{F}$), and put $\neg\neg$ in front of atomic formulas, after having replaced $(a \neq_\tau b)$ by $\neg(a =_\tau b)$. It is equivalent to leave $\bot$ unchanged and map $(a \neq_\tau b)$ to $\neg(a =_\tau b)$.

Let us briefly discuss Modified Realizability. To each closed formula A is associated a simple type A^* of potential realizers of A. Actual realizers of A are closed terms of type A^* satisfying a property, usually written $t \Vdash A$, defined by induction on A. Typical clauses are:

$$
\begin{array}{rclrcl}
t^\iota \Vdash \bot & := & \bot & t^\iota \Vdash (a =_\tau b) & := & (a =_\tau b) \\
t \Vdash (A \Rightarrow B) & := & \forall u(u \Vdash A \Rightarrow tu \Vdash B) & t \Vdash \forall x^\tau A & := & \forall x^\tau(tx \Vdash A) \\
t \Vdash (A \wedge B) & := & (\mathsf{P}_1 t \Vdash A \wedge \mathsf{P}_2 t \Vdash B) & t \Vdash \exists x^\tau A & := & (\mathsf{P}_2 t \Vdash A[\mathsf{P}_1 t/x])
\end{array}
$$

Note that this provides a realizer, written t_{IAC}, of intuitionistic choice $(\mathsf{IAC}^{\sigma,\tau})$[1]:

$$\lambda z.\mathsf{Pair}\,(\lambda x.\mathsf{P}_1(zx))\,(\lambda x.\mathsf{P}_2(zx)) \quad\Vdash\quad (\forall x^\sigma \exists y^\tau A) \Rightarrow \exists f^{\sigma\to\tau}\forall x^\sigma A[fx/y]$$

A proof in PA^ω of a formula A can be mapped to a realizer of the negative translation $A^\neg$ of A[2]. For $\mathsf{CAC}^{\iota,\tau}$, this leads (modulo the intuitionistic equivalence $\neg\forall\neg \longleftrightarrow \neg\neg\exists$) to find a realizer of

$$\forall x^\iota \neg\neg\exists y^\tau A^\neg \Rightarrow \neg\neg\exists f^{\iota\to\tau}\forall x^\iota A^\neg[fx/y]$$

It is well-known (see e.g. [3, 4, 9]) that such a realizer can be obtained by combining a realizer of $\mathsf{IAC}^{\iota,\tau}$ with a realizer of the *Double Negation Shift*

$$(\forall x^\iota \neg\neg B) \Rightarrow \neg\neg\forall x^\iota B \qquad (\mathsf{DNS})$$

for the instance $B := \exists y^\tau A$. Assuming Ψ realizes this instance of DNS, we get

$$\lambda z.\lambda k.\Psi z(\lambda a.k(t_{\mathsf{IAC}}a)) \quad\Vdash\quad \forall x^\iota \neg\neg\exists y^\tau A^\neg \Rightarrow \neg\neg\exists f^{\iota\to\tau}\forall x^\iota A^\neg[fx/y]$$

The reader can check that we obtain the following realizer of CAC:

$$
\begin{array}{rcl}
t_{\mathsf{CAC}} & := & \lambda z.\lambda c.\Psi(t_{\neg\neg\exists}z)(\lambda a.c(\lambda x.\mathsf{P}_1(ax))(\lambda x.\mathsf{P}_2(ax))) \quad \Vdash \\
& & \forall x^\iota(\forall y^\tau(A \Rightarrow \bot) \Rightarrow \bot) \Rightarrow \forall f^{\iota\to\tau}(\forall x^\iota A[fx/y] \Rightarrow \bot) \Rightarrow \bot
\end{array}
$$

with $t_{\neg\neg\exists} := \lambda a.\lambda x.\lambda k.ax(\lambda y.\lambda z.k(\mathsf{Pair}\,y\,z)) \Vdash \forall x^\iota \neg\forall y^\tau \neg A \Rightarrow \forall x^\iota \neg\neg\exists y^\tau A$

Realizers Ψ of DNS can be obtained by adapting Spector's *Bar-Recursion* to realizability [3, 4].

The purpose of this paper is to realize CAC using Bar-Recursion, directly in a language for classical proofs. We show that (the interpretation in a suitable model

[1] We use the λ-notation for individual terms in $\mathcal{I}$.

[2] To get extraction for Π^0_2-formulas, one can adapt Friedman's trick by defining $(t^\iota \Vdash \bot)$ as $\perp\!\!\!\perp(t)$, where $\perp\!\!\!\perp$ is a given predicate, see e.g. [4] and also Sect. 6.

of) t_{CAC} realizes $\mathsf{CAC}^{\iota,\tau}$, for a notion of realizability defined for (the interpretation in a suitable model of) an extension of Parigot's $\lambda\mu$-calculus [14].

Most non-degenerate models and operational semantics for the $\lambda\mu$-calculus rely on CPS translations (see e.g. [15]). If we CPS-translate Bar-Recursion we obtain a term of type

$$(\iota^\neg \to (\tau \to \iota^\neg) \to \iota^\neg) \to ((\iota^\neg \to \tau) \to \iota^\neg) \to \iota^\neg$$

with $\iota^\neg := (\iota \to \mathtt{R}) \to \mathtt{R}$. Obvious choices for $\mathtt{R}$ besides (a model of) ι, e.g. a one-point object, tend to give degenerated results: typically, in domains (and even predomains [18]), taking $\mathtt{R} = \{\bot\}$ ($\mathtt{R} = \emptyset$) gives a unique inhabitant in $\iota^\neg$. We use the fact, observed in [11], that in the coproduct completion (given by the Fam construction, see e.g. [1]) of Hyland-Ong innocent unbracketed games for PCF, the basic type of natural numbers is of the form $([\![\mathbb{N}]\!] \to \mathtt{R}) \to \mathtt{R}$, for the one-move game $\mathtt{R}$ and the countable family of empty games $[\![\mathbb{N}]\!]$ (see Sect. 4). We then reason using the usual argument [4, 3].

4 The Model of Hyland-Ong Games

In this section, we present the bare minimum we need on Hyland-Ong games. We use innocent unbracketed games, combined with the coproduct completion provided by the Fam construction. Details can be found in e.g. [8, 7, 11, 1].

4.1 Arenas and Strategies

Definition 4.1 (Arena). *An* arena *is a countable forest of* moves*. Each move is given a polarity O (for Opponent) or P (for Player or Proponent):*

- *A root is of polarity O.*
- *A move which is not a root has the inverse polarity of that of his parent.*

A root of an arena is also called an initial move. We will often identify an arena with its set of moves.

Definition 4.2 (Justified sequence). *Given an arena $\mathcal{A}$, we define a* justified sequence *on $\mathcal{A}$ to be a finite word s on $\mathcal{A}$ together with a partial* justifying function *$f : |s| \rightharpoonup |s|$ such that:*

- *If $f(i)$ is undefined, then s_i is an initial move.*
- *If $f(i)$ is defined, then $f(i) < i$ and s_i is a child of $s_{f(i)}$.*

We denote the empty justified sequence by ϵ. Remark here that by definition of the polarity, if $f(i)$ is undefined (s_i is initial), then s_i is of polarity O, and if $f(i)$ is defined, then s_i and $s_{f(i)}$ are of opposite polarities. Also, $f(0)$ is never defined, and so s_0 is always an initial O-move. A justified sequence is represented for example as:

If $\mathcal{A}$ is an arena, X is a subset of $\mathcal{A}$ and s is a justified sequence on $\mathcal{A}$, then $s_{|X}$ is the subsequence of s consisting of the moves of s which are in X.

Definition 4.3 (Play). *A* play *s on $\mathcal{A}$ is an even and alternating justified sequence of $\mathcal{A}$, i.e., for any i, s_{2i} is a O-move and s_{2i+1} is a P-move. We denote the set of plays of $\mathcal{A}$ by $\mathcal{P}_{\mathcal{A}}$.*

A play on an arena is the trace of an interaction between a program and a context, each one performing an action alternatively.

Definition 4.4 (Strategy). *A* strategy *σ on $\mathcal{A}$ is a non-empty even-prefix-closed set of finite plays on $\mathcal{A}$ such that:*

- *σ is deterministic*
- *σ is innocent*

The definitions of determinism and innocence are standard and can be found for example in [7, 8].

Cartesian Closed Structure. The constructions we use will sometimes contain multiple copies of the same arena (for example $\mathcal{A} \to \mathcal{A}$), so we distinguish the instances with superscripts (for example $\mathcal{A}^{(1)} \to \mathcal{A}^{(2)}$).

Let $\mathcal{U}$ be the empty arena and $\mathcal{V}$ be the arena with only one (opponent) move. If $\mathcal{A}$ and $\mathcal{B}$ are arenas consisting of the trees $\mathcal{A}_1 \ldots \mathcal{A}_p$ and $\mathcal{B}_1 \ldots \mathcal{B}_q$, then the arenas $\mathcal{A} \to \mathcal{B}$ and $\mathcal{A} \times \mathcal{B}$ can be represented as follows:

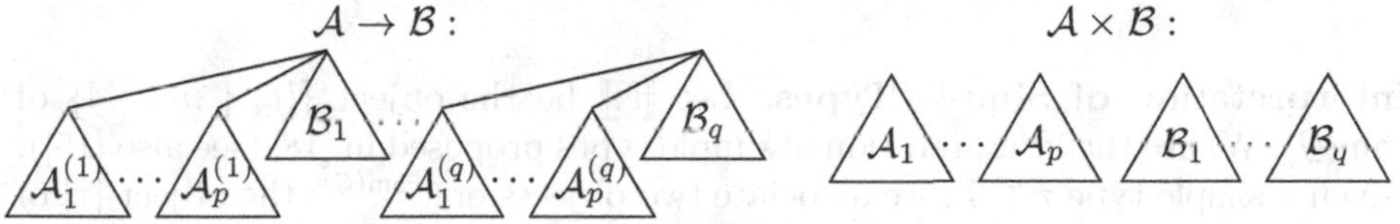

The constructions described here define a cartesian closed category whose objects are arenas and morphisms are innocent strategies. Details of the construction can be found in [7, 8]. In the following this category will be denoted as $\mathcal{G}$.

4.2 The Fam Construction

Our model is built as a continuation category [18]. In order to make explicit the double negation translation of the base types, we base the model on the category of continuations $\mathrm{R}^{\mathsf{Fam}(\mathcal{G})}$, where $\mathsf{Fam}(\mathcal{G})$ is a variant of the coproduct completion described in [1] applied to the category $\mathcal{G}$ defined in Sect. 4.1.

Definition 4.5 ($\mathsf{Fam}(\mathcal{G})$)**.** *The objects of $\mathsf{Fam}(\mathcal{G})$ are families of objects of $\mathcal{G}$ indexed by at most countable sets, and a morphism from $\{A_i \mid i \in I\}$ to $\{B_j \mid j \in J\}$ is a function $f : I \to J$ together with a family of morphisms of $\mathcal{G}$ from A_i to $B_{f(i)}$, for $i \in I$.*

See [5] for details on the differences with [1]. Note that $\mathsf{Fam}(\mathcal{G})$ is a distributive category with finite products and coproducts, and has exponentials of all singleton families. The empty product and terminal object is the singleton family $\{\mathcal{U}\}$, the empty sum and initial object is the empty family $\{\}$, and:

$$\begin{array}{rcl} \{A_i \mid i \in I\} \times \{B_j \mid j \in J\} & := & \{A_i \times B_j \mid (i,j) \in I \times J\} \\ \{A_i \mid i \in I\} + \{B_j \mid j \in J\} & := & \{C_k \mid k \in I \uplus J\} \text{ where } C_k := \begin{cases} A_k & \text{if } k \in I \\ B_k & \text{if } k \in J \end{cases} \\ \{B_0\}^{\{A_i \mid i \in I\}} & := & \{\Pi_{i\in I} B_0^{A_i}\} \end{array}$$

We fix once and for all:

$$\mathtt{R} \quad := \quad \{\mathcal{V}\}$$

which is an object of $\mathsf{Fam}(\mathcal{G})$ as a singleton family. $\mathtt{R}$ has all exponentials as stated above. Note that the canonical morphism $\delta_A : A \to \mathtt{R}^{(\mathtt{R}^A)}$ is a mono.

The category of continuations $\mathtt{R}^{\mathsf{Fam}(\mathcal{G})}$ is the full subcategory of $\mathsf{Fam}(\mathcal{G})$ consisting of the objects of the form $\mathtt{R}^A$. The objects of $\mathtt{R}^{\mathsf{Fam}(\mathcal{G})}$ are singleton families, and $\mathtt{R}^{\mathsf{Fam}(\mathcal{G})}$ is isomorphic to $\mathcal{G}$. We will consider that objects and morphisms of $\mathtt{R}^{\mathsf{Fam}(\mathcal{G})}$ are arenas and strategies and we will use the vocabulary defined at the end of Sect. 4.1 on $\mathtt{R}^{\mathsf{Fam}(\mathcal{G})}$ also.

4.3 The Type Structure

We use the lambda notation in $\mathtt{R}^{\mathsf{Fam}(\mathcal{G})}$, *i.e.* we build simply-typed λ-terms with constants in $\mathtt{R}^{\mathsf{Fam}(\mathcal{G})}$. We write them using bold symbols (such as $\boldsymbol{\lambda}$, $\langle \_, \_ \rangle$ etc) in order make no confusion with the syntactic $\lambda\mu$-terms of Section 5.

Interpretation of Simple Types. Let $[\![\mathbb{N}]\!]$ be the object $\{\mathcal{U}_n \mid n \in \mathbb{N}\}$ of $\mathsf{Fam}(\mathcal{G})$. We use the interpretation of simple types proposed in [18] (see also [15]). Given a simple type $\tau \in \mathcal{T}$, we associate two objects of $\mathtt{R}^{\mathsf{Fam}(\mathcal{G})}$: the object $[\tau]$ of *programs* of type τ, and the object $[\![\tau]\!]$ of *continuations* of type τ. We let

$$[\![\iota]\!] := \mathtt{R}^{[\![\mathbb{N}]\!]} \qquad [\![\sigma \to \tau]\!] := \mathtt{R}^{[\![\sigma]\!]} \times [\![\tau]\!] \qquad [\![\sigma \times \tau]\!] := [\![\sigma]\!] + [\![\tau]\!] \qquad [\tau] := \mathtt{R}^{[\![\tau]\!]}$$

Note that $[\![\sigma \to \tau]\!] = [\sigma] \times [\![\tau]\!]$, and moreover

$$[\sigma \to \tau] \quad = \quad \mathtt{R}^{[\sigma]\times[\![\tau]\!]} \quad \simeq \quad \mathtt{R}^{[\![\tau]\!]^{\mathtt{R}^{[\![\sigma]\!]}}} \qquad \text{and} \qquad [\sigma \times \tau] \quad \simeq \quad \mathtt{R}^{[\![\sigma]\!]} \times \mathtt{R}^{[\![\tau]\!]}$$

Representation of Arithmetic Constants. In $\mathsf{Fam}(\mathcal{G})$ a morphism from the terminal object $\{\mathcal{U}\}$ to $[\![\mathbb{N}]\!] = \{\mathcal{U}_n \mid n \in \mathbb{N}\}$ is given by a function from the singleton set to $\mathbb{N}$ together with a strategy from $\mathcal{U}$ to $\mathcal{U}$. Since there is only one such strategy, such a morphism is given by a natural number. We will call this morphism $\widetilde{n}$. Similarly a morphism from $[\![\mathbb{N}]\!]$ to $[\![\mathbb{N}]\!]$ is given by a function from $\mathbb{N}$ to $\mathbb{N}$. This leads to a morphism $\widetilde{\mathsf{succ}} : [\![\mathbb{N}]\!] \to [\![\mathbb{N}]\!]$ for the successor function on $[\![\mathbb{N}]\!]$.

Moreover, given $a : [\tau]$ (officially, $a : \{\mathcal{U}\} \to [\tau]$ in $\mathsf{Fam}(\mathcal{G})$), and $b : [\![\mathbb{N}]\!] \to [\tau] \to [\tau]$, we can define by induction on $n \in \mathbb{N}$ a morphism $\widetilde{r}_{a,b} : [\![\mathbb{N}]\!] \to [\tau]$ such that $\widetilde{r}_{a,b}\widetilde{0} = a$ and $\widetilde{r}_{a,b}(\widetilde{n+1}) = b\widetilde{n}(\widetilde{r}_{a,b}(\widetilde{n}))$. This leads to $\widetilde{\mathsf{rec}} := \boldsymbol{\lambda} a.\boldsymbol{\lambda} b.\widetilde{r}_{a,b}$ in $[\tau] \to ([\![\mathbb{N}]\!] \to [\tau] \to [\tau]) \to [\![\mathbb{N}]\!] \to [\tau]$.

We now discuss the object of $\mathsf{R}^{\mathsf{Fam}(\mathcal{G})}$ associated to the base type ι. We have:

$$[\iota] \quad := \quad \mathsf{R}^{\mathsf{R}^{[\![\mathbb{N}]\!]}} \quad = \quad \mathsf{R}^{\mathsf{R}^{\{\mathcal{U}_n \ \mid \ n\in\mathbb{N}\}}} \quad \simeq \quad \mathsf{R}^{\Pi_{n\in\mathbb{N}}\mathsf{R}} \quad \simeq \quad \{\mathcal{V}^{\Pi_{n\in\mathbb{N}}\mathcal{V}}\}$$

Note that this is the usual flat arena of natural numbers:

It is easy to see that $\boldsymbol{\lambda} k.k\widetilde{n}$ corresponds to the strategy answering n to the initial opponent question q. Moreover, the only inhabitants of $[\iota]$ are the empty strategy $\perp_{[\iota]}$ and the strategies $\boldsymbol{\lambda} k.k\widetilde{n}$ for $n \in \mathbb{N}$.

The arithmetical constants of System T will be interpreted in $\mathsf{R}^{\mathsf{Fam}(\mathcal{G})}$ using $\mathbf{succ} : [\iota] \to [\iota]$ defined as $\mathbf{succ} := \boldsymbol{\lambda} n.\boldsymbol{\lambda} k.n(\boldsymbol{\lambda} x.k(\widetilde{\mathsf{succ}}\, x))$ and $\mathbf{rec} : [\tau] \to [\iota \to \tau \to \tau] \to [\iota] \to [\tau]$ with $\mathbf{rec} := \boldsymbol{\lambda} u.\boldsymbol{\lambda} v.\boldsymbol{\lambda} n.\boldsymbol{\lambda} k.n(\boldsymbol{\lambda} x.\widetilde{\mathsf{rec}}\, u(\boldsymbol{\lambda} y.v^\bullet(\boldsymbol{\lambda} k.ky))xk)$, where $v^\bullet := \boldsymbol{\lambda} x.\boldsymbol{\lambda} y.\boldsymbol{\lambda} z.v\langle x, y, z\rangle$ (see [5] for details).

It is convenient to use the notations $(\_)^\bullet$ and $(\_)^\circ$ for resp. curryfication and uncurryfication. Note that as with $v^\bullet$ above, the amount to which an expression is curryfied/uncurryfied depends on the context, and moreover that in $\mathcal{G}$, $(\_)^\bullet$ and $(\_)^\circ$ are the identity.

5 Lambda-Mu-Calculus

We present here an extension of Parigot's $\lambda\mu$-calculus [14] that we will use as a programming language for our realizers. We begin by a basic language, which essentially adds pairs and products to the original calculus. We then present an extension with the arithmetic constants of Gödel's System T, which will be used for the realization of PA^ω. Finally, we discuss the interpretation, along the lines of [15], of the calculus in the model $\mathsf{R}^{\mathsf{Fam}(\mathcal{G})}$, and present an operational semantics using an abstract machine adapted from [18].

Syntax and Typing. We assume given two countable sets $\mathrm{Var} = \{x, y, z, \dots\}$ and $\mathrm{CVar} = \{\alpha, \beta, \gamma, \dots\}$ of respectively *term* and *continuation* variables. The $\lambda\mu$-terms are defined as follows:

$$t, u \in \Lambda \quad ::= \quad x \ \mid \ \lambda x.t \ \mid \ tu \ \mid \ \mu\alpha.v \ \mid \ \langle t, u\rangle \ \mid \ \mathsf{p}_1(t) \ \mid \ \mathsf{p}_2(t)$$

where v is a *named term*: $\quad v \quad ::= \quad [\alpha]t$

They are typed by extending Parigot's system [14] with rules for product types:

$$\frac{}{\Gamma, x:\tau \vdash x:\tau \mid \Delta} \qquad \frac{\Gamma \vdash t:\tau \mid \Delta, \alpha:\tau}{[\alpha]t : (\Gamma \vdash \Delta, \alpha:\tau)} \qquad \frac{v : (\Gamma \vdash \Delta, \alpha:\tau)}{\Gamma \vdash \mu\alpha.v : \tau \mid \Delta}$$

$$\frac{\Gamma, x:\tau \vdash t:\sigma \mid \Delta}{\Gamma \vdash \lambda x.t : \tau \to \sigma \mid \Delta} \qquad \frac{\Gamma \vdash t : \sigma \to \tau \mid \Delta \qquad \Gamma \vdash u:\sigma \mid \Delta}{\Gamma \vdash tu : \tau \mid \Delta}$$

$$\frac{\Gamma \vdash t:\tau \mid \Delta \qquad \Gamma \vdash u:\sigma \mid \Delta}{\Gamma \vdash \langle t,u\rangle : \tau \times \sigma \mid \Delta} \qquad \frac{\Gamma \vdash t : \tau_1 \times \tau_2 \mid \Delta}{\Gamma \vdash \mathsf{p}_i(t) : \tau_i \mid \Delta}\ (i=1,2)$$

Extension with Arithmetic Constants. We write Λ_T for the set of $\lambda\mu$-terms obtained by extending the grammar of Λ with the following productions:

$$t, u \quad ::= \quad \dots \quad \mid \quad \overline{n} \quad \mid \quad \mathsf{succ} \quad \mid \quad \mathsf{rec}(t,u)$$

where $n \in \mathbb{N}$. We extend the typing rules of Λ with the following ones:

$$\frac{}{\Gamma \vdash \overline{n} : \iota \mid \Delta} \qquad \frac{}{\Gamma \vdash \mathsf{succ} : \iota \to \iota \mid \Delta} \qquad \frac{\Gamma \vdash t:\tau \mid \Delta \qquad \Gamma \vdash u : \iota \to \tau \to \tau \mid \Delta}{\Gamma \vdash \mathsf{rec}(t,u) : \iota \to \tau \mid \Delta}$$

Interpretation in $\mathsf{R}^{\mathsf{Fam}(\mathcal{G})}$. The interpretation of Λ_T in $\mathsf{R}^{\mathsf{Fam}(\mathcal{G})}$ follows the lines of [15]. A term $\vdash t:\tau|$ is interpreted by $[t] \in [\tau]$. To make the presentation simpler, we use $\boldsymbol{\lambda}$-expressions in $\mathsf{R}^{\mathsf{Fam}(\mathcal{G})}$ build from the variables of Λ_T with the following convention: a term variable x of type τ (resp. a continuation variable α of type σ) in Λ_T becomes a variable x of type $[\tau]$ (resp. a variable α of type $[\![\sigma]\!]$) in the $\boldsymbol{\lambda}$-calculus of $\mathsf{R}^{\mathsf{Fam}(\mathcal{G})}$:

$$\begin{array}{rclrclrcl}
[x] & := & x & [\overline{n}] & := & \boldsymbol{\lambda}k.k\widetilde{n} & [\mu\alpha.[\beta]t] & := & \boldsymbol{\lambda}\alpha.[t]\beta \\
[\lambda x.t] & := & \boldsymbol{\lambda}\langle x,k\rangle.[t]k & & & [\langle t,u\rangle] & := & \boldsymbol{\lambda}k.\mathbf{case}\,k\{[t],[u]\} \\
[tu] & := & \boldsymbol{\lambda}k.[t]\langle [u],k\rangle & & & [\mathsf{p}_i(t)] & := & \boldsymbol{\lambda}k.[t](\mathbf{in}_i k) \\
[\mathsf{succ}] & := & \boldsymbol{\lambda}\langle n,k\rangle.\,\mathbf{succ}\,n\,k & & & [\mathsf{rec}(t,u)] & := & \boldsymbol{\lambda}\langle n,k\rangle.\mathbf{rec}\,[t][u]\,n\,k
\end{array}$$

Operational Semantics. We now present an operational semantics for Λ_T using an abstract machine. The machine is derived from the interpretation of Λ_T in $\mathsf{R}^{\mathsf{Fam}(\mathcal{G})}$, following the method of [18]. Our machine is actually an adaptation of the machine of [18] to a typed language with arithmetic constants.

The machine evaluates triples of the form (t, e, π), where t is a $\lambda\mu$-term, e is an environment and π is a stack. Environments map term variables to closures and continuation variables to stacks. Stacks, closures and environments are defined by mutual induction as usual:

$$\begin{array}{rrcl}
\text{Env.} & e \in \mathrm{E} & ::= & \varepsilon \mid (x,c) :: e \mid (\alpha,\pi) :: e \\
\text{Closures} & c \in \mathrm{C} & ::= & (t,e) \\
\text{Stacks} & \pi \in \Pi & ::= & \star \mid \langle c,\pi\rangle \mid \mathsf{kp}_i(\pi) \mid \mathsf{ksucc}(\pi) \mid \mathsf{krec}(t,u,c,\pi)
\end{array}$$

We let $e(x) := c$ if (x, c) is the first occurrence of the form (x, c') in e, and define $e(\alpha)$ similarly. Let $\mathrm{dom}(e)$ be the domain of the partial map $e(\_)$.

The evaluation rules are the following:

$$
\begin{array}{rcll}
(x, e, \pi) & \succ & (t, e', \pi) & \text{if } e(x) = (t, e') \\[1em]
(tu, e, \pi) & \succ & (t, e, \langle (u, e), \pi \rangle) & \\
(\lambda x.t, e, \langle c, \pi \rangle) & \succ & (t, (x, c) :: e, \pi) & \\[1em]
(\mu\alpha.[\beta]t, e, \pi) & \succ & (t, (\alpha, \pi) :: e, \pi') & \text{if } ((\alpha, \pi) :: e)(\beta) = \pi' \\[1em]
(\mathsf{p}_i(t), e, \pi) & \succ & (t, e, \mathsf{kp}_i(\pi)) & i = 1, 2 \\
(\langle t_1, t_2 \rangle, e, \mathsf{kp}_i(\pi)) & \succ & (t_i, e, \pi) & i = 1, 2 \\[1em]
(\mathsf{succ}, e, \langle (t, e'), \pi \rangle) & \succ & (t, e', \mathsf{ksucc}(\pi)) & \\
(\overline{n}, e, \mathsf{ksucc}(\pi)) & \succ & (\overline{n+1}, e, \pi) & \\[1em]
(\mathsf{rec}(t, u), e, \langle (v, e'), \pi \rangle) & \succ & (v, e', \mathsf{krec}(t, u, e, \pi)) & \\
(\overline{0}, e, \mathsf{krec}(t, u, e', \pi)) & \succ & (t, e', \pi) & \\
(\overline{n+1}, e, \mathsf{krec}(t, u, e', \pi)) & \succ & (u, e', \langle (\overline{n}, e), \langle (\mathsf{rec}(t, u)\overline{n}, e'), \pi \rangle \rangle) &
\end{array}
$$

The correctness of the machine (*i.e.* reduction preserves semantics) can be proved as usual[3] (see e.g. [18]). For extraction, we actually only need the property stated in Prop. 7.3, to be discussed in presence of Bar-Recursion.

6 Classical Realizability

In this section, we present our notion of realizability. It is highly inspired from Krivine's Realizability [10], but adapted to the simply-typed model $\mathtt{R}^{\mathsf{Fam}(\mathcal{G})}$.

The main idea, adapting Krivine's ideas to the typed continuation category $\mathtt{R}^{\mathsf{Fam}(\mathcal{G})}$, would be to fix a *Pole* $\perp\!\!\!\perp \subseteq \{[\overline{n}] \mid n \in \mathbb{N}\}$, and then associate to each formula A a type A^* and a set $\mathcal{A} \subseteq [\![A^*]\!]$ defined by induction on A. Realizers would then be strategies in $\mathcal{A}^{\perp\!\!\!\perp} \subseteq [A^*]$, the *Orthogonal* of $\mathcal{A}$.

We choose to have $\perp\!\!\!\perp \subseteq [\iota]$ to get extraction (see Prop. 7.4). This causes difficulties since $[\iota] = \mathtt{R}^{[\![\iota]\!]}$ is not a base type in $\mathtt{R}^{\mathsf{Fam}(\mathcal{G})}$. Roughly speaking, our choice for $\perp\!\!\!\perp$ leads to $\bot^* := \iota$, but there are not enough contexts in $[\![\iota]\!] = \{\bot_{[\![\iota]\!]}\}$, since applying $\bot_{[\![\iota]\!]}$ to a numeral $[\overline{n}]$ gives the empty strategy on $\mathtt{R}$. A solution is to add some space in the interpretations, and have $\mathcal{A} \subseteq [\![\iota]\!] \to [\![A^*]\!]$ and $\mathcal{A}^{\perp\!\!\!\perp} \subseteq [\![\iota]\!] \to [A^*]$ for a formula A. For instance, we can then have $\boldsymbol{\lambda} k.k$ as a basic context "at type" $[\![\iota]\!]$ (actually $[\![\iota]\!] \to [\![\iota]\!]$).

The definition of realizability involves two additional translations, that we present now. First, to each formula A, we associate the simple type A^*:

$$
(a^\tau \neq_\tau b^\tau)^* \;:=\; \iota \qquad \bot^* \;:=\; \iota \qquad (\forall x^\tau A)^* \;:=\; \tau \to A^*
$$
$$
(A \Rightarrow B)^* \;:=\; A^* \to B^* \qquad (A \wedge B)^* \;:=\; A^* \times B^*
$$

[3] Since the model $\mathtt{R}^{\mathsf{Fam}(\mathcal{G})}$ is typed, this would involve typing rules for environments and stacks.

Moreover, we map each individual term $a \in \mathcal{I}$ to a $\lambda\mu$-term $a^\dagger \in \Lambda_T$:

$$\begin{array}{rclrclrcl} x^{\tau\dagger} & := & x & (ab)^\dagger & := & a^\dagger b^\dagger & \mathsf{s}^\dagger & := & \lambda xyz.xz(yz) \\ \mathsf{k}^\dagger & := & \lambda xy.x & \mathsf{0}^\dagger & := & \overline{0} & \mathsf{S}^\dagger & := & \mathsf{succ} \\ \mathsf{Rec}^\dagger & := & \lambda xy.\mathsf{rec}(x,y) & \mathsf{Pair}^\dagger & := & \lambda xy.\langle x,y\rangle & \mathsf{P}_i{}^\dagger & := & \lambda x.\mathsf{p}_i(x) \end{array}$$

The Realizability Construction. To a formula A, we will associate two sets $||A|| \subseteq [\![\iota]\!] \to [\![A^*]\!]$ and $|A| \subseteq [\![\iota]\!] \to [A^*]$. These sets will only be defined for *closed* formulas. It is convenient (and necessary to deal with CAC in Sect. 7) to allow parameters in $\mathtt{R}^{\mathsf{Fam}(\mathcal{G})}$. In order to realize the induction axiom, we must restrict to the *total* elements of $\mathtt{R}^{\mathsf{Fam}(\mathcal{G})}$. For a simple type τ, the set $\tau^{\mathsf{t}} \subseteq [\tau]$ of its total elements is defined by induction on τ. Let $\iota^{\mathsf{t}} := \{[\overline{n}] \mid n \in \mathbb{N}\}$, and using curryfied notation:

$$\begin{array}{rcl} (\sigma \to \tau)^{\mathsf{t}} & := & \{a \mid \forall b \in \sigma^{\mathsf{t}},\ ab \in \tau^{\mathsf{t}}\} \\ (\sigma \times \tau)^{\mathsf{t}} & := & \{a \mid \mathbf{p}_1(a) \in \sigma^{\mathsf{t}} \ \&\ \mathbf{p}_2(a) \in \tau^{\mathsf{t}}\} \end{array}$$

Lemma 6.1. *For all $a \in \mathcal{I}_0^\tau$, $[a^\dagger] \in \tau^{\mathsf{t}}$.*

We now only consider closed formulas with parameters of the appropriate type in τ^{t} ($\tau \in \mathcal{T}$). Let $\perp\!\!\!\perp \subseteq \iota^{\mathsf{t}}$.

First, given $\mathcal{A} \subseteq [\![\iota]\!] \to [\![A^*]\!]$, we define $\mathcal{A}^{\perp\!\!\!\perp} \subseteq [\![\iota]\!] \to [A^*]$ as

$$\mathcal{A}^{\perp\!\!\!\perp} \quad := \quad \{a \in [\![\iota]\!] \to [A^*] \mid \forall b \in \mathcal{A},\ \boldsymbol{\lambda} k.ak(bk) \in \perp\!\!\!\perp\}$$

If moreover $\mathcal{B} \subseteq [\![\iota]\!] \to [\![B^*]\!]$, we let

$$\mathcal{A}^{\perp\!\!\!\perp} \cdot \mathcal{B} \quad := \quad \{\boldsymbol{\lambda} k.\langle ak, bk\rangle \in [\![\iota]\!] \to [A^*] \times [\![B^*]\!] \mid a \in \mathcal{A}^{\perp\!\!\!\perp} \ \&\ b \in \mathcal{B}\}$$

We now define the sets $|A| \subseteq [\![\iota]\!] \to [A^*]$ and $||A|| \subseteq [\![\iota]\!] \to [\![A^*]\!]$ for a formula A. We let $|A| \subseteq [\![\iota]\!] \to [A^*]$ be $||A||^{\perp\!\!\!\perp}$, and define $||A|| \subseteq [\![\iota]\!] \to [\![A^*]\!]$ by induction on A as follows:

$$\begin{array}{rcl} ||\bot|| & := & \{\boldsymbol{\lambda} k.k\} \qquad\qquad ||A \Rightarrow B|| \quad := \quad |A| \cdot ||B|| \\ ||a \neq_\tau b|| & := & \begin{cases} \emptyset & \text{if } [a^\dagger] \neq [b^\dagger] \\ \{\boldsymbol{\lambda} k.k\} & \text{otherwise} \end{cases} \\ ||A \wedge B|| & := & \{\boldsymbol{\lambda} k.\mathbf{in}_1(ak) \mid a \in ||A||\} \cup \{\boldsymbol{\lambda} k.\mathbf{in}_2(bk) \mid b \in ||B||\} \\ ||\forall x^\tau A|| & := & \bigcup_{a \in \tau^{\mathsf{t}}} \{\boldsymbol{\lambda} k.\langle a, bk\rangle \mid b \in ||A[a/x]||\} \end{array}$$

Realization of Equality and Arithmetic Axioms. We now discuss the realization of the axioms of PA^ω.

First, it is easy to see that all equational axioms (including reflexivity) are realized by the identity:

Lemma 6.2. *We have $\boldsymbol{\lambda} k.[\lambda x.x] \in |a =_\tau a|$. Moreover,*

$$\begin{array}{rr} \boldsymbol{\lambda} k.[\lambda x.x] \in |\mathsf{k}\,a\,b =_\tau a| & \boldsymbol{\lambda} k.[\lambda x.x] \in |\mathsf{s}\,a\,b\,c =_\tau ac(bc)| \\ \boldsymbol{\lambda} k.[\lambda x.x] \in |\mathsf{Rec}\,a\,b\,\mathsf{0} =_\tau a| & \boldsymbol{\lambda} k.[\lambda x.x] \in |\mathsf{Rec}\,a\,b\,(\mathsf{S}\,c) =_\tau bc(\mathsf{Rec}\,a\,b\,c)| \end{array}$$

where in each case, individuals a, b, c are in the appropriate τ^{t}, σ^{t}, ρ^{t}.

The realization of our version of Leibniz's scheme is obtained by applying realizers of the first premise to realizers of the second premise.

Lemma 6.3. $\boldsymbol{\lambda} k.[\lambda x.\lambda y.yx] \in |A[a^\tau/z^\tau] \Rightarrow \neg A[b^\tau/z^\tau] \Rightarrow a^\tau \neq_\tau b^\tau|$.

For the Arithmetic axioms, it is easy to see that $(\mathsf{S}a \neq_\iota 0)$ is realized by any natural number. As expected, the recursor $\mathsf{rec}(\_,\_)$ realizes induction.

Lemma 6.4. *(i) For all $n \in \mathbb{N}$ and all $a \in \iota^{\mathfrak{t}}$, we have $\boldsymbol{\lambda} k.[\overline{n}] \in |\mathsf{S}a \neq_\iota 0|$.*
(ii) $\boldsymbol{\lambda} k.[\lambda x.\lambda y.\mathsf{rec}(x,y)] \in |A[0/x] \Rightarrow \forall x^\iota(A \Rightarrow A[\mathsf{S}x/x]) \Rightarrow \forall x^\iota A|$.

Adequacy for Classical Proofs. Adequacy of the realizability interpretation is proved as usual.

Theorem 6.5. *Let Γ, A, Δ with $\Gamma = A_1,\ldots,A_n$, $\Delta = B_1,\ldots,B_m$, and such that $FV(\Gamma,A,\Delta) \subseteq \{x_1^{\tau_1},\ldots,x_k^{\tau_k}\}$.*
From a proof of $\Gamma \vdash A \mid \Delta$ in PA^ω one can build a term

$$x_1 : \tau_1,\ldots,x_k : \tau_k, y_1 : A_1{}^*,\ldots,y_n : A_n{}^* \vdash t : A^* \mid \alpha_1 : B_1{}^*,\ldots,\alpha_m : B_m{}^*$$

such that for all $c_1 \in \tau_1{}^{\mathfrak{t}},\ldots,c_k \in \tau_k{}^{\mathfrak{t}}$, all $a_1 \in |A_1[\boldsymbol{c}/\boldsymbol{x}]|,\ldots,a_n \in |A_n[\boldsymbol{c}/\boldsymbol{x}]|$, and all $b_1 \in ||B_1[\boldsymbol{c}/\boldsymbol{x}]||,\ldots,b_m \in ||B_m[\boldsymbol{c}/\boldsymbol{x}]||$, we have

$$\boldsymbol{\lambda} k.[t][\boldsymbol{c}/\boldsymbol{x}][a_1 k/y_1,\ldots,a_n k/y_n, b_1 k/\alpha_1,\ldots,b_m k/\alpha_m] \in |A[\boldsymbol{c}/\boldsymbol{x}]|$$

In particular, from a proof of $\vdash A|$ in PA^ω with A closed, one can build a term $\vdash t : A^*|$ such that $\boldsymbol{\lambda} k.[t] \in |A|$.

Extraction. Extraction of witnessing programs from realizable (and hence from provable) Π^0_2 statements is performed as usual. We come back on this point in Sect. 7 (Prop. 7.4) in presence of CAC and Bar-Recursion.

7 Realization of Classical Countable Choice

In this section we discuss the realization of the classical axiom of countable choice $\mathsf{CAC}^{\iota,-}$. Our realizer is based on Berger & Oliva's variant of Spector's Bar-Recursion [4].

Extension of the $\boldsymbol{\lambda\mu}$-Calculus with Bar-Recursion. We extend the set $\Lambda_{\mathcal{T}}$ with constants for bar-recursion: $t, u \in \Lambda_\Psi ::= \ldots \mid \Psi_\tau(t,u)\langle s_0,\ldots,s_n\rangle$, where $n \in \mathbb{N}$ and $\tau \in \mathcal{T}$.

These constants are typed as follows: $\Gamma \vdash \Psi_\tau(t,u)\langle s_0,\ldots,s_n\rangle : \iota \mid \Delta$ whenever $\Gamma \vdash t : \iota \to (\tau \to \iota) \to \iota \mid \Delta$, $\Gamma \vdash u : (\iota \to \tau) \to \iota \mid \Delta$ and $\Gamma \vdash s_i : \tau \mid \Delta$ for all $0 \leq i \leq n$.

The operational semantics uses some auxiliary terms. We define by induction on τ the terms $\vdash \mathrm{ex}_\tau : \iota \to \tau|$. Let $\mathrm{ex}_\iota := \lambda x.x$, $\mathrm{ex}_{\tau\to\sigma} := \lambda x.\lambda\_.\mathrm{ex}_\sigma x$ and $\mathrm{ex}_{\tau\times\sigma} := \lambda x.\langle \mathrm{ex}_\tau x, \mathrm{ex}_\sigma x\rangle$.

Moreover, given $n \in \mathbb{N}$, $s_0, \dots, s_n, t \in \Lambda_\Psi$, we let $\langle s_0, \dots, s_n\rangle @ t$ be a term (written using rec) such that for all $e, e' \in \mathrm{E}$, $\pi \in \Pi$ and $m \in \mathbb{N}$,

$$(\langle s_0, \dots, s_n\rangle @ t, e, \langle(\overline{m}, e'), \pi\rangle) \succ \begin{cases} (s_m, e, \pi) & \text{if } m \leq n \\ (t, e, \langle(\overline{m-(n+1)}, e'), \pi\rangle) & \text{otherwise} \end{cases}$$

The operational semantics of $\Psi_\tau(t,u)\langle s_1, \dots, s_n\rangle$ is given by:

$$\begin{array}{l}(\Psi_\tau(t,u)\langle s_0, \dots, s_n\rangle, e, \pi) \quad \succ \\ \qquad (u, e, \langle((\langle s_0, \dots, s_n\rangle @ \lambda\_.\mathrm{ex}_\tau(t\,\overline{n+1}\,\lambda x.\Psi_\tau(t,u)\langle s_0, \dots, s_n, x\rangle), e), \pi\rangle)\end{array}$$

The Bar-Recursor in $\mathsf{R}^{\mathsf{Fam}(\mathcal{G})}$. We now define the strategies interpreting Ψ_τ in $\mathsf{R}^{\mathsf{Fam}(\mathcal{G})}$. Fix $\tau \in \mathcal{T}$. First, given $a_0, \dots, a_n \in [\tau]$, and $b \in [\iota \to \tau]$, let

$$\langle a_0, \dots, a_n\rangle @ b \quad := \quad [\langle x_0, \dots, x_n\rangle @ y][a_0/x_0, \dots, a_n/x_n, b/y]$$

For each $m \in \mathbb{N}$, we will define by induction on m a family of strategies $(\widetilde{\Psi}^m_n)_{n \in \mathbb{N}}$. Each $\widetilde{\Psi}^m_n$ will be in $[\tau]^n \to \widetilde{\tau_\Psi}$, where $[\tau]^0 := \{\mathcal{U}\}$, $[\tau]^{n+1} := [\tau] \times [\tau]^n$ and

$$\widetilde{\tau_\Psi} \quad := \quad [\iota \to (\tau \to \iota) \to \iota] \to [(\iota \to \tau) \to \iota] \to [\iota]$$

We let $\widetilde{\Psi}^0_n := \boldsymbol{\lambda}\langle x_1, \dots, x_n\rangle.\bot_{\widetilde{\tau_\Psi}}$ and

$$\begin{array}{rcl}\widetilde{\Psi}^{m+1}_n & := & \boldsymbol{\lambda}\langle x_1, \dots, x_n\rangle.\boldsymbol{\lambda}b.\boldsymbol{\lambda}c.c^\bullet(\langle x_1, \dots, x_n\rangle @ \\ & & \qquad \boldsymbol{\lambda}\_.[\mathrm{ex}_\tau]^\bullet(b^\bullet\,\boxed{n+1}\,(\boldsymbol{\lambda}x.\widetilde{\Psi}^m_n\langle x_1, \dots, x_n, x\rangle\; b\; c)^\circ))\end{array}$$

Given $a_0, \dots, a_n \in [\tau]$, we now define a strategy $\widetilde{\Psi}^\tau_{\langle a_0, \dots, a_n\rangle}$ using the CPO structure on $\mathcal{G}$ (and hence on $\mathsf{Fam}(\mathcal{G})$). Note that the family $(\widetilde{\Psi}^m_{n+1}\langle a_0, \dots, a_n\rangle)_{m \in \mathbb{N}}$ is directed. We let $\widetilde{\Psi}^\tau_{\langle a_0, \dots, a_n\rangle} := \bigvee_{m \in \mathbb{N}} \widetilde{\Psi}^m_{n+1}\langle a_0, \dots, a_n\rangle$ and $[\Psi_\tau(t,u)\langle s_0, \dots, s_n\rangle] := \widetilde{\Psi}^\tau_{\langle [s_0], \dots, [s_n]\rangle}[t][u]$.

Realization of $\mathsf{CAC}^{\iota,-}$. We discuss here the realization of $\mathsf{CAC}^{\iota,\tau}$ using (the interpretation in Λ_Ψ) of the term t_{CAC} build in Sect. 3, where we take suitable instances of $\Psi_\tau(\_,\_)\langle\dots\rangle$ for Bar-Recursion. We let

$$\begin{array}{rrcl} & t^{\tau,A}_{\mathsf{CAC}} & := & \lambda z.\lambda c.\Psi_{\tau \times A^*}(t_{\neg\neg\exists}z, \lambda a.c(\lambda x.\mathsf{p}_1(ax))(\lambda x.\mathsf{p}_2(ax)))\langle\rangle \\ \text{where} & t_{\neg\neg\exists} & := & \lambda a.\lambda x.\lambda k.ax(\lambda y.\lambda z.k\langle y, z\rangle)\end{array}$$

Proposition 7.1. $\boldsymbol{\lambda}k.[t^{\tau,A}_{\mathsf{CAC}}] \in$
$|\forall x^\iota(\forall y^\tau(A \Rightarrow \bot) \Rightarrow \bot) \;\Rightarrow\; \forall f^{\iota\to\tau}(\forall x^\iota A[fx/y] \Rightarrow \bot) \;\Rightarrow\; \bot|$.

Contrary to e.g. [3, 4], we do not use the decomposition of CAC as IAC + DNS discussed in Sect. 3. Rather, we show directly that Bar-Recursion realizes a form of choice.

The main point is to decompose the notion of realizability proposed in Sect. 6 w.r.t. the relativization of quantifiers. We first extend the formulas:

$$A, B \quad ::= \quad \dots \quad | \quad \tilde{\forall} x^{\tau} A \quad | \quad (\mathsf{r}_{\tau}(a^{\tau}) \times A) \Rightarrow B$$

Hence, in extended formulas, the construction $(\mathsf{r}_{\tau}(a) \times A)$ is only allowed to appear to the left of an implication. Realizability is extended as follows:

$$\begin{aligned} \|\tilde{\forall} x^{\tau} A\| &:= \bigcup_{a \in \tau^{\mathfrak{t}}} \|A[a/x]\| \\ \|(\mathsf{r}_{\tau}(c) \times A) \Rightarrow B\| &:= \{\boldsymbol{\lambda} k.\langle \boldsymbol{\lambda} k'.\mathbf{case}\, k'\{c, ak\}, bk\rangle \mid a \in |A| \;\&\; b \in \|B\|\} \end{aligned}$$

Extended formulas and their realizability interpretation rely on ideas introduced in Krivine's Realizability [10] (see also [12]). We also extend the mapping $(\_)^*$: $(\tilde{\forall} x^{\tau} A)^* := A^*$ and $((\mathsf{r}_{\tau}(a) \times A) \Rightarrow B)^* := \tau \times A^* \to B^*$. The following is the key for Prop. 7.1. It is shown as usual, see e.g. [3, 4].

Lemma 7.2. *Let B such that $(B \Rightarrow \bot)$ is an extended formula. Assume $b \in |\forall x^{\iota}(\tilde{\forall} y^{\tau}(B \Rightarrow \bot) \Rightarrow \bot)|$ and $c \in |\tilde{\forall} f^{\iota \to \tau}(\forall x^{\iota} B[fx/y] \Rightarrow \bot)|$. Then $\boldsymbol{\lambda} k.\tilde{\Psi}^{B^*}_{\langle\rangle}(bk)(ck) \in |\bot|$.*

Computational Adequacy and Extraction. For extraction, we rely on the following property relating the evaluation of $\lambda\mu$-terms with their interpretation in $\mathsf{R}^{\mathsf{Fam}(\mathcal{G})}$.

Proposition 7.3. *(i) If $\vdash t : \iota|$ in Λ_{Ψ}, then for all $n \in \mathbb{N}$ we have $(t, \varepsilon, \star) \succ (\overline{n}, e, \star)$ if $[t] = [\overline{n}]$.*
(ii) Let $\vdash t : \iota \to \iota$ in Λ_{Ψ}. For all $n, m \in \mathbb{N}$, if $\boldsymbol{\lambda} k.[t]\langle[\overline{n}], k\rangle = [\overline{m}]$ then $(t\overline{n}, \varepsilon, \star) \succ (\overline{m}, e, \star)$.

Extraction of witnessing programs from realizable (and hence from provable) Π^0_2 statements is performed as usual:

Proposition 7.4. *From a proof of $\mathsf{PA}^{\omega} + \mathsf{CAC}^{\iota,-} \vdash \forall x^{\iota} \exists y^{\iota}(a =_{\iota} 0)$ (where $FV(a) \subseteq \{x, y\}$), we can extract a term $\vdash t : \iota \to \iota|$ such that for all $n \in \mathbb{N}$, there is $m \in \mathbb{N}$ such that $(t\overline{n}, \varepsilon, \star) \succ (\overline{m}, e, \star)$ and $[a^{\dagger}][[\overline{n}]/x, [\overline{m}]/y] = [\overline{0}]$.*

Proof (sketch). By adequacy, we get u s.t. $\boldsymbol{\lambda} k.[u] \in |\forall x^{\iota} \neg \forall y^{\iota}(a \neq_{\iota} 0)|$. Let $n \in \mathbb{N}$ and fix $\perp\!\!\!\perp := \{[\overline{m}] \mid [a^{\dagger}][[\overline{n}]/x, [\overline{m}]/y] = [\overline{0}]\}$. We thus have $\boldsymbol{\lambda} k.[u\overline{n}(\lambda x.x)] \in |\bot|$. This implies $[u\overline{n}(\lambda x.x)] = [\overline{m}]$ with $[\overline{m}] \in \perp\!\!\!\perp$. We conclude by Prop. 7.3.(ii). □

8 Conclusion

We presented a notion of classical realizability for $\mathsf{PA}^{\omega} + \mathsf{CAC}$ based on Hyland-Ong innocent unbracketed games for a simply-typed extension of Parigot's $\lambda\mu$-calculus. For PA^{ω}, these realizers seem to CPS translate to the same realizers as obtained by a negative translation from PA^{ω} to HA^{ω} followed by Friedman's translation and a realizability interpretation, as devised in Sect. 3 It is not clear whether this extends to the decomposition of CAC as IAC + DNS, because of the interaction of the CPS translation with Friedman's trick.

Further works will concern this question, a comparison with [17], where Bar-Recursion is used in an untyped Classical Realizablity model, as well as trying to extend the result to non-innocent games (along the lines of [5]), known to raise problems with Bar-Recursion [3].

References

[1] Abramsky, S., McCusker, G.: Call-by-Value Games. In: Nielsen, M. (ed.) CSL 1997. LNCS, vol. 1414, pp. 1–17. Springer, Heidelberg (1998)
[2] Amadio, R.M., Curien, P.-L.: Domains and Lambda-Calculi. Cambridge Tracts in Theoretical Computer Science. Cambridge University Press (1998)
[3] Berardi, S., Bezem, M., Coquand, T.: On the Computational Content of the Axiom of Choice. Journal of Symbolic Logic 63(2), 600–622 (1998)
[4] Berger, U., Oliva, P.: Modified bar recursion and classical dependent choice. Lecture Notes in Logic 20, 89–107 (2005)
[5] Blot, V.: Realizability for peano arithmetic with winning conditions in HON games. In: Hasegawa, M. (ed.) TLCA 2013. LNCS, vol. 7941, pp. 77–92. Springer, Heidelberg (2013)
[6] Griffin, T.: A Formulae-as-Types Notion of Control. In: POPL 1990, pp. 47–58. ACM Press (1990)
[7] Harmer, R.: Games and Full Abstraction for Nondeterministic Languages. PhD thesis, Imperial College, London (1999)
[8] Hyland, J.M.E., Ong, C.-H.: On Full Abstraction for PCF: I, II, and III. Information and Computation 163(2), 285–408 (2000)
[9] Kohlenbach, U.: Applied Proof Theory: Proof Interpretations and their Use in Mathematics. Springer Monographs in Mathematics. Springer (2008)
[10] Krivine, J.-L.: Realizability in classical logic. In: Interactive Models of Computation and Program Behaviour. Panoramas et synthèses, vol. 27, pp. 197–229. Société Mathématique de France (2009)
[11] Laird, J.: A Semantic analysis of control. PhD thesis, University of Edimbourgh (1998)
[12] Miquel, A.: Existential witness extraction in classical realizability and via a negative translation. Logical Methods in Computer Science 7(2) (2011)
[13] Oliva, P., Streicher, T.: On Krivine's Realizability Interpretation of Classical Second-Order Arithmetic. Fundam. Inform. 84(2), 207–220 (2008)
[14] Parigot, M.: Lambda-Mu-Calculus: An Algorithmic Interpretation of Classical Natural Deduction. In: Voronkov, A. (ed.) LPAR 1992. LNCS, vol. 624, pp. 190–201. Springer, Heidelberg (1992)
[15] Selinger, P.: Control Categories and Duality: on the Categorical Semantics of the Lambda-Mu Calculus. Mathematical Structures in Computer Science 11, 207–260 (2001)
[16] Simpson, S.G.: Subsystems of Second Order Arithmetic, 2nd edn. Perspectives in Logic. Cambridge University Press (2010)
[17] Streicher, T.: A Classical Realizability Model araising from a Stable Model of Untyped Lambda-Calculus (unpublished Notes, 2013)
[18] Streicher, T., Reus, B.: Classical Logic, Continuation Semantics and Abstract Machines. J. Funct. Program. 8(6), 543–572 (1998)
[19] Troelstra, A.S.: Metamathematical Investigation of Intuitionistic Arithmetic and Analysis. LNM, vol. 344. Springer, Heidelberg (1973)

Proofs, Upside Down

A Functional Correspondence between Natural Deduction and the Sequent Calculus

Matthias Puech

Department of Computer Science, Aarhus University, Denmark*

Abstract. It is well known in proof theory that sequent-calculus proofs differ from natural deduction proofs by "reversing" elimination rules upside down into left introduction rules. It is also well known that to each recursive, functional program corresponds an equivalent iterative, accumulator-passing program, where the accumulator stores the continuation of the iteration, in "reversed" order. Here, we compose these remarks and show that a restriction of the intuitionistic sequent calculus, LJT, is exactly an accumulator-passing version of intuitionistic natural deduction NJ. More precisely, we obtain this correspondence by applying a series of off-the-shelf program transformations *à la* Danvy et al. on a type checker for the bidirectional λ-calculus, and get a type checker for the $\bar{\lambda}$-calculus, the proof term assignment of LJT. This functional correspondence revisits the relationship between natural deduction and the sequent calculus by systematically deriving the rules of the latter from the former, and allows us to derive new sequent calculus rules from the introduction and elimination rules of new logical connectives.

1 Introduction

A typical introductory course to proof theory starts by presenting the two calculi introduced by Gentzen [9]: first *natural deduction*, that defines the meaning of each logical connective by its introduction and elimination rules, and then the *sequent calculus*, an equivalent refinement of the latter that makes it easier to search for proofs. Natural deductions admit a *bidirectional* reading: introduction rules are read bottom-up, from the conclusion, and elimination rules are read top-down, from the hypotheses. Sequent calculus is then presented as a response to this cumbersome bidirectionality, by turning all elimination subproofs upside down (fig. 1): introductions are renamed "right rules", upside-down eliminations become "left rules", and they operate directly on formulae in the environment Γ, instead of operating on the goal of their premises.

This kind of inversion of control is performed routinely by functional programmers: a piece of data traversed recursively might be turned upside down to be

* This work was carried out while the author was at Univ Paris Diderot, Sorbonne Paris Cité, PPS, UMR 7126 CNRS, PiR2, INRIA Paris-Rocquencourt, F-75205 Paris, France.

C.-c. Shan (Ed.): APLAS 2013, LNCS 8301, pp. 365–380, 2013.

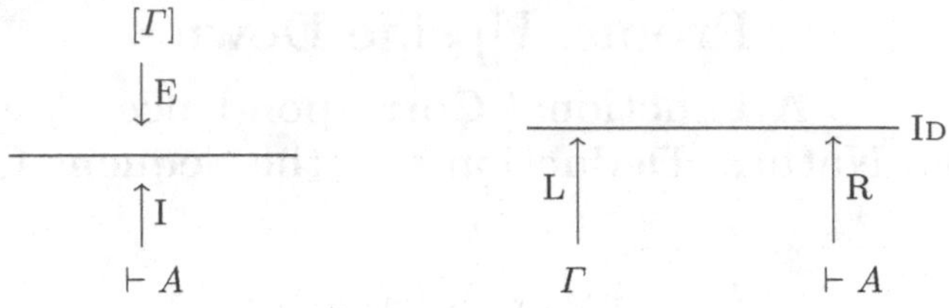

(a) natural deduction (b) sequent calculus

Fig. 1. From natural deductions to sequent-calculus proofs

traversed iteratively. For instance, a recursive function computing the exponent tower of a list (fig. 2) can be transformed in a tail-recursive function carrying an accumulator; only, in this case, the list must be reversed first (because exponentiation is not commutative) and the value for the base case, here 1, must be passed at the top level. Not only are these two programs equivalent, but one can always derive the second from the first.

The analogy is even clearer from the other side of the Curry-Howard looking glass. It is well known since Herbelin's work [10,11] that a restriction of intuitionistic sequent calculus LJ named LJT can be viewed as a type system for the $\bar{\lambda}$- or *spine*-calculus, a language in which consecutive eliminations are reversed with respect to the usual λ-calculus, the variable case being accessible at the top level. Recently, Espírito Santo lifted the restriction [7], and presented two isomorphic calculi corresponding to full LJ. Both authors posed a pair of calculi, respectively in natural-deduction and sequent-calculus style, and showed how to translate a given term from one to the other.

We propose here a method to systematically derive, not a particular proof, but the *inference system* of an intuitionistic sequent calculus itself from the rules of an intuitionistic natural deduction, by means of only off-the-shelf program transformations, in the style of Danvy and colleagues [1]: take NJ, presented as a recursive type-checking program for the bidirectional λ-calculus, turn it into an equivalent accumulator-passing style program, and you will get a type checker for $\bar{\lambda}$-terms, which are notations for LJT proofs. In other words, we show that LJT is precisely to NJ what `tower_acc` is to `tower_rec`. We conclude that, in the light of functional-programming techniques, we can reinterpret Gentzen's discovery of sequent calculus as a "compilation" of natural deduction.

```
let rec tower_rec = function
  | [] → 1
  | x :: xs → x ** tower_rec xs
let tower xs = tower_rec xs
```

(a) a recursive function

```
let rec tower_acc acc = function
  | [] → acc
  | x :: xs → tower_acc (x ** acc) xs
let tower xs = tower_acc 1 (List.rev xs)
```

(b) in accumulator-passing style

Fig. 2. From a recursive function to its accumulator-passing equivalent

In section 2, we present this transformation step-by-step, in OCaml:

- *CPS transformation*, showing that eliminations are head recursive,
- *lightweight defunctionalization*, reifying the continuations into *spines*,
- *reforestation*, decoupling the checking of a term from its reversal, and introducing an intermediate data structure: $\bar{\lambda}$-terms.

For the sake of conciseness, this transformation is performed in NJ with a restricted set of connectives; in section 3, we show that it is modular, i.e., that it applies to richer situations, by exhibiting example extensions.

2 The Transformation

2.1 NJ and the Bidirectional λ-Calculus

The starting point of our transformation is a standard type checking algorithm for NJ proofs of propositions built out of the following connectives (this choice is discussed in the next section):

$$A, B \ ::= \ A \supset B \mid A \vee B \mid A \wedge B \mid \mathsf{p}$$

The terms we assign to NJ proofs are not however those of the usual λ-calculus, but of a *bidirectional* extension of it [16,3] (fig. 3). Bidirectional typing was devised initially as a method for partial type inference. The idea is to judge differently two classes of λ-terms, those *checkable* (whose type is supposed to be an input of the type-checking algorithm) and those *inferable* (whose type can be synthesized by the algorithm).

This distinction can be reflected back syntactically by *stratifying* the syntax of terms (as in, e.g., [14]) into two categories: general *terms* M, N, whose checking requires to know their type, and *atomic terms* R, whose type can be synthesized. An atomic term is a term, since if we can infer its type, we can check that it is equal to a given type, hence the coercion from M to R and rule Atom.[1] Dually, every term can be made atomic provided we are given its expected type, hence the typing annotation construct $(M : A)$ and rule Annot. Variables are inferable since their type can be read off the environment. Eliminations are too, provided their principal premise is inferable, and its conclusion is a subterm of it; all other constructs are "only" general terms. Since the λ-abstractions are checked, they do not require type annotations (rule Lam; this omission was the original motivation of bidirectional type checking).

This stratification has another interpretation: one can see the bidirectional calculus as a reorganization of the syntax of the λ-calculus concentrating on *redexes*. In the λ-calculus, redexes are the combination of matching introductions and eliminations. Here, we restrict principal premises of eliminations to

[1] Often, you will find this rule restricted to atomic types, e.g., in [3], which ensures η-long canonicity. We are not concerned by this restriction here.

$$M, N ::= \lambda x.\, M \mid \mathbf{inl}(M) \mid \mathbf{inr}(M) \mid \langle M, N\rangle \mid \mathbf{case}\ R\ \mathbf{of}\ \langle x.\, M \mid x.\, M\rangle \mid R$$
$$R ::= R\, M \mid \pi_1(R) \mid \pi_2(R) \mid x \mid (M : A)$$

$\boxed{\Gamma \vdash M \Leftarrow A}$ Checking

$$\textsc{Lam}\ \frac{\Gamma, x : A \vdash M \Leftarrow B}{\Gamma \vdash \lambda x.\, M \Leftarrow A \supset B} \qquad \textsc{Inl}\ \frac{\Gamma \vdash M \Leftarrow A}{\Gamma \vdash \mathbf{inl}(M) \Leftarrow A \vee B}$$

$$\textsc{Inr}\ \frac{\Gamma \vdash M \Leftarrow A}{\Gamma \vdash \mathbf{inr}(M) \Leftarrow A \vee B} \qquad \textsc{Pair}\ \frac{\Gamma \vdash M \Leftarrow A \qquad \Gamma \vdash N \Leftarrow B}{\Gamma \vdash \langle M, N\rangle \Leftarrow A \wedge B} \qquad \textsc{Atom}\ \frac{\Gamma \vdash R \Rightarrow C}{\Gamma \vdash R \Leftarrow C}$$

$$\textsc{Case}\ \frac{\Gamma \vdash R \Rightarrow A \vee B \qquad \Gamma, x : A \vdash M \Leftarrow C \qquad \Gamma, y : B \vdash N \Leftarrow C}{\Gamma \vdash \mathbf{case}\ R\ \mathbf{of}\ \langle x.\, M \mid y.\, N\rangle \Leftarrow C}$$

$\boxed{\Gamma \vdash R \Rightarrow A}$ Inference

$$\textsc{Var}\ \frac{x : A \in \Gamma}{\Gamma \vdash x \Rightarrow A} \qquad \textsc{Pil}\ \frac{\Gamma \vdash R \Rightarrow A \wedge B}{\Gamma \vdash \pi_1(R) \Rightarrow A} \qquad \textsc{Pir}\ \frac{\Gamma \vdash R \Rightarrow A \wedge B}{\Gamma \vdash \pi_2(R) \Rightarrow B}$$

$$\textsc{App}\ \frac{\Gamma \vdash R \Rightarrow A \supset B \qquad \Gamma \vdash M \Leftarrow A}{\Gamma \vdash R\, M \Rightarrow B} \qquad \textsc{Annot}\ \frac{\Gamma \vdash M \Leftarrow A}{\Gamma \vdash (M : A) \Rightarrow A}$$

Fig. 3. The bidirectional NJ/λ-calculus

be other eliminations or variables, creating no redexes, or type annotation.[2] Consequently, to construct a bidirectional term with a redex, we *must* use the annotation, for instance $(\lambda x.\, M : A \to B)\, N$. Conversely, a term that does not use this construct is canonical; such a term can be seen as a notation for *intercalations* [19]. Note that there are more non-canonical bidirectional terms than there are equivalent λ-terms [6], since we can always add type annotations, e.g., $(x\ M : A \supset B)\ N$ instead of $x\ M\ N$. Note also that an atomic term has no more than one direct atomic subterm, since an elimination has no more than one principal premise; hence, we will sometimes call them *chains of eliminations*. A (general) term which has a direct atomic subterm, i.e., a coercion R or an elimination **case** R **of** $\langle x.\, M \mid y.\, N\rangle$, will be called a *full chain.*

Figure 4 is a transliteration of this algorithm into OCaml, a metalanguage more suitable for program transformations. For concision, we use pattern-matching failure to signal a typing error. Function `infer` is written in lambda-dropped

[2] Note that ∨-eliminations are *not* allowed as principal subterms of an elimination, since they could "hide" a redex (a *commutative cut*). The same remark would apply to e.g., ⊥ or ∃.

```
type a = At | Imp of a × a | And of a × a | Or of a × a
type var = string
type env = (var × a) list
type m = Lam of var × m | Pair of m × m | Inl of m | Inr of m
 | Case of r × var × m × var × m | Atom of r
and r = App of r × m | Pil of r | Pir of r | Var of var | Annot of m × a

let rec check env c : m → unit =
  let rec infer : r → a = function
  | Var x → List.assoc x env
  | Annot (m, a) → check env a m; a
  | App (r, m) → let (Imp (a, b)) = infer r in check env a m; b
  | Pil r → let (And (a, _)) = infer r in a
  | Pir r → let (And (_, b)) = infer r in b
  in fun m → match m, c with
  | Lam (x, m), Imp (a, b) → check ((x, a) :: env) b m
  | Pair (m, n), And (a, b) → check env a m; check env b n
  | Inl m, Or (a, _) → check env a m
  | Inr n, Or (_, b) → check env b n
  | Case (r, x, m, y, n), c → let (Or (a, b)) = infer r in
    check ((x, a) :: env) c m; check ((y, b) :: env) c n
  | Atom r, c → match infer r with c' when c=c' → ()
```

Fig. 4. Initial program, i.e., fig. 3 in OCaml (module Initial)

form, to emphasize that its recursive calls are in the scope of the same environment env and expected type c. It is only called in non tail-recursive position: its code begins by recursively descending all the way to the bottom of a chain of eliminations. Only then does it synthesize the type of the atomic term, "on the way back". Alternatively, we could traverse this chain in reverse order, accumulating the synthesized types. It is precisely what we embark on doing.

2.2 CPS Transformation

The first two steps of our transformation could be considered a unique, compound one called "algebraic CPS transform" since its popularization by Danvy et al. [5,1]. Its goal is to turn the recursive program above—it needs a stack, implicit in the metalanguage, to store intermediate results—into a deterministic state transition system, a simpler metalanguage where this stack is *reified.* Here however, we only perform this transformation selectively, on function `infer` but not on `check`, since we are only interested in reversing atomic terms.

The first step is to turn every call to `infer` into a tail-recursive one, by applying Plotkin's standard call-by-value CPS transformation [17] (we show only the modified lines).

```
let rec check env c : m → unit =
  let rec infer : r → (a → unit) → unit = fun r s → match r with
```

```
| Var x → s (List.assoc x env)
| Annot (m, a) → check env a m; s a
| App (r, m) → infer r (fun (Imp (a, b)) → check env a m; s b)
| Pil r → infer r (fun (And (a, _)) → s a)
| Pir r → infer r (fun (And (_, b)) → s b)
in fun m → (* ... *)
| Case (r, x, m, y, n), c → infer r (fun (Or (a, b)) →
    check ((x, a) :: env) c m; check ((y, b) :: env) c n)
| Atom r, c → infer r (function c' when c=c' → ())
```

We add an extra functional argument `s` to `infer`, which is called with its result; recursive calls "chain up" the computation to be done at return time. Consequently, all calls to `infer` are tail calls. Note the answer type of `infer`: it is fixed by the return type of `check`, which is `unit`. All calls to `infer` are done directly after pattern-matching: the function is *head recursive* (doing all the work "on the way back").

The CPS transformation trades one feature of the metalanguage—the ability to store intermediate results on a stack—into another—the ability to have functions as first-class values. Yet, in what follows, we map back such a higher-order program into a first-order one.

2.3 Lightweight Defunctionalization

The second step is a variant of *defunctionalization*, as showcased by Danvy and Nielsen [5], which takes a program with first-class functions and returns an equivalent one where these functions have been reified into purely first-order data. The idea is to replace every such inner function by a unique identifier (a type constructor in our case), and all application of a functional variable `f` by `apply f`, where `apply` is a "dictionary" mapping identifiers to the function they stand for. Each inner function can have free variables, so each constructor needs to be parameterized by the values of these free variables. *Lightweight* defunctionalization [2] restricts this set of parameters: free variables that are in scope of both introduction and elimination of functions do not need to be parameters. In our case, both `env` and `c` are "constant" throughout all recursive calls to `infer`, and need not be saved in constructors.

We thus introduce the type s of *spines*[3]: we call SCase, SAtom, SApp, SPil and SPir the respective continuations of the previous program. Then we transform our program accordingly, introducing function `apply`:

```
type s =
  | SAtom
  | SPil of s
  | SPir of s
  | SCase of var × m × var × m
  | SApp of m × s
```

[3] We motivate the choice of this name in section 2.5.

```
let rec check env c : m → unit =
  let rec apply : s × a → unit = function
    | SApp (m, s), Imp (a, b) → check env a m; apply (s, b)
    | SPil s, And (a, _) → apply (s, a)
    | SPir s, And (_, b) → apply (s, b)
    | SCase (x, m, y, n), Or (a, b) →
      check ((x, a) :: env) c m; check ((y, b) :: env) c n
    | SAtom, c' when c=c' → () in
  let rec infer : r → s → unit = fun r s → match r with
    | Var x → apply (s, List.assoc x env)
    | Annot (m, a) → check env a m; apply (s, a)
    | App (r, m) → infer r (SApp (m, s))
    | Pil r → infer r (SPil s)
    | Pir r → infer r (SPir s)
  in fun m → (* ... *)
    | Case (r, x, m, y, n), c → infer r (SCase (x, m, y, n))
    | Atom r, c → infer r SAtom
```

We uncurried `apply` on-the-fly for legibility. Note that defunctionalization preserves tail calls: function `infer` is still tail-recursive.

Because all inner functions transformed stemmed from CPS, `s` is the type of *reified continuations*. Because the original type checker traverses the whole term structure, these can be seen as the type of *zippers* [12] or *contexts* of atomic terms: a pair `(r, s) : r × s` determines uniquely an atomic position inside an atomic term $S[R]$. CPS and defunctionalization decomposed the recursive process in two parts: what is done "on the way down" of an atomic term traversal (function `infer`), accumulating a continuation `s`, and what is done "on the way back", (function `apply`), reading off this continuation in reverse order. Since `infer` was head recursive, our transformed `infer` is a simple *reversal* function that takes an atom to a spine, and eventually calls `apply` with this spine. Function `apply` now actually performs the type synthesis; the impatient reader can already interpret this function as the second judgment of fig. 7, but a final step is needed to reach our target.

2.4 Reforestation

This type checker is a strange hybrid: given a term `m`, it checks its type until arriving to a full chain (`check`), which it reverses into a spine `s` (`infer`), which in turn is type-checked (`apply`). In the last step, we decouple completely reversal and checking so that, given a term `m`, we can first reverse it completely, and only then check its type. The transformation comprises two *reforestation* steps. Reforestation is the inverse of Wadler's *deforestation* [20]: instead of eliminating intermediate data structure for efficiency by "chaining up" function calls, we reintroduce an intermediate data structure of reversed terms from "chained up" function calls.

The first reforestation concerns `infer`: it "lifts up" the computation done in its base cases (Var and Annot) outside it, at its call sites. To this end, `infer` needs to return an intermediate data structure, that we call a *head* h, representing algebraically the computation to be done in these two base cases, each parameterized by their free variables:

```
type h =
  | HVar of var × s
  | HAnnot of m × a × s
```

A new `head` function is introduced, that plays the same role as `apply` in the defunctionalization step: it maps an "algebraic base case" `h` to the computation it stands for. Previous call sites to `infer` now perform the composition of the new `infer` and `head` functions. It reads:

```
(* ... *)
  let head : h → unit = function
    | HVar (x, s) → apply (s, List.assoc x env)
    | HAnnot (m, a, s) → check env a m; apply (s, a) in
  let rec infer : r → s → h = fun r s → match r with
    | Var x → HVar (x, s)
    | Annot (m, a) → HAnnot (m, a, s)
(* ... *) in fun m → (* ... *)
    | Case (r, x, m, y, n), c → head (infer r (SCase (x, m, y, n)))
    | Atom r, c → head (infer r SAtom)
```

In Wadler's words, this program is not in "treeless form", because of these function compositions. Applying deforestation to it, we would get back the program of the last section. The type h of heads represents *reversed full chains*: if we were to construct a full chain out of thread and pearls (fig. 5), reversing it would amount to hold it, not by its top-level node (a Case or an Atom) but by its bottom node (a Var or an Annot) and letting all nodes hang loose underneath; the whole atomic spine would be reversed, top-level nodes becoming bottom nodes (SCase and SAtom) and bottom nodes becoming top-level nodes (HVar and HAnnot).

Interleaved checking and reversal are still not completely decoupled, so we perform one final reforestation, on function `check`. Again, we "lift up" the calls to `infer` in the base cases (Case and Atom) outside of `check`, at the top level. To this end, we introduce the intermediate data structure v of reversed terms, on the model of m but replacing constructors Case and Atom by a unique VHead constructor. Since `check`, `head` and `spine` are mutually recursive, so are the final types v, h and s. Function `check` is decomposed in two passes, one taking an `m` to an intermediate `v` (`rev`), and one actually checking the resulting `v` (`check`). The resulting code is shown on fig. 6. For better readability, we renamed `infer` into `rev_spine`, and `apply` into `spine`. Again, if we deforest this program, the intermediate data structure `v` vanishes, and both passes are merged into one and we get back the previous type checker.

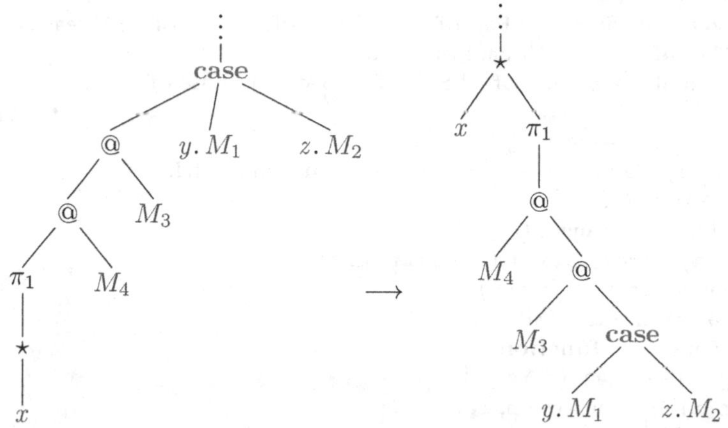

Fig. 5. Reversing a full chain into a head

The transformation is now over, and our goal is achieved: the resulting program `check` is the composition of reversal `rev` and checking `check`. Checking is more space-efficient than the original one, because we made function `infer` tail-recursive, with an accumulator storing the synthesized type. The top-level function is observationally equivalent to the original program: we traded stack space for an intermediate data structure of "reversed" terms.

Theorem 1. `Initial.check env c m` *is defined iff* `Final.check env c m` *is defined.*

Proof. By composition of the soundness of the transformations.

However, decoupling these two phases offers the opportunity to study the intermediate data structure unveiled.

2.5 LJT and the $\bar{\lambda}$-Calculus

Let us transliterate back data structures `v`, `h` and `s` and functions `check`, `head` and `spine` into BNF syntax and inference rules, a metalanguage more suitable for logical interpretation. fig. 7 presents this system[4]. It is precisely the $\bar{\lambda}$-calculus of Herbelin [10,11], a proof term assignment for LJT. LJT is a restriction of the sequent calculus LJ, with features of *focusing* [13].

Reversed terms V contain all introductions, and two "structural" constructs: variables and type annotations, both attached to a *spine* S of eliminations. This spine is terminated by a $\cdot$ ("nil"), or a **case** construct. When restricted to its implicative fragment, this calculus is sometimes called a *spine calculus* [3]: applications can be viewed as n-ary[5], i.e., applied to a list of arguments

[4] With two small differences: we inlined type h and function head for compactness, and lambda-lifted all inner functions.

[5] Note that partial application is still possible, since the length of this list can vary and the return type C in SAtom can be an arrow.

```
type v = VLam of var × v | VPair of v × v | VInl of v | VInr of v | VHead of h
and h = HVar of var × s | HAnnot of v × a × s
and s = SApp of v × s | SPil of s | SPir of s | SAtom | SCase of var × v × var × v

let check env c : m → unit =
  let rec rev_spine : r → s → h = fun r s → match r with
    | Var x → HVar (x, s)
    | Annot (m, a) → HAnnot (rev m, a, s)
    | App (r, m) → rev_spine r (SApp (rev m, s))
    | Pil r → rev_spine r (SPil s)
    | Pir r → rev_spine r (SPir s)
  and rev : m → v = function
    | Lam (x, m) → VLam (x, rev m)
    | Pair (m, n) → VPair (rev m, rev n)
    | Inl m → VInl (rev m)
    | Inr n → VInr (rev n)
    | Case (r, x, m, y, n) → VHead (rev_spine r (SCase (x, rev m, y, rev n)))
    | Atom r → VHead (rev_spine r SAtom) in
  let rec check env c : v → unit =
    let rec spine : s × a → unit = function
      | SApp (m, s), Imp (a, b) → check env a m; spine (s, b)
      | SPil s, And (a, _) → spine (s, a)
      | SPir s, And (_, b) → spine (s, b)
      | SCase (x, m, y, n), Or (a, b) → check ((x, a) :: env) c m; check ((y, b) :: env) c n
      | SAtom, c' when c=c' → () in
    let head : h → unit = function
      | HVar (x, s) → spine (s, List.assoc x env)
      | HAnnot (m, a, s) → check env a m; spine (s, a) in
    fun v → match v, c with
      | VLam (x, v), Imp (a, b) → check ((x, a) :: env) b v
      | VPair (v, w), And (a, b) → check env a v; check env b w
      | VInl v, Or (a, _) → check env a v
      | VInr w, Or (_, b) → check env b w
      | VHead h, c → head h
  in fun m → check env c (rev m)
```

Fig. 6. Final program, i.e., fig. 7 in OCaml (module Final)

$f\,(M_1, M_2, \ldots, M_n, \cdot)$, in contrast with the usual $(((f\ M_1)\ M_2)\ \ldots)\ M_n$ of NJ. Espiríto Santo [7] speaks of a difference of *associativity* of application. Generalizing to our extended fragment, the situation is more subtle: an elimination chain is piled up in reverse order, and its head construct, a variable or an annotated term that was buried under eliminations, is brought back at the top level. For example, the full chain **case** $\pi_1(f\ x)$ **of** $\langle x_1 . M_1 \mid x_2 . M_2 \rangle$ is now written with the head variable f first: $f\,(x\,(\cdot), \pi_1, \mathbf{case}\langle x_1 . M_1 \mid x_2 . M_2\rangle, \cdot)$.

As promised, the typing rules are in Curry-Howard correspondence with a sequent calculus-like system. Like the rules of fig. 3, they come in two judgments;

$$V, W ::= \lambda x. V \mid \langle V, W \rangle \mid \mathbf{inl}(V) \mid \mathbf{inr}(V) \mid x\,(S) \mid (M : A)\,(S)$$
$$S ::= V, S \mid \pi_1, S \mid \pi_2, S \mid \mathbf{case}\langle x. V \mid y. W \rangle \mid \cdot$$

$\boxed{\Gamma \vdash V \Leftarrow A}$ Right rules

$$\textsc{VLam}\ \frac{\Gamma, x : A \vdash M \Leftarrow B}{\Gamma \vdash \lambda x. M \Leftarrow A \supset B} \qquad \textsc{VPair}\ \frac{\Gamma \vdash M \Leftarrow A \qquad \Gamma \vdash N \Leftarrow B}{\Gamma \vdash \langle M, N \rangle \Leftarrow A \wedge B}$$

$$\textsc{VInl}\ \frac{\Gamma \vdash M \Leftarrow A}{\Gamma \vdash \mathbf{inl}(M) \Leftarrow A \vee B} \qquad \textsc{VInr}\ \frac{\Gamma \vdash M \Leftarrow B}{\Gamma \vdash \mathbf{inr}(M) \Leftarrow A \vee B}$$

$$\textsc{HVar}\ \frac{x : A \in \Gamma \qquad \Gamma \mid A \vdash S \Leftarrow C}{\Gamma \vdash x\,(S) \Leftarrow C} \qquad \textsc{HAnnot}\ \frac{\Gamma \vdash M \Leftarrow A \qquad \Gamma \mid A \vdash S \Leftarrow C}{\Gamma \vdash (M : A)\,(S) \Leftarrow C}$$

$\boxed{\Gamma \mid A \vdash S \Leftarrow C}$ Focused left rules

$$\textsc{SApp}\ \frac{\Gamma \vdash V \Leftarrow A \qquad \Gamma \mid B \vdash S \Leftarrow C}{\Gamma \mid A \supset B \vdash V, S \Leftarrow C} \qquad \textsc{SPil}\ \frac{\Gamma \mid A \vdash S \Leftarrow C}{\Gamma \mid A \wedge B \vdash \pi_1, S \Leftarrow C}$$

$$\textsc{SPir}\ \frac{\Gamma \mid B \vdash S \Leftarrow C}{\Gamma \mid A \wedge B \vdash \pi_1, S \Leftarrow C} \qquad \textsc{SCase}\ \frac{\Gamma, x : A \vdash V \Leftarrow C \qquad \Gamma, y : B \vdash W \Leftarrow C}{\Gamma \mid A \vee B \vdash \mathbf{case}\langle x. V \mid y. W \rangle \Leftarrow C}$$

$$\textsc{SAtom}\ \frac{}{\Gamma \mid C \vdash \cdot \Leftarrow C}$$

Fig. 7. The LJT/$\bar{\lambda}$-calculus [10]

unlike them, no judgment infers a type: both are in checking mode. This fact is a notable difference with the usual definition of spine-form calculi [3]: their restriction to negative connectives makes possible to infer the types of spines, which is impossible when extended with e.g., disjunction. The right rules are unchanged with respect to fig. 3, except for two new rules: HVAR, sometimes called FOCUS, which focuses on a particular premise (variable) and checks the attached spine, and HANNOT, which corresponds to the usual CUT rule. In "focused mode", all rules act on a distinguished premise A (the *stoup*) hence their names: left rules. Once focused on a premise, these rules oblige us to continue working on it until we can either close the branch by SATOM (usually called INIT) or by a "polarity switch", i.e., here when the stoup contains a disjunction. Tracing the stoup back through the transformations, it corresponds to the *accumulator* threaded in `spine` on fig. 6, which was the returned type of function `infer` on fig. 4. In other words, the focused hypothesis of a left rule in LJT corresponds to the principal premise of an elimination in NJ.

3 Extensions

Although we chose to start with a reduced set of logical connectives ($\wedge$, $\vee$, $\supset$), the same scheme extends to all connectives of intuitionistic predicate logic: $\top$, $\bot$, $\forall$, $\exists$, as well as variants of these and related systems.

3.1 Multiplicative Connectives

For instance, taking the *multiplicative* definition of the conjunction via the unique elimination:

$$\dfrac{\vdash A \wedge B \qquad \begin{matrix}[\vdash A] \quad [\vdash B] \\ \vdots \\ \vdash C\end{matrix}}{\vdash C}\ \textsc{ConjE'}$$

leads to the following normal term assignment (showing only the $\wedge$, $\supset$ fragment):

$$\begin{aligned} M, N &::= \lambda x.\, M \mid \langle M, N\rangle \mid \textbf{let } \langle x, y\rangle = R \textbf{ in } M \mid R \\ R &::= x \mid (M : A) \mid R\, M \end{aligned}$$

Note that the **let** construct is a general term, for the same reason the **case** construct was in section 2.1. Applying the same transform, we get the following term assignment:

$$\begin{aligned} V &::= \lambda x.\, V \mid \langle V, V\rangle \mid x\,(S) \mid (M : A)\,(S) \mid R \\ S &::= \cdot \mid M, S \mid \langle x, y\rangle.\, M \end{aligned}$$

where the top-level **let** gets buried under the chain of eliminations, and the corresponding checking rule:

$$\textsc{ConjL'}\ \dfrac{\Gamma, x : A, y : B \vdash M \Leftarrow C}{\Gamma \mid A \wedge B \vdash \langle x, y\rangle.\, M \Leftarrow C}$$

which is the usual left rule of the multiplicative conjunction. Note that the premise loses the focus on the hypothesis, just like for disjunction. The same system was proposed by Herbelin in his PhD thesis [11].

3.2 Modal Logic of Necessity

Pfenning and Davies [15] propose a reconstruction of modal logic in terms of the Gentzen apparatus. They present the necessity modality $\Box A$ (denoting the necessity for A to be true *under no hypotheses*) as a connective defined by the following introduction and elimination rules:

$$\frac{\Delta; \cdot \vdash A}{\Delta; \Gamma \vdash \Box A}\ \textsc{BoxI} \qquad \frac{\Delta; \Gamma \vdash \Box A \qquad \Delta, A; \Gamma \vdash C}{\Delta; \Gamma \vdash C}\ \textsc{BoxE}$$

The environment is split in two sets: Γ and Δ, *resp.* the true and the necessarily true assumptions. To use a necessary hypothesis, we add rule:

$$\frac{A \in \Delta}{\Delta; \Gamma \vdash A}\ \textsc{Meta}$$

The authors also propose a term assignment for these rules, that we easily make bidirectional by stratification (again, the $\supset$, $\Box$ fragment):

$$\begin{aligned} M &::= \lambda x.\, M \mid \mathbf{box}(M) \mid \mathbf{let\ box}\ \mathtt{X} = R\, \mathbf{in}\ M \mid R \\ R &::= (M : A) \mid x \mid \mathtt{X} \mid R\, M \end{aligned}$$

Note the new set of *metavariables* $\mathtt{X}$ referring to necessary hypotheses. Again, applying our transformation, we get the following reversed syntax:

$$\begin{aligned} V &::= \lambda x.\, V \mid \mathbf{box}(V) \mid x\,(S) \mid \mathtt{X}\,(S) \mid (M : A)\,(S) \mid R \\ S &::= \cdot \mid M, S \mid \mathtt{X}.\, M \end{aligned}$$

The associated rules for the new syntactic constructs are the left and right rules for necessity, and a focus rule for necessary hypotheses:

$$\frac{\Delta; \cdot \vdash M : A}{\Delta; \Gamma \vdash \mathbf{box}(M) : \Box A}\ \textsc{BoxR} \qquad \frac{\Delta, \mathtt{X} : A; \Gamma \vdash M : C}{\Delta; \Gamma \mid \Box A \vdash \mathtt{X}.\, M : C}\ \textsc{BoxL}$$

$$\frac{\mathtt{X} : A \in \Delta \qquad \Delta; \Gamma \mid A \vdash S : C}{\Delta; \Gamma \vdash \mathtt{X}\,(S) : C}\ \textsc{FocusM}$$

Seeing the stoup as a non-necessary hypothesis, and erasing all term information, this system is the sequent calculus proposed by the authors [15].

3.3 Full Sequent Calculus

As we noted previously, LJT is a focused system: it is equivalent to LJ in terms of provability but not all LJ proofs are represented. Espírito Santo [7] proposes two term assignments λ^{Gtz} and λ_{Nat} for *resp.* full LJ (without the focusing restriction) and its corresponding natural deduction. This pair constitutes an interesting test bed for the transformation. Let us start from λ_{Nat} (restricted to the $\supset$ fragment, but easily extensible):

$$\begin{aligned} M &::= x \mid \lambda x.\, M \mid M[x/R] \\ R &::= (M : A) \mid R\, M \end{aligned}$$

It generalizes the previous bidirectional calculus by replacing the coercion from M to R by a substitution $M[x/R]$.[6] This construct corresponds to the *cut* rule:

$$\textsc{Cut}\ \frac{\Gamma \vdash R \Rightarrow A \qquad \Gamma, x : A \vdash M \Leftarrow B}{\Gamma \vdash M[x/R] \Leftarrow B} \qquad \textsc{Annot}\ \frac{\Gamma \vdash M \Leftarrow A}{\Gamma \vdash (M : A) \Rightarrow A}$$

Transforming the corresponding type checker amounts to turn eliminations R upside down, putting annotation nodes at the top level and substitution nodes at the bottom:

$$\begin{aligned} V &::= x \mid \lambda x.\, V \mid (V : A)\,(S) \\ S &::= V, S \mid x.\, V \end{aligned}$$

Like in $\bar{\lambda}$, the annotation $(M : A)$ becomes a "focusing *cut*" $(V : A)\,(S)$; its "nil" construct $\cdot$ however is replaced by a new binder $x.\, M$ that allows losing the focus on the stoup:

$$\textsc{HAnnot}\ \frac{\Gamma \vdash V \Leftarrow A \qquad \Gamma \mid A \vdash S \Leftarrow B}{\Gamma \vdash (V : A)\,(S) \Leftarrow B} \qquad \textsc{Unfocus}\ \frac{\Gamma, x : A \vdash M \Leftarrow B}{\Gamma \mid A \vdash x.\, M \Leftarrow B}$$

It is precisely the calculus λ^{Gtz} of Espírito Santo.

4 Conclusion

We presented a modular, semantics-preserving program transformation turning a logical system presented in natural-deduction style into one in sequent-calculus style. It achieves the systematic and simultaneous derivation of the "reversed" term structure, the type checker (and thus the sequent rules) and the translation function from one to the other. In particular, starting from a *bidirectional* presentation of the λ-calculus, we ended up with the composition of a reversal function, taking λ-terms to $\bar{\lambda}$-terms, and a type checker for $\bar{\lambda}$-terms, in *accumulator-passing style.* The accumulator corresponds to the *stoup*, and is used to check spines. Spines are *contexts* of atomic terms, which are *checked* contrarily to previous presentations, and were evidenced by CPS and defunctionalization. These two steps can be seen as a form of (partial) *compilation*, since the computation

[6] Also, a variable is a general, checked term, and not an atom as before; this shallow difference only forces to put more type annotations to make it a bidirectional checking algorithm.

on spines is more direct than on atomic terms. Reforestation showed how spines "plug into" reversed terms, and evidenced the final structure of $\bar{\lambda}$-terms.

Composing CPS and defunctionalization has many well-documented applications: it turns evaluation functions into abstract machines [1], and exhibits the *zipper* [12], or *one-hole context* of a traversal [5]. Combined with deforestation, it turns small-step into big-step semantics [4]. This scheme was recently used to check types "by reduction" [18], but without the purpose of proof-theoretic interpretation. To the best of our knowledge, the present work is the first application of these techniques to proof theory.

One could rightfully argue that our starting point, the bidirectional λ-calculus, is only a notation for an *extension* of NJ, and is already an important step toward LJ. Indeed, it would be desirable to explain this extension similarly in terms of a systematic program transformation. Besides, we showcased the behavior of our transformation on a few known pairs of calculi; a natural continuation of this work will be to apply it to other logics, in particular to get a better understanding of focusing [13]. For instance, LJQ [11] is dual to LJT in that its focus is biased toward the conclusion, and not the hypotheses, and features a call-by-value semantics where LJT reduces in call-by-name. Still, we do not know what natural-deduction style calculus corresponds to LJQ [7]; applying our transformation backwards could help finding out. Finally, another interesting application concerns classical logic. In natural deduction it usually takes the form of a control operators (**call**/**cc**), whereas it appears as a facility to switch between multiple conclusions in sequent calculus. Will our transformation turn one presentation into the other? Answering these questions will require an analysis of bidirectional and canonical forms in these logics, that we leave for further investigation.

Acknowledgements. We are grateful to Pierre-Louis Curien, Olivier Danvy, Hugo Herbelin, Yann Régis-Gianas, and the anonymous reviewers for their valuable comments on various drafts of this document.

References

1. Ager, M.S., Biernacki, D., Danvy, O., Midtgaard, J.: A functional correspondence between evaluators and abstract machines. In: Miller, D. (ed.) PPDP, Uppsala, Sweden, pp. 8–19. ACM Press (August 2003)
2. Banerjee, A., Heintze, N., Riecke, J.G.: Design and correctness of program transformations based on control-flow analysis. In: Kobayashi, N., Babu, C. S. (eds.) TACS 2001. LNCS, vol. 2215, pp. 420–447. Springer, Heidelberg (2001)
3. Cervesato, I., Pfenning, F.: A linear spine calculus. J. Log. Comput. 13(5), 639–688 (2003)
4. Danvy, O., Millikin, K.: On the equivalence between small-step and big-step abstract machines: a simple application of lightweight fusion. Inf. Process. Lett. 106(3), 100–109 (2008)

[7] Espírito Santo [8] recently raised the question and conjectured a correspondence with his $\underline{\lambda}\mu\text{let}_Q$-calculus.

5. Danvy, O., Nielsen, L.R.: Defunctionalization at work. In: Søndergaard, H. (ed.) PPDP, pp. 162–174. ACM (2001)
6. Santo, J.E.: An isomorphism between a fragment of sequent calculus and an extension of natural deduction. In: Baaz, M., Voronkov, A. (eds.) LPAR 2002. LNCS (LNAI), vol. 2514, pp. 352–366. Springer, Heidelberg (2002)
7. Espírito Santo, J.: Completing Herbelin's Programme. In: Della Rocca, S.R. (ed.) TLCA 2007. LNCS, vol. 4583, pp. 118–132. Springer, Heidelberg (2007)
8. Santo, J.E.: Towards a Canonical Classical Natural Deduction System. In: Dawar, A., Veith, H. (eds.) CSL 2010. LNCS, vol. 6247, pp. 290–304. Springer, Heidelberg (2010)
9. Gentzen, G.: Untersuchungen über das logische Schließen. I. Math. Z. 39(1), 176–210 (1935)
10. Herbelin, H.: A λ-calculus structure isomorphic to Gentzen-style sequent calculus structure. In: Pacholski, L., Tiuryn, J. (eds.) CSL 1994. LNCS, vol. 933, pp. 61–75. Springer, Heidelberg (1995)
11. Herbelin, H.: Séquents qu'on calcule: de l'interprétation du calcul des séquents comme calcul de lambda-termes et comme calcul de stratégies gagnantes. PhD thesis, Université Paris-Diderot—Paris VII (1995)
12. Huet, G.P.: The zipper. J. Funct. Program. 7(5), 549–554 (1997)
13. Liang, C., Miller, D.: Focusing and polarization in linear, intuitionistic, and classical logics. Theor. Comput. Sci. 410(46), 4747–4768 (2009)
14. Löh, A., McBride, C., Swierstra, W.: A tutorial implementation of a dependently typed lambda calculus. Fundam. Inform. 102(2), 177–207 (2010)
15. Pfenning, F., Davies, R.: A judgmental reconstruction of modal logic. Mathematical Structures in Computer Science 11(4), 511–540 (2001)
16. Pierce, B.C., Turner, D.N.: Local type inference. ACM Trans. Program. Lang. Syst. 22(1), 1–44 (2000)
17. Plotkin, G.D.: Call-by-name, call-by-value and the lambda-calculus. Theor. Comput. Sci. 1(2), 125–159 (1975)
18. Sergey, I., Clarke, D.: A correspondence between type checking via reduction and type checking via evaluation. Inf. Process. Lett. 112(1-2), 13–20 (2012)
19. Sieg, W., Cittadini, S.: Normal natural deduction proofs (in non-classical logics). In: Hutter, D., Stephan, W. (eds.) Mechanizing Mathematical Reasoning. LNCS (LNAI), vol. 2605, pp. 169–191. Springer, Heidelberg (2005)
20. Wadler, P.: Deforestation: Transforming programs to eliminate trees. In: Ganzinger, H. (ed.) ESOP 1988. LNCS, vol. 300, pp. 344–358. Springer, Heidelberg (1988)

Author Index